D1287882

God's Will and Testament

God's Will and Testament

*Inheritance in the Gospel of Matthew
and Jewish Tradition*

Daniel Daley

BAYLOR UNIVERSITY PRESS

© 2021 by Baylor University Press
Waco, Texas 76798

All Rights Reserved. No part of this publication may be reproduced, stored in a retrieval system, or transmitted, in any form or by any means, electronic, mechanical, photocopying, recording, or otherwise, without the prior permission in writing of Baylor University Press.

Cover design and typesetting by Kasey McBeath
Cover art: *The Sermon on the Mount*, from the Sistine Chapel, c.1481–83 (fresco). Bridgeman Images.

The Library of Congress has cataloged this book under ISBN 978-1-4813-1552-4.

Library of Congress Control Number: 2021939843

Printed in the United States of America on acid-free paper with a minimum of thirty percent recycled content.

My wife, Brennen, made countless sacrifices so that this book could be written. I dedicate this book to her, with love and gratitude.

Contents

Acknowledgments   ix

1   Introduction: Matthew and Jewish Tradition   1
    1.1   Matthew and Sapiential Traditions   6
    1.2   Matthew and "Apocalyptic"   7
    1.3   Trajectories within Second Temple Literature   12
    1.4   God as Father   18
    1.5   Israel, Church, Jews, and Gentiles   20
    1.6   The Approach of This Study   37

2   Inheritance in the Hebrew Bible   45
    2.1   נחלה and Its Cognates as Inheritance   48
    2.2   Inheritance in the Hexateuch   50
    2.3   Inheritance in the Former Prophets   72
        JUDGES, SAMUEL, KINGS
    2.4   Inheritance in the Latter Prophets   92
        JEREMIAH, ISAIAH, EZEKIEL

3   Inheritance in the Second Temple Period:
Apocrypha and Pseudepigrapha   109
    3.1   1 Enoch   110
    3.2   Sirach   130
    3.3   Tobit   136
    3.4   Judith   139
    3.5   1 and 2 Maccabees   140
    3.6   The Psalms of Solomon   143
    3.7   Conclusions   149

4   Inheritance in the Second Temple Period:
The Qumran Literature   153
    4.1   Wisdom Compositions   158
        4QINSTRUCTION, BOOK OF MYSTERIES,
        THE SEDUCTRESS (4Q184), 4QBEATITUDES (4Q525)

    4.2   Qumran Compositions Concerned
        with Religious Law   216
           THE DAMASCUS DOCUMENT, THE COMMUNITY
           RULE, THE WAR SCROLL
    4.3   Conclusions   237

5   Inheritance in the Gospel of Matthew   **239**
    5.1   Inheritance in Matthew 5:5   239
    5.2   Inheritance in Matthew 19:29   306
    5.3   Inheritance in Matthew 21:38   321
    5.4   Inheritance in Matthew 25:34   337
    5.5   Conclusions   353

6   Conclusion: Matthew and the Promise of Discipleship   **357**

Bibliography   365
Subject Index   387
Ancient Sources Index   389

Acknowledgments

My wife, Brennen, and our three children, Eisley, Greyson, and Maeve-lynn, were a consistent source of joy during the course of writing and brought levity when the research and writing was at its most difficult. This project is the product of their labors as much as my own.

My parents, Ken and Kathy Daley, offered loving support and advice and provided considerable financial support in the completion of this project. My grandparents, Mike and Rosalie Dooley, and my wife's parents, Marlon and Elizabeth Gates, offered consistent prayers and encouragement. Considerable financial support was provided by Jason and Lindsay Spencer, Dave and Tamii Johnson, and Layton and Veronica Diament. Other consistent support was offered by the Turners, the Zions, the Cooks, the Bronsons, Mwongeli Mutua, the Detweilers, and the Kruths, and many other friends and family offered support when needs arose. We are forever grateful for your commitment to our family and our work.

Ben Wold made thoughtful and trenchant comments on the work and offered encouragement. Ben has been an excellent adviser, teacher, and friend. Others have also tilled the soil so that I would have a fruit-ful path forward as a scholar of the Bible, including Tony Slavin, Rex Koivisto, Brad Harper, Matthew V. Novenson, and Reimund Bieringer, and for that I am forever grateful. This book benefited, at various points, from thoughtful engagement by Elena Dugan, Michael Reed, Michael F. Bird, James K. Aitken, and Catrin H. Willaims. Needless to say, the book's shortcomings are my responsibility.

Finally, I would like to thank Cade Jarrell and the entire team at Baylor University Press. Cade is a gifted and thoughtful editor who has been insightful in his comments and supportive of my work. Baylor has been an excellent partner in getting this book into the world.

1

Introduction

Matthew and Jewish Tradition

Inheritance terms and concepts are ubiquitous throughout the Bible and the non-biblical Second Temple material. It is not controversial to state that, throughout the Hebrew Bible (hereafter HB), the Israelites believed themselves to be the people of God uniquely chosen from among the peoples of the earth and that this status as elected people guaranteed them certain privileges not granted to other peoples. One of these privileges was the right to an inheritance granted by God himself—a birthright that provided a sense of God's protection and an awareness of their relationship to God as a special people. Details regarding the nature of their inheritance—what it is, who receives it, and how their inheritance is obtained—appear in every strata and section of the Hebrew Scriptures, and in many Second Temple Jewish texts, and yet surprisingly little scholarly attention has focused on inheritance as a unique and crucial concept for Israelite and Jewish religious life and belief. Inheritance terms and concepts also appear frequently in the New Testament (hereafter NT), and focused scholarly attention in this group of texts has been only slightly more sustained. Most studies on inheritance in the NT have limited their focus to Paul's "core" letters, such as Galatians, 1 Corinthians, and Romans, while these concepts in other NT texts have largely been relegated to brief treatments in the commentaries.[1]

---

[1]   Major studies of inheritance in Paul include: James D. Hester, *Paul's Concept of Inheritance: A Contribution to the Understanding of Heilsgeschichte* (SJT 14; Edinburgh: Oliver and Boyd, 1968); Mark Forman, *The Politics of Inheritance in Romans* (SNTS 148; Cambridge: Cambridge University Press, 2011); and Caroline Johnson Hodge, *If Sons, Then Heirs: A Study of Kinship and Ethnicity in the Letters of Paul* (Oxford: Oxford University Press, 2007).

The paucity of attention to inheritance concepts in Matthew's Gospel is surprising for at least two reasons. First, Matthew is widely regarded as the most "Jewish" of the Gospel accounts, and inheritance terms and concepts are ubiquitous throughout Jewish literature.[2] The First Gospel frequently interacts with various texts from the HB as intertexts,[3] the concept of the fulfillment of these texts was clearly important to Matthew's writer,[4] and inheritance terms feature prominently in many of the antecedent texts with which Matthew interacts.[5] Providing a more focused account of Matthew's use of inheritance concepts will provide additional insights into Matthew's understanding of its Jewish milieu than has currently been offered.

Second, how one answers questions regarding who stands to inherit relates directly to one of the most important debates regarding Matthew's Gospel over the past few decades, namely, the dynamics between Jews and gentiles both within the content of the Gospel and among the perceived community from which the Gospel was produced. These questions concern identity, community dynamics, and the very nature of salvation and human relationship to Israel's God. The dynamic between Jews and

---

[2]   See Anthony J. Saldarini, *Matthew's Christian-Jewish Community* (Chicago: University of Chicago Press, 1994), 1, who writes that Matthew is generally considered the most Jewish of the Gospels "because it refers in a sustained and serious way to the Bible, to specific Jewish customs and beliefs, and to the general Jewish cultural and religious thought-world of the first century." See also Rodney Reeves, *Matthew* (SGBC; Grand Rapids: Zondervan, 2017), 20–21, who offers a brief account of Matthew's "implied readers" to suggest that the First Gospel is particularly concerned with "Jewish interests."

[3]   Various perspectives regarding Matthew's use of the Hebrew Bible are covered in most commentaries, but more sustained treatments have been offered. See, for example, R. H. Gundry, *The Use of the Old Testament in St. Matthew's Gospel: With Special Reference to the Messianic Hope* (NTS; Leiden: Brill, 1968); and Graham Stanton, *A Gospel for a New People: Studies in Matthew* (Louisville: Westminster John Knox, 1992), 346–63. See also the survey of the history of research in Richard Beaton, *Isaiah's Christ in Matthew's Gospel* (Cambridge: Cambridge University Press, 2002), 14–43. For the dynamics of Matthew's use of the Hebrew and the Septuagint, see M. J. J. Menken, *Matthew's Bible: The Old Testament Text of the Evangelist* (Leuven: Leuven University Press, 2004).

[4]   See, for example, Michael P. Knowles, "Scripture, History, Messiah: Scriptural Fulfillment and the Fullness of Time in Matthew's Gospel," in *Hearing the Old Testament in the New Testament* (ed. Stanley E. Porter; Grand Rapids: Eerdmans, 2006), 59–82.

[5]   The clearest example is Matthew's use of Ps 37, which uses inheritance terms and concepts as many as six times (Ps 37:9, 11, 18, 22, 29, 34). Psalm 37:11 reads, "But the meek shall inherit the land, and delight in abundant prosperity" (NRSV). Matthew appears to quote a portion of that verse in 5:5, "*Flourishing* are the meek, because they will inherit the earth." Other examples will be explored in ch. 5. The question regarding the translation of μακάριος is a matter of importance for interpretation. The decision to translate the term "flourishing" will be discussed in detail in 5.1.1.2.

gentiles is at the very heart of the human problem that Matthew's Gospel seeks to describe, and the sense of unity, inclusion, and togetherness is wrapped up in Matthew in an extremely nuanced and often paradoxical presentation of Jesus' intentions toward building a community based on his teaching and authority. There is a scholarly consensus that Matthew features the language of "othering," but much less clear is the identity of those who are "othered" and why, as well as the identity of those who stand to benefit from following Jesus and how their involvement might come about.[6] It will become clear throughout this study that Jewish/gentile relations is a prominent theme in inheritance contexts not only in Matthew but also throughout much of the relevant literature antecedent to Matthew. Therefore, understanding inheritance in both Matthew and the antecedent material is paramount to understanding the Jewish/gentile dynamic presented in the text. Conversely, understanding something about the Jewish/gentile dynamic is vital to understanding the nature of inheritance, so to some degree a circular approach is required. Needless to say, it would be difficult to understand inheritances without a proper account of who stands to receive them. Despite the obvious ways in which inheritances (monetary, cultural, familial, and otherwise) figure into the dynamics of identity and inclusion, and despite the large number of academic treatments of Jewish/gentile dynamics in Matthew, no treatment of which I am currently aware offers a direct focus on Matthew's use of inheritance concepts.

The intention of this study is to fill lacunae in research on Israelite/Jewish inheritance, and the potential for gentile inclusion in the inheritance, in at least three regards. First, much of the scholarly focus on inheritance has been limited to specific groups of texts; *either* the HB *or* certain NT texts or authors. While studies done on inheritance in Paul's letters have interacted to some degree with the HB and various Second Temple compositions, these interactions have been brief and reductive, offering an analysis only of inheritance contexts in which the scholar perceives there to be relevance.[7] In other words, such treatments are selective and therefore run the risk of missing important details. This study aims to bridge the gaps in inheritance research across the divides between the HB, the Second Temple period, and NT literature, by

---

[6]   See, for example, Anders Runesson, "Judging Gentiles in the Gospel of Matthew: Between 'Othering' and Inclusion," in *Jesus, Matthew's Gospel and Early Christianity: Studies in Memory of Graham N. Stanton* (ed. Daniel M. Gurtner, Joel Willitts, and Richard A. Burridge; LNTS 435; London: Bloomsbury, 2011), 133–51.

[7]   Forman, *Politics*, 80–84, surveys just a few examples of Second Temple compositions over five short pages. Hester, *Paul's Concept*, 22–36, limits his discussion of the Hebrew Bible and Second Temple compositions to just eight pages each.

offering as full a treatment of inheritance as space will allow across the entire spectrum of compositions. On the one hand, this will allow for a more comprehensive analysis of the way that inheritance concepts were used and developed by Jewish writers over time and from the perspective of various Jewish traditions; on the other hand, it will open new perspectives on Matthew's own theology by giving attention to the history of an idea and its place within the First Gospel.

Second, very little sustained attention has been given to inheritance concepts in Second Temple literature, across the Apocrypha, Pseudepigrapha, and the Scrolls discovered at Qumran. This study aims to present a fairly comprehensive picture of inheritance throughout these categories of compositions in order to better understand the dynamics, developments, and perspectives regarding inheritance throughout the various compositions associated with these textual groupings. The goal is not only to understand how these Second Temple traditions may have impacted the perspective found in Matthew's Gospel, but also to appreciate inheritance in the Second Temple period for its own sake, and possibly to use Matthew to gain insights into inheritance retrospectively into the Second Temple period.

Third, by the very nature of a study such as this, an ending point and clear objective to the collection of texts with which the researcher chooses to engage is needed. The NT text that serves as the climax of this study is Matthew, for at least three reasons:

1) The Gospels present a narrative account of the beginnings of the story of Jesus and his people, and among the Gospels, Matthew is often considered to possess the greatest level of continuity with its Jewish milieu. Understanding inheritance concepts within Matthew might contribute to our understanding of this continuity or discontinuity in ways previously not explored in detail.

2) Explorations into Matthew's use of inheritance concepts is surprisingly lacking.

3) Inheritance concepts feature in passages in Matthew that are important to the ongoing debate regarding Jewish/gentile dynamics in the text, but very little has been said about how inheritance may contribute to understanding these dynamics.

Matthew's Gospel features inheritance language on four occasions (Matt 5:5; 19:29; 21:38; 25:34). The first occurrence appears in the famed beatitudes, where Jesus tells his disciples, "Flourishing are the meek, because they will inherit the earth." The first instance is possibly connected to the second, where Jesus refers to "the renewal of all things" (Matt 19:28) and promises that everyone who sacrifices for his sake "will inherit eternal life." The third and fourth occurrences appear in contexts that lie at the center of the debate regarding Jewish/gentile dynamics in Matthew. In the parable of the wicked tenants (Matt 21:38), the tenants conspire to kill the son of the vineyard owner and steal his inheritance. As a result, Jesus declares that these tenants will have the kingdom of God taken away from them and given to others. It is not too much to argue that the interpretation of this parable is the linchpin of the entire discussion regarding Jews and gentiles in Matthew. The final occurrence is found in the Judgment of the Nations (Matt 25:34), where some "inherit the kingdom," and others do not.

As this study suggests, each of the four instances of inheritance terms in Matthew feature in contexts that intersect with certain relevant themes that also feature in inheritance contexts throughout the HB and Second Temple compositions. These themes include the nature of wisdom and sapientially oriented compositions, apocalyptic motifs, the trajectories of the convergence between wisdom and apocalyptic,[8] God's

---

[8]   It is important to recognize that the entire concept of "genre," and in particular the genres of "wisdom" and "apocalypse," have been problematized and reconsidered in some recent scholarship. Some scholars prefer to understand wisdom and apocalyptic as "modes of discourse" rather than as strict genres of literature, understood through a text's use rather than its ideology, vocabulary, or thought structure. This is true not only of genres as they have been traditionally conceived but also of the use of Torah in certain texts, as Torah may have been understood by some ancient writers, especially in the Second Temple period, as modes of Mosaic discourse rather than the Pentateuch or other specific texts. For the purposes of this study, genre is understood loosely and with porous boundaries. Wisdom and apocalypse are viewed primarily as "themes," "traditions," and "modes of discourse," though it is recognized that literary genre is still a valid and useful way to discuss texts. Helpful in this regard is Hindy Najman, "The Idea of Biblical Genre: From Discourse to Constellation," in *Prayer and Poetry in the Dead Sea Scrolls and Related Literature* (ed. Jeremy Penner, Ken M. Penner, and Cecilia Wassen; STDJ 98; Leiden: Brill, 2012), 307–21, who concludes that genre is a useful classification tool but that, particularly in the Second Temple period, Jewish literature did not adhere to restrictive prototypes. For examples of these porous boundaries, see Hindy Najman, "Jewish Wisdom in the Hellenistic Period: Towards the Study of Semantic Constellation," in *Is There a Text in This Cave?* (ed. Ariel Feldman, Maria Cioata, and Charlotte Hempel; STDJ 119; Leiden: Brill, 2017), 459–72, who notes Second Temple compositions which feature wisdom, liturgical, apocalyptic, prophetic, and legal discourses within the same composition. For discussions regarding wisdom as genre, see Stuart Weeks, *An Introduction to the Study of Wisdom Literature* (London: T&T Clark, 2010), 3–5, and Tremper Longman III, *The Fear of the Lord Is Wisdom: A Theological Introduction to Wisdom in Israel* (Grand Rapids: Baker Academic, 2017), 276–82. For a defense of "apocalypse" as a genre, see John J. Collins, *The Apocalyptic Imagination: An Introduction to Jewish Apocalyptic Literature* (Grand Rapids: Eerdmans, 2016), 1–17.

role as a father to his people, and as stated previously, the development of the dynamics between Israelites/Jews and gentiles. Before investigating inheritance terms directly, it is helpful to offer here a brief overview of these themes in Matthew. This overview provides a framework for many of the themes that frequently intersect with inheritance concepts throughout Jewish literature. Furthermore, explicit treatment of these themes anticipates the direction of analysis present in conclusions from this study, and in particular, discussions as found in chapter 5 regarding inheritance terms in Matthew.

1.1. Matthew and Sapiential Traditions

Ben Witherington III has argued that Matthew is best understood through "a complete sapiential reading" of the entire Gospel.[9] Witherington's proposal regarding a thoroughgoing sapiential reading of the text has been challenged as an overreading,[10] and some scholars have gone so far as to argue that wisdom is not an important theme in Matthew.[11] While many of the criticisms of Witherington's arguments are apt and provide a helpful caution against reading the entire Gospel as a "sapiential text," most scholars agree that Matthew makes extensive use of sapiential elements and that these elements are prominent enough to establish a point of connection with antecedent Jewish wisdom literature.[12] Key to Matthew's structure are its five major teaching blocks (5-7; 10; 13; 18; 23-25). Discipleship, or the teacher/student relationship, is an important theme throughout Matthew (e.g., Matt 10), as is the passing on of instruction related to ethics and deeds (e.g., Matt 5:19). Frequently noted is the way that Matthew refers to Jesus as wisdom

---

[9]   Ben Witherington III, *Matthew* (Macon, Ga.: Smyth & Helwys, 2006), 17. Every major section of Witherington's commentary argues for a sapiential background to the content of the Matthean passages discussed.

[10]   For an evaluation of Witherington's proposal, see Grant Macaskill, *Revealed Wisdom and Inaugurated Eschatology in Ancient Judaism and Early Christianity* (Leiden: Brill, 2007), 253–58.

[11]   See, for example, Celia Deutsch, *Lady Wisdom, Jesus, and the Sages: Metaphor and Social Context in Matthew's Gospel* (Valley Forge, Pa.: Trinity Press International, 1996).

[12]   See the brief review of Witherington's arguments by Daniel M. Gurtner, "The Gospel of Matthew from Stanton to Present: A Survey of Some Research Developments," in Gurtner et al., *Jesus, Matthew's Gospel and Early Christianity*, 36, who states that Witherington overplays his hand at times but that his scope is "breathtaking" and that his argument requires scholars to consider the implications of wisdom when deciding what type of document Matthew's writer intended to write.

personified (Matt 11:19),[13] followed by striking linguistic and thematic parallels between Jesus' instruction on the light burden of his teaching yoke in Matt 11:25-30 and the wisdom imagery found in Sir 51:23-30.[14] The sapiential emphasis in Matthew provides an important point of connection to relevant wisdom-themed compositions among Matthew's antecedent literature where inheritance terms are used.[15]

1.2. Matthew and "Apocalyptic"

There is wide scholarly agreement that Matthew makes use of apocalyptic elements. In fact, these elements are more common in Matthew than in the other Gospels, and when comparing parallel material with Mark, Matthew tends to heighten the apocalyptic language. There has been debate on defining the parameters of what constitutes "apocalyptic," both in Matthew and more broadly, and this has led to discussion regarding how prevalent apocalyptic elements are in Matthew, as well as regarding the function of such elements, the reasons for their use, and the antecedent traditions that may have led to Matthew's linguistic choices.[16]

Of particular concern has been the use of terms to describe the nature of apocalyptic material in a given composition. For example, it is widely agreed that Matthew is not an "apocalypse" in the proper sense of that term but that the Gospel features extensive use of apocalyptic

[13]   So John Kampen, "Aspects of Wisdom in the Gospel of Matthew in Light of the New Qumran Evidence," in *Sapiential, Liturgical and Poetical Texts from Qumran* (ed. Daniel K. Falk, Florentino García Martínez, and Eileen Schuller; Leiden: Brill, 2000), 236, who states, "Wisdom here is clearly identified with Jesus the man who performed these deeds. In this case Jesus is not portrayed as an exponent of or envoy for wisdom but is rather wisdom herself." See also Celia Deutsch, "Wisdom in Matthew: Transformation of a Symbol," *NovT* 32 (1990): 13–47, who argues that in Matthew Jesus takes the place of Lady Wisdom. Deutsch notes the significance of Matthew's transformation of the imaginary woman of the wisdom myth into a historical figure, Jesus. She argues that Matthew identifies Jesus with Lady Wisdom because he perceives that "many of the elements in the wisdom myth describe Jesus, his deeds and teaching."

[14]   Though not all accept the parallel. See, for example, the survey in Stanton, *Gospel*, 366–77.

[15]   See also M. Jack Suggs, *Wisdom, Christology and Law in Matthew's Gospel* (Cambridge, Mass.: Harvard University Press, 1970), one of the earliest and most influential extensive treatments of the sapiential aspects of Matthew.

[16]   See Donald A. Hagner, "Apocalyptic Motifs in the Gospel of Matthew: Continuity and Discontinuity," *HBT* 7, no. 2 (1985): 60–68, who demonstrates that apocalyptic motifs and language are present throughout every major section of Matthew, even in sections not traditionally considered to be apocalyptic in nature. David C. Sim, *Apocalyptic Eschatology in the Gospel of Matthew* (Cambridge: Cambridge University Press, 1996), 6–7, gives a brief overview of scholars who have downplayed the importance of both apocalypticism and eschatology in Matthew.

themes, motifs, and language. Furthermore, some scholars have argued that the social setting of the writer(s) and readers/hearers of Matthew formed an apocalyptically oriented community, which helps to explain why Matthew features more focused use of apocalyptic elements than the other Gospels.[17] There are ongoing discussions regarding each of these aspects, but the overall observation made by such debates is an important one: apocalyptic material is often found in texts and compositions not considered to be "apocalypses." Furthermore, apocalyptic is not, as some assume, limited to end-time, eschatological concerns, but rather makes use of a vast plurality of ideas and motifs.[18] In other words, apocalyptic categories for texts and communities are complex and multifaceted, so the terms used to explain this complexity must be carefully used and explained.

One often-used paradigm features a distinction between three key terms and the concepts they function to represent: *apocalypses, apocalypticism*, and *apocalyptic*. The term *apocalypse* refers to the literary phenomenon (often classified as a genre) that was prominent between 200 B.C.E and 200 C.E. Apocalypses are often understood to contain interpretations of earthly circumstances in light of the supernatural world, with an eye toward the future, and often contain (but are not limited to) ethical requirements for the faithful, sectarian language,[19]

---

[17]   The most thorough treatment of a socioreligious approach to apocalyptic in Matthew is Sim, *Apocalyptic Eschatology*, who argues that apocalyptic ideas in the text, as well as the fact that Matthew makes more frequent use of these ideas than the other Gospels, is best explained by an apocalypticism movement involved in the creation of the text. According to Sim, Matthew's apocalyptic worldview is distinctive and comprehensive and would have derived from a community rife with apocalyptic expectation.

[18]   Scholars frequently insist upon the need to distinguish consistently between "eschatology" and "apocalyptic," recognizing that eschatology is one aspect of an apocalyptic worldview but that apocalyptic is far more multifaceted than end-time concerns, and some apocalyptically oriented compositions make little use of explicitly eschatological themes. For comments on the distinction, see Daniel M. Gurtner, "Interpreting Apocalyptic Symbolism in the Gospel of Matthew," *BBR* 22, no. 4 (2012): 530. See also Christopher Rowland, "Apocalyptic, the Poor, and the Gospel of Matthew," *JTS* 45, no. 2 (1994): 505, who argues that too much is made of eschatology as an aspect of apocalyptic. He states, "Apocalyptic is not only about the end of the world, neither is it mere prediction. Of course, it speaks about the future, but it is a future—as well as a present—viewed in the light of the God who now reigns and will be seen to reign on earth."

[19]   The term "sectarian" is controversial, as is the relationship of sectarianism (however defined) to apocalypses. The link between apocalypses and sectarian social movements was made due to the nature of many apocalyptically oriented texts, based on the need of marginalized groups to critique the present and provide hopeful expressions for the future. However, scholars have recognized that apocalyptic material cannot be explicitly linked to protest movements, and such material was used by a plurality of communities and in a variety of different subjects and literary genres. See Christopher Rowland, "Apocalypticism," in *The Eerdmans Dictionary of Early*

various forms of dualism, a strong sense of "in-group" identity, and a particular view of divine revelation. The term *apocalypticism* describes the socioreligious aspect of communities. Rather than compositions, it refers to the groups of people who are formed by a common identity and interpretation of reality based on their view of God, the world, and divine revelation. The term *apocalyptic* refers to the worldview espoused by communities and in compositions. Rather than communities or the compositions they produce, apocalyptic is a term used to refer to the ideas themselves—theological perspectives held by the apocalyptically oriented communities, some of which produce apocalypses in order to codify their apocalyptic perspectives.[20] A vast number of proposals have been put forward describing the ideas that are most indispensable to an apocalyptic worldview, and space precludes a detailed account of these proposals. Concepts frequently argued for include criteria for judgment,[21] a reinforcement of group identity,[22] paraenesis against theological opponents, an emphasis of God's determination over the course of human events, various forms of dualism, the influence on the supernatural upon earthly circumstances, the fates of the wicked and the righteous, privileged revelation from God, and the imminence of the end.[23]

One important aspect of apocalyptic that receives very little attention, but is important for the use of inheritance concepts in apocalyptic literature, is an increasingly universal perspective on the coming salvation. Donald Hagner notes the use of this theme, arguing that in much Jewish apocalyptic material gentile inclusion comes into view through access to the elect community of Jews.[24] Hagner notes the use of this theme in Matthew in particular, but as we shall see in this study, gentile inclusion becomes prominent in much of the eschatological material of

---

Judaism (ed. John J. Collins and Daniel C. Harlow; Grand Rapids: Eerdmans, 2010), 345–48. Issues regarding the use of "sectarian" as an identifier are addressed throughout this study, particularly in chs. 1 and 4.

[20]   For an influential account of the terms, and defense of "apocalypse" as a genre, see Collins, *Apocalyptic Imagination*, 1–17. See also the discussion in Klaus Koch, "What Is Apocalyptic? An Attempt at a Preliminary Definition," in *Visionaries and their Apocalypses* (ed. Paul D. Hanson; London: SPCK, 1983), 16–36, on the problem with terms and the difference between apocalypse as a literary type and apocalyptic as a social movement.

[21]   Especially Daniel Marguerat, *Le Jugement dans l'Evangile de Matthieu* (Geneva: Labor et Fides, 1981).

[22]   See Hagner, "Apocalyptic Motifs," 58–59.

[23]   See Gunter Bornkamm, "End-Expectation and Church in Matthew," in *Tradition and Interpretation in Matthew* (ed. G. Bornkamm, G. Barth, and H. J. Held; London: SCM, 1963), 15–51.

[24]   Hagner, "Apocalyptic Motifs," 59.

the Latter Prophets of the HB, as well as apocalyptic material found in compositions such as the Book of the Watchers and the apocalyptically oriented aspects of 4QInstruction. This does not lessen the strong sense of in-group identity, but it does reconstitute the parameters of who can belong to the group. In Matthew in particular, Hagner notes that the Jewish-Christian community thought of themselves as a remnant demonstrating a particular commitment to God but that the salvation brought by God would concern the entire world. This study explores the ways that inheritance terms in Matthew illustrate this perspective.

Not all scholars are happy with the terms *apocalypse*, *apocalypticism*, and *apocalyptic*.[25] Some have argued against the very idea of using apocalyptic content to categorize texts into an apocalyptic "genre."[26] Although some of the criticisms against these terms, and against the genre of apocalypse, are valid, more satisfactory alternatives have yet to be presented or widely accepted, and these categories have merit in clarifying the complexity of the ideas that must be considered when making sense of apocalyptic compositions, communities, and ideas. Even if these terms and distinctions are to be accepted, David Sim is correct to caution against a necessary relationship between each of these categories. Sim argues that apocalyptic socioreligious movements are necessarily tied to apocalyptic worldviews, but this connection does not necessitate that communities with such perspectives be tied to compositions of the apocalypse genre, even as they may be responsible for compositions of other genres. He notes in particular that the community that made use of the Qumran site is thought to be, in some fashion, an apocalyptically oriented community, with apocalyptic worldviews, but while it collected and made use of apocalypses (e.g., Daniel, 1 Enoch), it likely did not produce an apocalypse of its own but used other literary forms to express its own theological convictions.[27] This observation is important for any discussion of apocalyptic material in Matthew. Some scholars have argued that every major section of the Gospel makes use of at least some apocalyptic literary features or theological perspectives, but the Gospel as a whole is not an apocalypse.[28] Furthermore, caution must be

[25]   See the critique in Sim, *Apocalyptic Eschatology*, 26–31, who argues that the cognate relationship of the terms implies a more necessary relationship between them than the evidence requires, which is bound to lead toward confusion. Sim highlights possible areas of confusion but does not propose a more appropriate set of terms.

[26]   See the review in Collins, *Apocalyptic Imagination*, 11–14.

[27]   This study recognizes that the relationship between the community that made use of the Qumran site, and the compositions often associated with them, is a matter of considerable debate. This will be addressed in detail in ch. 4.

[28]   See Gurtner, "Interpreting Apocalyptic," 531, who argues that apocalyptic elements permeate Matthew in a variety of literary forms, including pronouncement

observed even regarding Sim's argument that apocalyptic views must have a necessary relationship with an apocalyptically oriented socioreligious movement. For his own part, Sim bases his argument regarding apocalyptic features in Matthew on sociological explanations regarding the community to which the Gospel was written, and his understanding of the community is in large part based on his analysis of the material in the text. His argument of a necessary connection between apocalyptic ideas and a community who espouses them allows him to use the material to construct such a community. Other scholars have pointed out the speculative nature of such an enterprise.[29] Principally, not all scholars are convinced of the existence of a "Matthean community" in the first place, and if one existed it seems difficult to arrive at any sure judgments regarding that community from mining the text for certain features and assuming their direct relevance to the life and inner workings of that community. There are other possibilities, such as appealing to and applying antecedent literary traditions and linguistic features, as well as semiotics.[30] It stands to reason that, if the writer(s) behind Matthew's

---

stories, miracle stories, discipleship instructions, and more. Although Matthew features apocalyptic themes and motifs, scholars are agreed that the Gospel as a whole is not best described as an apocalypse. Prior to the twentieth century, many scholars described the Gospels as biographies of Jesus. In the early twentieth century, many scholars rejected this view due to the kerygmatic nature of the compositions, but recently, multiple scholars have reverted to the older view in a growing consensus that understands the Gospels as examples of Greco-Roman biography. See Richard A. Burridge, *What Are the Gospels? A Comparison with Graeco-Roman Biography* (Cambridge: Cambridge University Press, 1992); David E. Aune, "Greco-Roman Biography," in *Greco-Roman Literature and the New Testament: Selected Form and Genres* (ed. David E. Aune; Atlanta: Scholars Press, 1988), 107–26; Dale C. Allison Jr., *Studies in Matthew: Interpretation Past and Present* (Grand Rapids: Baker Academic, 2005), 142–55; and Stanton, *Gospel*, 59–71. While the parallels between the Gospels and Greco-Roman biographies are striking, Donald A. Hagner, *The New Testament: A Historical and Theological Introduction* (Grand Rapids: Baker Academic, 2012), 211–12, lists other possibilities and reasonably concludes that Matthew's Gospel contains a "multifaceted character," meaning that several ancient genres are equally incorporated into the First Evangelist's approach.

[29]   See, for example, Gurtner, "Interpreting Apocalyptic," 529–31, who critiques Sim's sociological approach on grounds that it speculates, rather than proves, that a Matthean community actually existed. Gurtner argues that rather than sociological explanations based on a possible community behind or in front of the text, apocalyptic in Matthew is best analyzed through narrative features within the text as well as its use of antecedent Jewish literary traditions. Apocalyptic material in Matthew is driven by making use of Jewish literary traditions to take advantage of the use of symbols in order to provide "some explanation or commentary on narrative events where a simple narrative description does not suffice."

[30]   See Rowlands, "Apocalyptic," who throughout his article appeals to antecedent Jewish traditions in order to explain Matthew's use of apocalyptic phrases and motifs.

Gospel was convinced that God had acted in a definitive way in Jesus, then a wide array of Jewish literary and textual traditions, linguistic features, theological motifs, and signs and symbols might be employed in order to communicate this to Jewish Christians. If God's definitive act in Jesus proposed a change to the present age that was influenced by otherworldly and eschatological realities, and the teaching of Jesus was understood to contain apocalyptic elements, then apocalyptic material being present in such an account is to be expected even if no apocalypticism movement stood in front of or behind the text.[31] As it stands, settling the debate regarding a possible apocalypticism movement as a "Matthean community" is not necessary for this study, as the focus here is on regarding only the potential influences on Matthew from its antecedent literature. It is important to recognize that such a community may have existed, and may explain much of the apocalyptic material in the Gospel, but that the establishment of a sociological profile for the community is not the only way to account for apocalyptic material in Matthew. The important thing here is simply to recognize that scholars are largely in agreement that Matthew features apocalyptic themes, motifs, and language. This study seeks to highlight the ways that a wide array of Jewish apocalyptic material features inheritance concepts, and chapter 5 is devoted to the ways that apocalyptic material intersects with inheritance concepts in Matthew's Gospel.

1.3. Trajectories within Second Temple Literature

It is widely accepted that Jewish literature from the Second Temple period influenced the writers, editors, and compilers of NT literature in various ways.[32] Although this reality needs little defense, it is helpful

---

[31] The nature of the teaching of the historical Jesus is a matter of considerable debate, and the literature on this debate is extensive. Such a debate is beyond the scope of this study, but many scholars have argued for an extensive use of apocalyptic material in Jesus' teaching. For a thorough account, see Dale C. Allison Jr., *Constructing Jesus: Memory, Imagination, and History* (Grand Rapids: Baker Academic, 2010).

[32] Though this recognition is not universally accepted. See, for example, Sungho Choi, *The Messianic Kingship of Jesus: A Study of Christology and Redemptive History in Matthew's Gospel with Special Reference to the Royal-Enthronement Psalms* (Eugene, Ore.: Wipf & Stock, 2011), 12–15, 34–35, who argues that extrabiblical sources from the Second Temple period are unreliable for the study of Matthew's Gospel. Choi argues that Second Temple literature is invaluable for understanding that period of Jewish history but that, despite some parallel use of language between Second Temple sources and NT sources, their theological and thematic contexts were far too divergent to be helpful. Choi argues that Second Temple Judaism and the writings of the NT show an "undoubtedly different theological ethos." He points specifically to the fact that Matthew never quotes extrabiblical sources in the way that he does biblical ones and argues that the

here to briefly highlight ways that Second Temple literature has been understood to have influenced the content of Matthew's Gospel.

A number of scholars have surveyed the ways that the Qumran Scrolls intersect with Matthew's Gospel and the life and teaching of Jesus.[33] Some of Jesus' words and deeds closely echo his contemporary Jewish teachings and practices, many of which appear in the Qumran Scrolls.[34] Much has been written regarding the possible connection between 4QBeatitudes and Matthew's beatitudes in Matt 5:3-12,[35] but there are other similarities besides. Richard Horsley argues that the primary parallels between the Scrolls and the NT texts regard the nature of the communities that produced them.[36] Although there are many differences between these communities, they share a number of common features that are unique enough to be suggestive of some manner of influence or shared thought-world. Horsley points specifically to the manner of protest and renewal apparent in both the Qumran community and the earliest Christians.[37] Both communities longed for fulfillment and wholeness, both incorporated community meals as acts of anticipation, both thought of themselves as engaged in a new Exodus and renewed Mosaic covenant, and both believed that they were fulfilling Isaianic prophecies. Both communities had a sense that God's decisive new action meant that a new age was imminent or at hand, and both responded to this belief with a renewed dedication to the covenant law.[38]

Dead Sea compositions are irrelevant due to their sectarian nature. I seek to demonstrate the following in this project: 1) a lack of direct citation has more to do with authority than it does influence and does not rule out influence and trajectory that contributes to a fuller understanding of Matthew, 2) Matthew's use of inheritance terms was undoubtedly influenced by the thought-world of the Second Temple period, and 3) the Dead Sea Scrolls were, in many instances, far less sectarian (and therefore more influential to the wider Jewish thought-world) than is often recognized by many NT scholars.

[33]   George J. Brooke, *The Dead Sea Scrolls and the New Testament* (London: SPCK, 2005), 20–24, helpfully lists the major ways that scholars have understood this intersection.

[34]   For example, Craig A. Evans, "The Synoptic Gospels and the Dead Sea Scrolls," in *The Bible and the Dead Sea Scrolls*, vol. 3: *The Scrolls and Christian Origins* (ed. James H. Charlesworth; Waco, Tex.: Baylor University Press, 2006), 75, states "All of the major themes or emphases in the Synoptics have close parallels in the Scrolls."

[35]   See ch. 5 of the present study.

[36]   Richard A. Horsley, "The Dead Sea Scrolls and the Historical Jesus," in Charlesworth, *The Bible and the Dead Sea Scrolls*, 3:37–60.

[37]   The present study recognizes that many scholars reject the idea that there was a singular community behind either the Qumran Scrolls or Matthew's Gospel. The potential for a Matthean community will be discussed in chs. 1 and 5. The problem of a singular Qumran community will be discussed in the introduction to ch. 4.

[38]   Horsley, "Dead Sea Scrolls," 44, points specifically to Matthew's Sermon on the Mount as an example.

In Horsley's view, both communities were anti-temple and dedicated to the renewal of Israel over against the temple and the high priesthood.[39] Horsley is careful to point out that these striking similarities often manifested themselves in different ways within these communities, but he argues that as long as the differences are kept in mind as a caution against overstating the case regarding possible direct influences, there are enough important parallels for the Qumran Scrolls to be instructive for understanding the teaching of Jesus and the Gospel traditions.[40]

Craig Evans demonstrates, in contrast to Mark and Luke, that Matthew is particularly fond of righteousness and its word group, and many of Matthew's uses of righteousness terms have close linguistic and theological parallels in the Scrolls.[41] Evans points out that the use of righteousness in Matthew also intersects with the evangelist's understanding of Scripture and fulfillment motifs, commenting that Matthew's hermeneutics of fulfillment are similar enough to those found in many of the Qumran Scrolls that comparisons between them are fruitful. The parallels regarding fulfillment hermeneutics have also been discussed by Loren Stuckenbruck, who notes the similar reading strategies of Matthew's Gospel with various compositions found at Qumran.[42] As

---

[39]   In recent scholarship there have been some attempts to establish that Jesus and the earliest Christians were pro-temple and continued to worship in the temple regularly. John W. Welch, *The Sermon on the Mount in the Light of the Temple* (Farnham: Ashgate, 2009), 42, argues for a "temple register" detectable throughout the Sermon on the Mount and that Jesus' declaration that he did not come to abolish the law but to fulfill it (Matt 5:17) includes pro-temple sentiment. The most recent example of this approach is Paula Fredriksen, *When Christians Were Jews: The First Generation* (New Haven: Yale University Press, 2018), 97, 123–25. Fredriksen addresses a number of passages in the NT that imply positive attitudes (or at least not overtly negative ones) toward the temple. However, she often overstates the positive stance toward the temple within these passages and ignores equally clear passages that feature overt criticism of the temple. For example, Fredriksen refers to Acts 2:46, which states that early Christians were "attending the temple daily and breaking bread in their homes," as evidence that temple worship continued as normal for the early Christian community. Commenting on this same passage, Horsley, "Dead Sea Scrolls," 48, convincingly argues that it hardly suggests "regular sacrificing and prayers" in the temple. Instead, the temple would have been the obvious place where the earliest disciples of Jesus would have gone to expand their movement by spreading the word about the renewal of Israel. In fact, it can be argued that criticism of the temple would make it an ideal place to proclaim a renewal movement.

[40]   One important difference pointed out by Horsley, "Dead Sea Scrolls," 50, considers the approach of each community to purity in light of their views toward renewal. The Qumran community intensified their concern for purity, whereas the Palestinian Jesus movement in many ways resisted the purity system in place in their towns and villages.

[41]   Evans, "Synoptic Gospels," 84–89.

[42]   Loren T. Stuckenbruck, "The Dead Sea Scrolls and the New Testament," in *Qumran and the Bible: Studying the Jewish and Christian Scriptures in Light of the*

a prime example, Stuckenbruck notes that both the *pesharim* and Matthew's Gospel relate their reading on the biblical tradition to a key figure that they believed was endowed with teaching authority: the Teacher of Righteousness in the case of the *pesharim*, and Jesus in the case of Matthew. Claims made about these central figures were bound up in the interpretation of authoritative texts whose initial contexts were not bound up with these figures. Instead, these interpretive strategies offer a cultural memory of these key figures to the followers they inspired. This extends beyond these figures to others associated with them. The *pesharim* relates sacred texts to figures such as the Wicked Priest, the Man of Lies, the Seekers of Truth, and others, while Matthew relates sacred texts to the twelve disciples, John the Baptist, Jesus' opponents, and others. The point of this example is not to attempt to draw parallels between Jesus and the Teacher of Righteousness but rather to suggest that the fulfillment hermeneutics of various Qumran Scrolls can shed light on the reading strategies found in Matthew's Gospel.[43]

Stuckenbruck also points to a number of instructions in various Qumran Scrolls that compare positively to many of the teachings of Jesus, such as their similar views on divorce, prohibitions against oath-taking, their exclusive use of the unique phrase "humble/poor in spirit,"[44] and similar approaches to intertextual interpretation of common passages such as Isa 61.[45] These comparisons are not strong enough to suggest direct literary dependence, but they do suggest a common thought-world by demonstrating that Jesus was concerned with similar issues to those posed by the Qumran Scrolls.[46] Although direct literary dependence between the Scrolls and Matthew is difficult to establish,

---

Dead Sea Scrolls (ed. Nóra Dávid and Armin Lange; Leuven: Peeters, 2010), 141–45. Stuckenbruck follows the well-known work of Krister Stendahl, who argued that Matthew's fulfillment hermeneutics were influenced by the interpretive methods found in the Qumran *pesharim*, though Stuckenbruck argues that these interpretive strategies can be found in Qumran texts other than *pesharim* and reflect a strategy that "was more widespread and, in any case, not confined to a particular genre."

[43]   Stuckenbruck, "Dead Sea Scrolls," 145.

[44]   See 1QM XIV 7; 1QH[a] VI 3; Matt 5:3.

[45]   Stuckenbruck, "Dead Sea Scrolls," 150–55.

[46]   Stuckenbruck, "Dead Sea Scrolls," 157, is careful to note differences, even to the degree where teaching appears to be in opposition to one another. One example he provides regards teaching concerned with finances and investment. Jesus' parable of the talents, although not about money per se, makes use of financial investment strategies to make a point about the kingdom of God. Investment appears cast in a positive light, which is also affirmed in the book of Tobit (1:14; 4:1-2). In the Scrolls however, in 4Q416 2 iii 3–5, the addressee is instructed that if he is given money, he should put it away and therefore be free of responsibility to it. There is no reason to suggest that Jesus was reacting to this passage in particular, but their approaches in this regard are very different.

such dependence is not necessary in order to establish influence in other ways, such as trajectories of themes and genres, as well as contributions to a common thought-world that would have impacted meaning and linguistic choices. Parallels are therefore mutually instructive for interpretation of texts and for understanding the development of both Jewish and early Christian thought.[47] As Evans reminds, these parallels are also close enough to suggest that the ideas found in the Qumran Scrolls are not as sectarian as is often assumed. Evans states, "Just as the parallels draw the Gospels back to Jewish Palestine, so also the parallels pull the Scrolls closer to mainstream Jewish ideas."[48]

One of the most important points of connection between the Second Temple literature and Matthew concerns the trajectory of sapiential and apocalyptic themes in Jewish compositions. For example, John Kampen notes the trajectory of the personification of wisdom. A prominent feature of Prov 1–9, personification is also taken up in Sir 51:23-27 and certain Qumran compositions such as the so-called 4QWiles of the Wicked Woman. While these compositions present wisdom personified as an agent of creation and something to be pursued, Kampen argues that Matthew develops this a step further, presenting Jesus to his community of followers not only as wisdom personified but also the hermeneutical principle for wisdom's own interpretation.[49] Kampen is careful to state that the evidence is not specific enough to suggest that Matthew is developing themes in direct interaction with these antecedent compositions, but there is enough evidence to suggest a mutual understanding of the trajectory and development of these themes over time.

The Second Temple period also saw a convergence of sapiential and apocalyptic material within certain compositions, which has led to an extensive body of literature analyzing the nature of the relationship of these themes to one another. For example, the compositions of 1 Enoch and 4QInstruction have often been compared to one another for their use of themes and certain linguistic features.[50] 1 Enoch has been regarded as an apocalyptic composition with strong sapiential elements, while

---

[47]   Stuckenbruck, "Dead Sea Scrolls," 170, states, "New Testament studies concerned with Jewish tradition cannot ignore the Scrolls without cutting out what has become both an essential source of information and launching ground for new and focused questions."

[48]   Evans, "Synoptic Gospels," 95. This issue will be discussed in detail in ch. 4.

[49]   Kampen, "Aspects of Wisdom," 236–38.

[50]   See, for example, Macaskill, *Revealed Wisdom*, who places 1 Enoch and 4QInstruction in conversation with Matthew and 2 Enoch. See also Loren T. Stuckenbruck, "4QInstruction and the Possible Influence of Early Enochic Traditions: An Evaluation," in *Wisdom Texts from Qumran and the Development of Sapiential Thought* (Leuven: Leuven University Press, 2002), 245–62.

4QInstruction has been regarded as a sapiential composition with an apocalyptic worldview. As Grant Macaskill argues, Matthew is the NT text that most exemplifies the convergence of wisdom and apocalyptic themes.[51] While Matthew is not principally understood as either a sapiential or apocalyptic text, both of these themes feature prominently, and it can be argued that Matthew represents a Jewish-Christian stage in the trajectory and development of the convergence of these themes in Jewish texts.[52] It is not only the case that Matthew, as a text, features both sapiential and apocalyptic elements, but there are pericopes in Matthew where these two converge. Matthew 11:25-30, often regarded as the primary wisdom passage in the Gospel, features the apocalyptic motif of hidden wisdom and special revelation. Only those who receive access to this revelation can know God's Son.[53] Wisdom and apocalyptic also converge in the beatitudes (Matt 5:3-12), a passage that features inheritance terminology. Beatitudes are, as a literary feature, largely regarded as sapiential, but Matthew's beatitudes are at once the declaration of a present reality and also "the promise of a reversal of the present order" through the use of future tense in the second clause of each beatitude.[54] The beatitudes make use of in-group language and an awareness of persecution, a promise of judgment and reward (Matt 5:10-12), and lead into descriptions of criteria

[51]   Macaskill, *Revealed Wisdom*, 15.

[52]   Relevant to Matthew's role in this trajectory is Matthew Goff's analysis of the convergence of wisdom and apocalyptic elements in the hypothetical sayings source Q, and the role of 4QInstruction in understanding the nature of this convergence. Goff addresses the view of some Q scholars that the wisdom and apocalyptic elements of such a collection of sayings would represent two, unrelated strata of development from within the Jesus tradition. Goff argues that 4QInstruction is a wisdom text with an apocalyptic worldview and that these elements were not developed as separate stages in the production of the composition but were incorporated together in the writing of the material as developments of both the sapiential and apocalyptic literary traditions as they were brought to bear upon one another. According to Goff, this lends support to the idea that it is unnecessary to propose that wisdom and apocalyptic in the Jesus traditions should be kept separate, as the convergence of these traditions in Q, or in the Gospels more widely, would best be understood as a further development of the convergence of these traditions that began centuries before the writing of the Gospel accounts. See Matthew J. Goff, "Discerning Trajectories: 4QInstruction and the Sapiential Background of the Sayings Source Q," *JBL* 124, no. 4 (2005): 657–73. In this study I affirm Goff's conclusions, with one important difference. Goff argues that there is a difference between 4QInstruction and Q in their eschatological presentations, as 4QInstruction features an entirely future eschatology in contrast to realized elements in Q. In ch. 4 I will explore 4QInstruction's eschatology in relation to inheritance terms and argue that Goff has missed important elements of realized eschatology in the composition. Macaskill, *Revealed Wisdom*, 229, also sees inaugurated eschatology as an aspect of 4QInstruction, though he discusses this under different themes than those explored in this study.

[53]   See Gurtner, "Interpreting Apocalyptic," 535.

[54]   See Hagner, "Apocalyptic Motifs," 64.

for judgment (Matt 5:19). In fact, much of the ethical instruction of the Sermon on the Mount is rife with apocalyptic language. Important for this study is the phrase "inherit the earth" in Matt 5:5, which is found in apocalyptic contexts in 1 Enoch and possibly 4QInstruction. The potential for a wisdom-apocalyptic trajectory between 1 Enoch, 4QInstruction, and Matthew is analyzed in chapters 3, 4, and 5.

1.4. God as Father

Explicit references to God as Father are infrequent in the HB (cf. Deut 32:4-6; Isa 63:16, 64:8; Jer 31:9). When such references appear, the principal concept is God's fatherhood over corporate Israel, a concept that is compounded implicitly by references to Israel as God's son (cf. Exod 4:22-23; Jer 3:19; 1 Kgs 8:36; Isa 61:7-9). Less frequently, God is also referred to as a father to the king of Israel (2 Sam 7:12-14). Despite the infrequency of references, Marianne Meye Thompson has argued persuasively that God as Father was an important concept to the ancient Israelites and that such a designation served to highlight three key activities of God in relation to his people. First, God as Father is the head of the clan or family of Israel and therefore Israel's chief ancestor. As such, it is God who is responsible to provide an *inheritance* to his heirs. Second, God the Father is one who cares for his children and provides for their protection and security. Third, God the Father is a figure of authority who must be honored and obeyed.[55] Although God is described as a father to Israel's king, Thompson argues that the concept of God as Father is primarily corporate, referring to his actions toward a people whom he creates and treats in a special way among the whole of humanity.[56]

References to God as Father are far more ubiquitous in the NT, especially in the Gospels (Matthew 44x, Mark 4x, Luke 17x, John 109x), where Matthew's portrayal of the concept stands out among the Synoptics.[57] Thompson argues that the portrayal of God as Father in the NT

---

[55]   Marianne Meye Thompson, *The Promise of the Father: Jesus and God in the New Testament* (Louisville: Westminster John Knox, 2000), 18.

[56]   Thompson, *Promise*, 20. See also Bruce Chilton, "God as 'Father' in the Targumim, in Non-Canonical Literatures of Early Judaism and Primitive Christianity, and in Matthew," in *The Pseudepigrapha and Early Biblical Interpretation* (ed. James H. Charlesworth and Craig A. Evans; JSPS 14; Sheffield: Sheffield Academic, 1993), 151–69, who argues that, in the Pseudepigrapha and Targumim, God was known as Father largely for the purposes of prayer and the dynamics of two-way discussion and relationship between God and his people.

[57]   For a source-critical analysis of God as Father in the Gospels, and a brief analysis of differences between the Gospels in their presentation of this theme, see H. F. D.

is far more continuous with the depiction found in the HB and Second Temple literature than it is discontinuous and that the three key activities of God as Father that she establishes for the HB are all still vital to the NT's portrayal.[58] Regarding Matthew in particular, Jonathan Pennington has argued that Jesus' depiction of God as Father in the First Gospel communicates the need on the part of Jesus' disciples for dependence upon God, affectionate intimacy, and obedience. God as Father in Matthew is a relational and identity term for Jesus, who consistently refers to God as "my Father," as well as for Jesus' disciples, to whom Jesus refers to God as "your Father."[59] Pennington refers to this as "insider language" that distinguishes Jesus and God's people from all others.[60] Throughout the Gospel Jesus and his disciples use God as Father as a motivating concept for their actions and sense of unity, and God as Father "in heaven" is consistently contrasted with the activities and identities of those on earth.[61] Donald A. Hagner notes the importance of God as "Father in heaven" for Matthew's Gospel when he argues that it is closely associated with Jesus' proclamation of the kingdom of God, which offers "the possibility of a new relationship with God." It brings about a new aspect of God's relationship with his people by simultaneously emphasizing the personal imminence of God as Father with the "otherness" of his heavenly nature.[62]

In chapter 5, more is said regarding the role of the "God as Father" concept in Matthew's Gospel, but it is important to establish here the particular relevance of this concept to "inheritance." Thompson emphasizes God's activity as the provider of an inheritance as a vital aspect of

---

Sparks, "The Doctrine of the Divine Fatherhood in the Gospels," in *Studies in the Gospels: Essays in Honor of R. H. Lightfoot* (ed. D. E. Nineham; Oxford: Basil Blackwell, 1967), 241–62.

[58]   Thompson, *Promise*, 19, 72. See also Jonathan T. Pennington, *Heaven and Earth in the Gospel of Matthew* (Grand Rapids: Baker Academic, 2009), 230, who agrees that there is greater continuity than discontinuity between the Hebrew Bible and the NT regarding God as Father but cautions that Jesus' usage of the concept, especially regarding his use of the phrase "my Father," does stand out as distinct. Pennington points out that there is no precedent for this exclusivity of usage.

[59]   See Stephen Westerholm, *Understanding Matthew: The Early Christian Worldview of the First Gospel* (Grand Rapids: Baker Academic, 2006), 113–17, who comments on God as Father as important to both Jesus and his disciples, while also distinguishing between the uniqueness of Jesus' personal address of God as "my Father" and the disciples' corporate identity as God's "children."

[60]   Pennington, *Heaven*, 250.

[61]   Jonathan T. Pennington, *The Sermon on the Mount and Human Flourishing: A Theological Commentary* (Grand Rapids: Baker Academic, 2017), 98–99.

[62]   Donald A. Hagner, *Matthew 1–13* (WBC 33A; Dallas: Word Books, 1993), 101.

his role as Father throughout the HB, Second Temple literature, and the NT. She goes on to argue that God as the giver of an inheritance makes the "God as Father" concept more ubiquitous than is usually argued, as the term for "father" need not be present to view God as Father in a given context. Anytime God is depicted providing an inheritance, one can argue that he does so as a father to his people even when he is not explicitly described as such.[63] This point is argued in detail throughout this study, with the aim to establish that inheritance concepts are vital to understanding the relationship between God and his people.

1.5. Israel, Church, Jews, and Gentiles

One of the most important scholarly debates regarding Matthew in recent years concerns the Gospel's presentation of the dynamics of the relationship between Jews and gentiles and the potential missions by Jesus' earliest followers to one or both of Israel and the other nations. The large number of questions concerning these issues has led to varying and often contradictory approaches among interpreters. These difficulties are illustrated by the near scholarly consensus that Matthew, across the full scope of the text, paints both a positive and negative picture of both Jews and gentiles. Often considered the most "Jewish" of the four Gospels, Matthew also submits piercing attacks against certain Jewish leaders.[64] Similarly, Matthew features material that portrays gentiles in a positive light and integrates them into important moments of the narrative,[65] and yet at other points gentile culture is set as an example to be avoided.[66] Matthew 10:5-6 portrays Jesus telling

---

[63]   Thompson, *Promise*, 39.

[64]   Matthew 23:1-36 functions as the climax of these attacks, but they are a consistent theme throughout the Gospel. See Matthias Konradt, *Israel, Church, and the Gentiles in the Gospel of Matthew* (Waco, Tex.: Baylor University Press, 2014), 101–66, who offers an extensive analysis of the conflict between Jesus and the Jewish authorities and demonstrates that these conflicts appear in every major section of Matthew. See also Reinhart Hummel, *Die Auseinandersetzung zwischen Kirche und Judentum im Matthäusevangelium* (Munich: Kaiser, 1963), 12–14.

[65]   See Donald Senior, "Between Two Worlds: Gentiles and Jewish Christians in Matthew's Gospel," *CBQ* 61, no. 1 (1999): 14–16, who details eighteen points at which gentiles are included in Matthew and argues that they appear in "every major segment of the gospel story." Although there are negative references to gentiles in Matthew, Senior argues that overall, the text's presentation of them is "positive and inclusive." See also Hagner, *Matthew*, lxvi, who details many moments of gentile inclusion in the narrative and argues that the theme of the kingdom of God is the key to a universalism throughout the text.

[66]   See, for example, Runesson, "Judging," 143, who states that "when non-Jewish culture and customs are addressed generally in the narrative, everything gentiles do must be shunned by Matthew's audience." Runesson notes anti-gentile sentiment in

his disciples to go nowhere among the gentiles and instead minister only to the "lost sheep of the house of Israel," while Matt 28:18-20 portrays Jesus sending out his disciples in order to make disciples of "all nations."[67]

How should we account for the seemingly divergent material? A number of scholars opt for socio-critical approaches in an attempt to reconstruct the Matthean community that may have either produced the text or been its intended audience. Other scholars favor intertextual and narrative approaches, arguing from Matthew's use of antecedent material and the flow of the arguments within the development of the text itself. These approaches seek to answer a number of important questions, such as:

• Was the Matthean community primarily Jewish, primarily gentile, or a blended community of both Jew and gentile?
• Did the Matthean community see itself as a messianic group from within Judaism, or had the community made a break with its Jewish associations and identities? In other words, do the conflicts within the Gospel describe those between two Jewish groups, or between Jews and Christians? Furthermore, did the Matthean community view themselves the same way they were viewed by others? If they viewed themselves as essentially a Jewish community, would other non-Christian Jews have accepted them as such?
• Does Matthew present "the church" as either a Jewish group, a replacement for Israel as the people of God, or something else entirely?
• How might the plurality of Judaism(s) in Matthew's time affect the way Jews are viewed in the Matthean narrative?
• Did a "Matthean community" actually exist, or was the Gospel written to be circulated to a wide group of people with broad and general applications?
• How can we reconcile the pro-Jewish and pro-gentile material with the material that is critical of those groups?
• What are we to make of the seemingly divergent missional statements by Jesus in 10:5-6 and 28:18-20? Did Jesus a) begin with a mission to Jews, only to replace it with a mission to gentiles? And if so, what motivated this shift? b) Expand the Jewish mission to

---

passages such as Matt 5:47; 6:7; 6:32; and 20:25-26 and notes that the text "others" even Jews who collaborate with gentiles (18:17).

[67]   Konradt, *Israel*, 1, opens his magisterial study of Matthew with the dilemma between Matt 10:5-6 and 28:18-20 and refers to this as "a central interpretive problem" for reading the whole Gospel.

include gentiles? c) Call for two distinct but complementary missions side by side, one to Jews and one to gentiles?

- Do Matthew's sharp criticisms of the Jewish leaders apply to those leadership groups alone, or do the Jewish leaders serve as ciphers for the whole of the Jewish people? In other words, does Matthew portray the Jewish leaders differently from "the crowds"?

Such a list of questions regarding this issue could be considerably longer, but these serve to illustrate the point: Matthew's portrayal of Jewish/gentile relations, and its portrayal of the nature of both Israel and the church in light of Jesus' ministry, is rather complicated, and these complications have led to understandably diverse reconstructions. Space here precludes a detailed account of the research that has been done regarding these issues in Matthew, but a brief sketch of representatives of some of the key ideas are indicative of the recent scholarly discussions.

Influential has been the work of Graham Stanton, who focuses largely on sociohistorical arguments. In Stanton's view, the Matthean communities have parted ways with Judaism and gentiles have already been accepted into these communities. He argues that Matthew features a rivalry between the church and the synagogue and that the Matthean communities arose out of God's rejection of Israel.[68] The evangelist considered his readers to be a blended community making up a "new people," or a "third race," over against both Jews and gentiles.[69] This largely accounts for the disparate portrayals of the missions given to Jesus' followers in 10:5-6 and 28:18-20. The mission of 10:5-6 was the original mission given to the disciples, but Jewish rejection of Jesus' messengers caused the original mission to be expanded into a gentile mission in 28:18-20.[70] The First Gospel is an apology of Christianity over/against Judaism, but Matthew's communities still hold on to hope that individual Jews will be converted.[71]

Stanton bases his view on a series of careful observations. First, he notes Matthew's sharp criticisms of the scribes and Pharisees and argues that these criticisms are evidence that there is a divide between church and synagogue. Second, Stanton argues that the worship and

---

[68]   Stanton, *Gospel*, 124.

[69]   Stanton, *Gospel*, 11–12. In agreement with Stanton is Pennington, *Sermon*, 96, who argues that Matthew has redefined the people of God in terms of faith response rather than ethnicity. Pennington goes as far as to argue that the term "gentile" is a negative term that applies equally to both Jews and gentiles who do not follow Christ. Gentiles are all people outside of the church.

[70]   Stanton, *Gospel*, 139–40.

[71]   Stanton, *Gospel*, 124.

descriptions attached to the church serve as a replacement for the worship of the Jews. The church features baptism as an entrance rite, and the promises made to the disciples regarding Jesus' ongoing presence with them are analogous to the ways that God was understood to be present in the temple and synagogue. The Jews continued to regard the temple as sacred, whereas Matthew describes in Jesus' coming something greater than the temple (Matt 12:6). Although Matthew affirms the law (Matt 5:17), Jesus' teaching takes precedent over the Torah, and the self-understanding of the Christian communities appear distinct from their Jewish counterparts. Third, Matthew focuses on the kingdom of God and its "transference" to a "new people" (cf. Matt 8:5-13; 15:13; 21:41-43). Paramount to Stanton's argument here is the parable of the wicked tenants (Matt 21:33-46), where the vineyard of the kingdom will be taken away from the Jewish leaders rejected by God and given instead to those who will yield proper fruit. Inheritance language features in the parable and will be important for our discussions regarding Matthew in this regard. Fourth, Stanton argues that Matt 28:15 expresses that the Jews and Jesus' disciples produced rival accounts of Jesus' resurrection, and therefore the Jews are set at a distance from the "new people" of God.[72]

Important for Stanton's arguments is an apparent assumption on his part that the Jewish leaders serve as a cipher for all Jews and that the Matthean polemic against the Jewish leaders equals a criticism of all Israel.[73] He argues that Matthew's community parted ways with Judaism after a prolonged period of hostility and persecution and that they were pained by Israel's rejection of Jesus and his messengers. The polemic against the Jews was a form of self-justification for its "position as a somewhat beleaguered minority 'sect' cut off from its roots."[74] However, this alienation did not only apply to Jews. Stanton accounts for the presence of both anti-Jewish and anti-gentile language in the Gospel by arguing that the community also felt cut off from the gentile world.[75] This offers a sociohistorical explanation for Matthew's emphasis of apocalyptic language. Matthew's community felt a sense of alienation from their roots and from the outside world and used apocalyptic language to reinforce group solidarity.[76]

[72]   These arguments are discussed in Stanton, *Gospel*, 126–31.
[73]   Similar is Ulrich Luz, *Studies in Matthew* (Grand Rapids: Eerdmans, 2005), 12, who argues that Matthew's rejection of the Jewish leaders eventually becomes a polemic against "the whole people led by the Scribes and Pharisees."
[74]   Stanton, *Gospel*, 156–57.
[75]   Stanton, *Gospel*, 160–61.
[76]   Stanton, *Gospel*, 162–63.

Stanton's arguments present the Matthean community *extra muros* in regard to Judaism. It was raised up in conflict with Judaism and as distinct and separate from it and constituted a "third race" based upon a commitment to follow Jesus. On the other end of the spectrum, there are scholars who argue that the Matthean community was *intra muros*; they were a messianic community that still considered itself to be completely Jewish.[77] The community's Judaism was qualified by the Christ event, but their Judaism was the foundation that defined the constitution of their discipleship. The *intra muros* position has been taken up in detail by scholars such as J. Andrew Overman, Anthony J. Saldarini, David C. Sim, and most recently, John Kampen.[78] Although each scholar nuances the *intra muros* position somewhat differently, a brief overview of Sim's arguments will suffice to understand aspects of the position.

Sim follows Overman and Saldarini in arguing that the Matthean community considered itself to be in continuity with Judaism. Sim agrees with Stanton that the community considered itself to be a sect,[79] but whereas Stanton emphasizes the distance between Matthew's community and its Jewish opponents, Sim argues for ideological similarities that place the Matthean community squarely within Judaism but in conflict with its local Jewish body.[80] He relies on comparisons with the Qumran community, which renounced mainstream Jewish society but certainly still considered itself to be Jewish. The sectarian nature of Matthew's community should be viewed the same way.[81] Matthew's conflict with the Jewish authorities is an internal Jewish debate between Matthew's community and representatives of "formative Judaism."[82]

[77]   So Saldarini, *Matthew's*, 1, who states that the Matthean community "are Jews who believe in Jesus as the Messiah and Son of God."

[78]   See J. Andrew Overman, *Matthew's Gospel and Formative Judaism: The Social World of the Matthean Community* (Minneapolis: Fortress, 1990); Saldarini, *Matthew's*; David C. Sim, *The Gospel of Matthew and Christian Judaism: The History and Social Setting of the Matthean Community* (Edinburgh: T&T Clark, 1998); and John Kampen, *Matthew within Sectarian Judaism* (New Haven: Yale University Press, 2019).

[79]   So also Overman, *Matthew's*, 16–19, who argues that Matthew's community used sectarian language to legitimate their own position.

[80]   So Overman, *Matthew's*, 4, who writes that Matthew's community "is a Jewish community, which claims to follow Jesus the Messiah, discovering that they are now different from what is emerging as the dominant form of Judaism in their setting."

[81]   This point is also taken up by John Kampen, *Wisdom Literature* (Grand Rapids: Eerdmans, 2011), 31–32, who argues that Matthew's particular use of wisdom motifs shows signs of sectarianism. Similarly to sectarian Second Temple texts, Kampen argues that Matthew uses exclusive wisdom and knowledge as a feature toward membership, which also explains Matthew's view of Jesus as a hermeneutical tool for interpreting Torah.

[82]   So also Overman, *Matthew's*, 1–5. It is for this reason that Sim argues the importance of labeling the group appropriately. Rather than "Matthean Christianity"

However, in agreement with Stanton, the community's conflict is not with Judaism alone but also with the gentile world. Matthew's group had been persecuted both by the local Jewish body and by gentiles during and after the Jewish war, cutting them off from mainstream groups in every direction. These conflicts motivated Matthew's use of apocalyptic motifs.[83] Sim takes this conflict further than Stanton by arguing that Matthew's Gospel is in fact an anti-gentile text and that his community had no interest in a gentile mission.[84] Any gentiles who entered the community would have done so as Jewish proselytes in keeping with the Scriptures.[85] This also would put the community in conflict with other Christians, as Sim argues that Matthew's community was at odds with what he called the "law-free" wing of the Jesus movement, which the Matthean community, as a law-abiding group, would have opposed.[86]

---

or "Jewish Christianity," Sim argues that an appropriate label for the group would be "Christian Judaism." Sim writes, "The all-important noun correctly defines the religion of these law-observant followers of Jesus as Judaism, while the adjective nominates their affiliation to the one they considered to be the Christ. Therefore, Christian Judaism is defined as a form of Judaism in the same way as we speak of Qumranite Judaism, Pharisaic Judaism and formative Judaism." See *Gospel*, 24–27.

[83]   See Sim, *Gospel*, 109–15, where he defines the basic features of their sectarianism. These features include dualistic language regarding righteousness and wickedness, the use and interpretation of the law, persecution, and hostility toward Jewish leaders. Despite these features Sim argues that the similarities between the Matthean community and formative Judaism kept the two groups in overall religious continuity. These similarities include monotheism, the importance of the covenant with God, a commitment to the Jewish Scriptures, and the observance of Torah. As with Stanton, Sim agrees that the community was alienated from places of Jewish worship and sought to legitimize its own beliefs and practices.

[84]   This is a consistent argument made throughout Sim's *Gospel*. For example, on page 152 he argues that, due to tensions in the aftermath of the Jewish war, it is unlikely that Matthew's Jewish community even associated with gentiles or had gentile friends. On pages 227–29 he surveys four passages (Matt 5:46-47; 6:7-8; 6:31-32; 18:15-17) which he considers to portray an all-encompassing rejection of gentiles by Matthew's entire community. Compare Runesson, "Judging," 140, 151, who agrees with Sim that gentiles are portrayed negatively in these passages, and he agrees that the Matthean community is embedded deeply within its Judaism. He states that the Matthean community understood Judaism to be the center of their world and that Jesus created for them "a centre within that centre." However, rather than a sect, Runesson argues that Matthew's community was radically externally focused on transforming the gentile world.

[85]   Similar is Runesson, "Judging," 146, who argues that gentiles must proselytize as Jews to be incorporated into restored Israel. Gentiles, who are "other" are then saved from their "otherness" through identification with Israel.

[86]   Sim, *Gospel*, 5–7. Sim appears to argue that Matthew's community is a law-abiding community in that they understand and observe the law the same way as Jews who do not follow Jesus. Different is Saldarini, *Matthew's*, 7, who argues that they observed the law as it was "interpreted through the Jesus tradition."

The strength with which Sim states his position that Matthew is anti-gentile is somewhat tempered by admissions that Matthew contains a mixture of both pro- and anti-gentile material, and he does admit that there are signs that Matthew envisions people of gentile origin having a share in God's kingdom.[87] However, even within these admissions Sim challenges many of the readings of Matthew that posit pro-gentile material, such as the significance of gentile women in the genealogy (Matt 1:1-17)[88] or the nature of the gentile mission of Matt 28:18-20.[89] In terms of the gentile mission, Sim admits that the presence of Matt 28:18-20 implies that the Matthean community accepted the validity of a mission to the gentiles, but he argues that the rest of the Gospel shows no signs that they ever participated in such a mission.[90] Their openness to a gentile mission means they would have accepted gentiles into their community as proselytes, but their sectarian nature would have prohibited them from seeking out gentiles actively.[91]

Sim's arguments offer many helpful critiques of the *extra muros* position. The most important critique may be a reconsideration of the parable of the wicked tenants (Matt 21:33-46). Traditionally, scholars have argued that the chief priests and Pharisees, represented by the wicked tenants, serve as ciphers for the whole of Israel. The kingdom of God is taken away from them and given to a "people" (ἔθνει) that produces proper fruit (Matt 21:43). Many scholars, Stanton included, have argued that this amounts to a rejection of all Israel. The new "people"

---

[87]   Sim, *Gospel*, 218.

[88]   Sim, *Gospel*, 218–20.

[89]   Sim, *Gospel*, 243–47.

[90]   Compare Runesson, "Judging," 151, who agrees with Sim that Matthew's community was *intra muros* but argues the opposite of Sim in regard to the gentile mission. Matthew, at its core, is a Jewish text that "others" gentiles, but the Matthean community inhabited a radical form of Judaism that sought to take on gentiles directly on a global scale in order to transform the empire.

[91]   Sim's argument in this regard relies on his previously argued socio-critical reconstructions of the Matthean community. While many of his arguments regarding the community are possible, his argument regarding the gentile mission has not won support. See, for example, the review by Mark Allan Powell, *HBT* 22, no. 1 (2000): 85–88, who questions why, if the Matthean community never intended to participate in a gentile mission, the Gospel would end so anticlimactically? Discipleship is a key Matthean theme. Ending the Gospel with an imperative not meant for the Gospel's audience is highly unlikely. Significantly, this is one place that Sim and Overman diverge, however slightly. Overman, *Matthew's*, 122, acknowledges the gentile mission but argues for a difference in character between the missions to the Jews and to the gentiles. To the Jews, the disciples practice healing, exorcism, and resuscitation. To the gentiles, there is only mention of teaching and education.

who receive the kingdom is either the church, the gentiles, or both.[92] However, Sim, among others recently, has challenged this position by arguing that the people of Israel are not represented by the wicked tenants in the parable but rather by the vineyard, which has done nothing wrong and is not to be replaced. It is the Jewish leaders who are represented by the wicked tenants and who are to be replaced by other leaders. These new leaders would likely come from within Matthew's community. The parable details the rejection of the Jewish leadership and does not suggest that God has rejected Israel as a whole.[93] This parable serves as a microcosm of the debate regarding the whole of Matthew; it should not be assumed that Jesus' conflict with the Jewish leaders amounts to a conflict with Israel broadly.[94] In fact, it is precisely because Matthew's community has not departed from Israel that Matthew's Gospel attacks its ineffective leaders so unreservedly.[95]

Although the *intra muros* position offers helpful critiques of the view that Matthew's community has left its Jewishness behind, it is not without its own extremities that have left it open to criticism. In an article focused on critiquing the views of Overman, Saldarini, and Sim, Hagner argues that they have overstated their case by neglecting the "newness" of Matthew and its many differences with the Judaism of its time.[96] Although Matthew is an exceptionally Jewish text that stresses its continuity with Judaism as much as possible, Hagner argues that it reflects its Christianity to a greater degree than

[92]   Stanton, *Gospel*, 11–12, 18, 152–53, in reference to Matt 21:43, argues that Matthew's readers viewed themselves "over against both Jews and Gentiles." In Stanton's view, this is not only a rejection of the leaders specified in the passage but a thoroughgoing anti-Jewish polemic. Similar is Hagner, *Matthew*, lxxi, who argues that the whole of Matthew presents a community that, due to the rejection of Jesus by unbelieving and hostile Jews, would have begun to think of itself as separate from, and opposed to, the rest of Israel. Hagner argues that Israel's rejection of God would have been followed by "God's rejection of Israel." This leads, in Matt 21:43, to a transference of the kingdom from Israel to the church. Matthew's community would have seen itself as the true fulfillment of Judaism but only as they had made a clean break from it.

[93]   Sim, *Gospel*, 148–49.

[94]   So Saldarini, *Matthew's*, 44, "The various leaders of Israel are the only groups unequivocally rejected by Matthew."

[95]   Following Overman, Saldarini, and Sim in the *intra muros* position is Charles H. Talbert, *Reading the Sermon on the Mount: Character Formation and Decision Making in Matthew 5–7* (Grand Rapids: Baker Academic, 2004), 1–7, who argues that Christianity sprung forth from within Judaism in the same way as Samaritanism, Pharisaism, Essenism, and others. Although Matthew's community saw itself as distinct from "formative Judaism," it still viewed itself as part of Judaism.

[96]   Donald A. Hagner, "Matthew: Apostate, Reformer, Revolutionary?" *NTS* 49, no. 2 (2003): 193–209.

its Jewishness.[97] Scholars widely recognize that Judaism in the first century existed in a plurality of local expressions, but there was a common set of elements that united them as distinctly Jewish, and in many ways the Matthean community "continued in a uniquely Jewish mode of existence."[98] Although these Jewish features are ubiquitous throughout the text, Hagner argues that the Matthean community "treasured a perspective that was dramatically new compared to anything else previously known in Judaism."[99] Due to this balance between the old and the new, it is too simplistic to see Matthew as *either extra muros* or *intra muros*. Instead, Matthew's community is best understood as representing one step within the "gradual transition" of the parting of the ways between Judaism and Christianity, and the aspects of old and new in the First Gospel reflect the ways that the community experienced their own part in that transition.[100]

Although Matthew balances old and new, Hagner argues that the new takes precedence. For example, in agreement with Sim, Hagner argues that the Torah is of importance to Matthew. However, in disagreement with Sim, Hagner argues that Matthew's community did not simply continue to view Torah in the same way as other first-century Jews. Instead, Matthew has a novel way of preserving both the gospel and the Torah by emphasizing Jesus' own authoritative interpretation of the law rather than the law itself. Jesus is the teacher *par excellence* (Matt 23:8-10), and his teaching of the law has a radical character to it.[101] In fact, the entire Gospel is filled with new things that are problematic for Judaism, including the eschatological announcement that the Messiah and kingdom had come, that this Messiah was a unique son of God, that the Messiah would die the death of a criminal, that obedience to God was now based on Jesus rather than Torah, that the new kingdom would involve

---

[97]   Hagner, "Matthew," 194, states that Matthew may even be as "Jewish" as, or more Jewish than, any manifestation of Judaism in the NT.

[98]   Hagner, "Matthew," 197. Common unifying features include, but are not limited to, monotheism, covenant, election, and Torah. The plurality of Judaism would have been present, but likely less pronounced, in Palestine. The plurality of Judaism(s) becomes more evident in the diaspora through social integration, language, education, and accommodation to diverse local communities. For a detailed account of this plurality, see John M. G. Barclay, *Jews in the Mediterranean Diaspora: From Alexander to Trajan (323 BCE–117 CE)* (Berkeley: University of California Press, 1996).

[99]   Hagner, "Matthew," 197.

[100]   Hagner, "Matthew," 200–201, argues that specific passages in Matthew detail the community's awareness of the conflict between old and new (9:16-17; 13:52). These passages portray a community making peace with both continuity and discontinuity with its Jewish past, and coming to an understanding of their dual identities as both Jewish and Christian.

[101]   Hagner, "Matthew," 202–3.

suffering, and many others.[102] Of principal concern would be Matthew's Christology. From the beginning of the Gospel, where Matthew presents Jesus as "Immanuel" (Matt 1:23), God with us, to the end of the Gospel where Jesus declares his unique authority (Matt 28:18-19), Matthew presents Jesus as a mediator between God and his people. It is Jesus who must be acknowledged in order for one to be right with God (Matt 10:32), Jesus is greater than Solomon (Matt 12:42), and Jesus is even greater than the temple (Matt 12:6). For Matthew, Jesus is the center of the story, and a Jesus-centered story forces a shift away from Torah and Judaism's common forms of worship. This Jesus-centrality affects other key aspects of Jewishness throughout the Gospel, including the election of Israel, views of ethnicity, and the temple. Furthermore, and key for our purposes regarding inheritance, these shifts in perspective have important ramifications regarding the Jewish focus on its land.[103] For Hagner, Matthew's Gospel may not present the radical break with Judaism for which the *extra muros* position often argues, but it does present a Jewish Christianity that is a perfection and fulfillment of Judaism. He argues that it is mistaken to assume that Matthew cannot maintain a "full Jewishness" while also introducing the "fully Christian identity of his community." The Matthean community would have regarded itself as loyal to Israel, its Scriptures, and its heritage, while also pointing to a "radical alteration of affairs" through its commitment to Jesus.[104]

Hagner is only one scholar among many to critique the extreme *intra muros* position. Donald Senior argues that Sim in particular glosses over passages in Matthew that present a positive view of gentiles (cf. Matt 8:10; 11:20-24; 12:38-42; 15:28) and argues that Sim's view that Matt 28:19 does not imply a gentile mission by the Matthean community "borders on the preposterous."[105] Ulrich Luz critiques the *intra muros* position on sociohistorical grounds, arguing that it is based less on the text of the Gospel of Matthew than on the way the text is read in light of speculative reconstructions of the Matthean community and early Christianity. The text is forced into these reconstructions and "ignores the conduit of the Matthean narrative in which everything flows toward the universal mission command." Regarding Sim in particular, Luz argues that many of his arguments are not plausible because he interprets the entire text "in terms of its beginning rather than its ending." By constructing a starting point for the community but ignoring the progression of the narrative, Sim is forced into the awkward position of arguing that

102   Hagner, "Matthew," 201.
103   Hagner, "Matthew," 204–6.
104   Hagner, "Matthew," 208.
105   Senior, "Between," 10–11.

Matt 28:18-20 is relatively inconsequential to the Matthean community.[106] In a similar fashion to Hagner, Luz challenges the very nature of the *intra/extra muros* debate by arguing that the Matthean community undoubtedly regarded itself as belonging to Israel but that their mission to Israel had come to an end and they no longer belonged to the Jewish synagogue. Luz notes the lack of "inside/outside" terminology in Matthew that one might find in the Gospel of John; the Jews are not the "negative other" and the church has not replaced Israel as the people of God, but Matthew's community, as followers of Jesus, have experienced a crisis of identity and Matthew was written to help them understand their own story.[107]

It is important to recognize that each of these positions relies principally on socio-critical reconstructions of the historical situation regarding the writer(s) of Matthew and the community to which the text was written. However, not all scholars accept the view that there ever was such a thing as a "Matthean community." In a volume edited by Richard Bauckham, a number of scholars contribute articles from different angles to argue that the Gospels were not in fact written to specific, closed communities whose historical situations can be reconstructed from aspects of each Gospel text.[108] As Bauckham argues in the introduction, the existence of a Matthean community is often assumed, but it is highly possible that the Gospels were all written as "open" texts which were intended to be circulated to a number of Christian communities in association with one another.[109] In his first of two articles in the volume, he continues this argument that the Gospel writers, including Matthew, likely expected their Gospels to circulate widely among many churches. The fact that Matthew and Luke both use Mark as their primary source proves that Mark was in wide circulation, and there are many clues that Matthew and Luke both used but expanded upon Mark because they each expected their own version of the Jesus story to surpass and replace Mark. The fact that Mark was in circulation presents the strong implication that Matthew and Luke assumed their Gospels might also reach a wide readership.[110] Furthermore, even if a Matthean community did exist, the fact that this community is

---

[106]   Ulrich Luz, *Matthew 1–7* (Hermeneia; Minneapolis: Fortress, 2007), 52.

[107]   Luz, *Matthew 1–7*, 54–55. This is not to state that Matthew does not feature "othering" language in any form. Runesson, "Judging," 143–45, details the use of gentile terms and customs to construct the concept of "the other," though the text does not exclude gentiles from the community or from salvation.

[108]   See Richard Bauckham, ed., *The Gospels for All Christians: Rethinking the Gospel Audiences* (Edinburgh: T&T Clark, 1998).

[109]   Richard Bauckham, "Introduction," in *The Gospels for All Christians*, 2.

[110]   Richard Bauckham, "For Whom Were the Gospels Written?," in *The Gospels for All Christians*, 11–13.

not explicitly mentioned in the text calls into question their hermeneutical relevance to its interpretation.[111] The views expressed by Bauckham and others in the volume must find room for reasonable accounts as to why each Gospel makes use of its specific unique features, why each Gospel writer shapes shared material in unique ways, and how we can account for the diversity between the presentations of the Jesus story between the Gospels.[112] However, their arguments do raise the possibility that understanding Matthew primarily through socio-critical reconstructions may lead to speculations which actually hinder our ability to understand the narrative of each Gospel properly.[113]

An important narrative and theological approach to Jewish/gentile dynamics in Matthew is that of Matthias Konradt. He welcomes the arguments of Overman and Saldarini that emphasize the central conflict

[111]   Bauckham, "For Whom," 44.

[112]   Bauckham, "For Whom," 47, recognizes the need to answer these questions. Another essay in the same volume, that of Loveday Alexander, "Ancient Book Production and the Circulation of the Gospels," 71–112, discusses the production and circulation of early Christian texts to demonstrate a model for the circulation of the Gospels. This point was taken up by Matthew D. C. Larsen, *Gospels before the Book* (Oxford: Oxford University Press, 2018), 100–114, who argues that Matthew's writer viewed his text as a new version of Mark and that the two texts existed within what Matthew's writer would have understood as a "fluid textual tradition." Within this relationship Larsen highlights the considerable similarities between Mark and Matthew to demonstrate that Matthew's writer saw his work as having a part within the Markan tradition rather than as two different books with separate agendas. If Larsen is correct, this tempers the role of a "Matthean community" as vital to understanding Matthew. Certainly, such a community might still account for some of the differences between Matthew and Mark within Larsen's model, but Matthew's role as a literary production within a specific tradition would be considerably more important to understanding the text than socio-critical reconstructions of the possible communities. On page 111, Larsen offers insights that would account for Matthew's changes and unique material: "The Gospel according to Matthew aims to narrow ambiguities in the Gospel according to Mark and direct the reader by limiting the number of possible meanings of a story or anecdote, supplying essential yet previously unspecified information." On page 12 he adds, "The textual tradition we now call the Gospel according to Mark makes assumptions, lacks clarity, and contains potentially ambiguous statements . . . the Gospel according to Matthew continues the text by seeking to clarify the gospel and remove its ambiguities." On page 14 Larsen argues that Mark and Matthew circulated without name attributions or titles because they were written to be circulated as contributions to a literary tradition.

[113]   See Craig S. Keener, *The Gospel of Matthew: A Socio-Rhetorical Commentary* (Grand Rapids: Eerdmans, 2009), 5, who argues that reconstructing Matthew's community(ies) can only be hypothetical. Based on patterns throughout the Gospel, certain details may be inferred, "but the fruits of such inferences are usually more slender than a historian would like." Keener suggests that a more helpful approach is to reconstruct what we know from the broader general milieu of the ancient Mediterranean world, and that such reconstructions shed helpful light on how Matthew's readers may have received it.

between Jesus and the Jewish authorities as indicative of competing claims of authority *within* Judaism, but he argues that the central weakness of the position is that it neglects the *theological* conception of Matthew's Gospel. Even as advocates of the *intra muros* position recognize the legitimacy of the gentile mission, they do not adequately describe the theological basis for such a mission, nor do they effectively pursue the relationship between Matt 10:5-6 and 28:18-20. According to Konradt, it is not enough to consider that Matthew does not reject Israel as the people of God; "one must also consider what both the formation of the ecclesia and the universal dimension of salvation at the end of the Gospel imply for the understanding of Israel (as the people of God)." In Konradt's estimation, establishing a path between Matt 10:5-6 and 28:18-20 is the key to understanding the dynamics between Jews and gentiles in Matthew's Gospel.[114]

Konradt's own study into these matters is extensive and insightful. Rather than exploring the debate through sociohistorical analysis, he approaches the problem through a detailed investigation into Matthew's theological concepts, its use of antecedent texts and traditions, and a narrative analysis of the development of themes within and throughout the text itself.[115] Konradt begins by recognizing that the majority of scholars have taken one of two positions: first, that Jesus and his disciples began with a mission to the Jews, who rejected Jesus and were in turn rejected by God. This led Jesus and his followers to *replace* the Jewish mission with one to the gentiles. Second, that Jesus and his disciples began with a mission to the Jews, and later *expanded* that one mission to also include gentiles. In this latter case, the distinction between Jews and gentiles would level out. The mission to Israel would continue, but its salvation-historical prerogative would be lost, and Jews and gentiles would be brought together equally under the same universal mission. One key purpose of Konradt's study is to offer a third alternative. He opens up the possibility that the Matthean community continued to distinguish between its two missions, one to Jews and one to gentiles, and that these parallel missions complemented one another and both missions endured. In this view there is room for Israel to maintain its special role among the nations.[116] The Jewish

---

[114]   Konradt, *Israel*, 12–14.

[115]   Konradt, *Israel*, 355–68, does engage very briefly with the matter of the potential of a "Matthean community," but his study largely eschews speculative questions regarding what the text might imply about its readers in order to focus on the explicit nature of Matthew as a story about Jesus and his first disciples.

[116]   Konradt, *Israel*, 2–6. Konradt makes the important distinction between "the nations" and the "the church." He recognizes that many scholars do not distinguish

mission is an early aspect of the ministry of Jesus and his disciples, but the gentile mission does not begin until after Easter. Despite the later start of the gentile mission, Konradt offers a compelling narrative and theological reading of the whole Gospel that seeks to demonstrate that the gentile mission was anticipated from the start and that the text features a narrative progression of gentile involvement that reaches its climax in Matt 28:18-20.

This narrative progression begins in Matthew's first verse. The genealogy is introduced with a double designation for Jesus' core identity as the Messiah; he is both the son of David and the son of Abraham. Konradt argues that this reveals two salvation-historical horizons; Jesus' Davidic sonship is connected to the promises of salvation to Israel, and his Abrahamic sonship is connected to the Abrahamic promise regarding Israel being a light to the nations and the inclusion of gentiles in salvation. The explicit mention of Abraham and David, with the whole of the genealogy, offers a history of God and his people in condensed form that also offers a compact presentation of the significance of Jesus.[117]

Konradt first discusses Jesus' focus on Israel. Not only is Jesus presented the son of David and the son of Abraham, but he is the unique son of God and the Messiah who is sent as a shepherd to guide the people of Israel (Matt 2:6; 10:5-6; 15:24). Jesus' role as shepherd speaks to God's favor of his people Israel over against the failure of the Jewish leaders.[118] Metaphorically, the scribes and Pharisees are blind guides (Matt 15:14; 23:16-26), and Matthew contrasts this with Jesus literally healing the blindness of some of his fellow Jews, a feat that angers some of his Pharisaic combatants (Matt 21:14-15).[119] In fact, the entire section of Matthew dedicated to Jesus' public ministry (Matt 4:17-11:1) summarizes his ministry *to Israel*; he has been sent to them as lost sheep in need of a shepherd (10:5-6).[120] This section serves as a summary of Jesus fulfilling Jewish Messianic expectations.

Key to Konradt's interpretation is the distinction between the Jewish leaders and "the crowds." The "lost sheep of the house of Israel" refers to the crowds who are viewed favorably in Matthew, while the

---

between the two, assuming a "double replacement thesis" in which the gentile mission replacing the Jewish mission amounts to the church replacing Israel as the people of God. Konradt argues that neither is the case but that a more nuanced approach to understanding the use of these terms is necessary for understanding Jewish/gentile dynamics in the text.

[117]   Konradt, *Israel*, 24–25.

[118]   Konradt, *Israel*, 29, 36–37. Konradt argues that Jer 23:1-4; 27:6; and Ezek 34 are likely influences on Matthew's presentation of the failure of Israel's shepherds.

[119]   Konradt, *Israel*, 45.

[120]   Konradt, *Israel*, 50–53.

Jewish leaders are hostile to Jesus and his disciples without exception.[121] The Jewish leaders are responsible for the hardships of the Jewish people and Jesus' presentation of the gospel of the kingdom is a response to their hardship. Therefore, it is not Israel as a whole who is viewed negatively in Matthew but rather the failed Jewish authorities, and Jesus and his disciples appear as new shepherds in competition with the failed Jewish leadership.[122] It is in this context that the contentious parable of the wicked tenants (Matt 21:33-46) is best understood; it is not all Israel that loses the inheritance of the kingdom but the Jewish authorities in particular. This explains why, as Jesus pronounces a series of woes against the scribes and Pharisees in Matt 23, he addresses the crowds along with his disciples rather than including the crowds in his criticisms (Matt 23:1). The crowds have a choice to make between following Jesus or the Jewish leaders, and this conflict lies at the center of much of Matthew's entire narrative.[123]

Konradt then turns his attention to the gentiles and the universal dimensions of the Matthean Jesus story. Although the mission to the

[121]   See also the extensive study on the crowds in Matthew by J. R. C. Cousland, *The Crowds in the Gospel of Matthew* (Leiden: Brill, 2002). Cousland, 301–4, concludes that the crowds and the Jewish leaders are distinct. The crowds serve as a microcosm of "the chequered history of Israel's involvement with Yahweh" and epitomize the rise and fall of the Jewish populace. The only time when the crowds are viewed negatively in Matthew is when they "serve as pawns to their leaders."

[122]   Konradt, *Israel*, 75–77, 85–91, 100–105. There is the matter of the crowds' reaction to Jesus in Matt 27:20; the Jewish leaders are portrayed as persuading the crowds in their favor. Konradt, 159–66, makes a careful distinction between a) the persuasiveness of the "old authorities" verses a truly negative portrayal of the crowds themselves and b) the difference between the crowds in Jerusalem versus the crowds Jesus interacted with more often throughout the narrative. The exception of 27:20 does not invalidate the general rule that the crowds are viewed positively in Matthew. The crowds in the passion narrative serve as a cautionary tale for those who favor the failed Jewish leaders and therefore follow the wrong path. See also Keener, *Matthew*, 48–49. Matthew writes to critique the failed Jewish leadership "just as Israel's prophets critiqued Israel from within" (48). "I find in the Gospel an author and audience intensely committed to their heritage in Judaism while struggling with those they believe to be its illegitimate spokespersons" (49). Matthew's Gospel regards the Jewish leaders as "illegitimate guardians of their heritage" (49).

[123]   Konradt, *Israel*, 126–48, especially 138, where Konradt states, "The central significance of the conflict between Jesus and the authorities in the Matthean Jesus story also places a greater weight on the crowds' tendency in choosing a side." Similar here is Daniel M. Gurtner, "Matthew's Theology of the Temple and the 'Parting of the Ways': Christian Origins and the First Gospel," in *Built upon the Rock: Studies in the Gospel of Matthew* (ed. Daniel M. Gurtner and John Nolland; Grand Rapids: Eerdmans, 2008), who argues that Matthew stresses the authority of Scripture, acknowledges the importance of the Sabbath, and is in favor of the existence of the temple as well as God's presence in it. There are a number of *intra muros* indicators throughout the Gospel, but Matthew's real conflict is squarely with the failed Jewish leadership.

gentiles is a post-Easter reality, the First Gospel sows the seeds of this mission throughout the narrative.[124] Universal salvation is anchored in Israel, which was always intended as an aspect of the Abrahamic promise.[125] Salvation to the nations does not replace salvation to the Jews, but rather salvation for the Jews is the first step toward the salvation of the other nations.[126] In fact, the gentile mission is so embedded into the entire salvation history of the Jewish Scriptures that to reject the mission is to depart from Scripture itself.[127] The theological foundation of the universal mission is the universal authority of the resurrected Christ, and the mission to the gentiles is not triggered by a Jewish rejection of Jesus but rather a fulfillment of Scripture.[128] *Contra* Sim's argument that gentiles can enter the community as proselytes, Konradt argues that the development of the church and the universal soteriological significance of Jesus' death brings a new salvation-historical situation. Jesus' universal authority that leads to the universal mission has little significance if gentiles, or the Matthean community for that matter, simply continued normal Jewish practice. As Konradt states, "The ecclesia does not seek proselytes but seeks, rather, to make disciples and integrate them into the ecclesia of Jesus through baptism." Disciples are incorporated into a salvation history that began with Abraham, and although Israel maintains its special role in the history of election, the mission to the gentiles implies an equality between gentiles and Israel. The gentiles join Israel

[124]   Konradt, *Israel*, 281, sums up this progression by stating that it is exposed in Matt 1:1, symbolically anticipated in 5:13-14; 8:5-13, 28-34; 15:21-28, and in signals and fulfillment quotations such as 4:15-16 and 12:18-21. These passages, among others, pave the way for the gentile mission, which does not explicitly factor into the narrative until 28:18-20.

[125]   Konradt, *Israel*, 265–72. Matthew's depiction of Jesus' Abrahamic ancestry continues to be an important theme throughout Konradt's arguments.

[126]   A sharp contrasting position is argued by Luz, *Studies*, 11–12. Recognizing the importance of the contrast between Matt 10:5-6 and 28:18-20, Luz argues, in a similar fashion to Konradt, that the Gospel builds progressively toward gentile inclusion. However, *contra* Konradt, Luz argues that the mission to gentiles is not a mere expansion of the Jewish mission but in fact replaces it. Matt 28:18-20 implies that Jesus' command of 10:5-6 is withdrawn and that the progression of gentile involvement in the text is literary preparation for the shift away from the Jewish mission and toward the mission to the gentiles. This shift in the mission corresponds with the Jewish Christian Matthean communities separating from Israel.

[127]   Konradt, *Israel*, 276.

[128]   Reeves, *Matthew*, 29, is similar on the first point, that Matthew includes subtle hints throughout the text to anticipate the gentile mission but that Jesus' first priority was the mission to his fellow Jews. However, Reeves argues that the gentile mission was a result of the Jews' rejection of Jesus. Konradt argues persuasively that the mission to the gentiles was not due to the Jewish rejection of Jesus but was instead motivated by a careful reading of certain scriptural texts.

under the Abrahamic promise, and although a distinction between them persists, the dividing line between Israel and the gentiles "loses its fundamental significance through the Christ event."[129]

Konradt is careful to distinguish between gentiles and the church. The church is not Israel, nor does it replace Israel, but rather it is a part of Israel that has recognized Jesus as Messiah. It is the part of Israel that has accepted Jesus' presentation of the kingdom and bears fruit accordingly. The church makes up the eschatological community gathered by Jesus within Israel but is open to people from all nations. Mission is the church's essential function, it is a gathered portion of humanity that "is itself the vehicle for further gathering."[130] The church does not replace Israel, but rather it replaces Israel's ineffective leaders[131] and forms as a community of people who have entered into discipleship and are tasked with passing on God's offer of salvation to both the Jews and gentiles. Jesus' disciples have exclusive claims to knowledge of God's will through Jesus' teachings, and they serve an intermediary function between Yahweh and the nations.[132] Although there is a sense in which Israel and gentiles are distinguished and Israel maintains its identity as "the people of God," salvation is found via entry into discipleship and the church. This is true for both Jews and gentiles.[133] The Matthean community therefore is not a sect that has withdrawn from surrounding Jewish and pagan environments, but the opposite, it is a community with a strong missionary orientation.[134]

Konradt closes his study by criticizing the very nature of the *intra/extra muros* debate. He argues that the Pharisees doubtless saw Matthew's community as Jewish but misguided. Matthew's community, on the other hand, did not see its faith as a break from Judaism, but in the move toward a universal mission they clearly experienced a fundamental change in their Jewish context. Due to the Matthean community's diaspora experience in Syria, many of the lines demarcating Jews from gentiles have lost their significance; therefore, determining the Matthean community's relationship to Judaism is extremely problematic. Instead, it is best to understand the conflict in Matthew specifically as one between believers in Christ and the Pharisaic synagogue.[135]

[129]   Konradt, *Israel*, 320–21.
[130]   Konradt, *Israel*, 336.
[131]   Konradt, *Israel*, 338, ties Matt 16:19 to 21:38-43 in this regard.
[132]   Konradt, *Israel*, 344–46.
[133]   Konradt, *Israel*, 350.
[134]   Konradt, *Israel*, 358–62.
[135]   Konradt, *Israel*, 363–65.

Konradt's arguments are helpful, particularly in the way they frame the conflict between Jesus and the Jewish leaders and differentiate between the Jewish leaders and the Jewish crowds. Discipleship is a central concern of the First Gospel, and identity and inclusion are largely decided by the choice one makes in whom they will follow—Jesus or the wayward Jewish leaders. Furthermore, Konradt's attention to the Abrahamic promise and Jesus as the son of Abraham are helpful not only to understanding the mission of Jesus' disciples toward the nations, but as we shall see throughout this study, the promises will be relevant to the entire Jewish presentation of inheritance across a broad scope of Jewish literature. The Abrahamic promises, each in their own turn, are relevant to inheritance at multiple points of the tradition. Many of the details of Konradt's arguments are open to question. For example, it is not always clear whether there is a demonstrable difference between either a Jewish mission that later includes gentiles, or a need to insist that the two missions are distinct but exist parallel to one another and are complementary. In the end, the result is largely the same: the two groups, Jews and gentiles, come into a saving relationship with God in Christ by virtue of joining the church. As it happens, it is not necessary in this study to solve the many nuanced aspects of Jewish/gentile dynamics in Matthew. The aim here is to understand precisely how these dynamics contribute specifically to our understanding of inheritance and to allow our understanding of inheritance to inform our views on the Jewish/gentile relationship. These themes will be taken up in chapter 5.

1.6. The Approach of This Study

Some comments are helpful in order to frame the approach toward the material that is analyzed. First, this study makes use of both synchronic and diachronic approaches to inheritance concepts. It is important to understand how a particular text or tradition used these terms and concepts for their own context, but for a study such as this, which seeks to understand Matthew's use of inheritance terms in light of antecedent traditions, an attempt must be made to offer suggestions as to how and why these terms and concepts developed over time before they influenced the writer of Matthew's Gospel. It is recognized that diachronic approaches to terms and concepts across biblical and other ancient material can be extremely problematic, primarily because the dating of various texts, or various recensions of texts over long periods of time, is both a speculative and controversial endeavor. For this reason, generalizations regarding developments are often necessary and certain conclusions must be held loosely, but both approaches are useful for our purposes.

Second, the approach to the texts treated, at relevant points, addresses important socio-critical questions, but no attempts are made to offer fresh socio-critical reflections or reconstructions for the communities behind or in front of the texts with which this study interacts. Each study, particularly regarding Matthew, is principally concerned with addressing questions reflected in the literary and narrative contexts of the texts themselves. The aim is to see how Matthew uses inheritance terms in its narrative, as well as to understand the antecedent texts and traditions that may have impacted the writer's thematic and linguistic choices.

Third, it is recognized that terms often cannot be equated with concepts. On the one hand, attempts are made to avoid equating the terms for inheritance with the concept of inheritance. On the other hand, it is largely accepted that the various concepts of inheritance are generally attached to the basic terms used to form those concepts, and the meanings of the terms are relatively straightforward. Furthermore, it is recognized that Hebrew words that lead to establishing certain concepts do not always correlate simply with the Greek words used to either translate the Hebrew terms or to continue in the establishment and continuation of those concepts.[136] However, in this instance, the primary Hebrew term for inheritance, נחל and its cognates, corresponds rather closely with the basic Greek term κληρονομία and its cognates, both in the way they are used in translation as well as in the development of common themes and concepts.[137] In both cases, it is argued that "inheritance" is the best word to translate both terms the majority of the time and that their use is relatively consistent with one another across the scope of Jewish and Christian literature. The purpose of this study is to understand inheritance as a concept history, rather than to define the terms themselves, but these terms present an overall consistency with the development of the concept over time.[138] In other words, it is important to recognize that

---

[136] See James Barr, *The Semantics of Biblical Language* (London: SCM Press, 1961), 8–45.

[137] The details are explored in ch. 2.

[138] The warning of Barr, *Semantics*, 206–11, is heeded in this regard. In Barr's trenchant criticism of *TWNT* he notes the failure of many exegetes to understand the difference between the definition of terms and the concepts that the terms are often used to describe. It is recognized here that there are many words that can be used to describe inheritance concepts and that inheritance terms do not always correspond to the concepts with which they are most often associated. See also the insightful discussion in Haley Goranson Jacob, *Conformed to the Image of His Son: Reconsidering Paul's Theology of Glory in Romans* (Downers Grove, Ill.: IVP Academic, 2018), 22–29. Jacob applies the linguistic concepts of semiotics to distinguish between signs/symbols, the concepts generated by use of those signs/symbols, and the sense of these things arrived at by an interpreter. Words are not identical with the objects to which they refer, which is made all the more problematic when interpreting the Hebrew Bible, which is full of poetic,

there is a difference between the precise definitions given to terms and the various ways that terms are used in given contexts. In this study, arriving at precise meanings is not the goal, as the meaning of the terms shifts over time and within certain contexts. This study will detail ways that the uses of inheritance terms are consistent within various texts and contexts and ways that the terms undergo shifts of usage and variations of meaning. Rather than singular, precise, unitary, and concise definitions, it is argued that inheritance terms in Jewish and Christian literature are used to convey associated themes, motifs, and ideas that are largely consistent within an overall theological concept. The goal is to understand how a diachronic study of these terms can help the reader to better understand the use and function of these terms across a full spectrum of the literature. No single definitions for these terms are offered because the meaning and use of these terms will somewhat vary from one text to another and from one time period to another. Inheritance terms have a range of meaning requiring different glosses in different contexts, and the reasons for which glosses are chosen are explained throughout the study of individual texts and passages. When major differences to the use of inheritance terms are detected across traditions, the argument is made that these differences are not separate uses of common terms but rather changes and developments to the same basic concepts that these terms describe.[139]

Despite the clarification that this study is focused on concepts and themes, rather than strictly being a word study, it is recognized that the bulk of the study is indeed focused on the uses of words. As mentioned above, this is largely because, in the case of inheritance, the concepts and words are tied together in an inextricable relationship. However, there are instances where the concept of inheritance is present even when the oft-associated terms are not. This is similar to the argument of Thompson, noted previously in this chapter, regarding God as Father. Although God's "fatherhood" is often tied to the terms used for "father," associated themes and motifs suggest that God's role as Father can be determined in contexts where the terms are absent. This is not often the case with inheritance concepts, as the concepts and uses of terms

---

figurative, analogous, and symbolic language. Understanding the path between symbols (terms), concepts, and interpretations helps to avoid an oversimplified approach. See also the helpful discussion in Pennington, *Sermon*, 21–22, who follows various works by Umberto Eco to distinguish between the dictionary model, where the understanding of language is relegated to the use of terms, and the encyclopedic model, where the use of terms is used to understand culture, history, and beliefs. "Concept histories" are attempts to use terms to understand larger realities based on their use in a cultural framework, as opposed to defining the terms themselves.

[139]   See the similar approach of Hester, *Paul's Concept*, vii–viii.

are closely aligned, but this study attempts to include notable instances where this does occur, such as in 4QBeatitudes, discussed in chapter 4.

A further difficulty in establishing meaning concerns the syntactic and thematic relationships between various terms that adjust meaning in given contexts. For example, the term נחל often appears alongside the term נתן (to give). When these terms appear together, they often highlight the aspect of giving (or gifting) as indelible to the concept of inheritance. But this does not exhaust the meaning of נחל, which also often appears alongside terms such as חלק (to divide, allot) and אחזה (possession), associations that highlight the dividing of a received inheritance or the possession of the inheritance itself. In these instances, the act of receiving is as important to inheritance contexts as the act of giving. The same is true for the Greek terms. The primary term for inheritance, κληρονομία, has as its root the term κλῆρος (lot, portion, share). The verb, κληρόω, can refer either to the casting of lots or the act of receiving them, depending on context. Although the κληρονομία word group often refers to the acquisition or reception of an inheritance or to the act of being an heir or beneficiary, terms in the group often appear alongside verbs such as δίδωμι (to give)[140] or λαμβάνω (to take, receive),[141] highlighting different aspects of meaning for the associated terms. In each case, although the range of meaning is manageable, context helps to dictate meaning, so that establishing short, precise meanings often remains problematic when one attempts to understand the broader concepts to which the terms refer. As this study demonstrates, the conceptual world portrayed by various texts also assists (and complicates) our understanding of meaning. For example, in the HB, Israel was in a national, covenantal relationship to their God, and they exhibited their commitment to their God, and established their inheritances, in unique ways, including the law, the temple, the land, etc. However, by the Second Temple period, some of these realities changed, and therefore the precise meanings and referents to inheritance terms underwent shifts, even though the broad theological categories for the uses of these terms remained consistent with historical uses of terms and concepts. This is explored in detail throughout the study.

Fourth, it is recognized that Matthew was written within a Roman imperial context. At points, this reality is addressed, particularly regarding the beatitudes. Pennington has argued effectively that the beatitudes reflect both Jewish wisdom and the Greco-Roman virtue tradition and that Matthew's use of ethical terms often reflects engagement with Greek

---

[140]   See Acts 7:5; 20:32.
[141]   See Col 3:24; Heb 9:15; 11:8.

and Roman ethical norms.[142] However, the considerable majority of this study focuses on Matthew's use of inheritance terms within its Israelite/Jewish milieu, as it is argued that its use of such terms was derived from Jewish traditions. The Roman political and cultural environment likely had an influence on Matthew's author(s), but in many ways it appears to have pushed him deeper into his own Jewish theological milieu as he sought to interpret his times through Judaism's Scriptures. Matthew's use of Scripture makes it abundantly clear that its author sought to explain Jesus' story through the cultural matrix of the biblical story, and this includes the way he uses inheritance terms. Roman understandings of inheritance are surveyed to interesting effect by Forman and Johnson Hodge in their studies on inheritance in Paul, but such contexts appear far less relevant to inheritance in Matthew's Gospel.

Finally, it is helpful to briefly comment on Matthew's sources and the place of Jewish texts in the world of the author. This study relies on analyzing texts across a broad spectrum of time and then makes suggestions that many of them, either directly or indirectly, influenced Matthew's theology and linguistic choices. Important questions arise in relationship to Matthew's sources. For example, did Matthew's writer make use of manuscripts, oral tradition, his own memory, or some combination of these? In other words, how did the writer receive texts and content found in what we now refer to as the HB or the Second Temple literature? Concerning those texts, which among them would Matthew's writer have considered Scripture, and which among them may he have viewed as helpful but something less than Scripture? Did first-century

---

[142]   See Pennington, *Sermon*, 29–40. A number of important studies have explored the Greco-Roman dimensions of Matthew's Gospel. See, for example, Wayne Meeks, *The Moral World of the First Christians* (Philadelphia: Westminster, 1986), 136–43; the essays in *The Gospel of Matthew in Its Roman Imperial Context* (ed. John Riches and David C. Sim; London: T&T Clark, 2005); Robert S. Kinney, *Hellenistic Dimensions of the Gospel of Matthew* (Tübingen: Mohr Siebeck, 2016), who argues that Hellenistic concepts permeate the whole of Matthew; Talbert, *Reading*, who analyzes the Greco-Roman aspects of the virtue tradition when discussing the Sermon on the Mount; and Jaroslav Pelikan, *Divine Rhetoric: The Sermon on the Mount as Message and as Model in Augustine, Chrysostom, and Luther* (Crestwood: St. Vladimir's Seminary Press, 2006), who argues that Greco-Roman rhetorical models were influential both on the Sermon on the Mount as well as the way it was interpreted in the early church. To suggest that Matthew is influenced by Greco-Roman language and concepts is not the same as suggesting that Matthew's theological concepts are consciously focused on the Empire. See Joel Willitts, "Matthew," in *Jesus Is Lord, Caesar Is Not: Evaluating Empire in New Testament Studies* (ed. Scot McKnight and Joseph B. Modica; Downers Grove, Ill.: IVP Academic, 2013), 82–100, who argues that Matthew's presentation of the restoration of the kingdom of Israel would present a perceived threat to any earthly kingdom but that Matthew shows no signs of critiquing Rome or singling it out uniquely.

Jews have anything like a closed collection of sacred texts from which to draw, and how differently did they treat those texts compared to non-scriptural compositions? How might these perceptions of authority have influenced the usage of the content when drawn upon?

A brief example illustrates the importance of these questions. It is argued in chapter 5 that Matthew's makarisms make use of lines and phrases from Isaiah and the Psalms and that the writer interweaves these lines and phrases to create composite quotations and allusions meant to draw the reader to the contexts and content of those references.[143] Are we to assume that Matthew's writer had copies of both Isaiah and the representative Psalms at his disposal? Did he create these composite references on his own, or were they already a part of the oral teaching or social memory of the community to which he belonged? Another example concerns Matthew's use of Mark's use of the HB. In Mark's version of the story of Jesus' entry into Jerusalem (Mark 11:1-10), Mark leaves the intertextual reference to Zech 9:9 unvoiced. However, when Matthew's writer draws on Mark to relay the same story (Matt 21:1-9), he removes the ambiguity by quoting Zechariah in full and adding details missing from Mark's account. Are we to assume that Matthew's writer had both texts, Mark and Zechariah, at his disposal, or is there some combination of the use of manuscripts, oral tradition, and social memory?

It is important to clarify here that this study is not overly concerned with source criticism, and most of these questions are not addressed in any detail. The goal here is to analyze the theme of inheritance across a broad spectrum of literature and to apply the findings from antecedent texts to Matthew's use of terms and ideas. Less important for this study is the exact manner in which those ideas came to the writer's attention. With that said (space precludes a full justification for the following statements), a few brief observations can be made.

Matthew's Gospel makes use of a repeated fulfillment formula.[144] This formula is used in reference to texts currently found in the HB but never for noncanonical texts. Furthermore, Matthew makes use of quotations or allusions from the HB but never from noncanonical texts. It is argued in this study that Matthew's writer was influenced, either directly or indirectly, by certain noncanonical compositions, and he was likely open to this influence and aware of it to some degree, but he displays a concerted engagement with certain texts, such as Isaiah and the Psalms, that certainly possessed a much greater authority in his theological

---

[143]   Matthew's Gospel makes use of these interwoven intertexts in multiple places throughout. See Richard B. Hays, *Echoes of Scripture in the Gospels* (Waco, Tex.: Baylor University Press, 2016), 187, for a list of examples.

[144]   E.g., 1:22-23; 2:15-18; 2:23; 4:14-16; 8:17; 12:17-21; 13:35; 21:4-5; 26:56.

matrix than texts that he does not cite or allude to directly. This does not mean other texts were not influential. Matthew's writer directly quotes the HB over sixty times, but this does not count the hundreds of allusions or echoes that can be detected. This study argues that the influence of many noncanonical compositions can be detected, either directly, or due to the nature of certain themes and ideas being "in the air" at the time. It is not controversial to suggest that noncanonical Second Temple compositions contributed to the social and symbolic world of Jews in the first century. Understanding these potential echoes can assist greatly in interpreting Matthew's Gospel. Nearly all of the often-discussed parallels between Matthew and its antecedent literature are limited to linguistic parallels, or citations, allusions, or echoes where direct textual dependence might be detected. Although linguistic parallels are noted in this discussion, the purpose here is not to argue that the First Evangelist knew or made use of every antecedent tradition that influenced the text. The aim of this study is to suggest that a necessary way forward in the discussion regarding the antecedent backgrounds of the Gospels is to move beyond discussions regarding direct literary and textual dependence in order to explore thematic and theological content that may have influenced the thought-world of the evangelists, especially regarding the history and trajectory of concepts within specific strands of Judaism that may have influenced the thinking of Jesus, his earliest followers, and the evangelists behind the Gospel accounts. This study aims to present a specific example of how these parallels might be considered. It is also important to note that the goal is not simply to shed light on the Gospels but to evaluate how the Gospels as one point in the trajectory might also illuminate the meaning of antecedent compositions that may belong to earlier points of development of their common thought-world.

It is likely that Matthew's author made use of both physical manuscripts and oral tradition. Social memory regarding certain ideas may have been composite in nature, but Richard B. Hays makes a compelling case that Matthew's writer is the author of his composite citations and interwoven material, based on the style, frequency, and unique application of his particular brand of intertextual hermeneutics.[145] Therefore, while it is possible that the material found its way to Matthew's writer through multiple mediums, the First Gospel portrays an author and editor with sophisticated hermeneutical sensibilities capable of utilizing received traditions to bolster his testimony of Jesus' story as it pertains to Israel's. This is also true of inheritance material, which derives its significance from Israel's Scriptures but is utilized to explain Jesus' significance.

[145]   Hays, *Gospels*, 186–87.

2

Inheritance in the Hebrew Bible

In the HB, the land of Israel is a pervasive and important theme. Landmark studies have been produced discussing everything from the prevalence of "the land" (הארץ) in texts across all eras of Hebrew scriptural composition,[1] to the theological significance of the land as it pertained to the relationship between God and his people.[2] The attention given to the land is with good reason. At one point in the tradition, Israel's greatest city, Jerusalem, was believed to be at the center of the earth (Ezek 5:5).[3] As W. D. Davies has written, "Israel, then, is the center of the earth, Jerusalem the center of Israel, Mt. Zion the center of Jerusalem,"[4] and all of this is both geographic and theological; the land of Israel has a prominent place within the Israelite worldview.[5] The HB is replete with descriptions of Israel containing sacred space and being home to the dwelling of God himself (e.g., Ps 43:3-4).[6] It is in Israel that God interacted with his people, blessed them, and kept them secure. The land is described as a gift from God (Deut 4:1), which God cared for

---

[1] For example, W. D. Davies, *The Gospel and the Land: Early Christianity and Jewish Territorial Doctrine* (Berkeley: University of California Press, 1974).

[2] For example, Walter Brueggemann, *The Land: Place as Gift, Promise, and Challenge in Biblical Faith* (Minneapolis: Fortress, 2002).

[3] See also 1 En. 26:1.

[4] Davies, *Land*, 8.

[5] See Norman Habel, *The Land Is Mine* (Minneapolis: Fortress, 1995), 2, who states: "In addition to being a physical entity, land is also a major symbol with a range of meanings reflected in the biblical texts. These meanings may be linked with economic, social, political, or religious contexts and interests."

[6] See N. T. Wright, *Finding God in the Psalms* (London: SPCK, 2014), 91.

and watched over (Deut 11:10-12). Israelite identity was tied to the land in ways not relevant to their life outside of it. Life in the land brought a sense of security and covenant location and was a key factor in the Israelites' understanding of their unique status as those in an exclusive relationship to their God.

However, missing from many studies is recognition that the land was not simply one gift among many, but it was a certain kind of gift—an inheritance.[7] The Israelites' belief that they had not only received the land from God, but inherited it, had a significant impact on shaping the way that the Israelites viewed the land, the way that they viewed their relationship to God, and the shape of their religious and social identity. Walter Brueggemann comes close to recognizing this when he writes, "and if God has to do with Israel in a special way, as he surely does, he has to do with land as a historical place in a special way. It will no longer do to talk about Yahweh and his people but we must speak about Yahweh and his people *and his land*."[8] There is a missing ingredient to this. Brueggemann attempts to answer *why* the land was viewed as such an important element in God's relationship with the Israelites. He understands the land's role in providing security and historicity to the Israelites, and he addresses the belief that this particular land had been the land promised to their ancestors,[9] but he does not discuss the method by which that promise was fulfilled. More precisely, he does not address why this particular land was so important as opposed to any other land where God certainly could have related to his people in precisely the same ways. This land was not just any land—it was *inherited* land. The Israelites viewed the land as their birthright. However, they had not only inherited the land from their ancestors but also believed they had inherited it from God himself. It was not a place whereupon they entered into a special relationship with God, but rather they believed that because they were already in that relationship they were able to enter the land. There is certainly evidence in the Hebrew Scriptures that the Israelites came to be enamored with the land for its own sake,[10] but initially it was nothing more than a promise, a by-product of the initiation by God of a

[7]   For example, in Davies' seminal study on the land he mentions inheritance just once, and that in a footnote, *Land*, 20, n. 12. In the note Davies admits that inheritance is an important theme, inseparable from discussions of the land, and yet he pays no further attention to it.

[8]   Brueggemann, *Land*, 5 (emphasis original).

[9]   Brueggemann, *Land*, 16–25.

[10]   See Moshe Weinfeld, *The Promise of the Land: The Inheritance of the Land of Canaan by the Israelites* (Berkeley: University of California Press, 1993), 183, who states, "No other people in the history of mankind was as preoccupied as the people of Israel with the land in which they lived."

relationship with their ancestors (Gen 15:1-21). Because they believed that God was *their* God, and that they were *his* people (Exod 6:7), it is the inheritance theme that provides significance to the land as something greater than simply geographic space. The language of giving and receiving is present in land contexts, but any kindness can motivate a gift, and anyone could give or receive a gift. In the Israelite worldview, an inheritance was a gift only given in kinsman-type relationships and signified a special tie that no other gift could; namely, there was something unique about the relationship that shaped the identity of those involved in the transaction. The land theme provided for the Israelites a sense of place, but the inheritance theme provides a sense that the Israelites belonged there; how they obtained the land says as much about their identity as the land itself. The Israelites viewed God as their "father," their chief ancestor, who brought the clan of Israel into being and gave them the land as their inherited birthright.[11] Considering that in many ways inheritance bolsters the meaning of the land, it is surprising that it has received so little attention in land studies.

The purpose of this chapter is to contribute to filling in this gap: the paucity of attention given to inheritance in studies regarding the land. The importance of inheritance to land has bearing on how the writer of Matthew's Gospel may have understood inheritance in the HB. The first section of this chapter analyzes inheritance in the Hexateuch, which is significant for at least two reasons. First, this is the foundational, opening section of the HB and many of the themes in this section set the tone for an Israelite worldview that may inform assessments of other antecedents of inheritance in Matthew's Gospel. Second, nearly half of all references to inheritance in the whole of the HB are found in this section. The goal here is to analyze relative terms and themes in order to better understand inheritance, what it was, who its intended recipients were, how it functioned, and to establish inheritance as one of the central themes of the Hexateuch for understanding Israelite social and religious identity. Although inheritance as a concept runs through every major section of the HB, its ongoing development remains largely reliant on the foundations of the Hexateuch. In addition to the Hexateuch, this chapter also focuses on inheritance in the monarchy period and the prophetic books, before concluding with a discussion on the major themes, trends, and motifs that surround the concept of inheritance.[12]

---

[11]   See Marianne Meye Thompson, *The Promise of the Father: Jesus and God in the New Testament* (Louisville: Westminster John Knox, 2000), 41.

[12]   Inheritance terms appear frequently in the Psalms (about 25x) and the Proverbs (about 9x). These uses are either so tied to the contexts of other HB compositions so as to be redundant, or so eclectic that they contribute little new information to

2.1. נחלה and Its Cognates as Inheritance

The noun נחלה and verb נחל are the primary terms used for inheritance in the HB. There has been some scholarly discussion regarding the most appropriate way to translate these words, rooted in the conceptual framework in which these terms can be found. The earliest influential examination of the relationship between נחלה and the land was undertaken by Gerhard von Rad.[13] His essay is limited to the Hexateuch and preoccupied with redaction-critical questions, but he concludes that נחלה primarily refers to the possession of hereditary land by tribes, clans, and families. According to Von Rad, many occurrences "are to some extent ambiguous,"[14] so that the precise interpretation and referent for נחלה depends on the perceived source of a given passage. For example, he argues that the Deuteronomist speaks of an "inheritance" for all Israel rather than individual tribes but that in a few instances this source also knows of tribal inheritance. The tribe was the ultimate trustee of the נחלה over and above the family.[15] Von Rad goes on to admit that the divisions between sources is not of decisive significance, as the Priestly writer would have gone on to adjust older material and that hereditary land was the principal concern in the use of נחלה in the Hexateuch.[16]

This notion of the נחלה as hereditary land was confirmed by Abraham Malamat in 1962.[17] In his analysis of the Mari documents, he found that several of them were concerned "with transfers of land in which there is no formal sale; the purchaser receives the property as a hereditary portion."[18] These transactions were designated by the term *nahalum*. One significant feature of this analysis was the notion of the land as inalienable, illustrated by one case in which a man became the legal son of another in order to obtain a portion of his landed property. Malamat offers "hereditary property, inherited portion, patrimony" as acceptable glosses for נחלה and argues that in both Mari and the HB the terms refer to "an essentially inalienable piece of land possessed solely by a gentilic unit" and that this land could not, in theory, be sold. The transfer of the

---

understanding inheritance as a "concept history." Therefore, this study does not feature a section on inheritance terms in these compositions, but relevant passages from both the Psalms and the Proverbs are discussed frequently throughout this study when relevant as a potential influence upon other texts.

[13]   Gerhard von Rad, "The Promised Land and Yahweh's Land in the Hexateuch," in *The Problem of the Hexateuch and Other Essays* (London: SCM Press, 1984), 79–93.

[14]   Von Rad, "Promised Land," 80.

[15]   Von Rad, "Promised Land," 86.

[16]   Von Rad, "Promised Land," 81.

[17]   Abraham Malamat, "Mari and the Bible: Some Patterns of Tribal Organization and Institutions," *JAOS* 82, no. 2 (1962): 143–50.

[18]   Malamat, "Mari and the Bible," 147.

land "could only be affected through inheritance."[19] Malamat suggests that this principle guarantees the stability of patriarchal-tribal organization and is further illustrated by the jubilee year, where a plot of land cannot be sold in perpetuity but only leased until the jubilee transferred the land back to its original owner.[20]

Some scholars have argued that "inheritance" is not the best translation of נחלה.[21] However, Christopher J. H. Wright argues effectively that "inheritance" is the best macro-term for נחלה. Of principal importance for Wright is the father-son relationship between Yahweh and his people, which is manifested at both the national (Exod 4:22; Deut 32:5, 6, 18, 19; Hos 11:1; Jer 31:9) and individual (Deut 14:1) level. Israel's sonship is indicated by their election, as they were brought into existence by Yahweh and chosen by him for his own possession. In this relationship "inheritance" is to be viewed as the most appropriate term for נחלה, "for in describing the land as Israel's *inheritance*, Deuteronomy must regard Israel as Yahweh's *son*" (emphasis his).[22] נחלה, then, signifies the unique relationship between Yahweh and his people.[23]

Wright also argues that the family unit was at the center of several spheres of life in Israel, including its landed property. Wright follows Malamat and the evidence from the Mari documents to illustrate that the passing of ancestral land is key to understanding the nuances of נחלה, including the inalienability of the land. He notes that there are no instances in the HB of an Israelite selling their land outside of the family unit and that the only way to dispose of land was to apportion it to legal family heirs.[24] The theological rationale for this comes from God's perpetual ownership of the land, most directly stated in Lev 25:23, "the land shall not be sold in perpetuity, for the land is mine; with me you are but aliens and tenants." Yahweh's relationship with the land is the fulcrum for Yahweh's relationship to Israel, and by extension, Israel's relationship to Yahweh's land.[25] In

---

[19]   Malamat, "Mari and the Bible," 149.

[20]   Malamat, "Mari and the Bible," 150.

[21]   For an example, see Habel, *Land*, 39–41. While Habel offers a detailed discussion on the idea of the land as a gift, he finds this simply to be a divine act that operates as a "conditional land grant." Yahweh has inalienable tenure over the land and he grants usage of the land to the Israelites as an allocation.

[22]   Christopher J. H. Wright, *God's People in God's Land: Family, Land, and Property in the Old Testament* (Grand Rapids: Eerdmans, 1990), 19.

[23]   Wright, *God's People*, 20, states, "It emerges, therefore, that the gift of the land, as a historical indicative which owes nothing to the action or merit of Israel, is directly related to the same unconditional feature of Israel's sonship; it is because Israel is Yahweh's firstborn son that the land is given as an inheritance. The bond between Israel's land theology and the status of the people's unique relationship with Yahweh is here seen at its closest—the one being, as it were, the tangible manifestation of the other."

[24]   Wright, *God's People*, 56–57.

[25]   Wright, *God's Land*, 59–60.

this, ancestral inheritance becomes the basis for understanding נחלה; Yahweh passes the land to his son(s) Israel, and Israel passes their apportioned land throughout the generations by way of patrimony within household units. The inalienability of the land ensures the security of each household, as they cannot be permanently alienated from their land.[26] This, in turn, ensures the permanence of their relationship to Yahweh.

There are several interpretive glosses that are appropriate for translating נחלה, depending on the context. As this study seeks to demonstrate, these include inheritance, portion, share, allotment, entitlement, possession, and heritage. At issue is whether a macro-term can be established to translate נחלה in a majority of instances that will reveal the conceptual framework behind the use of the word. Behind the singular term נחלה lies a conceptual framework for understanding its essential character; there are other words used in the HB for many of these glosses,[27] so the question may be asked, what distinguishes נחלה among them? A case is made that נחלה has an essentially *relational* character and that Wright is correct to emphasize Yahweh's fatherhood and election of Israel as important to understanding this term clearly. It appears as a key term in a threefold relationship; it emphasizes the *permanence* of Israel's relationship to Yahweh by highlighting: 1) the relationship of Yahweh to the land, 2) the relationship of Yahweh to his people, and 3) the relationship of Yahweh's people to Yahweh's land, which he gives to his people as a gift. Among the agreed upon translations for נחלה, "inheritance" is the best concept for describing the nature of these relationships. Essential to understanding inheritance is the relational aspect of the gift; Yahweh's relationship to his people, and by extension the people's relationship to Yahweh's land, is not primarily an administrative one but rather a familial one. Yahweh offers his land as an inheritance to his son(s) Israel. This study indicates when other glosses seem best in a given context, but the focus is primarily on "inheritance" as a macro-term for נחלה.

2.2. Inheritance in the Hexateuch

A study of the Hexateuch rather than the Pentateuch requires comment. One of the purposes of this study is to discuss Matthew's antecedents through a narrative and thematic framework, and at the close of the Pentateuch, the narrative regarding the theme of inheritance is left

---

[26]   Wright, *God's Land*, 63.

[27]   Frequently used terms are: חלק (share, portion); the verb is found 56x in the HB and the noun is found 32x. The term, like terms referring to inheritance, is most often tied to land portions allotted to Israel's tribes and clans. See *NIDOTTE*, 5 vols. (ed. William A. VanGemeren; Grand Rapids: Zondervan, 1997), 2:159 (Cornelis van Dam); and גורל (allotment), found 77x in the HB. The term refers mostly to the casting of lots but is frequently featured in land and inheritance contexts. See *NIDOTTE*, 1:826–27 (Cornelis van Dam).

incomplete. It is in Joshua that the reader finds narrative cohesion and completion of the Pentateuch regarding the theme of inheritance, with the content and nature of inheritance usage demonstrating a shift from Judges forward. There is no intent to support any particular documentary theories. The goal of this section is to evaluate how inheritance contributes to an understanding of the identity and worldview of the Israelites within a narrative framework and evaluating the Hexateuch as a complete narrative satisfies that goal.[28]

2.2.1. Relative Terms

2.2.1.1. נחלה and Its Cognates

The noun נחלה and verbal forms from the root נחל are the main words for inheritance in the Hexateuch and the whole of the HB. The noun is used 122 times (out of 220 total in HB), and the verb is used 34 times (out of 59 total in HB). In this section major elements of the use of נחלה and its cognates (i.e., what it is, who receives it, and how it functions) are considered, and important associated themes are turned to in a later section.

1. The Land as נחלה for Israel

The most common referent of נחלה is the land. Although not inseparable, the land and the inheritance are closely linked in a large number of contexts (e.g., Exod 23:30-31; Num 34:13-29). Within these contexts נחלה displays its broadest range of meaning (inheritance, possession, portion, and allotment)[29] and often, use of the term implies all of these. The following six points may be made regarding this usage.

First, foundational is the belief that God is the one who bestows the land as a נחלה. Leviticus 25:23 depicts Yahweh as declaring his ownership of the land, and the passage refers to the Israelites as תושבים (tenants). God prepared the land before the Israelites took possession of it (Exod 23:20); he directs the treatment and cultivation of the land to his own specifications (Exod 23:10-12). The land is consistently referred to

---

[28] Of course, if the goal were to track the *development* of the Israelite worldview regarding inheritance then documentary theories may become quite useful, although still largely speculative. Von Rad, *Hexateuch*, 80–82, argues that there is scant use of inheritance language for Israel as a whole in the pre-Deuteronomic writings but that the concept of inheritance is found in each source of the Hexateuch, and Israel as Yahweh's inheritance, or tribal inheritance of the land, are attested in the earliest sources. These distinctions within the range of the terms will be discussed below. For more regarding documentary issues in relation to the Deuteronomic History, see Thomas Römer, *The So-Called Deuteronomistic History: A Sociological, Historical, and Literary Introduction* (London: T&T Clark, 2007).

[29] Christopher J. H. Wright, *nāḥal*, in *NIDOTTE*, 3:77.

as a possession for the people of Israel, but despite the status of the land as an inheritance given over to the Israelites, God is never depicted as surrendering his ultimate ownership and control.[30] Because God maintains ownership, inheriting the land is not a one-time transaction but rather a continual one that signifies an ongoing relationship between God as the giver of the land and the Israelites as heirs and beneficiaries. God is the one who sets the boundaries of the land,[31] as well as the tribal borders (Num 34:1-12), and because of this the Israelites are never granted the right to move those borders (Deut 19:14). Once in the land, the Israelites are to worship Yahweh, not according to the ways of the former inhabitants of the land but according to the ways directed by God in response to his blessings (Deut 12:1-7).

Second, although the Israelites are consistently depicted as actors in obtaining their own נחלה, the verb נתן (to give) appears often in inheritance contexts to remind the reader that inheritance is, by its very nature, a gift (Deut 4:21). Regardless of the Israelites' involvement in securing the inheritance, without God as its guarantor they would be unable to receive it; indeed, they nearly do not. Deuteronomy 9:13-21 depicts the Israelites, prior to obtaining the land, worshiping a false idol in the form of a golden calf, which is an activity expressly forbidden once the Israelites entered the land (Deut 4:15-24). Moses is said to intervene with God, and he uses inheritance language to dissuade God from destroying the Israelites for their rebellion (Deut 9:25-29). The Israelites are referred to as God's own נחלה.[32] This story is set up with a recognition that God is gifting the land to the Israelites because the current inhabitants are

---

[30]   God's "perpetual ownership" of the land is not explicitly stated but is strongly implied by his role in securing the land, his continual rule over the land and its inhabitants, and his ability and right to take the land away from the inhabitants. For more on the theme of God's perpetual ownership of the land, see Habel, *Land*, 98; Von Rad, "Promised Land," 87; Davies, *Land*, 157. In order to solve the possible tension between God's gift of the land to the Israelites and his perpetual ownership of it, Wright, *God's Land*, 10, offers a commendable solution when he states, "Theologically, the land could be viewed from two angles. From Israel's point of view it was the land of promise and gift—the major theme of their historical traditions. From Yahweh's point of view it was the land that belonged in a unique sense to him, and his prior ownership of it must be acknowledged by Israel in cultic and legal institutions."

[31]   There has been some discussion regarding possible inconsistencies in the various descriptions in the Hexateuch of the borders of the land. The descriptions in Gen 15:18-21 and Exod 23:31 include a wider space than the description in Num 34. The precise dimensions of the land are an important consideration in land studies, but solving this issue is not necessary for understanding the theme of inheritance. For more, see Weinfeld, *Promise*, 52–75.

[32]   Moshe Weinfeld, *Deuteronomy 1–11* (AB 5; New York: Doubleday, 1991), 417, points out that the role of the Israelites as God's inheritance is addressed by Moses both at the start and end of his prayer in 9:26-29, which forms an inclusio around the

wicked and deserve to be driven out (Deut 9:4).[33] The Israelites are not inheriting the land due to their own righteousness, because they have none (Deut 9:6-8),[34] but rather they receive the inheritance as a gift from God despite themselves.[35]

Third, the primary way that נחלה is tied to the land is through tribal allotment.[36] In this sense, the land is regarded as *divided* as much as it is *received*. In fact, the verb נחל can refer to the process of "allotting," or "handing out" the land (Num 34:1-29).[37] Rather than the Israelites as a whole,[38] much of the discussion centers on hereditary portions of the land disseminated to both tribes and families (Josh 11:23).[39] The lot was divided to each tribe based on its size (Num 26:52-56; 36:54).[40] It

prayer. Moses appeals to God to allow the Israelites to remain in their inherited land despite their rebellion, due to their status as God's inherited people.

[33]   See John Van Seters, *The Pentateuch: A Social Science Commentary* (Sheffield: Sheffield Academic, 1999), 105–6.

[34]   This passage makes use of language also found in rebellion narratives in Exodus, connecting them. It is not simply the golden calf incident that demonstrates Israel's rebellion; this was their continual disposition. See S. R. Driver, *Deuteronomy* (ICC; Edinburgh: T&T Clark, 1895), 112, "Israel has never yielded itself readily to God's will."

[35]   Illustrating this further, the entirety of Moses' appeal to God in 9:26-29 places the Israelites on the receiving end of God's mercy and favor. Moses reminds God of the divine purpose, using both the patriarchs and the exodus as examples, and appeals to God's glory as justification for sparing the Israelites. For more, see Duane L. Christensen, *Deuteronomy 1–11* (WBC 6A; Dallas: Word Books, 1991), 191.

[36]   As Lawrence E. Stager notes in "Forging an Identity: The Emergence of Ancient Israel," in *The Oxford History of the Biblical World* (New York: Oxford University Press, 1998), 150, the Israelite "tribe" can be understood as kinship based on common descent. The precise boundaries and constitution of the Israelite "tribe" can be difficult to determine. As Stager describes, kinship is implied, but it is not sufficient to assume that the tribes were solely kin-based. Tribes were sociopolitical groups focused on allegiance and shared identity.

[37]   See Habel, *Land*, 34.

[38]   Gerhard von Rad, *Old Testament Theology*, vol. 1 (London: SCM Press, 1965), 224, detects a shift in focus on this point with the Deuteronomist. He argues, rightly, that the majority focus on tribal allotment is found in Numbers and Joshua; it is in Deuteronomy that the focus on inheritance lies with the whole of Israel. He sees this as an overall condition of Deuteronomy; Israel as a focus of the text as the tribes fade into the background.

[39]   See Von Rad, *Hexateuch*, 81.

[40]   Wright, *God's Land*, 48–53, describes the threefold division of Israel in relation to land allotment: the *tribe*, the *clan* (or, *kin-group*), and the *family*. The tribe was the trustee of the inheritance and held ultimate title to the land over and above the family units. The kin-group was an intermediate group between the tribe and the family, which constituted a social unit of closely related families from within a tribe. Wright argues effectively that this kin-group was the territorial unit within the system of land tenure, in that an individual Israelite became associated with the territory of their kin-group as their "geographical address." Kin-group names occasionally became interchangeable with the names of villages.

should be emphasized that, although "land" is the referent of נחלה in these instances, and although נחלה can mean "allotment" or "possession," נחלה is at times paired with other Hebrew words for these concepts (e.g., חלק, "allotment" in Deut 14:27-29; אחזה, "possession" in Num 27:7; 35:2), which clearly distinguishes between them. Dividing the land between the tribes as a possession allows them use of the land, but the concept of inheritance is what governs that use, beginning with the observation that the allotments are inalienable. Precisely because each allotment was given *as an inheritance*, the land cannot be permanently sold outside of the tribe to which it is allotted (Lev 25:23) and the borders cannot be moved (Deut 19:14).[41] Inheritance guarantees that the land will be passed down forever (Josh 14:9).[42]

Fourth, due to God's continued ownership of the land, in addition to maintaining its original borders, there were strict regulations regarding the way the land must be treated. Because the land was holy, these regulations included the development of cities of refuge for the perpetrators of unintentional killings. If the family of the victim arranged for retribution, and a murder was committed on inherited land, then the land would be stained with innocent blood. The cities of refuge were set aside as a place at which a perpetrator was able to flee (Deut 19:1-13). Furthermore, in warfare, when the Israelites were to engage an enemy from outside of the inherited land, they were to offer the enemy terms of peace (Deut 20:10), but when engaging the inhabitants of the land of promise they were not to offer peace, they were to completely cleanse the land of its inhabitants so that the inhabitants' practices would not be adopted by the Israelites (Deut 20:16-18) and therefore cause them to sin against God. The community itself was also tightly regulated for the strict purpose of maintaining the holiness of inherited land, including the offering of the first fruits of the land to God (Deut 26:1), the handling of capital punishment (Deut 21:23), and marriage (Deut 24:4). In the latter case, improper handling of divorce and remarriage is said to bring sin upon the land that God נתן לך נחלה (gives to you as an inheritance). These regulations are not described as protecting the land for its own

---

[41]   See Wright, *God's Land*, 55–58.

[42]   The inalienability of the land is often tied to the structure and purpose of the Jubilee legislation. Even if land were to change hands legally, God's ownership of the land, and demarcation of boundaries, requires that the land eventually revert back to the tribe and family that originally received it. See John Sietze Bergsma, *The Jubilee from Leviticus to Qumran: A History of Interpretation* (SVT 115; Leiden: Brill, 2007), 33–34, who also connects this idea to the need to maintain ancestral graves, which could not be done if a family was alienated from the land. This issue becomes relevant later in the chapter with our discussion on the books of Samuel.

sake but rather are due to the fact that God owns the land, the Israelites are merely heirs, and they receive the land as a gift.

Fifth, the Israelites are responsible to play a role in obtaining the נחלה, and each tribe bears responsibility to assist the others in taking possession of their land. This is a consistent theme but is most evident in the case of the Reubenites, Gadites, and the half tribe of Manasseh. Before taking the land promised to them, these three groups become interested in land not defined by the original borders (Num 32:1-5).[43] Due to the extra space they would need for their large number of livestock, they ask for land east of the Jordan, but Moses holds them accountable to their responsibility in the conquest. They must join the other tribes by taking up arms in order to dispossess the inhabitants of Canaan. Provided that the people of Reuben, Gad, and Manasseh fulfill this responsibility, Moses promises them the land of their request as their inheritance (Num 32:28-42).

Sixth, although the נחלה is not earned, it is a gift, God places a condition on it, namely, that if the Israelites will not be obedient to his commands, then they will not inherit the land (Deut 4:1; 12:9-12). When they enter the land, if they rebel against God, then the נחלה will not be retained. Obedience should be driven by God's goodness to the Israelites (Deut 4:20), and if the Israelites remain obedient, then they will be blessed in the land (Deut 15:6), which serves the purpose of displaying the glory of God to the surrounding nations (Deut 4:6-8). Indeed, as John Van Seters argues, the basis for the law itself is predicated on land inheritance. Van Seters states, "the whole of the law code, with its regulation of religion, government, the courts, taxes and social welfare, is viewed as a 'constitution' given through Moses in anticipation of their inheriting the land."[44] The Amorites were eliminated from the land by God because of their evil ways, as the land was delivered to the Israelites, but there is no guarantee that the Israelites will live any better. Van Seters states, "If the Israelites behave in the same way as the former inhabitants, then they, too, will forfeit their right to the land. So the gift of the land is conditioned upon obedience to the law (the covenant)."[45] Famously, the story of the Hexateuch depicts the wilderness generation as rebellious, and it is said that their generation would not be allowed to

---

[43]   The inalienability of the tribal allotments seems not to be an issue, as the actual borders and allotments for the individual tribes were not made until Num 34, when Moses recognizes that the tribes of Reuben, Gad, and the half tribe of Manasseh had already received their inheritance (34:13-15). See Baruch A. Levine, *Numbers 21–36* (AB; New York: Doubleday, 2000), 536.

[44]   Van Seters, *Pentateuch*, 105, points out that the giving of the law code in Deuteronomy is consistently accompanied by the phrase "when Yahweh brings you into the land that he is giving you . . ."

[45]   Van Seters, *Pentateuch*, 106.

partake in the inheritance (Num 32:10-15). Joshua is an exception, as he is consistently depicted as a hero who would lead the next generation to take possession of the נחלה (Deut 3:28; 31:7; Josh 1:6).

2. A נחלה for the Levites

A second major usage of נחלה and its cognates is not at all in reference to land but rather the lack of possessing it. The Levites were not given an allotment of the land as an inheritance; they were provided with land in which to live (Num 35:1-8), including cities and pastureland for their livestock, which were allotted to them out of the land inherited by the other tribes, and each tribe contributed according to the size of their own נחלה. In the Hexateuch, the נחלה of the Levites is described in at least four ways.

First, in Num 18:20-26 the Levites' נחלה is described as the tithe offered by the Israelites at the temple, and this is in return for the work that the Levites perform in service of the tent of meeting, in which they "spare the Israelites the risk of approaching the 'dangerous' sanctuary."[46] After receiving the tithe as a נחלה (portion), the Levites were to tithe off that to the priests as their own contribution (Num 18:26).[47]

Second, in Deut 18:1, in an anomalous usage in the Hexateuch, we find the phrase אשי יהוה ונחלתו יאכלון. Various translations render the referent of the pronominal suffix differently. The ESV translates this phrase "They shall eat the LORD's food offerings as their inheritance," referring to the Israelites as those who will receive the food offered to Yahweh as part of *their own* inheritance. This translation is consistent with the ideas of Num 18:20-26, but it is less natural than the NRSV rendering: "They may eat the sacrifices that are the LORD's portion." The third person, masculine, singular pronominal suffix ו- at the end of נחלתו suggests that the portion, or inheritance, in this verse belongs to God and not the Levites. "Portion" is a more natural gloss in this context than inheritance; however, in the following verse we find נחלה twice more, which refers to the Levites' non-land inheritance among the Israelites. They are to eat of the food of the offering since they have no נחלה of their own.[48] Similar to the land, the נחלה of the offering belongs to God and he gives it as a gift.

Third, Josh 18 describes the allotment of land to the final seven of the tribes who received their נחלה. These seven tribes were to divide

---

[46]   Martin Noth, *Numbers* (London: SCM Press, 1968), 137.

[47]   See Philip J. Budd, *Numbers* (WBC 5; Columbia: Thomas Nelson, 1984), 207.

[48]   See Peter C. Craigie, *The Book of Deuteronomy* (London: Hodder and Stoughton, 1976), 258.

their portions, but the Levites are not to receive one. Rather than the fruit of the priesthood, as in Num 18, the priesthood itself is described as their נחלה.

Fourth, and most importantly, the Levites receive Yahweh himself as their own inheritance. In Num 18:20b, Yahweh declares to the Levites, "I am your portion and your inheritance (נחלתך) in the midst of the Israelites." The idea that God is a נחלה to the Levites is also found in Deut 10:9 and 18:1-2. Precisely why the Levites are described as having Yahweh as their נחלה, when he is never described as such in relation to any of the other tribes, is never made explicit. He is described as a נחלה to a tribe that has none otherwise. The other referents for the נחלה in relationship to the Levites (i.e., the tithe, offerings, and priesthood itself) all find their value in the cultic practices and service to the tabernacle. Working in service to the regulation and ritual of worship placed the Levites in proximity to Yahweh in a way that nothing else could, and it was in him that they were expected to find their נחלה.

3. Yahweh's Own נחלה

Although small in number, there are a series of important and often anomalous instances in the Hexateuch describing the נחלה belonging to Yahweh himself. In Exod 15:17, there is a poetic reference to "the mountain," clearly a reference to the land, in which God is said to have made his dwelling. This mountain is referred to as God's נחלה, best understood in the context as his own "possession." The land as God's dwelling is directly connected to the ability of the Israelites to inherit the land in the future. Yahweh's ownership of the mountain as his own נחלה was an important expression of his sovereign reign over the land and its people.[49]

The principal usage of נחלה in relation to Yahweh regards God's people, the Israelites, as his own inheritance. Exodus 34 describes an interaction in which Moses asks God to pardon the Israelites of their sins and take them as God's own נחלה (34:9). God is said to make a covenant with Moses and the people (35:10), clearly signifying that he has responded favorably to this request to make them his inheritance.[50] In a similar occurrence, in Deut 9, God expresses his anger against the people for their rebellion (9:24) and decides to destroy them. Moses

---

[49]   See John I. Durham, *Exodus* (WBC 3; Columbia: Thomas Nelson, 1987), 208–9.

[50]   This passage is rhetorically linked to Exod 19:5, where God declares to Moses, "Now therefore, if you obey my voice and keep my covenant, you shall be my treasured possession out of all the peoples." Moses' request is a response to God's initial invitation. See Durham, *Exodus*, 455.

reminds God of his redemptive act of bringing the Israelites out of Egypt and refers to the people as God's נחלה (9:26). With the success of God's people, his own reputation is at stake (9:28). Moses never justifies the behavior of the Israelites but reminds God that הם עמך ונחלתך (they are your people and your inheritance) and that God has demonstrated his power to the world by redeeming them (9:29).

Deuteronomy 32 is an important passage for understanding the people as God's נחלה. Often referred to as "the Song of Moses," verses 8-9 in this poetic text read:[51]

> When the Most High[52] apportioned (הנחל) the nations,
>   when he divided humankind,
> he fixed the boundaries of the peoples
>   according to the number of the gods;[53]
> the LORD's own portion was his people,
>   Jacob his allotted share.

The term הנחל, the hiphil infinitive from the root נחל, is best translated "apportioned," because in the context the idea is not that the Most High is causing the nations to "inherit," but rather the nations are themselves being created and God is dividing one from another. The boundaries between them are being fixed. Although Yahweh is depicted as controlling the allotment of all nations, he then takes Israel (Jacob) as his own portion. Yahweh receives Israel as his own נחלה, clearly establishing a relationship with them that he does not have with the other nations.[54]

---

[51]   English translations of block passages from NRSV unless otherwise indicated.

[52]   There has been considerable discussion regarding possible polytheistic connotations in v. 8, revolving around the identity of עליון, "the most high." Some scholars have regarded עליון as distinct from יהוה of v. 9 and greater than יהוה. In this reconstruction, יהוה is equal to the other "divine beings" and receives Israel as his own portion from עליון. For a fuller discussion, see Paul Sanders, *The Provenance of Deuteronomy 32* (Leiden: Brill, 1996), 78, who convincingly argues that there is no basis for a separation of עליון from יהוה as different gods.

[53]   Establishing the wording of this text is infamously problematic. Where the NRSV reads "gods" in v. 8, the ESV reads "sons of god" and the NIV reads "sons of Israel." Notes in the NRSV and ESV give primacy to the LXX and Dead Sea Scrolls as the source of the reading, while the NIV gives primacy to the Masoretic Text. This is a complex problem, but solving it is not necessary in order to understand Yahweh's inheritance in this passage.

[54]   This idea is also communicated in Deut 14:1-2: "You are children of the LORD your God. You must not lacerate yourselves or shave your forelocks for the dead. For you are a people holy to the LORD your God; it is you the LORD has chosen out of all the peoples on the earth to be his people, his treasured possession." The word for possession in this passage is סגלה, rather than נחל, but clearly the context supports the idea that God has a special relationship with Israel that he does not share with the other nations.

2.2.1.2. ירש and Its Cognates

Another important term for understanding inheritance in the HB, and one given much less attention than נחלה, is the verb ירש. The term appears in the Hexateuch 131 times (out of 232 total in HB).[55] The lack of attention paid to this verb in the Hexateuch is surprising given its frequency and importance to inheritance contexts, especially regarding the ways in which it can provide nuances to inheritance that are unique and distinguishable from נחלה. Although the noun נחלה appears in Genesis, the verbal form does not; ירש is the only verb for inheritance found in Genesis, appearing ten times and covering a broad range of ideas related to inheritance. ירש appears in each book of the Hexateuch, with the majority of instances in Deuteronomy and Joshua.

There is no agreement on the etymological meaning of the root ירש; however, accepted translations are "inherit," "disinherit," "take or gain possession," and "dispossess."[56] The aspect of "disinheritance" and "take possession" are potentially the most important of the nuances regarding the difference in meaning between ירש and נחלה.

While נחלה carries connotations of giving and receiving, ירש connotes, in many instances, the opposite. It is a form of inheritance that describes a threat to a possession or inheritance or the taking of a possession or inheritance by force. This often includes the use of aggression and violence.[57] The primary contexts where this meaning becomes prominent are in regard to Israel's conquest of the land of Canaan and removal of the inhabitants, although there are contexts in addition to the conquest where ירש is used of force and the taking or losing of an inheritance. The conquest looms large over the inheritance and land themes of the Hexateuch. If the Israelites are to inherit the land, they must conquer and drive out the inhabitants in order to cleanse the land of their culture, false gods, and forms of worship. It is beyond the scope of this chapter to explore this idea exhaustively; however, one important example, where ירש and נחלה appear side by side, serves to demonstrate the point. Num 33:50-56 reads:

> In the plains of Moab by the Jordan at Jericho, the Lord spoke to Moses, saying: [51] Speak to the Israelites, and say to them: When you

---

[55]   The noun form, ירשה, appears twelve times (out of sixteen total in HB), but the noun exclusively refers to "possession" in the sense of occupation and provides little to the discussion regarding inheritance, so it will be left out of the discussion.

[56]   See Christopher J. H. Wright, "ירש (yarash)," in *NIDOTTE*, 2:539.

[57]   In my own analysis of each use of ירש in the Hexateuch, I regard 91 of the 131 instances to either explicitly state, or strongly imply, the taking or loss of a possession or inheritance by the use of force and violence, and another 15 where force is possibly implied as a subtext. Only 25 instances do not contain a discernable trace of force.

cross over the Jordan into the land of Canaan, [52] you shall drive out (הורשתם) all the inhabitants of the land from before you, destroy all their figured stones, destroy all their cast images, and demolish all their high places. [53] You shall take possession (הורשתם) of the land and settle in it, for I have given you the land to possess (לרשת). [54] You shall apportion (התנחלתם) the land by lot according to your clans; to a large one you shall give a large inheritance (נחלתו), and to a small one you shall give a small inheritance (נחלתו); the inheritance shall belong to the person on whom the lot falls; according to your ancestral tribes you shall inherit (תתנחלו). But [55] if you do not drive out (תורישו) the inhabitants of the land from before you, then those whom you let remain shall be as barbs in your eyes and thorns in your sides; they shall trouble you in the land where you are settling. [56] And I will do to you as I thought to do to them.

In this passage, cognates of ירש and נחלה are each used four times; in each instance where נחלה is used, the connotation is either the giving or receiving of the inheritance. In each instance where ירש is used, the connotation is force; the places of worship are demolished, the current inhabitants of Canaan are "driven out" (lit. disinherited/dispossessed), and the land is then possessed by the Israelites. Similar comparisons could be made regarding Deut 1:38-39 and 19:1-3. Additional passages where ירש clearly entails inheritance by force, or the violent disinheritance of the inhabitants of the land of Canaan, are Lev 20:24; Num 13:30; Deut 3:12-20 (occurs 3x), and Deut 20:16-18. Deuteronomy in particular makes it clear that dispossession does not simply entail "removal" of the inhabitants of Canaan but destruction through warfare.[58]

Furthermore, there are many passages where ירש is used to declare that God will assist the Israelites to disinherit and drive out the inhabitants of the land in order for Israel to inherit it (Deut 7:1-17, occurs 2x; 9:1-23, occurs 8x). In such passages, God is given credit for the success of dispossessing the inhabitants (Exod 34:24; Deut 4:32-38). ירש can be used to describe a lack of success on the part of the Israelites in driving out the Canaanites (Josh 15:63; 16:10; 17:12-18). In some instances, ירש is even used against the Israelites themselves; in Num 14:12, in

[58]   See Weinfeld, *Promise*, 76–98, who states that though this verb literally means to "cause to possess/inherit," it also "can mean simultaneously both expulsion and extermination" (83). Weinfeld points out that the language in most of the Pentateuch only requires that the Israelites "drive out" or "dispossess" the inhabitants from the land of Canaan. It is only in Deuteronomy that we find commands for the inhabitants to be annihilated (20:16-18) and that the Israelites "shall not let a soul remain alive" (20:16). He argues that this idea was written in retrospect, as the book of Deuteronomy was taking shape in the eight and seventh centuries B.C.E., and that later sources (e.g., 1 Kings, 2 Chronicles) reveal that this annihilation was never carried out.

response to the unbelief of the Israelites to God's many works on their behalf, God declares, "I will strike them with pestilence and 'disinherit' them" (אורשׁנו).

Disinheritance as a connotation of ירשׁ is also evident in contexts regarding inheritance where the conquest is not in view. In Gen 21, Sarah views Ishmael as an illegitimate heir (despite patrimonial custom) and does not want him to obtain any part of the inheritance (21:10). Although violence is not in view, force clearly is. Sarah views Ishmael as a dis-inheritor to Isaac, so she demands that Ishmael be dis-inherited. Other such examples abound, such as references to Abraham's offspring taking possession of the gates of their enemies (Gen 22:17; 24:60) and the descendants of Esau violently dispossessing the Horim from the land of Seir in order to take it as a possession of their own (Deut 2:12-31; Josh 24:4).

There are several unique occurrences of ירשׁ that continue to describe disinheritance or dispossession by force. In Gen 45:11, Jacob's family is described as being dispossessed from their land by famine. Leviticus 25:46 gives Israelites permission to pass slaves down through patrimonial inheritance as long as the slaves are not Israelites. In Num 27:11, Zelophehad's daughters have their father's inheritance threatened, due to a lack of a male heir, and they appeal to leaders of Israel for permission to obtain their family inheritance. Deuteronomy 28:15-68 describes exile for the Israelites as a curse if they disobey God's commands, and it is said that the land itself will act out against the Israelites, taking over and disinheriting them from the land (28:42).

There is reason to doubt that violence and aggression are germane to the definition of ירשׁ. There are passages where ירשׁ and נחלה appear together when the line between them is not clear. In Deut 31, Joshua is commissioned as the leader who will bring the Israelites into the land to possess it. Although the dispossession of the inhabitants is implied by the overall narrative of Deuteronomy, it is a mere subtext to this particular chapter, and ירשׁ (31:13) and נחלה (31:7) appear to be used in precisely the same way: to describe the simple possession of the land that God has sworn to give the Israelites. Similar comparisons could be made regarding Deut 15:4; 25:19; and 26:1. In fact, in many instances when ירשׁ and נחלה appear side by side, it is נחלה that carries the connotations of inheritance, and ירשׁ in those instances is best understood to connote "take possession of" or "occupy." There are also instances where ירשׁ is used on its own, but it carries similar nuances to נחלה, such as the land as a gift (Deut 5:31-33; 6:18; 10:11), the requirement of obedience for the Israelites to obtain the inheritance (Deut 6:1; 8:1; 11:8-9), and the blessing that obedience brings upon the inherited land (Deut 32:47). There are other examples of the use of ירש where force and aggression are not in view. Genesis 15:1-8 uses ירש to describe Abraham's lack of an heir to his estate. In Num 36:8, the daughters of Zelophehad are granted their father's inheritance and Deut 16:20 requires that justice be done in the land if the Israelites are going to inherit it.

Although force is not always in view regarding the use of ירש, examples abound to demonstrate that it is not only a clear connotation of the term's meaning but a rather dominant one depending on the context. This review reveals that the term is multifaceted. Although "inheritance" is an important concept in the range of meaning of ירש, it is certain that נחלה is the principal term for the concept. There are many instances, particularly in the infinitive, where the best gloss for ירש is "to take possession of" in the sense of ownership or occupation, and inheritance is not clearly in view (Deut 17:14; 21:1; 23:21). In many instances ירש and נחלה appear to be synonymous but function in different ways. נחלה is the far more relational term. ירש is the term used for inheritance when force, violence, or aggression is in view, and "possession" and "dispossession" are other important concepts in the term's range of meaning.

2.2.1.3. κληρονομία and Its Cognates

The LXX also requires attention here due to its relevance for Matthew's Gospel; moreover, the way that its translators have rendered terms of interest here illuminates their relationship to one another. The Greek noun for inheritance, κληρονομία, appears sixty-four times in the Hexateuch; fifty-six times for נחלה, and seven times for ירש. The verbal form, κληρονομέω, appears eighty-five times; seventeen times for נחל, and sixty-three times for ירש. A cognate, κλῆρος, which more precisely connotes the idea of a "lot," "portion," or "share" rather than an "inheritance," appears eighty-eight times. Ten times κλῆρος renders the Hebrew word גורל (lot), but forty-five times it renders נחלה and eight times it is used for ירש. The meaning of these Greek terms mirrors the Hebrew terms quite closely. Their usage serves to demonstrate the largely synonymous way that ירש and נחלה were received in interpretations of the Hexateuch's texts and demonstrates that, when interpreting inheritance in both Hebrew and the LXX, נחלה and κληρονομία function in a relatively synonymous fashion.[59]

[59] For more on statistics and translations, see *NIDNTTE*, 5 vols. (2nd ed.; ed. Moisés Silva; Grand Rapids: Zondervan, 2014), 2:693–96. It is the case that there are difficulties at times and in individual instances of justifying the translation choices of the LXX translators. There may be instances where Greek terms for "inheritance" are used to translate נחלה and ירש when other terms may be more appropriate, but these statistics

2.2.2. Inheritance and the Promise to Abraham

One of the most dominant themes related to inheritance in the Hexateuch is the Abrahamic promise. The inheritance and the promise are interwoven throughout the narrative of the Hexateuch; it is in the promise that the inheritance finds both its beginnings and much of the significance of its story, and it explains why any attempt to understand inheritance using the Pentateuch, and omitting Joshua, leaves the inheritance narrative without a conclusion. Attention is required both to the promise, its provenance and meaning, as well as to how this significant theme connects with the inheritance throughout the whole of the Hexateuch.

2.2.2.1. Genesis 12:1-7

The terms for "inheritance" and "promise" do not appear in Gen 12:1-7; however, in this passage themes begin to develop that will exert influence upon the narrative of the Hexateuch. God makes a covenant with Abram, not yet Abraham, which establishes the relationship between them. Abraham is to leave his homeland for a land he does not know. In so doing, he is to trust in the divine speech of God and devote himself completely to God's guidance,[60] as obedience to the command to leave his land was a necessity to obtaining the first aspect of the promise revealed in 12:2-3, "I will make of you a great nation, and I will bless you, and make your name great, so that you will be a blessing. I will bless those who bless you, and the one who curses you I will curse; and in you all the families of the earth shall be blessed." It was in this new land that Abraham would become "a great nation." The need for obedience is supported by the passage; the main verbs in 12:2-3 (make, bless, make great, be, bless, curse, find blessing) are all subordinate to the imperative "go" from 12:1. Abraham's obedience serves as a catalyst to receiving the promises.[61]

---

demonstrate the volume of instances where the Hebrew and Greek terms for inheritance line up, revealing that, for the LXX translators, these terms were viewed largely as synonyms. For more on the dynamics of the LXX as a translation of Hebrew, see Karen H. Jobes and Moisés Silva, *Invitation to the Septuagint* (Grand Rapids: Baker Academic, 2000), 86–102.

[60] See Gerhard von Rad, *Genesis* (London: SCM Press, 1961), 154.

[61] See Keith N. Grüneberg, *Abraham, Blessing, and the Nations: A Philological and Exegetical Study of Genesis 12:3 in Its Narrative Context* (Berlin: de Gruyter, 2003), 144–45, who correctly argues that "it is not to say that their fulfillment is necessarily dependent on his going, simply that the text does not discuss what might happen were he to remain in Haran." Though the construction of the text is not necessarily conditional, he goes on to state, "When the construction denotes a result, it is always an intended result."

The term ברך (bless) is the key term, appearing five times in 12:2-3 alone. Abraham is assigned the role of mediator in God's saving plan—God will bless Abraham, and through Abraham, others will be blessed. However, as seen later with regard to inheritance, God's people (in this case Abraham) serve a mediatory role. God maintains ownership and control of the blessings, and he is the one who receives credit for fulfilling the promises. Others will be blessed *through* Abraham, but they will be blessed *by* God. An additional aspect of the promise is then made in 12:7: when Abraham arrives in the new land, God promises "To your offspring I will give this land." In this passage, the promise comprises three basic elements: 1) Abraham will be made into a great nation, 2) his descendants will *inherit* the land to which Abraham has sojourned, and 3) many others will be blessed through Abraham.[62]

2.2.2.2. Genesis 15:1-7; 18

In Gen 15:1-7 and 18,[63] Abraham expresses concern regarding his lack of an heir to his household (15:2-3). God confirms to Abraham that his offspring will be as numerous as the stars (15:5), and as with his sojourn of Gen 12, Abraham trusts the divine voice (15:6). God reiterates his earlier promise (from 12:7) that he will give the land of Canaan to Abraham's offspring (15:7, 18).

It is with this passage that the reader finds the first occurrence of the pairing of inheritance terminology with the promise. The verb ירש appears five times in this passage, the first three in reference to an "heir" to Abraham's estate, the last two in reference to the land that Abraham's descendants are to inherit. Abraham assumes that Eliezer of Damascus, likely a servant in Abraham's home, is his only acceptable heir.[64] Genesis provides no evidence for the practice of adopting an

---

[62]   For a detailed account of the construction of this passage, see Grüneberg, *Abraham*, 142–52.

[63]   There has been significant debate regarding the date as well as the literary and compositional history of Gen 15. These issues need not concern us here. For purposes of this study, the majority of scholars would regard vv. 1-6, as deriving from a single source. Regarding the redactional layers, Benjamin Schliesser, *Abraham's Faith in Romans 4* (Tübingen: Mohr Siebeck, 2007), 98, has effectively demonstrated the "structural coherence" and "intentional character" of the entire chapter and regards it as a "compositional unity." For a detailed analysis of the history of scholarship on this chapter, see Schliesser, 82–117. For a shorter summary, see Claus Westermann, *Genesis 12–36* (London: SPCK, 1985), 214, who warns against subjectivity in dividing the text.

[64]   The precise relationship of Eliezer to Abraham is a matter of confusion, as the text of 15:2b is widely regarded as corrupt and impossible to accurately translate. The only certainty is that Eliezer is not a blood relative. For more on this, see Gordon J. Wenham, *Genesis 1–15* (WBC 1; Waco, Tex.: Word Books, 1987), 328.

heir; however, the Nuzi Tablets (mid-second millennium B.C.E.) provide evidence that the practice may have been in place in Abraham's culture. If an heir was lacking, a servant could become the heir to an estate for services rendered. However, if a son was born the adopted heir could not disinherit him.[65] The author of Genesis may have this practice in mind, however, as in 15:4 God reiterates to Abraham that his own son will serve as "your heir" (יִירָשְׁךָ). Not only will he have a son but many more descendants besides (15:5).

Because Abraham trusted the divine voice (15:6), and believed these things would come to pass, the Lord וַיַּחְשְׁבֶהָ לּוֹ צְדָקָה (counted it to him as righteousness). In the Hexateuch, the noun צְדָקָה (righteousness) normally refers to right moral conduct.[66] However, Abraham is not depicted as "doing" righteousness; his own belief was the desired response despite the fact that he was unaware of how these promises would come to be fulfilled (15:8). Rather than the promises themselves, Abraham believed by "fastening himself to the one who speaks."[67] Benjamin Schliesser argues persuasively that the term has a relational character, writing that, "in the anthropology of the Old Testament, the borderline between what a person does and what a person is lacks a clear definition." Therefore, a person's action and a person's being are intimately connected. Abraham's trust in God is what gives him right standing before God and reciprocates the relationship that God initiates through the promises. The contents of the promises in this passage are as follows: 1) a son will serve as Abraham's heir to his own household, 2) future descendants beyond his own son will continue Abraham's line, and 3) Abraham's descendants will possess the land of the Canaanites (15:7, 18).

2.2.2.3. Genesis 17:1-8

An important term for the whole of Gen 17 is בְּרִית (covenant), which appears thirteen times, four of which appear in the opening section (17:1-8). God makes a series of promises to Abraham, and the covenantal language provides Abraham with a binding assurance that God's promises will stand.[68] The covenant is dependent on Abraham's obedience but is still described as a gift from God (17:2). God establishes and maintains

---

[65]   See E. A. Speiser, "Notes to Recently Published Nuzi Texts," *JAOS* 55 (1935): 435–36.

[66]   See J. K. Bruckner, "Ethics," in *Dictionary of the Old Testament: Pentateuch* (ed. T. Desmond Alexander and David W. Baker; Downers Grove, Ill.: InterVarsity Press, 2003), 225.

[67]   Schliesser, *Abraham's Faith*, 137.

[68]   Hebrew does not have a specific term for "promise," but "covenant" works largely the same way. See Westermann, *Genesis*, 260.

the covenant, which will be an everlasting covenant throughout the generations of Abraham's offspring (17:7). In this passage, the covenant and the promise become one, and together they include assurances about 1) descendants for Abraham (17:2, 6), 2) land for Abraham's descendants (17:8), and 3) Abraham becoming not only the father of one great nation but also a multitude of nations (17:4-6). Later, there is also a reiteration of the promise from 15:4 that Abraham will have a son, Isaac (17:16, 19); however, this reiteration provides new information in terms of what it is that Abraham's heir stands to inherit. Isaac will not simply inherit Abraham's estate, as Abraham appears to have assumed in Gen 15:2, but he will also inherit the covenant itself as an everlasting covenant for his own offspring (17:19).

2.2.3. Inheritance and the Promise in the Rest of the Hexateuch

Throughout Genesis, the three most consistent aspects of the promise are 1) descendants for Abraham, 2) land for Abraham's descendants, and 3) the blessing of all nations through Abraham. Although the land promise is reiterated to Abraham's immediate offspring (Gen 26:1-5; 28:10-15), the promises are not meant to find their fulfillment in Genesis. Inheritance terminology is tied to the promise, specifically in reference to the land, once more in Gen 48:4-6, but the association between these concepts continues throughout the Hexateuch.

In Exod 32:13, in response to God's anger during the golden calf incident, Moses uses the association between the two concepts to quell God's wrath against the Israelites. In the story, Moses states, "Remember Abraham, Isaac, and Israel, your servants, how you swore to them by your own self, saying to them, 'I will multiply your descendants like the stars of heaven, and all this land that I have promised I will give to your descendants, and they shall inherit (נחלו) it forever.'" In response to this, God is said to relent from his plan to destroy the people.

In Deut 1:8 God commands the Israelites, "See, I have set the land before you; go in and take possession (רשו) of the land that I swore to your ancestors, to Abraham, to Isaac, and to Jacob, to give to them and to their descendants after them." In Deut 31:7-8 Moses declares to Joshua, "Be strong and bold, for you are the one who will go with this people into the land that the Lord has sworn to their ancestors to give them; and you will put them in possession (תנחיל) of it. It is the Lord who goes before you. He will be with you; he will not fail you or forsake you. Do not fear or be dismayed." Other instances appear in Deut 8:1; 9:5; 10:11; and 11:8-9. An important theme present in many of these contexts has been discussed throughout this section: Yahweh goes before the Israelites and because of his relationship to his people, he relents from disaster upon them in the midst of their disobedience and guarantees the success of their inheritance.

At the conclusion of Deuteronomy, the inheritance has not been received, which provides the reason why it became so important within the narrative of Joshua. In Josh 1:6, God is said to commission Joshua, declaring, "Be strong and courageous; for you shall put this people in possession (תנחיל) of the land that I swore to their ancestors to give them." Israelite participation with God toward the obtaining of the inheritance takes up a large portion of Joshua, with inheritance terminology appearing eighty-eight times, including contexts involving conquest (Josh 2–12), the allotment of the inheritance (Josh 13–19), and the regulation of the inheritance (Josh 20). At the end of the story, the themes of inheritance and the Abrahamic promise are brought together once more, declaring the enterprise a success. Joshua 21:43-45 states:

> Thus the LORD gave to Israel all the land that he swore to their ancestors that he would give them; and having taken possession (ירשו) of it, they settled there. [44] And the LORD gave them rest on every side just as he had sworn to their ancestors; not one of all their enemies had withstood them, for the LORD had given all their enemies into their hands. [45] Not one of all the good promises that the LORD had made to the house of Israel had failed; all came to pass.

2.2.4. Themes Associated with Inheritance

In light of this survey of the most significant passages featuring inheritance terminology, as well as attention to the development of a framework for understanding its usage, a number of important themes associated with inheritance may be observed that merit further consideration. These themes may be organized in two major categories: family politics and social identity.

2.2.4.1. Family Politics

In inheritance contexts that involve family dynamics, inheritance predominantly describes the passing down of goods and property from one generation to another. This was done through patrimony: the passing of an inheritance from a father to an heir, preferably a son. Victor H. Matthews argues that patrimony and the production of a proper heir was the primary purpose of marriage in ancient Israel and, although "primary" is debatable, there is no question that it would have been an important

motivator, especially for the wealthy.[69] Patrimony was the only way in
the ancient world to assure that a person's estate would remain within
the family lineage. As observed in the previous section, when Abraham
lacked an heir this was an issue of principal concern and motivated what
Matthews calls "creative legal strategies."[70] Abraham proposed that his
heir might be a household servant (Gen 15:2) and his wife offered a sur-
rogate to produce a proper heir (Gen 16:1-4).[71]

Patrimony may have ramifications for a number of particular family
dynamics. In Exod 20:14 and 17, it is largely the male head of household
who is protected. Although patriarchy motivates such wording, Matthews
argues that there was a need to ensure that a man's progeny was his own.
This may be the reason that Lev 20:10 describes capital punishment for a
man who sleeps with a married woman, and for the woman herself, but no
such punishments are offered for married men who commit adultery with
unmarried women. In Matthews' words, "The law did not ensure marital
fidelity on his part; its focus was paternity, not sexual ethics."[72]

There are other examples of inheritance having a significant impact
on family dynamics. In Gen 31, after Jacob's relationship with his
father-in-law Laban has soured, he decides to leave Laban's household
and return to the land of his own ancestors. Jacob is married to Rachel
and Leah, both daughters of Laban, who do not protest, because they
have no portion or "inheritance" (נחלה) with their father due to his ill
regard for them.

The daughters of Zelophehad, addressed in a number of passages
(Num 27:1-11; 36:1-12; Josh 17:4), are an important case. Zelophehad
has passed away without sons, but his daughters appeal to Moses and
Eleazar the priest to request their father's share in the coming land inheritance (Num 27:4).[73] Moses is said to bring the case before Yahweh,
who grants them a נחלה among their father's tribe. This case appears
to set a new legal precedent within the community, as a command goes

[69]   Victor H. Matthews, "Family Relationships," in *Dictionary of the Old Testament: Pentateuch* (ed. David Baker and T. Desmond Alexander; Grand Rapids: Zondervan, InterVarsity Press, 2003), 295.

[70]   Matthews, "Family," 295.

[71]   Patrimony may also motivate the concept of "levirate marriage," although
Deut 25:6 describes the need for an heir to continue the family name of the deceased,
not to pass on his estate. See Wright, *God's Land*, 57.

[72]   Matthews, "Family," 296.

[73]   George Buchanan Gray, *Numbers* (ICC; Edinburgh: T&T Clark, 1956), 398,
is right to point out the importance of the circumstances surrounding Zelophehad's passing. Were he "in the company of Korah" (Num 27:3), or guilty of some other exceptional
sin, his inheritance may have been forfeit, even for his progeny. His daughters appear to
be aware of this, and point to his death in the wilderness as a criterion for his inheritance
to remain within his household.

out prioritizing the recipients of an inheritance in cases where a man dies with no male heir.[74] Priority is based on family proximity: first the daughters inherit, and if a man has no daughter then it transfers to his brothers, and finally the nearest kinsman of his clan (Num 27:8-11). This arrangement guarantees a man's inheritance and prioritizes family lineage in all cases.

Due to the strict border arrangements given to clans and tribes by Yahweh, the arrangement providing Zelophehad's inheritance to his daughters concerned the leaders of the tribe of Manasseh, from which Zelophehad's family derived. If a woman marries outside of her own tribe, patriarchy required that the woman become a member of her husband's tribe. If the daughters of Zelophehad were to marry outside of Manasseh, then Zelophehad's share of the tribal inheritance would go with them, decreasing Manasseh's tribal inheritance decreed by God and increasing the share of another tribe (Num 36:5).[75] Moses then shares this concern and decrees that an inheritance cannot transfer between tribes; if a female heir is to maintain her inheritance she must be required to marry within her own tribe (Num 36:8-9).[76] Although progeny took the place of primacy in the decision of Num 27 to give Zelophehad's inheritance to his daughters, in Num 36 progeny becomes secondary to the tribal land allotments decreed by God.[77]

---

[74]   Levine, *Numbers*, 347, argues that the newness of the precedent is paralleled by a unique use of language to establish it. Numbers 27:8 uses the verb עָבַר, "to pass over," to describe the handing of Zelophehad's inheritance to his daughters. Levine argues that the verb here is best translated "to transfer" and stands out against the use of the verb נתן, "to give," which is used when male heirs receive an inheritance. He argues that the use of עבר in inheritance contexts is restricted to the present verse and states, "The implication is that something unusual is being prescribed, from a legal point of view."

[75]   As Gray, *Numbers*, 397, points out, this case further suggests Yahweh's perpetual ownership of the land, when he states, "According to the Levitical law this principle is based on the religious theory that all the land was Yahweh's, granted by him to the various families merely for use, and therefore inalienable by them."

[76]   Budd, *Numbers*, 390, notes the strategic placement of this story at the end of the book of Numbers, operating as an appendix to the book as whole, in order to capture an important theme, "The integrity of the tribes as distinct entities within the people of God must be preserved. This concern arises naturally from the principle enunciated in Num 26:52-56 that the land is to be divided among the tribes and an inheritance and an inheritance for each to be received."

[77]   See Itamar Kislev, "Numbers 36, 1-12, Innovation and Interpretation," *ZAW* 122, no. 2 (2010): 249–59, who argues that the concept of tribal allotment was an innovation at this point. The HB knows of personal and familial inheritance, and the concepts of the inalienability of the land and the Jubilee year are typically applied to clan and household inheritance rights. However, in this passage those same concepts are applied to the tribes for the first time (see especially 36:4).

2.2.4.2. Social Identity

Among all of the themes associated with inheritance in the Hexateuch, one of the most important is its impact on the social identity of the Israelites. This identity is rooted in three important concepts: election, redemption, and covenant; each of these is intimately linked to inheritance terminology and is therefore presented below.

Election and Redemption

The idea that God chose, or elected, Israel as a certain group of people to be *his own people*, one that has a unique relationship to him from among and out of all other people on earth, is a prominent feature of the book of Deuteronomy. Deuteronomy 7:6-8 states the idea clearly: God has chosen the Israelites out from among the nations as his treasured possession. Of this passage Ronald E. Clements writes that it communicates "a more conscious relating of this special bond between Yahweh and Israel to the existence of other nations." Moreover, election brought Israel together around such concepts as "land, freedom, holiness and its special destiny among the nations."[78] The election looks back to the works of God on Israel's behalf (Deut 7:8) and also has an eschatological element, guaranteeing Israel's success among the nations into the future. Deuteronomy 26:18-19 reiterates this point and adds the need for the Israelites to respond to their election through obedience to God's commandments. To be chosen by God as his own possession obligates Israel to right moral conduct, to be a holy nation (Deut 7:6; 14:2, 21; 26:19), the terms of this designation to be decided by God based on his own unique moral commands.[79]

Election and inheritance are closely related in a number of passages. In Deut 32:8-9, Yahweh apportions (בהנחל) the nations but takes Israel as his own inheritance. In Deut 7, Moses describes the process of God's removal of other nations from the promised land, and Israel's inheritance (רשתה) of that land, and uses Israel's election from among the nations as the justification for why the inheritance will belong to them. Extending from the concept of election is the idea that the Israelites have been redeemed by God from their previous, oppressive circumstances. Election and redemption are two sides of the same coin and appear together in a number of passages. Deuteronomy 7:8 states, "The LORD has brought you out with

---

[78]   Ronald E. Clements, *Old Testament Theology* (London: Marshall, Morgan & Scott, 1978), 89.

[79]   T. D. Alexander, *From Paradise to the Promised Land* (Grand Rapids: Paternoster Press, 2002), 266.

a mighty hand and redeemed you from the house of slavery, from the hand of Pharaoh king of Egypt." In Deut 9, when God decides to destroy the Israelites for the golden calf incident, election and inheritance are paired with God's act of redemption by Moses in his appeal to God for leniency; Deut 9:26 states, "Lord God, do not destroy the people who are your very own possession (נחלתך), whom you redeemed in your greatness, whom you brought out of Egypt with a mighty hand." God's people are unique to him as a "treasured possession" (Deut 14:2), and they are described as his children (Deut 14:1). It is in this context that the Israelites understood the נחלה: not simply as a gift but a certain kind of gift — an inheritance passed down from God to them, based on the unique, redeeming, kinsman-type relationship that they believed they had to God. Van Seters brings these ideas together when he states, "God's choice of Israel as his special people, the gift of the land to them and their faithful commitment to exclusive worship of Yahweh is the way in which Deuteronomy sets out their sense of identity."[80]

Covenant

The ties between inheritance and covenant were discussed in the preceding section on the Abrahamic promise; however, this concept also relates to election and requires further comment here. The Israelites' social identity was shaped by the fact that they believed they were in a covenant relationship with Yahweh, and that relationship, at its very core, contained the promise of inheritance. The covenant was freely offered and freely accepted not as an act of compulsion but the origination of a unique relationship between God and Abraham, the latter becoming the ancestral symbol of the people who would deal with God in this way for generations to come.[81] As Harry M. Orlinsky points out, this covenant is said to have been passed down from one generation to the next until it became a fluid aspect of nearly every tradition of the HB. The covenant began as an interaction between God and Abraham, but Israel received chronic reminders as to their own role as recipients of the covenant. On God's part, the covenant came with the promise of land. On the part of the Israelites, the covenant came with the responsibility to maintain an exclusive relationship to Yahweh as their God. As Van Seters states, "If the covenant is broken, even by a few, then they can lose the land. . . .

---

[80]   Van Seters, *Pentateuch*, 106–7.

[81]   Harry M. Orlinsky, "The Biblical Concept of the Land of Israel: Cornerstone of the Covenant between God and Israel," in *The Land of Israel* (Notre Dame: University of Notre Dame Press, 1986), 29–30.

The covenant includes the whole people, the nation, and does not admit individual exceptions."[82]

2.2.5. Conclusions

Ideas associated with the term נחלה are tied up with important themes associated with *relationship*. On a basic family level, an inheritance is the contents of an estate passed down through patrimony, and in this sense, נחלה signifies a relationship that is unique; patrimony only applies to familial bonds between fathers and their sons. This same terminology applies to the relationship between Yahweh and his people, and Yahweh and his land, and by extension, Yahweh's people to Yahweh's land, which also signifies a unique quality to these relationships. Whether the נחלה is land passed by Yahweh to his son(s) Israel as a gift, or is Yahweh giving himself as a נחלה to the Levites, or is the land passed down within Israel as an ancestral heritage, the nature of the terminology is more than administrative. The involvement of נחלה language with other concepts such as election and the promise between Yahweh and Abraham (and his descendants) serves all the more to illustrate the inherently *relational* nature of נחלה.

2.3. Inheritance in the Former Prophets

2.3.1. Judges

The book of Judges plays an important role in the Tetrateuch/Pentateuch/Hexateuch debate, and its references to inheritance have a direct impact on the way we view its relationship to other texts in the HB. As Klaas Spronk has argued, "There can be no doubt about it that the present form of the book of Judges is presented as a sequel to the book of Joshua."[83] He points out the noted parallels between Joshua and Judges and argues that Judges is dependent on Joshua in those cases. Furthermore, he echoes the opinion of many scholars that Judges is both pro-Judah and pro-monarchy, by portraying the sad state of Israel after the death of Joshua and before the establishment of a king. The repeated lament of a time with no king (17:6; 18:1; 19:1) leaves Israel vulnerable, where all the people "did what was right in their own eyes" (17:6); this lack of centralized leadership has led the Israelites not into liberty but chaos.

---

[82]   Van Seters, *Pentateuch*, 107.

[83]   Klaas Spronk, "Some Remarks on the Origin of the Book of Judges," in *The Land of Israel in Bible, History, and Theology: Studies in Honor of Ed Noort* (ed. Jacques van Ruiten and J. Cornelis de Vos; Leiden: Brill, 2009), 145.

In this way, Judges works not only as a sequel to Joshua but also as an introduction to Samuel and the monarchy. According to Spronk, the book of Judges was a late construct within the Former Prophets, written with Joshua and Samuel in mind and filling in the gap between them.[84]

Although Judges operates as a bridge between Joshua and Samuel, there are important points of disjunction between Joshua and Judges as it relates to inheritance. In conjunction with both Joshua and Deuteronomy, Judges locates inheritance within a tribal framework, a feature largely absent from inheritance contexts from Samuel moving forward.[85] As Philip R. Davies argues, this tribal setup led Israel to becoming a territorially defined nation, "where the promised-land belongs less to the nation as a whole and attaches to individual tribes." This leads to a degree of autonomy in Judges, with an increase in independent tribal activity and ultimately the dissolution of Israel as a unified whole.[86] In the Hexateuch, the tribes of Israel are depicted as a unified nation under a single leader. The inheritance of the land provides a place of liberty and security, where God's people benefit from his promises and are no longer threatened by their enemies. By contrast, in Judges they are responsible for their own inheritance. Rather than security and peace with their enemies, Judges presents the Israelites' position in the land as full of conflict and uncertainty.[87]

This disjunction is made immediately apparent at the opening of Judges. Joshua 21:43-45 depicts the conquest as a success: God has given Israel its land, they have taken possession of it and settled there. The tribes have been given rest from their enemies and all of God's promises have been fulfilled. Joshua 24 provides a warning that the Israelites must continue to obey Yahweh (24:27) but states that they did so during Joshua's lifetime (24:31).[88] This is set in contrast to the

---

[84]   Spronk, "Judges," 147–48. Spronk's article effectively demonstrates many thematic and linguistic links between Judges and Joshua and between Judges and Samuel.

[85]   Nili Wazana, "'Everything Was Fulfilled' versus 'The Land That Yet Remains,'" in *The Gift of the Land and the Fate of the Canaanites in Jewish Thought* (ed. Katell Berthelot, Joseph E. David, and Marc Hirshman; Oxford: Oxford University Press, 2014), 14, points out that even within Joshua the picture of inheritance and conquest is not unified. The first half of the book (chs. 1–12) presents a more "whole-Israel" approach to inheritance, whereas tribalism dominates the second half of the book (chs. 13–21).

[86]   Philip R. Davies, *The Origins of Biblical Israel* (New York: T&T Clark, 2007), 56–57.

[87]   See E. John Hamlin, *At Risk in the Promised Land* (Grand Rapids: Eerdmans, 1990). The unstable position of the Israelites in the land is a key theme of his treatment.

[88]   This is not to say that the picture of conquest and inheritance in Joshua was unified or smooth. Joshua 11:23 states that Joshua had taken the whole land and distributed it among the tribes and that Israel had rest from their enemies. However, in Josh

repeated refrain in Judg 1 that the various tribes לֹא הוֹרִישׁ, "did not drive out," the inhabitants of their allotted inheritance.[89] As Victor H. Matthews states, Judges "serves as a counterpoint to Joshua's exuberant accounts of total victory."[90] Judges 2:1-5 depicts the angel of Yahweh visiting Israel and declaring that God had been faithful to his end of the covenant he made to Israel's ancestors but that Israel had failed, and therefore the inhabitants of Canaan would be an ongoing snare to them.[91] Structurally and linguistically, Judges finds much in common with Deuteronomy and Joshua. The focus remains on tribal inheritance and the need to drive out the inhabitants of Canaan. However, narratively, Judges presents a sharp break with the story

---

13:1 Yahweh declares to Joshua that much of the land had yet to be possessed. There is a noted disjunction within Joshua itself. However, by the end of the book, the conquest is presented clearly as accomplished. See Davies, *Origins*, 57–58, who argues that the statement in 11:23 was provisional; occupation and subjugation are to be distinguished. Joshua 1–12 portrays occupation, and 13:1 introduces the need for subjugation of the land and its inhabitants. See also Iain Provan, V. Philips Long, and Tremper Longman III, *A Biblical History of Israel* (Louisville: Westminster John Knox, 2003), 167–68, who argue that the disjunction within Joshua is itself evidence that the disjunction between Joshua and Judges need not imply contradiction between the two texts. The difference between occupation and subjugation is present throughout both, and Joshua recognizes at the end of the book that some work regarding subjugation is yet to be accomplished.

[89] ירשׁ appears 27x in Judges. In conjunction with the Hexateuch, it almost always refers to the use of violence or force to drive out the previous inhabitants and dispossess them from the Israelites' inheritance. There are two exceptions; an instance in 14:5 is anomalous and best rendered as something like "impoverish," and an instance in 18:7 refers to the possession of wealth. However, in Judges the term is never best rendered "inherit" but is instead used as a complementary term to the story of inheritance in Judges that follows instances of the term נחלה (see, for example, their use in 2:6, where נחלה refers to inheritance and ירשׁ refers to the dispossession of the inhabitants). Therefore, in this section ירשׁ will not be treated on its own.

[90] Victor H. Matthews, *Judges and Ruth* (NBC; Cambridge: Cambridge University Press, 2004), 46–47. Matthews projects this forward, stating that the Deuteronomist Historian responsible for Judges intends to portray that "the failures of the settlement period contributed to the failures of the monarchy."

[91] Hamlin, *Promised Land*, 54, notes that the phrase כל־בני, "all the people," appears just twice in Judges, in 2:4 and 20:26, when referring to all of Israel. This is set in contrast to the fragmented activity of the tribes throughout the book. The contrast is cautioned by Davies, *Origins*, 61, who notes, "Judges is not entirely about individual tribal activity. There is a tension between the tribal and pan-Israelite perspectives throughout: although each tribe conquers its own territory alone, in the period that follows, the Judges are said to judge Israel as a whole, and it is also Israel, not the individual tribes, that sins, causing oppression (but only of a certain tribe or tribes) and then deliverance by a tribal hero who then becomes the next judge of Israel. The stories of individual tribes (occasionally helping out their neighbors) are thus interspersed by a story of a corporate entity with a single governance." Davies' caution is apt, but tribalism and a lack of centralized leadership are clear themes in Judges.

of inheritance in the Hexateuch, which was so cleanly concluded at the end of Joshua. The land is not secure, and in contrast with the theme of tribal cooperation found in the Hexateuch, the lack of centralized leadership leaves the tribes moving toward increasing levels of isolation.

The first two instances of נחלה in Judges appear in 2:6-10. Although Joshua is declared deceased in 1:1, in 2:6 he is alive and dismissing the Israelites to their נחלה in order to take possession of it (ירש). This raises a question of the coherence of the text. Judges 2:6-10 is mirrored by Josh 24:28-31. The majority of scholars argue that Judg 1:1–2:5 is a late addition, making 2:6 the original opening of Judges. In this view, Judges begins at 2:6 with a full quote from Josh 24:28-31 in order to link the two texts together, and a later redactor added 1:1–2:5 as a new introduction to the book.[92] Instead, Martin Noth argues that Judg 2:6 was originally used by the Deuteronomist as the continuation of Josh 23 and that Josh 24 and Judg 1:1–2:5 were later additions, meaning Josh 24 quotes Judg 2, rather than the reverse.[93] The difficulties in coherence are best solved by Barry G. Webb, who argues that Judg 2 quotes Josh 24 and that Judg 2:6 flows well syntactically from the previous verse, demonstrating unity between the units 1:1–2:5 and 2:6-10. According to Webb, 2:6 is a literary use of flashback, making strategic use of a temporal break to shift focus.[94] Where Judg 1 was "concerned primarily with the military and political aspects of the period in question," the angel of Yahweh's speech in 2:1-5 shifts to the religious implications by changing the point of view.[95] Webb states:

> In chapter 1 we see the period unfolding from the perspective of the Israelites themselves; in 2:1-5 we see it for the first time from Yahweh's perspective. In 2:6-10 the *whole* period is then reviewed from this new perspective. The religious question (Israel's relationship to

[92]   See Baruch Halpern, *The First Historians: The Hebrew Bible and History* (University Park: Pennsylvania State University Press, 1988), 136. Halpern challenges this view, noting that it does not solve the problem of coherence and renders the redactor clumsy. He instead argues that the chapters indicate an organic logic and that the complexity of the argument does not require composite authorship.

[93]   Martin Noth, *The Deuteronomistic History* (Sheffield: JSOT Press, 1991), 23–24. Noth argues, "The Deuteronomistically edited passages Josh. 24:1-28 and Judg 2:1-5 were added after the final chapter of the book of Joshua, ch. 23, and—later still—without any Deuteronomistic revision, the mass of all traditional fragments, which form the present Judges 1."

[94]   Similarly, see Halpern, *Historians*, 136–37, who argues that the narrative complexity is necessary for the complexity of the argument of the text.

[95]   Barry G. Webb, *The Book of Judges* (NICOT; Grand Rapids: Eerdmans, 2012), 134–35.

Yahweh) is now the focus of attention, and it is the military and political aspects of the period which are passed over in silence.[96]

As I argue above, the Israelites' inheritance of the land was a result of their relationship to Yahweh. As they failed to completely remove the inhabitants of their allotted land, their focus was on the land itself; but the writer of Judges presents Yahweh as far more concerned with the way in which their disobedience affects the covenant and his relationship with his people. In the Hexateuch, the covenant was tied to Israelite identity, and Judges records that the breaking of the covenant changed Israelite identity from this point forward. In Judg 3:1-6, the remaining inhabitants are used by Yahweh to test Israel, to see if they would obey the covenant; but some Israelite men married non-Israelite women and began to worship their gods. As Davies argues:

> This obviously undermines the distinction between a Canaanite and an Israelite population, on both genealogical and religious definitions. It also resolves the issue of incomplete settlement of the land: a population emerges that is not "Israelite" and not "Canaanite," in the terms employed by Deuteronomy and Joshua, but *undifferentiated* (emphasis his).[97]

This all brings added importance to Judg 2:6-9 and explaining the direct quotation from Josh 24:28-31. In Josh 24, Israel served Yahweh and had "known all the work that the LORD did for Israel" (24:31). By contrast, Judg 2:10 states that a new generation had arisen "who did not know Yahweh or the work that he had done for Israel" in the generation of their fathers. This leads to the apostasy of the people in 2:11-13, where the people abandoned Yahweh and did what was evil in his sight. Judges' use of Josh 24 is a callback, meant ultimately to contrast the two passages by way of the reaction of the people to Yahweh. The Hexateuch ends with an obedient Israel and their relationship with Yahweh intact; Judges begins with a rebellious and idolatrous generation who

---

[96]   Webb, *Judges*, 135. See also Trent C. Butler, *Judges* (WBC 8; Nashville: Thomas Nelson, 2009), 42, who notes that through these two perspectives, those of both Yahweh and the Israelites, "we discover one central truth: life is going to be more difficult in the promised land than we expected and than we experienced in most of the book of Joshua." Lillian R. Klein, *The Triumph of Irony in the Book of Judges* (Sheffield: Almond Press, 1988), 36, describes the irony of this change when she writes, "The disparity between the Israelite (human) and Yahwist (divine) perceptions shows the people to be narrowly fixed on occupation of the land at whatever cost, Yahweh is concerned with the integrity of the covenant. Accordingly, the human perception dwells at great length on details of occupation, while in Yahweh's perception the occupation is passed over in one verse (2:6) and emphasis is given to the change in relationship between Yahweh and his people during the generations that followed Joshua."

[97]   Davies, *Origins*, 62.

has forsaken their relationship with Yahweh, leading to a functional shift in Israelite identity. The use of the direct quote illustrates the power of the contrast.[98]

Although Judges uses the passage in Josh 24:28-31 to contrast the context of Joshua in regard to Israel's relationship with Yahweh, there is also an important change to the quotation that places it firmly in the context of the circumstances in Judges. Josh 24:28 states, וישלח יהושע את־העם איש לנחלתו (And Joshua sent away the people, each man to his inheritance). The inheritance was secure and settled. However, Judg 2:6 states, וישלח יהושע את־העם וילכו בני־ישראל איש לנחלתו לרשת את־הארץ (And Joshua sent away the people, and each man of the Israelites went to his inheritance *to take possession of the land*). In Judges, the inheritance has been allotted and settled in, but the dispossession of the inhabitants has not been completed.[99] Added weight is provided in Judg 2:7-9 by the reminder that under Joshua the people served Yahweh. Joshua lived to the age of 110, his long life implying Yahweh's approval of him. In Judg 2:9 the Israelites are reminded that Joshua has *his own* נחלה, granted to him in Josh 19:49-50 as a way of honoring his position. The quote is amended as though it is still the command of Joshua, a figure of considerable authority, that the conquest of the land should continue. The quotation has been reappropriated and given new life in a new context.[100]

Noteworthy is that the inheritance in Judg 2:6 is not likely an individual inheritance. Joshua's individual inheritance in 2:9 is a special case and is used to set him apart from the rest of the Israelites. Although "each man" is sent to his inheritance, the portions of the inheritance are defined corporately, first by tribe, then clan, then family. This is confirmed by the only use in Judges of the verb נחל, where Jephthah's expulsion from his family cost him a share in the inheritance (Judg 11:1-3).[101]

The following two instances of נחלה found in Judges both occur in 18:1. Judges 17:6 sets the context, reminding the reader that there was no king in Israel and that "all the people did what was right in their own eyes." Judges 18:1 begins with part of that refrain, "there was no king in Israel," likely calling back to the idea that the tribes, in this case the Danites, were acting on their own and without the accountability of

---

[98]   Webb, *Judges*, 136.

[99]   See Butler, *Judges*, 42.

[100]   See Butler, *Judges*, 38, who notes that the reference to Joshua also has a literary effect through Judg 3–16, contrasting Joshua with the less than perfect leaders recorded in the Judges period. Invoking Joshua has as much to do with dishonoring disobedient Israel as with honoring Joshua.

[101]   Webb, *Judges*, 137.

central authority in Israel.[102] According to Judg 1:34, the Danites had been given an allotment of the inheritance but failed to obtain it due to aggressions from the inhabitants. Judges 18 records their mission to take for themselves an inheritance from another location. In the Hexateuch, the borders of the inheritance were described as inalienable, but due to Dan's failure to obtain their allotment, they pursued Laish, a land outside of Israel's territory.[103] As Webb points out, Yahweh was with Israel in their attempts to obtain the promised land, but he was totally absent from the Danite campaign described in Judg 18.[104] He states, "Israel was advancing into the heart of the land to claim their promised inheritance; the Danites were withdrawing from theirs." Once again, a failure to obtain the inheritance led to negative consequences in the relationship between Yahweh and the Israelites. This leads to the Danites erecting an idol in the final scene of the episode (18:30).[105] Trent C. Butler argues that the Danites' relationship to their inheritance is further evidence in Judges of Israel's decline, through "a whole tribe's loss of territory, a theme that will then be trumped by the Benjaminites who almost lose their entire identity as a tribe. All this occurs with no king in Israel."[106]

It is to this tribe, the Benjaminites, that we now turn for the context of our final instances of נחלה in Judges. In Judg 19–20, a Levite enters the Benjaminite town of Gibeah with his concubine, who is raped and murdered by Benjaminites living there. In 20:6, the Levite alerts the other tribes by cutting his concubine into pieces and sending her body parts to the territories of each tribe's נחלה. The other tribes of Israel assemble and form an army, demanding that the perpetrators of the crime be surrendered, but the Benjaminites refuse to hand them over and form their own army in response. The Benjaminites are decimated in war with the other tribes, and the elders of Israel are forced to hatch a kidnapping plot to repopulate Benjamin. The surviving Benjaminites take new wives and are said to return to their own נחלה to rebuild their towns and cities (21:23). The rest of the Israelites then return to their own נחלה as well (21:24).

[102]   See Matthews, *Judges*, 174, who states that the repeat of a portion of the refrain indicates to the reader "that the episodes are related, at least to the extent of sharing a common social and political setting."

[103]   Webb, *Judges*, 434. This failure is described in the Hexateuch itself, which ascribes the newly sought territory as their inheritance; see Josh 19:40-48.

[104]   See also Matthews, *Judges*, 175, who states, "There is never any direct mention of divine aid or sanction for the activities of the spies or for the immigration of the tribe of Dan."

[105]   Webb, *Judges*, 453.

[106]   Butler, *Judges*, 389.

Once again, this story features callbacks to Joshua. Joshua 24:28 states, וישלח יהושע את־העם איש לנחלתו (And Joshua sent away the people, each man to his inheritance). In Judg 21:24, we read that the Israelites went out from these events by their tribes and families, איש לנחלתו (each man to his inheritance). Both Joshua and Judges conclude with the Israelites returning to their inheritance. As we have seen, Judg 2:6 also features the same phrase. The callback is meant to contrast the picture in Joshua, rather than complement it, as well as draw the reader back to the beginning of Judges and the failure of the mission to possess the land fully. In Josh 24, the Israelites are described in "whole-Israel" terms and are sent away after having renewed their covenant with Yahweh. In Judg 21, the Israelites have narrowly avoided the destruction of an entire tribe, and at no point have they asked Yahweh for directions on how to proceed. Butler argues that, "Throughout the entire book no narrative progress is made. Israel stands in the same position at the end of Judges as it did at the end of Joshua, people returning to live on their inherited land."[107] Without gaining new land, Israel fails the mission described by Judg 2:6. This is partly correct, but there is a sense in which the narrative progresses through the regression of Israelite society and identity. Joshua ends on the high note of a renewed covenant, while Judges ends with the culmination of one of its major themes: the increasing isolation of the tribes and the fragmentation of all Israel. The penultimate verse of Judges ends with the tribes retreating to their own inheritances, which is immediately followed by the final verse of the book, consisting only of the repeated refrain, "In those days there was no king in Israel, all the people did what was right in their own eyes." Judges sets the stage for Israel's need: unity through the influence of a strong leader.[108] The lack of human leadership is surpassed by the absence of Yahweh from key texts in Judges, and the Israelite shift in identity away from the Hexateuchal focus on the people's relationship to Yahweh is supported by Judges' hyperfocus on the land in a tribal framework, rather than the land and the Israelites as "Yahweh's inheritance." נחלה plays a key role in passages where these themes are established.

---

[107]   Butler, *Judges*, 468.

[108]   Judges features many leaders with varying degrees of quality and success. The failure of the judges to secure a unified Israel tempts the reader to see the book as arguing against a monarchy or centralized leadership. Butler, rightly, demonstrates that the judges are contrasted with the successful leadership of Joshua and therefore is best read as pro-monarchy. See Butler, *Judges*, 471.

2.3.2. The Books of Samuel

1 Samuel focuses on Benjamin a great deal, and this focus (along with Samuel's role as a judge) "furnishes a straightforward narrative continuity" between Judges and the books of Samuel.[109] However, the depiction of Israel changes drastically between the two books. Judges' focus on the individual tribes greatly diminishes, giving way instead to Samuel's focus on כל־ישׂראל (all Israel).[110] Samuel still presents Israel as fragmented; it is depicted by a few cooperating tribes and Benjamin and Judah are often singled out. However, as Davies states, "Saul's Israel is not the twelve tribe Israel of the Pentateuch or Joshua. Nor do we find twelve individual tribes, as in the core of judges."[111] The books of Samuel focus instead on the reunification of Israel under a monarch.

Cognates of נחלה appear seven times in Samuel; the noun appears six times and the verb once. There is a high degree of uniformity among these uses, but the verb, which appears in Hannah's Song in 1 Sam 2:1-10, stands out as unique. While the passage has a problematic textual history, the meaning of וכסא כבוד ינחלם (inherit a seat of honor, 2:8) is not controversial.[112] The main theme of the hymn is the holiness, reliability, and sovereignty of Yahweh that places Yahweh over the fortunes of humans. 1 Samuel 2:4-10 centers on Yahweh's right to intervene in the social order and direct the outcomes of those under his rule, which often leads to a reversal of fortunes, where the poor are raised from the dust and made equal to princes and the rich. Yahweh's enemies will be laid waste, but his faithful ones will be guarded.[113] The inheritance is the reception of favor granted by Yahweh.

The first appearance of the noun is found in 1 Sam 10:1. Saul is anointed by Samuel as the first king over Israel. Samuel declares that Yahweh has anointed Saul to be ruler over Yahweh's נחלה. David Tsumura argues, using parallels from other passages in the HB, that נחלה here refers both to Yahweh's people and his land.[114] In the MT, 1 Sam 10:1 is ambiguous and the exact meaning of נחלה is difficult to determine. The text in the LXX is much longer, with many scholars arguing that it preserves an older reading, theorizing that a good

---

[109]   Davies, *Origins*, 67.

[110]   This construction is used in Judges just twice, in 8:27 and 20:34. It is used in the books of Samuel 33x.

[111]   Davies, *Origins*, 67.

[112]   The textual history of the passage is detailed in Theodore J. Lewis, "The Textual History of the Song of Hannah: 1 Samuel II:1-10," *VT* 44, no. 1 (1994): 18–46.

[113]   See David Toshio Tsumura, *The First Book of Samuel* (NICOT; Grand Rapids: Eerdmans, 2007), 145–50.

[114]   Tsumura, *Samuel*, 282.

portion of the verse was lost in the MT due to haplography.[115] This longer reading provides clarity to the issue by focusing specifically on Saul's rule and responsibility over Yahweh's people. In the LXX two clauses are paralleled:

10:1b—Οὐχὶ κέχρικέν σε κύριος εἰς ἄρχοντα ἐπὶ τὸν λαὸν αὐτοῦ, ἐπὶ Ἰσραηλ

Has the Lord not anointed you to rule over his people, Israel?

10:1d—ἔχρισέν σε κύριος ἐπὶ κληρονομίαν αὐτοῦ εἰς ἄρχοντα

The Lord has anointed you to be ruler over his inheritance.

In 10:1d, κληρονομίαν corresponds to נחלה in the MT. Taking these two clauses together, it is best to regard the נחלה as Yahweh's people, whom he is trusting to the care of Saul as king. While the land may also be in view, it is the people that Saul is called to protect, and his victory over Israel's surrounding enemies is said to be the sign that Yahweh has anointed Saul to rule. The contrast with Judges is evident; rather than a focus on tribal land, Yahweh's concern here is depicted as the whole of his people.

There are four instances of נחלה in the books of Samuel that all occur in constructions where the term is paired with the divine name. 1 Samuel 26:19 and 2 Sam 20:19; 21:3 all feature the phrase נחלת יהוה, "Yahweh's inheritance," and 2 Sam 14:16 features the phrase נחלת אלהים, "God's inheritance." These are the only instances of these constructions anywhere in the HB, so each instance merits attention here before drawing conclusions regarding their meaning.

1 Samuel 26:19 occurs during Saul's pursuit of David. After sparing Saul's life, David questions the motivation behind Saul's pursuit and appeals for an end to their conflict. David laments that he has been driven outside of נחלת יהוה and forced away from Yahweh's presence. A number of interpreters have argued that the inheritance here refers to Yahweh's land.[116] This makes good sense considering the context; David laments being forced into foreign territory. This verse features the only occurrence in Samuel of the verb גרש (to drive out), which elsewhere in the HB usually signifies being driven out from land.[117] H. O. Forshey argues instead that the inheritance here is referring to the people

---

[115] See P. Kyle McCarter Jr., *II Samuel* (AB 9; New York: Doubleday, 1984), 171.

[116] See Hans Wilhelm Hertzberg, *I & II Samuel* (London: SCM Press, 1964), 210.

[117] Cf. Gen 4:14; Exod 6:1, 12:39, 23:28; Num 22:6; Judg 6:9. In many of these contexts, גרש functions the same way as ירש and refers to the dispossession of the inhabitants of Canaan from the land, often by force. גרש does appear in contexts where a person is driven out from the presence of another individual, such as Pharaoh (Exod 10:11) or in the case of divorce (Lev 21:7; Num 30:9).

of Israel, rather than the land. He focuses on the use of the verb ספח (to attach). David is being driven out from having a share/attachment in Yahweh's inheritance. This verb is used in the HB just five times,[118] and as Forshey argues, "A survey of these texts reveal that forms of *SPH* are used to express some kind of affiliation with a human community, formally or informally perceived." According to this evidence, Forshey argues, David's concern is that he is not cut off "from the community with its special relationship to Yahweh."[119]

The next instance of נחלת יהוה is found in 2 Sam 20:19, during the story of Sheba's rebellion.[120] Joab discovers Sheba in a northern border city called Abel, and Joab's forces begin battering the wall with intent to besiege the city to get to Sheba. A wise woman from Abel beseeches Joab to cease his destructive intent; she informs Joab that Abel had long been known as a peaceable place, where disputes were settled among the Israelites. The woman then asks Joab why he would seek to destroy נחלת יהוה. The story ends with the people of Abel cutting off the head of Sheba and delivering it to Joab so as to turn away their destruction. A. Graeme Auld argues that the נחלה here, best rendered "heritage," refers to some degree to the land (in this case Abel as a portion of the fuller נחלה), but he also sees a unique reference to the mothers and children within that land as a part of the נחלה that would be destroyed in Joab's assault on the city.[121] P. Kyle McCarter argues that the phrase אמוני ישראל found in verse 19 should be rendered something like "the architects of Israel" and is a reference to those from whom Israelite society was inherited. The wise woman of Abel would be among these. Although McCarter does not discuss the phrase נחלת יהוה specifically in this verse, if we follow his argument, to destroy these heirs of Israelite society would be to destroy those who are נחלת יהוה and therefore refers to specific people among the Israelites.[122] Forshey argues that נחלת יהוה "clearly designates the city Abel Beth-Maacah." He recognizes that the language

[118]   1 Sam 2:36, 26:19; Isa 14:1; Hab 2:15; Job 30:7.

[119]   H. O. Forshey, "The Construct Chain naḥalat YHWH / 'alōhîm," *BASOR* 220 (1975): 52.

[120]   This is the second appearance of נחלה in ch. 20. The other is found in v. 1, where Sheba announces to his followers that they have no נחלה with David. This appears to be used by Sheba as a rally cry for his revolt. This use of נחלה is anomalous, and few commentators make reference to it in relationship to the use of נחלה in the HB more broadly. In this context נחלה is best rendered something like "share" and refers to the fact that Sheba intends for his followers to separate from David as the king of all Israel.

[121]   A. Graeme Auld, *I & II Samuel* (Louisville: Westminster John Knox, 2011), 564. Auld appears to argue this based on the appearance of the term אם, "mother," in this verse, but he admits that the use of the term is ambiguous and its meaning difficult to determine.

[122]   McCarter, *II Samuel*, 430.

of the verse includes the people of the city but argues that "its primary reference would appear to be to the physical territory and the structures of the city." As such, Forshey argues that this verse is unique in the HB as a reference to נחלה that does not include either Yahweh's people or the land of Canaan as Yahweh's special possession.[123]

The third and final occurrence of נחלת יהוה appears in 2 Sam 21:3. Israel is said to experience a three-year famine. David inquires of Yahweh and is informed that the Gibeonites, described as Amorites cohabiting the land of Canaan with the Israelites, suffered under the hand of Saul, and the famine was due to Saul's unresolved bloodguilt. Most scholars focus on the placement of the story and the obscurity of its details, but these debates are unnecessary for informing the meaning of נחלת יהוה.[124] In the narrative, David summons the Gibeonites and asks what he might do in order to make expiation, so that the Gibeonites might bless נחלת יהוה. It is unclear if the Gibeonites are responding to this phrase in particular, or to David's overall question regarding expiation, but the Gibeonites clarify what they are *not* looking for, before stating what they do in fact require as satisfaction of Saul's offenses against them. They state that they do not require money, nor that any of Israel's people be put to death. It is possible that they respond this way in order to clarify that they do not mean to seek expiation against נחלת יהוה, but rather against Saul in particular, and that they understand נחלת יהוה to be his resources and his people. They state that Saul almost removed the Gibeonites from having their own place in the territory of Israel and that as vengeance they require the deaths of seven of Saul's sons. David complies with their request. When analyzing this passage, Auld points to a parallel in 1 Kgs 8:35-40. In that passage, Solomon is dedicating the temple and refers to a famine in the land due to the sins of Israel; the people are required to confess Yahweh and turn from their sin in order that the land may receive rain and the famine come to a stop. The land is referred to as a נחלה for the people, but it is also referred to in that passage as Yahweh's land (8:36).[125] This comparison is apt, considering that a famine in the land is precisely what David aims to negotiate in 2 Sam 21. Forshey agrees that the land is the focus here, pointing out that after the bloodguilt was satisfied, Yahweh heeded the supplications on behalf of the land (ארץ).[126]

---

[123]   Forshey, "Construct Chain," 51. See also A. A. Anderson, *2 Samuel* (WBC 11; Nashville: Thomas Nelson, 1989), 241.

[124]   See McCarter, *II Samuel*, 443–46.

[125]   Auld, *I & II Samuel*, 572.

[126]   Forshey, "Construct Chain," 51.

The fourth instance of נחלה in construct with the divine name is found in 2 Sam 14:16, but in this verse נחלה is paired with אלהים, the only appearance of the construction of the phrase נחלת אלהים found in the HB. In 2 Sam 13, David's son Amnon rapes his sister Tamar, and Absalom murders Amnon as an act of vengeance. Absalom flees to Geshur, remaining there three years (13:38). In chapter 14, Joab sends a widow to David to petition him for help, claiming that one of her sons has killed the other, and now her family wants the other son dead. Upon her appeal for help, David guarantees the safety of the remaining son. The story was a ruse set up by Joab, meant to illustrate to David that he must allow Absalom to return to Israel, which he does. Without considering the uniqueness of the phrase נחלת אלהים, Hans Wilhelm Hertzberg states that "the heritage of God" means "primarily the land—as God's fief to his people." נחלת אלהים is the land in its aspect of dual ownership.[127] Instead, Forshey finds parallels between this passage and the use of נחלה in 1 Sam 26:19; both passages feature appeals by dependent servants to their king. He argues that, as with David in 1 Sam 26, the widow is concerned that she and her remaining son be cut off from among the people.[128] A. A. Anderson admits the difficulty of identification for the phrase, arguing that it likely refers to the landed property specifically of the family of the widow in question, rather than the full land of Israel, but he admits that it could also refer to either the people of Israel or the land of Israel.[129]

Theodore J. Lewis gives the most thorough treatment to the consideration of נחלת אלהים as a unique phrase. He states his view that the three instances of נחלת יהוה in the books of Samuel all refer both to the land of Israel and its people but argues that נחלת אלהים refers to the "ancestral estate" of the widow and her family. He demonstrates that, in ancient Near Eastern literature, the term אלהים can simply refer to the dead. This is not always an attempt to deify the deceased but is "simply a way of getting at the preternatural character of the deceased."[130] The dead Samuel is referred to as אלהים in 1 Sam 28:13, and Isa 8:19-20 refers to the consultation of "ancestral spirits" (אלהיו)—the dead on behalf of the living. Lewis argues effectively that this interpretation fits

<hr/>

[127]   Hertzberg, I & II Samuel, 333. Auld, I & II Samuel, 493–94, also argues for the land as the referent.

[128]   Forshey, "Construct Chain," 53, appeals to the widow's concern that the death of her and her offspring would cut off her husband's name from the face of the earth.

[129]   Anderson, 2 Samuel, 189. McCarter, II Samuel, 346, also appears uncommitted, translating the phrase "Yahweh's estate," but following Forshey that the phrase could refer to the people of Israel, or of both the people and the land.

[130]   Theodore J. Lewis, "The Ancestral Estate (נַחֲלַת אֱלֹהִים) in 2 Samuel 14:16," JBL 110, no. 4 (1991): 602.

the context of the passage. The widow appeals to David on behalf of her dead husband; if she and her son were to be killed by their extended family, then the name and remnant of her deceased husband would be wiped from the face of the earth. Lewis then demonstrates that the שֵׁם (name) of deceased ancestors is often connected to a concern for an ancestral family's נחלה, such as in Ruth 4:5-10, where Boaz is said to marry Ruth in order to maintain the שֵׁם and נחלה of Ruth's deceased husband.[131] In Lewis' view, the unique construction of נחלת אלהים in 2 Sam 14:16 requires a referent for נחלה that is unique in the HB; it refers to the widow's concern for her deceased husband's link to the family estate rather than to the land as a whole, and אלהים would refer to the deceased husband rather than to God. In support of Lewis' view, 2 Sam 14:7 features one of only two uses of the verb ירש in the books of Samuel. As I argue above, this term usually refers to disinheritance through violence. Here the term refers to the violent cutting off of the family name were the widow's son to be killed.[132] In Lewis' view, the divine name does not feature in this construction, and this passage does not figure in to discovering the meaning of the phrase "Yahweh's inheritance" in the books of Samuel.[133]

The evidence suggests that there is clear uniformity to the use of נחלה in the books of Samuel. In six uses of the noun, three of them feature a unique construction, נחלת יהוה, found only here in the HB. In another instance, 1 Sam 10:1, the context is consistent with the others and the נחלה clearly belongs to Yahweh. This demonstrates the likelihood that the phrase, and the ideas behind it, were familiar to at least some Israelites at the time that the terms were recorded. In other words, there is good reason to look for uniformity of meaning between each instance.

Forshey argues that the use of נחלה in conjunction with the divine name does not present a unified picture of inheritance in the books of Samuel. At times, he argues, the referent is the land, and at times it is the people. He argues that 1 Sam 26:19 and 2 Sam 14:16, the two references to the people as נחלה, likely come from a later stage of the Deuteronomic material, after the Israelites lost the land. נחלה would come to refer to the community so that "Israel's relationship to Yahweh can

---

[131]   Lewis, "Ancestral Estate," 607.

[132]   The other is found in 1 Sam 2:7, where the meaning is something like "destroy."

[133]   A potential problem arises with Lewis' view when one considers that the significant manuscript group boc2e2 reads יהוה in 2 Sam 14:16 rather than אלהים. This could signify that 2 Sam 14:16 refers to Yahweh, as most commentators assume. Lewis recognizes this and challenges the problem by arguing that the scribe did not recognize the connotation "the spirit of the dead" and rendered יהוה on the false assumption that the verse referred to God. See Lewis, "Ancestral Estate," 603.

continue to be affirmed despite her alienation to her land."[134] While possible, this does not explain the uniformity of the construction of the terms. McCarter counters Forshey by arguing the equal possibility that the mixed results offered by a survey of נחלה in Samuel could "only have arisen at a time when the close identification of people and land could be taken for granted." Instead, McCarter appears to argue that to some degree "Yahweh's estate" refers to both land and people in all instances.[135] Tsumura likewise argues that each instance of נחלה in 1 Samuel "seems to refer both to Israel as the inherited land and to the people as the covenant community."[136] Even Forshey, despite drawing firm conclusions delineating between land and the people in each instance, admits that "one cannot separate completely the concepts of land and people."[137]

The evidence is tentative, and scholars are far from a consensus on the meaning of נחלה in the books of Samuel. One issue may be that some are demanding that the identification of referents for the term is too precise. In each case (save the possibility of 2 Sam 14:16, if Lewis proves to be correct), there are compelling reasons to argue in favor of the נחלה as referring to either the people of Israel, the land of Israel, some smaller portion of the land, or some combination of these. The most persuasive conclusion is that the phrase נחלת יהוה is a "catch-all" phrase that refers in the first instance to any and all things that belong to Yahweh. While this is the primary meaning, it does not exclude that the construct may also refer in an individual instance to one aspect of that which Yahweh possesses. That is, in each instance *both* meanings are in view simultaneously: as a macro-phrase it indicates all that belongs to Yahweh while also dealing with the individual aspect being emphasized. The phrase then refers in each instance to all of Yahweh's possessions while being applicable to contexts where one possession is emphasized much more than the others (i.e., people, land, a portion of the land) and explains why it is difficult in each instance that the term נחלה occurs to discover the precise referent. As such, being cut off from נחלת יהוה, as is so often the concern in these passages, is much more about being cut off from a relationship to Yahweh than an aspect of his possessions, which is a result that commentators fail to recognize.

---

134   Forshey, "Construct Chain," 53.
135   McCarter, *II Samuel*, 346.
136   Tsumura, *Samuel*, 605.
137   Forshey, "Construct Chain," 51.

2.3.3. The Books of Kings

If the books of Samuel focus on the creation of the monarchy, then the books of Kings focus on its dissolution. As Marvin A. Sweeney states, "1–2 Kings provides an account of the concluding stage of Israel's existence in the land of Israel."[138] Samuel took steps toward presenting a more unified Israel than could be found in Judges, but after this unification peaks under the reign of Solomon, Kings brings Israel toward a new mode of fragmentation under a divided monarchy. Kings takes the reader through the fall of Israel to Assyria (2 Kgs 17) and concludes with the roots of the exile of the Israelites from the land of Judah under the conquering hand of the Babylonians.[139] One of the chief concerns of the work is to explain exactly how Israel arrived at that point; the kings of Israel had led the people away from Yahweh.[140]

נחלה appears seven times in Kings in four different contexts. The first three instances appear in Saul's dedication of the temple in 1 Kgs 8, a passage that helps to illustrate the unique religious and political position of Israel under Solomon's rule. David's reign built toward unity but was always plagued by signs of tribal fragmentation, and following Solomon's reign, unity dissolves. There was a unity in Israel under Solomon not seen before or after. As Davies states, "First Kings 8 stands out as an extended account of a twelve-tribe kingdom of Israel. Perhaps we should connect this episode with the fact of Solomon's single coronation and read the narrative as implying that under Solomon alone such a unified kingdom of Israel once really existed."[141] This unity is illustrated by five appearances in 1 Kgs 8 of the phrase כל־קהל ישראל (all the assembly of Israel), a phrase used frequently in the Hexateuch but just three times in Judges and not at all in Samuel.[142] The phrase does not simply refer to all of Israel in a generic sense but portrays the unity of the tribes. At no point does Solomon even attempt to pay lip service to tribal autonomy; he assembles the heads of the tribes together as one.[143]

In Solomon's dedication speech, he recognizes the deeds of Yahweh on behalf of the exodus generation (8:16) and therefore does not repeat the mistake of the Israelites who failed to do so in the Judges period. He then petitions Yahweh directly, asking that the temple be a place of prayer, where Yahweh would hear his people and forgive their iniquities (8:30). His prayer recognizes the land as a gift to Israel's forefathers,

138 Marvin A. Sweeney, *I & II Kings* (Louisville: Westminster John Knox, 2007), 5.
139 1 Kgs 17:19-20 blames Israel in the north for Judah's demise.
140 Sweeney, *I & II Kings*, 6.
141 Davies, *Origins*, 71.
142 1 Kgs 8:14 (2x), 22, 55, 65.
143 Simon J. DeVries, *1 Kings* (WBC 12; Waco, Tex.: Word Books, 1985), xxiii.

potentially a reference to the Abrahamic promise (8:34), a gift given (נתן) to the people as a נחלה. The sins of the people could serve to alienate them from the land (8:35-40), but if the people repent and fear Yahweh, Solomon's prayer is that they be forgiven (8:40). The reference to נחלה in 8:36 is firmly at home in the Hexateuchal usage; it is a clear reference to the land as a gift from Yahweh to his people, likely drawing on aspects of the Abrahamic promise. There is no view here to tribal allotment, only the whole of the land as it is provided for the whole of the people based upon Yahweh's faithfulness to Israel's forefathers, with clear recognition of Israel's obligation to covenant faithfulness.

The Hexateuchal context continues for the other two uses of נחלה in 8:51, 53, but the referent of the נחלה changes. Beginning in 8:46, Solomon's prayer anticipates the exile, to a time when the people will sin against Yahweh and be carried off as captives to a foreign land. Solomon asks that, if the people cry out in prayer, they would be protected. Again, the land here is cast as a gift to Israel's forefathers (8:48), and Solomon references the exodus (8:51), but rather than referring to the land as the people's נחלה, Solomon appeals to Yahweh based on the people's position as the נחלה of Yahweh. Although the construction of terms between Samuel and Kings is slightly different, the referents are consistent between them, as well as similar uses stretching back to Deuteronomy, where there is an emphasis on Israel as a people set apart from other peoples of the earth as belonging uniquely to Yahweh.[144] As Simon J. DeVries states, "This plea is concluded by a pointed summation of Deuteronomistic theology, requesting Yahweh's attention on the ground of Israel's election."[145] Pointedly, Volkmar Fritz takes notice of the fact that Solomon does not petition Yahweh to return the Israelites to the land but instead asks that they receive compassion in the sight of their captors (8:50). Inheritance stresses God's relationship to his people and the protection he provides for them.[146] This protection is then celebrated by Solomon (8:55-56) in words that recall Josh 21:43-45, praising Yahweh for rest and the fulfillment of his promises and pointing to Yahweh's fidelity to the covenant.[147] Although the land is a consistent and important theme throughout Solomon's speech and prayer in 1 Kgs 8, the greatest emphasis in its use of נחלה is on its function as a relational term indicating the covenant between Yahweh and his people.

---

[144]   Cf. Deut 4:20; 9:29; 32:8-9. This concept is present prior to Deuteronomistic material, albeit without the use of נחלה as Yahweh's people in those instances. See Exod 19:5 and Lev 20:24.

[145]   DeVries, *1 Kings*, 126.

[146]   Volkmar Fritz, *I & II Kings* (Minneapolis: Fortress, 2003), 100.

[147]   See Sweeney, *I & II Kings*, 136.

The next passage to be discussed is 1 Kgs 21. In the narrative, a man named Naboth owns a vineyard near the home of Ahab, king of the northern tribes in Israel. Ahab approaches Naboth to inquire about acquiring the vineyard for himself, to be used as a vegetable garden. Naboth declines the king's offer, stating that he cannot part with נחלת אבתי, "the inheritance of my fathers" (21:3, then quoted back by Ahab in 21:4). Ahab and his wife Jezebel conspire to have Naboth killed, and then they take possession (ירש) of the vineyard. Elijah condemns Ahab on Yahweh's behalf, and Ahab later repents of his actions.

The נחלה of this passage is clearly linked to major Hexateuchal themes of inheritance. Ahab's offer would appear fair—the full monetary value or an even better vineyard—but Naboth's concern to maintain his ancestral inheritance is rooted in legal and religious contexts, thus his statement in 21:3, "Yahweh forbid," that he should surrender it. The phrase חלילה לי מיהוה (Yahweh forbid) is not simply colloquial; it is used in the books of Samuel three times (1 Sam 24:6; 26:11; 2 Sam 23:17), each time portraying actions that would be a direct affront to Yahweh.[148] Due to Yahweh's role as the perpetual owner and guarantor of the land, he forbade the sale or transfer of land allotments save for financial necessity (Lev 25:23-28), which did not appear to be a concern for Naboth. The land was allotted by tribe (Num 26:52-56) and perpetually passed down through patrimony. Yahweh's ownership of the land, gifting of the land, and the passing of the land down through ancestral inheritance, are all linked through the concept of נחלה. Naboth is of the tribe of Issachar, Ahab of the tribe of Manasseh, for Naboth's land to change hands it would pass from one tribe to another, extending Manasseh's holdings beyond tribal boundaries.[149] The case of the daughters of Zelophehad is especially instructive in Naboth's response. In Num 36, the phrase נחלת אבתינו (the inheritance of our fathers) also appears a number of times. The daughters are concerned that they stand a chance to lose their ancestral inheritance, so provision is made to ensure that it stay with them. Numbers 36:9 ensures that no ancestral inheritance shall transfer between tribes, guaranteeing that land allotments would stay with the tribes, and families, for which Yahweh intended them. Based on these factors, Jerome T. Walsh makes an important point regarding Naboth's unwillingness to part with his vineyard when he states, "Naboth reveals that his rejection of Ahab's offer is not a willful refusal but a matter of conscience, and he

---

[148]   On this phrase, see Mordechai Cogan, *1 Kings* (AB 10; New York: Doubleday, 2000), 478, who argues that it is akin to profanation and suggests that the sale would be a desecration.

[149]   See Sweeney, *I & II Kings*, 249.

establishes both a religious and a legal basis for his inability to accede to Ahab's request."[150] In other words, Naboth's rejection was nothing personal but rooted in legal and religious tradition and in effect out of his hands.[151] Ahab solves the problem through Naboth's murder. The oft-used Hexateuchal term ירש, which I argue above often appears alongside נחלה and in various inheritance contexts, appears five times in this chapter (21:15, 16, 18, 19, 26), four times to describe the violent way that Ahab "dis-inherits" Naboth from his ancestral property and takes it for his own possession.[152]

נחלה appears once, in 2 Kgs 21:14. Chapter 21 describes Manasseh's reign, the details of which are framed by the phrase "He did what was evil in the sight of the Lord" (21:2, 16). 2 Kings 21:2-9 lists the charges against Manasseh (i.e., he placed altars to false deities in the temple, among other serious crimes), and 21:10-15 declares Yahweh's verdict against him. Yahweh judges that Manasseh's crimes were worse than the pre-Israelite inhabitants of Canaan, inhabitants driven out from the land by Yahweh. As Robert L. Cohn states, "In this context Manasseh's acts are presented as a reversion to a wickedness that repudiates the entire history of Yahweh's relationship with Israel in its land."[153] This comparison provides Yahweh with the justification for his judgment; disaster will reign over Jerusalem and Judah, and Yahweh will forsake the remnant of his נחלה, allowing them to be handed over to their enemies. Judah is compared with Israel (21:13), which anticipates the exile by implying a similar fate. The נחלה in this verse belongs to Yahweh. Although the destruction of the land is important to the context of the passage, and possibly an aspect of Yahweh's נחלה, the "remnant" of Yahweh's נחלה is clearly a reference to his people in Judah, whose destruction is the result of their actions to forsake their relationship with him.

---

[150]   Jerome T. Walsh, *1 Kings* (Berit Olam; Collegeville, Minn.: Liturgical Press, 1996), 318. As Walsh points out, it is unclear whether these Hexateuchal laws were in use in Ahab's time, but the writer of the narrative is surely aware of them.

[151]   Stephen C. Russell, "Ideologies of Attachment in the Story of Naboth's Vineyard," *BTB* 44 (2014): 29–39, argues that, for Naboth, it was in fact a very personal matter. He traces evidence that suggests that Naboth's sole concern was his attachment to the ancestral land due to his attachment to his ancestry and the likelihood that the land would have contained the tombs and burial grounds of his ancestors. As we have seen, Lewis argues a similar case in regard to 2 Sam 14:16. The point is not to say that Naboth would have been otherwise happy to part with his land but rather that he had legal traditions available in order to decline the offer.

[152]   The first four of these instances are in this context. The fifth use of ירש in 21:26 describes the destruction of idols.

[153]   Robert L. Cohn, *2 Kings* (Berit Olam; Collegeville, Minn.: Liturgical Press, 2000), 147.

2.3.4. The Relationship between Judges, Samuel, and Kings

There are many narrative and linguistic features that link Joshua to Judges, Judges to Samuel, and Samuel to Kings, but there are also points of disjunction between them, particularly in the way they each present Israel's political structure, in terms of tribal autonomy and leadership, as well as the Israelites' relationship to Yahweh and to the land. The Hexateuch presents a נחלה for Yahweh—made up of both the land and his people—that serves to illustrate that his people are his own treasured possession. The people are separated out from the rest of the peoples of the earth and related to Yahweh through the covenant that he made with their forefathers. The Hexateuch also knows a נחלה for the people, principally their land, both as the whole of Israel and as the portions allotted to tribes and families. The borders of the land are decided by Yahweh and the allotments are apportioned by Israel's leaders. נחלה is a relational term; the land is an important aspect, but the primary concern is to illustrate the election and political and religious identity of the Israelites under Yahweh.

In Judges, the leadership structure of Israel deteriorates and with it the relationship between Yahweh and his people. Judges is focused on the land itself as a נחלה for the people and particularly emphasizes the tribal allotment and the fragmentation of a religious and political Israel through inter-tribal conflict. In Samuel–Kings, the entire focus of the נחלה shifts; although these texts know a נחלה as the people's land (1 Kgs 8:36), and as personal and ancestral property (1 Kgs 21:3), the majority of passages refer to the נחלה as belonging to Yahweh, made up of both his people and the land, and attention paid to the individual tribes all but vanishes from inheritance contexts. In all of this the term remains relational, but the referents shift from Judges, concerned with the land as a נחלה for the people, to Samuel–Kings, concerned with the people as a נחלה for Yahweh, and passages featuring נחלה reveal the decline of the relationship between Yahweh and his people.

In light of the foregoing observations, what explanations are available to account for this shift? The most likely solution lies in 1 Sam 10:1, the first appearance of the noun form of נחלה found in Samuel–Kings. As I argue above, the context is Samuel's anointing of Saul as Israel's first king. Samuel declares that Saul is to be ruler over Yahweh's נחלה, referring to Yahweh's people, but likely also implying the whole of his heritage. I argue this is the best way to understand the concept of Yahweh's נחלה in the books of Samuel. In the Hexateuch, the land was allotted to tribes, clans, and families, but the tribal structure broke down in Judges to a point that tribal autonomy was no longer

viable. Ultimately, the land always belonged to Yahweh, so the introduction of the monarchy allowed for the entirety of Yahweh's נחלה,
his land and people, to be subsumed under the monarch as the keeper
of the נחלה.[154] Tribal divisions were no longer an issue as far as נחלה
was concerned, nor was the נחלה that belonged to the people, because
it all now belonged to the monarch on Yahweh's behalf. The Naboth
incident illustrates that the allotments were still to be respected (i.e.,
the king did not have the right to simply take what land he desired),
but Samuel–Kings portrays a move by Yahweh to regain control of the
נחלה on his own terms. This reading is informed by the rebellion of
Sheba and Israel's rejection of Rehoboam. Sheba's rally cry, that he
and his followers have no נחלה with David (1 Sam 20:1), is taken up
by the Israelites who rebel against Rehoboam (1 Kgs 12:16). In both
cases, discontent is shown in the king, the one called and anointed by
Yahweh to be keeper of his own נחלה. For certain Israelites to declare
that they have no נחלה with Yahweh's king, the result is to have no
נחלה with Yahweh, the one the king represents. The נחלה of the king
and the נחלה of Yahweh are to be seen as one and the same.

2.4. Inheritance in the Latter Prophets

Inheritance in the Hexateuch and Former Prophets is particularistic.
Yahweh is viewed to maintain perpetual ownership of the land, his land,
and he elects the Israelites, his people, and through the conquest, he
brings his people into his land and offers it to them as their own inheritance, to be an ancestral heritage passed down through the generations
by patrimony. Deuteronomy 32:8-9 is indicative of many central themes
regarding inheritance in these texts: the nations are divided, boundaries
are fixed between them, and Yahweh takes his people as his own portion.
Moreover, he is to be a father to them (32:6) and Israel's sonship is a
status conferred as an aspect of their very creation.[155]

Although this particularism continues in the Former Prophets, the
referents of inheritance are altered by dynamic shifts in Israel's identity
and social situation. Rather than placing blame for covenant disobedience upon the people directly, as in Judges, the books of Kings place
this blame on the monarch, intensifying the relationship of the prophet
to the monarch amidst calls to a return to Yahweh and covenant faithfulness. The descent of covenant disobedience culminates in the exile,

[154]   For an extensive discussion regarding the relationship of the monarch to the
land as Yahweh's representative, see Habel, *Land*, 17–31.
[155]   See J. G. McConville, *Deuteronomy* (Downers Grove, Ill.: InterVarsity Press,
2002), 453.

the ramifications of which have an impact on the inheritance. The Latter Prophets describe these ramifications in great detail. The majority of references to נחלה appear in Jeremiah, Isaiah, and Ezekiel, therefore the discussion will focus on these three books.

2.4.1. Jeremiah

In language indebted to Deuteronomic literature, Jeremiah depicts Yahweh placing his judgment against Judah for worshiping and making offerings to foreign gods (1:16).[156] Although Jeremiah is to expect opposition, he is called to speak against the Judahites on behalf of Yahweh (1:17-19).[157] Much of the language regarding inheritance in Jeremiah is familiar. In their neglect of Yahweh and their pursuit of false gods, Israel had defiled Yahweh's land and made his נחלה an abomination (2:7).[158] Yahweh's people Israel is to avoid learning "the way of the nations" (10:2), for Yahweh belongs distinctly to Israel as their portion and Israel belongs distinctly to Yahweh as his own נחלה (10:16). But having gone after false gods (11:10), they have broken the covenant made between Yahweh and Israel's forefathers (11:8).[159] Therefore, Yahweh promises to bring disaster upon his own people (11:11), who will cry out to their foreign gods and receive no help (11:12).

Jeremiah 12 contains six of the book's fifteen instances of נחלה. These references oscillate between the people of Israel and the land as the referent of the נחלה; the people are clearly in view at the start of the poem, as Yahweh declares that due to the evil actions of Israel and their breaking of the covenant, Yahweh has abandoned his נחלה (12:7) and given Israel over to the hands of her enemies. The references in 12:8-9 follow suit in referring to the people, but a change in referent is apparent at 12:10-14, where many shepherds, a reference to foreign rulers, have destroyed Yahweh's vineyard, the land of Judah, and made desolate

---

[156] On comparisons with Deuteronomic linguistic choices, see Jack R. Lundbom, *Jeremiah 1–20* (AB 21A; New York: Doubleday, 1999), 244.

[157] See William L. Holladay, *Jeremiah 1* (Hermeneia; Minneapolis: Fortress, 1986), 31, who points out that the language in this passage is militaristic. Jeremiah is "being equipped by Yahweh for lifelong battle as a warrior in a holy war against his people." The war imagery is adapted for prophetic use and is followed by prophetic activity. See also William McKane, *Jeremiah*, vol. 1 (ICC; Edinburgh: T&T Clark, 1986), 23.

[158] See Lundbom, *Jeremiah 1–20*, 260, who demonstrates connections between Jer 2:7 and parts of Deuteronomy.

[159] The exact identity of which generation of "fathers" are in view is difficult to determine. The reference to Egypt assumes the exodus generation, but Holladay, *Jeremiah*, 354, argues that the focus is on Josiah and his generation. Precise identification is unnecessary; McKane, *Jeremiah*, 239, is likely correct that included is the "long history of apostasy extending to the present."

כל־הארץ (the whole land, 12:11).[160] כל־הארץ is the נחלה that Yahweh has given to his people Israel to inherit (הנחלתי). These mixed referents have led Jack R. Lundbom to observe that, although each usage of נחלה in this passage may refer singularly to either the people or the land, "Totality is achieved by accumulation," where the whole of Yahweh's possession, his land and his people, are in view.[161] The Israelites broke the covenant, so Yahweh surrendered the Israel of his own נחלה, both the land and the people, over to their enemies.

The slow burn of Yahweh's declaration of judgment against Israel makes use of repetition regarding Israel's sin, recounted again in the oracles of Jer 17. Judah, by its own act of continued idolatry in the land, has lost the נחלה that God has given to it, and the result will be exile to a land that they do not know. Jeremiah 17:1 (that their sin "is engraved on the tablet of their hearts") is likely a reference to the tablets of the commandments and Judah's covenant relationship with Yahweh. As Craigie et al. note, "Here it is Judah's sin, not her covenant love and faithfulness, that has been written upon the heart."[162] Judah has broken the covenant, and exile is the result.

Not all is to be lost forever. Jeremiah 33 reports an eschatological peace promised by Yahweh. Following Babylon's destruction of Jerusalem and casting of the Israelites into exile, Yahweh promises to bring Judah and Israel together to fight against the Babylonians and to restore the fortunes of his people, rebuilding them as they were before (33:1-8). Interestingly, Jeremiah proclaims a time when a restored Israel will be a sign to the nations (גוי) that God is good to his own people (33:9). Yahweh is said to promise that a Davidic king shall always sit on the throne of the house of Israel (33:17).

Jeremiah 32 declares that Yahweh will gather the Israelites from all of the lands of which they were exiled, and he will bring them back to Israel to dwell in safety (32:17). He will renew his covenant with them, despite their prior disobedience, and rather than their sin inscribed on their hearts, as in chapter 17, the fear of Yahweh will be inscribed on their hearts so that they will never again turn away from the covenant (32:36-41).[163]

---

[160] Some discussion has centered on the identity of the "shepherds." As a reference to foreign rulers, see Holladay, *Jeremiah*, 388. For the identification of the vineyard as Judah, see Peter C. Craigie, Page H. Kelley, and Joel F. Drinkard Jr., *Jeremiah 1–25* (WBC 26; Dallas: Word Books, 1991), 185.

[161] Lundbom, *Jeremiah 1–20*, 654.

[162] Craigie et al., *Jeremiah*, 223.

[163] See also Jer 31:33, where it is the law that is written on their hearts. The eschatological context between the two passages is the same.

The judgment of Babylon takes up the final chapters of Jeremiah, where the beginnings of the eschatological fulfillment are described. Judah and Israel are brought together to seek Yahweh and join in a covenant with him (50:4-5). Babylon's sins against Judah are detailed in oracles by Yahweh, first among them (50:11) is Babylon's guilt in "plundering my inheritance" (שׁסי נחלתי). In describing Babylon's destruction, Yahweh declares once again that Israel is his own inheritance (נחלתי), chosen by Yahweh from among the nations to be his unique people (51:19). Although the exile is a progression in Israel's historical narrative, most of the referents to נחלה in Jeremiah are to Yahweh's people, his land, or the land as the נחלה of his people—all of this is consistent with the predominant usage throughout the HB. The term נחלה is both relational and particularistic; Yahweh is the God of the Israelites, the Israelites are Yahweh's own people, and Yahweh dwells among his people in a unique way compared to the other nations, despite descriptions of the nations as belonging under Yahweh's sovereign control.[164]

There is, however, a new development in the Latter Prophets that is all but completely absent from the Hexateuch and Former Prophets. In Jer 3, Yahweh calls Israel to repentance, and refers to an eschatological reality in which he will forgive his people for their sins. Yahweh will return his people to Jerusalem from their places of exile, but in this passage they will not be alone. Jerusalem will be called the throne of Yahweh, and not just Israel, but "all nations" (כל־גוים) shall gather to the throne, in the presence of Yahweh, and no longer follow their own evil ways (3:17). The clear implication is that Yahweh will open access to himself and the city of Jerusalem to non-Israelites. The focus of the passage is primarily Israel, and it is to Israel that Yahweh declares himself as a father (3:19), but the nations are invited into this relationship through Israel in a way that opens a door toward a less particularistic relationship.[165] The nations are not invited on their own terms but come as those repenting of their own ways.

---

[164]   See, for example, the formula והייתי להם לאלהים והמה יהיו־לי לעם in Jer 31:33, "I shall be to them their God, and they shall be to me my people" and the same formula in 32:38, though with the clauses in the reverse order.

[165]   Holladay, *Jeremiah*, 121, notes that the phrase in 3:17, "walk in the stubbornness of their own evil heart," occurs seven times in Jeremiah, and each of the other six occurrences refers to Israel. For this reason, some scholars have argued for an emendation of כל־גוים to מכל־גוים, so that rather than the nations gathering to Jerusalem, it is the Israelites arriving *from* the nations to gather together before Yahweh. Holladay is right to argue that this change is without warrant and that the best way to see the use of terms is as the "author's adaptation of a stock phrase in the tradition, an adaptation in a universalistic direction." Yahweh's restoration of Israel is said to instill "fear and trembling" into the nations in 33:9, which may constitute motivation for the nations to pilgrimage into Jerusalem.

Yahweh will be enthroned in the common life of the reconstituted nation, and the nations will "stream into it for healing and enlightenment."[166] As discussed above, the culmination of the forgiveness offered by Yahweh is that he will once again place his people in the land that he gave to their forefathers as a נחלה (vv. 18-19), though, in this passage, the נחלה clearly belongs to the Israelites rather than the nations as a whole.

2.4.2. Isaiah

Isaiah is replete with this eschatological expectation of an inclusion of the nations. As James M. Scott writes, "Although the eschatological restoration is first and foremost for Israel, it will also affect all other nations . . . all other nations will participate in the eschatological pilgrimage to Zion."[167] This theme is strongly stated in Isa 2:2-4, where כל־גוים (all the nations)[168] will stream into Zion so that Yahweh may teach them his ways and they may walk in his paths (2:3).[169] This passage

---

[166]   McKane, *Jeremiah*, 77.

[167]   James M. Scott, *Paul and the Nations* (Tübingen: Mohr Siebeck, 1995), 72. Our purpose is to detail the specific ways that this theme relates to inheritance language. Scott surveys the theme of the nations in Isaiah and other prophetic literature in greater detail. Scott notes that there is also a negative response to the nations in the Latter Prophets, where the nations will be destroyed, and Israel alone will be saved (Ezek 30:3). He notes that two traditions are allowed to exist side by side, in tension—a universalistic one that envisions salvation for Israel and the nations together and a particularistic one that envisions salvation for Israel alone.

[168]   Some scholars are careful to distinguish between "eschatological" and "future-oriented" expectations in regard specifically to Isa 2:2-4. The time frame regarding "In days to come" (v. 2) is ambiguous, and many scholars reserve the term "eschatology" for a more distant future. See, for example, Joseph Blenkinsopp, *Isaiah 1–39* (AB 19; New York: Doubleday, 2000), 190. It should be noted that the distinction is helpful for the exegetical precision of specific passages, but the eschatological flavor of Zion pilgrimage passages in the Latter Prophets is generally accepted by scholars.

[169]   The eschatological expectation of the inclusion of the nations, as well as inheritance language, are found in each of the three major divisions of Isaiah. The discussion regarding the authorship of these sections, as well as the influence of the final redactor in each section, is complex, and options are many. For instance, regarding Isa 2:2-4, John D. W. Watts, *Isaiah 1–33* (WBC 24; Nashville: Thomas Nelson, 1985), 28, states the importance of the fact that a vision of Zion without nationalistic goals "belongs to Isaiah of eighth-century Jerusalem. It was not an invention of convenience by the postexilic community." However, see Marvin A. Sweeney, "Structure and Redaction in Isaiah 2–4," *HAR* 11 (1987): 407–22, for a discussion on Isaiah 2:2-4 and its place in "First-Isaiah." Sweeney surveys scholars who argue that Isaiah was the author of the passage but then argues that it is the product of the final redactor and therefore places it in the time of the Persian period. Brevard S. Childs, *Isaiah* (Louisville: Westminster John Knox, 2001), 28–29, argues that the evidence of authorship and provenance is inconclusive but that the passage is likely ancient while its position in the book is "surely redactional." H. G. M. Williamson, *Isaiah 1–27*, vol. 1 (London: T&T Clark, 2006), 176–77, notes the similarity between this

has a prominent place in Isaiah, setting up themes that will be echoed throughout the book, especially in the second half.[170] As Scott states, the goal of the restoration of Israel after the exile is "that Israel and the nations might worship the Lord together in Zion."[171]

The pilgrimage of Isa 2 is described in greater detail in Isa 14:1-2, a passage featuring the verbal form of נחל. In the preceding passage, Isaiah 13 is an oracle concerning Yahweh's judgment against Babylon for its oppression against Israel. It concludes by stating that judgment is coming near (13:22); 14:1-2 then shifts focus to Israel, whose salvation is tied intimately with Babylon's fall. Though the timing of Babylon's judgment is not to be prolonged, the passage reflects a seething tension that Israel must wait for Yahweh's redemption rather than follow into Babylon's example of violent rebellion.[172] God's intervention leads to a reversal of fortune and a new election of Israel, with a repeated pattern; as the first election led to the gift of land from Yahweh to his people, the second election will see Yahweh place the Israelites back in the land that is described both as their land (אדמתם) and Yahweh's (אדמת יהוה). Sojourners (גר) will attach themselves to the Israelites,[173] and the people of the nations will be responsible for repatriating the Israelites in the land.[174] The Israelites will be allowed to take captive their oppressors and rule over them. Each of these themes is repeated in second election passages throughout Isaiah.[175]

---

passage and Isa 40–55; 56:6-8; 60; 66:18-21; Jer 3:17; Hag 2:7-9; Zech 2:14-16; 8:20-23, which are all exilic or postexilic passages, but these clearly later passages all portray the nations joining Israel, where in this passage they pilgrimage to Israel but their religious commitment is ambiguous or absent. He argues then that this passage could be early and serves as a precursor to later tradition that makes the commitment of the nations to Yahweh more explicit but could just as easily fit into the later tradition. The precise timing of the composition of many of these passages does little to change the meaning of inheritance, or the relationship of the nations to Yahweh and Israel in a general sense, so rehearsing these debates in greater detail is not necessary for our purposes.

[170] See Williamson, *Isaiah*, 172.

[171] Scott, *Nations*, 73. It is unclear if Isa 2:2-4 is meant to imply proselytization. Childs, *Isaiah*, 30, does not think so, arguing that the passage makes no mention of religious function and refers only to instruction and "primordial harmony."

[172] See Watts, *Isaiah 1–33*, 203. These themes are repeated in another passage featuring נחלה, Isa 46–47. Babylon's judgment "is not far off," and Israel's "salvation will not delay" (46:13). Yahweh declares that he was angry with his people and profaned his own inheritance (נחלתי) by handing them over to the Babylonians (47:6), but Babylon's judgment is imminent.

[173] Otto Kaiser, *Isaiah 13–39* (London: SCM Press, 1974), 25, states that גר "does not refer merely to the Canaanites who lived among the Israelites. It can also refer at least to the non-Israelites who in the diaspora felt themselves drawn to Judaism."

[174] Cf. Isa 43:5-7; 49:22-23; 60:4.

[175] See Blenkinsopp, *Isaiah 1–39*, 282.

Isaiah 19:16-25 depicts a blessing being passed not only to Israel but to Egypt and Assyria as well. The choice of the cities is striking, as they both serve as two of Israel's greatest oppressors in the exodus and exile. The passage speaks of a highway between them, which is said to facilitate not trade or social and political communication but common worship of Yahweh. Where Isa 2:2-4 was ambiguous as to religious function, Isa 19 is clear, the Egyptians are said to engage in cultic practices and along with the Assyrians and Israelites they swear an allegiance to Yahweh. This is said to be in response to a savior who will deliver them from oppressors, and like the pilgrimage passage of Jer 3:17, non-Israelites come to Yahweh for healing. Verse 25 is key to our purposes; Yahweh declares Egypt to be עמי (my people), a phrase usually reserved for Israel and rife with covenant meaning.[176] The Assyrians are said to be the work of Yahweh's hands. Consistent with usage throughout the HB, only the Israelites of this trio are said to be Yahweh's inheritance (נחלתי). Due to the relational nature of this term, there is a sense in which Israel's unique relationship with Yahweh is maintained and even highlighted in this passage where other nations are said to belong to Yahweh. While other nations worship, Israel is still Yahweh's נחלה. As Blenkinsopp notes, "Israel still occupies the central position both geographically and symbolically as uniquely the possession of Yahweh."[177] However, Watts is right to suggest that this does not downplay the significance of this passage for the other nations; the titles applied to them here are also commonly reserved for Israel.[178] There is a multilateral relationship between these three nations that places them all under the care and blessing of Yahweh.

These themes come together with inheritance language once again in Isa 49. The speaker is commissioned in 49:1-6; he is to be a servant of Yahweh, but Yahweh declares that it is not enough that his servant only "raise up the tribes of Jacob and restore the survivors of Israel" (49:6a). The servant is also called to be "a light to the nations (גוים)," that Yahweh's salvation may "reach to the ends of the earth" (49:6b). To the astonishment of the rulers of the nations, Yahweh will restore Israel, this once defeated nation, and through Yahweh's power and faithfulness, Israel will begin anew (49:7). Yahweh will give the servant as a

---

[176] The LXX renders this verse "My people in Egypt," referring to the Israelites, rather than referring to the Egyptians as Yahweh's people. This is more consistent with the predominant usage of the HB but does not fit the syntax of the verse in MT and misses the direction of the theme of the nations through the second half of Isaiah and later Second Temple Jewish literature. See Watts, *Isaiah 1–33*, 260.

[177] Blenkinsopp, *Isaiah 1–39*, 320.

[178] Watts, *Isaiah 1–33*, 261.

covenant to his people, and the servant will establish the land once again and "apportion (הנחיל) the desolate inheritances (נחלות)" (49:8).

Many of the finer details of the passage are too ambiguous to identify with certainty. As Klaus Baltzer suggests, "light" (אור) here likely relates to justice and should be linked directly to salvation.[179] To be a light to the nations is to facilitate their deliverance. The nature of the deliverance is difficult to determine with certainty. Blenkinsopp notes that salvation elsewhere in Deutero-Isaiah deals not with righteousness, but victory, and is proclaimed when Yahweh establishes his kingdom and brings the world to order.[180] Goldingay and Payne associate the deliverance envisioned with the defeat of Cyrus and the restoration of the community of God.[181] Salvation is largely political and economic, and as Watts states, is the establishment of a stable rule that would "restore the nations' economies and social orders."[182] While these suggestions are agreeable, Claus Westermann is right to argue that the passage is cryptic but that there can be no doubt that the salvation of Israel is "extended to include the Gentile world."[183]

It is difficult to determine the degree to which this gentile inclusion might relate to the inheritance. The hiphil infinitive verb הנחיל (to apportion) in 49:8 signals causation and brings to mind Joshua's role in apportioning the inherited land. In the same way Joshua allocated the land, the servant is tasked with its reallocation. נחלות here is plural; the only other instance of the plural נחלה in the HB appears in Josh 19:51, the culminating passage after Joshua distributes land allotments to the heads of the tribes of Israel (Josh 13–19). This, coupled with the explicit mention of Israel in Isa 49:7, the preceding verse, indicates that despite gentile inclusion in the "day of salvation," the נחלה in this passage still refers to the land allotted to Israelites. The apportioning of the inheritances is connected to "the prisoners" and "those who are in darkness" (49:9), and

---

[179]   Klaus Baltzer, *Deutero-Isaiah* (Hermeneia; Minneapolis: Fortress, 2001), 311.

[180]   Joseph Blenkinsopp, *Isaiah 40–55* (AB 19A; New Haven: Yale University Press, 2002), 302.

[181]   John Goldingay and David Payne, *Isaiah 40–55*, vol. 2 (ICC; London: T&T Clark, 2006), 166. This possibility makes for an interesting reversal of fortune, as many scholars identify Cyrus himself as the servant of Isaiah 42, who is charged with largely these same tasks. The servant of Isa 42 is tasked with being a light to the nations and a covenant for the people (v. 6), bringing justice to the nations (v. 1). For the identification of Cyrus as the servant of Isa 42, see John D. W. Watts, *Isaiah 34–66* (WBC; Columbia: Nelson Reference, 2005), 649; Blenkinsopp, *Isaiah 40–55*, 299–300. Blenkinsopp argues that 49:1-6 provides a break with the previous commission; Cyrus failed and the commission of 49:1-6 is a prophet taking on this role based on Cyrus' failure to complete the tasks.

[182]   Watts, *Isaiah 34–66*, 737.

[183]   Claus Westermann, *Isaiah 40–66* (Philadelphia: Westminster, 1969), 212.

Yahweh's "highways shall be raised up" (49:11) so that those "from the north and from the west" (49:12) shall come to Yahweh for deliverance. These are all likely references to Israelites returning from exile.[184]

The narrative of the inclusion of the nations features strongly at the beginning of Third Isaiah in chapters 56–57. Yahweh's imminent "salvation" and "deliverance" are promised (56:1) but not to Israel alone. Yahweh is depicted as declaring, "Do not let the foreigner joined to the LORD say, 'The LORD will surely separate me from his people'" (56:3). To any foreigner (נכר) who holds fast to Yahweh's covenant (56:6), they will be brought into the presence of Yahweh, their sacrifices will be accepted, and the temple will be a house of prayer for כל־עמים (all peoples, 56:7). Yahweh will gather Israel but also others besides (56:8).[185] This oracle ties together themes from the first section of Isaiah. Although foreigners remained ethnically distinct from Israel, this passage relates to the pilgrimage passages (cf. Isa 14:1) where they were allowed to attach themselves to Israel as proselytes. The fact that foreigners have a part in worship in the temple "makes them members of the community in full standing," so that they "cease to be foreigners."[186]

Once again, inheritance language appears alongside these themes. Isaiah 57:13b states:

> Whoever takes refuge in me shall inherit the land (ינחל־ארץ)
> and possess (ייראש) my holy mountain. (My translation)

It is difficult to determine what relationship, if any, this verse has to the oracle of 56:1-8. Many scholars argue that these passages come from different strands in the tradition,[187] so the section of 57:1-13 may speak only of Israel and not to the more universalistic context of 56:1-8. A later passage, 60:21, refers to those who will possess the land forever (לעולם יירשו ארץ), referring specifically to Israel as a promise that they will never again be driven into exile.

Regardless of the potential for redactional layers in the book, the final form of the composition places 57:13 after the portrayal of foreigners as members of the community in full standing. This means that the final editor structured the book in such a way to open the text to such an

---

[184]   See Blenkinsopp, *Isaiah 40–55*, 306.

[185]   Many scholars have argued that 56:1-8 works as a thematic prologue to "Third Isaiah," introducing themes related to the nations that will find their culmination in chs. 65–66. Isaiah 65–66 is discussed extensively in chs. 3 through 5 of the present study on Second Temple literature and Matthew's Gospel. For more on Isa 56:1-8 as a prologue, see Childs, *Isaiah*, 454.

[186]   Westermann, *Isaiah 40–66*, 315.

[187]   See Westermann, *Isaiah 40–66*, 307.

interpretation, and subsequent readers would see the argument develop in such a way that the inclusion of foreigners would precede the statement that "whoever takes refuge" in Yahweh would "inherit the land." Rather than ethnic origins, those who inherit are defined by religious devotion.[188] As Isaiah reads from beginning to end, it increasingly offers the potential that the nations have a share in the inheritance. It is difficult to be sure of the strength of the relationship, but the universalism in Isaiah, paired with the character of the usage of inheritance terms, opens the reader of Isaiah to new interpretive possibilities that the nations, at the very least, have access to the נחלה of the land through Israel in a way that is absent from preceding traditions. This refers to the inheritance of allotted land, as Isaiah never places the nations in a context that allows them to be Yahweh's נחלה,[189] nor is Yahweh ever referred to as the נחלה of the nations.[190]

2.4.3. Ezekiel

The book of Ezekiel features eighteen instances of נחלה and its cognates, sixteen of which can be found in the temple vision of chs. 40–48, which are the focus here.[191] A number of scholars have raised questions as to the authorship of the temple vision and its overall consistency with Ezek 1–39, but John D. Levenson persuasively argues that, regardless of authorship and redaction questions, the vision is consistent with the book as a whole.[192] Key to the vision is Ezek 43:1-12, which

---

[188]   See also Watts, *Isaiah 34–66*, 832.

[189]   Though Isa 19:16-25 places Egypt and Assyria in a parallel relationship to Israel as Yahweh's נחלה, as we have seen. Also, Isaiah 54:17c references the נחלת of "the servants of Yahweh." Some scholars argue that this phrase introduces a trajectory toward gentile inclusion, in which case they would take part in the נחלה, referring to direct access to a relationship with Yahweh. For details, see Watts, *Isaiah 34–66*, 808–10; Joseph Blenkinsopp, *Isaiah 56–66* (AB 19B; New York: Doubleday, 2003), 33.

[190]   Though Isa 57:13 is the final occurrence of נחל and its cognates in Isaiah, inheritance concepts continue to feature through to the end of the book. The primary term for inheritance in Isaiah's final chapters is ירש, which features at key points in the narrative regarding exile, salvation, eschatology, and gentile inclusion (esp. Isa 60:21; 61:7; 65:9). These passages exerted significant influence over subsequent texts regarding inheritance, so they will be discussed in detail in chs. 3, 4, and 5.

[191]   The other two instances of the noun are found in 35:15 and 36:12, which refer to the land as the נחלה of the Israelites. These instances supply no new information to the discussion.

[192]   For differing views on the authorship and unity of Ezek 40–48, see G. A. Cook, *The Book of Ezekiel* (ICC; Edinburgh: T&T Clark, 1936), 425–29; Steven Shawn Tuell, *The Law of the Temple in Ezekiel 40–48* (Atlanta: Scholars Press, 1992); Moshe Greenberg, "The Design and Themes of Ezekiel's Program of Restoration," *Int* 38 (1984): 181–208.

answers Ezek 8–11 and God's abandonment of the defiled temple. Yahweh returns to the temple, which serves as the climax of the restoration vision of Ezek 40–48.[193] Moshe Greenberg also adds Ezek 20:40 and 37:24b-28 as precursors for the temple vision. He states, "Unlike God's past experience with Israel, the future restoration will have a guarantee of success, its capstone will be God's sanctifying presence dwelling forever in his sanctuary amidst his people. The vision of the restored temple (and God's return to it) in chapters 40–48 follows as a proleptic corroboration of these promises."[194] Levenson argues that the temple vision begins with a mountain that is typologically related to Sinai (40:2), "so that Ezekiel becomes a new Moses and the text itself the new תורה."[195] He points out that Ezek 40–48 is the only legislation in the HB that is not delivered by Moses, the purpose of the typology being the proper functioning of the liturgy. Levenson argues for an eschatological interpretation of the temple vision, relating it to Eden as a place with no historical association, where there is no "differentiation into nations and classes." Zion certainly is Israel-centric, but Ezekiel's temple vision is an attempt to realize the promise of Eden "without cancelling the divine singling-out of Zion and David. It is a program to depoliticize the monarchy through a new constitution."[196]

The expected timing of the prophecy's fulfillment is difficult to determine, as is the relationship of the vision to the expectation of a literal temple. *Contra* Levenson, Steven Shawn Tuell rejects an eschatological intention, arguing instead that the vision describes actual institutions dated to the Persian period.[197] He states, "Ezekiel 40–48 is the religious polity of the Judean restoration, a present tense description of the author's self-conception and their conception of God."[198] Tuell

[193]   John Douglas Levenson, *Theology of the Program of Restoration of Ezekiel 40–48* (Missoula, Mont.: Scholars Press, 1976), 10. Levenson argues for the unity of the vision with the previous chapters, stating that Ezek 43:1-12 is "the crown and consummation of Ezekiel's life's work." See also Tuell, *Ezekiel*, 175–76, who argues, "The core vision is concerned with the problem of the divine presence, which indeed could be said to be the uniting theme of the entire book of Ezekiel."

[194]   Greenberg, "Design," 182.

[195]   Levenson, *Ezekiel*, 37–49. This quote is taken from Tuell, *Ezekiel*, 13, who affirms the basic argument put forth by Levenson.

[196]   Levenson, *Ezekiel*, 33.

[197]   Scott, *Nations*, 70–72, helpfully points out that the restoration program is viewed from different perspectives in different strands of the tradition. In some exilic and postexilic texts, it is presented from a contemporary, theocratic perspective. In other texts, from an eschatological perspective. Although interpretations of individual texts may vary among scholars, both perspectives can be found in the traditions when taken as a whole.

[198]   Tuell, *Ezekiel*, 14.

recognizes that the dimensions of the temple make it unlikely that they were meant to be literal,[199] but rather he argues that the dimensions are a hybrid description from different structures that were intended to be symbols that speak to cultural realities. For Tuell, the temple vision is not a failed prophecy or flawed building project, nor is it to be relegated to some irrelevant eschatological future, but is meant to be a confession that Yahweh is close at hand through a restored cult in a restored temple.[200] Even if many of the descriptions are symbolic or typological, they represent the intention that the restoration plan points to "right worship in the right temple" for the contemporaries of the vision.[201] Similarly, Leslie C. Allen argues that even if a passage is eschatological in scope, it is best regarded as having first spoken to its own generation. Therefore, the temple vision is about reassurance, about presenting symbols of renewed social identity and fellowship with God.[202]

While it is possible that the temple vision is intended to present an eventual eschatological fulfillment in some respects, it is best to understand the contemporary relevance of its cultic and legal features. The passage portrays a new, idealized social reality for a postexilic community in need of a new exodus and serves to offer a renewed hope. It is in this context that נחלה interacts with the renewed community throughout the vision. One way that the temple vision seeks to offer a new hope is by appealing to the more historically stable elements of the past—a new exodus and new covenant by appealing to the old. The vast majority of the נחלה references fit into this mold.

When discussing rules for Levitical priests, Ezek 44:28 reiterates that the Levites will not inherit their own plot of land. In a context pulled from Hexateuchal usage, Yahweh states "This shall be their inheritance (נחלה); I am their inheritance (נחלתם). And you shall give them no holding in Israel, I am their holding." The details are also from the Hexateuch: the Levites will eat from the first fruits of the offerings of Israel and receive a plot of land set aside for them (45:1).

Cognates of נחלה appear six times in Ezek 46:16-18. In a new feature to land holdings in Ezekiel's account, portions of land are set aside for the "prince" (נשיא).[203] He is allowed to hand over his inherited property

---

199   Tuell, *Ezekiel*, 23.

200   Tuell, *Ezekiel*, 174–78.

201   Tuell, *Ezekiel*, 14.

202   Leslie C. Allen, *Ezekiel 20–48* (WBC 29; Nashville: Thomas Nelson, 1990), 215.

203   A great deal has been written about the identity of the נשיא. Levenson, *Ezekiel*, 111–15, argues that the נשיא is a stand in for the king (מלך), a person in a place of honor, but that there is no true analogy to be made between the נשיא and any figure in Israel's past. It is not necessary to identify specifics of the נשיא for our purposes.

to his own sons, which they are able to hold in perpetuity. However, if the prince gifts any of his inheritance to a servant, it must be returned to the prince's family on the year of liberty. What's more, the prince is not allowed to take the inheritance of the people, so that none shall be alienated from their own ancestral property. It is very possible that the writer has prior abuses in mind, such as that of Ahab and his confiscation of Naboth's vineyard (1 Kgs 21).

The division of inherited land occupies the entire ending of the temple vision, from 47:13–48:35. Ezekiel 47:13a states, "Thus says the LORD God: These are the boundaries by which you shall divide the land for inheritance (תתנחלו) among the twelve tribes of Israel." The reallocation of the inherited land, divided along tribal lines, is the climax and ultimate end game for the vision of Israel's renewed social existence. The new allocation is patterned off Joshua's allotment program (Josh 13–19) and as Levenson notes, takes the program back to a time before land boundaries were not yet "blurred by an ascending central government."[204] Levenson surely has in mind the suppression of tribal distinction run by Solomon, as I argue above was a feature of 1 Kings. Adding further to the idealized nature of the restorative effects of the vision, in Ezekiel all the tribes are allotted land west of the Jordan—a correction to three trans-Jordanian tribes of Reuben, Gad, and half-Manasseh, which received land across the Jordan in Num 32, with reluctance on the part of Moses. Ezekiel repositions these tribes in land that was meant for them, based on boundary descriptions more in line with the promises to the patriarchs.[205] In keeping with our understanding of the temple vision as symbols and types representing an idealized social situation, Levenson argues:

> The order of the allotments to the tribes is not in conformity with that in any period in Israelite history, nor is there evidence that it was even attempted upon the restoration. There never was a *status quo* for which this program could have been the rationalization. Instead, it is purely ideal, and its idealism, incidentally, argues strongly that it is the product of the exile.[206]

Likewise, Tuell writes, "The plan for the division of the land also sets out to right old wrongs. Every tribe is given the same inheritance. Regional hostilities are placated by moving the trans-Jordanian tribes west and Judah north. Thus, all Israel is placed on an equitable footing under God."[207] Although the representation of land allotments is an idealized symbol, the theological reality behind it is quite serious. The purpose is

---

[204]   Levenson, *Ezekiel*, 112.
[205]   See Walther Eichrodt, *Ezekiel* (London: SCM Press, 1970), 590.
[206]   Levenson, *Ezekiel*, 116.
[207]   Tuell, *Ezekiel*, 172.

egalitarian; all Israel stands before God as one, all tribes viewed equally. Ezekiel sets out a plan for a new understanding of Israelite identity. Ezekiel 47:14 states, "You shall allot them (נחלתם) equally."

It is in this egalitarian program that Ezekiel presents a unique feature to inheritance contexts. Alongside these passages drawing on key Israelite symbols of the past, Ezek 47:21-23 states:

> So you shall divide this land among you according to the tribes of Israel. You shall allot it as an inheritance (נחלה) for yourselves and for the aliens (גרים) who reside among you and have begotten children among you. They shall be to you as citizens of Israel; with you they shall be allotted an inheritance (נחלה) among the tribes of Israel. In whatever tribe aliens (גר) reside, there you shall assign (תתנו) them their inheritance (נחלתו), says the Lord GOD.

Although we have seen an openness to aliens, foreigners, and the nations in inheritance contexts in Isaiah and Jeremiah, and although generosity to resident aliens in Israel is a principle throughout the HB,[208] this sort of provision—that the aliens will be given an actual allotment of the נחלה—is unprecedented. In previous passages aliens always remain aliens, and the נחלה only ever belongs to the Israelites, but here aliens are to be considered among the Israelites as "native sons of Israel" (והיו לכם כאזרח בבני ישראל). They are coheirs and ethnic Israelites. This drastic step is a proper ending to Ezek 40–48; as Levenson states, "The program of restoration in these nine chapters seeks to remedy those inequalities which are associated with inequities," and must be understood as "the visualization of the ideal society not as (egalitarian) man conceives it, but as the God of history conceives it."[209] The exilic restoration project, were it to properly be conceived as a new reality of social identity, advances the prospects of all who live in the inherited land, including the גר who at one time had no rights to land ownership.[210] Ezekiel 48 closes out the section with details of the portions of the land for the tribes, with resident aliens receiving lots as coheirs with the tribes in which they reside. This places the גר in an entirely new sort of relationship with Yahweh.

2.4.4. Non-Israelites in the Latter Prophets

Walther Eichrodt argues that the resident alien in the HB saw a gradual shift in status, from outsiders to proselytes. They had always been protected against oppression (Lev 19:33), and were expected

---

[208] See Lev 19:33; Deut 24:17.
[209] Levenson, *Ezekiel*, 125.
[210] See Tuell, *Ezekiel*, 173.

to observe commandments (Lev 18:26), but it was not until Ezek 47:22-23 that they were able to enjoy full rights of citizenship.[211] Blenkinsopp notes that Yahweh was shared with the nations from quite an early point; examples abound of gentiles interacting positively with Israel and its God going back to Genesis.[212] In an interesting study, Scott demonstrates that positive gentile involvement with Israel goes back to the table of nations in Gen 10 and that the table tradition was developed in this regard throughout multiple strands of Israelite/Jewish literature.[213] As I argue above, the third major aspect of the Abrahamic promises was that Abraham's descendants would be a light to the nations.

However, although a positive attitude relating to gentiles can be found throughout all strands of the HB, as it pertains to inheritance, to gentile/alien acceptance as full coheirs to the land, and to their equal status with the Israelites in their relationship with Yahweh, there can be little doubt that these realities were not present until the Latter Prophets.[214] Favor toward gentiles was embedded from the earliest point in the traditions, but the explicit way in which gentiles/aliens would be blessed by interaction with Abraham's descendants does not become clear until quite late, as a need for a new social identity in Israel saw the liturgical community take precedent over the ethnic one. This is not to say that all presentations of gentiles in the Latter Prophets are positive. As we have seen, the wicked among the nations fall under judgment. However, a gradual development of gentile inclusion and the reshaping of Israelite identity to accept non-Israelites finds its fullest expression in restoration contexts.

---

[211]   Eichrodt, *Ezekiel*, 592.

[212]   Joseph Blenkinsopp, "Second Isaiah—Prophet of Universalism," in *The Prophets: A Sheffield Reader* (ed. Philip R. Davies; Sheffield: Sheffield Academic, 1996), 192–93, points to three examples, Jethro, Rahab, and Naaman, but states, "This list is not, of course, exhaustive. Rabbinic tradition, which traces the history of proselytism, by a remarkable paradox, back to Abraham, has no difficulty finding proselytes in biblical narrative for every kind of proselyte." See also Gordon Mitchell, *Together in the Land: A Reading of the Book of Joshua* (Sheffield: JSOT Press, 1993), 152–84, who lists a number of intriguing examples of gentiles living amongst and being accepted by the Israelites in the book of Joshua.

[213]   Scott, *Nations*, 5–56.

[214]   See Konrad Schmid and Odil Hannes Steck, "Restoration Expectations in the Prophetic Tradition of the Old Testament," in *Restoration: Old Testament, Jewish, and Christian Perspectives* (ed. James M. Scott; Leiden: Brill, 2001), 52, who recognize this when they argue, "the late period of prophetic tradition here adopts the positive aspect of an *orientation toward the nations* and an *inclusion of the nations* in salvation."

2.5. Conclusions

Inheritance concepts throughout the HB reveal both stability in meaning and intent as well as considerable diversity. Stability is provided by God himself, who is the primary provider of inheritances, even regarding those inheritances of land and property that are passed down in perpetuity by ancestors from within tribes, clans, and families. God was viewed as the father of Israel and the ultimate ancestor of every tribe, and all inheritances were ultimately initiated by him. These inheritances were, ideally, more important than the things being inherited, as the nature of inheritance signified something about God's relationship with, and disposition toward, those to whom he provided an inheritance. This positions the concept of inheritance as relational, as well as the term נחל when it is used in relationship to God and his interactions with his people.

The diversity regarding inheritance contexts can be seen primarily as one analyzes the use of such concepts across various traditions and compositional strata. In the Hexateuch, inheritance is relatively stable. The heirs are the Israelites, their inheritance is the land, and they receive it as a gift. The land is to be allotted to tribes and clans, but the gift is contingent on their obedience to take possession of the land from the prior inhabitants and their continued obedience to the covenant. There is diversity regarding certain features, such as the inheritance granted to the Levites or the portrayal of the relative success of the Israelites to obey God's instructions, but the overall picture of inheritance in the Hexateuch follows this basic narrative paradigm. An important aspect of inheritance in the Hexateuch concerns the Abrahamic promise, which posited that God's people, the Israelites, would receive a land of their own, where they would be a light to the nations of the earth.

Inheritance concepts experience a clear narrative shift in the Former Prophets. The book of Judges portrays Israel in moral and structural chaos, which leads to the monarchy. God entrusts his inheritance (his people, his land, and any and all things which belongs to him) to the king who is tasked with its oversight. The inalienable nature of the land inheritance depicted in the Hexateuch continues for families, but in many respects the Former Prophets flatten out distinctions between tribes and clans. The relational nature of the inheritance remains paramount, as being cut off from the inheritance is akin to being cut off from God himself.

Inheritance concepts experience yet another narrative shift in the Latter Prophets, and this shift is the most dramatic. The exile leads to a disruption and redefinition of Israelite social and individual identity as the writers of these compositions wrestle with their unsettled relationship with the land. The loss of land, threatened and then actualized, does not negate the concept of inheritance, which is further evidence to support the notion that inheritance and its relational significance transcends its land-based contexts. Although the relational aspects of inheritance remain, every other aspect undergoes adjustment. The Israelites are still recipients of the inheritance, but gentiles are envisioned as eventual coheirs. The land of Israel is still in view, but inheritance begins to take on further geographical connotations. The Israelites are still required to be obedient to God, but the need for his intervention in their affairs is heightened. Whereas the inheritance in the Hexateuch and Former Prophets is set in contemporary perspective, in the Latter Prophets the fuller inheritance becomes an eschatological hope. Many of these themes are most dramatically expressed in Ezek 47:21-23, where foreigners are included with the Israelites as coheirs and native sons. Ezekiel 40–48 visualizes an ideal society where tribal distinctions are negated, and foreigners are included in the inheritance. This offers a new reality of social identity under God. An important aspect regarding the diversity of the HB's narrative of inheritance is the attention given to the three aspects of the Abrahamic promise. Although the first two key aspects (i.e., Abraham as a father of many descendants and his descendants possessing a land of their own) receive a great deal of attention in the Hexateuch, and are stable and present in the Former Prophets, the third aspect (i.e., that Abraham's descendants would be a light to the nations) is all but neglected until the Latter Prophets, where it becomes a prominent feature.

3

Inheritance in the Second Temple Period

Apocrypha and Pseudepigrapha

The texts discussed here, typically categorized as apocrypha and pseude-pigrapha,[1] are those that feature inheritance terminology and offer a contribution to the discussion on the "concept history" of inheritance in Jewish literature. Organizing these compositions chronologically would be difficult, as the precise dates and provenance of many Second Temple texts are disputed, but they span a wide chronological spectrum, from the earliest portions of the Enochic literature in the third century B.C.E to the Psalms of Solomon, which derives from the first century B.C.E and possibly into the first century C.E. The use of inheritance terminol-ogy in this period is diverse. Some attempt is made to explain the rea-sons for the diversity and any development in the concept beyond its use in the HB; however, the important issues for our discussion center more on what the terms mean, how they were used, and how the concept of inheritance functioned in the literature. Exploring the reasons for devel-opment and diversity is largely limited to the pursuit for the meaning and use of the terms.

---

[1]   Whereas "apocrypha" is more straightforward, "pseudepigrapha" is problem-atic because not all compositions categorized as such are pseudonymously written or attributed. Moreover, the compositions discovered at Qumran contain many fragments from these pseudepigraphical texts that could, technically, be discussed in the following chapter on the Dead Sea Scrolls.

3.1. 1 Enoch

The book typically referred to as "1 Enoch" is a collection of compositions that date to a wide range of periods. There are five references to inheritance in 1 Enoch. Verbs appear four times: three in the Book of the Watchers (all in 5:5-9) and once in the Book of Parables (40:9). Nouns appear once in the Epistle of Enoch (99:14). Due to the possible late date of composition for the Book of Parables, its import for this discussion is minimal;[2] therefore this analysis is limited to references found in 1 En. 5:5-9 and 99:14, with reference to 40:9 where helpful for interpretation.

3.1.1. Establishing the Text of 1 Enoch 5:5-9

An important passage featuring inheritance terminology is found in 1 En. 5 (the Book of the Watchers). This chapter features an oracle of judgment against the wicked and blessings pronounced for the righteous chosen. The wicked face destruction, and the righteous are promised salvation. The wicked will perish, but the righteous will "inherit the earth." However, there are significant text-critical problems in the section of the chapter where inheritance language is found, which requires preliminary analysis before the phrase "inherit the earth" can be interpreted.

In the Greek tradition, Codex Panopolitanus (sixth century) is the only manuscript that preserves chapter five,[3] and it features the phrase κληρονομήσουσιν τὴν γῆν (inherit the earth) three times, once each in verses 6, 7, and 8.[4] However, the Ethiopic tradition, with dozens of manuscripts ranging from the fifteenth to the eighteenth centuries, preserves the phrase just once, in verse 7. This has led to some variation in English editions of the text. R. H. Charles translates the phrase one time, in verse 7, following the Ethiopic.[5] He regards a large portion of verse 6 to be the result of Christian interpolation and argues that the phrase "inherit the earth" both in verses 6 and

---

[2]   Dating the Book of Parables is a notorious problem. J. T. Milik, *The Books of Enoch: Aramaic Fragments of Qumran Cave 4* (Oxford: Clarendon, 1976), 96, famously dated it to the late third century C.E. Most scholars today reject such a late date but still regard it as much later than the other portions of 1 Enoch. For a detailed analysis by various scholars on the date of the Book of Parables, see "Part Six: The Dating" in *Enoch and the Messiah Son of Man: Revisiting the Book of Parables* (ed. Gabriele Boccaccini; Grand Rapids: Eerdmans, 2007), 415–96.

[3]   See Matthew Black, *Apocalypsis Henochi Graece* (Leiden: Brill, 1970), 7.

[4]   See Black, *Apocalypsis*, 20.

[5]   R. H. Charles, *The Book of Enoch* (Oxford: Clarendon, 1893), 61. Also following the Ethiopic is Michael A. Knibb, *The Ethiopic Book of Enoch: A New Edition in Light of the Aramaic Dead Sea Fragments*, vol. 2 (Oxford: Clarendon, 1978), 66; James H. Charlesworth, *The Old Testament Pseudepigrapha*, vol. 1 (New York: Doubleday, 1983), 15. Charlesworth bases his text on a single fifteenth-century Ethiopic manuscript, with assistance from Charles' text (10).

8 is a doublet of verse 7.[6] George Nickelsburg likewise omits the phrase from verse 8, citing it as a doublet. He cites the possibility that the phrase in verse 6 is a doublet, but translates it, so that his edition has "inherit the earth" twice in chapter 5, which does not follow either manuscript tradition.[7]

The Aramaic tradition, only extant in the Dead Sea Scrolls, does not provide any clarity. As Florentino García Martínez notes, the Aramaic Book of the Watchers is "substantially the same" as the Greek and Ethiopic versions,[8] but portions of chapter 5 are only extant in three manuscripts, and all of them either cut off before the use of our phrase or pick up after it would appear.[9] For example, 4Q201 1ii 14–17 preserve parts of 1 En. 5:5-6, but only the portion describing curses for the wicked, and then breaks off, with preserved text beginning again in 6:4.[10]

There are good reasons to argue for the presence of doublets. Although Charles does not clarify how he believes the doublets entered Codex Pan, the most likely scenario is that they were placed there, or in a parent manuscript, intentionally by a scribe desiring to preserve variant but plausible readings. The phenomenon of doublets is well attested and is made apparent when repetition creates redundant phrases or clauses that are nearly the same, close in proximity, and add nothing new to the context.[11] The passages in question in the Greek of 1 En. 5 are as follows:

v. 6c—ἔσται αὐτοῖς σωτηρία, φῶς ἀγαθόν, καὶ αὐτοὶ κληρονομήσουσιν τὴν γῆν

> They will have salvation, a good light, and they will inherit the earth.

v. 7a—καὶ τοῖς ἐκλεκτοῖς φῶς καὶ χάρις καὶ εἰρήνη, καὶ αὐτοὶ κληρονομήσουσιν τὴν γῆν

> And the chosen ones will have light and joy and peace, and they will inherit the earth.

v. 8a—τότε δοθήσεται τοῖς ἐκλεκτοῖς φῶς καὶ χάρις, καὶ αὐτοὶ κληρονομήσουσιν τὴν γῆν

> Then the chosen ones will be given light and joy, and they will inherit the earth.

---

[6]   R. H. Charles, *The Ethiopic Version of the Book of Enoch* (Oxford: Clarendon, 1906), 11.

[7]   George W. E. Nickelsburg and James C. Vanderkam, *1 Enoch: The Hermeneia Translation* (Minneapolis: Fortress, 2012), 22.

[8]   Florentino García Martínez, *Qumran and Apocalyptic: Studies on the Aramaic Texts from Qumran* (Leiden: Brill, 1992), 60.

[9]   Witnesses are 4Q201, 4Q202, and 4Q204. See *The Dead Sea Scrolls Study Edition* (ed. Florentino García Martínez and Eibert J. C. Tigchelaar; Leiden: Brill, 1999), 399–401.

[10]   See Milik, *Enoch*.

[11]   See Emanuel Tov, *Textual Criticism of the Hebrew Bible* (Minneapolis: Fortress, 1992), 241.

There are reasons to support Codex Pan: first, although Charles argues for interpolations and doublets in other places in the manuscript, these usually constitute just a few words. If we were to accept Charles' argument regarding the doublet in 5:6, then this would add thirty-six words to that verse, and in verse 8, an additional thirteen words.[12] These would be by far the largest additions in the entire manuscript, meaning that a pattern of such lengthy additions is not established by Charles.

Second, Charles argues that Codex Pan and the Ethiopic tradition are very close, to the point that they likely derived from the same ancestor manuscript, which he regards as the first Greek translation of the Semitic original.[13] In fact, according to Charles, Codex Pan is closer to the Ethiopic than any other Greek manuscript. Furthermore, as noted above, García Martínez states that the Aramaic manuscripts reveal that the Greek and Ethiopic traditions are consistent with the Aramaic manuscripts from Qumran. Therefore, it is not a settled matter that the Ethiopic form of chapter 5 derives more directly from the Semitic and that Codex Pan is the outlier. Even Charles points to instances where the Greek includes clauses that are omitted by the Ethiopic, but are likely genuine, meaning that the Ethiopic tradition likely dropped certain clauses over time.[14] It is possible that the phrases in question in chapter 5 were removed from the Ethiopic tradition, which is likely due to repetition.[15]

Third, there are other instances of repetition in Codex Pan. The Book of the Watchers makes frequent use of common terms and phrases where context dictates that a doublet is not to blame, so even cases of demonstrable redundancy are not out of the question. For example, in

---

[12]   Charles, *Ethiopic Version*, 11.

[13]   Charles, *Ethiopic Version*, xxvii, argues that the Semitic original of the Book of the Watchers was a mix of Hebrew and Aramaic, and that chs. 1–5, written after the rest of the book as an introduction, was written in Hebrew. This decision was made before the discovery of Aramaic manuscripts of ch. 1–5 at Qumran. Although there is a consensus that all sections of 1 Enoch derive from a Semitic source language, the debate regarding the use of Hebrew and/or Aramaic remains an open question. For more, see George W. E. Nickelsburg, *1 Enoch 1*, Hermeneia (Minneapolis: Fortress, 2001), 9.

[14]   Charles, *Ethiopic Version*, 5, n. 9, 15.

[15]   See Michael A. Knibb, "The Book of Enoch or the Books of Enoch?" in *The Early Enoch Literature* (ed. Gabriele Boccaccini and John J. Collins; Leiden: Brill, 2007), 29, who argues that the Ethiopic tradition reflects changes that are rooted not only in translation but in clear editorial intervention based on the development of the tradition in a Christian context. This is not to say that the Greek has not been the subject of similar intervention. It likely has been. But the extant Greek tradition is limited to the degree that establishing editorial changes is very difficult. For a fascinating account regarding scribal arrangement in Codex Pan, see the recent article by Elena Dugan, "Enochic Biography and the Manuscript History of 1 Enoch: The Codex Panopolitanus Book of the Watchers," *JBL* 140, no. 1 (2021): 113–38.

5:9 alone we find three very similar phrases used in an almost clumsy repetition:

πάσας τὰς ἡμέρας τῆς ζωῆς αὐτῶν (all the days of their lives)

τὸν ἀριθμὸν αὐτῶν ζωῆς ἡμερῶν (the number of the days of their lives)

ἐν πάσαις ταῖς ἡμέραις τῆς ζωῆς αὐτῶν (in all the days of their lives)

Repetition and a lack of precision are characteristic features of the Book of the Watchers. Nickelsburg recognizes this, arguing that this repetition often serves a structural purpose and in a few cases is employed simply for stylistic symmetry.[16] The three occurrences of "inherit the earth" in chapter 5 are similar enough that if two of the instances were in fact doublets, then it is difficult to see why the scribe(s) felt the need to include one at all, let alone two doublets of the same verse. Repetition and a lack of precision on the part of the author may make for a better explanation.[17]

In light of these three points, and without further witnesses from the Greek or Aramaic traditions, it seems that both scenarios are possible and there are no reasons to be dogmatic: the repetition of the phrase "inherit the earth" could be the result of doublets or couplets, or, all three could be original. However, between the composition of the Book of the Watchers and the fifteenth century, Codex Pan is the only extant manuscript in any language to contain 5:6b-8. To assume doublets and dismiss portions of verses 6 and 8 is to work on an assumption regarding the transcription tradition that has no evidence to support it. It is just as possible that the verses were a stable feature of the earlier tradition and were dropped by the Ethiopic tradition or even before the text began to be translated into Ethiopic.

Even if the verses are doublets, they were preserved for a very distinct reason, and we have no way of knowing the extent to which they may have been preserved elsewhere in the tradition or if the instance of verse 7 found in the Ethiopic is more original than those found in verses 6 and 8. Although the verses are similar, there are distinct

---

[16]   Nickelsburg, *1 Enoch 1*, 129.

[17]   The situation of the Enochic manuscripts bears some resemblance to the manuscript history of Tobit. There was a long-standing belief that the shorter versions of Tobit were closer to the original and that they had been expanded over time through changes and additions. This picture changed, however, with the discovery of Aramaic and Hebrew manuscripts at Qumran, which reflected the early character of longer readings. See Stuart Weeks, Simon Gathercole, and Loren T. Stuckenbruck, *The Book of Tobit: Texts from the Principal Ancient and Medieval Traditions* (Berlin: de Gruyter, 2004), 3.

features between them, specifically the appearance of the noun σωτη-ρία (salvation) in verse 6, and these features offer important insights. As argued above, in comparison with other doublets found in the manuscript by Charles, the addition of forty-nine words between verses 6 and 8 would prove to be excessive, calling the argument into question. However, even if they are doublets, the insertion of these variant readings serves to stress the importance of their content, and the anomaly of such excessive additions proves a compelling reason to engage with these verses as they are found in the manuscript in order to discover just why the scribe(s) felt the need to include them. With the manuscript tradition as we have it, discovering the so-called "original" reading is impossible, so engaging with this manuscript as it has come down to us will likely yield important insights into the meaning of the phrase "inherit the earth." Such engagement may provide clues about the importance that "inherit the earth" held for the scribe(s) of Codex Pan and may speak to the importance of the phrase at the time when the Enochic compositions were first written. The reasons for engaging with the phrase as it appears in Codex Pan are compelling, so it is to this version that we turn to below.

3.1.2. The Structure of 1 Enoch 5:5-9

The consensus among Enochic scholars is that the section containing chapters 1–5 was likely written independently. Although some have suggested that this section serves as an introduction to all of 1 Enoch,[18] it is much more likely that the introduction only serves the Book of the Watchers. As Nickelsburg observes, the whole section takes the form of a prophetic oracle and foreshadows the message of chapters 6–36 by employing its words, phrases, and motifs.[19] Some of the ways in which this is apparent are discussed below.

The introduction opens with the superscription in 1:1, which announces the coming judgment for all of humanity and anticipates the centrality of this theme throughout the book. There is a stark contrast between "the righteous chosen," who will be saved (σωθήσονται), and "the enemies," who will be removed. This theme is elaborated upon in 1:7-9, where, at the judgment, the earth will be cut off and torn apart and the wicked will be destroyed, but God will make peace with the righteous chosen. 1 Enoch 1:8 can be arranged in an a-b-b-a format with the first and last lines of the verse creating an inclusio, and in both structure and content it anticipates our passage in 5:5-9. 1 Enoch 1:8 reads:

---

18   Charlesworth appears to suggest this in *Pseudepigrapha*, 6.
19   Nickelsburg, *1 Enoch 1*, 132.

a—With the righteous he will make peace (εἰϱήνην),
  and over the chosen there will be protection,
  and upon them will be mercy (ἔλεος).
    b—They will all be God's,
    and he will grant them his good pleasure.
    b—He will bless them all,
    and he will help them all.
a—Light (φῶς) will shine upon them,
and he will make peace (εἰϱήνην) with them.[20]

1 Enoch 2:1–5:3 details the obedience of nature—how the created order does not alter its works from the words of God. By contrast, in 5:4, we are told that the sinners, unlike nature, have not stood firm in God's commandments, but have turned aside, and therefore will be denied the peace of God.[21] These themes culminate in 5:5-9, which serves as the concluding section of the introduction to the book. As stated previously, repetition is a key aspect of 1 En. 1–5, which serves here as a bracket in order to emphasize the point and elaborate upon it.[22] This repetition builds on the striking contrast between the sinners and the righteous in detailing the consequences of all that has been described in the book thus far. Verse 5 is set in obvious contrast to verse 9, where the sinners and the righteous are compared with strikingly similar language:

Of the sinners, 5:5 states:

"Then you will curse your days, and the days of your life will perish,
and the years of your destruction will increase in an eternal curse;
and there will be no mercy (ἔλεος) or peace for you."

Of the righteous, 5:9 states:

"But the number of the days of their life they will complete,
and their life will grow in peace, and the years of their joy will
    increase in rejoicing
and eternal peace all the days of their life."

These verses work as brackets to illustrate the message of this passage, and along with 5:8, verse 9 works as a reprise of 1:8, repeating the use of terms such as light (φῶς), mercy (ἔλεος), and peace (εἰϱήνη) being granted to the righteous by God. Verse 5 is the counterbalance, where the sinners and the righteous are separated as those who receive mercy

---

20   Translation by Nickelsburg, *1 Enoch*, 20.
21   For a detailed analysis of the role of nature in holding the sinners accountable in 1 En. 2:1–5:4, see Randal A. Argall, *1 Enoch and Sirach: A Comparative Literary and Conceptual Analysis of the Themes of Revelation, Creation and Judgment* (Atlanta: Scholars Press, 1995), 101–7.
22   On the use of repetition as literary brackets, see Nickelsburg, *1 Enoch 1*, 129.

and forgiveness and those who do not. The verses between the brackets compound this contrast by repeating it through the use of parallelistic poetry. The sinners are addressed directly in the second person, while the righteous are discussed in the third person.

Verse 5:6 states:

"Then you will leave your names as an eternal curse for all the
    righteous,
and by you all who curse will curse, and all the sinners and wicked
    will swear by you.
But the chosen will rejoice; and for them there will be forgiveness
    of sins
and all mercy and peace and kindness.

"For them there will be salvation, a good light, and they will inherit
    the earth.
But for you sinners there will be no salvation, but on all of you a
    curse will abide."

Verse 5:7 states:

"For the chosen there will be light and joy and peace, and they will
    inherit the earth.
But for you wicked there will be a curse."

The contrast between the righteous and the sinners does not continue in verse 8, because verses 8-9 serve to summarize and elaborate on the fate of the righteous. Verses 8-9a, however, continue the parallelistic structure, providing a mirror by which to interpret them. Verses 5:8-9a can be arranged in this way:

5:8a—Then light and joy will be given to the chosen, and they will
    inherit the earth.
5:8b—Then wisdom will be given to all the chosen;
        and they will all live,
        and they will sin no more through godlessness or pride.

5:8c—In the enlightened man there will be light,
        and in the wise man, understanding,
        and they will transgress no more,
5:9a—nor will they sin all the days of their life, nor will they die in
    the heat of God's wrath.

When reading verses 8a and 9a in parallel, we see that it is those who inherit the earth who, as a product of this inheritance, will not die in God's wrath. When reading 8b and 8c in parallel, we see that the chosen will live, and sin no more, because they have received wisdom and understanding. This is returned to below.

3.1.3. Interpreting "Inherit the Earth" in 1 Enoch 5:5-9

The language of 1 En. 1:1 closely resembles that of Deut 33:27-29, where God drives out the enemies of Israel and saves his people. However, in Deuteronomy it is all Israel who is chosen and saved. In 1 Enoch, God distinguishes between those within Israel; the righteous are a portion of the nation chosen over and against their enemies, "whether within or outside the nation."[23] Enoch's purpose is to speak on behalf of the elect (1:3) and to declare God's pleasure and blessing upon them (1:8).[24] According to 5:5, the sinners are then cursed, which leads to a shortening of their days and a lack of peace. Verse 5:9 then declares the fullness of life for the chosen and that their peace will extend all the days of their lives. 1 Enoch 5:6-9a describes how this peace is accomplished.

1 Enoch 5:6b states that the chosen will be forgiven of their sins. This motif is only present elsewhere in the Book of the Watchers in 12:5 and 13:4-6, where the Watchers request forgiveness and are denied, so the declaration of forgiveness of human agents in 5:6 is unique. It is not denied that the righteous do in fact sin, as their forgiveness is necessary. Their forgiveness serves to highlight their election; it is only the chosen who are forgiven. This forgiveness anticipates a moral effect in verse 9 when the righteous will no longer sin.

Forgiveness leads into the first refrain featuring inheritance language. Before we can interpret the phrase "inherit the earth," one more thing can be said regarding the number of times it appears in the composition. The reference in verse 7 was accepted by Charles as original due to its appearance in the Ethiopic witnesses, and the references in verses 6 and 8 were called into question. As I argue above, much of the repetition in the Book of the Watchers is stylistic, and whether the repetition regarding inheritance was designed by the author or the editor, the effect is clear: it serves to emphasize the importance of the phrase and the concepts attached to it. However, there are subtle but important differences between each of the three references in this passage, and recognizing these unique features is an important aspect of analyzing their contribution.

The reference in verse 6 is the only one that attaches the inheritance of the earth to the concept of salvation (σωτηρία), a concept that is central to the Book of the Watchers as it appears in the opening verse. As James Charlesworth argues, the postexilic literature portrays many Jews as concerned over the lack of purity of their fellow Jews, the frequent

---

23   See Nickelsburg, *1 Enoch 1*, 135.

24   The exact identity and social context of the two groups is difficult to determine, and such identifications are not necessary for the present study. For details of the discussion, see Nickelsburg, *1 Enoch 1*, 62–67.

prosperity of those living in disobedience to God, and the consistent condition of their land as it was ruled by foreign oppressors. Evil is a dominant force in the world because it has obtained the earth.[25] This is the context in which salvation is cast in the Book of the Watchers.[26] The forgiveness of sins allows the chosen to be regarded as righteous and separates them from those still regarded as sinners. The chosen will be saved from among their fellow Jews who prosper despite their disobedience, and they will be saved from foreign oppressors who rule their land.[27] The righteous will find peace with God, and they will inherit the earth. Salvation will be denied to the sinners, which constitutes a lack of peace with God and a denial of the inheritance. These themes are then emphasized in verse 7. Where the inheritance refrain in verse 6 attaches inheritance to salvation and light, verse 7 utilizes the concepts of joy and peace that also feature in the summary of the passage in verse 9. More will be said on the meaning of these terms below.

The inheritance refrain in verse 8 also adds a subtle but unique contribution: the idea that light and joy and the inheritance of the earth will be given by God as opposed to earned or taken by the righteous.

[25]   For examples in the literature, see Charlesworth, *Pseudepigrapha*, xxx.

[26]   Charlesworth's description is generic to the broader background of salvation in the Second Temple period and many of its texts but is not meant here to encapsulate the specificity of the background for the Book of Watchers, or the whole of 1 Enoch, in most respects. The background for each section of 1 Enoch is varied and requires a nuanced approach not necessary for our purposes in this discussion. For details of the possible backgrounds for the Book of the Watchers, see many of the essays in Boccaccini and Collins, *Early Enoch Literature*, particularly Martha Himmelfarb, "Temple and Priests in the Book of the Watchers, the Animal Apocalypse, and the Apocalypse of Weeks," 219–35, who argues that the temple imagery in 1 Enoch portrays a community critical of the Jerusalem temple and the temple priests; Patrick Tiller, "The Sociological Settings of the Components of 1 Enoch," 237–55, who sets the Book of the Watchers as a polemic against the rule of the Ptolemies and their local representatives; Pierluigi Piovanelli, "Sitting by the Waters of Dan, or the Tricky Business of Tracing the Social Profile of the Communities That Produced the Earliest Enochic Texts," 257–81, who disagrees with both Himmelfarb and Tiller and places the social background of the Book of the Watchers in Galilee. Piovanelli also disagrees with the thesis of Michael E. Stone, "The Book of Enoch and Judaism in the Third Century B.C.E.," *CBQ* 40, no. 4 (1978): 479–92, who argued that the authors of the Book of the Watchers were themselves disenchanted priests. Each of these essays point to the difficulties and speculative nature of pinpointing the community (if there was one) and social settings of any portion of 1 Enoch.

[27]   See Loren T. Stuckenbruck, "The Plant Metaphor in Its Inner-Enochic and Early Jewish Context," in *Enoch and Its Qumran Origins: New Light on a Forgotten Connection* (ed. Gabriele Boccaccini; Grand Rapids: Eerdmans, 2005), 210–12, who discusses the plant metaphor in 1 En. 93:10 and its relationship to other uses of the metaphor in Qumran texts, such as 4QInstruction. The details of the divide between the righteous and the sinners from *within* Israel offer a complex picture of the nature of election and Jewish identity in many Second Temple texts.

The righteous do not already possess the earth.[28] In 1 En. 5:8 we find two instances of the term δοθήσεται, the future passive of the verb "to give." It is God who grants the inheritance and associated gifts to the righteous at some future point.

In order to understand the phrase "inherit the earth," it is helpful to discuss the two main texts that the writer of the Book of the Watchers is possibly drawing on for his use of terms. The first is Ps 37 (Ps 36 in the LXX), which uses the phrase "inherit the earth/land" five times (vv. 9, 11, 22, 29, 34) and the noun "inheritance" one time (v. 18). Dating the Psalm is difficult, but its contents fit in well with the state of postexilic literature previously described by Charlesworth. As in the Book of the Watchers, the Psalm is committed to the contrast between the righteous and the wicked, and it is concerned with the perception that the wicked prosper while those who follow God are left to suffer. The Psalmist states that the righteous Israelites need not worry about the wicked, as they will soon fade like the grass (37:1). They will be cut off (37:9-10), and the righteous will be saved. The details of this Psalm bear a striking resemblance to 1 En. 1–5 in a number of ways, but here I will detail five of the most important, referring to Ps 36 in the LXX for a comparison of Greek terms:

1) When comparing Ps 36 to 1 En. 1:8, both passages promise protection for the righteous against the sinners (Ps 36:39-40), blessing (Ps 36:22), and help in a time of need (Ps 36:40). Both promise that a light (φῶς) will shine upon the righteous (Ps 36:6).

2) Both passages promise a quick and violent end to the days of the sinners (Ps 36:13-17; 1 En. 5:5), making use of the future middle indicative of the verb ἀπόλλυμι (to perish, Ps 36:20; 1 En. 5:5).[29] Conversely, both passages promise salvation (σωτηρία) to the righteous (Ps 36:39; 1 En. 5:6) and an extension of their days (Ps 36:27-29; 1 En. 5:9).

---

[28]   This is a theme described in great detail in the Book of Parables (1 En. 38:4; 48:8; 62:6; 63:1, 12; 67:12), where the land is possessed by the kings, the mighty, and the strong, all of whom are described as wicked. Although these references reveal something of the worldview regarding 1 Enoch in its final form, the relevance for interpreting the Book of the Watchers is limited, as the Book of the Watchers was likely written under Ptolemaic rule, and the Book of Parables was written later under a different administration.

[29]   Important to note is that equivalents of the verb "to perish" can be found in both the Greek and Ethiopic witnesses but not in the Aramaic fragments from Qumran. This places some question as to whether or not the verb is original.

3) Both passages feature the use of the phrase "inherit the earth" in repetition (Ps 36, 5x; 1 En. 5, 3x).

4) Although the book of Joshua portrays the inheritance of the land as having been realized by the Israelites (Josh 21:43-45), both of these texts fit with the postexilic circumstance that found the Israelites alienated from the land and no longer in control of it. In both cases the inheritance is a future promise, indicated by the use of the future tense verb, "will inherit."

5) The language attached to inheritance shows signs of dependence. For example, Ps 36:22 reads: "for those blessed by the Lord shall inherit the land (αὐτὸν κληρονομήσουσι γῆν), but those cursed (καταρώμενοι) by him shall be cut off." By comparison, 1 En. 5:7 reads: "For the chosen there will be light and joy and peace, and they will inherit the earth (αὐτοὶ κληρονομήσουσιν τὴν γῆν), but for the wicked there will be a curse (κατάρα)."

The relationship of these texts to wisdom is also an important point of unity. Peter C. Craigie argues that Ps 37 is one of the most striking examples of a sapiential Psalm, standing firmly in the wisdom tradition.[30] He states, "Like Proverbs, the Psalm is a kind of anthology of wisdom sayings . . . the instruction provided guidance concerning how to live a moral and God-fearing life, and set a broader context within which to understand the apparent success and prosperity of those who lived irreligious and immoral lives."[31] In the Psalm, this wisdom is connected to inheritance. Verses 29-31 state:

The righteous shall inherit the land,
    and live in it forever.
The mouths of the righteous utter wisdom,
    and their tongues speak justice.
The law of their God is in their hearts;
    their steps do not slip.

In this passage, the parallelism suggests that wisdom is equated with Torah (ὁ νόμος, v. 31), which coincides with the nature of the Psalm as

---

[30]   The use of "Wisdom Psalm" as a category has been challenged in recent scholarship, particularly by James L. Crenshaw, *The Psalms: An Introduction* (Grand Rapids: Eerdmans, 2001), 87–95. The categorization, however, still receives large support. See Walter Brueggemann, *Psalms* (Cambridge: Cambridge University Press, 2014), 184.

[31]   Peter C. Craigie, *Psalms 1–50* (WBC 19; Nashville: Thomas Nelson, 1983), 296–97.

an instructional poem.[32] The idea that the law is on the heart, and that one does not falter in adhering to it, is also connected directly with the inheritance of the land in Deut 30:11-20, where the Israelites are promised possession and blessing in the land as long as they follow God's commandments.[33] Like Ps 37 and 1 En. 5, Deut 30:18-20 also promises that those who disobey God will be cut off from the land and perish (ἀπολεῖσθε, fut mid of ἀπόλλυμι) but that those who obey God will be blessed with a lengthening of days in the land.

In comparison with Deut 30 and many other inheritance passages throughout the Hexateuch, it is clear that the inheritance in Ps 37 is the land of Israel, thus "inherit the land," rather than "inherit the earth," is the best translation of κληρονομήσουσι γῆν (Ps 36, LXX) and its cognates throughout the Psalm. However, in contrast to the Hexateuch, which promises the inheritance to all of Israel over and against the Canaanite inhabitants of the land, the early postexilic context of this Psalm places the conflict between those within Israel seeking to honor God and those prospering in the land by their disobedience to the law, whether from within the community of the Israelites or outside of it. Although the exact timing of the inheritance is unclear, the future tense of the verb "will inherit" is tempered by the anticipation that the wicked will be cut off "quickly/soon" (ταχὺ, v. 2). The Psalm is sapiential, not apocalyptic; the prosperity of the wicked will be short-lived and the Psalm is seeking to instruct the righteous regarding how to live until the wicked are removed.[34] The closest thing to apocalyptic language is found in 37:34-36, where the righteous are said to look upon the destruction of the wicked until they could no longer be found, but in conjunction with early postexilic literature, the Psalm anticipates a swift resolution to the circumstances of the righteous. Verse 37:3 promises that, if the righteous trust in the Lord and do good, they will find security in the land, but throughout the Psalm the condition of the land itself remains unchanged.

Later in the Second Temple period this optimistic perspective shifts, because time goes on, but the situation remains unchanged. This is demonstrated in the interpretation of Ps 37 in the Psalms Pesher, a commentary found among the Qumran Scrolls. The commentary downplays the Psalm's sapiential aspects and interprets it eschatologically.[35] The wicked are still in control of Israel at the time of writing

---

[32]   Craigie, *Psalms*, 299.

[33]   Charles Augustus Briggs and Emilie Grace Briggs, *The Book of Psalms* (ICC; Edinburgh: T&T Clark, 1906), 330.

[34]   Craigie, *Psalms*, 297.

[35]   See Nickelsburg, *1 Enoch 1*, 162.

and are made up both of the violent ones of the nations and the wicked of Israel. The wicked will be cut off forever and exterminated. "The congregation of the oppressed" are God's elect who do his will. Rather than Israel alone, the pesher concludes that the righteous will inherit "the whole earth."[36]

These aspects of wisdom and apocalypticism come together in the Book of the Watchers. 1 Enoch 5:8 states that the righteous chosen will be given (δοθήσεται) light and joy and the inheritance of the earth. They will also be given (δοθήσεται) wisdom.[37] They will no longer sin through godlessness or pride, a line that confirms that aside from their election they shared the condition of the wicked. The parallelism suggests that the granting of wisdom brings life; it is a saving wisdom that brings moral change.[38] As with Ps 37, this wisdom is contrasted with the behavior of the wicked that have not stood firm in God's commandments (5:4).

There is a potential difference between Ps 37 and 1 En. 5 regarding wisdom that should be addressed. As I argue above, wisdom and instruction in Ps 37 are directly tied to the law, to Torah. E. P. Sanders concludes that 1 Enoch, which also ties wisdom to commandments and obedience, is concerned with the covenant between God and Israel detailed in the Pentateuch, which is described as proffered by Moses on God's behalf. Sanders states, "Salvation depends on election and that what is necessary to maintain the elect state—to be righteous—is to maintain loyalty and obedience to God *and his covenant*" (emphasis mine).[39] Although Nickelsburg agrees that, in 1 En. 5:8, wisdom is related to Torah,[40] he argues (*contra* Sanders) that throughout 1 Enoch the writers are little concerned with Torah and the covenant. The covenant is mentioned in relationship to wisdom in one place, 1 En. 93:6-10, but Nickelsburg points out that 1 En. 5:4 uses the more general category of "his commandments" (τὰς ἐντολὰς αὐτοῦ), without reference to specific laws associated with the covenant.

---

[36]   Compare 4Q171 1+3 4iii 10 with 4Q171 1+3 4 10–11. For an English translation integrating the manuscripts of the Pesher, see Geza Vermes, *The Complete Dead Sea Scrolls in English* (London: Penguin Books, 2011), 521–22. For a critical edition of the Psalms Pesher, see *The Dead Sea Scrolls: Hebrew, Aramaic, and Greek Texts with English Translations*, vol. 6B: *Pesharim, Other Commentaries, and Related Documents* (ed. James H. Charlesworth; Tübingen: Mohr Siebeck, 2002), 6–33. The comments on inheritance in the pesher primarily concern Ps 37:22, 34.

[37]   See also 1 En. 93:10.

[38]   See Nickelsburg, *1 Enoch 1*, 163.

[39]   E. P. Sanders, *Paul and Palestinian Judaism* (Minneapolis: Fortress, 1977), 362.

[40]   Nickelsburg, *1 Enoch 1*, 163.

Therefore, it is difficult to determine exactly which commands the Book of the Watchers has in view. What is certain is that the centrality of judgment in 1 Enoch "implies a corpus or collection of laws and commandments that form the criteria for that judgment." However, Nickelsburg argues, although right actions are important, 1 Enoch's language places it clearly within the sapiential-apocalyptic tradition, where revealed wisdom operates as an epistemological category. For texts in this tradition, right action is only possible for those who are rightly informed.[41] Wisdom originates with God, and one can only obtain it through revelation.[42] Therefore, to turn aside from God is a hardness of heart (5:4), but receiving wisdom leads to understanding (5:8). This revealed wisdom, rather than the Torah, leads the righteous to transgress no more.[43] While 1 Enoch implies a tacit approval of Torah, it appears to be a subcategory subsumed under the

---

[41]   See Nickelsburg, *1 Enoch 1*, 50–51, as well as George W. E. Nickelsburg, "Enochic Wisdom and Its Relationship to the Mosaic Torah," in Boccaccini and Collins, *The Early Enoch Literature*, 83. See also Joseph Blenkinsopp, *Wisdom and Law in the Old Testament: The Ordering of Life in Israel and Early Judaism* (Oxford: Oxford University Press, 1995), who argues for a merging of the law and wisdom in much of the Second Temple literature. He writes of law codes at Qumran, "In their care to provide appropriate motivation for observing the laws and to promote a reflective approach to the moral life in general, they come close in several aspects to the teaching of the sages." See also Alice M. Sinnott, *The Personification of Wisdom* (Aldershot: Ashgate, 2005), 174, who argues not that wisdom and Torah have merged but that they are one in the same— that the Torah is identified as wisdom in texts such as Ben Sira and Baruch. A third option sees Torah and wisdom as separate categories in the Second Temple literature, which are brought together and placed in relationship to one another. The details of this relationship require a nuanced analysis in each text where this relationship appears. This issue factors into the discussion below, especially regarding Sirach.

[42]   See Christopher Rowland, "Apocalypticism," in *The Eerdmans Dictionary of Early Judaism* (ed. John J. Collins and Daniel C. Harlow; Grand Rapids: Eerdmans, 2010), 345, who argues that this reliance on revelation rather than reading and interpretation of texts is a distinguishing feature of apocalyptic literature.

[43]   See also John J. Collins, *The Apocalyptic Imagination: An Introduction to Jewish Apocalyptic Literature* (Grand Rapids: Eerdmans, 2016), 48–49, who argues that 1 En. 2–5 is not concerned with the law of Moses but rather the law of nature. He states, "There is no suggestion that Sinai is at variance with the laws of nature, but the ultimate authority is older than Moses and applies not only to Israel but to all humanity. The contrast between the order of nature and the disorder of sinful humanity forms the backdrop for the eschatological judgment." Andreas Bedenbender, "The Place of the Torah in the Early Enoch Literature," in Boccaccini and Collins, *The Early Enoch Literature*, 76, argues that the reference to Sinai in 1 En. 1:4 and the discussion of the law of nature which follows intends to "build a bridge between Enochic wisdom and the Mosaic Torah."

wisdom reported by Enoch,[44] which operates in the Book of the Watchers "as revelation of a higher kind."[45]

This revealed wisdom also defines at least one of the four uses of the term "light" (φῶς) found in 1 En. 5:5-9. In 5:8, the wise man is equated with the enlightened (πεφωτισμένῳ) man, and light is equated with wisdom and understanding. In the three refrains featuring the phrase "inherit the earth," the meaning of the three references to "light" is less clear. Nickelsburg suggests that it is a reference to the theophanic glory,[46] which would fit with the likely meaning of the term in 1:8, where light serves as the divine presence who makes peace with the righteous, and would make sense of the full phrase "the good light" (φῶς ἀγαθόν) in 1 En. 5:6. This also bears similarity to the clear meaning of light in Isa 60:19-22, where God serves as an everlasting light to the righteous, who "inherit the land forever" (αἰῶνος κληρονομήσουσιν τὴν γῆν).

The question regarding timing is where the sapiential and apocalyptic elements of the Book of the Watchers meet, in what Nickelsburg calls a "this-worldly apocalypticism." It is here that we must briefly analyze the second of the texts that 1 En. 5 is likely drawing on for its use of language: Isa 65–66. Isaiah 64:8-9 deals with the cry of the Israelites, who, in an act of penitence, ask God to remember that they are his people. God responds in Isa 65:1-14 by declaring his judgment that they have turned aside from his ways, and that only his chosen will inherit (κληρονομήσει, 65:9) Israel. The language of election is deliberate, as those who have forsaken God will be destroyed (65:11-12), but the chosen will be blessed (65:16).

1 Enoch 5:6ab likely borrows language directly from Isa 65:15-16.[47] Where 1 En. 5 moves directly from there into the inheritance of the earth, Isa 65:17-25 moves directly into an apocalyptic vision of the end of the current earthly circumstance and the creation of a new

---

[44]   Some discussion has centered on the exact role of the person of Enoch in relation to the wisdom revealed in the text. John J. Collins, *Seers, Sybils and Sages in Hellenistic-Roman Judaism* (SJSJ; Leiden: Brill, 1997), 340–43, argues that, at points, Enoch appears to play the role of scribe, whose job it is to record the information given him. However, because Enoch communicates teaching from heaven to earth, he functions as a seer, one who mediates divine revelation.

[45]   Bedenbender, "Enoch," 79. See also Nickelsburg, "Enochic Wisdom," 88–94, who argues that although 1 Enoch is not anti-Torah, it is concerned with issues of God's justice and human conduct that are rooted in the prophetic literature and in wisdom traditions that interpret the prophetic literature.

[46]   Nickelsburg, *1 Enoch 1*, 162.

[47]   See Nickelsburg, *1 Enoch 1*, 161.

heavens and a new earth.[48] The former things are cast aside in favor of a new relationship between God and his people. John D. W. Watts convincingly argues that this passage moves beyond a Deuteronomistic view of the participation and salvation of all Israel and into a new vision of God's relationship specifically with those who seek him. Israel is divided between the rebels and the servants, with curses for the former and blessings for the latter.[49] God's "people" are no longer delineated by birthright; they are those who seek God from within Israel but also those who seek him from among the nations.[50]

God's new people come with a new vision of temporal space. In the same way that in Gen 1:1 God created the heavens and the earth, in Isa 65:17 he declares his intention to create a new heavens and a new earth. Isaiah 65 describes an idyllic existence reminiscent of Eden, where the creation is at harmony and humans experience life at an optimum level: with the absence of violence and distress and a lengthening of the days of life to a peak number of years.[51] Although the term ארץ (land/earth) is often translated "land" in the HB, Watts points out that, when in parallel with שמים (heavens), the term gives a description of totality, encompassing the universe and the divine realm—so the entire earth rather than Israel alone is in view, with a new Jerusalem at the center of this new earth.[52]

1 Enoch imports this vision into its social milieu in order to present the righteous chosen with an apocalyptic hope. The sin and violence of the earth are blamed on unholy angels, who mated with women and taught humankind to sin (1 En. 7–9). The earth was filled with iniquity (9:9) and social conditions for the righteous were precarious; therefore, 1 Enoch presents salvation as yet future; it will be realized in a new Jerusalem and a renewed earth.[53] The description of this new creation begins

---

[48]   John D. W. Watts, *Isaiah 34–66* (WBC; Columbia: Nelson Reference, 2005), 924, argues that this new heavens and new earth is not eschatological, that Isaiah presents the new age as already present with the reign of Cyrus and the rebuilding of Jerusalem under the Persians. Claus Westermann, *Isaiah 40–66* (Philadelphia: Westminster, 1969), 408, rightly interprets it eschatologically but is careful to differentiate between apocalyptic (the destruction of one earth which is replaced by another) and eschatological (the miraculous renewal of this present earth).

[49]   Watts, *Isaiah 34–66*, 912.

[50]   Watts, *Isaiah 34–66*, 919. See also Joseph Blenkinsopp, *Isaiah 56–66* (AB 19B; New York: Doubleday, 2003), 275

[51]   Blenkinsopp, *Isaiah 55–66*, 287, points out the difficulty in establishing a dependence of this passage on Gen 1–3. Later interpreters have made the connection by way of similarity, but there are differences that make the argument for dependence questionable.

[52]   Watts, *Isaiah 34–66*, 924.

[53]   Nickelsburg, *1 Enoch 1*, 5.

in 1 En. 10:18–11:2, where the thematic and linguistic similarities to Isa 65–66 are clear. God declares that all perversity will be removed from the earth and that the deeds of the righteous will stand forever (10:16). Once again there is an emphasis on the lengthening of days for the righteous (10:17), and an idyllic existence is described where truth and peace will characterize the earth for all the days of eternity and through all of the generations of humanity (11:2). These themes are echoed in 1 En. 25:6, which says of the righteous:

> Then they will rejoice greatly and be glad,
>> and they will enter into the sanctuary.
> Its fragrances will be in their bones,
>> and they will live a long life on the earth,
>> such as your fathers lived also in their days,
>> and torments and plagues and suffering will not touch them.[54]

One of the most important points of connection between 1 En. 10 and Isa 66 concerns the identity of the righteous that stand to inherit. The book of Isaiah often includes non-Israelites with Israelites as those that gather to worship at the mountain of God (Isa 11:11-12; 56:1-8); Isa 66:18-21 famously expands on this theme, as God sends the survivors of his judgment to gather the nations and give them standing in his eschatological kingdom.[55] The people of the nations facilitate the return of diaspora Jews, some of whom are made priests and Levites.[56] Isaiah 66:22-23 then states that in the new heavens and the new earth "all flesh" shall worship before God. As Joseph Blenkinsopp notes, "One aspect of this eschatological scenario is that all humanity will worship the one true God, the God of

---

[54]   See Simon Gathercole, *Where Is Boasting? Early Jewish Soteriology and Paul's Response in Romans 1–5* (Grand Rapids: Eerdmans, 2002), 44, who states, "The life spoken of here is something entirely future and has not yet been attained: the food that is for the life of the elect cannot be touched until after the Great Judgment." It is important to note that the eschatological situation in 1 En. 25 is not identical to that of 1 En. 5:5-9. Chapters 24–26 portray Enoch before God's throne, which God will sit upon when he descends upon the earth in blessing. This passage relies on temple imagery rather than that of the restored earth depicted in 1 En. 5:5-9. The important point of connection lies in the way both passages describe the status of the righteous as an eschatological community. For more on the temple imagery in 1 Enoch, see David W. Suter, "Temples and the Temple in the Early Enoch Tradition: Memory, Vision, and Expectations," in Boccaccini and Collins, *Early Enoch Literature*, 195–218, who argues that the temple imagery in 1 Enoch is used to critique the Second Temple and that the book envisions a time when God's throne can be approached in a dwelling upon the earth.

[55]   Blenkinsopp, *Isaiah 55–66*, 313.

[56]   Watts, *Isaiah 34–66*, 940.

Israel, in Jerusalem."⁵⁷ This universalistic approach is taken up in 1 En. 10:21-22, when all the sons of men will become righteous, and all the peoples will worship and bless God in the renewed earth. Verse 22 then confirms that all the earth, not Israel alone, will be cleansed.

The righteous stand to receive an idyllic existence on a renewed earth, but 1 En. 5:5-9 presents inheritance as the specific access point through which that gift is received.⁵⁸ The inheritance leads to salvation and life, an idea present elsewhere in Second Temple literature. In 1 En. 40:9, part of the Book of Parables, those who repent "inherit everlasting life."⁵⁹ In the Psalms of Solomon we once again find a contrast between the righteous and the wicked, where the wicked will "perish" (ἀπόλοιντο), but the servants of the Lord stand to "inherit" (κληρονομήσαισαν) the Lord's promises (12:6).⁶⁰ Israel is presented as God's own inheritance (κληρονομία τοῦ θεοῦ ἐστιν Ισραηλ), while the wicked are denied by God (14:5). The sense is eschatological; the inheritance (κληρονομία) of the wicked is death and destruction, but on the day of mercy, the righteous "will inherit life" (κληρονομήσουσιν ζωὴν, 14:10). In 1 En. 5:8, the righteous inherit the earth and receive wisdom so that they may have life (ζήσονται), and throughout 5:5-9 the noun, ζωῆς, is repeated five times, providing a clear emphasis that the eschatological earth is inherited by the righteous, and this inheritance leads to life.

3.1.4. 1 Enoch 99:14

The second Enochic reference that requires attention is found in the Epistle of Enoch.⁶¹ Composed in the second century B.C.E., the epistle

---

⁵⁷   Blenkinsopp, *Isaiah 55–66*, 316.

⁵⁸   The connection between 1 En. 5:5-9 and the concept of the restoration of creation is one that has not received enough attention in scholarship. For example, David E. Aune, with Eric Stewart, "From the Idealized Past to the Imaginary Future: Eschatological Restoration in Jewish Apocalyptic Literature," in *Restoration: Old Testament, Jewish, and Apocalyptic Perspectives* (ed. James M. Scott; Leiden: Brill, 2001), 173–75, details the role of 1 Enoch in apocalyptic contribution to the concept of restoration and connects 1 Enoch to Isa 65–66, as I have done here, and yet he makes no mention of 1 En. 5:5-9.

⁵⁹   This reference is not found in the Greek witness. See Nickelsburg, *1 Enoch*, 55.

⁶⁰   For a critical edition, see Robert B. Wright, *The Psalms of Solomon: A Critical Edition of the Greek Text* (New York: T&T Clark International, 2007).

⁶¹   Found in 1 En. 92–105, though often discussed in accord with the narrative bridge of 1 En. 91. The Epistle itself is regarded as a redacted unit, with sections deriving from different authors. See the discussion in Loren T. Stuckenbruck, *1 Enoch 91–108* (Berlin: de Gruyter, 2007), 1–16. Stuckenbruck argues that the compilers of this section

features an appeal to the righteous to hold firm as they wait for the judgment and promises found in earlier parts of the Enochic corpus.[62] Enoch is a leader of "the whole earth" (92:1), universalizing the revelation as it "becomes a source for the righteousness of the whole human race."[63] The righteous are exhorted to await their eschatological vindication and the destruction of the sinners (99:1, 9, 16).

In 99:10 the only makarism in the epistle is found. It is sandwiched between a series of woes and forms an inclusio with 98:9. The two passages read:

> 1 En. 98:9: Woe unto you, fools, for you shall perish through your folly! You do not listen to the wise, and you shall not receive good things.

> 1 En. 99:10: In those days, blessed are they all who accept the words of wisdom and understand them, to follow the path of the Most-High; they shall walk in the path of his righteousness and not become wicked with the wicked; and they shall be saved.[64]

Jonathan A. Linebaugh argues that the woes function as a "judicial recalibration," a present representation of "the eschatological restoration of balance and justice." There is a moral logic that subverts the present with a future reality.[65] These verses represent the sharp contrast between those who do not listen to the wise, and so will perish (ἀπολεῖσθε, 98:9), and those who accept the words of wisdom, and so shall be saved. Interesting to note, in 99:10, righteousness is determined not by election but by adhering to instruction.[66] This opens the door for the previously mentioned universalism, explored in 1 En. 100:6, which states that the wise among all sons of the earth will see the truth, as long as they contemplate the words of this epistle.[67] The wisdom (truth) in question consists of the whole of Enoch's revelation.

1 Enoch 99:11 begins a new section of woes, focused on sinners' mistreatment of their neighbors. To mistreat a neighbor results in being slain in Sheol. The woe of verse 14 states:

---

knew and drew upon preexisting Enochic traditions, including the Book of the Watchers, and "attempted to find a literary or narrative rationale for the additions they were making." There is largely a thematic consistency between the Book of the Watchers and the Epistle of Enoch.

[62]   Nickelsburg, *1 Enoch 1*, 8.

[63]   Nickelsburg, *1 Enoch 1*, 53.

[64]   Translations for these verses taken from Charlesworth, *Pseudepigrapha*.

[65]   Jonathan A. Linebaugh, "Debating Diagonal Δικαιοσύνη: The Epistle of Enoch and Paul in Theological Conversation," *Early Christianity* 1 (2010): 111–12.

[66]   See Stuckenbruck, *1 Enoch*, 411. See also Gathercole, *Boasting*, 49, who states of this verse, "Their way of life is decisive for their salvation."

[67]   See Nickelsburg, *1 Enoch 1*, 497.

> Woe to those who reject the foundation and everlasting inheritance
> (τὴν κληρονομίαν) of their fathers; and a spirit of error pursues you;
> you will have no rest.

The exact nature of the "foundation" is unclear. It matches the building imagery of the previous two verses (99:12-13), but is this time tied to the inheritance. Loren Stuckenbruck connects this verse to our previously discussed passage in 1 En. 5:5-9, arguing that the foundation here refers to the sapiential character of 1 Enoch, the wisdom that the sinners should, but do not, share. The inheritance in 99:14 then refers directly to this wisdom, as is illustrated by the fact that, instead of wisdom, the sinners pursue a "spirit of error." However, Stuckenbruck also recognizes that in 5:5-9 the inheritance is land, a renewed, eschatological earth. He notes the parallels to the biblical tradition and suggests that the inheritance of land may also be implied in 99:14. In this case, in both passages, the inheritance is bound up with both Enochic wisdom and the eschatological possession of land.[68] This possible allusion to land in 99:14 is bolstered by a potential contrast with Sheol in 99:11. Furthermore, 99:14 contains a reference to rest. The lack of rest as a judgment mirrors the lack of peace in the previous verse (99:13), which together recalls the judgment of 1 En. 5:5. The lack of rest in 1 En. 5:5 is in direct contrast to the lack of ability to inherit the eschatological earth. While admittedly the reference to "the fathers" (τῶν πατέρων) draws on Israel's past, Stuckenbruck affirms that the author's ideology of community remains open (is nonsectarian) to all who pursue wisdom and is closed only to those who pursue error.[69]

3.1.5. Conclusions

In the view of 1 Enoch, contemporary Israel is made up of two primary groups: the sinners and the righteous. The sinners are cursed, meaning

---

[68]   Stuckenbruck, *1 Enoch*, 422.

[69]   Stuckenbruck, *1 Enoch*, 423. Stuckenbruck's view is contrasted with Nickelsburg, *1 Enoch 1*, 498, who argues that the "foundation and everlasting inheritance of the fathers" is a reference to Torah. The concept of Torah as an inheritance can be found in CD I 15–17, and the association of the Torah to "the fathers" can be found in T. Mos. 9:6 and 1 Macc 2:19-20. Nickelsburg admits that this would be exceptional, as the Enochic corpus attributes truth to Enoch's heavenly revelations rather than tradition from Israel's forebears, which leads him to refer to this reference as a "remarkable slip." However, T. Mos. refers to land in relation to "their fathers" in 1:8 and 2:1. It is possible that the author sees Enoch's everlasting wisdom as having roots in previous generations, and following Stuckenbruck, the inheritance as a reference to Enoch's wisdom and the eschatological earth fits the context of Enoch generally. This would fit with the possibility that the Enochic tradition may feature a merging (conflation) of Enoch's heavenly wisdom and Torah.

that their days will be cut short, and they will be denied access to God's presence and eschatological peace. The righteous are both the chosen within Israel and those outside of Israel from among the nations who come to worship God in Jerusalem. As Nickelsburg argues, this means that election in 1 Enoch is both exclusive and universal. It is exclusive because the definition of who constitutes "true Israel" is in the process of changing. It is not all Israel who is chosen but only those who "accept Enoch's version of law and wisdom" and live according to it. Election is universal because "Enoch's wisdom is made available to all of humanity."[70]

For the righteous, there is salvation from enemies and peace with God. The locus of salvation and life is the eschatological renewed earth; the wicked have been cut off from this earth and it has been cleansed from oppression. On this earth, the righteous receive wisdom and a full and abundant life. The means of obtaining this earth is through inheritance, a concept at home with election. In the common way that children inherit an estate from their father, the inheritance of the eschatological earth by the chosen as a gift from God signals something about the nature of their relationship; the chosen receive from God that of which no one else has claim. The inheritance of the earth in the Book of the Watchers is directly contrasted with the curse of the wicked in 5:6-7, and paralleled with life in verse 8, showing that life and an abundant future are a direct consequence of the inheritance granted to those whom God deems righteous. The inheritance in the Epistle of Enoch is primarily the reception of Enoch's heavenly wisdom but secondarily implies peace in the renewed earth.

3.2. Sirach[71]

The book of Sirach comfortably finds its place in the wisdom traditions of Israel.[72] Inheritance terms appear in the book thirty-three times, some

---

[70] Nickelsburg, *1 Enoch 1*, 54.

[71] Although Hebrew (called "Ben Sira") is the original language of the book of Sirach, portions of the Hebrew text are no longer extant. Translations follow the Greek and Syriac versions, and it is the Greek that was likely influential in the late Second Temple period and into the early Christian era. The Greek is the version that was handed down through most of the book's history, it is the version of the text featured in the LXX, and a number of scholars continue to use the Greek as the starting point in order to analyze and obtain a view of the complete book. For these reasons, it is with the Greek text that this study interacts. See Patrick W. Skehan and Alexander A. Di Lella, *The Wisdom of Ben Sira* (AB 39; New York: Doubleday, 1987), 51–62.

[72] Wisdom literature as "genre" is a disputed category; see Tremper Longman III, *The Fear of the Lord Is Wisdom: A Theological Introduction to Wisdom in Israel* (Grand Rapids: Baker Academic, 2017), 276–82.

of which are in direct relationship to wisdom. Many of the instances of inheritance language are anomalous and pragmatic and are not relevant to our discussion. Therefore, this section focuses on those instances that have bearing on inheritance as a specific theme in Sirach.[73] Before discussing inheritance in the book, two important things must be said about the way in which wisdom functions in Sirach.

First, the wisdom tradition in Israel is often regarded by scholars as distinct from other themes in Jewish literature. It is practical rather than theological and universal rather than particular to Israelite history and cultic practices.[74] Wisdom is often rooted in creation rather than Israel's election or covenant.[75] By contrast, as we shall see, Sirach "pays considerable attention to Israel and its Scriptures."[76] Although Sirach is modeled on the canonical book of Proverbs, it departs from Proverbs, and many other wisdom-themed texts, in the way that it focuses on salvation history and Israel's Fathers as a source of instruction.[77] Sirach focuses on "the right deeds, piety, and obedience of individual Israelites of renown."[78]

Second, Sirach makes a unique contribution to the relationship between wisdom and Torah. As with other Second Temple wisdom passages, such as those in the Enochic literature discussed above, wisdom is in some measure rooted in the sage at the head of the text. Unlike 1 Enoch, the sage in Sirach is a secondary source of wisdom as the place of primacy is granted to the sage's interpretation of the previous writings

[73]   Examples of these anomalous uses include 10:11, where dead bodies "inherit" maggots and worms, or the practical advice in 33:24 that in death, parents should distribute their "inheritance" to their children.

[74]   Longman, *Fear*, 163–75, has argued persuasively for a caution against this general consensus. In his view, wisdom in Israel is rooted in the expression "the fear of the Lord." He acknowledges that the relationship between wisdom and law and covenant is not a major theme in the wisdom tradition but that "the fear of the Lord" provides an implicit connection between wisdom and law/covenant, which grants a degree of particularity to wisdom's roots in the proper relationship between Israel and Yahweh.

[75]   See Longman, *Fear*, xiv.

[76]   John J. Collins, *Jewish Wisdom in the Hellenistic Age* (Louisville: Westminster John Knox, 1997), 44–45. Collins compares Sirach to Qoheleth, which he dates closely to Sirach, and points out that it does not make mention of the Law or the Prophets. By contrast, Sirach roots wisdom in the covenant and the law of Moses. See also Richard J. Coggins, *Sirach* (Sheffield: Sheffield Academic, 1998), 76, who points out that, in 24:23, personified wisdom "comes to be identified with the covenant of the Most-High God," an identification that "differs from anything we know of in the earlier wisdom tradition."

[77]   The close similarities between Sirach and the canonical book of Proverbs are well established. For more on the relationship between Sirach and Proverbs, see Longman, *Fear*, 221.

[78]   George W. E. Nickelsburg, *Jewish Literature between the Bible and the Mishnah* (London: SCM Press, 1981), 61.

of Israel, especially Torah. In Sirach, creation is still the chronological starting point, instead of historical events particular to Israel. However, as Nickelsburg argues, personified wisdom is brought to life and embodied in Torah, and it is in Torah's instruction where "she offers the dynamic for obedience and hence the possibility for life."[79] This is not to say that, in Sirach, wisdom and Torah are conflated. In the Torah itself wisdom is a minor theme, but law is always primary. Conversely, Collins makes a persuasive case that, in Sirach, the wisdom tradition is primary, and the sage defines the Mosaic covenant by the terms of the wisdom tradition. This is evidenced by the fact that Sirach does not cite biblical laws directly, draws on other sources of wisdom besides the Torah, and roots all wisdom, including the law, in the order of creation.[80] With this nuance of emphasis in view, Collins argues that it is best to see Sirach as "a wisdom teacher, not an exegete or expositor of the Torah."[81] With an understanding that wisdom is the overriding category of instruction in Sirach, and Torah is a secondary category subsumed by wisdom, it is still the case that Sirach places an emphasis on Torah as an essential aspect of wisdom that is neglected in many other wisdom-themed texts.[82] Understanding the unique role of Israelite history, as well as the Torah, is essential to interpreting texts in Sirach where inheritance terminology becomes important.

The relationship between wisdom and inheritance becomes apparent in the first instance of inheritance language in Sirach. Chapter 4 speaks of wisdom personified as a woman, a feature borrowed directly from

[79]   Nickelsburg, *Jewish Literature*, 61. Nickelsburg is careful to point out that Sirach is the earliest text to discuss the relationship between Torah and wisdom "in detail and in theory." As Collins, *Wisdom*, 15–16, points out, a relationship between wisdom and Torah appears briefly in texts such as Deut 4, Ezra 7, and the canonical Psalms 1, 19, and 119.

[80]   Collins, *Wisdom*, 55. See also Gerhard von Rad, *Wisdom in Israel* (London: SCM Press, 1972), 244. See also Samuel L. Adams, *Wisdom in Transition: Act and Consequence in Second Temple Instructions* (SJSJ; Leiden: Brill, 2008), 199, who argues that Sirach's allegiance to Torah "is a constituent element in a larger sapiential framework." This is contrasted with Skehan and Di Lella, *Wisdom*, 336, who argue for a conflation of wisdom with Torah in Sirach, based on their interpretation of 24:23.

[81]   Collins, *Wisdom*, 57.

[82]   It is important to note that not all scholars have agreed that Torah is important to Sirach. Von Rad, *Wisdom*, 247, for example, argues that Sirach makes use of Torah to interpret the concept of "the fear of God" but that Torah as a whole is not of interest to Sirach. Conversely, Nickelsburg, *Jewish Literature*, 59, argues that, for Sirach, the identification of wisdom and Torah is "the heart and dynamic of his thought" and that his primary concern is one's conduct in relation to the specifics of Torah. See also Adams, *Wisdom*, 199, who points out that Sirach's emphasis on Torah is "a major departure from Proverbs" and that its Torah engagement is likely due to engaging a later audience with an established legal corpus.

Proverbs (and utilized in other wisdom texts), where she is depicted as having been present with God at the creation of the world and utilized by God in his creative act (Prov 8:22-31).[83] Sirach 4:13 declares that whoever holds fast to woman wisdom "inherits glory" (κληρονομήσει δόξαν). What it means to inherit glory is difficult to determine from the context. It could refer to the benefits woman wisdom provides as described in the chapter, such as joy (4:12) and security (4:15). The phrase "inherits glory" is rare but appears in Prov 3:35, a passage featuring woman wisdom. There, a wise person "inherits glory" (δόξαν σοφοὶ κληρονομήσουσιν, LXX), but a fool receives disgrace. Again, Prov 3 details various blessings for the wise and curses for the foolish, so "glory" could simply refer to the reception of blessings and God's favor.

A further clue may be provided by T. Job 43, where Elihu is said to be evil. Because of his evil, Eliphas declares that Elihu will no longer be counted among the living. He will be cast into darkness, and those that receive him at the doorway into darkness will inherit his glory from him (κληρονομήσουσιν αὐτοῦ τὴν δόξαν, 43:6). The implication of Eliphas' hymn is clear: Elihu's loss of his glory is the loss of his life. This implication is drawn out in Sir 4:19, where to forsake wisdom is to be handed over to ruin. Similar is Sir 15:6, where the one who obeys the law receives wisdom and through wisdom inherits an everlasting name (ὄνομα αἰῶνος κατακληρονομήσει), as well as Sir 37:26, where the wise will "inherit value" (κληρονομήσει πίστιν) and receive an everlasting name. The phrase "inherits glory" is ambiguous enough that it possibly includes all that comes with God's favor, both blessings in life and a good name in death.[84] However, an argument is made in chapter 4 of the present study regarding the use of the phrase "inheritance of glory" in 4QInstruction, that inheriting glory is specifically about the elevation of a person's status from lesser glory to greater glory within their lifetime.[85] In the case of 4QInstruction the argument is made that the addressee has the opportunity to advance beyond his role as a student of wisdom to the role of a sage when he takes on the status of an authority figure in the community and upon the entire earth. Sirach 4

[83]   Longman, *Fear*, 19. Longman discusses "woman wisdom" throughout his book, as she appears in various wisdom-themed texts under his consideration.

[84]   Shannon Burkes, "Wisdom and Law: Choosing Life in Ben Sira and Baruch," *JSJ* 30, no. 3 (1999): 253–76, discusses the role of life and death in Sirach and other wisdom-themed texts, concluding that the terms often function as metaphors for human flourishing. Life refers to longevity as a consequence of good living, illustrated by Torah observance and obedience to wisdom. By shunning wisdom, a wicked person may hasten physical death but lives in ruin by failing to obtain the favor of the Lord. To "inherit glory" likely runs along these lines: to obtain God's favor and live in his blessings.

[85]   See 4.1.1.

may possibly have the same basic idea in mind: the one who holds fast to wisdom "inherits glory" (4:13), while two verses later it is said that the one who obeys wisdom "will judge the nations" (4:15). In keeping with the use of the phrase "inherit glory" in other contexts, it appears best to understand the inheritance of Sir 4:13 similarly: the one who "inherits glory" has their status elevated to a position of authority. Sirach 4:16 then promises that for those who are faithful, they will also inherit wisdom herself, and she will then be passed down as an inheritance to future generations.

Sirach 24 brings together all the various themes discussed thus far: woman wisdom, the law, Israelite history and identity, and inheritance. As is typical of the wisdom theme, woman wisdom is at first associated with creation; as in Prov 8 she is depicted as having been created by God and then present over all the earth. Her influence was universal, holding sway over "every people and nation" (24:6). However, particularism enters as woman wisdom seeks out a particular nation in which to abide (24:7), and the creator chooses for her Israel, which is given to her as her own inheritance (ἐν Ἰσραηλ κατακληρονομήθητι, 24:8). It is clear that this inheritance is referring to geographic space; the inheritance is a dwelling (24:8) and includes Jerusalem (24:11).[86] This usage of inheritance language diverges greatly from biblical usage, as Israel is given to someone other than God or the Israelites as an inheritance, but it is important to note that woman wisdom should not be regarded as a figure separate from God. Wisdom is personified, but it is the wisdom that belongs to God and originates from him.[87] It is through wisdom that God founded the earth (Prov 3:19). Woman wisdom inheriting Israel is best understood as an aspect of God's unique relationship to Israel and its people. According to Sir 24, wisdom has a part with every nation and every people, but God's wisdom abides with Israel in a way that is unique compared to any other nation.[88] Sirach 24:12 confirms this, as wisdom takes root with Israel's people, who are referred to as God's own inheritance (κληρονομίας αὐτοῦ). As with Sir 4:16, woman

---

[86]   See Skehan and Di Lella, *Wisdom*, 333, who note the parallelism between "Jacob" and "Israel," and "make your dwelling" and "make your inheritance." The physical space of dwelling explains the physical nature of the inheritance.

[87]   See Collins, *Wisdom*, 50, who points to the similarities of Sirach and Proverbs, and particularly passages such as Sir 24:3 and Prov 2:6, to demonstrate that woman wisdom is identified with "the word of God."

[88]   See Collins, *Wisdom*, 51, who equates woman wisdom in Sirach with "God's presence and agency." Sirach 24:1-8 bears remarkable similarity to Deut 32:8-9, where Yahweh selects Israel from among all nations as his own inheritance. Taking these passages together, wisdom functions in Sirach as the mechanism through which he chooses Israel for himself.

wisdom herself is offered to the people of Israel as their own inheritance (24:20); those who obey her will not be put to shame (24:22).

If woman wisdom has a part in every nation, in what way is she particular to Israel? According to Sirach, it is through the Torah. Sirach 24:23 states, "All this is the book of the covenant of the Most-High God, the law that Moses commanded us as an inheritance (κληρονομίαν) for the congregations of Jacob." The law itself is regarded as an inheritance for Israel, as instruction that will provide understanding (24:26) and be passed down through all future generations (24:33). As discussed above, there are no specific laws mentioned, and law and wisdom are not to be conflated, but obedience to the law is the way to obtain wisdom and all her blessings. Wisdom clearly preceded the law (24:3) and expressed herself in ways other than the law among various nations (24:6). However, in Israel it is primarily through the law that God's wisdom was made manifest to his own inheritance—his own distinct people—and it is through a proper relationship with God that a person can obey the law and become wise. The law then is not the only form of wisdom, even in Israel, but is a form of wisdom that connects God to a particular people in a particular way—through covenant. The law is the way that God's wisdom settles itself in the land.

The particularism of Sirach continues in chapter 36, where the Israelites call out to God to destroy his enemies among the nations for the sake of his people Israel (36:3). They ask God to put the nations in fear, in much the same way as the conquest under Joshua. Just as with the exodus and conquest, they ask God to perform signs and wonders (36:6), so that the nations will know that the Lord is the only God (36:5). To this point, the land of Israel has been depicted as the inheritance of both God and woman wisdom, but in 36:10,[89] the Israelites call for God to return the land to them as their own inheritance.[90]

Particularism takes its most specific form in the hymn of the ancestors of Israel found in Sir 44–50. As Collins notes, nothing like it is found in other wisdom-themed texts, with the history of Israel drawn out in detail to provide examples of instruction.[91] However, this particularism introduces key elements of universalism regarding inheritance. Sirach 44:19-21 extols the virtues of Abraham, praising him for keeping the

[89]   Sirach 36:16 in the NRSV.

[90]   Collins, *Wisdom*, 109–11, makes a compelling case that this chapter is likely a later addition to Sirach. Nowhere else in the book is antagonism expressed toward foreign nations, and the specifics of the chapter do not fit the time line of Sirach in terms of Jewish/gentile relations. If the chapter is not original to Sirach, Collins argues that its context would fit best during the Maccabean crisis.

[91]   Collins, *Wisdom*, 44.

law and proving faithful to the covenant. Because of Abraham's faith-fulness, he was granted the role of father to "a multitude of nations," so that through him, "the nations would be blessed through his offspring." The blessing to the nations is that God would "give them an inheri-tance (κατακληρονομῆσαι) from sea to sea, and from the Euphrates to the ends of the earth." As noted in our previous discussion on the HB, the Abrahamic promise in Genesis sees God promise Abraham three key things: that Abraham would have numerous descendants, that those descendants would receive a land of their own, and that through Abraham's descendants the nations of the earth would be blessed. Sirach 44:21 focuses almost exclusively on the third promise, and the blessing to the nations is explicit—they receive the earth as an inheritance. Sir-ach provides no clear description of precisely what it means to inherit the earth, and what this might mean for the relationship of God to the nations, but as with many of the other texts analyzed throughout our discussion, the inheritance here is a gift from God.

Inheritance terminology appears in the hymn eight more times, with the context of each taken directly from the Hexateuch. In the hymn for Aaron (Sir 45:20-22), inheritance appears five times to describe the inheritance of the priesthood. The inheritance of Aaron is the first fruits of the abundance of Israel's offerings (cf. Deut 18:1). The priests have no inheritance of land (cf. Josh 18), but their inheritance is the Lord himself (cf. Num 18:20). In the hymn of Joshua and Caleb (Sir 46:1-9), Joshua and Caleb are praised for their role in leading Israel against her enemies to obtain its inheritance of the land (cf. Josh 14:13-15; 19:49-51).

3.3. Tobit

Tobit is principally concerned with the plight of Israel and its ultimate fate in the postexilic dispersion. The book deals first with individuals, but the story of the characters parallels that of the nation, and the final two chapters of the book assure the reader that the problem of exile and dispersion is foremost on the writer's mind, as is the eschatological hope for the regathering of God's people into a newly constituted Jeru-salem.[92] The book is postexilic, but Tobit's understanding of the exile is strongly influenced by the Pentateuch and Deuteronomic theology.[93]

---

[92]   See Nickelsburg, *Jewish Literature*, 33.

[93]   See the detailed article by A. A. Di Lella, "The Deuteronomic Background of the Farewell Discourse in Tob 14:3-11," *CBQ* 41, no. 3 (1979): 380–89, where he argues primarily for the strong ties between Deuteronomy and the final chapter of Tobit but also comments that "A careful reading of Tobit will show that Deuteronomy provided background material for much of the rest of the book."

The book opens with an appeal to tribal social identity; Tobit's family is of the tribe of Naphtali (1:1), and the writer makes consistent use of narratives from the Pentateuch.[94] The God of Tobit is the creator of the world (3:11), the God of Israel (3:3-5), and the God of the law of Moses (6:13). Importantly for our purposes, Tobit presents God as a father and Israel as his children (13:3-4). God's providence is a major theme, as is the trust of the characters in God's providence throughout the story.[95] Inheritance terms appear in Tobit six times, and in nuanced ways each of these are rooted in the Pentateuch as well as influenced by the social changes among the Israelites during the exile.

There are two important issues regarding inheritance in Tobit that require discussion. The first concerns the references to Sarah as an inheritance for Tobias (3:17; 6:12). Inheritance in the context of a marriage union is a unique usage. On the surface, "inherit" appears to function as a synonym for "receive," but two important considerations root this marriage into the theology of inheritance. First, Tobias' reception of Sarah as his wife is listed in conjunction with his inheritance of her ancestral estate (6:12-13). The parallel usage of terms implies that Tobias' reception of Sarah and her father's estate be viewed in a synonymous way—as inheritances. Second, Raguel states that Sarah is being given to Tobias specifically as a gift from God himself (7:11).[96] For Jews in the diaspora, their inability to inherit landed property in Israel does not stop the practice of God granting to them inheritances, it simply changes the referent of the types of things to be inherited. As argued throughout this study, inheritance language is tied to God's relationship with his people, and his favor toward them. Sarah's prayer for God's intervention in chapter 3 leads to his response in the form of a unique mode of inheritance, in this case, a marriage union that perpetuates Sarah's family line. This mode of inheritance highlights the theme of God's providence in the story; their marriage was literally a match made in heaven.

The second issue involving inheritance that merits attention concerns the phrase "will inherit the land/earth" (κληρονομήσει γῆν) in 4:12. κληρονομήσει is a collective singular referring to the offspring of the patriarchs as those that *will inherit*. The verb is in the future tense. While it is possible that Tobit is referring to the more immediate offspring of the patriarchs, those that inherited the promised land after the conquest, and that the future tense verb implies a future inheritance *for*

---

[94] For examples, see Benedikt Otzen, *Tobit and Judith* (Sheffield: Sheffield Academic, 2002), 29.

[95] Otzen, *Tobit*, 27.

[96] See Joseph A. Fitzmyer, *Tobit* (Berlin: de Gruyter, 2003), 233, who points out that the verse is theologically passive; God gifts Sarah to Tobias.

them (meaning the patriarchal generations), it is important to note that Tobit ends with an eschatological expectation for the return of the Jews to a reconstituted Israel. From the perspective of the book of Tobit, the diaspora Jews are not in possession of the land, therefore the promise of the inheritance of the land is not yet realized. In Tobit's view, the Israelites were exiled due to their own rebellion against the commands of God (3:3-5). Tobit's final prayer calls for God's mercy, recognizing his fatherhood over his people Israel (13:1-5). Tobit calls for God's people to acknowledge him (13:8-10) and then turns his attention to the gentiles, who will come from all over the earth, bearing gifts for God and praising him in Jerusalem (13:11). Tobit imagines the reconstituted Israel as a city built with gold and precious jewels where God will be worshipped forever (13:16-17). In Tobit's final council to Tobias, he expresses his confidence in this eschatological reality where the Israelites are brought back into the land of Israel, and where the gentiles will be converted, abandoning their former ways (14:5-7). Tobit's eschatological vision shares many of these features with other important eschatological passages (e.g., Jer 3:17; Isa 2:2-4; Ps Sol 17:28-35), and some scholars have noted that the phrase κληρονομήσει γῆν in Tob 4:12 is a direct echo of Isa 60:21,[97] an eschatological promise that Yahweh's people will "inherit the land forever" (αἰῶνος κληρονομήσουσιν τὴν γῆν). Given the eschatological vision that concludes the book of Tobit, it is possible that the future tense reference to inherit the land in 4:12 is a foreshadowing of this eschatological vision. "Will inherit the land" in 4:12 is tied to Abraham's offspring, and in 14:7, Tobit refers to the reconstituted Israel as "the land of Abraham." God's people, the offspring of the patriarchs, are still in line to inherit a reconstituted Israel where Jews and gentiles come together in unified worship of Israel's God.[98]

This nationalistic inheritance is tied to the inheritance of Tobias and Sarah's marriage as the two stories parallel one another. In both inheritances, the providence of God plays a central role; it is God who determined the marriage of Tobias and Sarah (7:10-14), and God who will

[97]   See Fitzmyer, *Tobit*, 174; Carey A. Moore, *Tobit* (AB 40A; New York: Doubleday, 1996), 169.

[98]   Tying "will inherit the land" in 4:12 to chs. 13–14 is called into question if it can be demonstrated that chapters 13–14 are not original to the composition. See, for example, Frank Zimmerman, *The Book of Tobit: An English Translation with Introduction and Commentary* (New York: Harper and Bros, 1958), 21, who argues that chs. 13 and 14 are independent of one another and both later additions to the text. Recent evaluations have effectively engaged with concerns regarding the integrity of the text and demonstrated its unity. See, for example, Fitzmyer, *Tobit*, 45, who argues that "there is no serious reason to think that the Book of Tobit, as we have it today, is not integral or does not represent the original form of the account."

gather his chosen people from the nations in which they are scattered (13:5). The success or failure of both the nation and the marriage are conditional; they depend on obedience to the law of Moses. The vision for a restored Israel is a nationalist one, but the inclusion of the promises made to Abraham's offspring focus on the role of Abraham's offspring as a light to the nations (13:11), an aspect of the Abrahamic promises that finds its development in the prophetic eschatological tradition of which the book of Tobit is a part.

3.4. Judith

Although Judith takes place largely in a postexilic setting and was composed in the Hasmonean period, like Tobit, many of the events of the book are interpreted in Deuteronomistic terms.[99] This includes Judith's portrayal of God's attributes, the covenant, Jerusalem, and the temple and its functions. This has led Moore to note that nothing "about God's titles or attributes in the book of Judith or about the cultus or the religious practices of individuals is at all unusual or noteworthy."[100] This holds true for inheritance terms, which feature six times and are drawn from usage common to Deuteronomy and Joshua.

In Jud 4:12, as the Israelites were preparing for the approach of Holofernes and his armies, they cried out to God, asking that he not allow their children and wives to be taken, nor for the "the towns of their inheritance" (τὰς πόλεις τῆς κληρονομίας αὐτῶν) to be destroyed. Moore argues persuasively that this phraseology introduces an important theological idea found in inheritance passages throughout Judith; there is an emphasis upon the land of Canaan given by God to Israel as an inheritance, rather than acquired by the Israelites through force or merit. Israel's actions in the conquest are recognized (5:15), but when they lost the inheritance due to defeat in battle, the blame lay not within the context of war but due to departing from the ways of God (5:18). If the land is principally a gift of God, rather than a spoil of war, then God alone can ensure that the gift stays with the Israelites rather than being taken as a spoil by Holofernes and his

---

[99]   The setting is made difficult by Judith's well-known dubious historical value. The book interchanges details from preexilic, exilic, and postexilic contexts, leading Otzen, *Tobit*, 91, to refer to the book as a "meta-history," which purposely mixes details of history and topography from various periods to relativize the story as an eschatological epic on a wide scale. For a treatment of the various historical problems, see Carey A. Moore, *Judith* (AB 40; New York: Doubleday, 1985), 38–56; for dating the book to the Hasmonean period, see 67–70.

[100]   For details, see Moore, *Judith*, 60–61.

armies. The Israelites recognize this in their prayer.[101] Judith features a dual usage for inheritance terms, both of which are rooted in the Hexateuch. The references all refer either to the land as an inherited gift from God to his people (4:12; 5:15; 8:22; 16:21), or to Israel, primarily the people but by extension the land, as the inheritance of God himself (9:12; 13:5). In all cases, the references place the inheritances under the protection and control of God.

3.5. 1 and 2 Maccabees

If Judith's use of inheritance terms was directly in line with biblical usage, 1 and 2 Maccabees is largely the opposite. With a few exceptions, inheritance terms in these compositions are anomalous and, in some instances, generically refer to the passing of something from one person to another. In 1 Maccabees, inheritance terms appear seven times. One instance is a generic reference to the throne of Israel being "passed down to" (inherited by) David (2:57), though this reference shares a context of Caleb's inheritance of allotted land due to his faithfulness during the conquest (cf. Josh 14:6-15). The other five references are in contexts not common to texts post 300 B.C.E. They function as synonyms for the act of seizure or refer to the spoils of conflict. 1 Maccabees 1:32 refers to the seizure of livestock, and 6:24 refers to the seizure of property. Attaching the concept of seizure by force to the use of κληρονομία may be a Hebraism held over from the biblical use of ירשׁ, which, as I argue in chapter 2, was used in the Hexateuch to connote an inheritance taken by force. The notable exception to this is 1 Macc 15:33-34, which uses inheritance and the concept of seizure separately, as the inheritance is the thing being seized. The inheritance here is clearly a reference to the land, in this case primarily Jerusalem, and is tied to Israelite ancestry. The missing feature regarding inheritance in 1 Maccabees is any sense that the items seized were ever given, promised, or passed down. Nowhere is the concept of inheritance tied to God, not his oversight, protection, gifting of the inheritance, or his general involvement in any way. Inheritance in 1 Maccabees is dominated by concepts of conflict, and all of this is spoken of in purely humanistic terms.[102]

---

[101]   See Moore, *Judith*, 152.

[102]   Gathercole, *Boasting*, 52, notes the strong theology of rewards in the book, where glory is not given but earned by Torah observance and brave deeds in battle. 1 Macc 15:33-34 might be explained by parallels in Thucydides, 2.35–36 (Smith, LCL) and Demosthenes, 12.21–23 (Vince LCL), where inheritances are said to be rightfully obtainable either by ancestral inheritance or from conquest in war. This background explains why Simon and Antiochus VII both claimed rights over the territory.

2 Maccabees features inheritance terms just twice, both in chapter 2. The chapter begins by reciting a legend that the prophet Jeremiah took the tent and the ark of God to the mountain where Moses had seen "the inheritance of God" (τὴν τοῦ θεοῦ κληρονομίαν).[103] Jeremiah then seals the tent and the ark in a cave dwelling he finds on the mountain (2:4-5). It is possible that the relationship between the accusative, κληρονομίαν, and the genitive, τοῦ θεοῦ, is an attributive one, in which case the passage could refer to the story in Exod 33:18-23, where Moses is allowed to see the glory of God. "The inheritance of God," in this case, would refer to "God's glory." However, if the reference in 2 Macc 2:4 is to be considered as consistent with that of 2:17, a more likely interpretation is to see this as a genitive of origin; the inheritance that Moses saw is not that which *belongs to* God but rather that which *comes from* God.[104] In this case, inheritance in 2:4 likely refers to Deut 32:48-52, where Moses climbs Mount Nebo and sees Israel's inheritance, meaning the land, just before he passes away.[105]

Does this mean that the inheritance in 2 Macc 2:17 also refers to the land? God, having saved all his people, has "returned the inheritance to all" (ἀποδοὺς τὴν κληρονομίαν πᾶσιν, 2:17). This is an inheritance that at some point would have been given to the Israelites, and then lost for a time, only to be rediscovered.

In commenting on the passage in 2:17, Goldstein argues that the inheritance is the land. This fits with the concept in 2:17 of salvation, which, in Second Temple literature, is often tied to the restoration of the Israelites into the land and freedom from their enemies. The verse would then portray a fulfillment of God's promises, which includes the ingathering of the dispersed exiles.[106] There is a problem however with this interpretation. In 2:17, the aorist participle ἀποδοὺς implies that the inheritance has already been returned. In 2:18, the phrase "For we hope" (ἐλπίζομεν γὰρ) begins a new clause, in which a future tense verb reiterates a not yet realized desire that God "will gather" (ἐπισυνάξει) his people from the dispersion and bring them back into the holy place (i.e., the temple). If God has already returned the inheritance to all, but the people are still in the dispersion and hoping to be returned to the

---

[103]   For details regarding the history of this legend and its use, see Jonathan A. Goldstein, *II Maccabees* (AB 41A; New York: Doubleday, 1984), 182.

[104]   See Seth M. Ehorn, *2 Maccabees 1–7: A Handbook on the Greek Text* (Waco, Tex.: Baylor University Press, 2020), 50.

[105]   See Robert Doran, *2 Maccabees* (Hermeneia; Minneapolis: Fortress, 2012), 57.

[106]   Goldstein, *II Maccabees*, 188.

land, then in the context it is difficult to explain how the future hopes of the people could be equated with God's completed accomplishments.[107]

Another possibility is grounded in a parallel with Sir 24:23, discussed above. In that passage, the law itself was given by Moses as an inheritance to God's people. God gives Moses the law, who then places the tablets of the law into the ark, the same ark that Jeremiah then deposits on the mountain in 2 Macc 2:5. Moreover, the law is important to the context of 2 Macc 2:1-3, where Jeremiah delivers the law to those being sent into exile (2:2) and then exhorts them not to allow the law to depart from their hearts (2:3). The law as the inheritance also makes possible sense of 2:17, where the inheritance has been returned to the postexilic dispersion. As Goldstein notes, the term "to us all" follows the returned inheritance, rather than the entire list of God's restored gifts to Israel (i.e., the kingship, the priesthood, the consecration).[108] In other words, the verse is clear that the inheritance has already been returned, but the status of the other gifts listed in the verse is ambiguous. Following the list of gifts, 2:18 has the phrase "just as he promised through the law" (καθὼς ἐπηγγείλατο διὰ τοῦ νόμου). The law, therefore, would be the inheritance returned to all, which would promise the restoration of the kingdom, the priesthood, and the consecration upon the return of the dispersed exiles.[109] In this reading, the land is still included within the inheritance, as one element of the future hope of God's people, but the inheritance also refers to other promises found within the law, and therefore, to the law itself.[110]

Although the land as an inheritance has far greater biblical precedent, Sir 24:23 provides a clear Second Temple source for the law to be received as an inheritance. The circumstances of the Second Temple period also provide a justification for such a development. As John D. Hester argues, due to the exile, the Israelites never fully resettled

[107] This is a problem that Goldstein is aware of; see *II Maccabees*, 187.

[108] Goldstein, *II Maccabees*, 187. Goldstein offers that this was due to damage done to the text and that the phrase "will also restore" must have originally belonged to the verse before the list of restored gifts but had fallen out of the text. With no textual evidence for support, this view only makes sense upon a certain interpretation of the verse and relies upon conjecture.

[109] The verse is likely an allusion to Exod 19:5-6, "Now therefore, if you obey my voice and keep my covenant, you shall be my treasured possession out of all the peoples. Indeed, the whole earth is mine, but you shall be for me a priestly kingdom and a holy nation. These are the words that you shall speak to the Israelites."

[110] This fits the context of the book, in which the law figures prominently. Gathercole, *Boasting*, 53–54, notes that the law is arguably more important to 2 Maccabees than to 1 Maccabees and that resurrection depicted in the book (e.g., 7:9, 23) comes to those who are faithful to Torah.

themselves in a satisfactory way. As the land inheritance took on an increasingly eschatological character, it became natural for other more realized gifts from God to take on the status of inheritance. Few things were as important to the Jews as the law, and it was through observance of the law that the future land inheritance was to be realized, so the law took on, in at least a few instances, a present inheritance status as a guarantee of the future inheritance of the restored land.[111]

3.6. The Psalms of Solomon

Scholars widely regard the Psalms of Solomon to be a mid-first century B.C.E composition, written as a response to the capture of Jerusalem by the Romans.[112] Many of the psalms betray an apparently eyewitness account of the events and concern the "righteous," which are Jews remaining devout to Yahweh in the face of religious syncretism, and the "sinners," made up of both gentiles/Romans (ἔθνη) and Jews who have not been faithful to God's covenant.[113] Both sinful Jews and gentile sinners are accused of profaning Jerusalem and the temple (1:8; 2:1-18). God will destroy the sinners, but the devout will be cleansed of their sins and granted eternal life (ζωὴν αἰώνιον), where they will remain "in the Lord's light" (ἐν φωτὶ κυρίου, 3:8-12). Cognates of κληρονομία appear in the composition nine times.

Ps. Sol. 7:2. Psalm 7 entertains the possibility that the gentile sinners may overtake the devout. The devout call for God to protect them (7:1), and plead that he not allow the gentiles to "trample your holy inheritance" (κληρονομίαν, 7:2). Although the exact referent of the inheritance is left ambiguous in this psalm, the term πατέω, "to trample," is used in 2:2 to refer to the gentiles trampling upon the temple and in 2:19 to refer to their trampling down of Jerusalem. The κληρονομία here belongs to God himself and likely refers to either the temple, Jerusalem, or both.

---

[111]   James D. Hester, *Paul's Concept of Inheritance: A Contribution to the Understanding of Heilsgeschichte* (SJT 14; Edinburgh: Oliver and Boyd, 1968), 32–33.

[112]   Although likely composed in Hebrew, the text is extant in Greek and Syriac manuscripts. For an analysis of the manuscript history, see Robert R. Hann, *The Manuscript History of the Psalms of Solomon* (Chico, Calif.: Scholars Press, 1982). For the Greek text, see Wright, *Psalms*. For the Syriac text, see Joseph L. Trafton, *The Syriac Version of the Psalms of Solomon: A Critical Evaluation* (Atlanta: Scholars Press, 1985). The Greek text is widely regarded as the earliest translation from the Hebrew, and features the largest number of manuscripts. This analysis will extend from the Greek text.

[113]   See Robert B. Wright, "Psalms of Solomon," in Charlesworth, *The Old Testament Pseudepigrapha*, 639, the Roman occupation introduced "foreign cultic and social practices which corrupt many citizens."

Ps. Sol. 9:1. Psalm 8 details the sins of the Israelites, providing justification for their exile. In neglecting God, the Israelites were expelled from the κληρονομία. Again, the exact referent is unclear; judging by the Jerusalem-centric nature of the psalms, this could refer to the holy city alone, but the context also fits well with inheritance contexts of the HB and likely refers to the promised land as the inheritance of the people, lost as a result of their disobedience to the covenant.[114]

Ps. Sol. 12:6. Psalm 12 deals with the wicked and the devout, calling for the Lord to provide salvation and protection for his servants (12:6). Verse 6 calls for the wicked to perish (ἀπόλοιντο) and for the devout to "inherit the Lord's promises" (κληρονομήσαισαν ἐπαγγελίας κυρίου). The exact promises in view are left unclear, though this likely refers to the salvation called for by the psalm—that God will protect the devout and grant them life.[115] The timing of the inheritance of life is left open, but the context is eschatological.

Ps. Sol. 14:5-10. Psalm 14 contrasts the devout with the sinners; the sinners in this case clearly referring to apostate Jews. The sinners have forfeited their social identity by their disregard for the law, but because the devout have observed the law they are the Lord's paradise, his "trees of life" (14:2-3). The devout will be "firmly rooted forever," implying that the sinners will be uprooted (14:4), lost from among Israel and forever denied identification with it. The devout of Israel are "the inheritance of God" (κληρονομία τοῦ θεοῦ, 14:5), but the sinners are denied this identification. Instead, for the sinners, "their inheritance is Hades" (κληρονομία αὐτῶν ᾅδης, 14:9), but the devout "will inherit life in joy" (κληρονομήσουσιν ζωὴν ἐν εὐφροσύνῃ, 14:10).[116]

---

[114]   Gathercole, *Boasting*, 64–65, points out that, in this psalm, salvation is described in terms of just recompense, detailing both the nationalistic and individualistic need to repay God through righteous deeds.

[115]   Cf. 14:9-10. The term "promises" does not appear elsewhere in the Psalms of Solomon.

[116]   Some debate on this psalm has centered on the role of the law and the need for obedience for righteous Jews to be counted among God's inheritance. Sanders, *Judaism*, 392–93, recognizes the need for obedience in the psalm but notes an appeal to God's mercy in Psalm 15. He argues that obedience is important, and that God does reward obedience and punish disobedience, but that salvation is granted due to the mercy of God and not the obedience of the righteous. Similar is James D. G. Dunn, *The Theology of Paul the Apostle* (London: T&T Clark, 1998), 152–53, when commenting on Lev 18:5, and noting its parallel relationship to Ps. Sol. 14, who argues that life is not attained by obedience but is granted by God as a covenant status. Life is *maintained* by obeying the law, but is *attained* by inclusion in the covenant. However, Gathercole, *Boasting*, 67, is right to point out the future tense of κληρονομήσουσιν ζωὴν; the righteous have not already been granted the inheritance of life but "will inherit" life as an aspect of eschatological judgment. Gathercole acknowledges the important role of God's mercy in these

The context of this psalm clearly anticipates an eschatological judgment. The wicked will be cast into darkness "on the day of mercy for the righteous" (v. 9). Although it is not clear that the Israelites maintained a strict divide between the dead and the living, the contrast between hades and life goes beyond the "this-worldly" and looks for judgment in a more complete form. The wicked in the psalm "do not remember God," a feature of hades throughout the HB and Second Temple literature,[117] where the dead are cut off from the cult of Israel and any relationship with Yahweh.[118] The inheritance in this psalm refers both to Israel as the Lord's inheritance and life as the inheritance of Israel, while the wicked receive an inheritance of judgment and alienation from both God and their social identity.

Ps. Sol. 15:10-11. Again, the context of the psalm is eschatological judgment for the sinners and salvation for the devout. The context largely matches that of Ps. Sol. 14. The sinners' inheritance is destruction and hades, and the effects of their actions will be passed down to their children (15:10-11). While the sinners perish (ἀπολοῦνται) on the day of the Lord's judgment (15:12), the devout "will live" (ζήσονται) in the Lord's mercy forever (15:13).

Ps. Sol. 17:23. Scholars widely regard the seventeenth psalm to be the most influential and theologically central of the book.[119] Both eschatological and messianic, this psalm is the culmination of the eschatological portions of the collection, "the restoration of Jerusalem, which will be brought about by the Davidic messiah."[120] The psalm recounts both the illegitimacy of Israel's former leadership and the abuses of foreign rulers and casts them against the kingdom of God (ἡ βασιλεία τοῦ θεοῦ) that judges the nations (17:3).[121] The role of the messiah is

psalms but rightly argues, "The role of works in final vindication cannot be ruled out simply by asserting that the mercy of God is basic for life and salvation: both viewpoints are held simultaneously."

[117]   See Job 26:5-6; Ps 6:5.

[118]   See *NIDNTTE*, 5 vols. (2nd ed.; ed. Moisés Silva; Grand Rapids: Zondervan, 2014), 1:152–53.

[119]   See James H. Charlesworth, *The Pseudepigrapha and Modern Research* (Ann Arbor: Scholars Press, 1981), 196.

[120]   Collins, *Apocalyptic Imagination*, 176.

[121]   The exact identification of these groups with various passages in the psalm are difficult to determine. Wright, *Psalms*, 1, finds in the psalm both "the expulsion of foreign influences" and "the displacement of the corrupt administrators of state and temple." See also Kenneth Atkinson, "Herod the Great, Sosius, and the Siege of Jerusalem (37 B.C.E) in Psalm of Solomon 17," *NovT* 38, no. 4 (1996): 313–22, who argues for future judgment against both illegitimate Hasmonean leaders and foreign oppressors. However, Johannes Tromp, "The Sinners and the Lawless in the Psalm of Solomon XVII," *NovT* 35, no. 4 (1993): 344–61, identifies all sinners in the psalm as foreigners.

to purge Jerusalem of foreign rule, not with an army but "by the word of his mouth" (17:24).[122] Verses 21-23 sees the rise of the Davidic king (βασιλέα). He will rule over Israel, in a time chosen by God,[123] purging Jerusalem of the gentiles with wisdom (σοφία). He will drive sinners out from the inheritance (κληρονομίας), which along with 7:2, is clearly a reference to Jerusalem.

An important development in this psalm comes in verses 28-35. There is, however, an important translation issue in verse 28 that must be cleared up in order to analyze the passage properly.

In the Greek, verse 28 reads:

καὶ καταμερίσει αὐτοὺς ἐν ταῖς φυλαῖς αὐτῶν ἐπὶ τῆς γῆς,
καὶ πάροικος καὶ ἀλλογενὴς οὐ πάροικος παροικήσει[124] αὐτοῖς ἔτι.

In his critical edition of the Greek text, Wright translates the verse:

He will distribute them upon the land according to their tribes.
The stranger and the foreigner will no longer live with them.[125]

At first glance, this translation makes sense. It is certainly possible according to the syntax, and it fits with the context of the first half of the Psalm. The messiah's role is to purify Jerusalem from gentiles, a feature also found in other purification texts.[126] The nations (ἔθνη) are said to flee from his presence (17:25) as he gathers his holy people (17:26). The messianic king will distribute the people upon their land according to their tribes (17:28), a feature that fits in well with the Israel-centric land-allotment contexts of the Hexateuch. It is in this context that the verse, translated in this way, sees the strangers and foreigners cast away from Jerusalem as the land is reallotted to the tribes of Israel.

However, verse 28 is also a shifting point in the attitude of the psalm toward gentiles. It is said of the messiah that he will judge all the nations (ἔθνη) in wisdom (σοφία), and the nations will serve him (17:29). The people of the nations will come from the ends of the earth to facilitate the pilgrimage of the Israelites back into the land, and he will be king over not only the Israelites but over the nations as well.[127] The Israelites

---

[122]   Charlesworth, *Pseudepigrapha*, 196.

[123]   The passage makes use of the eschatologically significant phrase "In the time chosen by you." Cf. Ps 75:2; Zech 14:1.

[124]   Trafton, *Psalms*, 173, believes that πάροικος παροικήσει is a paronomasia. Wright, *Psalms*, 190, has only παροικήσει.

[125]   Wright, *Psalms*, 190.

[126]   Cf. Neh 13.

[127]   Joseph L. Trafton, "The Psalms of Solomon: New Light from the Syriac Version?" *JBL* 105, no. 2 (1986): 236, points out that the Syriac here has the nations bringing gifts to the Israelites, rather than bringing the Israelites themselves as a gift to the messianic king. He notes that the Greek, where the Israelites are the gifts, is an "odd

and the nations together will be taught by God, and they will walk in his ways (17:32). The nations will stand before him, and he will have compassion on them (17:34). There is remarkable consistency with this section of the psalm and many pilgrimage passages in the Latter Prophets. As I have argued in chapter 2, many of those passages portray a positive attitude toward the gentiles, allowing them to come in among the people of God and worship there (cf. Jer 3:17). Particularly striking is a comparison between this psalm and Isaiah 2:2-4a. In both passages, the nations stream into Jerusalem. They will come to be taught and judged, forsaking their own paths for the path laid out by Israel's God. Also significant is a comparison between this psalm and Isaiah 14:1-2. Both passages portray a return from exile for the people of God, with a resettlement of the land. Both passages portray gentiles as those responsible for the repatriation of the Israelites, and in Isaiah, the nations are not cast away, but join the Israelites, becoming servants as they do in 17:30 of this psalm.

This brings us back to the translation of 17:28, specifically the second half of the verse. Again, the Greek states, καὶ πάροικος καὶ ἀλλογενὴς οὐ πάροικος παροικήσει αὐτοῖς ἔτι. Wright translates the verse in reference to location, with the stranger being removed: "The stranger and the foreigner will no longer live with them." However, the future tense of the verb παροικέω, "to live as a stranger," appears with the negative οὐ just one time in the LXX, in Sir 38:32, referring to tradesmen and craftsmen living in the cities. In that passage, the tradesmen *will not* be removed, they are not to live *as strangers* in the cities, nor are they to leave (καὶ οὐ παροικήσουσιν οὐδὲ περιπατήσουσιν), but because of their contributions, they will always have a place. In fact, because of their presence, cities are inhabitable by others. The verb παροικέω can refer simply to the act of sojourning, but as in Sir 38:32, it can more directly refer to the act of being a stranger or living as a sojourner.[128] In combination with the negative, the verse then negates the act of living in that condition, and the adverb ἔτι with dative pronoun αὐτοῖς would refer both to location and association, placing the gentiles in the opposite position of that dictated by Wright's translation. A possible translation would then read: "The stranger and the foreigner will *no longer live as strangers* among them."[129]

---

concept." However, the concept is seen throughout pilgrimage passages in the Latter Prophets, so the Greek rendering fits within that tradition.

[128]   See *NIDNTTE*, 3:642.

[129]   As Wright, *Psalms*, 191, notes, this is closer to the Syriac, which reads "will live near them." This is not to say the Syriac was translated this way *from the Greek*. Trafton, *Psalms*, 206–7, notes the difficulty in demonstrating the vorlage of the Syriac manuscripts, arguing for a Hebrew vorlage, but noting that enough of the Syriac seems

Rather than being purged, the gentiles who assist in repatriating the Israelites would experience a change in position. If they repented of their old ways, they would be welcomed as servants of God, rather than rebuffed as foreigners. This would fit well with another passage analyzed in chapter 2, Ezek 47:21-23, which, like this psalm, is an eschatological passage portraying the reallocation of the land to returned exiles. In that passage, the resident aliens are not cast away, but are instead allowed to reside among God's people, and are no longer considered strangers and aliens, but are considered native born sons of Israel. In my reading of 17:28, the context is similar to Ezek 47:21-23, though extended beyond simply resident aliens; the land is redistributed, and the gentiles that stream into Jerusalem to repatriate the exiles are no longer strangers but rather welcomed as servants of God's messiah.[130]

If this is the case, then what are we to make of the negative attitude toward gentiles in the first half of the psalm? Joel Willitts offers a helpful distinction between two separate groups of gentiles portrayed in the text. The psalmist is careful to use important descriptive words of the gentiles who are cast out from Jerusalem and destroyed, such as "unrighteous" (17:22) and "unlawful" (17:24). Willitts argues, correctly in my view, that these statements are not aimed at gentiles in total, "but at the Gentile *oppressors* who are exercising political domination over Israel" (emphasis his). It is specifically the gentiles who have trampled upon Jerusalem and defiled the land that are to be destroyed.[131] The gentiles who facilitate the return of the Israelites to the land are received in a positive way. It is specifically the sinners (oppressors) who are driven out from the inheritance, but this psalm appears to make a way for gentiles to be welcomed among the Israelites as they re-inherit their land.

---

to derive from the Greek that it is likely the scribes consulted Greek manuscripts at certain points (to his point, most notably Ps. of Sol. 13). If Trafton is correct, this places the Greek and Syriac as largely independent witnesses to the Hebrew, with the Syriac shedding possible light on how the Hebrew may have read.

[130]   *Contra* Johannes Tromp, "The Davidic Messiah in Jewish Eschatology of the First Century BCE," in *Restoration: Old Testament, Jewish, and Christian Perspectives* (ed. James M. Scott; Leiden: Brill, 2001), 190–91, who argues that the Messiah's role in this psalm is to free the city from all foreigners and subdue the nations. In my view, the parallels with passages in the prophetic tradition do not guarantee literary dependency but suggest a similarly positive view of long-term gentile involvement with the people of God.

[131]   Joel Willitts, "Matthew and Psalms of Solomon's Messianism: A Comparative Study of First-Century Messianology," *BBR* 22, no. 1 (2012): 46–47. Willitts argues that the two perspectives show the psalmist is ambivalent toward gentiles, while my argument requires a more actively positive view toward the pilgrimage gentiles.

3.7. Conclusions

While there is diversity regarding the concept of inheritance in the apocrypha and pseudepigrapha, the diversity is largely confined to a few common and identifiable themes. Whereas in the HB the inheritance is largely confined to land, either promised, realized, or hoped for, or to the nature of the relationship between God and his people, in this literature the inheritance refers to a wider range of items and realities. Inheritance can refer to the land (Judith), or more particularly Jerusalem or the temple (1 Maccabees, the Psalms of Solomon). Rather than realized, the land is hoped for and often takes on an eschatological shape similar to the Latter Prophets, and like the prophets, the timing of the expectation can be either imminent or indeterminate (the Book of the Watchers, Sirach, Tobit), and either "this-worldly" (1 Enoch, Tobit, 1 Maccabees) or "other-worldly" (the Psalms of Solomon).[132] In some compositions,

---

[132]   The nature of the eschatological hope of a renewed/restored earth in these texts has often been categorized as either "prophetic," following on the heels of the Latter Prophets of the HB, or "apocalyptic," regarded as a newer development within the Second Temple literature. For example, Jill Hicks-Keeton, "Already/Not Yet: Eschatological Tension in the Book of Tobit," *JBL* 132, no. 1 (2013): 97–117, argues that Tobit's eschatological vision is consistent with the restorationist eschatology of the Latter Prophets. This includes the expectation that the exiles will be returned to the land of Israel, that Jerusalem and the temple will be rebuilt, that God's new salvific act will overshadow the old, and that the gentiles will come to worship the God of Israel. Tobit is not innovating in his eschatological expectations but rooting them in "long-standing biblical traditions and echoes of Israel's prophetic voices." She contrasts this with the widespread "apocalyptic eschatology" that was far more prevalent in Second Temple writings contemporary to Tobit. As one example, she compares Tobit to the *Apocalypse of Weeks*, which, in contrast to Tobit, "offers a radically different understanding of God's impending activity on behalf of Israel, one that diverges significantly from Israel's prophetic tradition." Konrad Schmid and Odil Hannes Steck, "Restoration Expectations in the Prophetic Tradition of the Old Testament," in *Restoration: Old Testament, Jewish, and Christian Perspectives* (ed. James M. Scott; Leiden: Brill, 2001), 47, define "prophetic" restoration as a return of the exiles to the land of Israel, where pious Israelites, joined by pious gentiles, would be separated from the wicked and join in a commitment to the law and right worship of Yahweh. The wicked are destroyed in final judgment. Aune, "Idealized Past," 148, more acutely defines the "apocalyptic" aspect of restoration as centered on God's intervention and rescue of his people in a saving act, where he punishes his enemies and restores the cosmic order by "recreating the cosmos to its original pristine perfection." He includes the Book of the Watchers in this description. The important difference between the prophetic restoration and the apocalyptic is the nature and extent of the restorative act. The prophetic restoration is largely focused on a reconstituted Israel, a regathering of the elect into the land, a rebuilding of the temple, and a recommitment to the law. Though gentiles are included, this is largely a particularistic picture of restoration, rooted in Israel's land and history. Apocalyptic restoration is universal and rooted in Eden and the creative act rather than Israel in particular. It imagines the recreation of the old into something new, not just a rebuilding but a new

inheritance terms are not used eschatologically, but historically, as they find their foundation in Israel's past (Sirach, Judith, 1 and 2 Maccabees). Inheritance in these texts is almost entirely corporate, rather than individualistic, as the regathering of the people is a key aspect of inheritance and restoration passages in the Second Temple period. Because the position of the Israelites in relation to the land was often in flux, other ideas began to take on the label of inheritance, such as wisdom (Sirach), the law (Sirach, 2 Maccabees), or even a marriage (Tobit). The key aspect of each of these, and the thing that binds them to the concept of inheritance going back to the Hexateuch and through the HB, is that in the majority of cases these inheritances were viewed as a gift from God and signaled something specific about the relationship between God and his people. The inheritances were often tied to the Abrahamic promise, a feature shared with inheritance in the HB, and were often tied to God's providence in his people's lives, as well as their election and salvation. Salvation centered on rescue—from enemies, exile, and a state of apostasy—and was tied to inheritance through a confidence in a return to God's gifts and promises. This salvation could refer to earthly blessing and long life (1 En. 5) or to an afterlife (the Psalms of Solomon). In these respects, inheritance is intimately tied to the confidence of the people in their individual and shared identity.

Inheritance in these texts often takes on a hybrid focus between mixed perspectives. For example, inheritance is often tied to election, as in Judith, where it can also be lost through disobedience. In 1 and 2 Maccabees, it is garnered through obedience, but these texts also feature a sharp focus on God's favor and providence as necessary for success. 1 Enoch 5 envisions the inheritance as a gift from God extended by his forgiveness, whereas 1 En. 99 extends the inheritance to those who adhere to instruction. Obedience itself is also varied, as Tobit, Judith, 1 and 2 Maccabees, and the Psalms of Solomon all envision the necessity of obedience to Torah, while the Book of the Watchers appeals to

---

creative act. These distinctions are helpful but can also be misleading. For example, as I argue here, Isa 65:17-25 introduces apocalyptic images into a representatively prophetic text. Conversely, 1 En. 5:5-9, largely categorized as apocalyptic, draws heavily on prophetic images from Isaiah and the Psalms, although it refits them into its own restoration program. The Psalms of Solomon may feature both aspects, as Pss. Sol. 14 deals in apocalyptic terms, but Pss. Sol. 17 is in many ways related to the prophetic. Finally, it is important to note that these distinctions are made specifically regarding an understanding of the concept of "restoration" and are not meant as a method of categorizing texts or understanding genres. That discussion is related but separate and has its own history; for a critique of the use of apocalyptic for organizing texts; see T. F. Glasson, "What Is Apocalyptic?" *NTS* 27, no. 1 (1980): 98–105. For a defense of the apocalyptic as genre, see Collins, *Apocalyptic Imagination*, 3–14.

an obedience to wisdom, and Sirach envisions both wisdom and Torah as two separate and unequal but important sides of the same coin. The inheritance can be presented either universally, to Jews and gentiles alike (1 Enoch, Sirach), particularly to Jews (Judith, 1 and 2 Maccabees), or feature a possible but ambiguous mixture of both universalist and particularistic language as it pertains to inheritance (Tobit, the Psalms of Solomon).

The Abrahamic promise continues to be an important theme to inheritance concepts in the Second Temple literature. Whereas the Hexateuch and Former Prophets focus almost exclusively on the first two aspects of the promise (i.e., that Abraham would have many descendants and that those descendants would multiply into a great nation), Sir 44:19-21 follows the development of the Latter Prophets to shift into a central focus on the third aspect: being the role of Israel as a light to the nations. In this instance, the nations themselves are said to anticipate their own inheritance from God.

4

Inheritance in the Second Temple Period

The Qumran Literature

Categorizing and grouping compositions discovered at Qumran can be a challenging enterprise. There is a temptation, at least as a starting point, to group *Yaḥad* compositions together and to discuss them in light of what we know about the Qumran site. These *Yaḥad* texts are often compared to other Qumran Scrolls in various ways, which is meant to enlighten both our understanding of the compositions as well as the various forms of Judaism existent at the time these works were composed and/or redacted. The problem, however, is the growing recognition of the extensive diversity of origins regarding the Scrolls. To begin with, it is not easy, nor desirable, simply to set compositions into categories of either *Yaḥad* or "mainstream." This would make use of an assumption that "mainstream" Judaism is discernible or that there even existed a majority form of Judaism at the time that could be set against various minority or "sectarian" Judaisms.[1] Furthermore, non-*Yaḥad* compositions could

---

[1]   Terms such as "mainstream" and "sectarian" have been extremely problematized in recent scholarship on the Dead Sea Scrolls. See, for example, Charlotte Hempel, "Qumran Communities: Beyond the Fringes of Second Temple Society," in *The Scrolls and the Scriptures: Qumran Fifty Years After* (ed. Stanley E. Porter and Craig A. Evans; Sheffield: Sheffield Academic, 1997), 47, who argues both that the Scrolls cannot simply be viewed as products of "fringe" communities but also that "mainstream" Judaism is a problematic concept. The problems defining "sectarianism" have been noted by a number of scholars, though see especially Jutta Jokiranta, *Social Identity and Sectarianism in the Qumran Movement* (STDJ; Leiden: Brill, 2013), who discusses the difficulty in defining sectarianism as well as distinguishing it from religious orders and voluntary associations. She argues that sectarians feature a higher tension and antagonism with the surrounding society. Although use of the term "sectarian" is problematic, "sect" and

fit into any number of categories, such as nonsectarian, pre-sectarian, sectarian but non-*Yaḥad*, pre-*Yaḥad*, and others besides.[2] There are also significant challenges to categorizing *Yaḥad* compositions. Some scholars have highlighted the possibility that the *Yaḥad* was not as monolithic of a community as once believed. It has been argued that the *Yaḥad* operated in various small communities throughout the region rather than being limited to involvement at the Qumran site.[3] Further complicating matters are challenges to the assumed models of sectarianism that dominate the interpretation of so-called *Yaḥad* material. There is an increasing awareness in Scrolls research that presuppositions regarding sectarian labels have potentially facilitated interpretations that are geared toward supporting such labels, rather than toward interpretations focused primarily on the content of the compositions in light of other evidence.[4] These concerns have led some scholars to highlight the way

---

"sectarian" are well-established concepts in early Judaism, and such terms are better defined than discarded completely. See, for example, Jutta Jokiranta, "Sectarianism," in *The Eerdmans Dictionary of Early Judaism* (ed. John J. Collins and Daniel C. Harlow; Grand Rapids: Eerdmans, 2010), 1209–11, who argues that, although any single "normative Judaism" has been widely rejected, it is still meaningful to speak of sectarian groups that stand in tension with wider society. She argues that some groups experienced a high-tension social differentiation with the wider majority. Regarding the potential of a Qumran community, the use of the term "sectarian" in this chapter refers to the long-standing associations with exclusive membership, some form of separation or isolation, and strict discipline, though it is recognized that such ideas are undergoing constant revision in Qumran scholarship and ultimately serve as heuristic terms to describe the interactions of specific groups with surrounding groups. The use of the term "sectarian" in reference to compositions serves to associate those compositions with the group(s) that produced them.

[2]   Various options have been highlighted by the work of Florentino García Martínez and Adam S. van der Woude, who proposed "the Groningen Hypothesis." This posits a pre-Qumranic stage of intellectual development in some of the literature, which was followed by a sectarian stage within the Qumran community. Although the Groningen Hypothesis is one account of the diversity of compositions among the Qumran Scrolls, and many scholars have argued against various aspects of the hypothesis, it presents clearly the diverse nature of the compositions found among the Qumran Scrolls. See Florentino García Martínez and A. S. van der Woude, "A 'Groningen' Hypothesis of Qumran Origins and Early History," *RevQ* 14 (1989–1990): 521–41.

[3]   See John J. Collins, "Beyond the Qumran Community: Social Organization in the Dead Sea Scrolls," *DSD* 16, no. 3 (2009): 351–69, who argues that it may be imprudent to even speak of a "Qumran community." Collins is not alone in this assessment. See, for example, Hartmut Stegemann, "The Qumran Essenes: Local Members of the Main Jewish Union in Late Second Temple Times," in *The Madrid Qumran Congress* (ed. J. Trebolle and L. Vegas Montaner; Leiden: Brill, 1992), 83–166.

[4]   See, for example, Gwynned de Looijer, *The Qumran Paradigm: Critical Evaluation of Some Foundational Hypotheses in the Construction of the Qumran Sect* (Atlanta: SBL Press, 2015), 139–40, who has argued that assumptions regarding sectarianism have motivated scholars to read certain compositions with a perceived

the Scrolls reflect the mainline traditions of Judaism.[5] Other scholars have questioned the very connection of the Scrolls to the Qumran site, arguing instead that the texts are simply the contents of various Jewish libraries stored there.[6]

To complicate matters further, even some individual *Yaḥad* compositions are no longer thought to be entirely so. A large number of hands were responsible for the manuscripts found at Qumran, with many manuscripts, including *Yaḥad* compositions, showing obvious signs of redaction.[7] This increases the likelihood that the *Yaḥad* may not have been responsible for large portions of the compositions most associated with them, though it is fair to assume they agreed with much of the content of the compositions they edited and copied.[8] These issues have

---

antagonism toward certain opponents, and content has been interpreted as different than, and opposed to, Jewish ideology in "the outside world." Assumptions of sectarianism have facilitated interpretations biased toward a "radicality" that influences the reading of terminology, style, beliefs, practices, and identity.

[5]   See Lawrence H. Schiffman, *Reclaiming the Dead Sea Scrolls: The History of Judaism, the Background of Christianity, the Lost Library of Qumran* (Philadelphia: JPS, 1994).

[6]   See Norman Golb, *Who Wrote the Dead Sea Scrolls? The Search for the Secret of Qumran* (New York: Scribner's, 1994). Golb's views have not gained wide support, but they highlight the problems that accompany many of the assumptions that come with the traditional views regarding the use of the caves for storing what are now referred to as the Dead Sea Scrolls. Golb's views have been challenged by, among others, Hempel, "Qumran Communities," 49, and Carol A. Newsom, "'Sectually Explicit' Literature from Qumran," in *The Hebrew Bible and Its Interpreters* (ed. William Henry Propp, Baruch Halpern, and David Noel Freedman; Winona Lake, Ind.: Eisenbrauns, 1990), 168–69.

[7]   Take, for example, the Damascus Document (CD). Once placed unquestionably into a category with other *Yaḥad* texts, studies such as those by Philip R. Davies, *The Damascus Covenant: An Interpretation of the "Damascus Document"* (Sheffield: JSOT, 1982), and Charlotte Hempel, *The Laws of the Damascus Document: Sources, Tradition and Redaction* (Leiden: Brill, 1998), have aptly demonstrated that possibly even the majority of CD's content is, at the most, pre-sectarian and that the composition was redacted for the purpose of fitting in with *Yaḥad* material. On Qumran texts more widely, including the Community Rule and the Temple Scroll, Hempel, "Qumran Communities," 47–48, argues that they resist the harmonization of early Qumran scholarship and exhibit diversity and complexity, not only from one composition to the next but also within individual compositions. Maxine Grossman, *Reading for History in the Damascus Document: A Methodological Method* (Leiden: Brill, 2002), x, has argued that many compositions within the Qumran Scrolls show signs of fragmentation, contradiction, and contestation, allowing for diversity and changes over time within communities that made use of the texts and copied the manuscripts.

[8]   See John Kampen, *Wisdom Literature* (Grand Rapids: Eerdmans, 2011), 20–21, who states, "The extensive, disparate, and fragmentary nature of the Qumran literature does not permit a simplistic or univocal description of the authors of these documents or their social setting." He goes on to state that the nonsectarian material "was considered important and was valued by the sectarians."

led Philip Davies to state, "To reduce the contents of the eleven manuscript caves to a 'Qumran Judaism' without rigorous method appears
impossible, and perhaps to try to reduce them to a single Judaism at
all is imprudent."[9] This imprudence appears, at least in some measure,
to extend to the way we group and read the compositions discovered
at Qumran.[10] Even different manuscripts of the same composition may
represent separate recensions of that composition, rendering the manuscripts as representatives of, in a technical sense, different "texts,"[11]
which may then highlight different historical and thematic realities.[12]
This has ramifications for the way one understands references to inheritance in so-called *Yahad* compositions, as these references may reflect
developments of the theme of inheritance not directly associated with
the *Yahad*, or any sectarian group. In other words, even references to
inheritance found in so-called *Yahad* or sectarian compositions may
reflect views of inheritance held during this period by Jews living in a
nonsectarian milieu. These issues led Davies to set aside any preconceived consensus on historical realities in favor of a more systematic
approach that analyzes texts in isolation before reattempting a synthe-
sis between them. Davies does not ignore the obvious links between
some compositions, such as shared calendars, light/dark dualisms, or
references to the Teacher of Righteousness, but he attempts to analyze

---

[9]   Philip R. Davies, "The Judaism(s) of the Damascus Document," in *The
Damascus Document: A Centennial of Discovery* (ed. Joseph M. Baumgarten, Esther G.
Chazon, and Avital Pinnick; Leiden: Brill, 2000), 28.

[10]   See, for example, Newsom, "'Sectually Explicit,'" 185, who argues that the
sectarian literature from Qumran is not sectarian enough to allow for a clear distinction.
Newsom states, "The question of determining what is sectarian or nonsectarian literature
from the Qumran library cannot be a matter merely of dividing the manuscripts into two
separate piles with appropriate labels." Multiple questions must be asked of each manuscript, and the question "is this sectarian?" cannot be answered with a simple yes or no.

[11]   Or, more precisely, different versions of the same composition.

[12]   See Grossman, *Reading*, ix–x, who argues along similar lines. Her study is
literary-critical, but she applies literary theory to reading toward a "new historiography,"
which makes use of interpretation as a method for analyzing "ranges" of probability in
regard to historical and social understanding. She problematizes reading for history at
face value, as well as the ability and value of discovering and reading for the original
intent of the "author." In Grossman's view, the Qumran Scrolls must be read not only in
light of composition, but also transmission and reception, so that both individual texts
as well as the individual manuscripts of those texts must be consulted for their diversity and contradictions rather than only their points of harmony. The character of each
manuscript has as much to say as a composite version of the text. When read this way,
the Scrolls do not reveal simple statements of fact but rather ideological constructions
of history. Grossman recognizes that this moves the interpreter away from readings of
history that are unitary and definitive but argues that ranges of probability are more
attainable than definitive data.

the manuscripts as discrete compositions, rather than based on shared characteristics.[13] I agree with the assessment of some scholars that certain so-called *Yaḥad* compositions are redacted versions of earlier, non-Qumran and even pre-sectarian compositions. Therefore, with Davies, I agree that preconceived notions of historical and social realities may, in many cases, serve to confuse careful analysis of the thematic content of many compositions. In light of these concerns, even grouping compositions in this chapter under the rubric of "The Dead Sea Scrolls" can be problematic, as in some cases the manuscripts are grouped this way not because of shared social or historical milieu but due only to the fact that they were discovered together in the caves near the Qumran site, and many if not all were likely used by a community that made use of the site. To be sure, the discovery of the manuscripts in close proximity to one another is significant, and the groupings are not without benefit, but the concerns of such a grouping should be noted. In light of the foregoing concerns, I have grouped the Qumran Scrolls into one chapter, without subdividing them according to historical or sociological categories. It is also due to these concerns that I spend some notable time discussing composition history in this chapter, rather than solely focusing on inheritance. These concepts will certainly contribute to the analysis of inheritance in individual compositions regarding the possible contexts from which inheritance language is derived.

None of this is to say that all categorical organization is unwise. In fact, some structure makes the analysis manageable. In this study I have adopted the approach of *The Dead Sea Scrolls Reader* and loosely ordered the compositions based on genre groupings.[14] Such a categorical approach is not without its own problems. Genre distinctions can be ill defined and either so rigid so as to exclude helpful examples or so loose so as to render the distinction meaningless. As George Brooke argues, "there are few, if any, pure examples of texts, not least because all genres evolve and such evolution introduces instability into generic definition."[15] We shall see early in this chapter that such evolution is possibly the defining feature of many compositions, such as 4QInstruction, which makes prolific use of themes and motifs associated with both "wisdom" and "apocalyptic" genres in a way that demonstrates an evolution in both genres. Like Davies, Brooke recommends that, to avoid this problem, one method would be to begin with single compositions

---

[13]   Davies, "Judaism(s)," 29.

[14]   Donald W. Parry and Emanuel Tov, eds., *The Dead Sea Scrolls Reader*, 6 vols. (Leiden: Brill, 2004), hereafter *DSSR*.

[15]   George Brooke, *Reading the Dead Sea Scrolls: Essays in Method* (Atlanta: SBL, 2013), xix.

and then move on to comparable ones.[16] Furthermore, any genre categorization must be viewed with porous boundaries and always be open to redefinition and new members.[17] With these concerns in mind, I have chosen not to group these compositions in a formal sense and instead treat them individually. This loose organization is based on a recognition that genre distinctions must not be held rigidly and that inheritance references are best analyzed in individual compositions in their individual contexts. Space precludes an analysis of every reference to inheritance found among the Qumran Scrolls. Many inheritance references are too fragmented or isolated to be analyzed with much fluency, and the relevance of many Qumran references to inheritance as a "concept history" is limited. Some minor occurrences will not be discussed at length, but many will be cited only as examples, such as inheritance references in "Bible apocalypses" (e.g., Ages of Creation; Apocalypse of Joseph).

4.1. Wisdom Compositions[18]

Defining wisdom literature can be notoriously difficult, due to the relatively arbitrary nature of such definitions.[19] Kampen has provided a helpful if relatively broad description as "instructional material that can be identified with the biblical tradition of wisdom, while not limited by it in form or content."[20] For example, this may include material concerned

---

[16]   Though it should be noted that Brooke favors another method, beginning with the larger corpus of compositions that share an agenda. As I have noted here, discerning such an agenda for the Qumran Scrolls is also problematic. Grossman, *Reading*, x, advocates for a multistage process of analyzing the Scrolls, the first of which is to read not only individual texts in isolation but individual manuscripts as well. This is done to recognize diversity from one manuscript to another and to sort out the ideological claims of each, looking for the selective use of Scripture, the choice of words and images, the constructions of history, and so on.

[17]   Although the concept of "genre" has been problematized, Hindy Najman, "The Idea of Biblical Genre: From Discourse to Constellation," in *Prayer and Poetry in the Dead Sea Scrolls and Related Literature* (ed. Jeremy Penner, Ken M. Penner, and Cecilia Wassen; STDJ 98; Leiden: Brill, 2012), 321, argues that genre distinctions for Second Temple sources should be used but that genre boundaries should be porous and that classifications of texts other than by genre are often helpful.

[18]   Unless otherwise noted, translations of wisdom compositions will be taken from Donald W. Parry and Emanuel Tov, eds., *The Dead Sea Scrolls Reader*, vol. 4, *Calendrical and Sapiential Texts* (Leiden: Brill, 2004).

[19]   See, for example, Hindy Najman, "Jewish Wisdom in the Hellenistic Period: Towards the Study of Semantic Constellation," in *Is There a Text in This Cave?* (ed. Ariel Feldman, Maria Cioata, and Charlotte Hempel; STDJ 119; Leiden: Brill, 2017), 464–65, who argues that Instruction is undoubtedly in the context of "wisdom traditions" but that it also "participates in liturgical, apocalyptic, prophetic, and legal discourses."

[20]   Kampen, *Wisdom*, 14.

with knowledge and truth, even if that material does not make consistent use of the accepted terms for "wisdom." This material is often (though not exclusively, or always) concerned with a sense of order established at creation, the recognition that God made the world, and the sense that humans are morally responsible agents who are held accountable for their response to the created order. Wisdom literature at Qumran is concerned with ethics and the extreme opposition between righteous and wicked forces in the world and the human behavior that follows. As this study addresses, the wisdom literature among the Qumran Scrolls features extensive use of apocalyptic themes, to the point that sapiential and apocalyptic, as categories, cannot be untangled.[21]

4.1.1. 4QInstruction[22]

Instruction is a substantial wisdom composition found among the Dead Sea Scrolls.[23] The composition was likely not a product of the Qumran community,[24] though the sheer number of manuscripts found at Qumran implies that it was popular among them,[25] and it shares a number of

---

[21]   See George W. E. Nickelsburg, "Wisdom and Apocalypticism in Early Judaism: Some Points for Discussion," in *Conflicted Boundaries in Wisdom and Apocalypticism* (ed. Lawrence M. Wills and Benjamin G. Wright III; Atlanta: SBL, 2005), 20.

[22]   Extant manuscripts of the text have been found only at Qumran and consist of the manuscripts 1Q26, 4Q415–18, 4Q423. It is known by many names, most often 4QInstruction. 4QInstruction can be a misleading title, due to the finding of a fragment in cave 1 at Qumran and the fact that most scholars now regard the text as originating prior to its use at the Qumran site. For this reason, I follow Kampen, *Wisdom*, 38, in using the title "Instruction." For publication of the Hebrew text with early extensive analysis, see John Strugnell, Daniel J. Harrington, and Torleif Elgvin, *Discoveries in the Judaean Desert XXXIV: Sapiential Texts Part 2, 4QInstruction* (Oxford: Clarendon, 1999), hereafter as DJD 34. The translation of *DSSR* followed in this study is taken from DJD 34.

[23]   It is the longest sapiential composition discovered at Qumran, and its length rivals that of the Temple Scroll and the Hodayot, two of the longest compositions at Qumran. Kampen, *Wisdom*, 12, argues that the text was the most "comprehensive and influential nonbiblical text within the circles that utilized these writings." For an analysis of the manuscripts that make up Instruction, see Matthew J. Goff, *4QInstruction* (Atlanta: SBL, 2013), 1–7.

[24]   Some scholars have argued that the text was a product of the Qumran community. For a brief survey of scholars who have argued along these lines, see Matthew J. Goff, *The Worldly and Heavenly Wisdom of 4QInstruction* (STDJ 50; Leiden: Brill, 2003), 222–24. Most scholars now regard the text as a product from outside of the community but that the texts were popular among the sectarian group at Qumran in a way similar to 1 Enoch and Jubilees. Most scholars date the composition to the late third or early second century B.C.E.

[25]   There are at least six copies and more than four hundred fragments, though the exact numbers are a matter of dispute. See the discussion in Goff, *4QInstruction*, 1–7. See Kampen, *Wisdom*, 40, who states that the manuscripts "point to a widespread use of

similarities with Qumran sectarian texts.[26] Like most wisdom compositions, Instruction does not have a clear structure, nor does it contain a definable internal logic or thematic progression.[27] Because of this, establishing the original order of the composition, or treating the pericope in a given order, is not necessary.[28] Although largely regarded as a wisdom composition and discussed from within the sapiential traditions of Jewish literature, much recent attention has been paid to the use of apocalyptic motifs that potentially place it upon a specific trajectory from within sapiential traditions.[29]

---

the text in the second half of the first century B.C.E., a period of extensive activity at the Qumran site and in the development of Jewish sectarian movements in Judea."

[26]   Goff, *4QInstruction*, 28–29. Daryl Jefferies, *Wisdom at Qumran: A Form-Critical Analysis of the Admonitions in 4QInstruction* (Piscataway, N.J.: Gorgias, 2002), 319–24, views the text as sectarian but not necessarily from Qumran itself. Kampen, *Wisdom*, 23, argues that most wisdom texts found at Qumran, including Instruction, are not sectarian in nature. They are examples of a particular trajectory of wisdom literature in Second Temple Judaism that sectarian authors found useful for interpretation and development.

[27]   Establishing structure and themes is made difficult by the fragmentary nature of the manuscripts. See Benjamin G. Wold, *4QInstruction: Divisions and Hierarchies* (STDJ 123; Leiden: Brill, 2018), 8, who notes that, after reconstructing the manuscripts, only about 30 percent of the original document survives. See Samuel L. Adams, *Wisdom in Transition: Act and Consequence in Second Temple Instructions* (SJSJ; Leiden: Brill, 2008), 217, who points out that though there is little apparent flow between sections, many of the individual units have an internal coherence.

[28]   See Daniel J. Harrington, *Wisdom Texts from Qumran* (London: Routledge, 1996), 40. See also Kampen, *Wisdom*, 39, who states, "A systematic reconstruction of a unified text incorporating all of the fragments is not possible." This has certainly not discouraged attempts to provide a structure for the text. Efforts began with DJD 34. Other notable attempts include Torleif Elgvin, "The Reconstruction of Sapiential Work A," *RevQ* 16 (1995): 559–80, and Eibert J. C. Tigchelaar, *To Increase Learning for the Understanding Ones: Reading and Reconstructing the Fragmentary Early Jewish Sapiential Text 4QInstruction* (Leiden: Brill, 2001). Benjamin G. Wold, *Women, Men, and Angels* (Tübingen: Mohr Siebeck, 2005), 38, notes that some value derives from these reconstructions. For example, many scholars agree that 4Q416 1 is the likely introduction to the document, and 4Q423 is located near the end. This means that the document would open with reflections on creation and the ordering of the cosmos and conclude with a section that rewrites Gen 2–4, increasing the likelihood that creation narratives are important for the text.

[29]   Significant studies detailing the merger between wisdom and apocalyptic in Instruction include Goff, *Heavenly Wisdom*, 28; 216–19, who argues that Instruction's author was steeped in the traditional wisdom of Israel but merged this wisdom with apocalyptic elements based on the influence of a trajectory of wisdom literature in the Second Temple period that finds other possible examples in some Enochic literature and sectarian texts at Qumran. The apocalyptic worldview was used by the author to provide a theological context to how the text's addressees should understand life and acquire wisdom. See also Adams, *Wisdom*, 273–77, who analyzes Proverbs, Ecclesiastes, Sirach, and Instruction, and argues for a steady "eschatologizing" of wisdom over time, toward a greater use of mystery language and concern for the afterlife and an otherworldly inheritance. Kampen, *Wisdom*, 44, on the relationship of apocalyptic to

Instruction is similar in form and content to wisdom texts, such as Sirach and parts of Proverbs,[30] and shares many thematic, linguistic, and theological features with apocalyptic compositions such as those found within the Enochic literature, though there are important differences between Instruction and each of these compositions.[31] Instruction is replete with instances of inheritance language, which makes it an ideal starting point for discussions regarding inheritance in the Dead Sea Scrolls. As Eibert J. C. Tigchelaar notes, נחלה is disproportionately frequent in Instruction, appearing more than thirty-five times versus just over forty-five instances for the rest of the Qumran literature combined.[32] Many of these instances intersect with several of the themes that scholars identify as the most important in the book. In order to provide context, an outline of some of the most important themes is offered here prior to analyzing passages featuring inheritance language.

4.1.1.1. Major Themes

1. The *raz nihyeh*

The רז נהיה, translated for this study as "the mystery of existence," is widely considered the most important concept in Instruction.[33] While

---

wisdom, states, "All the evidence points to Instruction as an early and significant work in a particular trajectory of wisdom literature in Second Temple Judaism." On page 23, he argues that this trajectory did not emerge out of a sectarian consciousness but was already existent when sectarian identity developed at Qumran. John J. Collins, *Scriptures and Sectarianism* (Tübingen: Mohr Siebeck, 2014), 252, argues that the debate on the origins of apocalyptic within wisdom literature is misleading. He argues that certain compositions, such as Instruction, were constructed from a diverse range of genres and themes and pulled from many different sources, so that the writer(s) of Instruction was influenced simultaneously by traditional biblical wisdom and apocalyptic motifs. Both traditions were well enough developed by the time Instruction was written.

[30]   Harrington, *Wisdom*, 40; Kampen, *Wisdom*, 36.

[31]   For a comparison of Instruction with 1 Enoch, see Loren T. Stuckenbruck, "4QInstruction and the Possible Influence of Early Enochic Traditions: An Evaluation," in *Wisdom Texts from Qumran and the Development of Sapiential Thought* (Leuven: Leuven University Press, 2002), 245–62. For a comparison with Sirach, see Daniel J. Harrington, "Two Early Jewish Approaches to Wisdom: Sirach and Qumran Sapiential Work A," *JSP* 16 (1997): 263–75.

[32]   Tigchelaar, *To Increase Learning*, 239. This takes into account the occurrences of overlapping manuscripts.

[33]   The translation of the phrase is not settled. *DSSR* has "the mystery that is to come." Goff, *Heavenly Wisdom*, 33–34, briefly describes various ways that the phrase has been translated. He lands on "the mystery that is to be" to emphasize the temporal sense of the phrase without incorrectly implying an exclusively future sense. Wold, *4QInstruction*, 3, translates the phrase "the mystery of existence," using lexicography, grammar, and syntax to argue that this best captures the breadth of the scope of the mystery, which "indicates temporal meaning that spans the entire plan of God from creation

the phrase has been the subject of much discussion, space precludes a description of the full range of possibilities as to its meaning and use.[34] Our purposes here are served by a general description of the meaning as agreed upon by most scholars.

Adams notes an important way that Instruction develops wisdom beyond the content of Proverbs and Sirach: first, by incorporating an otherworldly expectation into an ethical framework and second, by replacing "the fear of the Lord" as the focal point for learning wisdom with "the mystery of existence."[35] The term רז appears in Daniel and 1 Enoch, where it signifies "the revelation of divine knowledge and secrets" or the mysteries of the heavenly realm. The רז נהיה extends this to include the entirety of the creative work of God, positioning and rein-terpreting traditional wisdom within an apocalyptic milieu.[36] Although some instances of the phrase point toward exclusively future realities, other instances describe the unfolding of events throughout the ages in the past, present, and future (4Q418 123 ii 3–4).[37] As Adams states, the רז נהיה in Instruction appears to describe "God's eternal relationship with the universe, including the capacity for judgment."[38] The heart of the concept is an attempt to convey God's control of the cosmos.

"The mystery of existence" signifies the content of learning that must be the focus of the text's addressee. It is to be the object of study and devo-tion, with benefits passed to the addressee as a reward for proper learning and observance. An understanding of the רז נהיה provides the addressee with the knowledge of truth and falsehood, wisdom and folly (4Q417 1 i 6–7).[39] It allows for correct decision-making, opens an awareness of

---

to the end-time." Kampen, *Wisdom*, 48, also translates "the mystery of existence." Most scholars are quick to point out that the phrase is very difficult to render into English, and therefore all translations can be criticized, but I agree with Wold that "the mystery of existence" best captures the central point of the mystery, that it includes God's overall plan for the world, from creation to judgment.

[34]   For extensive discussion see Adams, *Wisdom*, 245–52, Goff, *Heavenly Wisdom*, 31–65.

[35]   Adams, *Wisdom*, 245. Adams translates the phrase "the mystery that is to be." See also Matthew J. Goff, *Discerning Wisdom: The Sapiential Literature of the Dead Sea Scrolls* (Leiden: Brill, 2007), 10, who argues that the רז נהיה and the themes of supernatural revelation and eschatological judgment are more in line with apocalypti-cism than traditional wisdom.

[36]   Although רז appears on its own in some texts, the full phrase רז נהיה appears only in Instruction (over 20x in the extant manuscripts), the Book of Mysteries (2x), and the Community Rule (1x).

[37]   See also Kampen, *Wisdom*, 48, who states of the mystery "The future unfolds as one begins to understand the natural world and the course of human history, which itself is developing in light of an inevitable future."

[38]   Adams, *Wisdom*, 248.

[39]   The text is likely intended for a community, with "the addressee" used as a rhetorical device.

eschatological judgment, and guarantees an eternal reward.[40] It is the content of heavenly wisdom that directly affects human behavior and is the key to a human understanding of the ways of truth and the order of the cosmos. By incorporating the past creation of God, the present behavior of humans, and the future judgment, the רז נהיה is wisdom instruction that provides a meeting place for the heavenly and earthly realms. Again, to quote Adams, an understanding of the רז נהיה gives the addressee "a better understanding of the divine plan, moral discernment, and eternal life."[41]

It is difficult to determine the medium by which the רז נהיה is to be communicated. The addressee is to invest himself in the study of, and adherence to, the mystery. Precisely how the addressee is to access the mystery is as much of a mystery as the mystery itself! Daniel J. Harrington has suggested that the "the mystery of existence" is an extrabiblical body of teaching (so not the Torah),[42] something like the "Instruction of the Two Spirits" in 1QS III 13-IV 26, the "Book of Meditation" referred to in 1QSa I 6–8, or the "Book of Mysteries" (1Q27, 4Q299–301).[43] However, other scholars have pointed out that there is no direct evidence in Instruction that "the mystery of existence" explicitly refers to a written text or group of texts.[44] It is possible that those responsible for the production of Instruction made use of written material in the process of training others in the study

---

[40]   Adams, *Wisdom*, 247.

[41]   Adams, *Wisdom*, 250.

[42]   Much discussion has centered on the relationship of the Torah to Instruction and the רז נהיה. Wold, *4QInstruction*, 146–95, argues that Torah is subordinate to, and supplanted by, "the mystery of existence." The author is familiar with Torah, and makes use of certain passages, but it is not of central importance and it is not thematized. Goff, *Discerning Wisdom*, 28–29, argues that the author considered Torah a source of wisdom but that there is not enough evidence to insist that the author considered it authoritative. He agrees with Wold that Torah is not a theme in its own right but states that it is assumed as a valid source of teaching. This makes it similar to the approach to Torah found in 1 Enoch and is contrasted with the view of Sirach. See also Kampen, *Wisdom*, 49.

[43]   Harrington, *Wisdom*, 49.

[44]   See John J. Collins, *Jewish Wisdom in the Hellenistic Age* (Louisville: Westminster John Knox, 1997), 123. Goff, *Discerning Wisdom*, 28, argues that, in a loose sense, all of the teachings in 4QInstruction could be considered as aspects of the "mysteries" to be engaged with and learned. Because the mystery is knowledge of all history and the created order, the mystery discloses knowledge about virtually any topic. Wold, *4QInstruction*, 174, argues that while 1 Enoch functions in a way that sees its composition as an aspect of the wisdom to be acquired, this is not the case with 4QInstruction. The text serves a pedagogic function in pointing to the רז נהיה but does not point to itself as an aspect of revelation. Kampen, *Wisdom*, 49, argues that the mystery is at least partly self-referential, suggesting that it includes a study of Instruction itself but that the mystery likely includes "the exploration, appropriation, and development of a unique, comprehensive worldview of which the authors of these texts only provided hints and clues, leaving the reader and/or adherent free to delve further into the revelation of the mystery."

of the mystery, but it could also include a series of other methods and mediums of study, including a mystical component.[45] Regardless of the medium of content, the text is clear that the mystery is passed on through formal and informal teaching, dialogue with neighbors, and instruction within families.[46] John Kampen argues that the mystery is at the very center of the identity of the group associated with Instruction. It is an important part of their oral tradition and is not public knowledge available to anyone but is exclusively available only to those who decide to join the group.[47]

2. Poverty

The addressee is consistently reminded that he is poor (e.g., 4Q416 2 ii 20; 4Q416 2 iii 2; 4Q416 2 iii 8; 4Q416 2 iii 19).[48] Scholarly debate has centered on the nature of this poverty, with arguments ranging from an emphasis on material poverty, spiritual poverty, the address-ee's social position, the addressee's standing with God, or some combination of these.[49] There is no doubt that, in some passages, material poverty is in view. Kampen has observed that poverty in Instruction offers "practical advice with regard to property, marriage, and borrowing money, it is employed to designate the addressee whose social location is one defined by want."[50] Tigchelaar has argued that this

---

[45]   Collins, *Wisdom*, 122, points to the esoteric nature of the mystery; encompassing the fullness of the divine plan, the mystery must be studied now but can only be comprehended in the end time. Adams, *Wisdom*, 251, points out that many scholars are hesitant to assign specific mystical elements to the instruction of the mystery but argues that possibilities include revelation, visionary experiences, meditation, rituals, words from angels, and access to heavenly tablets. Goff, *Discerning Wisdom*, 22, argues that unlike Daniel, where mysteries are disclosed by a heavenly figure, the רז נהיה is not delivered this way. It has already been revealed, and the addressee has a responsibility to gaze upon, grasp, meditate upon, and examine it.

[46]   Adams, *Wisdom*, 251–52. Kampen, *Wisdom*, 27, highlights the role of the teacher and student in the communication of the mystery. Unlike hierarchical teacher/student relationships found in Qumran texts, the relationship here appears entirely instructive. The teacher is tasked with instructing in basic issues of theology and history and advancing the understanding of the mystery. To a point, this view is challenged in this study under the discussion regarding 4Q418 81, where is it argued that the sage has an authoritative role within the community.

[47]   Kampen, *Wisdom*, 59.

[48]   The principal term for poverty in the text is מחסור. The term is rare in the Qumran literature, and in the HB is most common to Proverbs. See Kampen, *Wisdom*, 53.

[49]   Important studies on poverty in Instruction include C. M. Murphy, *Wealth in the Dead Seas Scrolls and in the Qumran Literature* (STDJ 40; Leiden: Brill, 2001), 163–209; Goff, *Heavenly Wisdom*, 127–67.

[50]   Kampen, *Wisdom*, 53.

poverty is conditional, meaning that the addressee is not necessarily poor but could become so.[51] Although this is plausible, Benjamin Wold questions this view by pointing out that the text places a present condition of poverty for the addressee in contrast to "nobility" (4Q415 6 2; 4Q418 177 5). As Wold states, these contrasts only make sense if poverty is a present reality and not an eventuality.[52] Goff points out that the text consistently associates the addressee with low social and economic status. Business transactions are discussed with the intent not for wealth, but to meet basic material needs, and the items being traded are modest.[53] The text is not concerned with economic class per se, as it does not criticize the wealthy, nor does it directly address the poor as an economic class, but it does offer a great deal of instruction regarding financial matters, especially regarding debt and surety.

More recent scholarship has centered on the metaphorical use of poverty language in the text. Wold has demonstrated that in some passages poverty places the addressee in contrast with angels. He states, "At times poverty functions as a metaphor for the *mēvîn's* own struggles to perfectly pursue wisdom in relationship to angelic beings."[54] The addressee is reminded through poverty language of his fatigable nature, that human beings are easily weary in their pursuit of wisdom, which stands in contrast to angelic beings who are models to be emulated (4Q418 69 ii).[55] Goff points out that poverty also connotes humility (4Q417 2 i 14), lowly status (4Q416 2 iii 15–16), and at times it represents an ethical ideal rather than an economic one. He argues rightly that this makes the best sense of the repeated use of the "you are poor" formula. The addressee is presumably aware of his material hardship, but the refrain does not only signify his economic realty. It also signifies his need to maintain an ethical disposition and a posture of humility and reverence.[56]

---

[51]   Eibert J. C. Tigchelaar, "The Addressees of 4QInstruction," in *Sapiential, Liturgical and Poetical Texts from Qumran* (STDJ 35; ed. Daniel K. Falk, Florentino García Martínez, and Eileen M. Schuller; Leiden: Brill, 2000), 62–75.

[52]   Wold, *Women*, 28. The contrast between poverty and nobility is discussed below, as this theme is important to some inheritance passages.

[53]   Goff, *4QInstruction*, 23.

[54]   See Wold, *4QInstruction*, 183–84, and Wold, *Women*, 155–56.

[55]   Wold, *4QInstruction*, 193.

[56]   Goff, *4QInstruction*, 25–26. Kampen, *Wisdom*, 25, writes, "The multivalent nature of the poverty and need addressed in the composition reframes the issues in light of heavenly and temporal realities in a manner familiar to us from apocalyptic literature."

3. Determinism and Dualism

Goff is representative of a majority view among scholars that Instruction possesses a deterministic worldview. According to Goff, the text portrays God as arranging in advance a divine plan that includes every deed, and this plan is revealed to the addressee through the רז נהיה. Anyone who studies God's predetermined plan will know how the mystery unfolds.[57] Goff notes the similarities between Instruction, the Community Rule, and the Hodayot to argue that the רז נהיה refers to an overarching divine plan that has been revealed only to the elect. The text possesses an apocalyptic epistemology, a central feature of which is the disclosure of heavenly knowledge to the elect and the assertion that history is ordained to have a predetermined end.[58] Goff argues that inheritance is a key aspect to this apocalypticism and determinism. Rewards and punishments are to be meted out after death, with some inheriting glory, while others inherit iniquity.[59] Everyone has an allotment from God, including angels, with each inheritance portrayed as an aspect of God's divine plan.[60]

Goff's view of determinism in the text appears to stem largely from his interpretation of the "Vision of Hagu" passage (4Q417 1 i 16; which is discussed in more detail below). His comments on this passage contribute to his view that the text possesses a dualistic anthropology based on a "spirit/flesh" dichotomy. Those of a "fleshly spirit" do not have access to the knowledge of good and evil and possess a predisposition toward wickedness. "Fleshly spirit" is a designation for those who are not among the elect, do not have access to divine revelation, and will not survive God's judgment. The "spiritual people," on the other hand, are like the angels. God fashioned them according to the likeness of the angels. They are the elect who receive revelation from God and are tasked with studying it closely. The "spiritual people" represent an ideal of humanity to which the addressee of the text is to aspire.[61] It is important to reiterate that, for Goff, the "spiritual people" and those of "fleshly spirit" represent two separate kinds of humanity, their status delineated by God as an aspect of his determined divine plan.

Despite arguing for a strong determinism and dualism in Instruction, Goff recognizes that the addressee has a responsibility to pursue wisdom and live ethically. The Addressee, writes Goff, "is in control of his own ethical conduct and the author of 4QInstruction wants him to

---

[57]   Goff, *Heavenly Wisdom*, 66–67.
[58]   Goff, *Heavenly Wisdom*, 37–41.
[59]   Goff, *Heavenly Wisdom*, 41.
[60]   Goff, *Heavenly Wisdom*, 67–68.
[61]   Goff, *Discerning Wisdom*, 33–36.

handle this appropriately." The knowledge of good and evil is provided to the addressee through the mystery, due to his elect status, but "His acquisition of the knowledge of good and evil is a sign that he has fulfilled the role that God has established for him." If this paradox between determinism and the effort of the elect is difficult to reconcile, Goff recognizes the difficulty when he writes, "In 4QInstruction the modern categories of free will and determinism are not fully distinct. Although living ethically is the responsibility of the addressee, 4QInstruction's ethical dualism is an aspect of its deterministic mindset."[62]

Goff's attempt at a measured balance between these themes is admirable, but it leaves open some important questions that he does not adequately attempt to answer. For example, as noted here, Goff argues that an inheritance of glory is determined according to God's divine plan and that the "spiritual people" are God's elect, imbued with a similar status to the angels as an aspect of their creation. However, in another place he also argues that the eschatological fate of the addressee is determined by his ethical conduct and that his "salvation" is not automatically guaranteed.[63] The addressee is exhorted to pursue wisdom, meaning he must be included among the elect who have access to revelation, in which case his inheritance should be determined. However, Goff admits that, though the addressee has been established among the elect, his ultimate rewards are not in fact determined, but rather he must earn them. The addressee must imitate the angels to be spared from eschatological judgment, and in fact the threat of judgment is the very thing that motivates the elect to pursue righteousness.[64] This seemingly disparate presentation of outcomes for the addressee stems from Goff's careful reading of separate pericope throughout the text, but Goff does not quite do enough to reconcile how a text can truly be described as deterministic and dualistic if outcomes remain conditional upon the addressee's actions. It might be enough to reconstruct Goff's view in this way:

> The "spiritual people" are God's elect who, by their elect status, have been created with the status of the angels and given access to the knowledge of good and evil through the mystery. God has determined that the elect have *the opportunity* to acquire an inheritance of glory through the pursuit and acquisition of wisdom and righteousness. The people of "fleshly spirit" are not elect and therefore are not given access to the mystery and do not have *the opportunity* to attain an inheritance of glory. God has determined that theirs is an inheritance of iniquity. The fate and inheritance of both groups is determined by

---

[62]   Goff, *Heavenly Wisdom*, 77–78.
[63]   Goff, *Heavenly Wisdom*, 171.
[64]   Goff, *Heavenly Wisdom*, 205–6.

God's judgment, but God's judgment of the elect is predicated upon the success of the elect in acquiring wisdom and attaining righteousness.

There is, however, a problem with this reconstruction. Goff does not appear to present the inheritance as an opportunity, but rather an inevitability, despite his admission that the addressee must be successful in order to receive eschatological rewards. It is difficult to square these disparate possibilities. Goff's admission of the difficulty is noted, and he is correct to state that we must avoid imposing modern conceptions of determinism and free will upon the text. However, while it is possible that the author(s) of Instruction offer an inconsistent presentation of ideas, it is difficult to believe that they meant to imply that the fate of the elect is both determined and not determined. Goff never argues that Instruction's presentation is inconsistent, nor does he attempt to reconcile these discrepancies.

Adams' views, in some regards, are similar to Goff's, but he also offers some important differences to Goff in the way he nuances Instruction's presentation. Adams agrees with Goff regarding the stark dualistic approach found in the "Vision of Hagu" pericope. He argues that the elect are the "spiritual people," and they alone have access to God and a program for maintaining their elect status. God withholds his wisdom from those of "fleshly spirit" and has done so since creation. Their lack of access to a knowledge of good and evil will impact them negatively at the final judgment. Failure is inevitable for this group, because they lack the ability to make correct choices in life.[65]

While recognizing that Instruction uses language that suggests determinism, Adams argues that both the determinism and the dualism of separate categories of people are less pronounced in Instruction than in Qumran texts such as 1QS. Adams argues that apocalyptic language and inheritance terms lead to an overstatement of determinism in the text. Rather than comparing Instruction's language and apparent categories to 1QS, as does Goff, Adams offers a comparison with Sirach, highlighting the fact that elect status only offers the *prospect* of ultimate deliverance.[66] Instruction does not signify a preordained status or offer an infallible guarantee of fellowship with the heavenly host. Like Sirach, Instruction portrays an intentional ordering of creation and favor toward a particular group (the "spiritual people"), but the text does not offer "a grand theological scheme based on rigid determinism."[67] Like Goff, Adams recognizes that the relationship between free will, determinism,

---

[65]   Adams, *Wisdom*, 256–63.
[66]   Adams, *Wisdom*, 264–67.
[67]   Adams, *Wisdom*, 265.

and divine agency is complex in ancient instruction texts. However, Adams avoids the strength of Goff's pronouncements of determinism as an ardent feature of the text's worldview. Instead, Adams makes the important point that deterministic language in ancient texts often served a pedagogical function to motivate pupils. Rather than a statement of ontology, such language often serves a rhetorical purpose to impress upon a pupil their special status and the way they should behave as a result. It is inclusion and identity language that serves as a framework for human behavior. Adams recognizes that Instruction makes use of deterministic language but is quick to point out that this is mitigated by other passages that indicate human agency and "the ongoing struggle within the heart of each individual." Based on the addressee's choices, he can either enjoy an inheritance of glory, or the inheritance can be forfeited leading to eternal torment.[68]

Wold has offered an extensive critique of the view that Instruction is deterministic and dualistic. He argues that the text portrays a distinction between a faithful community "digging laboriously for truth" and a group of "wayward ones who have failed in this task." There is an "in" group and an "out" group, but rather than having their fates determined, Wold argues that the distinction is based entirely on the degree to which individuals have sought and obtained understanding. Wold writes, "On the extreme end of the spectrum are those who have simply rejected the pursuit of wisdom, which results in an 'us' and 'them' scenario. Gradations within the community itself are expressed as individuals who are distinguished from one another based upon the extent to which they have obtained knowledge." In Wold's view, wisdom has been offered to all, and humanity as a whole is tasked with the pursuit of wisdom and the knowledge of good and evil. The distinction between "us" and "them" is a distinction among all humanity, between those who have acted wisely and those who have not.[69] There is no ontological distinction between types of humans, which provides greater weight to the warnings regarding the dangers of foolish choices. There are those from within the "in" group who are in danger of corrupting their spirit.[70] For Wold, this is one reason that the comparison between angels and humanity is so important. Angels never tire in their pursuit of truth. By comparison, humans are fatigable and in danger of falling away. One must always choose truth and seek righteousness. Wold argues that even the designations of "fleshly spirit" and "spiritual people" have been misunderstood. Rather than a "spiritual people," Wold argues that all of

---

[68]   Adams, *Wisdom*, 267.
[69]   Wold, *4QInstruction*, 18–19.
[70]   Wold, *4QInstruction*, 22.

humanity is in possession of a "spirit," but this spirit becomes "fleshly" when an individual is wayward and dispossessed of revealed wisdom. There is no ontological or predetermined distinction.[71] The wicked were originally fashioned to pursue righteousness and can be lifted from sinful mortality and separated from the "fleshly spirit" to a place with the righteous community, where they can enjoy God's secret counsel and receive God as an inheritance.[72] All eschatological judgment and reward is rooted in human activity.[73]

Each of these major themes—the "mystery of existence," poverty, and determinism and dualism—are featured prolifically throughout the composition. Though it is possible that deterministic and dualistic language is present for rhetorical reasons without making declarations regarding ontology, it must be emphasized that the issue regarding the presence or absence of determinism and dualism constitutes two entirely opposing ways to read Instruction. These themes will be carefully addressed through the analysis of inheritance terms in the text, and conclusions regarding these themes will be reserved for the end of the chapter at the conclusion of the analysis.

4.1.1.2. Instances of Inheritance in Instruction

There are nearly forty instances of inheritance terms in Instruction, but many of these are found in fragments that are far too damaged to contribute much to the discussion regarding the text's presentation of inheritance concepts.[74] Some of these fragments will be used for reference, but the major focus of the discussion will center on some of the larger fragments that have been important for scholars' understanding of the text.

1. 4Q416 2 ii[75]

This section is concerned with financial and material lack. God has the ability to extinguish life but chooses instead to be charitable. This charity does not bring abundance, but the text states that God is reliable to fulfill basic needs, and the addressee should be satisfied with what God

---

[71]   Wold, *4QInstruction*, 106.
[72]   Wold, *4QInstruction*, 75–78.
[73]   Wold, *4QInstruction*, 112.
[74]   See, for example, 4Q418 185a+b2, which refers to inheritance twice, including the phrase "inheritance of glory," as well as 4Q418 251 1, which refers to the "inheritance of Adam." Both of these phrases have important parallels in Instruction, but these fragments are far too damaged to be informative for exegesis.
[75]   4Q416 2 is the most substantial body of text, which remains in four columns, some of them rather full.

has provided. The passage concerns the addressee's debt to creditors but not because he borrowed on his own behalf; the addressee has performed an act of mercy and gone into debt on behalf of a neighbor who was in need (4Q416 2 ii 5). The passage cautions against such surety due to the consequences of what would befall the addressee should the neighbor not make good on the debt. If the addressee goes surety, and the neighbor defaults, this could lead the addressee into difficult financial circumstances.[76] Such financial difficulty is not an excuse to neglect "the mystery." Even in poverty the addressee is encouraged that the mystery must be pursued and observed (4Q416 2 ii 8–9).[77]

Line 6 states that the addressee must not "exchange" (מור) his "holy spirit" (רוח קודשכה) for a price. This is reiterated in lines 17–18, where the addressee is instructed not to sell his soul for money and that for no price should he sell his "glory" (כבד) or "inheritance" (נחלה). Goff argues that the loan, and its repayment, is of principal concern. The addressee is to speak honestly and directly with his neighbor, not the creditor, to stress the importance of repaying the loan so that the addressee can get his own treasures back.[78] Goff argues that the thrust of the passage is not only that unsound financial entanglements can threaten the addressee's financial well-being but also that such entanglements can lead to the loss of his elect status.[79] The addressee has a privileged place with God and a status among the angels, which is conveyed by reference to his "holy spirit," a phrase in Qumran literature that signifies the elect status of members of the Qumran community.[80] The selling of this status through surety means that the addressee's elect status is not guaranteed but predicated upon observing the teachings of the text, which includes avoiding surety.[81] However, on this point Goff's argument lacks clarity. At one point Goff argues that the passage is not written to the addressee to warn

---

[76]   See Goff, *4QInstruction*, 73–77, for a discussion on debt slavery and indebtedness in early Judaism.

[77]   Benjamin G. Wright, "The Categories of Rich and Poor in the Qumran Sapiential Literature," in *Sapiential Perspectives: Wisdom Literature in Light of the Dead Sea Scrolls* (ed. John J. Collins, Gregory E. Sterling, and Ruth Clements; STDJ 51; Leiden: Brill, 2004), 113–14, commenting on this passage and others in Instruction, argues that dealing with creditors and debt is one of the principal concerns of the entire text and that this likely reflects the social world of the author(s). In Wright's view, a major concern is the addressee remaining on equal social footing with his creditors.

[78]   Goff, *4QInstruction*, 72, finds a parallel with Prov 6:3, "So do this, my child, and save yourself, for you have come into your neighbor's power: go, hurry, and plead with your neighbor."

[79]   Similar is Wright, "Categories," 114, who states that for the addressee "by giving up his purse he has given away his life."

[80]   Goff, *4QInstruction*, 73.

[81]   Goff, *4QInstruction*, 72–73.

him of the *possibility* and dangers of becoming a debt-slave through surety but written as though this circumstance has already come into fruition.[82] Therefore, becoming a debt-slave through surety has cost him the freedom of his body, but he must *also* avoid selling his soul, causing him to forfeit his elect status.[83] At another point, Goff appears to argue that the addressee would forfeit his elect status (his glory and inheritance) through the act of going surety in itself.[84] Goff's account of the passage leaves a lack of clarity as to what exactly in the circumstances described would cause the addressee to lose his status. According to Goff, the text instructs that the addressee, because of his connection to the heavenly world, is to serve well in his role as a debt-slave, but Goff does not clarify well enough if failure in this task, or the act of becoming a debt-slave in the first place, will lead to the loss of elect status.[85] Furthermore, Goff does not clarify how, in a dualistic understanding of the text, a person can be born among the elect and share a status with the angels and yet forfeit that status through financial entanglements.

Wold offers a different reading. Although the root word מור does invoke a financial transaction (the addressee should not "exchange" his holy spirit for a price), the financial aspects are less of a concern than the behavior of the addressee toward his neighbor. The addressee is warned not to belittle his own spirit through improper speech toward his neighbor (1. 6). He must maintain healthy relations with his neighbor in the midst of complex financial circumstances. It is not going surety or becoming a debt-slave that are the primary ways one exchanges his holy spirit but rather "how one attends to a relationship with a fellow member of the community when dealing with poverty." Preserving a neighbor's dignity and coming to their aid in need are valuable acts, but when entanglements arise, the addressee must behave in a way befitting one who holds a heavenly status.[86]

Wold's reading has much to support it. The passage is concerned at multiple points with the behavior of the addressee toward others. Line 3 instructs the addressee not to make the poor stumble because of their poverty and instructs him to hide his face because of the poor person's

---

[82]   Goff, *4QInstruction*, 84, "Since this passage is written to a debt-slave, line 17 may also mean that one should not exchange his soul *in addition to* having already handed over his body (to a creditor) to work as a slave" (emphasis his). See Harrington, *Wisdom*, 46, who argues that the text itself is unclear: "Whether this refers to going into debt or selling oneself into slavery is not clear; perhaps the latter is only the extreme case of the former."

[83]   Goff, *4QInstruction*, 84.

[84]   Goff, *4QInstruction*, 85.

[85]   Goff, *4QInstruction*, 85.

[86]   Wold, *4QInstruction*, 137–38.

shame. This is likely done to secure the poor person's dignity. Kampen argues that "holy spirit" in line 6 is about "the spirit of your holiness," referring not to elect status but rather retaining integrity and "their own spiritual identity." He argues that a "holy spirit" is resident in each person engaged in the process of learning discernment.[87] Line 7 instructs the addressee to seek the presence of his neighbor through proper speech in order to find favor with him, and by so doing the addressee will conduct himself well. In this sense, it is not that the addressee must avoid exchanging his holy spirit for money in itself, but rather that financial entanglements, regardless of the price involved, are not worth compromising the addressee's right conduct toward others.[88]

This theme of right conduct continues throughout the passage. The addressee is instructed to work well for his creditor (l. 9), with humility and leaving none of his work undone (l. 10). The addressee is not to debase himself before one who is less than he, so that he may become like a father to those beneath him. If the addressee were to smite one beneath him, it would lead to his own shame (l. 16). The addressee is instructed not to attempt to live above his means (ll. 19–20) and to honor his own wife (l. 21). The conduct of the addressee toward others is far more of a concern in the passage than the material results of his poverty, and it is through improper conduct, not his compromised financial situation, that the addressee is in danger of exchanging his holy spirit for a price. The material aspects are important: the greater the level of financial loss and hardship for the addressee, the greater the risk of the addressee falling into improper conduct as a response to that hardship. This is signified by the fact that the addressee is also warned of the opposite reaction; he is instructed not to esteem himself highly because of his poverty, taking pride in his impoverished state as though it were a badge of honor (l. 20). If the addressee pursues wisdom and observes the instruction regarding his conduct, economic and otherwise, then he will not lose his glory or inheritance. This is the reason that maintaining a focus on the mystery despite his poverty is so important. Even in poverty the addressee can observe the "mystery of existence" and conduct himself with wisdom toward others, maintaining his glory and inheritance.[89]

---

[87]   Kampen, *Wisdom*, 67, appears to relate the line entirely to behavior and does not address "elect status" at all in relation to this column.

[88]   So Kampen, *Wisdom*, 70, the lines are an injunction that the addressee "not abandon his own principles."

[89]   See Adams, *Wisdom*, 254, a person's status does not negate their ongoing need to study the mystery and become a wiser person. The addressee must exercise restraint in daily activities and gaze upon the mystery.

How are we to interpret the terms "glory" and "inheritance"? Goff understands inheritance terms in Instruction through the rubric of determinism and dualism. They are terms that signify elect status. However, the fact that the addressee can forfeit these things through unwise behavior at least opens the possibility that these terms refer to real world circumstances rather than to anthropological nature.[90] There is one possibility that neither Goff nor Wold explores that functions as a *via media* between certain aspects of their arguments regarding this column. With Wold, the instruction that the addressee not "exchange his holy spirit" has ethical connotations; the addressee is to conduct himself wisely and ethically toward all with whom he comes into contact. However, with Goff, the column reads most clearly if the addressee's conduct toward debtors and the possibility of debt-service are a primary concern. I submit that, if נפש in line 17 refers to the self, then the context of line 17 is best read to refer to the addressee's *vocation* in particular—the addressee is to regard himself as a servant in *spirit only*, but in body he is to serve freely. Lines 18–19 flow logically from this concern; to sell one's "glory" and "inheritance" is to exchange one's status as a free worker and bring ruin on one's own body. One's vocation is one's status, and to enter debt-slavery is to have this status removed. This also makes the best sense of line 15, wherein the addressee is told not to lower himself to "whatever is not worthy of you," as well as lines 18–21, where he is instructed to live within his means and not to overindulge in ways that might compromise his ability to maintain the free status of his vocation.

In order to justify this reading, it is important to establish that terms for "glory" and "inheritance" often refer to vocation, status according to earthly circumstances, and one's financial position. Precisely such arguments have been made by Haley Goranson Jacob. Jacob argues that, in the majority of instances where כבוד is associated with mankind, it refers to honor, repute, respect, esteem based on earthly possessions, the importance of one's achievements, or the virtue and qualities of one's character (Gen 45:13; Job 19:19: Ps 49:16-17).[91] Glory often relates to vocational status with royal figures (Ps 8:5) but is also used in direct correlation with the activities of hired workers (Isa 16:14;

---

[90]   Reward and punishment is certainly within the purview of the text. See Cana Werman, "What Is the Book of Hagu?" in Collins et al., *Sapiential Perspectives*, 131, who argues that one of the tasks of the addressee is to survey the scope of history in order to understand the way that punishment and reward had been meted out for human conduct in the past. This would direct the addressee toward proper behavior and qualify him for his own rewards.

[91]   Haley Goranson Jacob, *Conformed to the Image of His Son: Reconsidering Paul's Theology of Glory in Romans* (Downers Grove, Ill.: IVP Academic, 2018), 29.

21:16). Jacob states, "In association with mankind and objects, the noun כבוד means riches, material greatness, and honor."[92] Jacob argues that the situation is largely the same when considering the use of δόξα in the LXX and NT.[93]

It is important to recognize the way in which glory relates to inheritance, considering the close relationship between the two in Instruction. Two illustrative examples are discussed in this study. The first example, found in 1 Sam 2:1-10, refers to Yahweh, who makes poor and rich, who brings low and exalts (2:7). 1 Samuel 2:8 states that Yahweh "raises the poor from the dust," and makes them "sit with nobles and inherit a seat of glory" (כסא כבוד ינחלם). To inherit glory/honor in this passage is to have one's status elevated from poverty to nobility.[94] The second example is found in Sir 4:13-15, which states that the one who holds fast to wisdom "inherits glory" (κληρονομήσει δόξαν, 4:13). Those who inherit glory will take on a position of authority and judge the nations (4:15).[95] A third example is argued by Jacob that, in Dan 12:1-13, glory is tied to an allotted inheritance that constitutes a reward or the reception of honor as an exalted status rather than an indicator of resplendence or anthropological nature. This is one of the rare instances in Daniel in which glory does not refer to rule or governance (i.e., vocation) but rather refers to those who will rise to eternal life rather than shame.[96] As seen below, the ideas of eternal life versus shame also take up residence in glory and inheritance contexts within Instruction. But the point remains: terms for glory in the HB, LXX, and NT are best understood as either indicators of earthly status and circumstances, or as rewards, and not as elect status or other anthropological realities.

It is possible to argue that an elevated status based on wealth would likely not fit the context of Instruction, considering the predominant theme regarding poverty and the fact that the addressee appears to be of relatively modest means. However, this consideration must be placed within the concerns of Instruction's theology, which does not consider wealth to be a particular virtue. In the context of this column, the important point for the addressee is, first, that he maintain a life of proper ethical conduct toward those with whom he comes into contact. Second, the addressee must maintain independence and economic freedom not for the purpose of material glory for its own sake but rather that he maintain the glory of the status afforded to a free person working within

---

[92] Jacob, *Conformed*, 31–32.
[93] Jacob, *Conformed*, 33.
[94] See 2.3.2.
[95] See 3.2.
[96] Jacob, *Conformed*, 57–58.

the inheritance of his vocation so that he is unhindered in his pursuit of the "mystery of existence." If the addressee is able to obtain wisdom in keeping with the mystery, then according to Instruction's particular theology this is where true glory and elevated status is found. Further investigation into glory and inheritance concepts throughout the rest of the composition is required before we can confirm this theory.

2. 4Q416 2 iii 5–12

In the following column, the theme of concern regarding financial entanglements continues. Lines 1–3 are likely in continuity with 4Q416 2 ii, which dealt with poverty. The term רש (poor) appears in the passage several times (ll. 6, 11, 12, 15, 19, 20), and the passage begins with the refrain וזכור כי ראש אתה (remember that you are poor). Such reminders of the addressee's poverty appear a number of times (ll. 2, 8, 12, 19).[97] In some sense this repeated refrain is meant to signify the addressee's material lack, but as seen below, in this passage it likely also serves as a metaphor for nonmaterial concerns.

Line 5 begins a new unit with the term וגם (and also). The addressee is told not to receive loans from those he does not know, but if he does, he is to take charge of repaying the loan so that his spirit is not corrupted (l. 6). If the addressee handles the loan properly in life, then in death he will "inherit joy" (ll. 7–8). Like 4Q416 2 ii, it is not the loan itself that corrupts the addressee's spirit but rather the addressee's lack of faithfulness in exhibiting right behavior in his dealings with others. If he deals well with his creditors, then he can die with the truth and be remembered well in death (l. 7).[98] As Goff states, the goal is that the addressee "enjoy a good death, with his reputation intact as an upright person."[99]

In lines 7–8, the phrase ואחריתכה תנחל שמחה (and in the end you shall inherit joy) has a few potential meanings. The term אחריתכה literally means "your end." Strugnell and Harrington translate the term as "your posterity," implying that it is the children of the addressee who inherit joy, rather than the addressee himself.[100] The further implication is that inheriting joy is the state of relief from the burden of the debt, since the addressee has taken care of the debt in his own lifetime. This

---

[97]   Goff, *4QInstruction*, 95.

[98]   As with the previous section, Goff, *4QInstruction*, 99, asserts that the financial entanglement in question could cause the addressee to forfeit his elect status. However, in this section Goff is clear that it is the lack of repayment of the loan, and not the loan itself, that is of greatest concern. He argues that repayment of the loan "helps him maintain his dignity and self-worth while in a difficult situation of indebtedness."

[99]   Goff, *4QInstruction*, 100.

[100]   *DSSR*, 97.

interpretation is unlikely, as the surrounding lines concern the death and reputation of the addressee and do not otherwise portray a concern for his surviving family members. Furthermore, the other uses of the root נחל in this passage clearly refer to the inheritance of the addressee rather than his posterity. The term could be rendered something like "in the end," which would highlight the eschatological aspects of Instruction, and the inheritance of joy would refer to a spiritual state after judgment.[101] While possible, line 7 appears concerned with the state of the addressee at the time of his death. The line could be read to separate the state of his remembrance shortly after his death from the inheritance of joy as a post-judgment condition, but the exact timing of the inheritance in this line is unclear.

While it is possible that to "inherit joy" is simply to be remembered well in death, a comparison with other passages suggests that the benefit being presented to the addressee is one of continued life after death. This appears to be the meaning of many inheritance passages in Instruction. Furthermore, 4Q417 2 i 10–12 promises the addressee "eternal joy," which is clearly a reference to eternal life. 4Q418 126 ii 7–8 promises to raise up the heads of the poor in "glory everlasting and peace eternal." This has led Collins to state of this passage and others in Instruction that "There seems little doubt that the elect are promised a blessed after-life."[102] If the addressee conducts himself well in his affairs, in terms of his behavior toward those in which he is engaged, then he will inherit joy in the afterlife.[103] Collins offers "in your hereafter" as a possible translation of אחריתכה, which highlights this dynamic. The text portrays a blessed afterlife for the addressee signified by the phrase "inherit joy."[104]

Lines 8–12 make up a unit, and line 8 once again reminds the addressee that he is poor. Interpreting lines 8–10a depends largely on how one translates certain prepositions and pronouns. It is helpful to compare the translations of Strugnell and Harrington, Goff, and Wold to survey some of the possibilities.

[101]   See Adams, *Wisdom*, 230.

[102]   John J. Collins, "The Eschatologizing of Wisdom in the Dead Sea Scrolls," in Collins et al., *Sapiential Perspectives*, 56.

[103]   Similar is Sir 7:32-36, where the reader is instructed to remember the end of his life. Considering his own end will decide the way in which he treats people while living.

[104]   Collins, "Eschatologizing," 56. Collins argues that this fits within the text's frequent comparisons with angels and does not include any sense of bodily resurrection. Collins compares these passages with Jub 23:31, which states, "their bodies will rest in the earth and their spirits will have much joy." Similar is Goff, *4QInstruction*, 100, who refers to "inherit joy" as "The anticipation of postmortem rewards," and Adams, *Wisdom*, 230–31, who states that the addressee receives "heavenly existence with the angels."

8 שמחה vacat אביון אתה אל תתאו זולת נחלתכה ואל תתבלע בה פן תסיג

9 גבולכה ואם ישיבכה לכבודכה התהלך וברז נהיה דרוש מולדיו ואז תדע

10a נחלתו

Strugnell and Harrington's translation states:

> 8. joy. *vacat* Thou art needy; do not desire something beyond thy *share/inheritance*, and be not *thou confused* by it, lest *thou* displace
>
> 9. thy boundary. *But if* (men) *restore thee to splendor* (?), walk in *it* (i.e., in thy נחלה) and *by* the רז that is to come study *the origins* thereof (i.e., of the mystery). And then thou shalt know
>
> 10a. what is *allotted to it*[105]

Strugnell and Harrington's rendering in *DSSR* infers that, despite the material poverty of the addressee, he must not desire any means other than his own share. If he does, then the boundary of his share may be moved, potentially implying a loss of the share he already possesses. However, other humans may restore the inheritance of the addressee, and if they do, he should walk in this restored inheritance. The addressee must also study the mystery to discover its origins. In this rendering of the passage, it is unclear how the mystery and its origins is connected to the inheritance, and the inheritance appears to refer predominately to the material/financial status of the addressee.

Goff translates:

> 8. joy. *vacat* You are poor, desire nothing except your inheritance. And do not be confused about it lest you move
>
> 9. your boundary. And if he restores you to glory, walk in it and through the mystery that is to be study its origins. And then you will know
>
> 10a. its inheritance.[106]

As Goff does throughout the composition, he argues that the inheritance in this passage is not the reception of goods or material wealth, but rather it signifies the elect status of the addressee.[107] Likewise, the poverty of the addressee is not only material but also signifies his

---

[105] *DSSR*, 97. All italics and parentheses are theirs.

[106] Goff, *4QInstruction*, 93.

[107] See Jean-Sébastien Rey, *4QInstruction: Sagesse et eschatologie* (STDJ 81; Leiden: Brill, 2009), 56–57, 102, who argues that the inheritance is both material wealth and holiness allocated to the addressee.

status through various circumstances discussed throughout the text. The text consistently indicates that the addressee should not let his circumstances keep him from studying the mystery.[108] Goff argues that the antecedent of "its origins" is "glory." *Contra* Strugnell and Harrington, the addressee is not to study the mystery to discover the origins of the mystery itself but rather to discover the origins and nature of his own elect status, referred to here as his inheritance and glory. By studying the mystery, the addressee can know if he is included among the elect and is qualified for an inheritance established for him before his birth.[109] Goff's view is deterministic and dualistic. Because the inheritance of glory was reserved for the addressee before his birth, he is qualitatively different from the wicked who cannot attain to the inheritance of glory.[110]

Goff argues that although the addressee's elect status is appointed to him, and although he can know the nature of his status by studying its origins, the terms "inheritance" and "glory" also signify postmortem rewards that in some measure are meted out in response to the addressee's ability to live according to the teachings of the mystery while living. The exhortation to understand the inheritance "lest you move your boundary" derives from passages in the HB discussed in chapter 2 of this study (cf. Deut 19:14; 27:17).[111] Because Instruction shows no concern for inherited land boundaries described in the Hexateuch, Goff argues that the text reformulates this tradition as a metaphor to teach the addressee to remain within his assigned elect status. This implies that, through improper action, this status can be moved. For Goff, these lines are not hypothetical instruction should the addressee falter in his actions, but rather they indicate that the addressee has already faltered. Rather than humans restoring the addressee, as Strugnell and Harrington have rendered the passage, it is God who restores the addressee to his glory.[112] When he does, the addressee has a responsibility to התהלך (walk) according to his inheritance as described by the mystery. This return to

---

[108]   Goff, *4QInstruction*, 100.

[109]   Goff, *4QInstruction*, 102–3.

[110]   Goff, *4QInstruction*, 102–3. Goff argues that the addressee can understand his elect status by knowing his own origins, meaning the time of his birth. His ultimate fate is predetermined by his own birthtime. Matthew Morgenstern, "The Meaning of בין מולדים in the Qumran Wisdom Texts," *JJS* 51 (2000): 141–44, provides support for this view using ancient horoscopes. Kampen, *Wisdom*, 109–10, argues that it is possible that these references to horoscopes are not as significant for Instruction as has been assumed and that the terminology in this fragment may refer to "origins" rooted in creation rather than birthtimes. This is the view of Wold, *Women*, 88.

[111]   See 2.2.1.1.

[112]   See also Wright, "Categories," 115, who argues persuasively for this position.

glory is not only about eternal life and postmortem rewards but about the ability of the addressee to live righteously according to his status.[113] Wold translates:

8. joy. *vacat* You are poor, do not desire anything except your inheritance, and do not be confused by it, lest you move

9. your boundaries, and if He has restored you to glory, walk in it, and by the mystery of existence seek its origins/birthtimes, and then you will know

10a. its inheritance.[114]

The translations of Goff and Wold are very similar, but they diverge in their position on some important points. Wold does not read Instruction in a deterministic or dualistic manner, meaning that "inheritance" and "glory" are not representative of elect status, and seeking "its origins" through study of the mystery has nothing to do with the birthtimes and appointed status of the addressee. Wold appeals to the end of the fragment, in lines 15–18, where he argues that the fragment teaches dual creators over the formation of humanity. In the same way that a father and a mother both take part in the natural birth of a person, God and the angels both have a role in the creation of that person as well.[115] Therefore, Wold argues, the exhortation to study one's origin in line 9 does not refer to the need to understand the time of one's birth in order to discover whether or not one is elect, but rather it is an exhortation to discover the angelic origins of all of humanity in order to model one's pursuit of wisdom after the nature of the angels. Like the addressee, the angels are tasked with the pursuit of wisdom and the attainment of an inheritance.[116] However, the angels are depicted as indefatigable in their

[113] Goff, *4QInstruction*, 103. Kampen, *Wisdom*, 54, highlights התהלך as a key term in Instruction, featuring 34x in extant fragments and pointing to the ethical standards described in the text.

[114] Wold, *4QInstruction*, 85.

[115] Goff, *4QInstruction*, 110, translates אדנים in line 16 as "the lord." He argues that the passage makes use of a parallelism comparing God to both the father and the mother in order to offer a theological rationale for filial piety. For Goff, it is God alone who creates humankind and the addressee was formed by his parents. Wold, *Women*, 149–55, surveys other ST literature where אדנים is used of angels, and he argues compellingly for a translation of אדנים as "angels." The column is to be understood in light of Gen 1:26, where the plural "us" is a reference to the creation of humankind by the dual participants of God and angels. The plural אדנים, literally "the lords," refers to the angels that served as a pattern by which to fashion humanity (see l. 17). This is heightened by comparison with 4Q417 1 i 17, which more clearly states that humans were fashioned after the pattern of the angels. Kampen, *Wisdom*, 74, follows Wold in translating "angels."

[116] Wold, *Women*, 157.

pursuit.[117] By contrast, humans are deficient and mortal in their pursuit of wisdom. Human conditions and circumstances often pose a threat of distraction toward a pursuit of wisdom, which leads to the warnings in this fragment that poverty must not detract from the study of the mystery. If the addressee pursues the mystery, he will understand that, if God were to restore him to an inheritance of glory, he would have the ability to pursue wisdom in light of his origins, which includes the example of the angels that played a role in his creation.[118]

For Wold, this also explains the poverty of the addressee in this passage. The insistence of the addressee's poverty includes material circumstances but more importantly refers to anthropological concerns; by comparison with the angels, the addressee is fatigable and beset with human limitations.[119] The addressee cannot use these limitations as an excuse to neglect the mystery, but instead he must be vigilant in his pursuit of wisdom and knowledge based upon the model of the angels.

Lines 11–12 provide the most help of any in 4Q416 2 ii–iii toward an understanding of the nature of inheritance in these fragments. Through to the *vacat* in line 12, these lines read, "and always praise His name, for from poverty He lifted your head, and with the nobles He made you to dwell, and in the inheritance of glory He placed you in authority, diligently seek His good will always."[120] Goff and Wold have both argued effectively that the term "nobles" here is a reference to angels.[121] In the midst of the constant reminders that the addressee is poor, he is told that he can walk in righteousness (l. 10), because God has seated him among the angels and lifted him from poverty into an inheritance of glory (ובנחלת כבוד).[122]

Goff's view that the inheritance of glory signifies the elect status of the addressee extends to these lines, where the addressee is to praise God in response to learning of his elect status through the mystery. Being

[117]   Wold, *Women*, 157–61.

[118]   Wold, *Women*, 161, points out that the angels are not depicted as perfect in their pursuit. They are also referred to as poor (4Q416 1). Compared to the fatigable nature of humanity their pursuit is exemplary.

[119]   Wold, *Women*, 180, argues that this reading is substantiated by a comparison with 4Q418 55 and 69, where the fatigable and mortal deficiency of the addressee is stated with more clarity.

[120]   Wold's translation, *4QInstruction*, 86.

[121]   Goff, *4QInstruction*, 105. Wold, *4QInstruction*, 85–90. See also Kampen, *Wisdom*, 76.

[122]   Wright, "Categories," 115–16, is among those who regard the passage as dealing with material poverty and social status among human nobles. He views the actual advancement in social status for the addressee as problematic but argues that the rather than constituting a claim of actual social advancement, the passage expresses confidence that such a circumstance is possible with God.

lifted from poverty is not to be understood as a literal rescue from material hardship, as the addressee is constantly reminded that he is still poor.
Instead, metaphorically speaking, he is wealthy because he has an elect
status. His elect status is more valuable than material wealth. Although
his status is allotted to him now, Goff argues against a "realized eschatology" in the passage; his status will not be fully realized until after
death when he receives eternal life with the angels. In the meantime, the
addressee is to praise God, walk in righteousness, and pursue wisdom
through the mystery.[123]

Wold, like Goff, argues that the addressee's head being lifted from
poverty is metaphorical. His material lack continues, but he has received
a greater status than wealth, namely, a seat among the angels. However, *contra* Goff, Wold does not see here a predetermined status for
the addressee, nor does he see the realization of the addressee's status as entirely eschatological. Poverty takes on a dual meaning: neither
material nor metaphorical poverty is ideal, but metaphorical poverty
functions as a cipher for the fatigable human condition, with the proper
response being a pious and humble attitude. Being lifted from metaphorical poverty is reserved not for an elect group but rather for those
who pursue wisdom, maintain a humble disposition before God, and live
faithfully among those in his community. It is in these engagements that
the addressee enjoys present participation with the angels by pursuing
wisdom in accord with the model of the angels.[124]

There are important questions that Goff's arguments do not adequately address. For example, why would the addressee's knowledge
of his predetermined elect status help him to find favor with God? In
what way would this knowledge change his need to pursue wisdom as
has been instructed by the mystery? Furthermore, the addressee is given
"authority" (l. 12) over his inheritance of glory. If the "inheritance of
glory" signifies elect status, does the addressee gain authority over his
own elect status, or something else? If something else, then what?

The logic of fragments 4Q416 2 ii–iii follows easier if the "inheritance of glory" is understood as both the elevation of the addressee's
present earthly status and a reward for the addressee rather than a signifier of a predetermined elect status. Instructive are comparisons between
4Q416 2 iii 11 and 1 Sam 2:8 discussed above. The similarities in these
lines are striking.

---

[123]   Goff, *4QInstruction*, 104–6. Collins, "Eschatologizing," 57, takes the same
position. He refers to a present participation with the angels as "less than conclusive,"
and considers most passages in *Instruction* "as anticipating future glory, rather than
enjoying it in the present."

[124]   Wold, *4QInstruction*, 90–94.

1 Sam 2:8c reads:

להושיב עם־נדיבים וכסא כבוד ינחלם

4Q416 2 iii 11 reads:

עם נדיבים הושיבכה ובנחלת כבוד המשילכה

In 1 Sam 2:8, it is said that God exalts the poor from the dust and the poor are made "to sit with nobles and inherit a seat of glory." In 4Q416 2 iii 11 God lifts the addressee's head from poverty, and the addressee is told "with the nobles he made you to dwell/sit, and in the inheritance of glory he placed you in authority." As discussed above, to "inherit glory" in 1 Sam 2:8 is to have one's earthly status elevated. It appears best to understand being seated with the nobles in 4Q416 2 iii (angels in this context) as an elevation of earthly status rather than an indicator of predetermined status or nature.

Sirach 4:13-15 is also instructive in understanding 4Q416 2 iii as the elevation of status and the reception of a reward. In Sir 4:13-15, it is the one who pursues wisdom that receives an elevated status of authority. Goff himself has argued that the addressee must be successful in pursuing wisdom and living in accord with the mystery for eternal life to be secured, but when one sees the inheritance as a reward, appeals to deterministic language in these fragments are found unnecessary. If Wold's argument regarding the angelic role in the origins of humanity is proven correct, then appeals to anthropological dualism suffer the same fate. The open questions are best addressed when the fragments are understood to communicate that the addressee must understand his own angelic origins for the purpose of viewing a specific model by which to pursue wisdom. To be given authority over the "inheritance of glory" is to understand that the inheritance of glory is a present participation in a future reward that the addressee has been given stewardship over, a reward granted to the addressee based on his success in pursuing the mystery, living with humility before God, and living well within the community.[125] The purpose of understanding the mystery is not to understand one's predetermined status but rather to understand the difference between truth and iniquity (l. 14). As I argue above, to "inherit joy" is to inherit the rewards of eternal life.[126] There is no reason to view the

---

[125] See Adams, *Wisdom*, 228, who states, "the author implies that the addressee will receive the same 'inheritance' as the angels, *if* he first spends a lifetime honoring them and committing himself to the content of these teachings" (emphasis his).

[126] Adams, *Wisdom*, 229, while using the same deterministic terminology as Goff, agrees that the inheritance is best understood as a reward for behavior when he states, "When considering the text as a whole, the addressee's eternal glory will only follow a righteous existence. A person's earthly behavior determines the true reward, and the 'inheritance of glory' promised to the righteous will more than compensate for current

future aspects of the "inheritance of glory" by other terms. Being seated with the nobles is not granted to one with elect status as signified by the "inheritance of glory," but rather, being seated with the nobles is an aspect of the inheritance itself—the reward of present participation with the angels as an inaugurated aspect of the fuller inheritance, which is eternal life among God and the angels in the afterlife.

The meaning of the phrase "inheritance of glory" in 4Q416 2 ii–iii is potentially clarified when one considers the present vocational aspects of the addressee's circumstances. Kampen offers an insightful summary of lines 8–9 that differs from Strugnell and Harrington, Goff, and Wold in one important regard. Rather than translating the verb בלע as "to confuse," as have the others surveyed here, Kampen argues that the verb can be translated "to be consumed" and that this better fits the context. He argues that these lines portray the paralyzing effects of lust.[127] To lust after wealth that is not available to the addressee will consume him and therefore move his boundary. In his summary, the addressee will move his boundary if his aspirations change and he becomes enamored with his financial position in life. Rather than concern himself with finances, which are in God's hands, the addressee must instead focus on discernment and walking in righteousness. If he does, then God will grant him a place of honor.[128] When interpreting lines 8–13, aspects of Kampen's arguments fit nicely with the view that the inheritance of glory refers in part to the present work with which the addressee has been given by God. The addressee is needy but is not to pursue or be consumed with any role but that which God has given him (l. 8). Rather than cross his boundary due to a desire for financial gain, the addressee should consider his present vocation to be a place of honor and conduct himself accordingly (l. 9). The addressee's vocation has kept him in poverty, but it is one in which he will be honored by others (l. 10) and it has given him a share with the angels (l. 11). The addressee has been given authority over his inheritance of glory, and therefore, despite his poverty, he serves in a vocation that allows him to seek knowledge and the "mystery of existence." The question remains: Are there any indications within Instruction regarding the

---

struggles." On page 242 he further argues that the "inheritance of glory" as a reward for the faithful pupil is a move that the author of Instruction has to make. The present life is beset with material lack, but the inheritance provides an apocalyptic framework for otherworldly prosperity and justice.

[127]   Kampen, *Wisdom*, 73.

[128]   Kampen, *Wisdom*, 57, does however disagree with Wold on the metaphorical and spiritual use of poverty in this passage. He argues instead for a material need on the part of the addressee.

details of this vocation? Further analysis of other columns is required before we can answer that question.

3. 4Q417 1 i

This fragment has been the most influential in developing deterministic and dualistic approaches to Instruction. These issues are important for how we view inheritance both in this passage and in the composition as a whole. The content on this fragment can be broken into four sections: lines 1–5 describe the fact that the "mystery of existence" reveals knowledge of the past, present, and future. Lines 6–13 discuss God's creation of, and plan for, the world. Lines 13–18 discuss the distinction between types of people—those who follow the mystery and those who do not. And lines 18–27 urge the addressee to pursue the mystery and thereby avoid iniquity. As with the previous two fragments, surveying the views of Goff and Wold are instructive in understanding the two major and widely disparate approaches to the issues raised by this passage.

In Goff's view, this passage reiterates the idea that the mystery "contains knowledge about God's orchestration of the cosmos, from creation to judgment."[129] God is sovereign over the whole of history and is executing his divine, predetermined plan. The addressee is tasked with consistent study of the mystery in order to "acquire knowledge about God's mastery over the created order."[130] Goff consistently argues for the passages' portrayal of God's deterministic plan as it relays his control over all the cosmos, including God's plan for final judgment. The mystery not only reveals God's plan, but God made use of the mystery in the act of creation itself (ll. 8–9).[131] A full understanding of creation is available only through supernatural revelation; the mystery "denotes both God's act of creation and the means by which the addressee can attain knowledge of this deed." God's plan is made intelligible to the addressee so that he can successfully live in harmony with it, acting ethically and walking in an upright manner. Line 12 refers to the secrets of God's plan. Goff compares the term מחשבה (plan) to its use in "The Treatise on the Two Spirits" (1QS III:15–16), where he argues that the term is used in a decisively deterministic way.[132]

[129]   Goff, *4QInstruction*, 143.

[130]   Goff, *4QInstruction*, 147.

[131]   Goff, *4QInstruction*, 150–51, relates this to Prov 3:19, where it states that "The Lord by wisdom founded the earth" (NRSV).

[132]   Goff, *4QInstruction*, 153.

A great deal of attention has been paid to lines 13–18, often described as the "Vision of Hagu" passage.[133] Line 14 features an imperative for the addressee to "inherit" his reward, an imperative that Goff understands as relating to the addressee's determined elect status. The reward is the addressee's ability to survive the coming judgment.[134] The nature of the "Vision of Hagu" referred to in line 16 is difficult to determine, but Goff is reasonable to argue that it relates to (or is a veiled reference to) the "mystery of existence."[135] An important question regarding this passage concerns who does and does not have access to the vision. Line 16 states that God has given the vision itself "as an inheritance" (וינחילה) to אנוש עם עם רוח. Goff translates the first instance of עם as the preposition "with," and the second instance of עם as the term "people." He translates this portion of the phrase עם עם רוח as together with a spiritual people. These "spiritual people," he argues, refers to those created in the likeness of angels and are therefore similar to angels. This does not refer to all humans but rather a subset of humanity created with a special, elect status. The term אנוש often refers to "humanity,"[136] but Goff argues that translating the full phrase "humanity together with a spiritual people" is unintelligible. If Goff is correct that the "spiritual people" serves as a category of people and a subset of humanity, then it would make little sense to state that the vision would be given to them if it was given to humanity in general.[137] Goff, following Collins, argues that אנוש is a reference to Adam.[138] In this understanding, Adam was the first to possess knowledge of the vision, and he is often associated in Jewish literature with angels and heavenly knowledge. Due to this model of creation, the "spiritual people," like Adam, have access to the vision and are given the intellectual ability to study and understand it. These "spiritual people" are contrasted with those of "fleshly spirit" (רוח בשר), who were not given access to the knowledge of good and evil (l. 17), keeping them in the dark on God's deterministic plan and forbidding them the ability to

---

[133]   For a brief bibliography of important contributions to the study of this passage, see Goff, *4QInstruction*, 155.

[134]   Goff, *4QInstruction*, 156.

[135]   Goff, *4QInstruction*, 162.

[136]   See *NIDOTTE*, ed. William A. VanGemeren (Grand Rapids: Zondervan, 1997), 1:447 (Victor P. Hamilton).

[137]   Goff, *4QInstruction*, 163.

[138]   See John J. Collins, "In the Likeness of the Holy Ones: The Creation of Humankind in a Wisdom Text from Qumran," in *The Provo International Conference on the Dead Sea Scrolls: Technological Innovations, New Texts, and Reformed Issues* (ed. Donald W. Parry and Eugene Ulrich; STDJ 30; Leiden: Brill, 1999), 609–18. Collins argues on the basis of Gen 1–3 and 1QS III 17. Goff, *4QInstruction*, 163–64, follows Collins. Kampen, *Wisdom*, 101, also follows Collins and states that the term "refers to Adam and the tradition that the knowledge of good and evil originates with the first man."

choose right from wrong. The "spiritual people" have the ability to gain eternal life, while those of "fleshly spirit" do not.[139] For Goff, this is all indicative of the determinism in Instruction, which states that God has set forth a divine plan for all creation, as well as dualism, which argues that God's determined plan extends to the very creation of humans.[140] The designation and status of the "spiritual people," as well as those of "fleshly spirit," is an aspect of their creation. These categories were set at the birth of each individual and their fate was determined at birth. It is only the "spiritual people" who were fashioned after the pattern of the angels, and the people called "fleshly spirit," by their very nature, do not have access to truth nor the ability to understand it.[141]

The final reference to inheritance in the passage comes in line 24, which refers to the "inheritance" of the wicked. The addressee is instructed to live righteously because the wicked will be punished "according to his inheritance." According to Goff, Instruction teaches that each person is given a particular inheritance by God as an aspect of his determined plan and their allotment as either "spiritual" or "fleshly." In other words, the inheritance of the wicked is that they will be judged according to their wickedness, which was established by their birth as an aspect of God's deterministic plan. Goff states that the exhortation to remain ethically vigilant "implies free choice" but that the text "also understands a person's conduct as divinely established."[142]

Wold addresses the apparent "spirit" and "flesh" dichotomy and views the passage very differently than Goff. He argues that the sage at the head of the text writes to a community of students that desire to grow in their understanding of the mystery but that the text deals with a spectrum of students at varying levels of success. Merit plays an important role in one's place within the community, as does one's level of acquisition of wisdom. Wold recognizes that both free will and determinism are present in early Jewish literature, and although these ideas are not to be viewed as incompatible, Instruction does not view people through a determined dualistic anthropology. The categories of the righteous and the wicked are not determined by birth but "by virtue of an individual's acquisition of insight, actualization of wisdom, and a

139   See also Adams, *Wisdom*, 256, who states that those of "fleshly spirit" are "unfortunate souls" who do not have access to knowledge.

140   See also Kampen, *Wisdom*, 100, who states that Instruction "presents two contrasting types of humankind, the spiritual people and the fleshly spirit."

141   Goff, *4QInstruction*, 162–65. See also Collins, "Eschatologizing," 55, who likewise argues that the "spiritual people" are the elect and enlightened, a disposition given to them at their birth. The vision, therefore, is not for humanity at large, or even for all Israel, but only for those whose predetermined lot is eternal life.

142   Goff, *4QInstruction*, 170.

dint of discipline."[143] The concept of deeds is emphasized in connection with the knowledge of good and evil. It is important to understand God's plan through a study of the mystery, but this is not to understand one's own predetermined status. This primarily concerns an understanding of deeds and their consequences and the way those consequences relate to punishment and reward for righteous and foolish behavior (ll. 12–13).[144]

Wold argues that there is no spirit/flesh dichotomy in 4Q417 1 i. He points out that viewing עם רוח as a distinct people group, the "spiritual people," would be a *hapax legomenon* not just in Instruction but in the whole of ancient Hebrew literature. Rather than viewing the עם רוח and the רוח בשׂר as distinct groups of humanity, Wold argues that the text presents them as two distinct types of spirits.[145] As shown above, Goff translates the phrase לאנוש עם עם רוח in line 16 as "to Adam together with a spiritual people," emphasizing that אנוש and the "spiritual people" are distinct from one another. Among Goff's arguments is an attempt to avoid the repetition of viewing אנוש as humanity and then the spiritual people as a subset of humanity, as though the text referred to all of humanity receiving the vision and then clarifying that only the spiritual people had done so. Instead, Goff argues that Adam received the vision, as do the spiritual people designated such at birth.[146] Wold, however, argues that אנוש is best translated as "humanity," which is well attested in Instruction (4Q416 2 ii 12; 4Q418 77 3).[147] He follows Werman in viewing the first עם in this line as attributive of אנוש, and the second עם as the preposition "with." Translating the phrase "people with a spirit," rather than "together with a spiritual people," removes the tautological problem of viewing עם and אנוש separately. Wold translates the phrase "He made humanity, a people with a spirit."[148] If this translation is correct, then there is no distinction to be made for a "spiritual people," and instead the phrase refers to all of humanity that is in possession of

143   Wold, *4QInstruction*, 95–96.
144   Wold, *4QInstruction*, 102.
145   Wold, *4QInstruction*, 99.
146   Goff, *4QInstruction*, 139.
147   Adams, *Wisdom*, 259, challenges Wold's translation of אנוש as "humanity," but mainly on the basis of viewing the "Vision of Hagu" pericope through dualistic lenses. If Wold is correct that the dualistic approach to the passage should be contended with, the criticism holds less weight.
148   Wold, *4QInstruction*, 105–6, points out that this reading is supported by a similar construction in 1QH[a] XI 23–24. See also the translation of Werman, "Book of Hagu," 137. It should be noted that, despite her translation, Werman interprets the passage in a dualistic manner. On p. 138, she argues that the ability to look into the vision "was not given to all but only to the one who was created with a spirit patterned after the angels. The fleshly spirit, on the other hand, is not capable of meditating and hence cannot differentiate between good and evil."

a spirit. A segment of humanity, the רוח בשר, are not those designated so at birth, but are those who have corrupted their spirit through wayward behavior and have been dispossessed of revealed wisdom.[149] This is supported by line 17, which states that those of "fleshly spirit" are "no longer" (ועוד לוא) given access to the vision, which implies that they once had it.[150] If those of "fleshly spirit" had been created separately, then they would never have had access to the vision and it could not be stated that they "no longer" possess it. Therefore, Wold writes, "there is no ontological and predetermined distinction between spiritual and fleshly people in 4QInstruction; in fact, there are no 'people of flesh,' only a *spirit* that is labeled 'fleshly.'"[151] This is supported by lines 17–18, which state that those of "fleshly spirit" lost access to the vision because they did not distinguish between good and evil according to their spirit. The "fleshly spirit" is designated so because their spirit has been corrupted, but the understanding ones are those that continue to gaze upon the mystery and walk according to it (l. 19). Furthermore, it is not only a subset of humanity that are fashioned after the pattern of the angels, but all humanity is fashioned so and given the ability to understand the created order and live accordingly.[152] The distinctions become appropriate for those who fail to live well and pursue the mystery and instead fall victim to their fatigable nature.

Wold's arguments have much to commend them. First, as we have seen above, Instruction views all of humanity, and not just a subset of humanity, as having been fashioned after the pattern of the angels (4Q416 2 iii 15–18). The text follows Gen 1:26 in presenting a dual

[149] This is also the view of Loren T. Stuckenbruck, "The Interiorization of Dualism within the Human Being in Second Temple Judaism," in *Light against Darkness: Dualism in Ancient Mediterranean Religion and the Contemporary World* (ed. Eric Myers, Armin Lange, and Randall Styers; Göttingen: Vandenhoeck & Ruprecht, 2010), 158. Stuckenbruck argues that rather than focusing on the contrast between "spirit" and "flesh," the authors of Instruction and other Qumran Scrolls were concerned with distinguishing one type of spirit from another and that these spirits correspond to obedience and submission to God. All humans with a spirit are vulnerable and subject to corruption. The spirit is not anthropological but ethical. It is neutral in that it is capable of being directed by the human will.

[150] Goff, *4QInstruction*, 139, agrees that "no longer" is the correct translation of this phrase.

[151] Wold, *4QInstruction*, 106 (emphasis original).

[152] Wold, *4QInstruction*, 104. On this point there is another key difference between the views of Goff and Wold. As demonstrated above, Goff argues that understanding the created order is possible only through supernatural revelation. Wold, 103, 115–19, argues that creation and the mystery are separate forms of revelation in Instruction and that creation reveals truth in a way that is available to all of humanity. He supports this view through a helpful comparison between Instruction and Paul's view of creation in Rom 1.

origin for humanity between God and angels. This is not the same as being seated with the angels, which is an aspect of the inheritance given to those who observe the mystery (4Q416 2 iii 11). All of humanity has been fashioned after the pattern of the angels, which allows for participation with the angels in a heavenly existence to those who obtain wisdom and walk according to it.

Second, Instruction is beset with passages that demonstrate that the goal of the mystery is that the addressee study it and keep it and walk according to its instructions. A failure to do so has already been described as a forfeiture of the inheritance of blessing through the moving of the "boundary" by a corruption of the spirit and the ability of the boundary to be restored by God if the addressee walks faithfully (4Q416 2 iii 6–9). There is an important parallel between the moving of the boundary in 4Q416 2 iii and living according to the "fleshly spirit" in 4Q417 1 i. Furthermore, Wold's argument, that those of "fleshly spirit" are those who have had their spirit corrupted, is supported by 4Q416 2 ii 6 and 2 iii 6, where the addressee is warned that aspects of his behavior can cause him to "exchange his holy spirit." There is an important parallel between exchanging one's holy spirit and corrupting one's spirit and therefore rendering it "fleshly."

Third, God having a plan, and having dominion and mastery over that plan, does not require a rigid determinism and anthropological dualism regarding humanity. Goff argues for his view of determinism in Instruction in part by pointing to parallels with "The Treatise on the Two Spirits," but Goff himself admits that the parallels are not exact.[153] Unlike the Treatise, Instruction never states that God's plan predates the creation of the world. Goff argues that 4Q417 1 i 11–12 implies such a view.[154] I agree with Goff that this passage portrays God's dominion over a divine plan, but for Instruction I argue that included within that plan appears to be an insistence that humanity study and observe the mystery and that an awareness that ethics and merit, rather than dualistic distinctions between humans, determine the inheritance. *If* the addressee succeeds, it is God's plan that he has a share in the inheritance of an honored vocation and blessed afterlife. *If* he fails, it is God's plan that he share in the inheritance of the wicked.[155]

---

[153]   See also Adams, *Wisdom*, 264, who points out that Instruction does not share dualism in a way as pronounced as the "Treatise on the Two Spirits." The categories of people are not developed in Instruction, especially in the way that Instruction does not contain the same light/dark contrasts found in the Treatise.

[154]   Goff, *4QInstruction*, 154.

[155]   Wold, *4QInstruction*, 53.

So, what are we to make of inheritance terms in 4Q417 1 i? The first instance comes in line 14 with the phrase "inherit your reward" (רוש פעלתכה).[156] The term "inherit" in this passage, however, is not from the root נחל as are the other instances of inheritance terms in Instruction. The term here is רוש. Goff points out the oddity of the form but argues that it likely comes from the term ריש, which is equivalent to ראש, meaning "poverty," or "origin." The connection within Instruction is obvious, as ראש is a key word across the entirety of the text and both poverty and origins are important concepts to its discourse. However, Goff does not explain why the term should be translated "inherit" in this line other than an appeal to context.[157] I argue that, rather than ראש, the form is an imperative of ירש, a term that, as we have seen extensively in this study, means "inherit" and has a close association with נחל. While it is unclear why the author would choose this term for inherit rather than נחל, two possibilities are likely. First, it is possible that the author had in mind a play on words with ראש, both for its frequency of use in Instruction and for the relationship between the two terms.[158] Second, ירש is a term for inheritance that often implies the taking of an inheritance rather than the reception of one. A better translation of the phrase might be *"take possession of your reward,"* as a way to emphasize the need of the addressee to play an active role in the acquisition of his reward.[159]

The second instance of inheritance language is found in line 16, "He gave it [the vision] as an inheritance (ינחילו) to humanity." In the reconstruction of the passage argued for here, this line refers to the vision and the revelation of the mystery as an inheritance to all of humanity and not, as Goff argues, to a subset of humanity. This usage is not completely in keeping with other uses of נחל in Instruction, as it does not refer to inheritance as a *reward* for the acquisition of wisdom and actualization of a life lived in accord with the mystery, but rather it refers to the very thing that will assist the addressee in acquiring the "inheritance of glory." Important

---

156   As translated by Goff, *4QInstruction*, 156.
157   Goff, *4QInstruction*, 156.
158   See *NIDOTTE*, 2:539 (Christopher J. H. Wright), which points to the use of both terms as a play on words in Prov 30:7-9.
159   The verb root ירש is also found in Instruction in 4Q416 2 ii 18; 4Q417 1 i 14; 4Q418 43 45 i 10; 4Q418 81+81a 3. There is no apparent uniformity to the use of this verb in Instruction. In 4Q416 2 ii 18, the term refers to the exhortation to the addressee not to dispossess (bring ruin upon) his own body through financial entanglements. In 4Q417 1 i 14, the term refers to the inheritance of a reward described by the book of remembrance. 4Q418 43 45 i 10 is derived from 4Q417 1 i. 4Q418 81+81a 3 will be discussed below; it is in the context of inheritance but appears in association with נחלה and refers to God giving an inheritance to all people. The term appears in the imperative form in CD III 7 in reference to taking possession of the land in a way that is consistent with my argument here.

to point out, in accord with the inheritances explored throughout this study, is that the inheritance of the vision is given by God.

The final use of inheritance language in this fragment comes in line 24, "According to his inheritance (נחלתו) he shall be treated as wicked." This relates closely to the inheritance of line 14, as well as those of the fragments so far discussed. Whereas 4Q416 2 ii–iii described the "inheritance of glory" as a reward for the addressee should he pursue and live according to the mystery, 4Q417 1 i describes the inheritance for the wicked. For those contaminated by evildoing, they will be treated as guilty (ll. 23–24) and face judgment (l. 18).[160] This line rules out a rigid determinism in the passage, suggesting that the addressee's status as righteous is dependent upon his ability to avoid a contamination of his spirit.[161]

4. 4Q417 2 i 7–18[162]

Similar themes to those discussed thus far are covered in 4Q417 2 i 7–18. Lines 7–17 are primarily concerned with ethical behavior in the context of eschatological judgment and feature a warning to the addressee to be wary of people "of iniquity." Punishment follows iniquity, so the addressee is to walk carefully amongst those guilty of wicked behavior (ll. 7–8). The most important feature of the passage concerns the behavioral "dispositions" that the addressee must cultivate: the inherent

---

[160]   Line 19 is often translated to describe God as "appointing" deeds. See, for example, Kampen, *Wisdom*, 63, who argues that the term פקד is deterministic and assigns the fate of the human situation. Wold, *4QInstruction*, 53, argues effectively that the term is better translated "examining." This further argues that status is based on ethics and merit. The addressee is not to understand through the mystery the deeds that have been appointed, but rather he is to explore the mystery in order to examine which deeds in the past have been worthy of the inheritance of glory and which have led to the inheritance of the wicked. By such an examination, the addressee will make good decisions regarding his own conduct. Werman, "Book of Hagu," points out that this is a feature of Qumran sapiential literature when she writes, "By studying how the world was created and by looking at historical events the wise person can deduce laws and rules according to which he should live" (128). She goes on to state regarding Instruction that the addressee "is instructed to look at human conduct during every period of world history and at the rewards and punishments meted out for the past, present and future. From this a person can deduce which deed is good and which is bad" (131). The goal is not to understand God's plan of appointed deeds but rather which types of deeds he rewards and which he punishes.

[161]   See Adams, *Wisdom*, 265–66.

[162]   The inheritance reference in line 18 of this column is anomalous to those discussed in this study and does not require much attention. Line 18 warns the addressee to look out for his own welfare when in the marketplace, taking his own share while being careful not to take more than he needs. See Adams, *Wisdom*, 234.

qualities of mind and character that precede and ultimately lead to certain actions toward others. The cultivation of these dispositions extends from a careful study of the "mystery of existence."

Because of his poverty, the addressee is צעיר (lowly, l. 10). Despite his lowly state, the addressee is to remain charitable and generous (ll. 8–9). Goff notes that the term צעיר has a positive connotation, relating to humility (Jer 30:19; Zech 13:7; CD XIX 9). It refers to an ethical disposition that the addressee must adopt; in his position as lowly and poor he may face grief and suffering, and yet, he is called to a life of generosity and humility in the face of those struggles.[163] Building on his lowly disposition, the addressee is described as being in "mourning" (l. 10). He is not to rejoice in his mourning as it may lead to trouble. However, it is those who mourn that will receive blessing. Rejoicing has been reserved for the "broken of spirit" (l. 11), and all those who mourn will receive "eternal joy" (l. 12).[164] Eternal joy is an eschatological reward offered to those whose present conditions of poverty and mourning lead not to wickedness but to generosity and humility. As befits the overall context of Instruction, the juxtaposition of mourning and joy portrays the deficient circumstances of this present life as unworthy of those living in God's good favor but tolerable in light of the value of the reward to come. Mourning and joy are placed in opposition to highlight the contrast of two fates; eternal joy is a future hope for those in present struggle.[165] This echoes the words of Isaiah 61:1-7, where Isaiah declares that God will "comfort all who mourn" (v. 2) and that "everlasting joy shall be theirs" (v. 7).

Lines 10–11 exhort the addressee to gaze upon the "mystery of existence" and "comprehend the origins (מולד) of salvation" in order to know who will "inherit glory" (נוחל כבוד) and who will inherit "toil" (עמל). As with 4Q416 2 iii 9, Goff argues that the term מולד here relates to the birthtimes of the addressee, indicating that the timing of his birth will inform him as to whether or not he can be included among the saved.[166] However, Goff admits that in this dualistic understanding of

[163] Goff, *4QInstruction*, 194.
[164] The phrase "broken of spirit" is fragmentary but has been reconstructed based on a parallel with 1QH^a XXIII 16. See Kampen, *Wisdom*, 105. DJD 34 has "contrite of spirit."
[165] See Goff, *4QInstruction*, 195.
[166] Goff, *4QInstruction*, 199–200, relates this to other passages in Instruction, such as 4Q415 11 11 and 4Q416 2 iii 20. However, Wold, *Women*, 88, 105–6, 201, has aptly demonstrated that these passages and others related to birthtimes often refer to the hierarchy in the relationship between husbands and wives rather than discovering the birthtimes of elect status. Many instances of מולד relate to the creation accounts in Genesis, in particular of the origins of the woman and her place in the created order.

the term the text provides no insight into *how* a person can know they are among the elect based on their time of birth.[167] This is resolved if, as with 4Q416 2 iii 9, we understand the exhortation to relate to "origins" rather than "birthtimes." Through the "mystery of existence," the addressee is to understand the origins of salvation, being the wisdom and dispositions taught by the mystery. This qualifies the addressee for the reward, being the "inheritance of glory" previously defined. This is supported by the parallel uses of the term עמל (toil) in lines 10 and 11. The one who rejoices in their mourning will "toil" in life (l. 10), just as the one who fails to understand the mystery will inherit "toil" (l. 11). However, juxtaposed with toil is the reward of the one who comprehends the mystery—the ability to "inherit glory," which leads to eternal joy.[168] This parallels with the need to understand the difference between truth and iniquity in 4Q416 2 iii 14–15 and 4Q417 1 i 6–7. The one who is foolish is punished for eternity, as with the one who inherits toil. In this passage, comprehending the mystery leads to dispositions such as lowliness, humility, and generosity, which leads to rejoicing for the broken in spirit.

5. 4Q418 55 1–12 & 69 ii 1–15

4Q418 55 and 69 are often studied together, due to their similar use of rhetoric, shared terminology, common use of the second person plural (which is rare in the rest of Instruction), and the prominence of angels in both passages.[169] As with 4Q416 2 iii, there is an emphasis on angels as a model for conduct. The addressees must be like the angels, who seek truth. 4Q418 55 introduces a "we" group, and a "they" group, who appear to be distinguished by their success at pursuing truth in a way patterned by the angels. 4Q418 55 3 uses the nifal verb נכרה, (to dig), to refer to the excavation and exploration of truth. This highlights the pedagogical emphasis of both this fragment and Instruction as a whole.[170] The "we" group and the "they" group are both a part of

---

[167]   Goff, *4QInstruction*, 200.

[168]   The concepts of joy and eternity are brought together in other Second Temple texts, such as 1QS IV 7; Jub 23:30-31; T. Jud 25:4. See Goff, *4QInstruction*, 196.

[169]   These and other similarities are described by Tigchelaar, *To Increase Learning*, 208–24. While angelology is an important theme in other fragments, these deal with this theme more extensively than any other. Wold, *4QInstruction*, 14–25, has argued effectively that the shared rhetorical features between these two fragments, particularly regarding direct and indirect speech, are not as similar as some have supposed, calling into question certain points of unity between them.

[170]   See Goff, *4QInstruction*, 214. The verb נכרה is rare but is also found in 4Q525 to refer to the acquisition of wisdom.

the community, but the "we" group pursues wisdom while the "they" group refuses to do so. Wold is correct that the distinction between the "we" group and the "they" group is not one of ontological nature and it is best not to view them dualistically. The text portrays a single community digging laboriously for truth. The "they" group has failed in this task, and the "we" group must live with the tension that the pursuit of the mystery and of knowledge is "a perpetual undertaking with the risk of failure."[171] 4Q418 69 ii contains a description of universal judgment also described in 4Q416 1 and very similar in many ways to the judgment depicted in 1 En. 1–5 discussed in chapter 3. While those who pursue truth will receive eternal life, those who neglect it will be cast into the "eternal pit" (1. 6).[172]

The ability of the addressees to participate with the angels is highlighted by the use of inheritance terms in these fragments. Those who pursue wisdom are נוחלי אמת (those who inherit truth, 4Q418 55 6).[173] The addressees would do well to emulate the angels who are models of pedagogical conduct (4Q418 55 8–12; 4Q418 69 ii 13–14). In order for the angels to serve as models, they are seen, like the addressees, to be students. Indeed, they are the ideal students.[174] Because of their success in diligently pursuing knowledge, the angels will be rewarded (4Q418 55 9–10). Humans, in contrast to angels, are fatigable and prone to laziness.[175] The speaker is concerned regarding the shortcomings of the human condition, but if the addressees pursue wisdom after the pattern of the angels, then they will "inherit (ינחלו) an eternal possession" (4Q418 55 12). The inheritance of the addressees is mirrored by the revelation that the angels themselves are also rewarded with an

[171]   Wold, *4QInstruction*, 18.

[172]   These themes have resonance with 4Q416 iii, where the head of the addressee is lifted from poverty and is seated with the nobles, and 4Q418 126 ii 7–8, which states, "And to shut the door on the wicked, but to raise up the head of the poor . . . in glory everlasting and peace eternal, and to separate the spirit of life from every spirit of darkness."

[173]   Goff, *4QInstruction*, 217, as with the whole of the composition, interprets line 6 deterministically. Whichever path one decides to take, between the "we" group and the "they" group, "God has determined the outcome." Goff states that the student "must choose a life of study and contemplation to achieve postmortem rewards such as life after death, but his elect status has been established by God." This elect status is signified by being one who inherits truth. On inheriting truth, see also the extremely fragmented 4Q416 4 3, "And thou, O understanding one, rejoice in the inheritance of truth."

[174]   Angels as students is rare in early Judaism. In texts such as the Book of the Watchers and Jubilees angels are portrayed as teachers. The role of angels as students in Instruction is a product of the need for the addressee to understand his ability to enter into participation with the angels in a pursuit of wisdom and a heavenly existence, which is presented in juxtaposition to his status as poor.

[175]   Wold, *4QInstruction*, 16.

inheritance in 4Q418 69 ii 13–14. Angels do not tire of the pursuit of truth but work toward it always. They walk in glory (כבוד) and their inheritance (נחלתם) is "eternal life." The pursuit of wisdom on the part of the angels and the addressees is ultimately portrayed as a pursuit of God himself, who never tires of knowledge and truth but delights in them eternally (4Q418 69 ii 12). The angels and the pursuers of truth are united in their shared "inheritance" and "glory," which are terms reflective of their elevated status as servants of God (i.e., vocation) who stand to receive an eternal reward. Although these terms are largely eschatological, they do not rule out the inaugurated aspects of the inheritance as a present participation between the addressees and the angels. They are both present participants of wisdom who share in a future glory.[176] Alexander Rofé comments on the participation of the human and the angelic in 4Q418 when he states, "These godly gifts make human beings equal to angels, not only in terms of status, but as one sacred community. . . . These two go hand in hand very well: divine, inspired wisdom and communion with heavenly beings—a choir of angels and mortals."[177]

4Q418 69 ii 10 features the phrase "the chosen ones of truth." The term בחיר (chosen) often denotes elect status in the HB but also describes individuals chosen to function in specific roles, such as the priesthood, servants, or the monarchy, and it serves as an inclusion and identity term as much as it does a term to describe a determined choice.[178] At Qumran, the term is used as a common designation for the members of the sect (e.g., 1QS XI 16; 1QpHab V 4; X 13; 1QM XII 4). It is possible that the phrase "chosen ones of truth" is intended as an identity term in this passage, but due to the dearth of explicit election language in Instruction, or of terms referring to Israel, it is important to understand the term in the context of these fragments. 4Q418 55 5 states that the "foolish of heart" are those who have not pursued knowledge and have not "sought" (שחרו) after understanding. They are part of the "they" group and have not "chosen" (בחרו) God's good pleasure. Those who inherit truth are those who are vigilant to pursue it. In 4Q418 69 ii 10, the "chosen ones of truth" are those who "seek" (שחר) understanding. Considering these lines in parallel, the emphasis is not on an ontological

---

[176]   Wold, *4QInstruction*, 24.

[177]   Alexander Rofé, "Revealed Wisdom: From the Bible to Qumran," in Collins et al., *Sapiential Perspectives*, 2–3. See also Harrington, *Wisdom*, 58, who argues that the Qumran community saw angelic existence as the ideal mode of existence for human life on earth. Heaven, then, is the extension of life on earth, only without the distractions of everyday life.

[178]   For a description of the full range of usage, see *NIDOTTE*, 1:628–31 (Emile Nicole).

difference between those who inherit truth and those who do not but rather on a difference regarding their choice to either pursue truth or neglect it. Although 4Q418 69 ii 10 makes use of the noun form "chosen ones," this term is best understood in this passage as an identifier for those who have chosen truth as opposed to a term describing predetermined status or nature.[179] The inheritance in these fragments belongs both to the angels, who are diligent to pursue truth, and to the members of the community who pursue truth in the same vein. The inheritance refers to a role in God's service, eternal life, and participation in the heavenly community.

6. 4Q418 81+81a 1–14

The addressee is to bless the angels and to praise God for separating him from a spirit of flesh (l. 1). The addressee must separate himself from everything that God hates (l. 2) and consecrate himself to God (l. 4). God has magnified the glory of the addressee and promised to give him good things (ll. 5–6), and if the addressee walks faithfully God will bless his deeds (ll. 6–7). The addressee is to love God and show mercy to those who keep God's words (l. 8). God has opened insight for the addressee and tasked him with turning away God's wrath from the community (l. 10). The section ends with a second call for the addressee to glorify the angels (ll. 11–12).

This fragment follows the "Vision of Hagu" passage as an important one for those arguing that Instruction features determinism and anthropological dualism. The addressee is described by a number of important phrases, such as "eternal spring" (l. 1), "most holy one" (l. 4), "firstborn son" (l. 5), and "eternal planting" (l. 13). Goff argues that each of these phrases refer not only to the elect status of the addressee but also to the fact that he has been separated from the rest of humanity.[180] Goff connects each of these phrases with potential parallels within the Dead Sea Scrolls and aptly demonstrates that they are similar to phrases that often denote an elect community. However, there are also important differences between similar phrases in the Scrolls and the use of these phrases

---

[179] Wold, *4QInstruction*, 21–23, translates the phrase "choosers of truth." Rather than denoting elect status, he argues that the term "choosers" refers to those who pursue and seek knowledge. See *NIDOTTE*, 1:631 (Nicole), which comments that the verb form was common in the HB but was generally supplanted by the nominative noun in the Second Temple period.

[180] Goff, *4QInstruction*, 243, argues that elect status, and the declaration that the addressee is different from the rest of humanity, is the main focus of the first 14 lines of this column.

in Instruction, and these differences should give the interpreter pause before accepting their relevance too easily.[181]

Wold argues effectively that this column refers to the elevated status of the addressee but not through elect status or anthropological dualism. In fact, all of Instruction is not addressed to a monolithic group, such as "elect ones" who all enjoy a similar status, but rather, it is addressed to a variety of students of wisdom who vary in status in their efforts to become sages themselves. 4Q418 81+81a offers instructions to those at the pinnacle of their pursuit of wisdom, and the addressee's status is due to his becoming a liturgical leader within the community.[182] The addressee has become a sage, and as such has been given authority within the community and been made a "most holy one" by God, which signifies his new position. As such, the addressee has been granted the status of "firstborn son" of God.[183] This status as a sage allows the addressee to intercede with God on the community's behalf and turn away God's wrath.[184] The addressee becomes a sage by merit of faithful pursuit of the "mystery of existence."[185] Due to his success in obtaining wisdom, God has magnified the addressee's glory, and the addressee is exhorted to consecrate himself to God and he is promised God's "good things." By becoming a sage, the addressee has his lot cast with the angels (ll. 4–5).[186]

---

[181]   Principally, as has been noted here, Instruction is not a *Yaḥad* composition. This means that terms and phrases in Instruction can be effectively compared to *Yaḥad* texts in many regards, but such comparisons must be done with a degree of caution. For example, Instruction does not feature terms such as "light" and "dark," nor does it feature the binary and dualistic language found throughout many *Yaḥad* texts to which Instruction is often compared.

[182]   Wold, *4QInstruction*, 80.

[183]   Goff, *4QInstruction*, 251, agrees the phrase "firstborn son" denotes the addressee's relationship to the angels. However, he attaches this to the addressee's elect status as one who receives a "special inheritance" from God. Wold, *4QInstruction*, 42–51, connects "firstborn son" here to his argument regarding the firstborn referred to in 4Q416 2 ii 13. Although Goff and *DSSR* both translate 4Q416 2 ii with a view that the firstborn there places the addressee in a firstborn son relationship to his creditor, Wold argues that this is unintelligible to the context of Instruction and does not make the best sense of the use of terms in that passage. The relationship between the creditor and the debtor in Instruction cannot take on such familial terms, as the creditor is outside of the community. Furthermore, in all the relevant literature the term "firstborn" always refers to one with an elevated status. In Wold's view, both instances of "firstborn" in Instruction refer to the addressee's relationship with God upon successful observance of the mystery.

[184]   Tigchelaar, *To Increase Learning*, 235, notes something similar. The statement that the addressee can "turn away anger" "may indicate that the addressee of this section is some kind of intercessory leader in the community."

[185]   Wold, *4QInstruction*, 74.

[186]   Wold, *4QInstruction*, 75.

Wold's argument is important, as it not only helps to make sense of this column, it also explains this column's use of phrases that are both similar to, and different from, the use of similar phrases in the Scrolls, and it better fits the overall context of Instruction. As we have seen, Instruction is rife with descriptions of reward and punishment for the success or failure of the addressee to pursue wisdom, it is highly pedagogical, and participation with the angels is an important theme. It is helpful to detail two important features in this column before drawing conclusions regarding the use of inheritance: the addressee's participation with the angels and the use of the phrase "eternal planting."

Participation with the angels. The addressee is urged to bless the angels. Although angel veneration is rare in Jewish sources, it is attested, and in Instruction it logically derives from the pedagogical nature of the composition as angels serve as models of the pursuit of wisdom.[187] By becoming a sage, the addressee's lot is cast with the angels, and he shares their status. Wold comments on the use of perfect verbs throughout the column to demonstrate that the addressee has been "placed" as a most holy one, his glory has been "multiplied," and he has been "placed" as a firstborn son. The verbal forms make these actions past and completed, meaning that the status that the addressee enjoys as one who participates with the angels is not only about future glory but about participation as an aspect of the addressee's present occupation.[188] Wold compares this interpretation with several other texts found throughout the Scrolls[189] and finds a close parallel in the Thanksgiving Hymns. 1QH^a XIX 12–18 states that to be in a lot with the angels is to be lifted from sinful, fleshly mortality to a place with the righteous community to whom are revealed truth and mysteries. Being lifted from sin and set with the angels is a present condition with eternal consequences. 1QH^a XIV 14–16 refers to a holy community that enjoys God's secret counsel, where there is no need for an intermediary between the righteous community and the heavenly throne room. These passages closely parallel the status of the addressee in 4Q418 81+81a, who was separated from a "spirit of flesh" and given a shared status with the angelic host. Wold comments, "Having one's lot cast with angels is part of a much more complex depiction of a conjoined community of righteous humans and angelic beings."[190] God shares his insights

---

[187]   See Loren T. Stuckenbruck, "Angels and God: Exploring the Limits of Early Jewish Monotheism," in *Early Jewish and Christian Monotheism* (ed. Loren T. Stuckenbruck and Wendy E. S. North; London: T&T Clark, 2004), 43–70.

[188]   Wold, *4QInstruction*, 75–76.

[189]   1QS^b III 22; IV 25–26; 1QH^a XIX 12–18; XIV; 4Q511 2 i.

[190]   Wold, *4QInstruction*, 77.

with the blended community of humans and angels, and the addressees venerate the angels as superior pursuers of wisdom.

Eternal planting. Line 13 refers to God placing the majesty of his glory before an eternal planting (מטעת עולם). The plant metaphor in some form shows up in various places throughout Jewish literature[191] and at times refers to Israel or a select community.[192] In the Qumran Scrolls the term refers to the *Yaḥad*,[193] but as a non-*Yaḥad* composition the identity of the community referred to in Instruction might be found elsewhere. I propose that the key to understanding the reference lies in the association between the addressees and the angels in 4Q418 81+81a and throughout Instruction. As we have seen, the angels themselves inherit an eternal possession (4Q418 55 12), and their lot is eternal life (4Q418 69 ii 13). Likewise, humans who inherit glory will receive eternal joy (4Q417 2 i 12). Humans who pursue wisdom, along with the angels, experience eternality as an aspect of their reward and obtain the status of the angels. 4Q418 81+81a 1 refers to the lips of the addressee as an eternal spring that blesses the angels and praises God, with the spring metaphor closely related to the concept of "planting." As Stuckenbruck comments, the eternal spring is the fountain "which feeds or waters the eternal plantation."[194] Stuckenbruck concludes that the planting metaphor in this column refers to the human community *only* insofar as it participates in the angelic community in anticipation of eternal life,[195] but it is reasonable to take this a step further and

---

[191]   In the HB, Isa 5:7; 60:21; 61:3. Also, 1 En. 10:3, 16; 84:6; 93:5, 10; 4Q423 1–2 i 7; 1QS VIII 5; XI 8; 1QH XIV 15; XVI 6.

[192]   The term "planting" is used to refer to Israel in Isa 61:3, a passage that has resonance with portions of Instruction. Stuckenbruck, "4QInstruction," 249–57, notes that this term is open to several interpretations in Instruction but that reference to an "elect human community" is among the possibilities. If so, Stuckenbruck admits that the nature of the community is unclear. Torleif Elgvin, "The Mystery to Come: Early Essene Theology of Revelation," in *Qumran between the Old and New Testaments* (JSOT 290; ed. F. H. Cryer and T. L. Thompson; Sheffield: Sheffield Academic, 1998), 125, argues that the metaphor refers to a "remnant community" of elect ones among humanity who have been given insight by God. These see themselves as a nucleus of the future restored Israel. Kampen, *Wisdom*, 135, points to the parallels with Jubilees to argue that the phrase in Instruction likely refers to Israel in association with God and/or angels but that this was later picked up and appropriated by the Qumran community to refer to the *Yaḥad*.

[193]   See Goff, *4QInstruction*, 257, who highlights the parallels with *Yaḥad* texts to argue that eternal planting in 4Q418 81+81a refers to elect status.

[194]   Stuckenbruck, "4QInstruction," 252.

[195]   Stuckenbruck, "Angels," 65–66. See also Wold, *4QInstruction*, 78, who states, "the elevated figure joins with the angelic community in the present and looks forward to eternal life and the continuation of these activities."

view the eternal planting as the blended community of angels and the humans in participation with them.[196]

Inheritance. In line 3 inheritance terms appear four times: three times the root נחל and once the root ירש. The relevant portion of the line reads that God "has given (יורישם) to each man his own inheritance (נחלתו), but he is your portion and your inheritance (ונחלתכם) among the children of mankind, and over his inheritance (נחלתו) he has set you in authority."[197] This line highlights the deeply theological significance of inheritance in Instruction in a way that is consistent with all of Jewish literature; the inheritance is not just a practical possession but is given by God as a relational aspect of his interaction with humanity. Line 3 makes use of Num 18:20, in which God states to Aaron, "You shall have no allotment (תנחל) in their land, nor shall you have any share among them; I am your share and your possession (נחלתך) among the Israelites." As discussed in chapter 2, Num 18:20 indicates that, as the tribes of Israel received their allotments of land as an inheritance from God, the Levites were denied a tribal allotment due to their occupation as priests. Instead of land, *their inheritance was the vocation itself* and the unique status that came with that vocation: a role as a liturgical leader within the community as well as a special relationship with God as those who represent the people to God. One important function of the priests was to offer sacrifices on behalf of the people to turn away God's wrath toward them.

The use of Num 18:20 in this passage, along with descriptive terms for the addressee such as "holy" and "son," has led some interpreters to conclude that the addressees in this column are priests.[198] Rightly, Goff rejects this view, arguing instead that the use of Num 18:20 is

---

[196]   See Goff, *4QInstruction*, 245, who comments that there are so many similarities between the angels and the intended audience of Instruction that there exists an intended ambiguity between them. Both are referred to as "holy ones," highlighting both their special relationship between them as well as their shared relationship to God. Instruction contains many features that present angels and the addressees as a shared community.

[197]   Wold's translation, *4QInstruction*, 73.

[198]   See Armin Lange, "The Determination of Fate by the Oracle of the Lot in the Dead Sea Scrolls, the Hebrew Bible and Ancient Mesopotamian Literature," in Falk et al., *Sapiential, Liturgical and Poetical Texts from Qumran*, 39–48. Tigchelaar, *To Increase Learning*, 236, argues that the different sections of Instruction are directed toward varying addressees, which allows for priests to be the audience of 4Q418 81+81a even while the rest of the composition contains hardly any priestly language at all. Torleif Elgvin, "Priestly Sages? The Milieus of Origin of *4QMysteries* and *4QInstruction*" in Collins et al., *Sapiential Perspectives: Wisdom Literature in Light of the Dead Sea Scrolls*, 82–83, argues that the language in this column "indicates that we have here symbolic language, not an address directly to priests."

metaphorical. He points to the inheritance of the Levites in Numbers as that which distinguishes them from the rest of Israel, whereas in Instruction, Num 18:20 is appropriated to distinguish the addressee from the rest of "humankind." Land allotments and the role of priests in Israel are not in view in Instruction. However, Goff then argues that the use of the Numbers passage in 4Q418 81+81a relates to the elect status of the addressee. Goff argues that it is possible that some of the addressees were priests but that there were a variety of vocations among them and that vocation was not the concern regarding the use of Num 18:20.[199]

Wold's view of the column explains the use of Num 18:20 as metaphorical (not taking literally the role of priests from the original context), while still demonstrating a view toward vocation. The vocation here is the role of the sage attained by the addressees who have become "most holy ones" by virtue of their successful pursuit of wisdom. These "firstborn sons" have received God as their inheritance. They have entered into a special relationship with God as they serve the community as liturgical leaders, and through their role in instructing the community in the "mystery of existence" they turn away God's wrath. God's own inheritance is humankind, which the addressees of this column have now been given authority over. As Wold states, "this reworking of Numbers functions to universalize the role of the sage." The role of the sage is extended, in theory, "even to the nations." Wold is careful to clarify that this does not imply that the sage has authority over humankind in a secular sense but that it refers to the role of the sage as an intermediary between "the children of mankind" and the "men of good pleasure," as well as between earth and the heavenly realm.[200] As we have seen throughout Instruction, all people are given an inheritance of some kind by God.[201] Those who successfully obtain wisdom receive an inheritance of glory, and those who neglect the mysteries receive an inheritance of toil. 4Q418 81+81a 3 insists that those who ascend to become sages receive an inheritance that is distinct from all others: God himself is their inheritance as they take on the role of liturgical leader and receive authority as an intermediary between God and man, not as priests but in analogous fashion.[202] Line 11 calls back to line 1, stating that before the

---

[199]   Goff, *4QInstruction*, 247–48.

[200]   Wold, *4QInstruction*, 80–82.

[201]   See for example 4Q416 3 2, "For from him comes the inheritance of all that lives."

[202]   See also 4Q423 4 3, which states "I am your portion and your inheritance among the sons of Adam. I will magnify you in the presence of all." Possible is Tigchelaar's suggestion that the first use of inheritance in this column, "He has given each man his own inheritance," relates not to the inheritances of glory and toil mentioned previously in the composition but to vocation. One's inheritance would refer to one's

addressee can gain his inheritance (נחלתכם) from the hand of God he must glorify the angels.

Line 14 is fragmented and the relevance of the line to the overall context of the column is unclear. However, the line contains a phrase of interest for our discussion, as it refers to those who are נוחלי ארץ (inheritors of the land/earth), followed immediately by a fragmented reference to שמים (heaven). As we have seen, the HB often describes the land as the inheritance of the Israelites, but the verb root נחל in construct with ארץ to form the construct phrase "inherit the land/earth" is extremely rare.[203] In the Qumran Scrolls this is the only time the construct phrase appears.[204] Also rare is the phrase "inherit the land/earth" in Greek.[205] In this line, translating the term ארץ as "earth," rather than "land," is to be preferred for at least three reasons. First, Instruction shows no real interest in the land of Israel in particular. Second, this column shows signs of universalism, appropriating Num 18:20 to refer not to Israelites but to "humankind," and the addressee has been appointed a "most holy one" over all the earth (l. 4). Third, the reference to "heaven" in line 14 is telling, as it sets a contrast between the earthly and heavenly realms.

As discussed in chapter 3, the phrase "inherit the earth" in 1 En. 5:6-8 is presented as a promised hope. Here the tone appears more assumed; the phrase might possess eschatological connotations, but the emphasis is on those who are already set to inherit in the present.

"position and tasks in life." In this suggestion, when lines 1–2 states, "He has separated you from every fleshly spirit," the phrase "fleshly spirit" is synonymous with "children of mankind" in line 3 rather than indicating those who neglect the mystery. In other words, all of humankind is given a vocation, but the addressee has been separated out from humankind and given a vocation separate from the others. See Tigchelaar, *To Increase Learning*, 232. The likelihood of this interpretation is increased by the use of inheritance in line 20 of this column, where the context is more clearly the vocation of those participating in manual labor. It is said that God distributes an inheritance (vocation) to every living being.

[203]   The phrase appears just once in the HB in construct form, in Isa 57:13 in reference to the land of Israel. "Inherit the earth" appears more often as a construct with ארץ and the root verb ירש, though it is still rare. It appears in Lev 20:24, where "land" is preceded by the direct object את in reference to the land belonging to the Canaanites, who the Israelites are to dispossess from the land. The construct with ירש is found four times in Ps 37 (vv. 9, 11, 22, 29), while the root נחל is found in v. 18 of that chapter but not in construct with ארץ.

[204]   The term ארץ appears in construct with the root verb ירש just four times, all in the Psalms Pesher of Ps 37, which I have detailed in the discussion on 1 Enoch in ch. 3.

[205]   The phrase appears in the LXX in Tob 4:12 (κληρονομήσει γῆν), Ps 24:13 (κληρονομήσει γῆν), Ps 36:9, 11, 22, 29 (κληρονομήσουσι γῆν), Isa 61:7 (κληρονομήσουσιν τὴν γῆν). It also appears three times in 1 En. 5:6-8 (κληρονομήσουσιν τὴν γῆν), and once in Matt 5:5 (κληρονομήσουσιν τὴν γῆν). See also a similar use of the phrase in Jub 17:3; 22:14; 32:19.

Because of the fragmentary nature of the line the antecedent is difficult to determine, but there is no good reason to believe that those who inherit the earth are different than the "eternal plantation" of line 13. By glorifying the angels, the addressee will receive his inheritance (l. 11), which refers to his own role as a liturgical leader in the community. However, by turning away God's wrath he opens a spring for *all the holy ones*, for everyone called by his name (l. 12), so that the glory of God's majesty may be manifest to an "eternal plantation" (l. 13), which I argue is the blended community of those who are righteous and the angelic host. This may be further confirmed by the use of the hitpael verb from the root הלך (to walk) in line 14, which has ethical connotations. The line ends with a reference to heaven, possibly denoting that those who inherit the earth walk upon the inherited earth in a way that accords with the heavenly realm. The addressees are being instructed on how to live in the present earth, in the same way as those who are in heaven (angels), and their present inheritance of the earth then accords with their status as a sage with authority.[206] As we have seen in our discussion in the Latter Prophets, 1 Enoch, and the Psalms Pesher, the phrase "inherit the earth" is an eschatological phrase that carries with it a universalism and a view toward this-worldly renewal. It is not entirely clear if the same sense of renewal is in view in Instruction. As Goff notes, Instruction never explicitly describes a restored and purified earth where the righteous live in a blessed existence. However, the use of the phrase "inherit the earth," coupled with Instruction's proclamations of final judgment, means that a transformation of the world is potentially implied.[207] In Instruction there is a contrast between the ethics and pursuit of wisdom by those of the earth, who are fatigable and distracted, and those of the heavenly host, who do not tire in their pursuit of wisdom in accordance with God's standards. Those who inherit the earth in this column are likely those who walk *according to heaven*, both the angelic host and those like the addressees of this column who have been successful in being lifted to an angelic status through their pursuit of the mystery.[208] As a liturgical leader, the addressee plays a role in leading others toward a status of "holy ones" and fellowship with the eternal plantation, and the reference to the inheritance of the earth coupled with the addressee's

---

[206]   See, for example, the idea in Matt 6:10, "Your kingdom come, your will be done, on earth as it is in heaven."

[207]   Goff, *4QInstruction*, 257.

[208]   We have already seen that, like the humans, the angels are described by this composition as those who receive an inheritance (4Q418 55 12; 69 ii 13).

role on behalf of humanity strongly implies that this fellowship is universally applied.[209]

7. 4Q423 5 3

Portions of 4Q423 are concerned with the garden of Eden as a metaphor for the condition of the addressees. It features a use of themes from Gen 1–3, though it reappropriates these themes to insist that gaining wisdom and insight from the tree(s) is a positive development.[210] The addressee has authority over the garden of Eden, and every tree in the garden has the ability to bestow knowledge.[211] The addressee has authority to serve and till the garden (4Q423 1 2), "serve" and "till" implying that maintaining authority in the garden requires work. This extends the metaphor to include the necessity on the part of the addressee to obtain wisdom through study of the mystery and live according to its ethical standards.[212] The addressee is said to rule over the garden (4Q423 1, 2 i 2), but he is also warned that the garden can produce thorns and thistles and fail to sprout forth its yield if the addressee is unfaithful (4Q423 1, 2 i 3–4). As Goff states, "Eden is used as a metaphor for the human condition. Both the right path and the wrong path are represented by Eden."[213]

4Q423 5 is fragmented and the context is often difficult to determine. Line 3 states that God "divided the inheritance (נחלת) of all rulers." Wold's suggestion is reasonable, that this line relates to the context of 4Q423 1, 2 i 2, where the addressee is regarded as ruler over the garden.[214] This relates to the vocation of the addressee in 4Q418 81+81a, who has become a sage and a representative of humankind, mediating between the earthly and heavenly realm. As the garden of Eden serves as a metaphor for the human condition, the sage is given an inheritance of authority within it.

---

[209]   Similar is Stuckenbruck, "4QInstruction," 248–49, who argues that, at the very least, those who inherit the earth are the addressees of the column. Stuckenbruck goes on to argue that the angels may also stand to inherit the earth along with the sage and the righteous community, drawing on the fact that Instruction regards the privilege of the addressee as a participation in the privileges accorded to the angels. Stuckenbruck notes the important difference between Instruction and 1 En. 5 in this regard; 1 En. 5 does not feature the direct analogy between the humans and the angels. Furthermore, 1 En. 5 is more eschatologically directed toward a future hope, whereas Instruction leaves the impression that the community anticipates the inheritance in the present. Despite the differences, Stuckenbruck notes that these are the only two instances of "inherit the earth" in the literature of the entire period, increasing the possibility that there may be a direct relationship between the traditions.

[210]   For an extensive analysis of the use of Gen 1–3 in 4Q423, see Wold, *Women*, 113–21.

[211]   Goff, *Heavenly Wisdom*, 100.

[212]   Goff, *Heavenly Wisdom*, 102.

[213]   Goff, *Heavenly Wisdom*, 103.

[214]   Wold, *Women*, 120.

4.1.1.3. Conclusion

Instruction is a composition best not interpreted through a lens of rigid determinism or anthropological dualism. This is not to suggest that some deterministic language is not present in the document. In fact, much of the language, especially when considered alongside *Yaḥad* compositions from Qumran, certainly details God's sovereignty over his plans for the world. However, such language in this composition points more toward inclusion and identity language that serves as a framework for human behavior than it does a rigid determinism. Furthermore, anthropological dualism is not found in the composition when the concepts of "people with a spirit" and "fleshly spirit" are correctly understood. Rather than ontology, these terms serve a pedagogical function to detail the success or failure of humans in obtaining wisdom and observing the "mystery of existence."

Inheritance in Instruction is multifaceted, but its various dimensions are all aspects of a singular approach by the author(s) of the composition. At points in the document, the "mystery of existence" reveals a path to inheritance, and in one passage the mystery is itself the thing being inherited (4Q417 1 i 16). The phrase "inherit joy" describes the future reward of a blessed afterlife for those who are successful in obtaining wisdom and observing the mystery. Inheritance also describes the fate of the wicked, who receive an inheritance of toil and stand to face judgment.[215] The "mystery of existence" is the centerpiece of the community and the key to the various descriptions of inheritance in the composition. The inheritance can be gained and lost as one chooses to either pursue or neglect the mystery. Even as the addressee participates in the acquisition of the inheritance, it is always described as being given by God.

Key to the inheritance is the origin of humanity, who were fashioned after the pattern of the angels. Despite this origin, angels are tireless in their pursuit of wisdom, while humans are fatigable and prone to distraction. If humans pursue wisdom and follow the mystery, they are elevated from their *status* of poverty (though not from economic poverty itself), which serves as a metaphor for their frail human condition, and given the status of the angelic host of heaven. Obtaining a place among the angels provides a future reward with an inaugurated aspect: the addressee participates presently with his heavenly status as a sage. In this, "inheritance" and "glory" function as *vocational* terms, where those who receive an elevated status are those who possess dispositions such as humility, generosity, and lowliness. This vocational aspect of

---

[215]   See the Ages of Creation (4Q180 1; 4Q181 2), which states that the angelic being Azazel taught wickedness to Israel and that the wicked of Israel passed on this wickedness as an "inheritance."

the "inheritance of glory" is somewhat veiled in earlier columns but becomes more explicit in 4Q418 81. The literal economic poverty of the addressee is a constant reality, but the addressee is not to be concerned by it. Instead, he is able to be elevated above the metaphorical poverty of his fatigable nature in order to receive a new status and an eschatological reward, the value of which surpasses material wealth. Those of broken spirit inherit participation in the glory of God, and material poverty becomes manageable in light of the reward to come.[216]

4.1.2. Book of Mysteries[217]

Like Instruction, Mysteries features a strong integration of wisdom and apocalypticism.[218] Both texts emphasize the "mystery of existence,"

---

[216] If the arguments regarding Instruction presented here are found persuasive, then there are a number of interesting parallels between the ideas in Instruction regarding inheritance, glory, and vocation with the arguments of Jacob, *Conformed*, 64–121, regarding these same themes in Paul's letter to the Romans. In Instruction, anyone who does not pursue the mystery is counted among those who have gone astray from the ways of God and neglected a chance to be counted among the heavenly community. The addressee must maintain his focus on his vocation and his pursuit of knowledge and the mystery. If he falters, God can restore him to his glory. The addressee's glory is an elevation of status above his fatigable nature to a place of authority among the liturgical community as well as a place of authority upon the earth itself, which may refer to a restored creation. Part of the role of the addressee as sage is to turn back the wrath of God against the community and possibly the earth itself. Jacob argues, contrary to the majority of Pauline scholars, that glory in Romans also refers to an elevated status and a renewed vocation. Those who have sinned are those who have neglected their vocation to properly rule over the creation, but through redemption they can be restored by God to their vocation and an elevated status of glory. Glory in Romans refers to humanity's exaltation to a renewed status and position of honor as one with a share with Christ in his reign over creation. Redeemed humanity takes on a role as viceregents who intercede on behalf of the creation and are given a place of authority upon the earth itself from within the kingdom of God. These viceregents do not only represent God to the creation but also intercede on behalf of the creation to God. In Jacob's view, glory is not simply the expression of an anthropological reality, but rather it is indicative of "vocational participation" that is expressed as a lived reality.

[217] Made up from MSS 1Q27, 4Q299, 4Q300, 4Q301. There has been discussion regarding the status of 4Q301 as a manuscript of the Book of Mysteries, though solving this identification has little impact on the discussion regarding inheritance. The text appears to have been quite large, but it is extremely fragmented, making interpretation difficult for several lines and overall contexts. For a brief summary of the issue regarding the status of 4Q301, see Kampen, *Wisdom*, 192–93.

[218] The text has at times not been viewed as an example of sapiential literature. Geza Vermes, *The Complete Dead Sea Scrolls in English* (London: Penguin Books, 2011), 408–9, categorized it as apocalyptic. Recent discussions have highlighted the similarities with Instruction and the semantic domain of wisdom terms in the text to designated it as a sapiential text which makes use of the apocalyptic tradition, similarly to Instruction.

though the focus in Mysteries is more on eschatological events, where Instruction highlights the "mystery of existence" as God's guiding plan through all of history from creation to judgment.[219] The eschatological focus of the "mystery of existence" in Mysteries ties wisdom to salvation, where dualistic categories such as "light" and "dark" are used to describe those who do good and are included among the righteous and those who are wicked and will ultimately be vanquished forever.[220] Wisdom in the text is conceived as a form of revelation from heavenly sources that is tied to the natural order; there is an "inclination of understanding" for those who pursue wisdom, and this understanding has implications for the possibility of the understanding person to exhibit morally upright behavior that accords with the order of the world (1Q27 1 i 5; 4Q299 8 6–7.)[221]

Although Mysteries and Instruction contain a number of important similarities, the potential for deterministic and dualistic language is greater in Mysteries.[222] Kampen comments, "I find this dualism to be more marked than that of Instruction, suggesting that its composition is closer to an actual division within the religious institutions and communities of Israel."[223] Even Mysteries, when compared with the "Treatise of the Two Spirits," contains deterministic and dualistic language that is far less explicit than the Treatise, suggesting a potential line of development from Instruction to Mysteries to the Treatise in terms of deterministic and dualistic concepts regarding language and the conceptions of group identity.[224]

Like Instruction, the upholding of the righteous and the punishment of the wicked is among the key concerns of the Book of Mysteries. However, whereas Instruction anticipates a blessed afterlife for the

---

[219]   See Goff, *Discerning Wisdom*, 75.

[220]   See Kampen, *Wisdom*, 191.

[221]   See Goff, *Discerning Wisdom*, 81–83.

[222]   The similarities and differences between Instruction and Mysteries have been compared in multiple studies. For a comparison between the texts, see Goff, *Discerning Wisdom*, 101–2; Elgvin, "Priestly Sages," 71–73, who also notes the many similarities between Mysteries and the book of Daniel; and Kampen, *Wisdom*, 195–96.

[223]   Kampen, *Wisdom*, 194.

[224]   As Goff, *Discerning Wisdom*, 100, notes, Mysteries, like Instruction, was likely not a product of the Qumran community but was brought there and used to develop the ideas of the Dead Sea sect. Goff follows Lange in noting that "the Treatise expands ideas and themes found in *Mysteries*." Furthermore, despite all the similarities between Mysteries and Instruction, their differences are instructive and make it unlikely that they derived from the same community. Mysteries likely postdates Instruction and shows signs of making use of similar themes and language, possibly deriving from a similar thought-world but developing the more malleable aspects of Instruction's ideas. Concerning the use of language as a strategy of polarization for strengthening the identity of an in-group, see A. Klostergaard Petersen, "Wisdom as Cognition: Creating the Others in the Book of Mysteries and 1 Cor 1–2," in *Wisdom Texts from Qumran* (ed. C. Hempel, A. Lange, and H. Lichtenberger; Leuven: Leuven University Press, 2002), 405–32.

righteous in participation with the angels, Mysteries looks forward to a utopian existence on a purified earth where the wicked will disappear from the presence of the righteous in the same way that darkness disappears from the presence of light (1Q27 1 i 1–12; 4Q299 1 1–9; 4Q300 3 1–6). The world itself will be transformed and wickedness will vanish.[225] This is similar to "the new heavens and the new earth" of Isa 65:17-25 and the renewed earth of 1 En. 10:20-21, both discussed in chapter 3 of this study.[226] These passages demonstrate the way that the wickedness of humanity is at odds with God's intent for creation and the constancy of nature and leaves humans at odds with creation and creator. Kampen comments, "When the creator ultimately wins and harmony is restored, only that portion of human society that has recognized this reality will be a participant in this restoration, a 'new creation.'"[227]

The only extant occurrence of inheritance language is found in 4Q299 3a ii b 14. The context is fragmented and difficult to determine fully. Line 13 refers to the origins of God's plan before line 14 declares that for those who have had their hearts tested by God, God will cause them to inherit (ינחילנו) something. The hiphil verb is transitive, as God tests the heart he causes them to inherit (i.e., be "heirs"), but the direct object is missing from the manuscript.[228] The origin of the inheritance is clear, it is from God and is based on his evaluation of their righteousness. The line is too fragmented to make proper sense of the nature of the inheritance, but it is reasonable to correlate it to the overall intention of the composition and the surrounding context. For the righteous, like light, their inheritance is to remain, and assumedly they will have a part in the renewed earth when it is cleansed from the presence of the wicked. The wicked will inherit ruin and will "vanish forever" (1Q27 1 i 6). Instruction features the phrase "inherit the earth" without explicit descriptions of a purified earth, though I argue above that this purified earth may be implied by the phase "inherit the earth." In Mysteries we have the opposite condition; the purified earth is paramount to the text without an explicit reference to "inherit the earth." It is reasonable to hypothesize that 4Q299 3a ii b 14 has this manner of inheritance in mind.

---

[225] See Menahem Kister, "Wisdom Literature and Its Relation to Other Genres: From Ben Sira to *Mysteries*," in Collins et al., *Sapiential Perspectives*, 27, who helpfully establishes this dynamic by pointing to the language of "mysteries of transgression" and "eternal mysteries" in the text (1Q27 1 i 2; 4Q300 1b 2). The work contrasts wisdom with counter-wisdom, where counter-wisdom is destined to perish and eternal wisdom is destined to prevail.

[226] See Goff, *Discerning Wisdom*, 86–88.

[227] Kampen, *Wisdom*, 196.

[228] The hiphil of the root verb נחל is relatively rare in the Qumran Scrolls. The most instructive reference, which will be discussed separately below, is 1QS XI 7, where God has made the chosen heirs of an eternal inheritance.

4.1.3. The Seductress (4Q184)[229]

The Seductress, a composition arranged in poetic format, details the attempts of an allegorical female figure making use of a variety of methods to lure righteous men away from the path of wisdom. Those who associate with her are resident in Sheol and are on the path to death and darkness. Although scholars have attempted to identify the specifics of the allegory and posit a polemical opponent for the text, Kampen persuasively argues that such an identification is not likely possible and is unnecessary to understand the major point.[230] In fact, it may be that no specific opponent was ever in view, as the objective appears to center on building ideological cohesion among the members of the community to which the text is directed.[231] As with Instruction and Mysteries the text makes use of terms and motifs integral to wisdom literature while also demonstrating a cosmological framework familiar to apocalyptic texts.

The seductress depicted in the text bears a number of similarities to "the strange woman" of Prov 1–9, and most scholars regard the latter as the inspiration for the former. There are however important differences; three

[229]   This composition survives in six fragments of a single manuscript (4Q184). A common title for the text, 4QWiles of the Wicked Woman, was first applied by John M. Allegro, "Wiles of the Wicked Woman: A Sapiential Work from Qumran's Fourth Cave," *PEQ* 96 (1964): 53–55. Although this title is still in use, many recent scholars have noted the inappropriate nature of the title in relationship to the content. Goff, *Discerning Wisdom*, 109, uses the title but notes that it is misleading. Kampen, *Wisdom*, 233, uses the title "The Evil Seductress." I have used here the title suggested by Vermes, *Complete Dead Sea Scrolls*, 417.

[230]   Suggestions include that the seductress is an allegory for Rome, that she is the wicked woman of Prov 1–9, that she is Simon the Maccabee, that she represents the dualistic ideology of the Dead Sea sect, that she represents the sect's fear of women, that she is a demonic figure, or that she is the full personification of evil. These possibilities are described by Ananda Geyser-Fouché, "Another Look at the Identity of the Wicked Woman in 4Q184," *HTS* 72 (2016): 1–9, who also entertains the possibility that the seductress represented the city of Jerusalem before concluding that the seductress is an allegory for foreign wisdom that would lead the righteous along the wrong path toward false instruction. Such an idea was also proposed by Martin Hengel, *Judaism and Hellenism*, 2 vols. (Philadelphia: Fortress, 1973), 1:156. Matthew J. Goff, "Hellish Females: The Strange Woman of Septuagint Proverbs and 4QWiles of the Wicked Woman (4Q184)," *JSJ* 39 (2008): 20–45, is right to point out that the text is simply not clear enough to view the seductress as a stand in for a specific abstract idea. She represents the wickedness that leads to death, but the definition of such wickedness is left open. Scott C. Jones, "Wisdom's Pedagogy: A Comparison of Proverbs VII and 4Q184," *VT* 53 (2003): 65–80, in a comparison between the seductress of this text and the strange woman of Proverbs, argues that the seductress in 4Q184 is best viewed as a teaching device to help students remain on the path to righteousness.

[231]   Kampen, *Wisdom*, 234–35. Kampen is in line with most recent scholarship in arguing that the text was not a product of the Qumran community and that the specifics of the community behind the text are out of reach.

in particular should be mentioned here. First, the depiction of the strange woman in Proverbs is more sexually explicit, whereas the depiction of the seductress in this text relies heavily on images of darkness and death such as "the pit" (l. 5), "darkness" (ll. 4–6), "ruin" and "destruction" (ll. 8–9), and "gates of death" and "Sheol" (l. 10).[232] There are references to the clothing and body parts of the seductress, but the emphasis is clearly on her role as a figure associated with death. Second, where Proverbs balances the figure of the strange woman with "lady wisdom," there is no competing figure presented in the extant material of The Seductress. Third, the targeted victims of the two texts are very different. The targets of Prov 1–9 are portrayed as fools who are simpleminded and without sense (Prov 7:7; 9:16). By contrast, the targets in The Seductress are the righteous who walk in an upright manner (ll. 13–15). As Goff states, "They are currently on the right path and the woman intends to make them stumble and veer off course."[233]

Inheritance terms appear three times: once each in lines 7, 8, and 11.[234] Translators often render the noun in line 7 (נחלת) as "inheritance" and the participles in lines 8 and 11 (נוחלי) as "possession."[235] This is reasonable from the context, as the thrust of lines 8 and 11 are not that the wicked will receive the seductress as their inheritance but rather that possessing her will lead to ruin. The concepts of inheritance and possession are related but not synonymous, as one leads to the other. The language is striking; the seductress dwells in beds of darkness and she rules the night (l. 6). The inheritance of line 7 is set in a stark contrast between wisdom and counter-wisdom. The seductress dwells in tents of silence in the midst of "an eternal fire," and she has no part (inheritance, נחלתה) with those who dwell in light. Although there is no figure of light or wisdom to compete with the seductress in this passage, there is an explicit contrast between competing forms of inheritance. There are those who possess the seductress and therefore participate in the path of sin and enter her gateway toward death (ll. 9–10), and there are those who "shine brightly" (l. 8) and walk in righteousness. Inheritance as a form of afterlife is not explicitly described by this text, but the description of the seductress dwelling in "eternal fire" implies a form of punishment after death.[236] This then suggests a blessed

---

[232]   See Goff, *Discerning Wisdom*, 112–14. Sheol is also depicted in Proverbs; see, for example, 5:5; 9:18.

[233]   Goff, *Discerning Wisdom*, 116–17.

[234]   Of note is the use of the Qal participle in lines 8 and 11, which is extremely rare. It is found one other time in the Qumran Scrolls in an extremely fragmented context, in 4Q525 13 5.

[235]   See *DSSR*, 285; Kampen, *Wisdom*, 238.

[236]   See Goff, *Discerning Wisdom*, 115, who relates this to similar descriptions in the Habakkuk Pesher 10:13 and the "Treatise on the Two Spirits" (1QS IV 13), where similar language describes punishment after death.

afterlife for the righteous in a way similar to the descriptions of Instruction, but such a postmortem blessing is not explicit in the text.[237] Also a point of interest is that God is not mentioned as a facilitator of such blessings or punishments in the text; they are predicated on the way one possesses or resists the seductress.

4.1.4. 4QBeatitudes (4Q525)[238]

Like the other wisdom texts discussed in this study, 4QBeatitudes is likely not a product of the *Yaḥad*.[239] Due to a lack of clear historical references it is difficult to date, but many scholars place it sometime in the middle of the second century B.C.E. Unlike the other wisdom texts discussed here, 4QBeatitudes displays a focused interest in Torah.[240] In fact, this interest is the goal of the composition: to encourage the pursuit of wisdom, which is equated with Torah. This equation is more pronounced than Sirach, which includes Torah among the various methods of gaining wisdom but does not equate the two. In 4QBeatitudes, Torah and wisdom are largely one and the same, and no source of wisdom other than Torah is ever mentioned.[241]

---

[237]   Kampen, *Wisdom*, 243, argues that the phrase "those who shine brightly" in lines 7–8 shine presumably because they are in the company of angels or the divine, implying either participation with the heavenly realm, an eternal reward, or both.

[238]   One manuscript (4Q525), a lengthy document made up of more than fifty fragments. The most substantial fragments are 2, 3, 5, and 14.

[239]   Jacqueline C. R. de Roo, "Is 4Q525 a Sectarian Document," in Porter and Evans, *The Scrolls and the Scriptures: Qumran Fifty Years After*, 365–66, argues that 4QBeatitudes is a product of the Dead Sea sect. She points to the similarity of terms between this composition and *Yaḥad* texts. However, although 4Q525 is written to a specific community, Goff, *Discerning Wisdom*, 227–28, is right to argue that there is no compelling reason to associate this text directly with the Dead Sea sect. The similarities of language are outweighed by much more compelling linguistic and thematic differences. See also Kampen, *Wisdom*, 308, who argues that the text features no "sectarian indicators," and Elisa Uusimäki, *Turning Proverbs towards Torah* (Leiden: Brill, 2016), 256, who notes that the rhetoric, function, and language would have appealed to a sectarian audience, but that the text was almost certainly pre-sectarian.

[240]   Kampen, *Wisdom*, 310, notes the remarkable contrast between 4QBeatitudes' use of Torah and the relative absence of Torah in other wisdom texts found at Qumran but notes that even in 4QBeatitudes, where Torah is instrumental to the very nature of the text, it shares with other wisdom texts at Qumran a relative absence of legal traditions.

[241]   For an analysis of the association between wisdom and Torah in 4QBeatitudes, see Elisa Uusimäki, "Happy Is the Person to Whom She Has Been Given: The Continuum of Wisdom and Torah in *4QSapiential Admonitions* (4Q185) and *4QBeatitudes* (4Q525)," *RDQ* 26, no. 3 (2014): 345–59. Uusimäki argues that the feminine suffix ה is used as a literary device to refer to both wisdom and Torah as "her," so that the text does not allow for making clear distinctions between them. Instead, the text posits an inseparable connection between wisdom and Torah. Uusimäki points out that this does

4Q525 2 ii + 3 features beatitudes (from which the composition derives its name) that pronounce the conditions of those who flourish. Wisdom is to be pursued with pure hands and an honest heart (l. 3). The attainment of wisdom is equated with following the law (ll. 3–4).[242] These beatitudes find an important parallel in Sir 14:20-27, a beatitude where the one who flourishes is the one who meditates on wisdom (v. 20). The one who obtains wisdom is the one who holds to the law (Sir 15:1).[243] Another potential parallel, which has been the subject of a great deal of scholarly attention, considers 4QBeatitudes in relationship to the beatitudes of Matthew's Gospel (5:3-12). These potential parallels are discussed in chapter 5, but it is worth mentioning here that Matthew's beatitudes share some structural and thematic similarities to 4QBeatitudes. Although the law is not mentioned in Matthew's beatitudes themselves, the law is an important theme in the immediate context of the Sermon on the Mount (Matt 5:17-20), and the beatitudes there also feature an important reference to inheritance (Matt 5:5).[244]

Although inheritance terms do not appear in 4Q525 5, there are associative terms in line 8 that call back to the inheritance contexts of the Hexateuch. The audience is instructed not to abandon their "portion" (חלק) to strangers or their "lot" (גורל) to foreigners. These terms fit comfortably in the context of Israel's elect status and the land-based inheritances of the Hexateuch, but due to damage to the fragment it is difficult to determine to what degree the writer had these things in mind. In the extant context there is no mention of land; the focus instead is on Torah observance. The use of terms strongly suggests a view of Israelite identity similar to Deuteronomy, where Israel constitutes an elect community from which gentiles are largely excluded as foreigners.[245] However, "portion" and "lot" as a reference to land in accordance with Deuteronomy is not likely.[246] Given the position of the Israelites to the land in the

not necessarily relate the Torah to the Pentateuch, as the concept of Torah in 4QBeatitudes lacks concrete references to specific laws and instructions but may refer to a more generalized view of Torah instruction. See also William A. Tooman, "Wisdom at Qumran: Evidence from the Sapiential Texts," in *Wisdom and Torah: The Reception of Torah in the Wisdom Literature of the Second Temple Period* (ed. Bernd U. Schipper and D. Andrew Teeter; Leiden: Brill, 2013), 212, who states that, according to 4QBeatitudes, "Torah is the source of wisdom, and Torah piety is its sign and substance."

[242] "Walking" in it, from the root הלך.

[243] For more on this parallel, see Goff, *Discerning Wisdom*, 208–9.

[244] See 5.1.2.3 on Matthew's Gospel for examples of this scholarship.

[245] See Goff, *Discerning Wisdom*, 218–19.

[246] Similar is De Roo, "4Q525," 355, who argues that "lot" here refers to behavior, though she does not mention Torah as a source for conduct in accordance with this term. Uusimäki, *Turning*, 250, argues that the lot is a reference to wisdom in general as something that belongs only to devout Jews.

second century B.C.E., these terms may refer instead to the law itself as a uniquely Jewish conception of wisdom that belongs to their community. This would be in line with the description in Sir 24:23 and 2 Macc 2 of the law itself as an inheritance. According to line 13, those who love God will, with humility, walk in the ways of Torah.

Cognates of נחל appear in 4Q525 13 2–5; 14 i 26; 14 ii 1–14; and 33 1.[247] The contexts of 14 i 26 and 33 1 are too fragmented to contribute anything to the discussion. Although 13 2–5 is extremely damaged, it does provide one important detail to the use of inheritance terms in the text. Line 2 mentions the possibility that the reader might "inherit evil" (תנחל ברעי), and line 4 describes the one who "inherits pride" (תנחל גאוה). The context appears to be entirely negative, with reference to the "mouth," as well as holding on to grudges and the shedding of blood. The nature of the inheriting is impossible to determine, but the terms are used in the text to describe negative consequences, almost certainly for those who use their speech to destructive ends.[248]

The negative context of fragment 13 is juxtaposed with the hopeful encouragement of fragment 14 ii. The reference to inheritance in line 1 is too fragmented to add much to understanding the passage, but the following lines are relatively full. Rather than inheriting evil, as in fragment 13, the reader here will be delivered from evil (רע) by God (l. 12). God will fill his days with good and he will walk (הלך) in peace. This encouragement is likely due to the reader's potential vocation as a teacher of wisdom and Torah.[249] The passage is replete with second masculine singular nouns and verbs to describe the conditions and declarations regarding the reader. The reader is told that because of him, others will "raise up your head" (l. 3). It is because of "your word" that others will be made strong (l. 4). Wise, Abegg, and Cook translate תהלל in line 4 as a piel, "you shall praise,"[250] but translating the verb as a pual, "you shall be praised," makes better sense of the context. The reader will contribute words to others that will strengthen them, and because of his teaching he shall be praised by others. The reader shall be blessed and find support from the reproach of the enemy (ll. 7–8). It is because of the reader's commitment to wisdom and teaching others that he can

---

[247]   Cognates of ירש also appear in 14 ii 13 and 15 6.

[248]   The term פה, "mouth," is also found in 4Q400 1 i 17 to describe the tongues of knowledge used to teach precepts to "the holy ones."

[249]   Goff, *Discerning Wisdom*, 226, argues that the text provides the reader with the prospect that they can be teachers later in life. He argues the plausibility that the text was written to a scribal retainer class, much like Sirach, and that the readers of the text were training to become wise men.

[250]   See *DSSR*, 4:255.

anticipate walking in peace (l. 13). Not only is he to walk in peace, but it is said that others will "walk together" (יתהלכו) in "your teaching" (תלמודכה). Line 14 states that the reader, as a teacher, will "inherit glory" (תנחל כבוד).

As we have seen, the inheritance of glory is important to inheritance usage in other wisdom texts found at Qumran. However, texts such as Instruction and Mysteries are steeped in the apocalyptic milieu, and this cannot be said of 4QBeatitudes, so the interpreter must resist uncritical comparison of this familiar phrase. Inheriting glory in Instruction refers to rewards for the one who successfully pursues wisdom and becomes a teacher himself. He will enjoy participation with the angels in the afterlife in the heavenly realm. "Glory" in Instruction refers to participation with the presence of the divine. However, from the limited extant material, it is not clear to what degree 4QBeatitudes features an explicit eschatological outlook, nor is it clear that it contains explicit references to the afterlife.[251] The context of fragment 14 is in regard to the way that the reader, upon becoming a teacher, will be honored by others for the effect of his teaching. Line 14 refers to "eternal rest," but this serves as a euphemism for death rather than the afterlife. When the reader dies, and his students will walk together in his teaching and mourn his passing (ll. 15–16), they will "remember you in your ways" (l. 16). The inheritance of glory here refers to the honor he will enjoy among his students after his passing, not to rewards in the afterlife. The passage concludes with the reader being instructed by his own teacher, the writer of the passage, in the ways of becoming a teacher himself. He is to mediate on wisdom and teach with humility (ll. 19–20), avoiding obscenity and being careful not to cause offense (ll. 26–28).

---

[251]   Goff, *Discerning Wisdom*, 217–23, argues that eschatology in the text is present but muted. The author likely believed that his students should be aware of final judgment and that those who do not heed wisdom will face divine punishment. Goff argues that judgment in the text likely refers more to natural death than eschatological punishment and that the fate of the righteous after death is not a focus of the text. In this it is closer to traditional biblical wisdom than apocalyptic. Many of the fragments that appear to contain possible eschatological references are too damaged to be sure of their content. Kampen, *Wisdom*, 307, identifies judgment as the focus of fragment 10, line 3, where judgment faces those who give in to the seductions of counter-wisdom. Kampen also finds in fragment 15 explicit descriptions of judgment used for refining, modeled after Ezek 22:17-22 and Isa 1:21-26. De Roo, "4Q525," 343, finds explicit statements of eschatological judgment in the fragmentary contexts of fr. 15, 21, and 22, and she compares these fragments to the eschatology of the book of Joel. De Roo, 345, goes so far as to state that 4Q525 features a "high concentration of eschatological elements," which separates it from traditional Jewish wisdom literature.

4.2. Qumran Compositions Concerned with Religious Law[252]

The three principal compositions considered here, the Damascus Document, the Community Rule, and the War Scroll, are often considered "foundation" texts for the community associated with the Qumran site. Grossman helpfully defines "foundation" texts as "the texts upon which communities—including sectarian movements—ground their group identity and understanding of authority."[253] These compositions are of primary importance to a community; they speak of admission requirements, authority structures, and ethics. They trace group origins, state expectations for members, and speak to their God-given identity and future destiny. As seen below, the nature of each of these compositions, including their origins, their relationship to one another, their perceived role as "foundation" texts, and their potential connection to a particular sectarian community, have become matters of considerable debate, but these compositions continue to be discussed in light of one another due to their potential use as key documents for the group most associated with the Qumran Scrolls.[254]

4.2.1. The Damascus Document[255]

In early Qumran research, the Damascus Document (hereafter CD) was typically considered a unitary composition and grouped among

---

[252]   Unless otherwise noted, translations of law compositions will be taken from Donald W. Parry and Emanuel Tov, eds., *The Dead Sea Scrolls Reader*, vol. 1, *Texts Concerned with Religious Law* (Leiden: Brill, 2004).

[253]   Grossman, *Reading*, 30.

[254]   The formation of identity, and specifically sectarian identity, is a complex issue. Identity is influenced by affinities, estrangement and marginalization, exchanges of social discourse, common habits, liturgies, and other cultural norms, shared values, and other concerns. At times, sectarian identity is constructed by polemical language, such as "we" and "they" language, but it is also deeply affected by positive exchanges of shared qualities. Various elements and theories regarding sectarianism in the Qumran Scrolls have been put forth, and while one of the arguments of this study is that "inheritance" terms are "identity" terms that are used in the shaping of shared religious values and social community, a detailed analysis of identity formation in the Qumran Scrolls is beyond the scope of this study. Many perceptive studies on identity formation in the Second Temple period have been produced, with a wide variety of conclusions. See Carol A. Newsom, *The Self as Symbolic Space: Constructing Identity and Community at Qumran* (Leiden: Brill, 2004); Florentino García Martínez and Mladen Popović, eds., *Defining Identities: We, You, and the Other in the Dead Sea Scrolls* (Leiden: Brill, 2008); Jokiranta, *Social Identity*.

[255]   Now often referred to as the Damascus Document, this composition was originally published in 1910 by Solomon Schechter under the title *Fragments of a Zadokite Work*. This consisted of three fragments of two recensions of a document found in the genizah of a Qaraite synagogue in Old Cairo. Fragments of the document were then

sectarian texts that described the historical and social conditions of the Qumran community.[256] The unitary nature of the composition has been challenged, as has its relationship to other sectarian documents among the scrolls discovered at Qumran.[257] The increasing awareness of redacted layers in the composition has called into question the relevance for some of CD's content for setting its ideas within the social and historical milieu of the Qumran site and the possible community (or communities) that made use of the site.[258] There are no easy solutions to

---

discovered at Qumran, with the Cairo fragments adopted into Qumran research and critical editions of the document. Prior to the Qumran discoveries, scholars had insufficient evidence regarding the identity and character of the community responsible for the document. Upon the discovery of the Qumran Scrolls, the document was quickly subsumed under research concerned with the Qumran community, though recent scholarship has cast doubts upon certain aspects of that association. Some scholars use the abbreviation "CD" to refer to the Cairo fragments alone, and "DD" to refer to those discovered at Qumran, though many scholars use either "D" or "CD" to refer to the document as a whole based on critical editions. Following the lead of the majority of scholars surveyed in this study, this section features the abbreviation CD, and the edition consulted is *DSSR*, vol. 1. For an extensive review of the manuscript history and early research on the document, see Davies, *Damascus*, 1–48.

[256] Representative of this approach is Vermes, *Complete Dead Sea Scrolls*, 26–90, who at times nuances the differences between CD and other so-called *Yaḥad* texts but utilizes CD as a unitary witness to the organized social and religious life of the community. Davies, *Damascus*, 16–20, argues that the social and historical milieu of the Qumran community was not read *out of* the composition but rather read *into* it by those who assumed its place as a *Yaḥad* composition. Davies notes multiple differences between CD and other key Qumran Scrolls.

[257] An influential source-critical study on CD that argues forcefully against the unity of the composition is that of Jerome Murphy-O'Connor, "An Essene Missionary Document? CD II, 14–VI, 1," *RB* 77 (1970): 201–29; "A Literary Analysis of Damascus Document VI, 2–VIII, 3," *RB* 78 (1971): 210–32; "The Critique of the Princes of Judah (CD VIII, 3–19)," *RB* 79 (1972): 200–216; "A Literary Analysis of Damascus Document XIX, 33–XX, 34," *RB* 79 (1972): 544–64; "The Essenes and Their History," *RB* 81 (1974): 215–44. Similar redaction-critical approaches to that of Murphy have been offered in the laws by Hempel, *Laws*; and in the admonitions by Davies, *Damascus*. Davies, 1–48, offers an extensive review of scholarship on CD, including various approaches to source and redaction criticism. The unity and single authorship of the composition has recently been defended by Ben Zion Wacholder, *The New Damascus Document: The Midrash on the Eschatological Torah of the Dead Sea Scrolls; Reconstruction, Translation and Commentary* (STDJ 56; Leiden: Brill, 2007), 9–12. Wacholder argues for the unity of the text based on vocabulary, literary style, theology, eschatology, and messianism, though he does not offer a response to the views of source and redaction scholarship specifically.

[258] For a review of these issues, see Hempel, "Qumran Communities." Also, Davies, "Judaism(s)," 36, who argues that the composition was largely composed prior to the formation of the Qumran community but edited by them. Manuscripts found at Qumran represent redactions "by one group of a document that substantially comprises the ideology of another."

these problems, and solving them is not within the scope of this study. However, it is important to be aware of these issues when analyzing CD's use of inheritance terms.

The composition is generally organized into two sections, the admonitions (I–VIII; XIX–XX) and the laws (IX–XVI). Inheritance terms appear six times: the root נחל appears twice (I 16; XIII 12), and the root ירש appears four times (I 7; III 7; VIII 14; XIX 27); all but one of these references appear in the admonitions. While Second Temple references of ירש are not always directly applicable to the concept history of inheritance, the references in CD are directly in line with the use of ירש in the Hexateuch. The community behind CD was well versed in Scripture, and the appearances of ירש assist in underscoring this point.[259]

CD focuses on the events following the Babylonian exile and on a repentant remnant that has formed a covenant group standing in opposition to a rebellious group of apostates. Grossman points out that the text interweaves sectarian and national/universal histories—sectarian because the covenant community of the text sees themselves as the "true Israel" and national/universal because God's anger is portrayed as being directed not only to the apostates within Israel, but toward "all humanity" (I 2).[260] The first admonition (I 1–II 1) focuses on the origins of the covenant group and makes use of Israel's history and scriptural themes to locate their own identity. God brought a remnant of Israel out from the exile and grew them up as a "root of planting" (שורש מטעת), a covenant community to "inherit his land" (לירוש את ארצו).[261] This inheritance functions as a historical callback to Israel's beginnings: the land is their gift from God by virtue of being his covenant people, and God

---

[259]   This is noted by Grossman, *Reading*, 2, who points specifically to the use of Scripture in the laws, as well as to constructed communal history, by making use of scriptural motifs such as the priesthood, the covenant, the exile, and the nature and identity of the "true" Israel.

[260]   Grossman, *Reading*, 108. See also her discussion on pp. 24–30, where she situates CD into common understandings of sectarianism. The community behind CD views its status through identity and the use of language and history rather than through social status and function in relation to Israel widely. The composition portrays a community that is, at least at the time of composition, open to new members.

[261]   Davies, *Damascus*, 53, identifies the reception of the land by the community, the "true Israel" as a key plot to CD. The land is desolate and inhabited by those God has rejected, but when the "true Israel" comes out from the exile they will receive the land and the wicked will be destroyed. The first admonition then offers the audience an invitation to join the "true Israel." Wacholder, *New Damascus*, 146, argues through reference to Ezek 47 that the inheritance of the land in this verse is a yet to be realized eschatological promise. In his view the appointment of the teacher of righteousness is also eschatological.

intends the land to be a place where his people would prosper (I 8).[262] He would test the heart of this community and raise up for them a teacher of righteousness to guide them in his ways (I 7–11). The final portion of the admonition speaks of those who rebel against God and sway from the paths of righteousness as it pronounces their destruction (I 12–II 1).

The composition begins with God's motivation for bringing a remnant community out from the exile—he remembered his covenant with "the first ones" (ראשנים). In the first admonition, these first ones are almost certainly the patriarchs, specifically Abraham, Isaac, and Jacob. God's covenant with Israel's forefathers provides the source of salvation for the remnant community (I 4).[263] A "man of mockery" appeared, who led Israel into rebellion (I 14–16). This rebellion shifted the "boundary markers" that "the first ones" (ראשנים) had set up to mark their inheritance (נחלתם). The relationship of boundary markers and inheritance has clear roots in the Hexateuch, where the inheritance refers to the land allotments given to tribes and families. Consider the linguistic similarities between CD I 16 and Deut 19:14:

> CD I 16—[the rebellious ones] "moved (לסיע) the boundary markers (גבול) which the first ones had set up (אשר גבלו ראשנים) to mark their inheritance (נחלתם)"

> Deut 19:14—"You must not move (תסיג) your neighbor's boundary marker (גבול אשר גבלו), which the first ones had set up (אשר גבלו ראשנים), on the inheritance (נחלתך) of land which you shall inherit (תנחל), which the LORD your God is giving you to inherit (לרשתה)."

Deuteronomy and CD's first admonition both make use of a combination of נחל and ירש to highlight the covenant community's inheritance and possession of God's gift to them. There are other important thematic and linguistic links between CD's first admonition and inheritance contexts in the Hexateuch. Like the Hexateuch, CD envisions the land (ארץ) as a gift from God where his covenant people will flourish (I 8), and all those who break the covenant will be barred from participation with the covenant community. These parallels are striking and lead the reader

---

[262] See Grossman, *Reading*, 179.

[263] Grossman, *Reading*, 111, argues for a multivalent use of ראשנים throughout the composition, noting that it is not always used positively. In the third admonition the term is used in a negative and dismissive way, pointing to the role of earlier generations of Israelites in breaking God's covenant. Because of this, God's covenant had been taken away from Israel and given to the remnant community in view in CD. This remnant has replaced the "old Israel." However, in the first admonition the term us unquestioningly positive and used as a motivation for God to save the remnant community as a way to honor is covenant with the patriarchs. This is an example of the diversity within the text for which Grossman argues.

toward land-inheritance associations. These associations are further encouraged by the other three appearances in CD of the verb ירש; CD III 7 refers to the failure of the Israelites to properly inherit the land at the time of the conquest, and CD VIII 14 (paralleled by XIX 27) directly quotes Deut 9:5 and refers to Moses encouraging the disinheritance of the Canaanites from the land so that the Israelites could fulfill God's land promise to them. The reference to ירש in III 7 is particularly important because the failure of the Israelites to first secure and then to keep the land is used in CD as a justification for the reception of the land for CD's covenant community.[264]

Despite the thematic and linguistic parallels to Hexateuchal contexts on land and inheritance, the "boundary markers" and "inheritance" in CD I 16 are best *not* viewed as references to land allotments. Although the reception of land for the remnant community is in view in the first half of the admonition, the second half is concerned with covenant breaking, which connects to the beginning of the admonition where God remembers his covenant with the patriarchs. The inheritance of I 16 is the covenant itself, the boundaries of which can be moved by those who forfeit (i.e., depart from) the boundaries of the covenant through their rebellion.[265] They are guilty of "specific transgressions against the traditions of the covenant" and attempting to alter the boundaries of the covenant with God.[266] This highlights what is often the strategy of CD's use of Scripture; making use of old, familiar scriptural concepts but appropriating them to explain and come to grips with their contemporary sectarian experience.[267] As Grossman explains, for those who wrote and read CD, communal identity was an issue of primary concern, which required that the community distinguish themselves from the wicked outside the community. As Grossman states, to construct these distinctions the community employed "scriptural themes and multivalent

---

[264]   See Grossman, *Reading*, 179. Wacholder, *New Damascus*, 243, when remarking on CD VIII 14, draws attention to the promise to the patriarchs and the audience of CD, who are compared favorably as having equal value. The followers of the teacher of righteousness take part in the promise and will receive the land.

[265]   See Mark J. Boyce, "The Poetry of the *Damascus Document* and Its Bearing on the Origin of the Qumran Sect," *RevQ* 14 (1990): 628, who compares the apostate of CD to the "wandering heifer" of Hos 4:16. This imagery is helpful for understanding the role of the apostate in attempting to move the boundaries of the covenant. Similar is Albert I. Baumgarten, "The Perception of the Past in the Damascus Document," in *The Damascus Document: A Centennial of Discovery* (ed. Joseph M. Baumgarten, Esther G. Chazon, and Avital Pinnick; Leiden: Brill, 2000), 6, who argues that this refers to those who disregarded "the bounds of Torah." This would refer to villains from outside of the community whose rebellion would require "the drawing of new boundaries and the establishment of new refuges of purity."

[266]   Grossman, *Reading*, 149.

[267]   Grossman, *Reading*, 124–26.

language to articulate a sense of communal identity."[268] Making use of common scriptural themes allowed them to be open to new converts, and appropriating those themes for their own experience allowed them to understand their self-perception as a new Israel.

Communal identity is also important to the only other appearance of נחלה in the composition (XIII 12), though this reference is not rooted in Israel's past. As Hempel has argued, the laws of CD (XIX–XVI) do not typically make use of a polemical or rhetorical style and show few sectarian features.[269] This is not the case with XIII 7–XIV 2, which Hempel argues has been heavily redacted, with its latest features, including the use of נחלה, merged with earlier material to bring it into line with the Community Rule.[270] Although Hempel's specific delineations regarding strata are difficult to prove with certainty, her argument highlights the way the rhetorical use of נחלה stands out in this passage.

CD XIII 7–XIV 2 describes the duties of the overseer of the camp. The overseer leads the camp both in pragmatic and pastoral leadership, organizing the structure and membership of the camp while also shepherding the members and instructing them in God's ways.[271] New members are, at this point, still allowed into the camp but only by permission of the overseer. Once new members are admitted the overseer is tasked with observing them according to their actions, intelligence, and other factors that would influence their involvement in the camp.[272] Based on these observations the overseer includes these new members in their "inheritance in the allotment of light." There is one feature of CD XIII 12a that is rooted in the language of Israel's history. As discussed in chapter 2 of this study, the Hexateuch makes frequent association between נחלה and the term גורל (lot, allotment).[273] In Numbers and Joshua, גורל is often used to denote the boundaries and allotments of land given as an inheritance to the tribes of Israel, but in CD, גורל and נחלה are brought together as a callback to Israel's inheritance to refer to the boundaries of the covenant community. Rather than land, new members of the community are given an inheritance in the allotment of "light" (אור). Receiving an allotment of light shares obvious similarities to dualisms in the Community Rule

---

268   Grossman, *Reading*, 162.

269   Hempel, *Laws*, 19–20, questions whether any whole document from Qumran can be described as sectarian. In her view, many of the key documents from Qumran are composite documents, and regarding CD in particular she argues that little of the document is sectarian. At 191 she argues instead that, rather than simply copying CD, the sectarian community brought it up to date with their views.

270   Hempel, *Laws*, 114–30.

271   Cf. 1QS IX 18.

272   Cf. 1QS V 23.

273   Cf. Num 26:55; 33:54; 34:13; 36:2; Josh 14:2; 17:14; 19:1.

where members of the covenant community are referred to as "children of light" (בני אור) and contrasted with the wicked, referred to as "children of darkness" (בני חושך).[274] Davies notes several differences between the "Judaism(s)" of CD and 1QS, so a one-to-one correlation between the precise nature of the communities described by each should not be assumed, but the use of the term אור in each composition is similar; light refers to the covenant community over against those outside of the boundaries of the community.[275] CD XIII 12 uses "light" as a way to describe entrance and communal identity as the inheritance of new converts who have been evaluated and accepted.

While the use of ירש for inheritance in CD is connected to Israel's historical land-inheritance framework, נחלה is appropriated in both instances (I 16; XIII 12) as an identity term to refer to the covenant of the community. The first instance, CD I 16, is a negative use to describe the way the wayward have moved the boundary of the covenant through their rebellion. The second instance, CD XIII 12, is a positive reference describing the acceptance of new members into the covenant community and their inheritance as members in "the allotment of light." The associations with land are still apparent, as those who receive the inheritance of membership in the camp are in line with the community to receive the land as participants in the "true Israel."

4.2.2. The Community Rule[276]

The situation regarding the Community Rule (hereafter S) is in many ways similar to that of CD. For many years, scholars operated within a

---

[274]   1QS I 8–10. See also 1QS III 17–26.

[275]   Davies, "Judaism(s)," 37–38, notes specifically that "Israel" is maintained as a more distinct category in CD, whereas Israel is not the focus of opposition in 1QS and there is no opposition described between Israel and the nations. Also, Davies argues that determinism merely plays "on the fringes" of CD, while it is central to the descriptions of light and dark dualisms in 1QS III–IV. Davies, *Damascus*, 25–43, argues that the community behind the core text that served as the structure of CD represents a pre-Qumran movement from which the Qumran community splintered. This was a non-sectarian, postexilic community. Similar to Davies is Hempel, *Laws*, 150, who argues that the community behind CD "differs in numerous respects from the community as described in the Community Rule." She argues instead that the community behind CD is a parent community to the *Yaḥad*. On pp. 25–70, Hempel also discusses the Halakhic material in CD and notes that it is free of polemics and is applicable to Israel widely.

[276]   The Community Rule is extant in one nearly complete manuscript from cave 1 (1QS) and at least ten manuscripts from cave 4 (4QS[a–j]). For a complete account of these manuscripts, see Philip S. Alexander and Geza Vermes, *Qumran Cave 4: Serekh Ha Yaḥad and Two Related Texts* (DJD XXVI; Oxford: Clarendon, 1998), 1–4. For a detailed introduction to the S material, see Sarianna Metso, *The Serekh Texts* (London: T&T Clark, 2007).

framework that regarded the *Yaḥad* as a self-designation for the group that made use of the Qumran site, often referred to as "the Qumran community."[277] Scholars have long recognized some differences between CD and S but have often flattened out those differences by pointing to the many similarities as a way to associate both compositions with the same community. CD and S were both widely regarded as compositions that originated within that community and served as foundation texts for their practices and ideology.[278] If this scenario reflected reality, then compositions such as CD and S would be important for understanding the practices and ideology of the Qumran community, but the relevance of these compositions for the wider Jewish experience would be questionable.[279]

However, as with CD, the relationship of S to the Qumran community has been challenged. John Collins has been representative of these challenges, arguing that S existed in different recensions and was copied repeatedly.[280] He argues that there are differences and contradictions between the various copies of S and that these contradictions sometimes appear in different sections of the same manuscript. These differences are the product of various recensions that reflect the developments of decisions and traditions within the communities that edited and copied the rules, and therefore these various recensions do reflect community life. However, these recensions likely do not reflect the development of a *single* community but many.[281] Furthermore, Collins argues that the

---

[277] See, for example, Russell C. D. Arnold, *The Social Role of Liturgy in the Religion of the Qumran Community* (STDJ 60; Leiden: Brill, 2006), 33, who states that the term *Yaḥad* "not only expressed their unity, but also distinguished them from everyone outside their community." Arnold notes that the use of the term as a designation for a community was unique to Qumran. Such a description assumes that the "Qumran community" and the *Yaḥad* should be considered synonymous and that the *Yaḥad* did not function outside of the Qumran site.

[278] See Arnold, *Social Role*, 29–33. Arnold recognizes and catalogues many of the differences between these compositions, but he still regards CD and S as the two foundational texts among the Qumran Scrolls to discuss "the Qumran community's social reality."

[279] So Arnold, *Social Role*, 31, who comments that S portrays a "strictly bounded and separated community."

[280] Collins, "Beyond," 354. See also John J. Collins, "The *Yaḥad* and the 'Qumran Community,'" in *Biblical Traditions in Transmission: Essays in Honor of Michael A. Knibb* (ed. C. Hempel and J. Lieu; Leiden: Brill, 2006). The views of Collins described here have been echoed and expanded by other scholars. See, for example, Alison Schofield, "Rereading S: A New Model of Textual Development in Light of the Cave 4 *Serekh* Copies," *DSD* 15 (2008): 96–120.

[281] Collins, "Beyond," 355. See also Schofield, "Rereading," 97–99, who follows Collins. She argues that the cave 4 manuscripts complicate the picture of the relationship of S to the Qumran site. In Schofield's view, all of the sectarian texts derive from a diverse population. Scholars tend to read the Qumran site into these texts, without warrant. Different versions of S do not reflect a single Qumran scribal tradition.

differences between CD and S are more instructive than many scholars often recognize and that CD and S were likely not first composed by the same community.[282] CD portrays an older, simpler community structure, while S is more developed. To be clear, there was no schism between the communities behind CD and S, but S is based on developments within communities that became stricter and more demanding.[283]

Collins' challenges to the editorial history of S extend into his understanding of the *Yaḥad* itself. In Collins' view, the presence of the *Yaḥad* reached into various locations so that the *Yaḥad* cannot only be associated with the one community in the wilderness often referred to as "the Qumran community." The *Yaḥad* were dispersed in various settlements among various small communities in villages and towns throughout the region, not at Qumran alone. Therefore, the different recensions of S were likely brought to the Qumran site from these various *Yaḥad* settlements, each of which would have been operating with different versions of S that had been edited in ways that reflect the developments from within each of these *Yaḥad* communities.[284] Different recensions and copies of S certainly would have applied to the *Yaḥad* community that made use of the Qumran site, but this group would not have been the one that produced each manuscript.[285] To complicate matters further, Collins argues that, although the site at Qumran was a sectarian site, the *Yaḥad* was likely not the only group to make use of the site. For

---

[282]   The many differences between CD and S have been described in detail by Sarianna Metso, "The Relationship between the Damascus Document and the Community Rule," in Baumgarten et al., *The Damascus Document: A Centennial of Discovery*, 85–94, who argues that the diversity within the 4QS material made it impossible to use it simply to supplement the CD and 1QS material. Metso argues that it is problematic to understand those behind CD and S as two monolithic groups: one behind CD and another behind S. The composite nature of each composition stresses that they have complex redactional histories.

[283]   Collins, "Beyond," 357–58.

[284]   Collins, "Beyond," 358–60. See also Schofield, "Rereading," 103–7, who argues that the different versions of S developed independently of one another. Because of this, there is no clear vorlage for S and it is problematic to look for historical correlations behind various recensions of the composition.

[285]   This view is in contrast to the long-held view of scholars that each of the manuscripts of S were copied by a single community making use of the Qumran site. Representative is Alexander and Vermes, *Cave 4*, 9, who state that the site was home to a single group, "the Qumran sect," and that S was a central text, containing the sect's "fundamental beliefs and practices." Alexander and Vermes recognize the diversity between the various manuscripts of S but argue that this was based on a long process of literary development *within* the community. Based on the paleographic range of the manuscripts, Alexander and Vermes argue that the development lasted throughout the entire period of the community's existence, where deliberate and recensional changes were made.

this reason, Collins argues that the interpretation of any of the Scrolls should not be tied too closely to our understanding of the site. S was not written specifically for the community(s) that made use of the Qumran site, even if it applied to them and was edited by them to some degree. In fact, because the *Yaḥad* was not an isolated monastic community, but was spread widely throughout the region, and because the site at Qumran likely had many users other than the *Yaḥad*, Collins argues that we should stop referring to a "Qumran community" altogether.[286]

These concerns highlight the difficulty in reading historical or social circumstances into the S material. Chief among composite sections of S is the so-called "Treatise on the Two Spirits" (III 13–IV 26), which is important for our discussion as four of the five occurrences of inheritance terms in the S material appear in that section (IV 15, 16, 24, 26). The Treatise is widely regarded as both edited into the surrounding material in the 1QS manuscript and is itself the product of an editorial process.[287] Further complicating interpretive matters is the possibility that the Treatise predates its use at the Qumran site, making its origins difficult to determine.[288] None of this is to suggest that the Treatise is entirely out of place. The editorial process of the composition was intentional, and the Treatise was meant to function within the S material. As Alexander and Vermes argue, despite the separate origins of blocks of S material,

---

[286] Collins, "Beyond," 368–69. Also Schofield, "Rereading," 97–99. As noted by De Looijer, *Qumran Paradigm*, 11–13, certain aspects of Collins' proposal have been met with skepticism by scholars of the Community Rule, but there is wide agreement even among these critics that the *Yaḥad* can no longer be viewed as a singular sectarian movement. This is further supported by archaeological evidence regarding pottery and agriculture that have led to yet further reevaluations of the use of the Qumran site. The site is likely less isolated than many scholars have previously recognized and may have been integrated into the wider regional economy.

[287] See the discussion in Alexander and Vermes, *Cave 4*, 10, who state that the Treatise is "an autonomous unit with no internal links either with what precedes it or with 1QS Vff." The Treatise has an independent character that circulated independently before being incorporated into the Community Rule.

[288] See the discussion in Sarianna Metso, *The Textual Development of the Qumran Community Rule* (STDJ 21; Leiden: Brill, 1997), 137–38. Metso notes attempts by some scholars to use chiastic structures to argue in favor of the Treatise as a literary unity, but she argues forcefully that these attempts fail when one compares the 1QS material to the evidence from cave 4. Metso argues that the evidence demonstrates the redacted nature of the Treatise and suggests that the Treatise possibly has its origins outside of Qumran. See also John J. Collins, *The Apocalyptic Imagination: An Introduction to Jewish Apocalyptic Literature* (Grand Rapids: Eerdmans, 2016), 193, who notes that the Treatise was an independent composition that was edited into the S material, but he finds the argument that the Treatise is "pre-Essene" to be problematic. Collins argues that the Treatise is the culmination of ongoing development but that it was likely complete in the early first century B.C.E.

these sections serve a thematic and functional purpose, highlighting key doctrines, practices, and customs for those that used the composition.[289] Precisely how important the Treatise's doctrines were to the communities that used it is a matter of debate. While the Treatise was once thought to be an important text for the *Yahad*, this view has been challenged in recent years.[290] The majority of attention paid to the Treatise has regarded its use of dualisms. Jörg Frey argues that the occurrences of dualistic language in the Scrolls are extremely limited, calling into question the importance of dualistic thinking by the communities that made use of the manuscripts. Furthermore, when the Scrolls do convey dualisms, they contain a variety of differences in content and the use of terminology.[291] In agreement with Frey, Hempel also notes that some of the cave 4 manuscripts of S do not contain the Treatise and that while it is safe to assume that the communities at Qumran studied the material, other Scrolls also make use of competing ideological and theological ideas.[292] In other words, the use of the Treatise and its dualisms is not nearly uniform enough to consider them a central feature of the group(s) that made use of the material. Despite these concerns, understanding inheritance language in the Treatise is important for at least two reasons: first, the composite nature of the Treatise, as well as the potential that much of the material was composed and circulated prior to and outside of *Yahad* and/or sectarian communities, implies that the material may reflect important developments among Second Temple Jews more broadly;[293] and second, as noted in our discussion

[289]   Alexander and Vermes, *Cave 4*, 10.

[290]   See, for example, Arnold, *Social Role*, 73–74, who argues that the treatise functioned as a sermon delivered by the Maskil to initiates to the *Yahad*, instructing them on life in the community in opposition to the world outside. This would place the Treatise in a foundational role within the community, instructing initiates on core ideologies found within the Treatise as a matter of first importance.

[291]   Jörg Frey, "Different Patterns of Dualistic Thought in the Qumran Library: Reflections on Their Background and History," in *Legal Texts and Legal Issues* (ed. M. Bernstein, F. García Martínez, and J. Kampen; Leiden: Brill, 1997), 278.

[292]   Charlotte Hempel, "The Treatise on the Two Spirits and the Literary History of the Rule of the Community," in *Dualism in Qumran* (ed. Géza G. Xeravits; London: T&T Clark, 2010), 102–20. See also Stuckenbruck, "Interiorization," 161, who argues that the Treatise was not initially composed by the community(s) at Qumran and "does not formally summarize or immediately reflect the group's ideology." In terms of dualisms, Stuckenbruck argues that those in the Treatise more closely resemble those in sapiential compositions than they do those found in compositions unambiguously connected to the Qumran community.

[293]   This point is not to deny the sectarian features of the Treatise but only to suggest that it may contain nonsectarian material. Although its sectarian character has been tempered in recent scholarship, it still portrays sectarian tendencies. See the nuanced approach of Thomas P. Dixon, "Knowledge and Deeds in the Two

regarding Instruction, the Treatise bears a number of linguistic and thematic similarities to other important Second Temple compositions. This means that understanding inheritance language in the Treatise may reveal ideas contained within it that were more ubiquitous than a discussion on dualisms would suggest.

The Treatise refers to the Maskil, whose role it is to instruct the "sons of light" as to the fate of humankind, especially concerning humankind's spirits and deeds (III 14). God is the creator and ruler over all things, and humankind is to walk according to one of two spirits that have been created by God: either the spirit of truth or the spirit of falsehood (III 18–19). Those who walk according to the spirit of truth are allied with and assisted by the angel of light, and those who walk according to the spirit of falsehood are aligned with the angel of darkness. The spirits of light and darkness are the cornerstone of every deed and the impetus for every inclination (III 21–26). All humankind are the recipients of eschatological promises. To the sons of light go promises of healing, peace, long life, eternal blessings, everlasting life, and a crown of glory. To the sons of darkness go eternal damnation, God's wrath, and eternity spent in outer darkness with no hope of rescue (IV 6–14). The fate of all humankind resides with these two spirits. It is said of the spirits themselves that God has caused them to "inherit/take possession of" all humanity (וינחילן לבני איש), and in doing so God has decided the fate of all people by the measure of which spirit predominates within them until the time of judgment (IV 26). All of humankind "inherits" a spirit based on these divisions (כול בני איש ובמפלגיהן ינחלו), and this "inheritance" (נחלה) dictates the outcome of every deed (IV 15–16). All people walk in both wisdom and foolishness, to some degree partaking in each of the two spirits, but those who walk in truth will do so in proportion to their "inheritance" (נחלה) of truth (IV 24). God has appointed these spirits to exist side by side until the last age, when they will be divided for all eternity (IV 17). In the last age, darkness will be destroyed, and truth will triumph across the earth (IV 19). At that time, God will purify all human deeds (IV 20), and those God has chosen for an eternal covenant will be made wise (IV 22).

Spirits Treatise," *JSP* 24, no. 2 (2014): 72, who applies a "minimalist" definition of sectarianism to the Treatise. This definition recognizes that the Treatise has a sectarian rhetorical purpose but does not presuppose a provenance at the Qumran site or with the *Yaḥad*. Instead, it recognizes that the text demonstrates a separation from a larger body of Israel "to pursue special piety within Judaism." Dixon recognizes that the dualism between "the sons of light" and "the sons of darkness" represents a sectarian consciousness, "regardless of who authored the text and what kinds of communities used it."

It is easy to see why dualism has been the focus of much of the research that has been done on the Treatise. The dichotomy between the "sons of light" and the "sons of darkness" is an important and compelling feature of the text. However, a close analysis resists simplistic explanations as to how dualisms are used. Mladen Popović has defined dualism as "two fundamentally opposed, causal principles" that "underlie the existence of the world and its constitutive elements."[294] In the Treatise, the nature of the opposition between light and dark must be refined, precisely because the causal dualistic forces in the text are themselves caused and directed by the single force of God. As such, these dualistic forces are only as opposed, and as equal, as God directs them to be. God is portrayed as the singular cause and power behind the dualisms in the text, and rather than causes, the forces of "light" and "dark" function only as mechanisms for God to carry out his plan. The opposition between "light" and "dark" is only potent as long as they are useful to God, but their opposition will run its course when the plan reaches its eschatological climax and the forces of darkness will be destroyed. As Popović notes, God himself is "the onto-logical basis of everything and everyone."[295] The potency of the dualisms is tempered by the fact that everything will ultimately happen according to God's plan, meaning that the concept of dualism appears far less import-ant to the author(s) of the Treatise than the need to emphasize the eschato-logical fate of those who belong to God's covenant community. Dualistic ideology is not itself the point, which may explain why dualisms are not ubiquitous throughout the Qumran Scrolls. The dualisms are a rhetorical device set to the task of motivating at least three other realities: 1) God's deterministic plan for his covenant community, 2) the eschatological fate of the "sons of light," and 3) motivation to good deeds that accompany covenant identity.

That dualisms in the Treatise are best viewed as a rhetorical device, rather than a vital aspect of the author(s) and/or community's ideology, is further illustrated by the fact that dualisms in the Treatise are not used in a uniform way. Instead, dualisms are employed to serve a rhetorical purpose in favor of a larger point. Frey has identified at least ten "dimen-sions" of dualistic thought in ancient religious thought, and scholars have identified as many as four of these categories in the Treatise alone.[296] These dimensions of dualism are interwoven in the Treatise and progress

---

[294]   Mladen Popović, "Light and Darkness in the Treatise on the Two Spirits (1QS III 13-IV 26) and in 4Q186," in Xeravits, *Dualism in Qumran*, 149.

[295]   Popović, "Light and Darkness," 151.

[296]   Frey, "Different Patterns," 282–85. These "dimensions" are broadly labeled as metaphysical, cosmic, spatial, eschatological, ethical, soteriological, theological, physi-cal, anthropological, and psychological.

from one section of the text to another. Stuckenbruck has argued for three dimensions of dualism in the text, and he has suggested a helpful outline regarding their progression: the first is cosmic dualism (III 18–IV 1), followed by ethical dualism (IV 2–14), and finally psychological dualism (IV 15–26). Despite their contrasts, these three spheres are bound up with and modify one another.[297] The key terms in the Treatise that demonstrate the use of cosmic dualism are "light" and "dark." According to Frey, the forces described by a cosmic dualism are neither coeternal nor causal. Although the description of these forces relies heavily on the first section of the Treatise, the aspect of God's dominion over them runs through the end of the text.[298] The second section features an ethical dualism that focuses on the division of humanity into two groups based on virtues and vices and makes use of ethical-dualistic terms such as "righteousness" and "wickedness." While ethics is primarily the focus of the second section of the text, these ethical terms are interwoven with cosmic terms: righteousness with light and wickedness with darkness. The third section of the text, where all four references to inheritance are found, makes use of psychological dualism. In this dimension, the opposition is not between two types of people but between principles or impulses at war within each individual.[299] In the case of the Treatise, the human being is a "locus of conflict" between light and dark, but it is the person's deeds, not the person themselves, which are assigned to one of the two divisions.[300] Previously, in the discussion regarding Instruction, it was noted that some scholars have argued in favor of an anthropological dualism in the Treatise. These scholars then note the similarities between the language of the Treatise and Instruction in order to argue that the latter also makes use of anthropological dualisms regarding the separation of humankind into two groups, based on possessing one of two kids of spirits. In regard to Instruction, I argue that this composition does not feature anthropological dualistic language; the same may be said of the Treatise. The Treatise does not simply separate people into two groups based on the spirits assigned to them but notes the struggle that goes on within each individual, including those categorized as the "sons of righteousness."[301] According to the Treatise, God has

---

[297] Stuckenbruck, "Interiorization," 162.

[298] Frey, "Different Patterns," 292.

[299] Frey, "Different Patterns," 285.

[300] Stuckenbruck, "Interiorization," 164.

[301] So also Frey, "Different Patterns," 294, who argues that there is not the slightest notion of anthropological dualism in the Treatise. The allocation of the spirits is not based on birth but on God's predestination expressed by God throwing the lot (IV 26). It should be noted that the Treatise is not altogether clear on how these spirits are applied. Popović, "Light and Darkness," 155, notes the difficulty when he argues that tensions

allowed righteousness and perversity to exist side by side within each person until the visitation, when wickedness will be destroyed and those belonging to God's covenant will be given the wisdom of the angels in a perfect way (IV 22–26). This dualism is psychological because it is individuals who serve as "the battleground where the conflict between opposing spirits is carried out."[302]

The dualisms in the Treatise confirm God's eternal plan and are further aimed toward expressing two important realities. The first concerns the importance of good deeds, focused specifically on the contrast between virtues such as humility, patience, and compassion (IV 3) and vices such as lying, pride, deceit, and foolishness (IV 9–11). As Dixon argues, the Treatise does not simply describe the eschatological purging of wicked people, but of deeds themselves, so that specific deeds described "provide a window into the unfolding of God's plan in creation and history."[303] Deeds also serve to foreground human nature, as the ebb and flow of good deeds by the individual exposes the struggle within each person.

The second reality concerns the eschatological fate of all humankind. As Stuckenbruck argues, the Treatise resists a simplistic delineation between the "sons of light" and the "sons of darkness." The Treatise recognizes that the righteous can and do fail, and the present age is one of uncertainty.[304] On the cosmic level God assigns the angels of light and darkness, but on the psychological level these cosmic spirits war within each individual so that at the ethical level the individual must be aware of which deeds accord with the angel of light.[305] The eschatological emphasis in the Treatise uses these rhetorical frameworks to edge the student toward the consciousness of a group identity on the basis of the ethics that correspond to a righteous community. As Stuckenbruck notes, these various dualities only exist temporarily, until they

---

in this regard remain in the final text of 1QS and that these tensions may be a result of recensions of the Treatise over time. On the one hand, the text describes human beings as rigorously assigned to one spirit or another. In this regard the dualistic approach appears to be anthropological. However, on the other hand, both spirits are portrayed as battling within people's hearts, suggesting that all individuals partake of the struggle between both spirits. This approach appears to be psychological. These two ideas are in opposition and the tensions are not easily solved.

[302]   Stuckenbruck, "Internalization," 164–65.

[303]   Dixon, "Knowledge and Deeds," 94.

[304]   Stuckenbruck, "Internalization," 165.

[305]   See Frey, "Different Patterns," 294, who argues in favor of these same dimensions of dualistic thought in the Treatise: cosmic, ethical, and psychological. Frey argues that the cosmic classifications of light and dark come together with the ethical terms of truth, justice, and wickedness and that these deeds take root within the psychological level of every individual.

are "wiped away at the appointed time of God's visitation" and the conflict between the two spirits is eliminated.[306] 1QS IV 25 states that the spirits will cease to be equals at the time of "renewal" (חדשה). The exact nature of the renewal is left ambiguous. As Albert Hogeterp suggests, it could refer to a purified life in the final age, and possibly afterlife, but at the very least it signifies the expectation of a new creation based on the eschatological promises of 1QS IV 6–8.[307]

It is in the progression and entanglements of the dualisms that inheritance terms in the Treatise are best understood. Even within the use of inheritance terms, which occur in relatively close proximity, there is diversity that has the initial appearance of conflict. On the one hand, all people are said to exhibit deeds that accord with the spiritual inheritance that they received (IV 16). On the other hand, each person is said to exhibit deeds that accord with both spirits but that the proportion of their deeds will accord with the measure of their inheritance of each spirit (IV 24). This is a difficult puzzle to solve, but it is possibly clarified by keeping in mind the progression of the Treatise's argument. The point regarding inheritance is to understand the deeds associated with the group identity, deeds that accord with God's covenant people. When the battle for righteous deeds wages within an individual, they are encouraged to understand deeds on a sliding scale that might motivate a course correction toward deeds that are appropriate for a member of the righteous community. This serves a rhetorical purpose because it allows for any individual to see their apparent failures in relative terms, believing that they can still be corrected toward a measure of righteousness that outweighs the foolishness they are tempted toward. If an individual is convinced they are an heir of righteousness, this serves as a motivating factor and a guarantee of success. Therefore, inheritance in the Treatise is an identity term, delineating those who have inherited a position as "sons of light" and motivating the deeds that accompany such an inheritance.

The only other appearance of inheritance language in S occurs in 1QS XI 7. As with the Treatise, the similarities between this section and Instruction, particularly 4Q418 81, are striking. The Instruction column refers to a heavenly community called an "eternal planting," which I argue refers to a mixed community of God's "holy ones," which are the angels, and the students of the Maskil who obtain wisdom and are elevated to a position of participation with the heavenly host. Instruction makes use of a watering metaphor for the establishment and growth of

---

[306]   Stuckenbruck, "Interiorization," 166.

[307]   Albert Hogeterp, *Expectations of the End: A Comparative Traditio-Historical Study of Eschatological, Apocalyptic, and Messianic Ideas in the Dead Sea Scrolls and the New Testament* (STDJ 83; Leiden: Brill, 2009), 287.

the community to which the planting metaphor applies. 1QS XI 7 makes use of similar language to make largely the same point, although the community in view is certainly rooted in a different sociological context than the community in view in Instruction.[308] 1QS XI refers to God's chosen, the *Yaḥad*, as recipients of an "eternal possession." God has caused his chosen ones to "inherit" (ינחיל) a lot with the "holy ones," the angels. The *Yaḥad* and the angels have been united as an "assembly of holiness" and an "eternal planting," and the planting metaphor, as in Instruction, is supported by an elaborate use of watering metaphors with the phrases "spring of righteousness" (1QS XI 6) and "reservoir of strength" (1QS XI 6–7).[309] The phrase "eternal planting" appears in one other place in S, 1QS VIII 5, where it refers to the *Yaḥad* alone. In this context the planting metaphor relies to some degree on its foundations in biblical texts such as Isa 60:21; 61:3, but S interprets and appropriates the metaphor to refer to the *Yaḥad* as the remnant of Israel.[310] They see themselves as a restored, righteous community, the plant of God, established and tended to pursue righteous deeds and future growth. However, in 1QS XI 7 it is not only the *Yaḥad* who are the "eternal planting," but as with Instruction the metaphor has a view toward the mixed community of humans and angels, and the *Yaḥad* have inherited participation in a blended community with the angels as an aspect of their eschatological blessing realized in the present remnant community.[311] This participation with angels is also hinted at in the Treatise, as those who have a lot with the "sons of righteousness" receive the wisdom of the angels at the time of the visitation (1QS IV 22). That eschatological vision is applied to the present participation.[312] The planting metaphor is not the only way that the passage connects the remnant community with Israel's authoritative scriptural past, as 1QS XI 7 makes use of a number of key words

[308]　See Patrick A. Tiller, "The 'Eternal Planting' in the Dead Sea Scrolls," *DSD* 4, no. 3 (1997): 334, who argues that the referents to the planting metaphor across Second Temple literature are relatively fixed, though the communities making use of the metaphor are not always the same or even connected or directly influenced by one another. He argues that this suggests a "common cultural and historical matrix" from which the metaphor was applied in various compositions.

[309]　See Cecilia Wassén, "Visions of the Temple: Conflicting Images of the Eschaton," *Svensk exegetisk årsbok* 76 (2011): 55.

[310]　See Tiller, "Eternal Planting," 334, who argues that all Second Temple references to "planting" are in some measure interpretations of the biblical material that makes use of the metaphor, with Isa 60:21 and 61:3 being the principal passages of engagement.

[311]　See Tiller, "Eternal Planting," 329.

[312]　Wassén, "Visions," 51, argues that this eschatological awareness is also present regarding the "eternal planting" in 1QS VIII, where the community is associated with atonement and the judgment of the wicked.

associated with the inheritance of land throughout the Hexateuch: terms such as נתן (to give), אוחזת עולם (eternal possession), and גורל (lot). As we have seen throughout this study, these terms are prolifically connected to inheritance concepts throughout Jewish literature, and they function the same way in 1QS XI 7 as they do in the Hexateuch, although appropriated to new ends. God is the one who gives the inheritance, he gives it as an eternal possession, and in his own plan he determines the lot of all who receive an inheritance from his hand. However, in 1QS XI it is not land that is inherited by God's covenant people but rather a more secure place: a place among the angels in the heavenly community.

4.2.3. The War Scroll[313]

The situation regarding the War Scroll (1QM) and the various "War Texts" (hereafter M) found at Qumran is relatively similar to that of the CD and S material. 1QM, shortly after publication, was regarded as a unified account written by a single author, and the material was thought to represent the views of the Qumran sect.[314] With new evidence provided by an analysis of the M material from cave 4, and a closer examination of the content of 1QM, the text is now regarded as a composite work made up of various sources, and its transcription history reveals various stages of recension and a complex redactional history.[315] Exploring this textual history is not necessary for this study, as the basic purpose of 1QM is relatively straightforward and terms for inheritance are best understood in light of the composition's narrative intent.

1QM is a description of eschatological war. The remnant of Israel, the "sons of light," are to fight a war against their enemies, "the sons

---

[313] For a detailed introduction to the war texts found at Qumran, see Jean Duhaime, *The War Texts* (London: T&T Clark, 2004). There is some debate regarding which manuscripts represent recensions of the War Scroll and how the content of the manuscripts might fit together. See especially pp. 12–43.

[314] See, for example, Yigael Yadin, *The Scroll of the War of the Sons of Light against the Sons of Darkness* (Oxford: Oxford University Press, 1962). Although Yadin regarded the text as derived from a single author, he argued that the text would have been reworked and arranged from various separate sources.

[315] An early extensive analysis was undertaken by Philip R. Davies, *1QM, the War Scroll from Qumran: Its Structure and History* (BibOr 32; Rome: Biblical Institute Press, 1977). Duhaime, *War Texts*, 53–59, argues that, due to the presence of varied material in M texts, the genre, purpose, and function of the M material may have changed with different recensions. However, he argues that despite the redaction process the final form of 1QM reads as a largely coherent document. Likewise, Brian Schultz, *Conquering the World: The War Scroll (1QM) Reconsidered* (Leiden: Brill, 2009), 86, notes that upon an initial reading, 1QM's themes appear to be presented in an incoherent manner but that the text makes use of a careful logical progression of the material.

of darkness." The "sons of light" engage in this war in participation with God and the angelic host in order to reestablish Israel's place in their land and establish their dominion over the nations of the earth. Before the war, the "sons of light" regard themselves as exiles. The war brings the remnant back into the land, ends their exile, brings Israel into dominion over the earth, and ushers in the messianic age.[316] These details imply a sharp divide between Israel and the gentile world and portray a nationalistic, rather than sectarian, worldview within the M material. The description of the war features a series of battles, tactical strategies, weaponry, and speeches and liturgical prayers to be recited before, during, and after battle.[317]

An important feature of 1QM is the way it uses Israel's Scripture. In particular, the composition makes frequent use of the Pentateuch in order to look to the past and strengthen the convictions of the community. The text also, at times, provides an eschatological context to Scripture where there was not one previously, in order to situate Israel's history in the context of a positive outlook toward the eschatological conflict.[318] As Jean Duhaime states, "Their dreams have been shaped by the memory of historical antecedents of salvation as well as by the prophetic expectations of victory. Their beliefs and hopes have repeatedly been expressed with the very words of their forerunners in faith."[319] It is in this dual focus of both looking back to the history of salvation and forward to the expected future victory that both references to inheritance in 1QM find their meaning.[320]

---

[316]   See Schultz, *Conquering*, 168–69.

[317]   The sequence of the battle, and the outline of the material, are matters of debate. Of principal concern has been the apparent discrepancy between columns 1 and 2. It has long been argued that the descriptions of war in columns 1 and 2 are contradictory and cannot be completely reconciled. Column 1 features only the three southern tribes going to war with the Kittim, whereas column 2 describes the remnant of the whole of Israel going to war with the entire gentile world. It has been argued that this discrepancy is the result of the editorial process of the M material. Shultz, *Conquering*, esp. 236–39, argues instead that columns 1 and 2 describe separate stages of the same war and that the details are complementary. Column 1 describes the "War of the Kittim," which is an initial stage of the war, and involves only Israel's neighbors. The details of this war are heavily influenced by Dan 11:40-45. Column 2, "the War of the Divisions," describes a second stage of the war with the rest of the nations. Due to the involvement of the angels in the first stage of the war, and the recapturing of Jerusalem, the outcome of the second stage of the war is an inevitable victory for the "sons of light."

[318]   See Duhaime, *War Texts*, 103, 113–14.

[319]   Duhaime, *War Texts*, 114.

[320]   Technically there are four inheritance references, 1QM X 15; XII 12; XIX 4, and 4Q492 1 4. However, 4Q492 1 4 is a duplicate of 1QM XIX 4, and 1QM XIX 4 is reworked material from XII 12, which features slight variations but is undoubtedly the same material reproduced. See Duhaime, *War Texts*, 20; Shultz, *Conquering*, 87. As Shultz

Both references to inheritance are found in columns X–XIV, which is an independent liturgical unit featuring speeches and prayers to be said at war.[321] These prayers focus on praising God and appealing to his covenant with Israel, as well as the dual focus of looking back into Israel's past redemption at the hands of God and forward to a greater redemption in the future.[322] 1QM X 10–15 appeals to the covenant and to God's complete control over creation, praising him for his power and his works to dictate human affairs, including in X 15 God's allocation to his people of "the inheritance of lands" (נחלת ארצות). This section is replete with references to Hexateuchal contexts, including to creation, Babel, and the establishment of clans and holy festivals. The inheritance here is clearly looking backwards to God's gift of the land to his covenant people. Column XII then looks to the future and calls on God to act on behalf of his covenant people. God is the hero of the war, directing his angels in battle (XII 4–5). The prayer asks God to crush the nations (XII 11) and fill God's land with glory and his inheritance (נחלת) with blessing. The inheritance here is God's own, and the antecedent of inheritance is his land. The glory of his land is described in terms of utopian blessing, such as cattle in the fields, gold in the palaces, and songs of rejoicing sung throughout the cities of Judah (XII 12–13).

There are two important features in 1QM to consider in relation to this study. First, as with many Second Temple texts discussed in this study, 1QM is set in the context of a community devoid of any military power and looking at inheritance in light of the loss of access to Israel's ancestral lands. In many texts, this shifts the view of inheritance toward other concerns, such as the law, wisdom, or an entirely eschatological renewed earth. Much of this shift in focus allows for the inheritance to be granted universally to gentiles. However, 1QM keeps the focus of Israel's inheritance squarely on the land, both the past allocation and the future reacquisition. An important purpose of the M material was to instill in the communities that used it a belief that God and his heavenly armies would destroy evil and restore them to their land.[323] Second, the community(s) in view in the M material is described as "poor" (אביונים). As we have seen, אביון has been used

---

argues, there is little rationale behind the reproduction of the material from column XII into column XIX. This study will focus only on the two unique references to inheritance.

[321]   For an extensive analysis of the use of 1QM as liturgy, see Daniel K. Falk, "Prayer, Liturgy, and War," in *The War Scroll: Violence, War and Peace in the Dead Sea Scrolls* (ed. Kipp Davis, Dorothy M. Peters, Kyung S. Baek, and Peter W. Flint; STDJ 115; Leiden: Brill, 2016), 275–94.

[322]   Schultz, *Conquering*, 258.

[323]   See Duhaime, *War Texts*, 60.

to describe the poor in other compositions among the Qumran Scrolls, principally for our purposes it (along with synonyms for "poor") is used throughout Instruction (cf. 4Q416 2iii 8–12; 4Q417 2i 17). In Instruction the poor are described as those who are elevated above their poverty to positions of honor and participation with the angelic host as teachers of wisdom and the "mystery of existence." This elevation, and the texts of Instruction in their entirety, are entirely peaceful, where the focus is on ethics and participation in a righteous and humble community.[324] However, in the M material, it is the poor who have been redeemed and rescued by God (XI 9), and it is for the poor that God will deliver his enemies toward destruction (XI 13), all through the context of a violent eschatological conflict.[325] The poor in the M material have little power to contribute, but participation with God and the angelic host in the destruction of enemies through battle is the means of their future elevation. The tone of the two presentations could not be more disparate.

[324]   See John Kampen, "Wisdom, Poverty, and Non-Violence in *Instruction*," in Davis et al., *War Scroll*, 215–36. Kampen cycles through the violent contexts of some of the Qumran Scrolls and then states that, in the midst of these descriptions, sits Instruction, a significant and influential composition that addresses real-world concerns "in a non-confrontational manner." Instruction certainly portrays postmortem judgment for the sons of iniquity (see 4Q418 69 ii), but there are no descriptions of violence toward oppressors or others in positions of power, and Instruction encourages a posture of humility toward the wealthy. Rather than overthrowing imperial rule, Instruction reveals practical ways to live a life devoted to God and patterned after the angels in the context of poverty and an imperial reality. The community's view as to the timing of the eschaton may have something to do with these emphases. Collins, *Scriptures*, 249, notes that within Instruction's apocalyptic elements, it never recognizes that the end is near. The end is assured but not imminent. As one waits for the end, regardless of timing, those who inherit glory are those who live wisely.

[325]   This is not to suggest that those behind the M material were themselves violent or even that they expected the violence to mirror that described in the "War Texts." Alex P. Jassen, "Violent Imaginaries and Practical Violence in the *War Scroll*," in Davis et al., *War Scroll*, 175–203, argues that the violence depicted in 1QM is an "idealized fantasy of eschatological retribution." This does not at all mean that the communities making use of the material were not anticipating a war. In fact, they most certainly were. This is to suggest, however, that the description of the war in 1QM served a largely rhetorical function to empower the communities making use of the material and that the descriptions of war were not meant to be considered realistic, even if the war was real. In fact, the religious elements of the texts reflect not a war manual but the opposite: the views of a group that lacks the ability to wage a war and instead must call on God and his angelic host. 1QM, then, is a composition where "imagination meets anticipation," and propaganda is used to legitimate impending violence against their enemies. See the Apocalypse of Joseph (4Q372 3), where God's covenant to Joseph's descendants is eternal, and God will protect his "inheritance," meaning his covenant people, from the nations by destroying all of Israel's enemies.

4.3. Conclusions

In many ways, inheritance contexts in the Qumran Scrolls mirror those of other Jewish compositions discussed from the HB and other Second Temple sources. Rather than used as a pragmatic term relating to the passing and acquisition of land property and goods from within families, inheritance terms more often refer to the gifts and blessings bestowed by God upon his covenant people. In other words, inheritance terms are more often theological than pragmatic, more often rooted in identity than property. Inheritances are bestowed by God, to his covenant people, as an aspect of his relationship with them. Although much of inheritance terminology in the Qumran Scrolls often takes linguistic cues from the Hexateuch, the Hexateuchal literary traditions are usually appropriated toward new aims. Indicators of God's relationship to his people are largely the same, but although land is in view in 1QM, more often the inheritance focuses on the community's membership boundaries, social identity, social status, ethical conduct, acquisition of wisdom, and eschatological postmortem fate. The way that sapiential and apocalyptic themes come together is instructive in this regard: wisdom acquisition, ethical conduct, and ultimate fate take precedent over issues regarding basic property, to the point that poverty, in certain compositions, becomes the norm, while the pursuit of wisdom and righteousness becomes an issue of central concern. Inheritance terms take on a more rhetorical role, important more for what they signify than what they provide in practical ways. Ultimately, the primary focus of inheritance in the Scrolls (esp. Instruction, 4QMysteries, the Community Rule) is on the ability of those who pursue God and his wisdom and righteousness to become members of the heavenly community and have a share in a reconstituted earth. As chapter 5 will demonstrate, these trajectories observed in Second Temple period compositions would take further shape in the Gospel of Matthew.

5

Inheritance in the Gospel of Matthew

5.1. Inheritance in Matthew 5:5

μακάριοι οἱ πραεῖς, ὅτι αὐτοὶ κληρονομήσουσιν τὴν γῆν.
Flourishing are the meek, because they will inherit the earth.

5.1.1. Matthew's Makarisms

Very few aspects of Matthew's makarisms have enjoyed scholarly consensus. Scholars are divided on their form, sources, meaning, number, and role within the Matthean narrative; even the translation of the term μακάριος is a matter of debate.[1] For scholars who argue that the makarisms are "blessings," discussions have centered on the nature of the blessings in view in Matthew. There are examples of makarisms

---

[1]   The issue regarding the translation of μακάριος will be discussed in 5.1.1.4. The issue regarding the number of Matthew's makarisms is not of particular relevance for this study. Most scholars entertain only the possibility of either seven or eight (see, for example, Robert A. Guelich, "The Matthean Beatitudes: 'Entrance Requirements' or Eschatological Blessings?" *JBL* 95, no. 3 [1976]: 415), with some scholars arguing for eight comprising two groups of four (see the discussion below 5.1.1.2). Dale C. Allison Jr., *The Sermon on the Mount: Inspiring the Moral Imagination* (New York: Crossroad, 2016), 29, argues effectively that Matt 5:11-12 functions as an extended ninth beatitude. Charles Quarles, *Sermon on the Mount: Christ's Message to the Modern Church* (Nashville: B&H, 2011), 40–41, recognizes nine statements but argues for eight makarisms with the ninth statement offering extended commentary on the eighth makarism. Hans Dieter Betz, *Essays on the Sermon on the Mount* (Philadelphia: Fortress, 1985), argues in favor of ten makarisms, with an initial series of eight in parallel form, with two further makarisms added secondarily, but this view has not found support.

in Jewish literature that speak of those who are blessed *because* of the positive nature of their current condition (cf. Prov 3:13). Conversely, there are examples in which future blessings are promised *despite* current circumstances, offering an eschatological reversal of unfortunate present conditions (Tob 13:14).[2] A growing number of scholars have challenged the long-assumed correlation between μακάριος and the concept of "blessing," arguing that rather than "divine favor," μακάριος refers to human flourishing and the fulness of an earthly life. In this instance, makarisms can still anticipate divine favor and eschatological blessings but they take on a decidedly ethical flavor as their primary emphasis.[3]

Further compounding the difficulties in interpretation are discussions regarding the differences between the makarisms in Matthew and the corresponding list in Luke 6:20-23. The potential relationship between these two lists often influences the way scholars view the nature of Matthew's makarisms, with many interpreters arguing that Luke's list features a more apparent design toward eschatological reversals, while Matthew features a more ethical and sapiential flavor.[4] Luke features four makarisms, with four corresponding woes (Luke 6:24-26), and each of the four Lukan sayings is represented in Matthew, albeit with some differences in form and vocabulary.[5] Matthew features nine sayings. The corresponding woes, which are considerably different than Luke's, have been moved to a much later place in the narrative (Matt 23). These differences are apparent within the first makarism in each list, when comparing Matt 5:3 with Luke 6:20. Matthew 5:3 is addressed in the third person plural and refers to those who are "poor in spirit," who will receive "the kingdom of heaven." Luke 6:20 is addressed to the second person plural and refers to those who are "poor," who will receive "the kingdom of God." These differences are not merely cosmetic. Scholars have long addressed the way that such differences affect meaning

[2]   On the distinctions between these two types of makarisms, see Allison, *Sermon*, 41–44.

[3]   For a detailed discussion regarding this option, see Jonathan T. Pennington, *The Sermon on the Mount and Human Flourishing: A Theological Commentary* (Grand Rapids: Baker Academic, 2017), 41–67.

[4]   See, for example, Georg Strecker, *The Sermon on the Mount: An Exegetical Commentary* (Edinburgh: T&T Clark, 1988), 30, who recognizes the considerable eschatological dimension of the Matthean makarisms but notes that Matthew's list presents an ethical intention not as apparent in Luke. Few scholars would deny that Matthew's and Luke's makarisms each contain both ethical and eschatological dimensions, but considerable discussion centers upon the distinct emphasis of each Gospel. This will be addressed in detail in 5.1.1.2.

[5]   Helpful is the distinction by Guelich, "Matthean Beatitudes," 419, who recognizes all four of Luke's makarisms in Matthew's list but describes the correlation between Luke 6:21b and Matt 5:4 as "indirect."

and reveal the interests of the writers and possible social conditions of the potential respective audiences.[6] Debate continues regarding the sources for the makarisms, including whether either Matthew's or Luke's can be said to be more "original" than the other. Discussions regarding the tradition history of the makarisms, as well as their differences in form, have largely centered on questions related to the synoptic problem, including the use of "Q," the potential influence of various Q recensions, development of the oral tradition, and the redactional activity of the evangelists themselves.[7] It is not necessary here to detail the precise relationship between Matthew's and Luke's makarisms, nor does this study require an analysis of the source-critical issues that exist between them, but certain aspects of the dynamics between Matthew's and Luke's lists are relevant to the discussion below, especially as certain comparisons between them illuminate meaning in Matthew's version. Section 5.1 discusses many of these issues, as well as potential antecedent traditions that may have influenced Matthew's thought-world, followed by an analysis of the role of inheritance in Matt 5:5.

[6]   This is the subject of the article by Thomas Hoyt Jr., "The Poor/Rich Theme in the Beatitudes," *JRT* 37, no. 1 (1980): 31–41. Hoyt argues that Luke is writing for a largely gentile audience and therefore omits much of Matthew's concern for the law. Matthew's and Luke's makarisms, as well as the sermons that contain them, focus on separate themes. Matthew's sermon is focused on righteousness and Scripture fulfillment, as well as Jewish piety. Luke is concerned with charity, concern for the poor and lonely, and love of enemies. Hoyt focuses on the differences between the first makarism, in particular, and argues that Luke 6:20 is primarily concerned with economic poverty, whereas the Matthean redactor added "in spirit" to redirect poverty into a religious dimension. See also Strecker, *Sermon*, 31–32, who argues that Luke 6:20 addresses the poor in a material sense and excludes the rich. Conversely, Matt 5:3 situates poverty within the context of the human spirit, referring to insight, feeling, and will. The goal of Matt 5:3 is to counter the high self-estimation of the scribes and Pharisees and encourage those who are humble. The possibility that Matthew's makarisms are designed to counter the behavior of the scribes and Pharisees will be discussed in detail in 5.1.1.3. Regarding Matthew's de-emphasis of material poverty in Matt 5:3, Hoyt, "Poor/Rich," 39–40, argues that Matthew's community may have been wealthy and that the writer therefore downplayed the economic aspects in order not to offend them. He argues that, contrary to Luke, Matthew's Gospel does not focus on criticism of the rich.

[7]   See Ulrich Luz, *Matthew 1–7* (Hermeneia; Minneapolis: Fortress, 2007), 186–87, whose brief discussion on backgrounds for the makarisms as a unit is limited to source-critical issues. See also the comparison between Matthew and Luke from a source and redaction-critical analysis in Guelich, "Matthean Beatitudes," 419–31, as well as Hoyt, "Poor/Rich," 33–34, for notes on the differences in vocabulary. Donald A. Hagner, *Matthew 1–13* (WBC 33A; Dallas: Word Books, 1993), 89, questions whether a common source could be behind either the Matthean or Lukan list. Even where the two overlap, there are differences, and a common source would raise too many questions regarding why the two lists are not more similar regarding what Hagner calls "irresistible material." He proposes instead the possibility of independent but overlapping oral traditions that would have circulated among various Christian groups.

5.1.1.1. The Character of Matthew's Makarisms

μακάριος appears seventy times in the LXX. It is the standard rendering of אשרי, which refers to a state of being blessed, happy, or fortunate.[8] Scholars agree that makarisms have their foundation in wisdom texts,[9] where they initially appeared as single sentences or groupings of two, offering praise to the prudent and extolling earthly blessings, prosperity, and a wise life to those who trust in God and keep his commandments.[10] Makarisms in the LXX refer principally to those who have a right relationship with God.[11] While makarisms continued to appear in wisdom texts in the Second Temple period, they increasingly began appearing in prophetic-apocalyptic contexts as well. Klaus Koch states that these blessings are directed at those who will be saved in the last judgment, "and who will participate in the new world because they have remained true to their faith."[12] According to Robert A. Guelich, the tone of prophetic-apocalyptic makarisms is based more on "consolation and assurance" than on the parenetic exhortation of those found in the wisdom literature.[13] Rather than ethics, makarisms of the prophetic-apocalyptic tradition are more concerned with reward and the reversal of unfortunate circumstances.

The majority of scholars place Luke's makarisms within the prophetic-apocalyptic tradition.[14] Luke's list fits the prophetic-apocalyptic style in both form and content.[15] This includes Luke's second person construction, its direct address (as opposed to addressing humankind in general), and a more obvious reversal of unfortunate

[8]   See Eugene H. Merrill, "אשרי," in *NIDOTTE*, ed. William A. VanGemeren (Grand Rapids: Zondervan, 1997), 1:561.

[9]   Especially the Psalms (25x) and Sirach (11x).

[10]   See Klaus Koch, *The Growth of the Biblical Tradition: The Form-Critical Method* (London: Adam & Charles Black, 1969), 7, who states that makarisms in the HB wisdom literature refer to "worldly well-being" for those who live in "conformity with the principles prescribed by God and the wise." See also Guelich, "Matthean Beatitudes," 416–17.

[11]   See "μακάριος," in *NIDNTTE*, 5 vols. (2nd ed.; ed. Moisés Silva; Grand Rapids: Zondervan, 2014), 3:207.

[12]   Koch, *Growth*, 7, refers to these as "apocalyptic blessing" and cites Dan 12:12; 1 En. 81:4; 82:4; 2 Bar. 10:6; 11;6; 14:10; Tob 13:14; Pss. Sol. 14:26; 17:50; 18:6; 2 En. 42:6-14; 52:1-16.

[13]   Guelich, "Matthean Beatitudes," 417.

[14]   So Hoyt, "Poor/Rich," 37, that the reason for Luke's makarisms is to offer confidence that "earthly conditions and roles would be reversed in the new age."

[15]   Though notable is Darrell L. Bock, *A Theology of Luke and Acts* (Grand Rapids: Zondervan, 2012), 202, who notes the eschatological reversal motif of Luke's makarisms but also argues that they are placed in an ethical context. The makarisms themselves stress the "present situation," and that "all will be changed later," but these reversals precede the primary ethic of the community (Luke 6:27-36), that they should love all, including their enemies. The disciples are to live well (Luke 6:43-44) and respond to Jesus' teaching with wisdom (Luke 6:46-49).

conditions (poverty, hunger, weeping, persecution).[16] Although form-critical observations are helpful, and Luke's writer does appear to have eschatological reversals in mind, Guelich is right to note that the form of Matthew's makarisms is not as easily placed within either sapiential or prophetic-apocalyptic traditions through form-critical analyses. Matthew's list appears to preserve an element of eschatological focus in the makarisms it shares with Luke, but its third person address, elaboration of lines (e.g., "poor in spirit" rather than "poor"), and aspects of virtue instruction place Matthew's makarisms in the path of wisdom instruction.[17] Matthew's writer appears to be building upon received literary traditions, but strictly speaking, the form and content of his makarisms are without parallel.[18] Matthew's makarisms are filled with new content in what Guelich argues is "comparable to new wine in old wine skins." As Guelich states, "A form-critical analysis may help us set the beatitudes within their cultural milieu, but ultimately it is not sufficient to explain their meaning and intent."[19]

Matthew's idiosyncratic presentation has led many scholars toward discussions regarding the relationship between Matthew, Luke, and the potential for Q and other sources, in an effort to determine the originality of each list and the redactive tendencies and purposes of each evangelist. Such concerns need not detain us here, but it is important to note that for many years scholars tended to place the Matthean and Lukan makarisms into one of two categories: either they reflected entrance requirements for the kingdom (ethical) or eschatological blessings/reversals in the midst of unfortunate circumstances (apocalyptic). In the early twentieth century, many scholars

---

[16]   See Guelich, "Matthean Beatitudes," 417–19, who summarizes this view by following the arguments of Eduard Schweizer, "Formgeschichtliches zu den Seligpreisungen Jesu," *NTS* 19, no. 2 (1973): 121–26. Guelich notes the form-critical success of Schweizer's analysis but argues that content and context are a greater influence on the makarisms than Schweizer recognizes.

[17]   See Hans Windisch, *The Meaning of the Sermon on the Mount* (Philadelphia: Westminster, 1951), 175–76, who argues that Matthew's first four makarisms refer to the hope of salvation in the age to come, and the second set of four refers to a religious attitude in line with wisdom instruction.

[18]   See R. T. France, *The Gospel of Matthew* (Grand Rapids: Eerdmans, 2007), 160, who argues that, while makarisms are normally single statements, antecedent literature shows no close parallel to Matthew's structure. France recognizes that Sir 14:20-27 and 25:7-11 use makarisms in conjunction with longer strings of statements regarding those who are happy/blessed but argues that the forms of these statements are not similar enough to compare with Matthew's makarisms.

[19]   Guelich, "Matthean Beatitudes," 419. See also Eduard Schweizer, *The Good News According to Matthew* (Atlanta: John Knox, 1975), 81, the HB presents makarisms as earthly blessings, while later Jewish literature emphasizes those who are blessed in the coming age of salvation. "Jesus' Beatitudes are totally new in taking a future blessing and declaring it as right now present."

argued that Luke fits nicely into the apocalyptic tradition and that Matthew "ethicized" Luke's makarisms, modifying them to include wisdom instruction. Rather than reversing the fortunes of Luke's "poor," Matthew's "poor in spirit" became an ideal to be emulated.[20] For many years, entrance requirements to the kingdom and eschatological reversals were the only two options that scholars entertained, though, helpfully, recent years have seen scholars bring more nuance into the discussion.[21] There are now at least six major possibilities addressed in recent scholarship integrating form and content toward interpreting the Matthean makarisms. A brief description of each of these six possibilities is helpful toward establishing an approach regarding the interpretation of inheritance in Matt 5:5.

1. Entrance Requirements

According to this view, Matthew's list is primarily concerned with ethics, and these ethics function to present entrance requirements into the kingdom of heaven for the disciples to whom the Sermon on the Mount is addressed. Typical of this position is Hans Dieter Betz, who argues that Matthew's makarisms function as a standard of initiation for those who wish to enter the community of Jesus' disciples.[22] The

---

[20]   See the discussion in W. D. Davies and D. C. Allison Jr., *Matthew 1–7* (ICC; London: T&T Clark, 1998), 439–40.

[21]   The limited scope of possible options is recognized by Pennington, *Sermon*, 62. Pennington notes that these two options draw a sharp distinction between wisdom and apocalyptic traditions and that entrance requirements and eschatological reversals are often presented as the only possible, and incompatible, options. He states, "These two categories become the primary means of interpreting and making sense of what Jesus is saying, and commentators fall on either side, though most commonly on the side of eschatological blessings." Pennington is one of the recent scholars who have recognized that a more sophisticated and nuanced approach is required. He states that limiting interpretation to these two options creates a strong dichotomy that, "like most dichotomies in complex situations, proves to be false." Scholars who appear to entertain only these two options for Matthew's makarisms include Davies and Allison, *Matthew 1–7*, 439; Guelich, "Matthean Beatitudes," 419; Charles H. Talbert, *Reading the Sermon on the Mount: Character Formation and Decision Making in Matthew 5–7* (Grand Rapids: Baker Academic, 2004), 47; Warren Carter, "Narrative/Literary approaches to Matthean Theology: The 'Reign of the Heavens' as an Example (Mt 4:17–5:12)," *JSNT* 67 (1997): 25. Similar is France, *Matthew*, 162, who does not equate ethics with "entrance requirements" but notes only two basic options between Luke and Matthew: that Luke's list is "radicalized" and Matthew's list is "spiritualized." Luke's list is concerned with "the situation in which the disciples find themselves," and Matthew's list is concerned with ethics. Such a clean and sharp distinction is also found in C. H. Dodd, *More New Testament Studies* (Manchester: Manchester University Press, 1968), 4–5, who argues that Luke's makarisms "announce an impending reversal of conditions," while Matthew's list "brings exclusively into relief the ethical quality of the martyr's sufferings."

[22]   Betz, *Essays*, 26–30. Other notable scholars who argue that the makarisms in Matthew function as entrance requirements include Windisch, *Meaning*, 26–27, 87–88;

list refers to the sort of righteousness that is rewarded in the hereafter and possesses a universal appeal; humanity in general is miserable, but the kingdom of heaven is promised to those who "measure up to the required righteousness here and now."[23] It is important to note that the majority of scholars who hold this position do so based on the view that wisdom traditions lie in the background of Matthew's list. This is not the case with Betz, who argues that the concept of "makarisms as standards of initiation" is rooted in apocalyptic writings such as 1 Enoch and 4 Ezra.[24] He argues that Matthew "introduces the ethical-paraenetic dimension" that is "laid down for admission into paradise" and that Matthew has in fact "wiped out the entire apocalyptic framework."[25] Matthew 5:3 is the foundation of the rest of the makarisms, and even the whole of the Sermon on the Mount, and contains all that a person needs to pass through this life into paradise. The entrance requirements are developed in Matt 5:4-12, which constitutes the "self-consciousness of the community," and the rest of the Sermon elucidates the meaning of the first makarism. Betz argues that interpretive traditions that see an antithesis between law and gospel do not do justice to Matthew's makarisms, as law and gospel are intertwined in order to present a "better righteousness" within Judaism.[26]

Strecker, *Sermon*, 25–61. See also Hoyt, "Poor/Rich," 32, who argues that the whole of Matthew's sermon, as opposed to Luke's, "consists of ordering the righteousness which God ordained as a condition for entrance into the kingdom."

[23]   Betz, *Essays*, 34.

[24]   Betz, *Essays*, 28–30.

[25]   Betz, *Essays*, 34. Similar is Strecker, *Sermon*. Unlike Betz, Strecker does not downplay the eschatological focus of Matthew's list and in fact views the eschatological elements as significant. However, he argues that the ethical admonitions amount to "eschatological demands" (26) and that Matthew is responsible for the sapiential aspects of the list in order to present Jesus as a wisdom teacher. Strecker argues that Matthew brings these two elements together so that "wisdom teaching can be expressed as eschatological proclamation," and "eschatological assertions appear in the form of wisdom instruction" (31). Strecker compares Matthew's makarisms to virtue lists in the HB, which must be fulfilled to enter the holy of holies, and argues that Jesus' "eschatological virtues" function the same way, as entrance requirements for the kingdom of heaven. Strecker argues for a difference in intent between Matthew's list and Luke's. Luke's list is concerned with hope and consolation, while Matthew's list is imperative; they are ethical demands that delineate the requirements for life in the *eschaton* (p. 33).

[26]   Betz, *Essays*, 35–36. Luz, *Matthew 1–7*, 189, recognizes an interpretive option for the makarisms that he calls "regulations for the life of the community," which he attributes in varying degrees to Zinzendorf, Windisch, Bonhoeffer, and Luther. Luz argues that these scholars present the makarisms as standards for how to deal with others in the community and includes attitudes and activities for life within the group. This is similar to Betz's standards of initiation, though Betz presents the makarisms as standards for entering into the group, whereas Luz notes that some scholars see the makarisms not as entrance requirements *per se* but as standards for those living within the community of disciples.

Davies and Allison are among those who argue against the makarisms as entrance requirements. They note that the makarisms do not actually contain any imperatives save Matt 5:11-12, where the hearer is called to rejoice and be glad. The commands do not follow along ethical lines. It is in these same verses, Matt 5:10-12, where Davies and Allison argue that ethics do not fit the context, as those who are persecuted should not see such a state as an ethical condition in which to enter. Instead, persecution is a state of suffering and in need of consolation; no change of behavior is envisioned. These observations, among others, lead Davies and Allison to conclude that, rather than ethical requirements, the makarisms are best understood as "eschatological reversals."[27]

2. Eschatological Reversals

Rather than striving for positively oriented ethical standards, many scholars argue that some of the first clauses of Matthew's makarisms promise eschatological reversals of negative personal and social circumstances. Rather than ideals to be emulated, the character of the makarisms present unfortunate realities.[28] Typical of this position is the work of Davies and Allison, who recognize that the makarisms do contain an ethical element. There is an implied ethical imperative to be "pure in heart" (Matt 5:8) and "peacemakers" (Matt 5:9).[29] However, they argue that the ethical dimension is subtle and does not overshadow the elements of consolation and promise. Rather than present moral guidelines, Matthew's list exists to bless the faithful within their current circumstances as they face the difficulty of everyday life.[30]

[27]   Davies and Allison, *Matthew 1–7*, 439–40.

[28]   See, for example, Mark Allan Powell, "Matthew's Beatitudes: Reversals and Rewards of the Kingdom," *CBQ* 58, no. 3 (1996): 463–67, who numbers Matthew's makarisms at eight and splits them into two stanzas of four. Each of the two stanzas have a distinct character, the first stanza presenting eschatological reversals to those who are unfortunate. For example, in Matt 5:3 he rejects the argument that "poor in spirit" refers to the humble and instead argues that it refers to those who are living with the negative spiritual consequences of economic poverty. The "meek" in Matt 5:5 are in a synonymous condition.

[29]   Davies and Allison, *Matthew 1–7*, 467, note in particular that many of the designations of the makarisms' first clauses present dispositions that were present in Jesus' own manner throughout the rest of the Gospel. Jesus was meek (Matt 11:29), he mourned (Matt 26:36-46), he was righteous (3:15; 27:4, 19), he showed mercy (Matt 9:27; 15:22), he was persecuted (Matt 26–27). In some fashion this feature presents Jesus as a model to be imitated, even if the dispositions in Matt 5:3-12 are largely negative in terms of their circumstances.

[30]   Davies and Allison, *Matthew 1–7*, 439–40. See also Scot McKnight, *Sermon on the Mount* (SGBC; Grand Rapids: Zondervan, 2013), 29–36. McKnight's view, in my

Davies and Allison argue that the differences between Matthew's and Luke's makarisms are therefore only stylistic and that the sense of each list is the same.[31] To be poor in spirit, to be meek, to mourn, to be persecuted; these are all unfortunate circumstances that have befallen the hearers, but there is hope, because "when the eschatological reversal takes place, the sick are made well, the humble are exalted, and the poor are made rich."[32] Recognizing that Matt 5:3 and 5:10 promise the kingdom of heaven in the present tense, and that there may be some present sense of the kingdom that can be received now, they note that these two verses work as an inclusio that brackets and explains the future tense promises of the other makarisms. Therefore, they argue that the present tense offers comfort and confidence but that these verses should be taken as examples of the "futuristic present" in which the blessings offered are still eschatological in nature.[33] The promised blessings in Matt 5:4-9 feature future-passive verbs; the future tense is eschatological in nature and the passive voice is a "divine passive," which guarantees that, on the last day, the hearers will be satisfied by

---

estimation, is less clear than that of Davies and Allison but appears to follow along similar lines. The makarisms do have an ethical element; they refer to people marked by special attributes or characteristics and to those who were "living out the kingdom vision." However, Matthew's list refers not to "a virtue list by which to measure moral progress." Jesus' focus is on future blessing to console the oppressed and not on desirable ethical traits. McKnight's view lacks clarity regarding those to whom the blessings are directed. On pages 30–31 he argues that the makarisms are a redefinition of the Jewish remnant and "radical revisioning of the people of God," implying that all of God's people are in view. However, on page 34 he argues that the makarisms are addressed to "people groups," which include the down-and-out and the oppressed—those who are "living properly, regardless of their circumstances and conditions." It is unclear if McKnight views all of God's people as "down-and-out and oppressed" or if the makarisms are addressed to a subset of God's people living in that condition and are therefore not relevant to Jesus' followers not characterized by Matthew's list. Moreover, if Matthew's list refers not to dispositions to be pursued but rather to people who happen to be living within the circumstances listed, then what does this mean for those who desire the kingdom but are living within more favorable circumstances?

[31] Davies and Allison, *Matthew 1–7*, 446. Similar is Leonhard Goppelt, *Theology of the New Testament*, vol. 1 (Grand Rapids: Eerdmans, 1981), 68, who argues that both Matthew's and Luke's lists refer to eschatological reversals, but there is still a difference regarding the nature of that which is reversed. For example, Luke's hunger refers to bread, whereas Matthew's refers to righteousness. This places the evangelists on two sides of the same basic reality: the dawn of salvation.

[32] Davies and Allison, *Matthew 1–7*, 443. They argue (449) that meekness is not the avoidance of hubris, but a state of powerlessness, and therefore rather than ethical it is an undesirable condition. See also McKnight, *Sermon*, 33.

[33] Davies and Allison, *Matthew 1–7*, 446. See also page 460, where they argue that this suggests that all of the makarisms function as different ways of expressing a single reality, namely, that "theirs is the kingdom of heaven."

God.[34] The purpose of Matthew's makarisms is to pronounce the outcome of the last judgment, that in the future the poor will possess the kingdom and that the world will be turned upside down; those who are at the bottom in this current life will one day reach the top.[35]

There is one further element that is an important feature of Davies and Allison's presentation. Although the reversals are eschatological, they are promises made based on the present grace of God and his present favor and blessings in the lives of the hearers. The future blessings are pronouncements that indicate a present reality and therefore function as a "practical theodicy." The makarisms "possess a secret vision and hope that makes powerlessness and suffering bearable."[36] This is illustrated by the place of the makarisms in Matthew's overall narrative, as it follows upon descriptions of Jesus as healer (Matt 4:23–5:2) and precedes the call for the disciples to be salt and light (Matt 5:13-16). The purpose is to place these passages before the imperative-oriented content of the rest of the Sermon on the Mount to place grace before demand and to use the makarisms to highlight not ethics but God's good favor and blessing.[37] This particular argument is similar to the next interpretive option, which sees Matthew's makarisms less as either ethics or reversals and more as descriptions of God's good favor toward his people.

3. Evidence of God's Favor

This position is similar to the eschatological reversals view. Both views reject the idea that the first clauses of Matthew's makarisms present "entrance requirements" into the kingdom of God; both views understand the second clauses as "divine passives," which place the hearer under the grace of God; and both views understand God's favor as the motivating factor in the reception of his blessings. The principal difference between the two views is that, for the "evidence of God's

[34]   Davies and Allison, *Matthew 1–7*, 453.

[35]   Davies and Allison, *Matthew 1–7*, 448, "God's own are on the bottom, the wicked are on top. So mourning is heard because the righteous suffer, because the wicked prosper, and because God has not yet acted to reverse the situation . . . the righteous therefore cannot but mourn. Until the eschatological reversal takes place, it is not possible to be content with the status quo." See also Goppelt, *Theology*, 68, who argues that Matthew's and Luke's list each provide nuances of this reversal, Matthew's being spiritual and Luke's being physical. He states, "The kingdom of God brings both a physical and spiritual dawn of salvation, i.e., regarding the end result a new world without want and suffering, a world of peace and righteousness."

[36]   Davies and Allison, *Matthew 1–7*, 467.

[37]   Davies and Allison, *Matthew 1–7*, 440. See also McKnight, *Sermon*, 35–36, who argues that the blessings are not for those who pursue wisdom or obey Torah but rather are for the one who "enjoys God's favor."

favor" position, it is not necessary to understand the first clauses of the makarisms as representative of unfortunate circumstances in need of reversal. Neither ethics nor eschatological reversals are the central point of the makarisms, rather, the central point is that the hearers understand that they have God's good favor upon them and a right and secure position as his children.

Typical of this position is Charles L. Quarles, who does view the makarisms as ethical, but states that, rather than entrance requirements, "the commandments define the character and conduct of those whom God has already claimed as His children."[38] The makarisms are ethical principles followed by rewards (as opposed to reversals of unfortunate circumstances), but that is not their primary characteristic. Instead, their focus is to pronounce salvation and present Jesus' disciples as the new Israel.[39] The makarisms function to introduce God's mercy and saving activity prior to detailing the commands of the rest of the Sermon on the Mount.[40] The makarisms do not gain one entrance into the kingdom, nor do they secure the divine blessing, but rather those who have already been blessed by God are qualified for rewards and will live ethically in light of their position as those favored by God.[41] In this view, there is a sense in which the state of being favored by God almost guarantees the desired result of ethical conduct.[42] Quarles argues this when noting the

[38]   Quarles, *Sermon*, 40.

[39]   Quarles, *Sermon*, 39. Similar is Hagner, *Matthew 1–13*, 91, who notes both ethical and eschatological dimensions to Matthew's makarisms but states, "This aspect of the beatitudes is decidedly secondary to the clear and grace-filled affirmation of the deep happiness of the recipients of the kingdom."

[40]   Quarles, *Sermon*, 40, follows the arguments of Davies and Allison, *Matthew 1–7*, 466, in this regard.

[41]   Using Matt 5:3 as an example, Quarles, *Sermon*, 44, states that the "poor in spirit" are those who understand themselves as spiritual paupers and that "there is nothing good in them that deserves God's love and forgiveness." They are to depend on God's grace alone, and those who receive it will enter the kingdom and a right disposition before God.

[42]   Similar is Carl R. Holladay, "The Beatitudes: Happiness and the Kingdom of God," in *The Bible and the Pursuit of Happiness* (ed. Brent A. Strawn; Oxford: Oxford University Press, 2012), 149–50. When discussing the "entrance requirements" position, Holladay notes that the scholars who support it view the two clauses of the makarisms through an if/then relationship. Under the "God's favor" position, the two clauses are best viewed through a declaration/promise relationship. The first clause, rather than a prerequisite for a reward, is viewed as an unexpected and unmerited offer of grace. He states, "Rather than stipulating entrance requirements for the kingdom, the first clauses are profiling the attitudes and experiences of those already in the kingdom." This is similar to Quarles, with one important difference. Rather than ethics, Holladay notes that the first clauses could still be viewed to depict unfortunate circumstances, which makes the pronouncement of the blessing sound unlikely. This compounds the quality of God's favor.

position of the makarisms at the beginning of the Sermon on the Mount when he states, "this order suggests that the righteousness described in the sermon is a result of divine blessing rather than a requirement for divine blessing."[43] The divine blessings of the makarisms pronounce God's favor over the disciple, who is then enabled to live in light of the commands of the rest of the sermon.

A similar view is argued by Guelich, who understands the makarisms as the *results* of the eschatological orientation of the kingdom of God. Guelich argues in favor of the prophetic-apocalyptic character of Matthew's makarisms but also understands ethics to be important. Rather than entrance requirements or eschatological reversals, Guelich argues that the eschatological nature of the kingdom was inaugurated with Jesus' ministry and that this eschatological reality changes conduct in the present. The righteousness spoken of in Matt 5:6, and throughout Matthew, refers to conduct and relationships based on the "promised age of salvation, the presence of the kingdom." With the dawn of the age of salvation, "a new relationship with God began for those whose lives were touched by Jesus' person and ministry." This new relationship, and the coming of the kingdom, changes one's conduct. The favor of God, and relationship with him, precedes and motivates ethics. Therefore, kingdom-oriented conduct is "the product of, not the entrance requirements for, the kingdom."[44] The kingdom, ethics, and the meeting of one's needs—these things all come from God as a gift. God-pleasing conduct is brought about by a new relationship with God and the presence of the kingdom in such a way that it *enables* one to do God's will. Therefore, righteousness in Matthew is a relational concept that motivates ethical conduct and results in the eschatological gift, but without the nature of the eschatological gift impressing itself upon the present, right conduct is not possible.[45]

Pennington critiques the "God's favor" position, and Quarles in particular, on two grounds. First, Pennington argues that many who view the makarisms this way do so upon the view that "blessed" is the best

---

[43]   Quarles, *Sermon*, 42.

[44]   Guelich, "Matthean Beatitudes," 429.

[45]   Guelich, "Matthean Beatitudes," 430. The needs of the "poor in spirit" and "those who mourn" are not met by "resolute determination to carry out the will of God in one's own strength" but rather by God, who "will satiate their earnest desires by accepting them into a new relationship with himself and enabling them in keeping with the presence of the age of salvation, to accomplish that for which they long, i.e. the will of God." Similar on this point is Allison, *Sermon*, 44, who states, "It is only after hearing the comforting words of 5:3-12, words that tell of rewards that human beings cannot create for themselves but can only receive as gifts from God, that one is confronted by the Messiah's demands." The result is not the burden of moral imperatives but compensation for those who are suffering.

translation for μακάριος, a translation that Pennington challenges. Second, Pennington argues that to view both the first and second clauses of makarisms as the *results* of God's favor is to misunderstand the function of makarisms in the antecedent literature and in Matthew's Gospel.[46] Pennington has been a forceful proponent of the "virtue-ethics" position, to which we now turn.

4. Virtue-Ethics

Pennington argues that the makarisms, and the entirety of the Sermon on the Mount, are best understood through what he calls an "encyclopedic context," which understands the terms and ideas of the makarisms through the nexus of two cultural paradigms, both of which point to virtue-ethics and human flourishing as the key backgrounds for Matthew's structure and intent. The first requires a thoroughgoing accounting of the historical, literary, and theological story of Israel through both the HB and the non-biblical Second Temple literature. Much of Israel's history, and especially the prophetic and sapiential writings, depicts the trustworthiness of God to bring about restoration for Israel and all of humanity into a redeemed, proper relationship with God and one another, "experiencing the flourishing life."[47] Of particular importance to Pennington's approach is to understand the integrative relationship of wisdom motifs with those of an eschatological and apocalyptic nature. The ethics of the Bible are tied to the story of redemption and God's relationship with humanity; wisdom provides practical reflections on human flourishing, which signals the coming time of restoration. Eschatological restoration is inaugurated into the life of God's people in the present, which reinforces and informs moral tradition. Repentance, moral instruction, and discipleship are informed by end-of-age perspectives on practical matters. The makarisms manifest a "genetic relationship to the perspective of this Second Temple apocalyptic wisdom . . . providing a vision for virtue that is oriented to God's restorative kingdom, and is given to those who have ears to hear and build their lives wisely upon Jesus's teaching."[48] Matthew's makarisms refer to virtue formation informed by eschatological hope.

The second cultural context that is important for understanding the makarisms is the Greco-Roman virtue tradition. Pennington argues that much of the language and concepts present in the Sermon, including the

---

[46]   Pennington, *Sermon*, 58–60.

[47]   Pennington, *Sermon*, 25, on this point cites Exod 15:1-18; Isa 51:3, 11; 52:7; 54:10; 55:12-13; 65:17-25; 66:12; Ezek 34:25; 36:35; 37:26.

[48]   Pennington, *Sermon*, 28–29.

makarisms, connects to and overlaps with Greek moral philosophy.[49] One key point of connection is the relationship between the term μακάριος and the term τέλειος, which is found in Matt 5:48. τέλειος in Matt 5:48 is usually translated "perfect,"[50] but it is a Greek ethics term that often connotes the concepts of wholeness and completion. Many scholars have noted the connection between these terms and another Greek virtue-ethics term, εὐδαιμονία (not found in the NT), which connotes the idea of human flourishing.[51] Pennington argues effectively that these three terms all share common connotations and were used to illustrate the same basic ideas regarding the intentional pursuit of virtue and learned practical wisdom.[52] We will revisit the connection between these terms below when discussing the best gloss for μακάριος, but it is important to note here that the close relationship between these terms contributes toward Pennington's argument regarding the virtue-ethical nature of the makarisms.

According to Pennington, both traditions, the Jewish sapiential-apocalyptic tradition and the Greco-Roman virtue tradition, emphasize human agency as the focus of morality and flourishing. Circumstances and fortunes are not determinative but rather "whether the agent orients his or her life virtuously." It is the ethics of virtue that result in "flourishing and happiness."[53] Pennington notes that the Second Temple wisdom literature does put the onus on God to bring the time of restoration but that those who flourish in that time are those who live virtuously in

---

[49]   Pennington, *Sermon*, 31–35, surveys some of the ways in which Second Temple and first-century Judaism was influenced by interactions with Greek and Roman culture.

[50]   So RSV, NRSV, NIV, ESV, KJV, NLT.

[51]   See, for example, Betz, *Essays*, 32. Also Luz, *Matthew 1–7*, 190, who suggests that the relationship between μακάριος and εὐδαιμονία is so close that the two terms can hardly be distinguished one from the other. Jaroslav Pelikan, *Divine Rhetoric: The Sermon on the Mount as Message and as Model in Augustine, Chrysostom, and Luther* (Crestwood: St. Vladimir's Seminary Press, 2006), 8, notes that in Aristotle's framework εὐδαιμονία refers to wisdom, virtue, and goodwill.

[52]   Pennington, *Sermon*, 31–35. Central to the argument is that the core approach of Greco-Roman philosophy toward virtue-ethics is the discovery of happiness and human flourishing and that this approach was exemplified in Aristotle but taken up by the majority of thinkers in the Greco-Roman tradition. This point is also made by William C. Mattison III, "The Beatitudes and Moral Theology: A Virtue-Ethics Approach," *Nova et Vetera*, English Edition 11, no. 3 (2013): 822–23, who notes that both Aristotle and Cicero devoted significant attention to the idea of human flourishing and that discussion surrounding virtue-ethics were equated with discussions on thriving and being happy. Mattison notes the connection between μακάριος and εὐδαιμονία and argues that for anyone schooled in classical culture, they would have understood the makarisms "in the context of the enduring question of how to live a happy life." He notes that many early Christian thinkers understood Matthew's makarisms this way.

[53]   Pennington, *Sermon*, 36.

alignment with God's will. In this way, the redemptive-historical perspective of the eschatological story of Israel is brought into alignment with the virtue-ethics approach of Greco-Roman philosophy.[54]

Pennington rejects the ethics approach, which regards the makarisms as entrance requirements. However, he also laments the way scholars often react to such an approach by rejecting or neglecting the ethical dimensions and instead arguing in favor of eschatological blessings as an exclusive and opposite interpretive solution. Pennington regards this as an unhelpful dichotomy. He agrees with the prophetic-apocalyptic approach, which views the restorative kingdom as a backdrop for the makarisms, but he argues that this backdrop works in conjunction with a wisdom-oriented virtue-ethics reading.[55] This places Matthew as a key point on the trajectory of the convergence of sapiential and apocalyptic traditions that began to take shape in the Second Temple period. In Matt 5:3-12, the wisdom tradition and the apocalyptic tradition are "inextricably interwoven."[56] Matthew's Gospel is an important point along this trajectory, and the makarisms function to present both an ethical vision for human flourishing *and* a future-oriented eschatological hope. In this regard Pennington places Matthew's makarisms along a direct line of tradition development with 1 Enoch and Instruction. Pennington states, "Jesus is offering a vision for a way of being in the world that will result

---

[54]   Pennington, *Sermon*, 37–38.

[55]   See also Mattison, "Beatitudes," 841, who notes that the majority of scholars argue that Matthew's makarisms are either ethical or eschatological but that this is an unhelpful dichotomy. In his view, ethics and eschatology need not be dichotomized. Matthew's makarisms are characterized by both ethical exhortations and eschatological deliverance. Mattison differs from Pennington in that he regards the ethics of the makarisms as signaling entrance requirements. A similar approach to Pennington is taken by Talbert, *Reading*, who offers a virtue-ethics reading of the entire Sermon on the Mount influenced by both Jewish and Greco-Roman sources, as well as integrating both a virtue-ethical and eschatological blessing approach to the makarisms. Talbert states, "The Beatitudes cannot be regarded as entrance requirements but rather as promises of eschatological blessings" (47), as well as "The unit is shaping character. . . . They sketch the outlines of a good person, a person of piety toward God and right behavior toward other humans" (57).

[56]   Similar is Luz, *Matthew 1–7*, 187–88. Luz notes that in the Jewish tradition makarisms were above all "wisdom paranesis as an expression of the connection between a person's deeds and what happens to the person." However, due to the rise of apocalypticism, makarisms took on the eschatological sense "when it was possible to formulate the deed-result connection by including the eschaton." Luz goes on to state, "Jesus' beatitudes are part of this transformation in apocalypticism of what was originally a wisdom genre." See also Ben Witherington III, *Matthew* (Macon, Ga.: Smyth & Helwys, 2006), 114, who argues that all of Matthew 5–7 fits within the wisdom tradition but that it does so with "counter-order" wisdom, as all of the teaching is delivered with a view toward God's eschatological reign as it breaks into the present.

in true human flourishing, precisely in the context of forward-looking faith in God eventually setting the world to rights."[57] Pennington argues that this makes the best sense of the way that "the kingdom of heaven" serves as an inclusio for the makarisms, as well as the relationship between the makarisms' first and second clauses. The kingdom functions as a "spatial metaphor and metonym for human flourishing." The first clauses of each makarism describe those who flourish in the kingdom and it is they who stand to receive the eschatological blessings of the second clauses.[58]

The core of Pennington's view is that the best reading of Matthew's makarisms combines and keeps in balance both the wisdom tradition (both Jewish and Greco-Roman) and the Second Temple apocalyptic tradition on eschatological blessing. In this way, he argues, the entire Sermon on the Mount "presents itself as an eschatological wisdom teaching on virtue."[59] The point here is that Pennington rejects the ethics approach, which views the first clauses as entrance requirements, but he also rejects the "evidence of God's favor" approach. The ethical dispositions presented by Matthew's makarisms are not requirements to earn entrance into the kingdom, but they are still virtues for which the disciples must strive.[60] In other words, they are not dispositions the disciples simply passively receive as recipients of God's favor, they are dispositions that must be actively cultivated if one desires to flourish and live in step with God's will. Those who live in this way stand to be rewarded with blessings.[61]

[57]   Pennington, *Sermon*, 63–64.

[58]   Pennington, *Sermon*, 66.

[59]   Pennington, *Sermon*, 66–67.

[60]   See Neil J. McEleney, "The Beatitudes of the Sermon on the Mount/Plain," *CBQ* 43, no. 1 (1981): 11, Matthew's makarisms "take on overtones of virtuous dispositions to be acquired within the church" and "exemplify the dispositions and virtues Christians need to practice the better righteousness demanded of them." D. A. Carson, *Jesus' Sermon on the Mount: And His Confrontation with the World* (Grand Rapids: Baker Books, 1987), 16–17, comes close to the "evidence of God's favor" position when he states that the makarisms refer to those "approved by God," but he realizes the ethical dimension by understanding the relationship between the first and second clauses of the makarisms. The blessings are not arbitrary because the promises of the second clauses flow from the character of the first; e.g., it is the merciful who are shown mercy. The makarisms are not entrance requirements but they are "the norms of the kingdom."

[61]   Pennington, *Sermon*, 160–61, notes the theological entanglements that often motivate these two readings. Scholars often draw theological lines regarding justification by faith versus salvation by works. Those emphasizing justification feel pressure to resolve the makarisms by arguing that they are grace-based and given by God to those who already believe. However, Pennington argues that Matt 5:3-12 presents commands without such theological influence. His question is not whether one must earn their way in, or receive God's favor because they are already in, but rather he presents virtue-ethics

The major interpretive approaches to Matthew's makarisms consider them to be either entrance requirements, eschatological blessings/ reversals, evidence of God's favor, or ethics for human flourishing. Although scholars who represent these approaches nuance their views in varying ways, most can be subsumed under one of these options. However, there are two further approaches to be addressed briefly, both of which rely on the structure of the makarisms as a list to interpret each individual makarism. Scholars who represent the following two approaches agree that individual makarisms are best interpreted by one of the previous four approaches, but they understand the structure of Matthew's list in such a way that the list lacks uniformity, and therefore the interpretation of each makarism does not always coincide with the others in the list. The first of these options understands Matthew's list broken into stanzas, while the second disregards any strict uniformity of intent among any of the makarisms on the list.[62]

5. Dividing the Makarisms into Two Stanzas

Mark Allan Powell has argued that the Matthean makarisms are a single, coherent unit but that they are structured as two distinct stanzas: the first describing eschatological reversals for present unfortunate conditions and the second describing rewards for ethical behavior.[63] Powell argues that Matthew's list has a structure that appears intentional, and therefore we should expect an overarching framework but that certain dispositions are best viewed as unfortunate (e.g., mourning, Matt 5:4), while others are best viewed as virtuous (e.g., peacemaking, Matt 5:9). Powell argues that, in

---

simply motivated by encouraging the disciples and the crowds to live in accordance with a flourishing life. Similar is Andrie B. du Toit, "Revisiting the Sermon on the Mount: Some Major Issues," *Neot* 50 (2016): 80–81, who notes the either/or nature of the discussion. Du Toit argues that to limit the Matthean makarisms to either entrance requirements or blessings based on God's favor is to misunderstand that they are "laudatory in nature." Noting the link with Isa 61, he argues that Matthew's list pronounces blessings based on God's grace but that the makarisms are also "soft imperatives" that appeal to the audience to take upon themselves the dispositions described in the list. The makarisms are not entrance requirements, but they are "urging, calling, inviting." Similar in this regard is Davies and Allison, *Matthew 1–7*, 439, who argue against the ethics approach but recognize "implicit" imperatives; e.g., "be pure in heart, be a peacemaker."

[62]   A third structural possibility useful for interpretation is offered by McKnight, *Sermon*, 37–38, who groups the makarisms into three groups of three: humility (5:3-5), justice (5:6-8), and peace (5:9-12). He argues that this summarizes the three moral themes of the makarisms as humility, justice, and peace.

[63]   Powell, "Matthew's Beatitudes," 460. This is also the view of David E. Garland, *Reading Matthew: A Literary and Theological Commentary on the First Gospel* (New York: Crossroad, 1993), 54, who argues that the first four makarisms pertain to one's disposition toward God, while the second four pertain to one's demeanor toward others.

Hebrew poetry, synonymous parallelism can be found in groups of either two, three, or four lines and that Matthew's list is best understood to make use of a form of parallelism that would "display internal consistency and contribute to the overall thought of the unit as a whole."[64]

Powell's position requires two things. First, his position is dependent upon a certain structure for Matthew's list. He argues that the makarisms of Matt 5:3-10 number eight, and should be kept separate from 5:11-12 when determining the structure.[65] Powell's arguments would not work for a structure that views Matthew's list as containing seven, nine, or ten makarisms. Second, Powell's argument requires that dispositions such as "poor in spirit" and "meek" be viewed as unfortunate circumstances rather than virtues. Powell recognizes that many scholars regard these dispositions as signifiers of humility and dependence upon God, but he argues instead that they refer to one who is dispossessed or despondent. For Powell, the poor in spirit are those who have no hope in this world.[66] Likewise, the meek are those who are oppressed or powerless.[67] Powell addresses the phrase "inherit the earth" in Matt 5:5 and argues that this confirms his interpretation, because an inheritance is not something one earns by being virtuous, but it is "a gift for which one must only wait."[68] Therefore, if the powerless only wait on God, they will eventually have their powerlessness reversed and they will inherit the earth. Matthew 5:7-10 then details virtuous dispositions such as mercy and peacemaking, and the second clauses of these verses offer rewards, rather than reversals, to the virtuous.[69]

---

[64]   Powell, "Matthew's Beatitudes," 461.

[65]   Powell, "Matthew's Beatitudes," 461–62, argues that Matt 5:3-10 makes a structured use of the third person and are bracketed by the kingdom of heaven in 5:3 and 10. Verses 11-12 are in the second person and are distinguished from 5:3-10 in length, meter, and use of the imperative mood. Allison, Sermon, 29, has argued for a ninth makarism in Matt 5:11-12 by demonstrating that other collections of makarisms in the ancient world often add emphasis to the concluding member of the series by making it longer and irregular to the rest of the list.

[66]   Powell, "Matthew's Beatitudes," 463–64.

[67]   This is also the view of John Nolland, The Gospel of Matthew: A Commentary on the Greek Text (NIGTC; Grand Rapids: Eerdmans, 2005), 201–2, who argues that πραεῖς refers to a state of powerlessness. Nolland recognizes that the singular πραΰς is used of Jesus in Matt 11:29 and 21:5 and that in the case of Jesus "powerlessness" would be an inappropriate understanding of the term, but he argues that it is in the plural form that the term implies a limitation of power rather than an honorable virtue. Nolland's argument appears speculative. It may be of note that 1 Pet 3:4 uses the adjective πραέως to refer to gentleness as a positive and honorable trait, so there is precedent for cognates of this term in the NT to be used in this way.

[68]   Powell, "Matthew's Beatitudes," 467.

[69]   Powell, "Matthew's Beatitudes," 470. Similar is Carter, "Narrative/Literary," 24–26.

Powell's argument is problematic at points. His proposed structure of eight makarisms is possible but still a matter of significant debate. At least two other issues can be raised here. First, for Powell's argument to work, one must view those "who hunger and thirst for righteousness" (Matt 5:6) as those in an unfortunate circumstance. Powell admits that the best argument for this is that it allows the verse to fit into the structure he has proposed, but he also argues that Matthew's Gospel places practice over intention and that the *longing* to do God's will, as opposed to the *actuality* of doing it, is foreign to the rest of the text. Therefore, the hunger and thirst of this verse refers to deprivation.[70] However, as we saw in chapter 1 of this study, much of Matthew's Gospel is concerned with the debate over discipleship and the correct way to follow God. Throughout the Gospel the crowds are placed at the center of this debate and they are presented with two mutually exclusive options: following the path of Jesus and his disciples or following the path of the scribes and Pharisees. The disciples and the crowds are encouraged to strive for a greater righteousness than that of the scribes and Pharisees (Matt 5:20), so to hunger and thirst for righteousness is best viewed within this context—the crowds must desire a greater righteousness (i.e., the righteousness of God), and it is only by this righteousness that they can be filled. This implies ethical connotations for Matt 5:6.

Second, Powell argues that the inheritance in Matt 5:5 must be viewed as a gift and that virtue cannot contribute to the reception of that gift. As we have seen throughout this study, this is simply not the case. The very foundations of inheritance concepts in the Hexateuch immediately introduce matters of participation by the Israelites in obtaining their inheritance, and literature antecedent to Matthew often describes conditions by which inheritances can be forfeit through ungodly and unethical behavior. Ethics are often directly tied to obtaining inheritances from God, even as those inheritances are viewed as a gift based on relationship with him.

Although Powell's structure brings difficulty regarding some of its details, there are other scholars who have struggled to find alignment regarding either ethics or blessings within Matthew's makarisms. This has led some scholars to question whether Matthew's list has any uniformity at all in this regard or whether each makarism is best interpreted independently of the others.

---

[70]   Powell, "Matthew's Beatitudes," 468.

6. No Standard Structure

Typical of this position is Luz, who argues that Matthew's makarisms are best viewed based on the redactional stages from which they appeared in the list. The most original makarisms (Matt 5:3, 4, 6) have as their background a hope in the eschatological reversal of conditions. The remainder of the makarisms were Matthean additions that were ethicized. As the Matthean list was compiled from lines drafted in various stages and from various sources, there is no single unified meaning to be found among them, and they are best viewed independently.[71]

7. The Character of Matthew's Makarisms

Limiting our approach to Matthew's makarisms to either "entrance requirements," "eschatological reversals," or "evidences of God's favor" is problematic. These positions are largely influenced by later theological debates regarding grace vs. works, and such a dichotomy does not factor into the teaching of Jesus in Matthew or into Matthew's intent and construction of his makarisms. The context leading up to Matt 5 (Matt 4:23-25) provides evidences of God's grace, and Davies and Allison are correct to point out that this intentionally precedes the ethics-driven instruction of the Sermon on the Mount in order to highlight the role of God's grace as a precursor to the imperatives. Within the makarisms, Matt 5:3 and 10 serve as an inclusio that positions the full list of makarisms as exposition upon the nature of the kingdom, and the absence of direct moral imperatives in Matt 5:3-10 makes it unlikely that entrance requirements into the kingdom are in view. However, the language of these makarisms parallels that of virtue-ethics contexts too closely for the ethical character of Matthew's list to be ignored or de-emphasized. Of course, one must argue that terms and phrases such as "poor in spirit," "mourn," and "meek" carry virtuous connotations and are not best read as unfortunate circumstances. Below, an effort is made to account for this reading, especially regarding "the meek" and the way that Matt 5:5 fits into an ethical reading.[72] With respect to these makarisms, Matthew's Jesus is not concerned with "how to get

---

[71]   Luz, *Matthew 1–7*, 186–90. See also Witherington, *Matthew*, 119–20, who notes the difficulty in finding uniformity. He argues in favor of the eschatological character of Matthew's list but still sees in certain makarisms a correlation between behavior and the ability to receive rewards in the future. Witherington argues that the list is carefully arranged in terms of the form, but he does not attempt a uniform explanation in terms of intent and character. Hagner, *Matthew 1–13*, 90–91, argues for the "evidence of God's favor" perspective but notes the difficulty in uniformity when considering the nature of ethics and blessings.

[72]   See 5.1.2.4.

in," he is concerned with the lives, character, and ethical dispositions of those who follow him and, in particular, the way that his followers' lives exceed those of Israel's current leaders in terms of obeying God and living according to the ethics of his kingdom.

Although the interpretive approach taken in this study, when interpreting Matthew's makarisms, is largely that of the virtue-ethics approach, there are important insights offered by the other approaches that are best integrated into a virtue-ethics understanding. Davies and Allison reference Matt 4:23–5:2 to submit that God's grace is a motivating factor for the makarisms as a "practical theodicy" that possesses "a secret vision and hope that makes powerlessness and suffering bearable."[73] This relates closely to the approach that views the dispositions and rewards of the makarisms as an "evidence of God's grace"; those who are already recipients of God's grace are qualified for rewards and will live ethically in light of their position as those favored by God.[74] In this view, there is a sense in which the state of being favored by God almost guarantees the desired result of ethical conduct. While I agree that God's grace is a motivating factor in obedience, and I agree that the placement of Matt 4:23–5:2 cannot be a coincidence and is therefore vital in understanding God's grace in the context of his blessings in Matthew's makarisms, I submit that a more important point of reference is the preceding pericope of Matt 4:18-22. It is here that Jesus offers his first disciples a chance to "follow me" (δεῦτε ὀπίσω μου), and they leave their vocation to do so.[75] God's grace to the first disciples is proffered through Jesus when they are called to follow, and as they make the appropriate sacrifices, they are promised eschatological rewards as a result (5:3-12). Therefore, contained within the offer of following Jesus is God's grace in the form of *possibility*. Those who accept the call and follow Jesus and his teachings are then *described* by the virtuous dispositions contained within the makarisms, and it is to those so described that eschatological promises are made. God's grace does not *produce* righteousness as an inevitable result, but it does make obedience *possible* and *motivates* obedience to Jesus' teachings.

The interpretive approach taken in this study, when interpreting Matt 5:5, is largely that of the virtue-ethics approach as it intersects with

---

[73] Davies and Allison, *Matthew 1–7*, 467.

[74] Quarles, *Sermon*, 44.

[75] See Davies and Allison, *Matthew 1–7*, 398. "Jesus' words, which contain no why, are not invitation. They are unconditional demand." Grammatically this is the case, but this is likely so for narrative purposes, as a similar call to "follow me" is made to the rich man (δεῦρο ἀκολούθει μοι, 19:21), who does not respond favorably. The demand can be resisted and is understood as an offer to become a disciple of Jesus.

260 God's Will and Testament

eschatology. It is reasonable to assume that the varying approaches to the makarisms extend from the difficulties inherent when attempting to understand their complex structure, intent, and use of antecedent traditions and that each approach represents aspects of the truth. Pennington's caution is apt; there is no need to dichotomize wisdom and apocalyptic, ethics and eschatology. The integration of these themes and motifs is apparent in the antecedent literature, as well as throughout Matthew's Gospel. Throughout the text God's grace is an apparent theme that motivates the disciples and presents offers of eschatological blessings, but this does not lessen the clear directives throughout the Gospel for the disciples to flourish by choosing to live righteously and in line with God's will. Furthermore, the crowds are offered the opportunity to flourish by following Jesus' teachings and the example of the disciples rather than the alternative example of the scribes and Pharisees, and these exhortations are clothed in virtue-ethical language. The crowds, largely a neutral party prior to Matt 27:15-26, must decide between the righteousness of the scribes and Pharisees or the righteousness of Jesus and his disciples that surpasses that of the scribes and Pharisees (Matt 5:20).[76] Matthew's makarisms serve as a microcosm toward understanding the character of this righteousness in all of its counterintuitive nature, as well as understanding the nature of the kingdom of God and the rewards of those who live according to its directives. The makarisms describe this greater righteousness through the wisdom instruction of Jesus as the authoritative apocalyptic sage *par excellence*, and this wisdom leads to kingdom living and human flourishing. This reading is further supported by an understanding of the ethical connotations of the terms and structure of Matthew's makarisms, which will be discussed in the following section.

It is important to clarify that a virtue-ethics reading does not exclude an element of the anticipation of eschatological reversal as an aspect of anticipated rewards. Although it is argued here that to be "poor in spirit," to "mourn," and to be "meek" (humble) are virtuous dispositions rather than unfortunate circumstances, it is also important to recognize that they are dispositions that are only appropriate and necessary prior to the eschaton. The earliest Christians longed for a time when those who are humble would be exalted (cf. Matt 23:12) and when mourning would no longer be necessary (cf. Rev 21:4). The important difference between a virtue-ethics approach and the common eschatological reversal approach is that, while some of the disciples may be helpless,

[76]   See Matthias Konradt, *Israel, Church, and the Gentiles in the Gospel of Matthew* (Waco, Tex.: Baylor University Press, 2014), 159–66, who argues that the crowds of Matt 27:15-26 are a cautionary tale of those who follow the scribes and Pharisees rather than Jesus and his disciples.

oppressed, and destitute, the makarisms present the virtuous aspects of those who are humble and those who mourn over the sins of Israel and their false shepherds. Rather than focusing on helplessness, the disciples participate with Jesus in their desire for the world to be set to rights (cf. Matt 23:37-39). The hope for the disciples is not only that they will receive blessings in the *eschaton*, but that the eschatological hope motivates their active participation with Jesus, and that such participation is then met with the guarantee of eschatological rewards. These are dispositions to be entered into: those that would be unnecessary in an ideal world but are ideal in a world that has not been fully reconciled to God. These dispositions place the disciples in a position that is both counterintuitive and countercultural when compared with the dispositions that are valued by those in the world in which they live.[77] These themes will be explored more fully in the following sections.

5.1.1.2. Translating μακάριος

Matthew 5:3-12 is often referred to as Matthew's "beatitudes." The term "beatitude" comes from *beatus*, the Latin translation of μακάριος, meaning "happy, blissful, fortunate, or flourishing."[78] Nearly every English Bible translation renders μακάριος as "blessed," implying the active divine favor of God, which is passively received by the subject of each makarism. Some scholars have argued that the translation of μακάριος affects the interpretation of the entire list and is therefore a matter of first importance.[79] R. T. France is among a minority of scholars who have argued that "happy," rather than "blessed," is a better English rendering for μακάριος. France argues that, rather than the Hebrew term בָּרוּךְ, meaning "blessed by God," the Hebrew equivalent of μακάριος is אַשְׁרֵי, meaning "happy, fortunate." France admits that "happy" is a gloss with its own problems. Μακάριος is not meant to describe a person who *feels* happy but rather a person who is in a happy situation. Rather than a passive blessing, makarisms are "descriptions, and commendations, of the good life."[80]

---

[77]   See Pennington, *Sermon*, 156. Flourishing are those who possess an awareness of how not right the world is.

[78]   See Pennington, *Sermon*, 42.

[79]   See, for example, McKnight, *Sermon*, 32, who argues that interpreting the entire passage stems from a proper understanding of this one word. He states, "Get this word right, the rest falls into place; get it wrong, and the whole thing falls apart."

[80]   France, *Matthew*, 160–61. Other scholars who render μακάριος as "happy" include Luz, *Matthew 1–7*, 185, 190, who notes, like France, his dissatisfaction with both "blessed" and "happy" as English renderings, and Hagner, *Matthew 1–13*, 87–88, 91, who clarifies that μακάριος as happy does not refer to happiness in a mundane sense

Quarles argues, against France, that "blessed" is still the best translation. He contends that "happy" is misleading because the makarisms
do not refer to emotions based on circumstances but rather to "those to
whom Jesus spoke as privileged recipients of God's favor."[81] Similar is
Scot McKnight, who argues that "blessed" denotes a "richer, covenantal,
and theological" context. He refers to "happy" as the "only real alternative" and argues against its use due to its psychological connotations.[82]

The translation issue has been addressed in detail by Pennington.
Based on an analysis of the form and function of various makarisms, he
argues that a makarism is "a pronouncement, based on an observation,
that a certain way of being in the world produces human flourishing and
felicity."[83] Pennington agrees with France that אשרי is the best Hebrew
equivalent of μακάριος and that this supports his virtue-ethics reading
of Matthew's list. In the HB, when אשרי is featured in makaristic formulas, it does not simply describe those who are blessed, or happy in their
circumstances but those who are in a happy state specifically due to their
wise choices. Makarisms do not refer to wise choices themselves, but
are observations, made by a third party, of those who make wise choices
and flourish due to them.[84] God's grace is an important factor, as those
who live wisely can only do so in response to his covenant faithfulness
and their reverence for him, but אשרי statements refer to the practical
wisdom that cultivates strong character, which results in flourishing.[85]
Pennington notes that it is rare to find a one-to-one correspondence
between Hebrew terms and Greek equivalents in the LXX, but that אשרי
is always rendered as μακάριος, and that the relationship between these
terms "overlap[s] with little remainder." Therefore, μακάριος communicates the same ideas of human flourishing as אשרי. Pennington states
that, due to the relationship between אשרי and μακάριος, "it becomes

---

but rather to those who now begin to experience salvation in this life. See also Mattison,
"Beatitudes," 822, who takes a virtue-ethics approach to Matthew's list and argues that
ethics in Greco-Roman culture sought to define the parameters and qualities for happiness. Because happiness was the defining factor in living a good life, μακάριος is best
understood in relation to this pursuit.

[81]   Quarles, *Sermon*, 42.

[82]   McKnight, *Sermon*, 36, argues that a fulsome rendering would be something
like "God's favor is upon."

[83]   Pennington, *Sermon*, 42.

[84]   Pennington, *Sermon*, 49. See also K. C. Hanson, "How Honorable! How
Shameful! A Cultural Analysis of Matthew's Makarisms and Reproaches," *Semeia* 68
(1994): 84, who argues effectively that makarisms are not only observations of flourishing made by a third party, they are affirmations of honor that challenge the reader/hearer
to respond favorably.

[85]   Pennington, *Sermon*, 44–47, such as being married, having children, and living with earthly well-being, riches, honor, and wisdom.

clear that something other than a pronouncement of divine blessing is at hand." Matthew is making an appeal "for what true well-being looks like in God's kingdom."[86]

Pennington is careful to point out that there is an organic, close relationship between אשׁרי and ברוך, which leads to much of the confusion between "flourishing" and "blessing." In much of the biblical literature, one can only flourish if one is in a covenant relationship with God, which includes his blessings and favor. However, the two terms are not synonyms, and Pennington argues that makarisms, when properly understood, do not function as blessings.[87] Instead, makarisms (e.g., Ps 1) often function as implicit invitations to pursue wisdom and living a certain way.[88] This is highlighted by the relationship between makarisms and their corresponding negatives. In ancient Near Eastern literature, the corresponding negative to a blessing is a curse. However, makarisms are not contrasted with curses but rather with woes.[89] This relationship is more pronounced in Luke's list, which places the makarisms and woes in direct contextual relationship. In the following section, it will be argued that, although Matthew's woes are strikingly different than Luke's and placed much later in the narrative, the makarisms of Matt 5 and the woes of Matt 23 are still meant to function in a contrasting relationship with one another. Woes are not intended as maledictions but rather calls to repent.[90] They expose a life of grief and destruction. As makarisms describe the flourishing life, woes describe the lives of those who are not flourishing and instead are choosing a life that lacks wisdom. As Pennington states, "Makarisms and woes are invitations to living based on sapiential reflections, not divine speech of reward or cursing."[91]

[86]   Pennington, *Sermon*, 47. Similar is Craig S. Keener, *The Gospel of Matthew: A Socio-Rhetorical Commentary* (Grand Rapids: Eerdmans, 2009), 165, who states that the makarisms declare, "It will go well with the one who . . . for that one shall receive . . . ."

[87]   Pennington, *Sermon*, 50. See also Hanson, "How Honorable!" 81–85, who argues that English Bible translations have blurred the distinction between blessings and makarisms. He provides a brief review of scholars who have failed to understand the distinction and argues similarly to Pennington and France that אשׁרי and μακάριος are related to, but distinct from, the concept of blessing.

[88]   See, for example, Prov 3:13, "Flourishing are those who find wisdom, and those who get understanding." See also Keener, *Gospel*, 165.

[89]   See Hanson, "How Honorable!" 85–89, who analyzes the relationship between blessings and curses and offers numerous examples from the HB and Second Temple literature. Similarly to Pennington, Hanson concludes that, despite some important similarities, makarisms and woes function differently than blessings and curses.

[90]   See Hanson, "How Honorable!" 84, woes are "reproaches" that challenge one's honor.

[91]   Pennington, *Sermon*, 53. See also Hanson, "How Honorable!" 91–92, who argues that makarisms are value judgments, made by individuals and communities,

Important for Pennington's argument is the relationship between μακάριος and two other Greek ethics terms, τέλειος and εὐδαιμονία.[92] Rather
than "perfect," as τέλειος is often translated in Matt 5:48, he suggests that a
better gloss would be "whole," "complete," or "virtuous." The term τέλειος
has an organic relationship with εὐδαιμονία, which many scholars translate as "flourishing."[93] This "teleiosity," or, "flourishing," described in Matt
5:48 runs like a thread through the Sermon on the Mount, which consistently calls for a greater righteousness for those who enter the kingdom of
heaven (Matt 5:17-20). The Pharisees, described as hypocrites, live in the
opposite direction of this sort of flourishing, and this is epitomized by the
opposite visions of Godward virtue presented in Matt 5:3-12 and 23:1-36.[94]
In this way, the makarisms are meant to describe not entrance requirements,
or the reception of blessings, but rather a "wholehearted orientation toward
God."[95] The makarisms begin the Sermon on the Mount by detailing the
character dispositions of those who stand to live in light of the moral

---

which imputes esteem based for demonstrating "desirable behavior and commitments." Makarisms "articulate the values of the community, sage, or teacher" upon
the subject.

[92]   The relationship between these terms was noted in 5.1.1.1. Betz and Luz
make note of the correlation between these terms. See also Mattison, "Beatitudes,"
822, who follows others and agrees that μακάριος and εὐδαιμονία are best regarded
as synonyms, and both contribute toward an understanding of the virtue-ethical pursuit
of a good life. Hanson, "How Honorable!" 93, produces an important example from
Josephus' Antiquities, in his account of Judah Maccabeus' speech to his troops, which
places μακάριος and εὐδαιμονία in a near synonymous relationship, by describing the honor and prosperity that comes from following laws and ancestral customs:
"Since, therefore, at the moment it lies in your power either to recover this liberty and
regain a prosperous (εὐδαιμονα) and honorable (μακάριον) life—by this he meant
one in accordance with the laws and ancestral customs—or to endure the shame, and
to leave your people without descendants by being cowardly in battle. You yourselves
must fight, then, since those who do not fight will also die; believing that suffering for
such great causes—freedom, patrimony, laws, worship—secures you perpetual honor"
(Ant. 12.7.3).

[93]   This begins with Aristotle, who related τέλειος, the complete attainment of
a goal, with εὐδαιμονία, the flourishing that results in such an attainment. See John
M. Cooper, Reason and Human Good in Aristotle (Cambridge, Mass.: Harvard University Press, 1975), 89–92. Cooper notes that many scholars of Greek philosophy have
translated εὐδαιμονία as "happy" but that this translation falls short, because εὐδαιμονία is not a subjective, emotional, or recurrent psychological state. It is not about
brief moments in time but rather sustainable living in light of a bright future. Cooper
connects εὐδαιμονία to τέλειος and explains that "teleiotation" is the "ultimate end,"
and εὐδαιμονία is the flourishing life that leads one there. Therefore, Cooper translates
εὐδαιμονία as "human flourishing."

[94]   See McKnight, Sermon, 30, who argues that Matthew's makarisms provides
"a list of the good guys," and that Matt 23 provides, "an alternate list of bad guys."

[95]   Pennington, Sermon, 74–80.

imagination that the Sermon aims to inspire.[96] Those who flourish are those who are poor in spirit, those who mourn over the state of Israel, those who are meek, etc., and it is those who flourish in these ways who can observe the greater righteousness of the Sermon (Matt 5:20) and be whole as their heavenly Father is whole (Matt 5:48). Due to these factors, Pennington offers "flourishing" as a translation for μακάριος. His arguments are convincing enough to determine that "flourishing" better captures the virtue-ethical character and intent of the makarisms than alternatives such as "blessed" or "happy," therefore this study adopts the translation of "flourishing," and its corresponding virtue-ethics approach, for Matthew's makarisms.

5.1.1.3. Matthew's Makarisms as Dispositions for the Model Disciple

An important factor in establishing a virtue-ethics reading of Matthew's makarisms is an understanding of their place within Matthew's narrative, both in the immediate context and in the Gospel as a whole. An understanding of the flow of the narrative not only highlights the role of the makarisms in detailing human flourishing in a general sense but specifically as dispositions for the model disciple.

As Jesus begins his earthly ministry (Matt 4:1-17), he calls his first disciples (Matt 4:18-22), and begins to appeal to the crowds, healing their sick and proclaiming the good news of the kingdom (Matt 4:23-25). Jesus then addresses both the crowds and his disciples (Matt 5:1-2), lists the makarisms (Matt 5:3-12), describes the purpose of true discipleship (Matt 5:13-16), affirms God's law (Matt 5:17-20), and then details his interpretations of various laws as the ethics of the kingdom (Matt 5:21–7:29). A number of linguistic and thematic inclusio feature throughout the narrative, bracketing important portions of text that all point to establishing an important meta-theme across the First Gospel: Jesus is establishing two competing modes of discipleship, and making an appeal to the crowds, offering them a choice between these two competing visions.[97] Jesus' vision for his own disciples is *teleiosity*, or wholeness (Matt 5:48), which is found by those who accept and enter into his vision of human flourishing and true righteousness. Jesus' vision of true righteousness is contrasted with that of the Jewish leaders, most often amalgamated by the designation "scribes and Pharisees," who are false shepherds leading

[96] The phrase "moral imagination" is taken from Allison, *Sermon*; it features in the subtitle of his book and runs as a theme throughout.

[97] See Rodney Reeves, *Matthew* (SGBC; Grand Rapids: Zondervan, 2017), 102–3, who argues that Jesus' intent was "to make disciples of the crowd." He was making disciples that would assist him in bringing the kingdom to earth, and "to extend his messianic work through his disciples," so that they might "help him do God's will on earth as it is in heaven."

Israel astray.[98] If one wishes to be a disciple of the kingdom that Jesus describes, their righteousness must line up with Jesus' vision (Matt 5:19) and therefore exceed the righteousness of the scribes and Pharisees (Matt 5:20).[99] At the center of these two competing visions are "the crowds" (τοὺς ὄχλους) who are introduced in Matt 4:25, at the very start of Jesus' ministry, and who enter the narrative as a neutral party, remaining that way until late in the Gospel.[100] While the Jewish leaders have authority among the crowds, Jesus' words and actions offer a compelling and competing vision against their authority (Matt 7:28).[101]

[98]   This point is made prolifically throughout Konradt, *Israel*, 37, 45, 75–77, 90–91, 102, 114–18. The Jewish leaders, as shepherds, have failed (Matt 10:6; 15:24), and Jesus has replaced them as the shepherd of Israel. Konradt argues effectively that the Jewish leaders are described as blind (Matt 15:14; 23:16-26) as a metaphorical way to refer to the enlightenment of Jesus' disciples as Israel's new models. Jesus sends his own disciples as a response to the hardship of his fellow Jews. Konradt argues that, although Matthew's writer surely understood the differences between the various authority groups in Israel (Sadducees, Pharisees, scribes, etc.), their differentiations recede from view and they are regarded as a single failed character throughout the narrative. The point regarding the amalgamation of the Jewish leaders is also made by David E. Garland, *The Intention of Matthew 23* (Leiden: Brill, 1979), 43–46, who argues that Matthew uses the various groups of Jewish leaders homogeneously as a collective literary convention, in order to present "the entire process of the history of Israel whose leaders have always been false." See also Janice Capel Anderson, *Matthew's Narrative Web: Over, and Over, and Over Again* (JSNTS 91; Sheffield: JSOT Press, 1994), 97–98, who argues that all of the Jewish leadership subgroups are indistinguishable in order to form a character who represents "the Jewish establishment." An important collection of articles on the reception of the Pharisees is *In Quest of the Historical Pharisees* (ed. Jacob Neusner and Bruce D. Chilton; Waco, Tex.: Baylor University Press, 2007), and in particular the article by Martin Pickup, "Matthew's and Mark's Pharisees," 67–112.

[99]   Kyle Keefer, *The New Testament as Literature: A Very Short Introduction* (Oxford: Oxford University Press, 2008), 31, points to the dualisms used throughout Matthew to illustrate this point of division between those who listen to Jesus and those who do not (cf. narrow and wide gates, Matt 7; house on rock and house on sand, Matt 7; parable of wheat and weeds, Matt 13; parable of foolish and wise bridesmaids, Matt 25; allegory of sheep and goats, Matt 25).

[100]   So Konradt, *Israel*, 100–105, 159–66. The crowds are set apart from both the disciples and the Jewish leaders and are presented throughout the narrative with a choice of allegiance between the two competing visions. The first negative depiction of the crowds is in Matt 27, where certain members among them have joined with the Pharisees. Even in this depiction, Konradt argues, there is a difference between the crowds in Galilee, which are always depicted positively, and those in Israel, which join with the Jewish leaders. Konradt argues effectively that this may be a reason why Matthew's resurrection narratives focus on Galilee as opposed to Jerusalem.

[101]   So Garland, *Intention*, 39–40. The crowds are under the authority of the Jewish leaders, but in Matthew they are "on the brink of acknowledging Jesus as God's son." They have a choice to make between Jesus as the son of David or casting their lot with "blind guides."

One often noted inclusio is Matt 4:23 and 9:35, two nearly identical verses that detail Jesus' teaching and healing throughout Galilee. These verses serve as a bracket to summarize these two actions; Jesus teaches (Matt 5:3–7:27) and he heals (Matt 8:1–9:34).[102] Each of these two sections is in turn bracketed by descriptions of the crowds as the intended audience of Jesus' actions: "When Jesus saw the crowds, he went up on the mountain," where he began to teach them, and at the conclusion of the Sermon on the Mount, Jesus encourages his audience to build their lives on his teaching, and to follow him (Matt 7:24-27), leaving the crowds astounded at his authority and doubting the teaching of their own scribes (Matt 7:28-29). When Jesus comes down from the mountain, the crowds follow him (Matt 8:1). He has compassion on the crowds, and it is among them that he begins to heal (Matt 8:1-4). Because of the ineptitude of the scribes and Pharisees, Jesus regards the crowds as sheep without a shepherd (Matt 9:36). The crowds need a true shepherd of Israel, so he gathers disciples to himself in order to make his message and healing ministry known (9:35–10:42),[103] training them to be models of his vision for true righteousness and obedience to God (Matt 5:16).[104] Jesus' preaching of the kingdom is that the

[102]   Konradt, *Israel*, 53, argues that this bracket provides a summary of Jesus fulfilling Israel's messianic expectations. For a different view on the use of these two parallel verses (Matt 4:23 and 9:35), see Talbert, *Reading*, 17, who argues that these passages introduce the following teaching discourses rather than serving as a bracket for Matt 5–9. Talbert's view is possible but does not take into account that these parallel verses both feature teaching and healing, which makes better sense of the material that comes in between them, rather than as introductions to teaching discourses only.

[103]   This theme in Matthew is more apparent when comparing Matthew's presentation of both the disciples and the Jewish leaders to the presentation of these two groups in the other Gospels. For example, Warren Carter, *Telling Tales about Jesus: An Introduction to the New Testament Gospels* (Minneapolis: Fortress, 2016), 134–44, points out that Matthew largely sanitizes the folly of the disciples portrayed in Mark. This allows the disciples to embody the descriptions of true righteousness as they follow Jesus' example. Conversely, Matthew's sustained negative portrayal of the Jewish leaders is largely consistent with that of Mark, but he heightens the criticism of the scribes in particular. Ulrich Luz, *Studies in Matthew* (Grand Rapids: Eerdmans, 2005), 120–21, cautions against overstating this point by arguing that Matthew has only "improved" the status of the disciples above their portrayal in Mark regarding the motif of understanding. In Matthew, the disciples understand better than in Mark, but in other ways Luz argues that the portrayal is largely the same between the two Gospels.

[104]   So Konradt, *Israel*, 75. Jesus sends out his disciples due to the hardship of the crowds. The disciples join in Jesus' pastoral ministry, as their ministry is meant to "continue the Messianic ministry of the shepherd of Israel to his flock by healing the sick and proclaiming the good news of the kingdom." See also Garland, *Intention*, 37–39, who argues that the disciples of Jesus, although often included alongside the crowds as an audience for Jesus' teachings, are not just followers but are meant themselves to become "the shepherds of a scattered flock." Garland follows the arguments of Paul S.

eschatological light has dawned in the present (Matt 4:12-17), bringing a wisdom-driven appeal to repentance and true righteousness. The crowds are prominently included both in the brackets over the entire narrative section (Matt 4:23; 9:35-36) and at the beginning and end of each sub-section (teaching, Matt 5:1; 7:28; healing 8:1; 9:36).[105]

Davies and Allison convincingly argue that the imperatives of Jesus' teaching in the Sermon on the Mount are preceded by healing and acts of God's grace (Matt 4:23-24); however, it does not necessitate that the makarisms also be viewed only as evidences of this grace.[106] I would argue instead that a more fluid transition is in view: Matthew's Jesus uses his proclamations of the kingdom and his healings to draw the crowds (e.g., Matt 4:24, "So his fame spread throughout all Syria"; Matt 8:1, "When Jesus had come down from the mountain, great crowds followed him"), and before introducing them to the ethics of this kingdom, he details for them examples of the character traits, or "dispositions," that aid true disciples in their efforts to live in light of kingdom norms. God's grace is the necessary appeal to gain the crowds' attention, but, to use Allison's phrase, their "moral imagination" is inspired by the honorable traits that the makarisms describe.[107] The first clauses of each makarism

---

Minear, "The Disciples and the Crowds in the Gospel of Matthew," in *Gospel Studies in Honor of Sherman Elbridge Johnson* (ed. Massey H. Shepherd Jr. and Edward C. Hobbs; *Anglican Theological Review*, Supplementary Series 3, 1974), 28–44. See also Dale C. Allison Jr., *Studies in Matthew: Interpretation Past and Present* (Grand Rapids: Baker Academic, 2005), 151, who demonstrates many of the ways that Matthew's Gospel "goes out of its way to make the twelve disciples emulate their Lord in numerous particulars." Allison parallels many passages in which Jesus is portrayed as healing, teaching, casting out demons, raising the dead, being handed over to authorities, and being associated with the devil by his enemies, with numerous examples of the disciples doing and experiencing these same things.

[105]   Davies and Allison, *Matthew 1–7*, 419–20, note several important functions of the crowds in Matthew. Their presence highlights the charisma of Jesus, they are open and receptive to Jesus' message, they are contrasted against, rather than included with, the Jewish leaders, and they are distinguished from the disciples. Davies and Allison state, "They are presented in a more or less positive light." The crowds are "not true followers of Jesus; yet they are also not in the same league with Jesus' opponents, the chief priests, the elders, and the Pharisees. The crowds fall somewhere in between." Davies and Allison argue that the crowds are a neutral party used to highlight the ineptitude of the Jewish leaders when they state, "the blame is to be laid squarely at the feet of their misguided leaders."

[106]   Davies and Allison, *Matthew 1–7*, 440. See the discussion here in 5.1.1.1.

[107]   It is important to point out that Allison, *Sermon*, 11, applied this phrase to the Sermon on the Mount as a whole, while viewing the makarisms as eschatological reversals. The full sermon was intended to inspire a "moral vision," meaning the principles and qualities brought about "through a vivid inspiration of the moral imagination." My argument here is that this description is apt for the makarisms as well as the Sermon as a whole.

describe the model disciple, and the second clauses describe the motivations for the disciples to manifest such dispositions. The inclusio found within the makarisms contributes to this understanding. The poor in spirit (Matt 5:3) and those who are persecuted for proper righteousness as defined by Jesus' teachings (Matt 5:10) are flourishing and therefore the kingdom of heaven is theirs, and these two makarisms encapsulate the meaning of the others: those who flourish are those who mourn, are meek, hunger and thirst for righteousness, are merciful, are pure in heart, and are peacemakers, and because they are flourishing they will inherit the earth, be filled, receive mercy, see God, and become children of God. Those who exhibit kingdom-oriented dispositions are flourishing and will receive the benefits of the kingdom. The full benefits are eschatological in nature but can be experienced in the present as a result of such flourishing, by virtue of being true disciples of Jesus and joining him in his messianic mission.[108]

One of the most important brackets for understanding the theme of competing visions of discipleship is the placement of the First Gospel's makarisms in relationship to its woes (Matt 23). The relationship between these two passages is not always appreciated.[109] For example, Davies and Allison note some of the linguistic parallels between the two passages, as well as the fact that the parallels appear in the two chapters in precisely the same order (kingdom of heaven, 5:5; 23:23; mercy, 5:7; 23:23; purity, 5:8; 23:25-26; persecution, 5:10-12; 23:34; prophets, 5:12; 23:34). Furthermore, they note that Matt 5:3-12 and 23:13-39 both end with the theme of the martyrdom of the prophets. Nevertheless, despite these intriguing parallels, Davies and Allison argue that these connections may be nothing more than coincidence and assume that even more points of connection would be likely if Matthew's writer intended these two passages to be viewed in light of one another.[110]

---

[108]   The makarisms are not soteriological but refer to discipleship. McKnight, *Sermon*, 1, states that the Sermon on the Mount "is the moral portrait of Jesus' own people." I argue that this is appropriate for the makarisms, which demonstrate dispositions appropriate for kingdom living.

[109]   See, for example, Guelich, "Matthean Beatitudes," 419, who, when comparing Matthew's list to Luke's, notes that Matthew's list shows "no trace" of the prophetic-apocalyptic woes of Luke's list. It is difficult to determine from Guelich's comments if he disassociates Matthew's makarisms from its woes or simply argues for a difference in character between the woes of Matthew and Luke. See also Garland, *Intention*, who in a lengthy study of Matt 23 does not make an explicit connection between Matthew's makarisms and woes, and France, *Matthew*, 162, who notes the relationship between makarisms and woes in Luke but adds that Matthew has "no parallel" in regard to this balance. Hagner, *Matthew 1–13*, 89, simply refers to the Lukan woes as "omitted" in Matthew and does not note any connection between Matt 5 and 23.

[110]   Davies and Allison, *Matthew 1–7*, 440–41.

More recently some scholars have appreciated the connection between these two Matthean passages by noting the intrinsic relationship between makarisms and woes. Pennington notes that a contrast between these two motifs is expected: makarisms describe flourishing, and woes provide an expected counterexample of dispositions that do not result in flourishing but in grief and destruction. Pennington admits that Luke's list follows the more expected pattern by placing its makarisms and woes in direct comparison but that the separation between Matthew's makarisms and woes does not negate their function as a literary pair. Pennington suggests that Matthew's writer placed the makarisms at the start of Jesus' first block of teaching, which was critical of the Jewish leaders (Matt 5:20), and the woes form a bookend with his final week of teaching, where Jesus' critiques of the Jewish leaders reaches a climax.[111] Jesus' disciples are to be pure in heart (Matt 5:8), but the Jewish leaders are hypocrites who pursue external righteousness without purity of heart (Matt 15:6-20; 23:25-28). The Jewish leaders are whitewashed tombs that appear beautiful on the outside but are internally unclean (Matt 23:27-28).[112] Pennington defines righteousness in Matthew as "whole-person behavior that accords with God's nature, will, and coming kingdom." The righteous person is the one who follows Jesus toward such flourishing and does God's will both externally and from the heart; a call to righteousness that contrasts and conflicts with the external and hypocritical righteousness of the scribes and Pharisees. Because this conflict continues throughout the narrative, it makes sense for Matthew to detail true righteousness at the start of Jesus' instruction in the Gospel and to bring his instruction to an end with the climactic expression of the counterexample.[113]

---

[111]   Pennington, *Sermon*, 55. See also Robert H. Gundry, *Matthew: A Commentary on His Handbook for a Mixed Church under Persecution* (Grand Rapids: Eerdmans, 1994), 69, who argues for the intrinsic connection between makarisms and woes but that Matthew's writer separated them as a function of the narrative. In Matt 5, Jesus is focused on his disciples and maintains that focus by moving the woes to ch. 23 for a sustained attack on his opponents. Despite this narrative distance between them, Matthew maintains a "fidelity" to the connection between makarisms and woes as a literary unit.

[112]   Pennington, *Sermon*, 84.

[113]   This point, that the leaders of the Jewish people are presented in Matt 23 as the antithesis of Jesus' disciples, is made by Sjef van Tilborg, *The Jewish Leaders in Matthew* (Leiden: Brill, 1972), 26, 98; Garland, *Intention*, 118. Graham Stanton, *A Gospel for a New People: Studies in Matthew* (Louisville: Westminster John Knox, 1992), 156–57, argues against this point because he does not see the scribes and Pharisees as a literary foil but rather an actual threat which represents the rejection of Matthew's community among their fellow Jews. However, Stanton does not consider two things: first, the scribes and Pharisees can be both a threat to the community and a literary foil *based upon* their socioreligious circumstances, and,

The truly righteous person hungers and thirsts for righteousness with a pure heart (Matt 5:6, 8), and their righteousness must surpass that of the scribes and Pharisees (Matt 5:20) whose righteousness is impure and full of hypocrisy (Matt 23:25-28).[114]

K. C. Hanson has also argued for the intrinsic connection between makarisms and woes, providing a number of important examples among a plurality of Jewish compositions.[115] He states that woes are "the antithesis and antipode of the makarism formula."[116] Makarisms serve to uphold the values of the community or a particular sage or teacher. They describe a righteous person who fears God and exhibits honorable social behavior. Conversely, woes serve to challenge disreputable behavior and the public honor of the perpetrators. Hanson emphasizes the public and social character of these formulas, noting that many of the woes were intended as oral reproaches uttered by an entire community.[117]

Regarding Matthew's makarisms, Hanson argues that the first clauses serve as value judgments, while the second ὅτι clauses function as "motivational clauses."[118] The third person construction, which is ideal for makarisms, allows honor to be attributed to anyone who behaves in like manner. This allows the makarisms to serve as appeals

---

second, the importance of the intrinsic relationship between the woes of Matt 23 and the makarisms of Matt 5.

[114] Pennington, *Sermon*, 91. See also Jack R. Lundbom, *Jesus' Sermon on the Mount: Mandating a Better Righteousness* (Minneapolis: Fortress, 2015), 11, who argues that the makarisms and woes are meant to balance one another out. Matthew 5–7 is meant to focus on those entering the kingdom, and 23–25 focuses on the kingdom in the coming days. Kenneth G. C. Newport, *The Sources and Sitz im Leben of Matthew 23* (JSNTS; Sheffield: Sheffield Academic, 1995), 157–75, notes numerous parallels between Matt 23 and the Sermon on the Mount, though he spends little time on the makarisms in particular. Anthony J. Saldarini, *Matthew's Christian-Jewish Community* (Chicago: University of Chicago Press, 1994), 49, notes that the woes contain a contrast between inner attitudes and outward behavior, that this contrast is also used to describe the Jewish leaders in the Sermon on the Mount, and that these criticisms are used by Matthew's writer to expose the Jewish leaders as a counterexample to Matthew's own community.

[115] Hanson, "How Honorable!" 95–96. Hanson argues that "honorable" is the best gloss for both μακάριος and אשרי and that "shame" is the best gloss for both οὐαί and הוי. On the intrinsic nature between makarisms and woes, he provides as examples Isa 3:10-11; Qoh 10:16-17; Luke 6:20-26; 1 En. 99:10-16; 1 En. 103:5-6; 2 En. 52:1-15; 2 Bar. 10:6-7.

[116] Hanson, "How Honorable!" 96.

[117] Hanson, "How Honorable!" 97–98, argues that this is true in both prophetic and sapiential contexts. The prophets would employ these formulas "in relation to the social ethos, in line with the concerns of the sages." Even in prophetic literature Hanson argues that makarism/woe formulas maintain their "didactic wisdom settings."

[118] See also Pennington, *Sermon*, 155. The ὅτι clause, which he translates "because," provides the explanation and causal grounds for the apparent paradoxes in the first clauses.

to the crowds and disciples.[119] The second clauses ascribe honor to those who act appropriately, and the two clauses are brought together by an act/consequence logic. Personal conduct results in public validation.[120]

Hanson argues along similar lines as Pennington regarding the placement of Matthew's makarisms in relationship to its woes. The makarisms open Jesus' first teaching block, the Sermon on the Mount, which describes the ethics of the kingdom. Although the second through the seventh makarisms (Matt 5:4-9) are in the future tense, the present tenses of the first and eighth (Matt 5:3,10) function as an inclusio that reveals that the motivations of the second clauses "may be realized within the community, and in this life."[121] The makarisms are not formal blessings, nor are they entrance requirements, they "express the conditions and behaviors which the community regards as honorable." They are in the tradition of the sages and point to "ideal character."[122]

Matthew's woes, on the other hand, are in the second person and directed at specific groups; the scribes and Pharisees. The woes are not legal and do not describe threats, rather they are aimed at uncovering shameful behaviors. The scribes and Pharisees are hypocrites, blind guides, blind fools, blind ones, and sons of those who killed the prophets. In the same way that Matthew's makarisms open Jesus' first block of teaching, its woes come at the end of Jesus' public ministry. This aspect is important for understanding the function of the woes and the role of the crowds and disciples. Although the woes are addressed *to* the scribes and Pharisees, they are not *for* them. Jesus' judgment against them has been passed. The true audience of these judgments is the crowds, who are given one final opportunity to enter into discipleship and see the error of the scribes and Pharisees and the hypocritical path that comes with

[119]   See Pennington, *Sermon*, 143. While Matthew does at points distinguish between the crowds and the disciples, in Matt 5:3-12 all are welcome to respond. The passage is "a general call to all people" as it epitomizes Jesus' teaching on the kingdom. This is *contra* McKnight, *Sermon*, 34, among others, who appears to present the makarisms as declarations of those already so constituted, rather than as appeals to those who are not. The list refers to those whom God knows to be living properly, because of God's omniscience of knowing "who is in and who is out."

[120]   Hanson, "How Honorable!" 100.

[121]   So Pennington, *Sermon*, 158. Matthew's makarisms are "invitations to flourishing in light of God's coming eschatological kingdom."

[122]   Hanson, "How Honorable!" 100–101. See also Pennington, *Sermon*, 159, the beatitudes are "a summary description of the character of the true disciple," and Luz, *Matthew 1–7*, 187, who points to the sapiential character of the makarisms as a didactic genre that serves to instruct. They are wisdom paraenesis that connects a person's deeds with what happens to them.

following them.[123] The crowds are mentioned for the first time in Matt 4:25, just before the dispositions of the makarisms are revealed, but the last time Jesus addresses this group is here, in Matt 23:1. Jesus addresses the crowds and the disciples when pronouncing woes against his opponents, but hereafter he only directly addresses his disciples (24:1, 3; 26:1, 8, 10, 20-21, 26, 31, 36, 38, 45). Hanson argues that this places an inclusio around Jesus' public ministry; there is an antithetical character to the makarisms and woes that encapsulates Jesus' entire ministry toward offering the crowds two competing visions of righteousness.[124] In the same way that Luke 6:20-26 offers corresponding makarisms and reproaches, Matthew's Gospel employs two series as brackets around Jesus' public teaching. The two units provide value judgments, "which constitute the positive and negative values of the kingdom." The crowds must choose, and once the final pronouncement of woes has been made, Jesus focuses on his disciples through his final block of teaching (Matt 24–25) and the final portions of the narrative (Matt 26–28).[125] In Jerusalem in particular, many among the crowds have cast their lot with the Jewish leaders (Matt 27:20, 24).[126] To strengthen Hanson's argument regarding the connection between Matt 5:3-12 and 23:13-31, he goes beyond the parallels noted by Davies and Allison and argues that the structure of the formulas, the role of the crowds and disciples, and the structure of the lists within the narrative of Matthew all point to a connection. As true disciples will be

[123]   See Garland, *Intention*, 118–20, who argues effectively that when the woes begin in Matt 23:13, "there is no explicit shift in the audience from that of the crowds and disciples mentioned in Matt 23:1."

[124]   To view Matt 5:3-12 and 23:1–24:2 as an inclusio around Jesus' ministry is not to suggest that Matt 23 opens Jesus' final teaching block in the same way that Matt 5:1-12 opens his first. Scholars are divided as to whether the woes of Matt 23 should be included with the teaching block of Matt 24:3–25:46 as a single teaching unit. As France, *Matthew*, 857, notes, many scholars argue that the change in location to the Mount of Olives, and the removal of the crowds among the audience, separates Matt 24:3 from what precedes it. France notes that Matt 24:3–25:46 follows a classic discourse pattern and therefore treats Matt 23 as a separate unit. Gundry, *Matthew*, 453, noting the connection between the makarisms and woes, treats Matt 23–25 as a single unit, as does Pennington, *Sermon*, 108. For a survey of scholars who view Matt 23–25 as a single unit, see Jason B. Hood, "Matthew 23–25: The Extent of Jesus' Fifth Discourse," *JBL* 128, no. 3 (2009): 527–43, especially p. 529. For a survey of varying views regarding Matt 23's place within the whole of the Gospel, see Davies and Allison, *Matthew 1–7*, 58–72. It is not necessary to solve this issue here, as Hanson's argument refers to the confines of Jesus' ministry rather than the precise structure of Matt 23–25 as blocks of teaching. Matt 4:25 and 23:1 form an inclusio regarding Jesus' address and approach to the crowds.

[125]   Pennington, *Sermon*, 143, "The hearing, understanding, and obeying moves one from being part of the crowd to being a disciple."

[126]   Hanson, "How Honorable!" 101–3.

"sons of God" (Matt 5:9), the scribes and Pharisees are instead "sons of hell" (Matt 23:15). In Hanson's view, "The antithetical parallels between the two could hardly be accidental."[127]

Hanson's argument regarding the social aspects of the makarisms has been emphasized by Francois P. Viljoen.[128] Viljoen agrees that the makarisms reveal a new way of life and call the hearers/readers to respond with right conduct. He states, "By revealing this new way of life, the beatitudes affect moral behavior. The addressees have to respond with adequate attitudes, actions and thoughts that are different to conventional ways of behavior. Therefore, the set of beatitudes describes the way of life of faithful disciples of Jesus." Ethical exhortations are embedded along with future blessings in a way that allows eschatological judgment to affect the present. According to Viljoen, this appeal is not merely individualistic but affects the "parameters of conduct" for Matthew's entire community. Matthew's makarisms are employed to reinforce the social identity of the group. By describing their state of flourishing, Matthew's Gospel separates true disciples from all other groups, and those who endure suffering for the sake of the group (Matt 5:10-11) will flourish in this life and be rewarded in heaven (Matt 5:12). "In this way," Viljoen writes, "the beatitudes constitute and affirm the community's unique identity and practices." They expect final vindication while living a righteous life under God's transforming kingdom.[129]

5.1.1.4. Conclusion

Following the work of Jonathan Pennington, I have argued here that "flourishing" is the best English translation of μακάριος. This gloss best represents a virtue-ethics approach to Matthew's makarisms, which understands the first clauses as positive dispositions for those who seek to be disciples of Jesus and enter the kingdom. The makarisms represent human flourishing and true righteousness. The second clauses of the makarisms represent corresponding benefits of the kingdom for those who live in light of Jesus' teaching, which are eschatological benefits available to Jesus' disciples in the here and now. These dispositions and benefits are offered to individuals, but they also represent the parameters of conduct for the entire community of disciples and therefore detail the honored values and social identity of all who constitute the group. The social identity of Jesus' community is contrasted with the Jewish

---

[127]   Hanson, "How Honorable!" 102.

[128]   Francois P. Viljoen, "Righteousness and Identity Formation in the Sermon on the Mount," *HTS* 69, no. 1 (2013): 1–10.

[129]   Viljoen, "Righteousness," 4–5.

leaders, who represent a counterexample to Jesus' teaching on righteousness. The scribes and Pharisees are set up as the foil to Jesus early in the narrative (Matt 5:20), and the rest of the Gospel refers to their hypocrisy and failure often (Matt 6:1-5, 16; 7:24-29; 15:1-20; 23:1-36). These competing visions of true discipleship are an important aspect of interpreting both Matthew's makarisms as well as many other important passages throughout the Gospel.

5.1.2. Interpreting Matthew 5:5

Understanding the character of Matthew's makarisms is an important first step toward interpreting each of them. With a virtue-ethics perspective in view, and understanding the contrasting dynamic between Jesus' disciples and the Jewish leaders, we can now interpret Matt 5:5 in context, especially regarding the role of inheritance in this verse and within the whole of Matthew's Gospel.

5.1.2.1. Matthew 5:3 and 5:5 in Comparison

Although Matt 5:3 is a shared makarism with Luke 6:20, there are differences between Matthew's and Luke's versions, especially Matthew's addition of τῷ πνεύματι (in sprit) to the phrase "flourishing are the poor," as it is found in Luke.[130] Scholars have argued that the phrase πτωχοὶ τῷ πνεύματι (poor in spirit), possibly derived from Second Temple literature,[131] was employed by Matthew's writer to explicate the

---

[130] Other grammatical differences include Matthew's third person plural compared to Luke's second person plural and Matthew's use of "kingdom of heaven" compared to Luke's "kingdom of God." There are other differences besides, depending on how one reads the purpose and meaning of the beatitudes in each Gospel. For example, the argument of this chapter has been that the tone of the beatitudes between Matthew and Luke is quite different. Matthew presents the opening clauses as qualities to be commended that are essentially spiritual and ethical, whereas Luke's presentation is that of concern regarding the situation in which the disciples find themselves. France, *Matthew*, 162, argues that in Luke terms such as poor, hungry, weeping, and hated are literal, whereas in Matthew key terms in the first clauses of each makarism have been spiritualized. Because of this, Matthew's makarisms promote the good life of the kingdom of heaven, but Luke's makarisms speak instead of "material and social disadvantage as a result of following Jesus."

[131] The phrase "poor in spirit" is a *hapax legomenon* in the canonical material (though the "contrite spirit" of Ps 34:18 comes close) but many scholars have argued that precedent for the phrase is found in the Qumran literature. 1QM XIV 7 and 1QS IV 3 feature the phrase poor/humble in spirit and this phrase is contrasted in 1QS XI 1, which refers to the "lofty in spirit." In these instances, the focus is not on those who are weak in character but rather refers to the person's relationship with God. As France, *Matthew*, 165, has stated, the humble in spirit in the Qumran literature "is a positive

meaning of Luke's "poor,"[132] which is largely focused on sociological and economic concerns.[133] Although Luke's use of πτωχός does not necessarily exclude the religious dimension of poverty, his makarism and its corresponding woe exhibit a decidedly more economic flavor, and Luke is generally more concerned than Matthew with charity, economic disadvantage, and critiquing the rich.[134] As Matthew's Gospel is more concerned with discipleship, ethics, and greater righteousness, specifically in contrast to the actions of the scribes and Pharisees, a religious emphasis of poverty is more in keeping with Matthew's overall message, and the addition of the phrase "in spirit" is often seen as a product of this emphasis.[135] In Matthew, it is argued, the poor are not those who are economically oppressed or destitute but rather those who remain faithful to God and thrive in the midst of their oppression. Rather than economic connotations, Matt 5:3 primarily refers to ethical and religious concerns.[136] The "poor in spirit" are those who are humble before God and submit to his will, realizing their need of him and dependence upon his grace and rule.[137]

---

spiritual orientation, the reverse of arrogant self-confidence." See also Craig A. Evans, *Matthew* (Cambridge: Cambridge University Press, 2012), 104, the "poor" in 1QM XIV 7 refers to those who stand opposite of those with a hard or haughty heart. It is a way of referring to those who are righteous, who "rely upon God and not upon power, wealth, or reputation."

[132]   So Hoyt, "Poor/Rich," 38. See also Allison, *Sermon*, 48, who does not commit to Matthew's writer as the source of this addition but states that Matt 5:5 was "added at some point in the tradition as an attempt to clarify 5:3" as an "accurate exposition." Whether "in spirit" was added by Matthew's writer or is the product of a pre-Matthean addition to the Q source is an open question. Although, see H. Benedict Green, *Matthew: Poet of the Beatitudes* (JSNT 203; Sheffield: Sheffield Academic, 2001), 27–36, 270–83, who dispenses with Q and argues that Matthew's makarisms are the most original between Matthew and Luke. Matthew's writer constructed his list as a structured poetic composition, and Luke's list is a secondary "radical scaling down" of Matthew's.

[133]   As indicated by Luke's corresponding woe in 6:24, "Woe to you who are rich, for you have received your consolation."

[134]   See Hoyt, "Poor/Rich," 38–41.

[135]   Contrasted with the scribes and Pharisees in Matt 23:12, who exalt themselves.

[136]   This is argued convincingly in Green, *Matthew*, 182–84. Green argues that the history of the Hebrew words used for "poor" is complex and underwent significant development over time. By the Second Temple period the poor became a self-designation for those practicing "corporate submission to the will of God" and denoted ethical and religious concerns. Rather than "subjection," the poor came to refer to "submissiveness." See also Hoyt, "Poor/Rich," 38–39. Keener, *Gospel*, 168–69, argues along these lines, stating that "poor in spirit" refers to those who are economically poor but do not use their poverty as an excuse to pursue wealth and instead express their reliance on God alone.

[137]   For a contrary argument, see Powell, "Matthew's Beatitudes," 464, who argues that "poor in spirit" holds entirely negative connotations. It refers to those with

For many scholars, Matt 5:5 was added, either by Matthew's writer or by pre-Matthean tradition, to provide a parallel to Matt 5:3 and further explicate its meaning.[138] According to this view, Matt 5:3 and 5:5 are essentially synonymous.[139] This could have been done to bring Matthew's makarisms further into line with its sources,[140] to establish a tighter structure for Matthew's list,[141] or simply to pro-

---

no hope and who are on the verge of giving up due to the oppression they face. Luz, *Matthew 1–7*, 190–93, notes that the phrase can reasonably be interpreted either way, either to refer to those who are despairing and despondent or those who are humble. Luz notes the tendency to ethicize Matt 5:3 but states, "We cannot determine unequivocally where the evangelist belongs in this development." On page 194 he appears to side with the latter based in the ethical connotations of the other makarisms, especially 5:5.

[138]   Guelich, "Matthean Beatitudes," 423–26, argues that Matt 5:5 is the product of a pre-Matthean addition to the Q material. The core of Matthew 5:3, 4, 6 par. Luke 6:20b-21 reflects Jesus' teaching, while Matt 5:11-12 was added to bridge the makarisms with the themes of the Sermon. Matt 5:5, 7-9 relied on the Psalms for their language and the rest of the Sermon material for their content, and Matt 5:5 was added to parallel Matt 5:3 to interpret it and protect its religious meaning. See also Davies and Allison, *Matthew 1–7*, 449, who argue that Matt 5:5 was added to the Q tradition by a pre-Matthean editor to "explicate the first beatitude." See McEleney, "Beatitudes," 12, for the view that 5:5 was added by a Matthean redactor as the last stage in the development of Matthew's list, in order to balance the list into two sets.

[139]   So Guelich, "Matthean Beatitudes," 425–26; Davies and Allison, *Matthew 1–7*, 449; Allison, *Sermon*, 48; Hagner, *Matthew 1–13*, 92. See also Green, *Matthew*, 181–82, who argues that Matthew's makarisms feature synonymous parallels through alternating pairs and that Matt 5:3 and 5:5 are paired within this structure. According to Green, although Matt 5:3 and 5:5 are synonymous parallels, and there is a great deal of similarity between "poor in spirit" and "meek," the two verses are not identical twins, as their second clauses provide different emphases.

[140]   Discerning this process is somewhat complicated by the fact that, while most manuscripts have the order "poor in spirit," "mourn," and then "meek," some witnesses flip the second and third makarisms, placing 5:3 and 5:5 together. Guelich, "Matthean Beatitudes," 427, argues that despite the parallelism between 5:3 and 5:5, the common order preserves the order of its source in Isa 61:1-7, which refers to the poor (Isa 61:1) and those who mourn (Isa 61:2) before Isa 61:7, which shared a common bond with which Matt 5:5. Davies and Allison, *Matthew 1–7*, 436, express doubts regarding Guelich's position, as well as the likelihood that 5:5 originally followed 5:3. Allison, *Sermon*, 48, argues that the synonymous nature of 5:3 and 5:5 implies that there is "a good chance that that was the original sequence." Bruce M. Metzger, *A Textual Commentary on the Greek New Testament* (Stuttgart: UBS, 1994), 10, argues the unlikelihood that a scribe would divide the rhetorical antithesis of heaven (5:3) and earth (5:5) and that it is more likely that second century copyists reversed the order of 5:4 and 5:5 to bring together "poor in spirit" and "meek." The question regarding the original order remains open and solving it is not necessary for interpretation.

[141]   For example, see Luz, *Matthew 1–7*, 187, who argues that Matt 5:5 may have been added to establish a π-series (πτωχός, 5:3; πενθέω, 5:4; πραΰς, 5:5; πεινάω, 5:6). He argues that the alliteration may have owed its form to oral tradition and that the oral and written tradition developed side by side, influenced by Isa 61:1-7 and various Psalms.

vide greater clarity,[142] but when comparing Matt 5:3 and 5:5, many scholars argue that "No real difference in meaning between the two is to be discerned."[143] In this view, πραΰς (the meek) is synonymous with, and explicates the meaning of, πτωχός (poor), and "inherit the earth" is synonymous with, and explicates the meaning of, "theirs is the kingdom of heaven."[144]

The relationship between πτωχός (poor, humble) and πραΰς (meek, humble) is incredibly close.[145] It is often compared to the relationship between the Hebrew terms עָנָו and עָנִי, which many scholars argue are virtually synonymous,[146] though the terms have developed over time to carry distinct nuances.[147] The πτωχός of Isa 61:1 (LXX), which lies behind Matt 5:3, and the πραΰς of Ps 36:11 (Ps 37:11 HB), which lies behind Matt 5:5, both have עָנָו behind them in the Hebrew. While in preexilic times the Hebrew cognates עָנָו and עָנִי applied to economic exploitation, the exile widened the range of meaning so that in postexilic literature these terms came to refer to Torah observance and submission to the will of God.[148] As H. Benedict Green argues, with עָנָו as the term behind both Matt 5:3 and 5:5, and considering the development of the term by the time it was used in Isaiah and the Psalter, the root meaning of these terms is "humble."[149] This reading is further confirmed by the Matthean motif of applying each of the makarisms to Jesus at later points in

[142]   So Gundry, *Matthew*, 69, who argues that the two are not synonymous but that 5:5 does explicate the meaning of 5:3. Meekness implies an acceptance of the lowly position indicated by poor in spirit.

[143]   Davies and Allison, *Matthew 1–7*, 449.

[144]   So Allison, *Sermon*, 47. "Poor in spirit" and "meek" are both ways of describing those who avoid hubris and are powerless in the eyes of the world. "The kingdom of heaven" and "inherit the earth" are terms relating to the future state.

[145]   On πτωχός, see *NIDNTTE*, 4:181. On πραΰς, see *NIDNTTE*, 4:123.

[146]   So Gundry, *Matthew*, 69. "Meek" correlates to עָנָו, and "poor" correlates to עָנִי, but the two terms are "virtually synonymous." See also Guelich, "Matthean Beatitudes," 425, the terms in the HB are "essentially synonymous, each sharing a socio-economic as well as religious meaning," but this close relationship broke down in later Judaism, especially in rabbinic literature. He states, "It is all but impossible to pinpoint when such a shift took place."

[147]   See *NIDOTTE*, 3:451 (W. J. Dumbrell).

[148]   See Green, *Matthew*, 182–83, who cites 1 QS V 7–11 and the Psalter as examples.

[149]   Green, *Matthew*, 184. See also *NIDOTTE*, 455, and Witherington, *Matthew*, 121, who recognizes that "poor" and "meek" go back to the same Hebrew root and argues that these terms do not refer to weakness but to "total dependency on God." Lundbom, *Jesus' Sermon*, 109, states that the meek are "not proud and not given to violence." For an opposing view, see Powell, "Matthew's Beatitudes," 463–67, who argues that, rather than humility, these terms in Matthew refer to those who are dispossessed, abandoned, powerless, and without hope, but who trust in God for their rescue. Similar is Davies and Allison, *Matthew 1–7*, 442–49. Powell and Davies and Allison

the Gospel. In light of this motif and the connection of these phrases to the similar phrases at Qumran, the phrases "poor in spirit" and "meek" would correlate with the references to Jesus' humility (πραΰς) in Matt 11:29 and 21:5.[150]

While it is true that the first clauses between Matt 5:3 and 5:5 are closely related, this is not the case with the second clauses. Rather than viewing "inherit the earth" as nearly synonymous with "theirs is the kingdom of heaven," it is better to view the inheritance of the earth as *an aspect of* the reception of the kingdom.[151] The inclusio of references to the kingdom in Matt 5:3 and 5:10 encapsulate each of the second clauses of the other makarisms as aspects of the kingdom belonging to those described by the first clauses.[152] The second clauses of each makarism are not to be understood as realities that are separate and unrelated to one another but rather as various aspects of the one reality that is the kingdom of heaven. In other words, the inheritance of the earth is closely related to the kingdom, but only in the same way as being comforted, filled, receiving mercy, etc., and not in synonymous fashion. The second clauses feature various benefits of the kingdom, so that those who receive the kingdom will inherit the earth, but the earth and the kingdom are not identical. The kingdom is the greater reality of which the inheritance of the earth is a part.[153]

---

do not take into account the shift in meaning of these terms across various stages of Israelite/Jewish literature.

[150] See Strecker, *Sermon*, 35–36. See also Davies and Allison, *Matthew 1–7*, 443–44, who argue that the religious meaning does not require an exclusion of the economic, but rather the two often go together. With many in Jesus' audience, the religious state of poverty was likely matched by an outward condition. "They knew the meaning of need because they were poor in spirit and poor in fact." Conversely, Hoyt, "Poor/Rich," 39, argues that Matthew's writer may have added "in spirit" in order not to alienate the wealthy members of his community. He argues that, in comparison to Luke, Matthew shows no real signs of critique against the wealthy. Matthew's motif of positively attributing many of the dispositions of the makarisms to Jesus is not accounted for by Powell, "Matthew's Beatitudes," 467, when he argues that "meek" is a negative circumstance.

[151] *Contra* Allison, *Matthew*, 47, who argues that both refer synonymously to the "ideal future state."

[152] So Goppelt, *Theology*, 68. See also Davies and Allison, *Matthew 1–7*, 446, who connect Matt 5:3-12 to 4:23 as an encapsulation of Jesus' proclamation of the kingdom.

[153] Green, *Matthew*, 182, argues for the synonymous nature of the first clauses of Matt 5:3 and 5:5 but recognizes that this does not extend to the second clauses. See also Alan Hugh McNeile, *The Gospel According to St. Matthew* (Grand Rapids: Baker Book House, 1980), 51, inheritance supplies "another aspect of the possession of the kingdom."

This is supported by Pennington's research regarding Matthew's use of the heaven-and-earth word pair. As is well known, in many places where Mark and Luke feature the phrase "kingdom of God," Matthew features the phrase "kingdom of heaven." Such is the case when comparing Matt 5:3 with the parallel makarism in Luke 6:20. Matthew uses the phrase "kingdom of heaven" thirty-two times, and the phrase is found nowhere else in all of Jewish and Christian literature.[154] A comparison between Matthew's "kingdom of heaven" and Mark's and Luke's "kingdom of God" reveals the phrases to be essentially synonymous.[155] The majority of scholars, noting that Matthew is often considered to be the most "Jewish" of the Gospels, explain away Matthew's unique phrase by regarding it as an honorary circumlocution on the part of the evangelist to avoid making use of the name of God.[156] The evangelist's linguistic choices are often considered to be motivated by the plural use of "heaven" in both Hebrew and Aramaic as a Semitic idiom. Pairing the term "heaven" with the kingdom was likely inspired by the evolution of similar phrases found in Second Temple compositions, such as "king of heaven" in 3 Macc 2:2, "sovereign of heaven" in 2 Macc 15:3-4, "God of heaven" in Jdt 6:19, and the many associations between heaven and God as king and lord throughout Daniel 2–7.[157]

There are scholars who are dissatisfied with the common explanation that Matthew's use of "kingdom of heaven" is an honorary circumlocution. Such a view is difficult to defend when one considers that Matthew does in fact use the term θεός on a number of occasions, including the full phrase "kingdom of God" at least four times.[158] Pen-

---

[154]   Jonathan T. Pennington, *Heaven and Earth in the Gospel of Matthew* (Grand Rapids: Baker Academic, 2009), 3.

[155]   See Hagner, *Matthew 1–13*, 48; France, *Matthew*, 101; Luz, *Matthew 1–7*, 135. Luz argues that, because no discernable theological difference appears present between the two forms of the phrase, Matthew's version may be guided by the usage of the Matthean community. Theological justification for Matthew's usage is provided below.

[156]   So Lundbom, *Jesus' Sermon*, 99; Hagner, *Matthew 1–13*, 47–48.

[157]   Including 2:28; 4:34-37; 5:23. See the discussion by Pennington, *Heaven*, 285–93, who regards Daniel 2–7 as the primary background for Matthew's use of "kingdom of heaven." See also Craig A. Evans, "Daniel in the New Testament: Visions of God's Kingdom," in *The Book of Daniel: Composition and Reception*, vol. 2 (ed. John J. Collins and Peter W. Flint; Leiden: Brill, 2002), 490–527.

[158]   So France, *Matthew*, 101, who states, "Since Matthew seems to have no inhibitions about speaking of God by name elsewhere, this is hardly an adequate explanation." He argues instead that Matthew's "kingdom of heaven" may be nothing more than a stylistic preference that requires no explanation. See also Gundry, *Matthew*, 43, who disregards the circumlocution argument, instead arguing that Matthew's writer was influenced by Dan 3:31–4:34 in order to highlight "God's universal dominion."

nington has made a compelling case that although "kingdom of God" and "kingdom of heaven" refer to the same kingdom, Matthew's unique version of the phrase is not an honorary circumlocution but rather Matthew's way of highlighting theological aspects of the kingdom that are important to themes and ideas throughout the First Gospel. "Kingdom of heaven" is used by Matthew when it functions as a comparison or contrast with "the earth," and throughout Matthew heaven and earth function as a word pair to draw attention to these comparisons and contrasts. Matthew's use of heaven in the singular refers to the visible realm, but heaven in the plural, rather than reflective of a Semitic idiom, refers to the divine and invisible realm and its bearing upon the visible earth. It is worth quoting Pennington at length regarding Matthew's use of the heaven-and-earth word pair:

> They emphasize a very important theological point: the tension that currently exists between heaven and earth, between God's realm and the ways of humanity's, especially as it relates to God's kingdom (the kingdom of heaven) versus humanity's kingdoms. This tension will be resolved at the eschaton—in the new Genesis (19:28)—that has been inaugurated through the life, death, and resurrection of Jesus Christ. In fact, only by recognizing the intensity of the tension that currently exists between heaven and earth can we fully appreciate the significance of the eschaton in which the kingdom of heaven will come to earth (6:9-10).[159]

This heaven-and-earth word pair as a Matthean feature relates directly to Matt 5:3 and 5:5. In Matt 5:5, a makarism not shared with Luke, Jesus quotes Ps 37:11 (36:11, LXX), promising that the meek will "inherit the earth." Matthew 5:3 is in the present tense, the poor in spirit presently participate in the kingdom of heaven. However, God's heavenly kingdom is very different from the earthly kingdoms. The promise to inherit the earth is future tense and eschatological; as the kingdom of heaven comes to bear upon the earth, those presently participating in the heavenly kingdom will inherit the earth as a result. The values presented in the entirety of Matthew's makarisms demonstrate that the values and social order of the heavenly kingdom and the present earthly order are incompatible. The ways of the earth are typified by the Jewish leaders throughout Matthew's Gospel, and the broader Greco-Roman society may also be in view.[160] Those flourishing in the heavenly kingdom are the poor in spirit who are elevated to a heavenly status and the meek who will inherit the earth in the future age. The inheritance of the earth is yet

[159]   Pennington, *Heaven*, 7.
[160]   Pennington, *Heaven*, 343, "The heaven and earth theme *emphasizes the universality of God's domain*" (emphasis his).

future because the values of the kingdom must come to bear upon the earth before it can be fully handed over to Jesus' disciples (Matt 6:10), and the heaven-and-earth theme "provides solace and hope for the disciples" while they await the time when the realities of heaven will come to bear upon the earth.[161] While they wait, Jesus' followers are called to live within God's ethical standards, which are both counterintuitive and countercultural when compared with the standards of the earth.[162] Rather than viewing the kingdom of heaven and the inheritance of the earth as virtual synonyms, Matt 5:5 is better viewed as a functioning addition to the heaven-and-earth word pair where the inheritance of the earth is an eschatological, spatial, and this-worldly reward for present kingdom participation. With Matthew's heaven-and-earth word pair in view, it is best to recognize both that Matt 5:3 and 5:5 carry similar connotations while also recognizing that Matt 5:5 carries its own theological weight.

5.1.2.2. Recognized Traditions Antecedent to Matt 5:5

A number of antecedent texts and traditions have been proposed as an influence both on the makarisms as a whole and on each individual makarism. Here I will trace the most frequent proposals regarding Matt 5:5, and in the following section I will propose traditions that might lie in the background of this makarism that are not often considered.[163]

1. Isaiah 61:1-7

One of the most frequently discussed texts as an influence on Matthew's makarisms is Isa 61:1-7. The parallels between these two passages are extensive,[164] and the majority of scholars agree that, at some point in the development of Matthew's list, Isa 61:1-7 influenced its linguistic features and word order.[165] This is especially important considering

---

[161]   Pennington, *Heaven*, 344.

[162]   As described by the rest of the Sermon and in contrast to the ways of the scribes and Pharisees. Pennington, *Heaven*, 346–47.

[163]   It is widely recognized that Matthew's makarisms, as a whole, are replete with examples of influences and parallels with the LXX. Green, *Matthew*, 264–67, argues that nearly every clause has a counterpart in the LXX text, and he provides a detailed chart to suggest such possible counterparts. Detailing many of these connections is beyond the purview of this study. This section largely remains focused on Matt 5:5 and in particular those passages that are relevant to inheritance.

[164]   See Davies and Allison, *Matthew 1–7*, 436–37, for a detailed list of parallels.

[165]   Guelich, "Matthean Beatitudes," 427, 431–33, argues that Matthew's writer likely added features to bring his list into line with the Isaianic passage. Conversely, Davies and Allison, *Matthew 1–7*, 437–38, argue that the influence of Isaiah is seen only in the earliest stratum of Matthew's list, those makarisms that belong to Q. Therefore, it was in Jesus' teachings where Isa 61:1-7 can most clearly be detected, and Matthew's

that many scholars find the influence of this passage to be absent, or faint, in Luke's version.[166] There is disagreement on the extent of Isaiah's influence on Matthew's makarisms and the point at which the parallels with Isaiah entered the tradition, and there is disagreement regarding whether or not the linguistic parallels require a parallel in meaning and intent, although scholars are nearly unanimous in arguing for a linguistic correlation between the two passages. The clearest parallels concern Matthew's first two makarisms regarding the poor and those who mourn, which were likely influenced to some degree by the same terms and word order in Isa 61:1-2. Of particular interest to Matt 5:5 is Isa 61:7, where those who are called priests of God are offered a double portion of the land inheritance, by which they shall have everlasting joy. Both verses feature the phrase κληρονομήσουσιν τὴν γῆν (LXX, they will inherit the earth) in the future tense, a phrase that is extremely rare in extant Greek Jewish and Christian compositions, but which is also found in Isa 60:21.[167]

---

writer did nothing to accentuate the connections between his makarisms and Isa 61:1-7. Precisely when Isa 61 entered the tradition regarding Matthew's list remains an open question, but its influence is widely accepted.

[166]   So Guelich, "Matthean Beatitudes," 431. However, see Davies and Allison, *Matthew 1–7*, 438, who argue that aside from Matt 5:3-12, Matthew shows no real interest in Isa 61, but Isa 61 can be detected in Luke 7:22, illustrating Luke's interest in that text. They argue that Isa 61 stands at the front of the makarism tradition, rather than with Matthew's writer, and that Jesus likely associated the makarism form with good news for the poor. If this is the case, then Isa 61 would also stand behind Luke's list.

[167]   In compositions that were written in Greek, or in those translated into Greek and in which the Hebrew vorlage is now unknown, the phrase appears with the article only three times in 1 En. 5:6-8 (κληρονομήσουσιν τὴν γῆν) and once in Matt 5:5 (κληρονομήσουσιν τὴν γῆν). It appears without the article in Tob 4:12 (κληρονομήσει γῆν). See also a similar use of the phrase in Jub. 17:3; 22:14; 32:19. κληρονομέω appears in close connection with γῆν a number of times in the LXX (37x, according to Luz, *Matthew 1–7*, 186), when translating both נחל and ירש in conjunction with ארץ, but these instances are rarely in construct form in Hebrew. The vast majority of instances are found in the Hexateuch, in the aorist tense, when referring directly to the inheritance of the land as a promise or result of the conquest (cf. LXX, Gen 15:7; 28:4; 47:27; Exod 23:30; Lev 20:24; Num 21:35; 26:53; Deut 1:8; 2:31; 3:12; 4:1). Some instances appear in the future, still clearly in relationship to the conquest (cf. LXX, Num 14:24, 31; 18:20; 26:55; 34:17; Deut 4:22; 5:33). The precise phrase κληρονομήσουσιν τὴν γῆν, in the fut, act, ind, 3, plu, construction, when a prophetic-eschatological intention is present in the context, is found only in 1 En. 5:6-8, Matt 5:5, and Isa 60:21; 61:7. Psalm 36:11 (LXX) from which Matt 5:5 draws most directly, features κληρονομήσουσιν γῆν without the article. The phrase "inherit the earth" appears just once in the HB in construct form with נחל, in Isa 57:13 in reference to the land of Israel. "Inherit the earth" appears more often as a construct with ארץ and the root verb ירש, though it is still rare. It appears in Lev 20:24, where "land" is preceded by the direct object את in reference to the land belonging to the Canaanites, who the Israelites are to dispossess from the land. The construct with ירש is found four times in Ps 37 (vv. 9, 11, 22, 29), while the root נחל is found in v. 18 of that chapter but not in construct with ארץ.

In both Isaiah passages, κληρονομέω translates ירשׁ rather than the more common נחל. In this instance the meanings are synonymous and may be nothing more than stylistic, as ירשׁ also stands behind κληρονομήσουσιν γῆν throughout Ps 36 (9, 11, 22, 29), as well as κληρονομήσει γῆν in Ps 24:13, while the noun κληρονομία translates נחלה in Ps 36:18 to the same basic effect.[168] In Isa 60:21, the righteous will "inherit the land forever." Blenkinsopp argues that this verse may draw directly on Ps 37 (Ps 36, LXX), where those who will inherit the land are those who trust in God and wait for him. In Isa 60:21 this is acknowledged as righteousness.[169] In Isa 61:1-7 these righteous ones have the good news proclaimed to them. They are the ענוים, those who are poor and those who mourn, who will inherit a double portion of the land. Blenkinsopp notes that, by the time Third Isaiah was composed, ענוים had maintained much of its economic connotation while shifting to a more religious meaning. The poor are, above all, those who seek God, and their opponents are the proud and godless. Based on the context of all of Third Isaiah, Isa 61 is situated within its portrayal of the Jewish community as those who find themselves in unsatisfactory circumstances. The hope of Isa 56–66 is that God will reverse those circumstances and bring history as they know it to an end.[170] Watts makes an important point regarding the term משׁנה (double portion). In the HB, this term can denote a recognition of status (e.g., Deut 21:7), or compensation for damages (e.g., Exod 22:4, 7, 9). It is possible that, in Isa 61:7, it refers to both: the status of the ענוים as righteous and future compensation for their present lowly position.[171]

Less frequently discussed is the possible relevance of the fuller inheritance context of Isaiah, and in particular Third Isaiah, to Matthew's use of inheritance terms. It is widely recognized that Isaiah stands in the background of Matthew's entire narrative.[172] As I argue in chapter 2, Isaiah's universalist eschatological vision is tied tightly to its presentation of inheritance concepts (cf. Isa 2:2-4; 14:1-2; 19:16-25; 49:1-8; 56-57), and as Richard B. Hays observes, Isaiah's universalist vision lies in the

---

[168]   Though note Davies and Allison, *Matthew 1–7*, 450, who argues that with ירשׁ as the background inheritance is possibly best rendered as "possess" or "acquire."

[169]   Joseph Blenkinsopp, *Isaiah 56–66* (AB 19B; New York: Doubleday, 2003), 218.

[170]   Blenkinsopp, *Isaiah 56–66*, 224–25.

[171]   John D. W. Watts, *Isaiah 34–66* (WBC; Columbia: Nelson Reference, 2005), 874.

[172]   See, for example, Richard B. Hays, *Echoes of Scripture in the Gospels* (Waco, Tex.: Baylor University Press, 2016), 175–85, who notes Isaiah's influence on Matthew's universal themes, and Pennington, *Sermon*, 145–46, who briefly summarizes the connections between Isaiah and a number of Matthean passages.

background of multiple Matthean passages (cf. Isa 60:1-6 w/ Matt 2:1-12; Isa 8:23–9:1; 42:1-7 w/ Matt 4:12-17; 12:15-21).[173] While it is likely that Isa 61:7 influenced Matt 5:5, and it is possible that Isa 60:21 did as well, it is important to see how these passages fit into the overall narrative regarding inheritance throughout Isaiah and especially Third Isaiah.

In chapter 3, Isa 64–66 was discussed in detail, and its relevance is important here. While the Deuteronomistic view of salvation included the participation of all Israel, Isa 64–66 features a new vision of God's relationship specifically with those who seek him. Israel is divided between the rebels and the servants, with curses for the former and blessings for the latter. God's "people" are no longer delineated by birthright; they are those who seek God from within Israel but also those who seek him from among the nations. God declares his intention to create a new heaven and a new earth. Isaiah 65 features the term ארץ (land/earth), but its pairing with שמים (heavens) encompasses the universe and the divine realm—so the entire earth rather than Israel alone is in view. This is the climax Third Isaiah builds toward. Craig Evans comes close to recognizing this when he cites the relationship between Matt 5:5 and Isa 60:21 and 61:7. Based on this relationship, Evans argues that Matthew's third makarism speaks to Israel's hope for national renewal, which includes, in some instances, "regaining the land itself." He recognizes that, in Jesus' day, many Jews were poor and disinherited and that Matt 5:5 is an allusion to re-inheriting the land.[174] While I agree that Matt 5:5 draws on these themes, the heaven-and-earth word pairing between Matt 5:3 and 5:5 suggests that τὴν γῆν in Matt 5:5 refers not to the land of Israel alone but to the earth and the eschatological renewal of all things. This is supported within Matthew by the anticipation of cosmic renewal (Matt 19:28)[175] and the fact that, in the majority of instances in Matthew, γῆν appears to refer to the earth rather than the land of Israel (c.f. Matt 5:18, 35; 6:10, 19; 9:6; 11:25; 12:42; 16:19; 18:18-19; 23:9; 24:30; 28:18).[176] This reading is also supported by Third Isaiah; although Isa 60:21 and 61:7 refer to the eschatological renewal of the land, the climax of the composition promises an entirely new creation, illustrated by the heaven-and-earth word pair (Isa 65:17).[177] The use of the heaven-and-earth word pair, as well as Matthew's consistent

---

[173]   Hays, *Gospels*, 175–85.

[174]   Evans, *Matthew*, 106. See also Davies and Allison, *Matthew 1–7*, who argue that, when using Isa 61, Jesus was "using the text as others before him."

[175]   Matthew 19:28 is discussed in 5.2.

[176]   With Matt 27:45 as an exception. See Davies and Allison, *Matthew 1–7*, 450.

[177]   See Luz, *Matthew 1–7*, 195, n. 94, who argues that the wording of Isa 60:21 and 61:7 is that of the "cosmic expansion of the promise of the land."

use of γῆν to refer to the earth, suggests that Matt 5:5 makes use of Isa 60:21 and 61:7 by drawing upon their themes but doing so within the wider presentation of eschatological renewal within Third Isaiah. In other words, the themes of Isa 60:21 and 61:7 are present but have been appropriated for a more universalistic purpose, which is in keeping with the trajectory to which Third Isaiah itself contributed.[178]

2. Psalm 36 and Psalm 32:12 (LXX)

Scholars widely regard Matt 5:5 as a quote of Ps 36:11 (Ps 37:11, MT).[179] The affinities are obvious:

Ps 36:11a: οἱ δὲ πραεῖς κληρονομήσουσιν γῆν.

Matt 5:5: μακάριοι οἱ πραεῖς, ὅτι αὐτοὶ κληρονομήσουσιν τὴν γῆν.

The Psalm uses the phrase "inherit the earth/land" five times (36:9, 11, 22, 29, 34), and the noun "inheritance" one time (36:18). Although dating the Psalm would be difficult, it probably predates (and possibly influenced) Isa 61, but the postexilic contexts of both passages are similar. The Psalm is committed to the contrast between the righteous and the wicked, and it is concerned with the perception that the wicked prosper while those who follow God are left to suffer. The Psalmist states that the righteous Israelites need not worry about the wicked, as they will soon fade like the grass (36:1). They will be cut off (36:9-10), and the righteous will be saved. The text fits the postexilic circumstance that found the Israelites alienated from the land and no longer in control of it. The inheritance is a future promise, indicated by the use of the future tense verb, "will inherit." As I argue in chapter 3, the Psalm is an anthology of wisdom sayings concerning a moral and God-fearing life. The inheritance referred to is the land of Israel, as opposed to "the earth," but rather than Israel as a whole, the inheritance is promised to those within Israel seeking to honor God. Relatively ignored in scholarship regarding Matthew's possible use of this Psalm is the shift in meaning that this Psalm took on late in the Second Temple period. Psalm 37 in the Psalms Pesher downplays the Psalm's sapiential aspects and interprets

---

[178]   See James M. Scott, *Paul and the Nations* (Tübingen: Mohr Siebeck, 1995), 13–14, 73, who argues that Isaiah, in many passages, stands among a tradition of HB texts that present a positive eschatological expectation for all nations.

[179]   Though see Davies and Allison, *Matthew 1–7*, 451, who argue that, although Matt 5:5 quotes Ps 37:11 more directly, it appears to recall Isa 61:7 to a great degree. This is due to the other connections between Isa 61 and Matthew's list and to the fact that Matthew and Isaiah agree, against the Psalm, with the use of the definite article before γῆν.

it eschatologically.[180] Rather than Israel alone, the Pesher concludes that the righteous will inherit "the whole earth," introducing an important point of connection with Matt 5:5.[181]

Psalm 32:12 (LXX) is also noteworthy, because it features both μακάριον and κληρονομίαν. Those who flourish are those who belong to God as his own inheritance.[182] It is possible that this verse influenced Matt 5:5 in placing inheritance in a makaristic formula, and the people belonging to God as his inheritance offers an important point of connection between this same theme in inheritance contexts throughout the HB (cf. chapter 2) and Matt 5:9's statement that the peacemakers will be called "children of God."[183]

3. Isaiah 61:1, Psalm 36:11 (LXX), and the עניים

The dual impact of Isa 61:1-7 and Ps 36 on Matthew is pronounced. The sapiential aspects of Ps 36 are reinterpreted in the Psalms Pesher with an eschatological flavor, and Third Isaiah describes the righteous as those who stand to receive an eschatological reward. The combination of these passages, with both sapiential and prophetic elements, are brought together in Matthew's list. As discussed in this chapter, both πτωχός in Isa 61:1 and πραΰς in Ps 36:11 have the עניים as their background.[184] In each of these passages, there is an element of reprieve for the destitute, and some scholars have insisted that such reprieve is in view in Matthew's makarisms.[185] As I argue above, there is a sense in which this is true. Those who are humble certainly hope to be exalted, and those who mourn long for a day when such mourning will no longer be necessary. In this, the original contexts of Isa 61 and Ps 36 have not lost their meaning. However, there are reasons to view the use of these terms in Matthew's makarisms through a more virtue-ethical lens, four of which I will mention here.

First, although the background of the עניים as destitute and economically disadvantaged cannot be ignored, Matthew's Jesus uses πτωχός and πραΰς both in a makaristic formula as well as the broader context of

---

[180]   See George W. E. Nickelsburg, *1 Enoch 1*, Hermeneia (Minneapolis: Fortress, 2001), 162, and Evans, *Matthew*, 105.

[181]   See Evans, *Matthew*, 106.

[182]   This potential point of connection is noted by Green, *Matthew*, 266.

[183]   See Ps 32:12 (LXX), λαός, ὃν ἐξελέξατο εἰς κληρονομίαν ἑαυτῷ (the people whom he has chosen as his own inheritance).

[184]   See 5.1.2.1.

[185]   So Davies and Allison, *Matthew 1–7*, 438–39, who argue that Jesus made use of Isa 61 in order to associate himself with that text as an "eschatological herald." They argue that Jesus made use of the text in its Isaianic context.

the Sermon on the Mount, which highlights the virtue-ethical connotations. Second, Third Isaiah and Ps 36 both feature a postexilic context, where those who are righteous and faithful to God are those who inherit the earth/world, and the עניים are to be understood in this context. As discussed above, in the postexilic era the עניים came to refer to the faithful and not only those in a difficult situation. Third, when πραΰς is used to translate ענו, it is usually understood in the sense of an ethical attitude.[186] Fourth, Matthew's makarisms, in line with wisdom contexts, are constructed in the third person, presenting a life of flourishing that is universally open to all who seek righteousness and exhibit these kingdom dispositions. Although there is an element of universality to Isa 61, Matthew's Gospel stands at a further point in the trajectory of this focus, which allows πτωχός and πραΰς to take on even further virtue-ethical connotations. Matthew's Gospel shows little interest in the land of Israel itself, so rather than maintaining the HB's focus on the עניים and their longing to be reconciled to the land, Matt 5:5 universalizes its context in both respects: all are invited to a life of humility and dependence on God, and the humble will inherit the earth.[187] In this way, the language of Isa 61 and Ps 36 is appropriated ethically for greater universalistic purpose.[188]

5.1.2.3. Previously Unexplored Traditions Antecedent to Matthew 5:5

Although a number of important antecedent traditions that were potentially influential on the theology and linguistic choices of Matthew's author(s) have been proposed, there are textual traditions that have received little to no attention. This could be simply an oversight, but some traditions have been ignored largely due to methodological

[186]   So Luz, *Matthew 1–7*, 194, who states, "Hence we may not simply read πραΰς with ענו and then equate it with 'powerless.'"

[187]   See Luz, *Matthew 1–7*, 195, it is the earth, not the land of Israel only, which belongs to the humble. "The traditional promise of land had long since been transposed into the cosmic realm."

[188]   Also worth mentioning is the view of N. T. Wright, *The New Testament and the People of God* (Minneapolis: Fortress, 1992), 384–90, who argues that Deut 27–34 is a theological and thematic influence over Matthew's Gospel, including the makarisms. Wright's argument contains many compelling features regarding the whole of the First Gospel, but its relationship to the makarisms is questionable due to his reliance on the association between "blessings" and "curses." See Charles Quarles, "The Blessings of the New Moses: An Examination of the Theological Purpose of the Matthean Beatitudes," *JSHJ* 13 (2015): 307–27, who largely affirms Wright's view but argues that it is plagued with "lexical problems," primarily Wright's connection between blessings and makarisms. Quarles notes that the only actual makarism in Deut 27–34 is in Deut 33:29, which is not featured in Wright's argument.

concerns. There is often hesitancy to make theological or "thought-world" connections if there are not a number of clear direct linguistic indicators. It is important to recognize that, without citations, allusions, or other clear linguistic indicators, it is extremely difficult to be *certain* of influence; nonetheless, making connections based on compelling thematic and theological affinities still offers the potential for exploring influences that may be relevant, and such affinities may offer valuable insights into the theological and linguistic matrices from which certain texts are derived. The linguistic indicators discussed in this section are not as clear as those reviewed in the previous one, but I argue that the thematic and theological parallels of the antecedent traditions focused upon in this study are compelling enough to explore their possible relevance for a better understanding of Matthew's Gospel.

1. The Abrahamic Promise

Matthew's Gospel begins its account of the story of Jesus with a theologically structured genealogy. It recalls, in familial terms, the history of God's people.[189] Much has been made regarding the aspects of the genealogy that foreshadow gentile involvement or inclusion in the First Gospel,[190] but of principal concern here is the reference in the first verse to Jesus as "the son of Abraham" (υἱοῦ Ἀβραάμ) and Abraham as the starting point to Jesus' genealogy (Matt 1:2, 17).[191] The writer's goal

---

[189]   So Luz, *Matthew 1–7*, 82, who states of Jesus, "He is Abraham's son and royal Messiah and thus the bearer of all Israel's messianic hopes in accordance with God's plan."

[190]   For example, the mention of four gentile women, often considered an entry point into Matthew's pro-gentile narrative, so Luz, *Matthew 1–7*, 85. This detail has been the subject of considerable debate. Space precludes a detailed account, though see David C. Sim, *The Gospel of Matthew and Christian Judaism: The History and Social Setting of the Matthean Community* (Edinburgh: T&T Clark, 1998), 218–20, who argues that it is uncertain that all four women were gentiles, and if they were, it is possible that a reason other than their gentile origins best explains their inclusion in the genealogy. Some scholars, such as McNeile, *Gospel*, 5, and Raymond E. Brown, *The Birth of the Messiah: A Commentary on the Infancy Narratives in the Gospels of Matthew and Luke* (New Haven: Yale University Press, 1999), 74, argue that their inclusion is better explained by the scandalous nature of their unions with their partners (which represents Mary's story more than that of the gentiles). Konradt, *Israel*, 271–81, recognizes that it is possible to see the gentile origins of the four women as less important if they are viewed only as proselytes, as Jews have always been open to non-Jews in this way. However, Konradt argues that universal salvation is grounded in Jesus as Abraham's son and that the universal aspects of Matthew's Gospel throughout the narrative are strong enough that the gentile origin of the four women is likely an important factor in the mention of their names as a foreshadowing of a gentile mission.

[191]   As opposed to Luke's list (3:23-28), which reaches back to Adam.

is to situate Jesus as the culmination of a particular trajectory. Konradt summarizes this idea when he states, "The history of salvation, which began with the calling of Abraham, leads up to its culmination in Jesus."[192] By invoking Abraham, Matthew's writer draws attention to the Abrahamic promises: Jesus is included among Abraham's descendants, is therefore an heir to the inheritance, and consequently plays a role in being a light to the nations.[193] That all three aspects of the Abrahamic promise had long been tied both to gentile and "whole-earth" inheritance is demonstrated by Sir 44:21, where the inheritance is not the land of Israel alone, but the whole earth, just as in Matt 5:5. Abraham is situated near the beginning of Sirach's account of Israel's heroic ancestry (44–50), where it states that Abraham's descendants would be as numerous as the dust and that the nations "would be blessed by his offspring." This blessing comes about for the "nations" (ἔθνη) as "an inheritance" (κατακληρονομῆσαι) from sea to sea and from the Euphrates "to the ends of the earth" (ἄκρου τῆς γῆς). As an heir to Abraham, the promises are now mediated through Jesus, which includes the inheritance itself with a view toward universalism.[194]

2. Jesus as the Heir of David

Not only does Matthew's genealogy refer to Jesus as the υἱοῦ Ἀβραάμ but also the υἱοῦ Δαυὶδ (son of David, Matt 1:1), so that Jesus is not only the heir to the Abrahamic promise, but he is heir to the throne of David

---

[192]   Konradt, *Israel*, 25.

[193]   Cf. Gen 17:4-6; Exod 32:13; Isa 49:1-8; and the discussions in 2.2.3, 2.2.4, and 2.4.4. Konradt, *Israel*, 26, 265–67, recognizes that some scholars have argued that the references to Abraham in Matt 1:1, 2, and 17 may refer only to Jesus' role in the salvation story of Israel or to Jesus as the "ideal Israelite." However, Konradt argues, based on references to Abraham in Matt 3:9 and 8:11, that gentile inclusion is in view regarding references to Abraham in Matthew's Gospel. He states, "Matthew sought to indicate the universality of salvation in Jesus in 1:1 as well as with the reference to his Abrahamic ancestry" (267). In this regard, Matthew's use of the Abrahamic tradition is in line with representations in other early Christian texts (Acts 3:25; Rom 4; Gal 3). See also Davies and Allison, *Matthew 1–7*, 158, that "son of Abraham" "probably also serves to announce the evangelist's interest in the salvation of the Gentiles"; and Luz, *Matthew 1–7*, 85, who connects the four gentile women to Abraham in the genealogy as clues to a universalistic undertone. Speaking of the connection between Abraham and Jesus in the genealogy, Luz states, "The movement of Israel's salvation to the Gentiles, a dominant theme of the Gospel of Matthew, is already declared in its opening text."

[194]   Evans, *Matthew*, 106, recognizes this in part when he relates the inheritance of Matt 5:5 to the inheritance aspect of the Abrahamic promise in Gen 15:7; 28:4. He states that Matt 5:5 "recalls God's promise to Abraham," as well as the inheritance of the land in Exod 23:30 and Deut 4:1. However, Evans does not recognize Jesus' relationship to Abraham and therefore Jesus' role as the heir and mediator of the inheritance.

as well.[195] Although there are no direct linguistic links between the kingly traditions regarding "Yahweh's inheritance" in 1–2 Samuel and inheritance contexts in Matthew's Gospel, thematic connections abound and the nature of ownership and possession of the inheritance is largely the same. In the Hexateuch, God maintains perpetual ownership of the inheritance, which he gives to his people as a gift. In 1–2 Samuel, God mediates the inheritance through Saul (1 Sam 10:1) and then all kings that come after Saul.[196] God entrusts his own inheritance (his people and his land) to a king for oversight, and to be cut off from God's inheritance is to be cut off from relationship with God, as well as God's people. These themes are relevant to inheritance contexts throughout Matthew, as Jesus the messianic king and heir to the Davidic dynasty is now the one through whom the inheritance is gifted and obtained.[197] In Matt 5:5, it is Jesus who has the authority to declare that the meek will inherit the earth, and that by doing so, they shall also have a share in the kingdom of heaven (Matt 5:3, 10).[198] Those who exhibit the dispositions of the makarisms will be persecuted on Jesus' account (Matt 5:11), meaning that the exhibitors of the makarisms are united to Jesus as the king and guarantor of the inheritance, as well as united to one another as members of Jesus' disciple community. Those of the community are therefore united to heaven through rewards (Matt 5:12) and to God himself as his children (Matt 5:9).

3. God as Father

The fatherhood of God is rooted in inheritance contexts from the Hexateuch through the whole of the HB and into the Second Temple period, and it features in the makarisms as well. Matthew 5:9 declares

[195]   See Dale C. Allison Jr., "The Embodiment of God's Will: Jesus in Matthew," in *Seeking the Identity of Jesus: A Pilgrimage* (Grand Rapids: Eerdmans, 2008), 122, "David" is the key term in the genealogy. It brings royal connotations to the fore, occurring at 1:1, 6, and 17. It lets the reader know that the kingdom belongs to Jesus, that he sits on the throne, and that he will judge and rule (19:28; 25:31-40). So also Konradt, *Israel*, 23–49; Luz, *Matthew 1–7*, 70; Hagner, *Matthew 1–13*, 9; France, *Matthew*, 32; and Davies and Allison, *Matthew 1–7*, 156–57.

[196]   See 2.3.2.

[197]   See Joel Willitts, "The Twelve Disciples in Matthew," in *Jesus, Matthew's Gospel and Early Christianity: Studies in Memory of Graham N. Stanton* (ed. Daniel M. Gurtner, Joel Willitts, and Richard A. Burridge; LNTS 435; London: Bloomsbury, 2011), 167, as the son of David, "Matthew's Jesus is the king over an eschatologically restored kingdom of Israel who will rule both Israel and the nations."

[198]   Similar themes are found in other NT writings. For example, Haley Goranson Jacob, *Conformed to the Image of His Son: Reconsidering Paul's Theology of Glory in Romans* (Downers Grove, Ill.: IVP Academic, 2018), 82, 138–39, argues that, in Romans, the inheritance belongs to Jesus, and to receive a part in the inheritance is to participate with Jesus in his reign as a coheir.

that those who exhibit the makarisms will be called "children of God" (υἱοὶ θεοῦ). The concept of God's people as his children, and the inheritance, are tied together more intrinsically in the Hexateuch than they are here in Matt 5:3-12,[199] but Matthew's list brings them together in a relationship close enough to suggest that a similar concept is in view: God is a father to his people,[200] which in Matthew's text refers to Jesus' disciples, and it is they who stand to receive his inheritance, in this case the whole earth.[201] In both contexts, that is, the Hexateuch and Matthew's makarisms, the inheritance is guaranteed by God himself as a gift. In the Hexateuch this is illustrated by the consistent use of the verb נתן (to give) in conjunction with inheritance contexts;[202] in the makarisms, this is illustrated by the use of the divine passive. Regardless of the involvement of God's people in participating in the acquisition of their inheritance, such inheritances would be unattainable without God's favor and role as the giver. The permanence of the inherited and renewed earth ensures the permanence of their relationship to God. The use of relational genitives is important: Jesus is υἱοῦ Δαυὶδ υἱοῦ Ἀβραάμ (Matt 1:1), which gives him authority over the inheritance and the responsibility to offer it universally, and those who become υἱοὶ θεοῦ (Matt 5:9) are those who receive the inheritance (Matt 5:5).

Although the language of inheritance and the fatherhood of God find their roots in the Hexateuch, there is one striking difference between the Hexateuchal contexts and that of Matt 5:3-12. In the Hexateuch, the Israelites were tasked with participating in the acquisition of their inheritance (the land) through force, by engaging the inhabitants of the land in a forcible and violent conflict. It is said that the inhabitants of the land deserved to be driven out due to their own wickedness (Deut 9:4); however, regardless of the

[199]   On the relationship between God as Father and the theme of inheritance in the Hexateuch, see 2.1.

[200]   So Davies and Allison, *Matthew 1–7*, 458–59, who state, "Believers in Jesus are, in Matthew, already sons of God (5:45), whom they call Father (6:9)." This guarantees both 1) a degree of intimacy with God and 2) a likeness to him.

[201]   On the Hexateuchal context as a background for Matt 5:9, see Evans, *Matthew*, 108; Talbert, *Reading*, 53. The connection of these themes is found elsewhere in NT literature, perhaps most prominently in Rom 8, where those who are adopted into the family of God become υἱοὶ θεοῦ, and by virtue of being children, they become κληρονόμοι (heirs/inheritors) of God and συγκληρονόμοι (joint heirs) with Christ (8:12-16) over a creation that awaits the redemption of God's children (8:21). Both Matt 5:11-12 and Rom 8:17-18 honor those who suffer on Jesus' account, and both promise future glory to those who do so. Both Matt 5:5 and Rom 8:27 reward those who wait on God for future glory.

[202]   See 2.2.1.1.

justification provided, the acquisition of the inheritance through violence and force is still a sanctioned practice (Num 33:50-56).[203] It is
striking that, in Matt 5:3-12, the exact opposite is in view. Whereas
the language of the second clauses of Matt 5:5 and 5:9 can be traced
back to the Hexateuch, the first clauses of those same verses promise the inheritance to "the meek" (5:5) and "the peacemakers" (5:9).
The peacemaking of Matt 5:9 presents a stark opposition to war-
making themes, as it refers to "someone who is reconciled to God,
knows God is for peace, and seeks reconciliation instead of strife
and war."[204] The same can be said of "the meek." The use of πραεῖς
implies a gentility and unassertiveness toward the acquisition of the
inheritance; it is not taken by force but belongs to those who exhibit
the humble disposition of reliance upon God alone for their eschatological blessing. Although McKnight does not juxtapose the meek of
Matt 5:5 with conquest contexts, he does recognize the opposition to
acquisition through violence, when he argues:

> Meekness is framed over against wrath, anger, violence, acquisitive-
> ness, rapaciousness, theft, violent takeovers, and brutal reclamations
> of property. The meek are unlike the Zealots, who used violence to
> seize the land. The meek choose to absorb unjust conditions in a form
> of nonviolent, nonretaliatory resistance that creates a calm, counter-
> cultural community of love, justice, and peace.[205]

Framing the reception of inheritance through peacemaking and meekness echoes Isaiah and Second Temple sources rather than the Hexateuch. Isaiah 9:7 states that the coming king of the throne of David will
establish "endless peace," and in Ps 37, it is those who are meek (37:11)
and who wait on Yahweh (37:9) who stand to inherit.[206]

---

[203]   See 2.2.1.1.

[204]   McKnight, *Sermon*, 46. McKnight (48) goes on to state that "son of God" in
5:9 denotes "someone who is on God's side," implying that "God is a God of peace."
Similar is Davies and Allison, *Matthew 1–7*, 458, "In being a peacemaker, the disciple is
imitating his Father in heaven."

[205]   McKnight, *Sermon*, 42. That "peacemakers" is deliberately counteracted
against the militarism of "the Zealots" is also the view of Hagner, *Matthew 1–13*, 94.
Luz, *Matthew 1–7*, 198, ties peacemaking to the love of enemies (Matt 5:44-48), and is
persuasive that the directive is focused not only on peacemaking within the community
of Jesus' followers, or not only between God and people, but also has a "life beyond the
boundaries of the community."

[206]   See also Keener, *Gospel*, 168, who argues that most Jews had long expected
a war against the gentiles. See, for example, 4.2.3 of this study, where such a war was
both expected and connected to inheritance themes in 1QM. However, Keener argues,
Jesus subverts this expectation in Matt 5:3-12 by promising the kingdom not to those
who force God's hand but to people of peace, which is connected to Isaiah throughout
(cf. Isa 25:6-9; 26:8; 30:15, 18; 40:30-31; 49:23; 50:10-11; 57:13; 64:4).

4. Instruction

It would be difficult to demonstrate that the First Evangelist knew or made use of Instruction in a direct way, but many thematic and theological parallels between the two compositions have been suggested.[207] Matthew is indebted to literary tradition that cannot always be proven through direct literary dependence, so it is important to explore thematic and theological content that may have influenced the writer's thought-world. While many of the proposed parallels between Matthew and Instruction are striking and already demonstrate the potential that they contributed to a common thought-world and theological milieu, there are further parallels between Instruction and Matt 5:3-12, in particular, which are illuminating and have yet to be explored.

First, as discussed in chapter 1,[208] it has been argued by some scholars that Instruction and Matthew are two of the few compositions in the Second Temple period that best illustrate the trajectory of sapiential and apocalyptic elements converging upon one another to establish a particular Jewish worldview influenced deeply by both traditions.[209] Both compositions feature an inaugurated eschatology whereby those who pursue wisdom and observe a greater righteousness can participate in the future blessings and inheritance in the present. In Instruction those who pursue wisdom through the mystery are contrasted with the wicked who will face judgment, referred to as those with a "fleshly spirit." In Matthew those who pursue a greater righteousness through Jesus are contrasted with the scribes and Pharisees (5:20). In both cases those who pursue a greater righteousness are in a state of religious poverty and are elevated above that poverty to a status and present participation with the heavenly realm as they await a fuller eschatological reward (cf. 4Q416 2 iii; Matt 5:3). In both compositions, this reward includes the right to "inherit the earth," and these are two of the few compositions in all of the extant Jewish and Christian documents to use that precise phrase

---

[207]   See, for example, Grant Macaskill, *Revealed Wisdom and Inaugurated Eschatology in Ancient Judaism and Early Christianity* (Leiden: Brill, 2007), who places 1 Enoch and Instruction in conversation with Matthew and 2 Enoch; Loren T. Stuckenbruck, "4QInstruction and the Possible Influence of Early Enochic Traditions: An Evaluation," in *Wisdom Texts from Qumran and the Development of Sapiential Thought* (Leuven: Leuven University Press, 2002), 245–62; Matthew J. Goff, "Discerning Trajectories: 4QInstruction and the Sapiential Background of the Sayings Source Q," *JBL* 124, no. 4 (2005): 657–73; John Kampen, *Wisdom Literature* (Grand Rapids: Eerdmans, 2011), 28–29.

[208]   See 1.3.

[209]   See Kampen, *Wisdom*, 28–29.

(cf. 4Q418 81+81a 14; Matt 5:5).[210] Furthermore, in both compositions the phrase "inherit the earth" is set alongside the plural form of
heaven in a thematic word pair.

Second, both compositions make use of a set of parallel key terms
that highlight ethical norms for faithful communities. In Matthew's case
this becomes more evident when all of its makarisms are considered.
Both feature the use of inheritance in important contexts, and both use
terms such as "poor," "mourn," "meek/humble," and "righteousness"
(see esp. 4Q417 2 i 7–18).[211] In both compositions, these seemingly dis-
paraging terms actually possess positive connotations. In Instruction,
despite his lowly state, the addressee is to adopt the virtuous dispositions
of remaining generous and humble, and he must mourn over wickedness.[212] It is those who mourn that will receive the blessing of "eternal joy" (4Q417 2 i 12). Similar dispositions are featured in Matthew's
makarisms. Some of these parallels may be no more than evidence that
both compositions were influenced by Isaiah and in particular Isa 61:1–
7. At the very least this may serve to demonstrate that they belong to a
common tradition that used that passage as a key text for ethical norms,
but it might be telling that both Instruction and Matthew's makarisms
make use of largely the same linguistic features from Isa 61 and also
ignore the same portions of the Isaiah passage.

Third, as discussed in detail in chapter 4,[213] poverty, both economic
and metaphorical, is a key theme throughout the whole of Instruction,
and this dual focus on being poor is found not only in Matt 5:3, but as
the first makarism, the concept of being "poor in spirit" establishes a
thematic framework for interpreting the rest of the makarisms. Although
many Jewish and Christian texts refer to poverty with the dual focus
of both economic and religious poverty, not all texts emphasize the

---

[210]   See 4.1.1.2. The phrase "inherit the earth" will be discussed in more detail
below.

[211]   Instruction also potentially features the phrase "contrite/broken of spirit,"
which would provide a parallel with Matt 5:3, though as discussed in 4.1.1.2, this phrase
in Instruction is fragmented and reconstructed by the editors of DJD 34.

[212]   Davies and Allison, Matthew 1–7, 449, are persuasive that "mourn" in Matt
5:4 has similar connotations. The mourning in view is likely a reference to the state
of mourning specifically over wickedness in Israel, as opposed to mourning in a more
general sense. I would disagree however with Davies and Allison's conclusion regarding
the nature of mourning as a disposition. They argue that the evangelist could not see
mourning as a good thing and is therefore best viewed as an unfortunate condition from
which to be rescued. There is a sense in which this is true, as God often promises to turn
sorrow into joy (Isa 60:20; 66:10; Rev 21:4). However, while the necessity to mourn is
not, in itself, positive, the act of doing so for the right reasons and in the right way can
still be viewed as a positive disposition, which I argue is likely the intent of Matt 5:4.

[213]   See 4.1.1.

religious sense the same way. As we have seen, most scholars argue that Luke places a greater emphasis on the economic aspect, and his Gospel offers a critique of wealth. While economic poverty is a theme for both Instruction and Matthew, neither composition is particularly concerned with economic class, and neither offers a critique of wealth. In both compositions, economic poverty is a factor in driving the faithful toward a religious poverty that manifests itself in full devotion and dependence upon God. In both compositions, the focus is not on poverty itself but on the way that one conducts oneself in the midst of non-ideal circumstances. The addressee of Instruction, and the disciples and crowds in Matthew, are to transcend their economic disadvantage in order to depend upon God, exhibit righteousness before him, and exhibit proper conduct toward others. Both compositions insist that the reader/hearer can flourish in the eyes of God while appearing not to flourish in the eyes of humanity, and therefore, both present a subversive and countercultural understanding of living within an impoverished or disadvantaged state. The addressee in Instruction has been given a seat among the angels, and the disciple in Matt 5:3-12 has been given a reward in heaven (5:12) and a place within the kingdom of God (5:3, 10); therefore, both compositions insist that the reader/hearer should behave in a way befitting one who holds a heavenly status.

The theme of proper conduct in the midst of poverty extends to the concept of *vocation* in both compositions. Throughout Instruction, the addressee is exhorted not to allow anything to distract him from pursuit of wisdom, righteousness, and "the mystery of existence." He is not to exchange his glory for a price (4Q416 2 ii 6), meaning, he is not to pursue wealth or become embroiled in financial entanglements that would distract him from the mystery or disqualify him from devoting himself to his vocation, in his case, becoming a sage and liturgical leader within the community. In Matthew, wealth and its pursuit are likewise viewed as a distraction from embracing one's full vocation as a disciple. This is presented clearly in the story of "the rich young ruler" (Matt 19:16-30), where a young man of wealth is instructed to sell his possessions, give his money to the poor, and follow Jesus as a disciple. As the young man goes away grieving due to his concern for his great wealth, Jesus instructs his disciples on the difficulty of wealthy people devoting themselves fully to God and entering his kingdom (19:24).[214] The terminology of Instruction might be appropriate of the young ruler: that he "exchanged his spirit for a price" and surrendered an opportunity of a

---

[214] This passage features a use of inheritance language in 19:29 and is discussed in more detail below.

God-oriented vocation for one of financial advantage. This same theme is present in the makarisms and throughout the Sermon on the Mount: a disciple of Jesus is not to be concerned with storing up treasures on earth (6:19-21), or being devoted to the pursuit of money (6:24), or searching for security by improving his financial position (6:25-34). Instead, a disciple of Jesus is in a state of flourishing if he is poor in spirit (5:3), meek (5:5), pursuing righteousness (5:6), being salt and light (5:13-16), and relying on God alone. In Instruction, wealth is an unnecessary pursuit that may distract one from the vocation of becoming a sage. In Matthew, wealth is an unnecessary pursuit that may distract one from the vocation of being a disciple.

Fourth, both compositions feature a participation with heaven for those who enter into their role, and this participation is an inaugurated aspect of future glory and promises. In Instruction, the addressee, by becoming a sage, has his lot cast with the angels, and he shares their status. The use of perfect verbs throughout 4Q418 81+81a demonstrates that the addressee has been "placed" as a most holy one, his glory has been "multiplied," and he has been "placed" as a firstborn son. The verbal forms make these actions past and completed, meaning that the status that the addressee enjoys as one who participates with the angels is not only about future glory but about participation as an aspect of the addressee's present occupation as a sage (the inheritance of glory). In Matthew, the disciple awaits certain promises as an eschatological reality (e.g., the inheritance of the earth), but the present tense of Matt 5:3 and 10 demonstrates that the disciple participates with the kingdom of heaven as a present reality. This theme of present participation with heaven on earth is further illustrated in Matt 6:10, as Jesus instructs his disciples to pray that God's will would be done "on earth as it is in heaven."

There are, of course, some key differences between these parallel concepts. Whereas Instruction views the addressee's participation with heaven through direct relationship with the heavenly host, Matthew refers to this participation as with God's kingdom, and angels are not mentioned in the immediate context. This difference may be tempered by the fact that angels play a more prominent role in Matthew than any other canonical Gospel (mentioned thirteen times). They play a role in separating those who are evil from those who are good (13:49), and the disciples are compared with angels favorably (22:30).[215] Another

---

[215] An important key difference being that, in Instruction, the addressee takes on the status of the angels and participation with them as a present, lived reality. In Matt 22:30, it is said that people will be like the angels "in the resurrection," referring to a postmortem reality. See France, *Matthew*, 839.

key difference is the precise nature of poverty in the two compositions. Instruction, like Luke's makarism in 6:20, views poverty as a vulnerable condition from which one will be rescued. Metaphorical poverty in Instruction is a cipher for human inadequacy. The addressee is to pursue wisdom and right conduct despite his poverty. Conversely, Matthew's makarisms, including 5:3, possess a decidedly greater ethical flavor. Although "poor in spirit" is a disadvantaged condition in the eyes of those in the world who possess wealth and comfort, it is still presented in Matt 5:3 more as a virtue for flourishing within the social context of Jesus' community rather than an unfortunate circumstance from which the disciples are waiting to be rescued.

Certain differences are to be expected, considering the roughly 300 years between the composition of Instruction and Matthew. It bears repeating that the purpose of this comparison is not necessarily to suggest any direct textual or linguistic dependence on Instruction by those responsible for Matthew's Gospel. The goal here is to suggest thematic and theological parallels that suggest that the two may belong within certain points along a trajectory of a common stream of tradition, which may have led to indirect influence. When Instruction and Matthew are read alongside one another, we are provided insights that are otherwise not available in regard to how both compositions operate with a view of inaugurated eschatology while offering paraenesis regarding how to conduct oneself. At the very least, these parallels may serve to help us better understand both compositions in light of one another.

5. Inherit the Earth in the Second Temple Period

The Hexateuchal traditions regarding the inheritance of the land of Israel are likely in the background of the Matthean Jesus' use of the phrase "inherit the earth," but this tradition has also been appropriated in a new covenantal context to describe the coming of a new creation rather than a focus on the land of Israel alone (Matt 19:28). The inheritance of the earth broadens the scope of both the covenant and the land inheritance in keeping with the way both have been appropriated into an eschatological framework; Israel is still Jesus' concern (Matt 10:5-6), but a universalistic concern for both the earth and the nations is not far behind (Matt 28:16-20), and Jesus' disciples are invited to anticipate and participate in that future in the present (Matt 5:5). The transitions between the inheritance of the land and the inheritance of the earth can be seen in some Second Temple material. In addition to the phrase "inherit the earth" in Ps 37 (Ps 36 LXX) and the Psalms Pesher previously discussed,[216] there are two other instances of the phrase in the Second Temple literature that deserve comment: one that features the phrase in Greek and the other in Hebrew.

As discussed in chapter 3, 1 En. 5:5-9 features the use of the phrase κληρονομήσουσιν τὴν γῆν three times.[217] This exact construction of the phrase in Greek, featuring the future, active, indicative, third person, plural form of the verb κληρονομέω with the article before the noun, is extremely rare in extant literature, found only in 1 En. 5, Isa 61:7, and Matt 5:5.[218] Although 1 En. 5:5-9 features a linguistic connection to Matt 5:5, themes associated with the inheritance in 1 En. 5 are relevant to Matthew's entire narrative of inheritance, which becomes clear below. For example, both 1 En. 5 and Ps 36:22 (LXX) declare that those not included in the inheritance will be cut off. Psalm 36:22 reads: "for those blessed by the Lord shall inherit the land (αὐτὸν κληρονομήσουσι γῆν), but those cursed (καταρώμενοι) by him shall be cut off." By comparison, 1 En. 5:7 reads: "For the chosen there will be light and joy and peace, and they will inherit the earth (αὐτοὶ κληρονομήσουσιν τὴν γῆν), but for the wicked there will be a curse (κατάρα)." This juxtaposition of the inheritance for those who experience God's favor versus being cut off from the inheritance for those who do not is strongly implied in Matt 5:5, as the inheritance is promised to those who follow Christ and is made explicit in each of Matthew's other inheritance contexts (19:29; 21:38; 25:34). In this way, in each passage, to inherit the land/earth is to be included and to be found within the identity of those connected to God. To be left out from the inheritance is to be excluded from identifying with God's people.

1 Enoch 5 and Matthew also fit, to some degree, with the postexilic circumstance that found the Israelites alienated from the land and no longer in control of it. In both cases the inheritance is a future promise, indicated by the use of the future tense verb, "will inherit." The lack of control of the land places the audiences of both compositions in a place of dependence upon God for future vindication. As discussed in chapter 2, the land was more than geographic space, it was a place of security and a signifier of the identity of God's people as those uniquely chosen by him. In contrast to the Hexateuch, which promises the inheritance to all of Israel over and against the Canaanite inhabitants of the land, the postexilic context of both 1 En. 5 and Matthew's Gospel places the conflict between those within Israel seeking to

---

[216] See 5.1.2.2.

[217] See 3.1.

[218] The use of the phrase throughout Ps 36 in the LXX does not feature the article. Tobit 4:12 is similar (κληρονομήσει γῆν), but the verb is singular and the article is not featured. Tobit refers to the descendants of Abraham who will "inherit the land."

honor God and those within Israel who are not doing so. In 1 En. 5, there are those prospering in the land by their disobedience to the law. In Matthew, the conflict is with the Jewish leaders in particular, who have followed God in a way defined by hypocrisy. As the parameters used to define and identify God's people have shifted, the nature of the land inheritance has shifted as well, and it is in this way that both 1 En. 5 and Matthew are likely influenced by Isa 56–66: in Isa 65:17 God declares his intention to create a new heavens and a new earth. Isaiah 65 describes an idyllic existence reminiscent of Eden, where the creation is at harmony and humans experience life at an optimum level. Isaiah 65 features the term ארץ (land/earth) in parallel with שמים (heavens), which describes totality and encompasses the universe and the divine realm—as such the entire earth rather than Israel alone is in view.[219] 1 Enoch imports this vision into its social milieu in order to present the righteous chosen with an apocalyptic hope. Matthew 5:3-12, like Isa 65, brings the land/earth together with the plural use of "heaven" (οὐρανῶν) to the same effect; reconstituting the people of God around Jesus as their messianic king comes with a new vision of temporal space. It is also argued in chapter 3 that the Book of the Watchers opens the possibility of the inheritance of the earth being received by gentiles, which was possibly influenced by Isa 66:18-23. As argued throughout this chapter, the universal application of "inherit the earth" is likely in view in Matthew as well.

The second instance of the phrase that requires discussion is found in Instruction. 4Q418 81+81a 14 states that those who are נוחלי ארץ (inheritors of the earth) יתהלכי (shall walk), which is followed immediately by a reference to שמים (heaven). The line is fragmented, and the full context is difficult to determine. As discussed in chapter 4,[220] the phrase might possess eschatological connotations, but the emphasis is on those who are already set to inherit in the present. The use of the imperfect hitpael verb from the root הלך (to walk) in line 14 likely has ethical connotations, and paired with the reference to heaven, likely means that those who inherit the earth are those who walk upon the inherited earth in a way that accords with the heavenly realm. The addressees are being instructed on how to live in the present earth, in the same way as those who are in heaven (angels), and their present inheritance of the earth then accords with their heavenly status. As we have seen in our discussion in the Latter Prophets, 1 Enoch, and the Psalms Pesher, the phrase "inherit the earth" is most often an eschatological phrase that carries with it a universalism and a view toward this-worldly renewal. To a degree, this may be in view in Instruction, but the context here

---

[219] Watts, *Isaiah 34–66*, 924.
[220] See 4.1.1.2.

emphasizes the ethical aspect of the inheritance; those who inherit the earth are likely those who walk *according to heaven*. The inheritance of the entire earth coupled with the addressee's role on behalf of humanity strongly implies that the inheritance is universal.

Like 4Q418 81+81a, Matt 5:3-12 features the heaven-and-earth word pair in an ethical context. Both passages offer the inheritance of the earth universally, and both offer it to those who conduct themselves toward God and others in an ethical way. In Instruction, those who inherit the earth are those who are given authority over it as sages and liturgical leaders in the community, and although this is less immediately apparent in the context of Matt 5:5, it is relevant to the role of the disciples throughout Matthew, who are given authority upon the earth (Matt 10:1). The important difference between these examples is that, in Instruction, the inheritance of the earth is a reference to authority *in itself*, while in Matthew, those in authority participate with the kingdom of heaven in the present but are given the inheritance of the earth as an eschatological promise and reward.

There are some important common threads related to "inherit the earth" contexts. In each case, the promise of the earth is made by one with ultimate authority over the earth (usually God, but in the case of Matthew, Jesus acting on God's behalf). In all cases except for possibly Instruction, the earth is a renewed and reconstituted earth, and in all cases except for possibly Instruction, the promise of the inheritance of the renewed earth is largely eschatological but imbibed with inaugurated significance. In all cases, the inheritance of the earth is open to all of humanity universally, and in all cases, it is promised to those who follow God and live in an ethical way. In the cases of the Book of the Watchers, Instruction, and Matthew's Gospel, the phrase is found in contexts that contribute to the trajectory of the convergence of sapientially and apocalyptically oriented literature.

6. Inheritance and Makarisms in the Second Temple Period

Considerable attention has been paid to certain parallels between Matthew's makarisms and 4QBeatitudes (4Q525).[221] Space precludes an analysis regarding the parallels and the possible influence of the latter upon the former, but it is enough to state here that, despite some

---

[221] See George Brooke, "The Wisdom of Matthew's Beatitudes (4QBeat and Mt. 5:3-12)," *Scripture Bulletin* 19, no. 2 (1989): 35–41; James H. Charlesworth, "The Qumran Beatitudes (4Q525) and the New Testament (Mt 5:3-11, Luke 6:20-26)," *RHPR* 80 (2000): 13–35; Émile Puech, "The Collection of Beatitudes in Hebrew and Greek (4Q525 1–4 and Mt 5:3-12)," in *Early Christianity in Context: Monuments and Documents* (ed. F. Manns and E. Alliata; SBF 38; Jerusalem: Franciscan Printing Press, 1993), 353–68; Evans, *Matthew*, 101–3.

similarities, there are important differences that call direct influence into question.[222] More specifically, although both texts feature makarism lists, and both feature terms for inheritance, 4QBeatitudes does not feature inheritance terminology within its makarism list itself, but rather, inheritance is referred to in another fragment.[223] Moreover, inheritance in 4QBeatitudes contains certain similarities with inheritance in other Second Temple compositions, such as Instruction, but not in ways that intersect with Matthew's use of the term. It is unclear if 4QBeatitudes features any notion of eschatology, and the inheritance of glory in 4QBeatitudes refers to the honor the addressee will enjoy among his students after his passing, not to rewards in the afterlife.

Closer to Matthew may be the list of woes in 1 En. 98:9–99:16, with its singular makarism in 99:10. The makarism states that those who flourish are those who obtain wisdom, obey God's commandments, and walk in the ways of righteousness. Righteousness belongs to those who adhere to instruction. Inheritance appears in a woe rather than a makarism (99:14), where a woe is pronounced upon those who reject τὴν κληρονομίαν τῶν πατέρων αὐτῶν τὴν ἀπ᾽ αἰῶνος (the everlasting inheritance of their fathers). As discussed in chapter 3,[224] the inheritance here recalls Israel's forefathers and the Abrahamic promise, while also connecting to 1 En. 5 in the way that it anticipates a renewed, eschatological earth. While the reference to "the fathers" (τῶν πατέρων) draws on Israel's past, Stuckenbruck argues persuasively that the author's ideology of community remains open (is nonsectarian) to all who pursue wisdom and is closed only to those who pursue error.[225] Like Matthew's list, this leaves the makarism and woes open to the response of the reader/hearer.

5.1.2.4. The Meaning of Matthew 5:5

In light of the preceding discussion regarding the character of Matthew's makarisms and antecedent traditions, attention may now be turned to an interpretation of Matt 5:5. The goal of Matthew's makarisms, as a whole, is to detail certain dispositions that describe an ideal disciple, a proper relationship to God and others, and reveal the experience of a flourishing life. Wisdom and eschatological motifs come together to reveal that

---

[222]   See Evans, *Matthew*, 102, who notes the lack of eschatology in 4Q525 as the principal difference.

[223]   The makarisms of 4QBeatitudes are found in 4Q525 2 ii, while inheritance terms are found in 4Q525 13, 14 i and ii, and 33. See 4.1.4.

[224]   See 3.1.4.

[225]   Loren T. Stuckenbruck, *1 Enoch 91–108* (Berlin: de Gruyter, 2007), 423.

eschatological restoration is inaugurated into the life of God's people in the present, which reinforces and informs moral tradition. Repentance, moral instruction, and discipleship are informed by end-of-age perspectives on practical matters. Matthew's makarisms refer to virtue formation informed by eschatological hope. The dispositions described by Matthew's makarisms do not only describe states in which the disciples may be found, or dispositions from which they can expect to be delivered, but they are dispositions that must be actively cultivated if one desires to flourish and live in step with God's will. Those who live in this way stand to be rewarded with blessings. This is particularly relevant to the way that the makarisms are contrasted with the woes of Matt 23 and the behavior of the scribes and Pharisees, who live as hypocrites, and for their own glory, rather than as those who exhibit meekness, peace-making, and purity of heart. The hope for the disciples is not only that they will receive blessings in the eschaton, but also that the eschatological hope motivates their active participation with Jesus, and that such participation is then met with the guarantee of eschatological rewards.

Although "meekness" does not initially strike one as a virtuous disposition, and even though the disciples hold out hope that they will one day be exalted, it is by being humble, meek, and relying on God alone that exaltation will one day come to fruition. It is in this way that "meekness" is a virtue: one must rely on God, rather than one's own strength or positive circumstances,[226] and serve God in the midst of trial and persecution (Matt 5:10-12).[227] These meek are the ones who will "inherit the earth." Being meek is not an entrance requirement into the inheritance, nor is it simply a response to salvation; in fact, soteriology is not the goal of the makarisms at all. Meekness, and the other makarisms, are meant to describe "the kind of people who will make up the kingdom of heaven."[228]

---

[226]   Talbert, *Reading*, 51, cites 2 En. 50:2, where one is commanded to "Live in meekness" so that they may "inherit the endless age that is coming." See also France, *Matthew*, 166, who argues that "meek" refers not only of the disadvantaged but also those who are humble and live well among other people and with a proper relationship to God. Wesley G. Olmstead, *Matthew 1–14: A Handbook on the Greek Text* (Waco, Tex.: Baylor University Press, 2019), 77, points to the use of πραεῖς to describe Jesus in Matt 11:29 and 21:5 and equates meekness with gentleness.

[227]   Convincing is Reeves, *Matthew*, 102–5, who adds Isa 53:3-4 and other prophetic traditions regarding Israel's rejection of its prophets as a possible background to the makarisms. Jesus expects the disciples to be persecuted in the same way that Israel's prophets were maligned by Israel's inept leaders.

[228]   Reeves, *Matthew*, 98, states as much regarding the entire Sermon on the Mount, but it is an apt description of those who exhibit the makarisms. Reeves is careful to point out that the Sermon is not meant to describe individuals but rather the righteousness of a people group.

The nature of the inheritance of the earth is more difficult to determine. McKnight argues that the inheritance refers to geographic space, but that τὴν γῆν refers not to the whole earth, but rather the land of Israel alone. He cites linguistic connections with the Hexateuch and Ps 37 to argue that "there is little likelihood that Jesus would have 'world' in mind." Due to the Jewish nature of Matthew's narrative, he argues that it is best to view τὴν γῆν as a reference to the land, as Israel itself is the only geographic space with which a first-century Jew would be concerned.[229] However, Charles Talbert is right to acknowledge that viewing the inheritance as "whole-earth" is the most Jewish interpretation, when one considers the trajectory of inheritance concepts throughout the Second Temple period,[230] many examples of which have been discussed in this chapter.[231] In particular, the "whole-earth" inheritance in Instruction, and its relationship to Matthew, have never been explored in the way offered here, and the parallels between these two compositions provide striking evidence that Jews in the Second Temple period envisioned a "whole-earth" fulfillment of the inheritance. Furthermore, the heaven-and-earth word pairing between Matt 5:3 and 5:5 suggests that τὴν γῆν in Matt 5:5 refers not to the land of Israel alone but to the earth and the eschatological renewal of all things. This is supported within Matthew by the anticipation of cosmic renewal (Matt 19:28) and the fact that, in the majority of instances in Matthew, γῆν appears to refer to the earth rather than the land of Israel (cf. Matt 5:18, 35; 6:10, 19; 9:6; 11:25; 12:42; 16:19; 18:18-19; 23:9; 24:30; 28:18).[232] Matthew 5:5 is best viewed as a functioning addition to the heaven-and-earth word pair (with Matt 5:3) where the inheritance of the earth is an eschatological, spatial, and this-worldly reward for present kingdom participation.[233]

---

[229]   McKnight, *Sermon*, 42–43. Similar appears to be Evans, *Matthew*, 106, who argues that the Jews of the first century hoped for "national renewal," and that "the promised re-inheriting of the land would strike a hopeful chord in the hearts of his hearers." This is also the position of Nolland, *Matthew*, 202, who argues that the land in view is "clearly the land of Israel, in the context of God's covenant promise to his people." Nolland argues this on the basis of interest in the land in Matt 4:25 and the postexilic context of Matthew.

[230]   Talbert, *Reading*, 52, appeals specifically to 2 En. 50:2, the Pesher of Psalm 37 from Qumran, and Paul's expectation in Rom 4.

[231]   Cf. Isa 60:21 and 61:7, which refer to the eschatological renewal of the land. The climax of the composition promises an entirely new creation, illustrated by the heaven-and-earth word pair (Isa 65:17). See Luz, *Matthew 1–7*, 195, n. 94, who argues that the wording of Isa 60:21 and 61:7 is that of the "cosmic expansion of the promise of the land."

[232]   With Matt 27:45 as an exception. See Davies and Allison, *Matthew 1–7*, 450.

[233]   There are scholars who have proposed that "inherit the earth" is best viewed as a spiritual, rather than special/geographical reality. See, for example Klaus Haacker,

The promise to inherit the earth is future tense and eschatological; as the kingdom of heaven comes to bear upon the earth, those presently participating in the heavenly kingdom will inherit the earth as a result. The inheritance is guaranteed by God himself as a gift, through Jesus, who is included among Abraham's descendants. Jesus is therefore an heir to the inheritance, and therefore plays a role in being a light to the nations, which highlights the universal aspect of the offer of inheritance. The inheritance is promised to those who follow God and live in an ethical way.

"What Must I Do to Inherit Eternal Life? Implicit Christology in Jesus' Sayings about Life and the Kingdom," in *Jesus Research: An International Perspective* (ed. James H. Charlesworth and Petr Pokorný; Grand Rapids: Eerdmans, 2009), 148, who does not mention Matt 5:5 but does refer to other Matthean passages regarding inheritance and argues that inheritance/entrance passages regarding the kingdom of God/heaven are used metaphorically: "The kingdom of God is not a territory but an age to come" and is synonymous with "eternal life." This is also the view of Davies and Allison, *Matthew 1–7*, 450, who argue, "Because the kingdom is already in some sense present, the βασιλεία is necessarily spiritualized and divorced from geography. It would seem to follow, then, that in Mt 5:5 'to inherit the land' has been spiritualized, and 5:5b is no more concrete than any other promises made in the beatitudes. It is just another way of saying, 'The one who humbles himself will be exalted (in the kingdom of God).'" This argument is based on the view of Davies and Allison that Matt 5:3 and 5:5 are best viewed synonymously. The "spiritual fulfillment" view is surveyed by Joel Willitts, *Matthew's Messianic Shepherd-King: In Search of "The Lost Sheep of the House of Israel"* (Berlin: de Gruyter, 2007), 157–62. Willitts critiques the spiritual fulfillment view, and rightly argues that Second Temple Jews, and Matthew's Gospel, retain a focus on actual territorial fulfillment. However, he specifically critiques a supersessionist version of the spiritual fulfillment perspective that views the lack of focus on the land of Israel in Matthew as a result of the Jews losing their status as the people of God. While Willitts rightly argues against a supersessionist perspective, and in favor of a territorial fulfillment to promises regarding the kingdom of God/heaven, he argues in favor of "the land of Israel," extended to include its "ideal" northern border, as the focus of Matthew's territorial expectations. Willitts connects this to Jesus' mission in 10:5-7 on "The lost sheep of the house of Israel" (172). While Willitts does recognize that views on territory fulfillment in the Second Temple period were diverse, and that there is evidence of a "whole-earth" tradition, he only provides evidence to support his Israel-specific view and does not survey Second Temple traditions that might undermine his position. Furthermore, he does not portray an awareness of inheritance contexts in the Second Temple period, does not mention the dynamics of the heaven-and-earth word pair, and does not survey most of the passages within Matthew that feature the term γῆν. Finally, Willitts does not entertain the possibility of a "third-way," which rejects supersessionist views of Matthew, rejects a solely spiritualized interpretation of the land and the kingdom, affirms the territorial aspect, and still argues that Matthew's Gospel views the territorial fulfillment as the whole earth, which includes Israel. An argument has been made throughout this study that, rather than synonyms, 5:5 is best viewed as a spatial/geographic aspect of the kingdom, which fulfills the promise to God's people of a home consisting of geographic space, but as with Isa 55–66, sees this territorial fulfillment as extending beyond Israel alone.

5.2. Inheritance in Matthew 19:29

καὶ πᾶς ὅστις ἀφῆκεν οἰκίας ἢ ἀδελφοὺς ἢ ἀδελφὰς ἢ πατέρα ἢ μητέρα ἢ τέκνα ἢ ἀγροὺς ἕνεκεν τοῦ ὀνόματός μου, ἑκατοντα-πλασίονα λήμψεται καὶ ζωὴν αἰώνιον κληρονομήσει.

And all who abandon houses or brothers or sisters or father or mother or children or fields for the sake of my name, will receive a hundred-fold and inherit eternal life.

5.2.1. The Rich Man

The phrase "inherit eternal life" (ζωὴν αἰώνιον κληρονομήσει) is found in Matthew's version of the story of "the rich man."[234] Before interpreting "inherit" in the passage, it is helpful to analyze some of the salient features of the story and then offer suggestions regarding possible antecedents to inheritance in this context that have not been addressed in previous studies.

5.2.1.1. Competing Modes of Discipleship

Mark's version of the story begins with a rich man approaching Jesus (10:17), calling him "good teacher" (διδάσκαλε ἀγαθέ), and asking him how he can "inherit eternal life" (ζωὴν αἰώνιον κληρονομήσω). Matthew's version begins with the man approaching Jesus (19:16), and calling him "teacher" (διδάσκαλε), but the adjective ἀγαθὸν is the accusative direct object of ποιήσω (work) rather than διδάσκαλε.[235] In other words, Mark's version of the story has the rich man calling Jesus "good teacher" and asking what he must do to inherit eternal life. Matthew's version of the story has the rich man calling Jesus "teacher" and asking what "good deed" he must do to have eternal life. In Matthew, "good" modifies the deeds required rather than Jesus' status as a teacher. In Mark, Jesus responds to "good teacher" by asking the rich man: "Why do you call me good? No one is good but God alone." In Matthew, the focus remains on the deeds themselves, as Jesus responds: "Why do you ask me about what is good? There is only one who is good." In both versions, Jesus then lists certain recognizable command-ments as requirements to inherit eternal life.

The majority of scholars argue that Matthew avoids the rich man's address of "good teacher" in order to avoid the christological ambiguity

---

[234]   See also the versions in Mark 10:17-31 and Luke 18:18-30.

[235]   See Wesley G. Olmstead, *Matthew 15–28: A Handbook on the Greek Text* (Waco, Tex.: Baylor University Press, 2019), 114.

of Jesus' answer in Mark: "Why do you call me good? No one is good but God alone."[236] This is certainly possible. France has argued that Matthew's writer/editor made the minimal changes required to avoid this ambiguity and achieve a shift in emphasis, which points to the writer's motive as "a deliberate apologetic device" to preserve Jesus' goodness (and possibly his divinity).[237] However, this shift in emphasis would also have been accomplished had Matthew's writer simply omitted the question "Why do you call me good?" from Mark. With this change, the ambiguity would have been avoided, and Jesus would still be referred to as "good teacher."

There is another important change between the two stories to which commentators pay far less attention. In Mark, the rich man "ran" to Jesus (προσδραμών) and "knelt" before him (γονυπετήσας). In Matthew, the man simply "approached" Jesus (προσελθών). The posture and enthusiasm with which the man approaches Jesus is entirely adjusted for Matthew's version. At the very least, Matthew's writer may have adapted the story to serve as an aspect of his narrative of competing forms of discipleship, in which case the rich man is at minimum a cipher for the neutral and inquisitive crowds (as opposed to the enthusiastic seeker portrayed in Mark's version), and it is possible that Matthew's writer shapes the narrative just enough to associate the rich man with the scribes, Pharisees, and other Jewish leaders his Jesus opposes throughout the narrative. A few important features speak to this possibility.

Matthew's version of this story is structured similarly to the story at the beginning of the chapter where Jesus engages with some Pharisees regarding his teaching on divorce. In the discussion with the Pharisees:

a) They begin by asking Jesus a question concerning matters of law (19:3).

b) Jesus answers their question with his own interpretation (19:4-6).

c) The Pharisees ask a clarifying question (19:7).

d) Jesus clarifies further (19:8-9).

e) The disciples, who witnessed the discussion, ask their own question regarding Jesus' interpretation (19:10).

---

[236] Cf. Donald A. Hagner, *Matthew 14–28* (WBC 33B; Nashville: Thomas Nelson, 1995), 555; Keener, *Gospel*, 474; Evans, *Matthew*, 344.

[237] France, *Matthew*, 731–32. France argues that, because the divinity of Jesus is not an aspect of the context of the story, Mark and Luke likely did not intend the ambiguity, which would only become a matter of possibly embarrassment in later Christian interpretation. Matthew's writer noticed the ambiguity and attempted to avoid it.

f)   Jesus recognizes that not everyone will accept his teaching (19:11).

g)   Jesus makes a bold statement regarding the need for those who live for the sake of the kingdom of heaven to make exceptional sacrifices (19:12).

Matthew's version of the story of the rich man follows this same narrative structure. The rich man asks Jesus a question, and in an important detail, rather than focusing on Jesus as a "good teacher," the focus of the rich man's question is on "good deeds." This story is structured to revolve around the law, and Jesus' interpretation of the law, in order to mirror Jesus' previous interaction with the Pharisees:

a)   The rich man asks a question concerning the law in relationship to eternal life (19:16).

b)   Jesus' offers his interpretation (19:17-19).

c)   The rich man asks a clarifying question (19:20).

d)   Jesus clarifies further (19:21).

e)   The disciples, who witnessed the discussion, ask their own question regarding Jesus' interpretation (19:25).

f)   Jesus recognizes that not everyone will accept his teaching (19:23-24, 26).

g)   Jesus makes a bold statement regarding the need for those who live for his sake to make exceptional sacrifices (19:29).

While it is the case that Mark also features Jesus' discussion with the Pharisees regarding divorce immediately prior to his version of the story of the rich man, there is a difference between Mark's and Matthew's versions of that story that also speaks to the First Evangelist's intention to make discipleship the key aspect of his version: following his discussion with the Pharisees, the Matthean Jesus' entire description of the length to which one must be willing to go to be a disciple of the kingdom (Matt 19:10-12) is missing from Mark's version. As with so much of Matthew's overall narrative, these stories concern the nature of true discipleship versus false discipleship.[238] The Pharisees

---

[238]   Keener, *Gospel*, 470, argues that 19:10-12 addresses disciples who are "able to bear" Jesus' teaching. He also notes the discussion in scholarship regarding the nuances of the structure of this discussion between Jesus and his disciples, a structure uncommon in other Matthean discourses but possibly shared with Matthew's story of the rich man (19:16-30).

and the rich man queried Jesus' interpretation of the law, and they were unable to accept kingdom-oriented discipleship on Jesus' terms. Sandwiched between these two stories is the short pericope about the kingdom of God belonging to little children; the Pharisees and the rich man would have been better off embracing the kingdom with childlike faith (19:13-15).[239]

The association between the rich man and the Pharisees is potentially called into question when one considers that the rich man, in Matthew, leaves his discussion with Jesus "grieving" (λυπούμενος). This is not necessarily the reaction one would expect from Jesus' opponents in the Gospel. However, this reservation may be tempered by the fact that, in Mark's version, the rich man was also "sad/appalled" (στυγνάσας). Matthew's writer leaves out this heightened emotional response, thereby softening the emotional aspect of the story.[240] When this is coupled with the fact that the rich man in Matthew's version does not "run" to Jesus, does not "kneel" before him, and does not call him "good," the First Evangelist is making a concerted effort to create personal and emotional distance between Jesus and the rich man. The Pharisees and other Jewish leaders referred to Jesus as "teacher" in other parts of the Gospel,[241] but it is inconceivable that they would kneel before him or refer to him as "good teacher." Although the rich man knows his lack (19:20), and appears genuine (19:22), the First Evangelist relays another incident where a scribe (γραμματεὺς) approaches Jesus in earnest, refers to him as "teacher" (διδάσκαλος), and states his willingness to follow him, only for Jesus to challenge him with the exceptional commitment required (8:18-20). In a way that mirrors the story of the rich man, the scribe in Matt 8:18-22 is left to face the prospect of a penniless existence, but it is to the disciples that Jesus commands: "follow me" (ἀκολούθει μοι).[242] The pericope in Matt 8:18-22 is missing from Mark entirely, and in Luke 9:57, it is not a "scribe" who expresses interest in following Jesus but the generic "someone" (τις). Matthew's writer appears to have made a concerted effort to portray the scribes, Pharisees, and other Jewish leaders as particularly unwilling to count the cost of following Jesus, which heightens the narrative contrast between the disciples, who surrender all to

---

[239]   Keener, *Gospel*, 473. If the kingdom is to be received by humble dependents, such as children, then those accustomed to power might find it difficult to enter the kingdom.

[240]   See W. D. Davies and D. C. Allison Jr., *Matthew 19–28* (ICC; London: Bloomsbury, 1997), 50.

[241]   Cf. 9:11; 12:38; 22:16.

[242]   Compare Matt 8:22 with 19:21, 28.

follow Jesus, and the Jewish leaders, who do not. The story of the rich man slots into this overall Matthean narrative motif.[243]

That the story of the rich man is best understood as an aspect of Matthew's competing visions of discipleship, and therefore connected to the scribes and Pharisees as the counterexample, is also indicated by certain shared features with other parts of the Gospel. The connections with aspects of the Sermon on the Mount are striking:

a) It is those who forego the pursuit of wealth, live meekly, and rely on God alone who will "inherit (κληρονομήσουσιν) the earth" (5:5). If the rich man foregoes his wealth, and relies on God alone, he will "inherit (κληρονομήσει) eternal life" (19:29).[244]

b) Jesus states that those who live "on my account" (ἕνεκεν ἐμοῦ) will be rewarded.[245] This includes those who are persecuted (5:10-11), with many scholars arguing that Matthew's Jesus had the scribes and Pharisees in mind as potential persecutors. Jesus states that those who live "on account of my name" (ἕνεκεν τοῦ ὀνόμα-τός μου) will be rewarded (19:29).

c) It is only those whose righteousness exceeds that of the scribes and Pharisees who will "enter into the kingdom of heaven" (εἰσέλ-θητε εἰς τὴν βασιλείαν τῶν οὐρανῶν, 5:20). The rich man states that he has followed the commandments, but Jesus calls him to a

---

[243]   Keener, *Gospel*, 274–77, argues that the First Evangelist's identification of a scribe in Matt 8:18-20 heightens the drama of the story. For a scribe, the cost of following Jesus would be particularly high, as this would cost him his popularity, and it would be particularly humiliating for a scribe to forego his previous training in order to live a penniless existence as one of Jesus' disciples. Jesus' demands would require that the scribe forego social obligations. Precisely these same basic arguments are made by David Crump, *Encountering Jesus, Encountering Scripture* (Grand Rapids: Eerdmans, 2013), 51–70, regarding the rich man. Analyzing the story from Mark's version, Crump asserts that Jesus' demands amounted to a thorough disruption of cultural conventions and would cause the rich man to deconstruct every aspect of his life. The point here is that in these two stories, Jesus did not ask this of those who would be seen as being in need of such deconstruction. Both the scribe and the rich man would have likely been considered law-observant Jews who had been blessed by God.

[244]   Technically, the rich man's immediate question concerns how he can "have" (σχῶ) eternal life, and Jesus uses the term "inherit" at the end of the story as he describes the parameters for the inheritance to his disciples. However, Matthew's "have" coincides with Mark 10:17, "What must I do to inherit (κληρονομήσω) eternal life?" The majority of scholars regard Matthew's "have," "enter," and "inherit" as synonymous for the purposes of this story. See 5.2.1.2 for details.

[245]   This is a common refrain uttered by Jesus in discipleship contexts; see Matt 5:10-11; 10:18, 39; 16:25; 19:29.

greater form of righteousness. The rich man must give all he has to the poor and follow Jesus. When the man is unwilling, Jesus states that it is difficult for the rich to "enter into the kingdom of heaven" (εἰσελεύσεται εἰς τὴν βασιλείαν τῶν οὐρανῶν, 19:23).

d) Jesus' commands regarding almsgiving are often considered to be a direct criticism of Jewish leaders in the synagogues (6:1-4), including his teaching that Jesus' disciples should store up "treasures in heaven" (θησαυροὺς ἐν οὐρανῷ, 6:20),[246] a phrase directly related to the giving of alms as opposed to building personal wealth.[247] Jesus' command to the rich ruler to almsgiving is so that he could store up "treasure in heaven" (θησαυρὸν ἐν οὐρανοῖς, 19:21).

It is important to recognize that in both Jesus' command that his disciples' righteousness must exceed that of the scribes and Pharisees, and in the story of the rich man, Jesus does not state that either have failed to live righteously according to the standards of the law.[248] The implication of Matt 5:20 is that the Pharisees have observed the law according to their interpretation, and in the story of the rich man Jesus does not question the man's sincerity that he has observed the laws to which Jesus refers. The question in both instances is not only in regard to following the law, but to following Jesus, observing his particular interpretation of the law, and completely committing oneself to serving God's kingdom. For Jesus, the entrance point is not law observance but "follow me" (ἀκολούθει μοι). "Greater righteousness" acknowledges that Jesus often asks his followers to break with cultural conventions and live in ways not easily described by law.[249] Greater righteousness, following Jesus, and living for the sake of Jesus' name is not a matter of simple obedience to the law; it includes things like loving one's enemies (5:43-48) and giving up the aspects of one's life that may keep them from following Jesus in quite the way that he requires (19:29).

Many of these same themes are also prevalent in Jesus' critique of the scribes and Pharisees in Matt 23. Jesus affirms that their teaching of the letter of the law is correct and worthy to be followed; however, it is in practicing "greater righteousness" that they fail and are not to

---

[246] Though see the discussion in Davies and Allison, *Matthew 1–7*, 581, who note some differences between Matt 6 and the nature of the Pharisees' hypocrisy as described in Matt 23.

[247] See Davies and Allison, *Matthew 1–7*, 631.

[248] So Crump, *Encountering*, 64–65.

[249] See Crump, *Encountering*, 58; France, *Matthew*, 732, Hagner, *Matthew 14–28*, 558.

be emulated. Rather than setting aside honor, they pursue it (23:6), and they are more concerned with material matters than the weightier matters of the law, such as justice and mercy (23:16-24).[250] Jesus affirms that they should have practiced such weightier matters without neglecting the portions of the law to which they were committed (23:23). Their hypocrisy led them to greed and self-indulgence (23:25),[251] the very matters that may have driven Jesus to command the rich man to set aside his material wealth in order to follow him.[252] The scribes and Pharisees asserted their own position, but to be disciples of Jesus, they needed to submit themselves to him as their teacher (23:8-12). Their failure to do so, and their failure to exhibit justice and mercy toward others, leads to Jesus' declaration that the scribes and Pharisees would not enter the kingdom of heaven (23:13). Due to the emotional distance between the rich man and Jesus created by Matthew's version of the story, it is at least likely that the rich man functions as a cipher for the crowds, who are neutral, interested observers throughout most of the narrative, following Jesus enough to consider the cost of his mode of discipleship. However, the structure and position of the story in Matthew's overall narrative, and the linguistic and thematic connections to Jesus' criticisms of the scribes and Pharisees elsewhere, open up the possibility that the rich man is meant to serve as a foil in similar fashion to the Jewish leaders: as a counterexample to true discipleship.

5.2.1.2. Salient Features of the Story for Interpreting Inheritance

There are a number of features in the story of the rich man that are important for understanding the story, and in particular the function of inheritance.

1) In Mark 10:17 the rich man asks what he must do to "inherit eternal life" (ζωὴν αἰώνιον κληρονομήσω). In Matt 19:16 he asks what he must do to "have eternal life" (σχῶ ζωὴν αἰώνιον). However, in Mark 10:30 those who follow Jesus will "receive" (λάβῃ)

---

[250]   Keener, *Gospel*, 551, provides examples of Jewish teachers who recognized distinctions in the law and argued that some were "weightier" than others. Various sources describe their own judgments regarding the weightier matters. Matthew 23:16-24 details Jesus' interpretation.

[251]   Davies and Allison, *Matthew 19–28*, 298, the accusation of 23:25 charges the scribes and Pharisees with economic and sexual sin.

[252]   See Helen K. Bond, *The Historical Jesus: A Guide for the Perplexed* (London: T&T Clark, 2012), 125, "Jesus criticized the Pharisees' love of money, presumably indicating that some at least were affluent."

eternal life in the age to come (ἐν τῷ αἰῶνι τῷ ἐρχομένῳ ζωὴν αἰώνιον) while in Matt 19:29 those who follow Jesus will "inherit eternal life" (ζωὴν αἰώνιον κληρονομήσει). Both versions also refer to the difficulty with which wealthy people will "enter into the kingdom of God" (εἰς τὴν βασιλείαν τοῦ θεοῦ εἰσελθεῖν). For the purposes of this story, it is best to view "inherit," "receive," and "enter" as synonyms, as well as "eternal life" and "the kingdom of God/heaven." They are used synonymously within each story, as well as interchangeably between Mark's and Matthew's versions.[253]

2)   Mark 10:30 refers to eternal life "in the age to come" (ἐν τῷ αἰῶνι τῷ ἐρχομένῳ), a phrase not found in Matthew's version, while in Matt 19:28 Jesus offers a reward to his disciples "at the renewal" (τῇ παλιγγενεσίᾳ),[254] a phrase not found in Mark's version. Both phrases are eschatological in nature and likely refer to a similar reality, though with different emphases. In Mark, "the age to come" is usually understood to refer, in ambiguous fashion, to "the age that will follow the present one."[255] Three possible interpretations have been offered for the term παλιγγενεσία in Matthew: 1) a renewed Israel,[256] 2) the age to follow this present one,[257] 3) a recreated heaven and earth.[258] David Sim has argued effectively, using Matt 5:18 and 24:35 as parallels, that Matthew's writer had the third option in mind.[259] Of all of the Gospels, Matthew is most concerned with the parousia of Jesus and the judgment that it brings (cf. 7:15-23; 13:24-30, 36-43,

---

[253]   So also Haacker, "What Must I Do," 145; Hagner, *Matthew 14–28*, 564; Keener, *Gospel*, 473.

[254]   The term παλιγγενεσία is found only one other place in the NT literature, Titus 3:5. Most scholars argue that the term was brought in from its more extensive use in stoic writings. See *NIDNTTE*, 1:569.

[255]   See David C. Sim, "The Meaning of παλιγγενεσία in Matthew 19:28," *JSNT* 50 (1993): 5.

[256]   So Gundry, *Matthew*, 392.

[257]   So Fred W. Burnett, "παλιγγενεσία in Matt 19:28: A Window on the Matthean Community?" *JSNT* 17 (1983): 62. τῇ παλιγγενεσίᾳ refers "to the consummation of the age but not the end of the world." See also Schweizer, *Matthew*, 390, "Matthew speaks of the end of the eon but never the end of the world."

[258]   So McNeile, *Gospel*, 281; Evans, *Matthew*, 347; Hagner, *Matthew 14–28*, 565; Keener, *Gospel*, 480; France, *Matthew*, 743.

[259]   Though see France, *Matthew*, 743, who agrees with Sim's basic argument but questions his emphasis on the importance of 5:18 and 24:35 to Matthew's overall eschatology.

47-50; 16:27-28; 25:31-46).[260] In Matt 19:28, τῇ παλιγγενεσίᾳ refers not only to the age to follow this one but to the passing away and recreation/renewal of the cosmos.[261] This renewal includes, but is not limited to, a restored Israel.[262]

3)   When Jesus lists the laws that the rich man needed to follow in order to have eternal life, he refers to laws found in the second half of the Decalogue; laws referring to the manner in which people must treat one another. Many of these laws are also discussed by Jesus throughout the Sermon on the Mount and further indicate that Jesus was not concerned as much with perfect law obedience as he was the aspects of the law that related to justice, mercy, and living righteously toward others.[263] Many Jews at the time would have known the laws, and maintained a proper understanding of God and worship, but Jesus wanted disciples who lived out the implications of their religious devotion.[264]

4)   The fact that Jesus appears to have accepted the rich man's claims of law obedience, and still demanded further action, demonstrates that law obedience in itself, and the act of almsgiving, were not the ultimate conditions for entrance into the kingdom.[265] The entrance point into the kingdom is one's willingness to follow Jesus.[266] This

---

[260]   Sim, "Meaning," 7–10.

[261]   See Olmstead, *Matthew 15–28*, 122: τῇ παλιγγενεσίᾳ is temporal and refers to "an era involving the renewal of the world."

[262]   So Davies and Allison, *Matthew 19–28*, 57–58, who are ambiguous as to whether τῇ παλιγγενεσίᾳ refers only to a new age or to the recreation of the cosmos. They argue that Matthew's writer was not interested in the details but only in describing a world where Christ reigns, which includes a redeemed Israel.

[263]   So Hagner, *Matthew 14–28*, 558; Davies and Allison, *Matthew 19–28*, 43. Garland, *Reading*, 200, relates Jesus' demands with Micah 6:8, "What does the LORD require of you but to do justice, and to love kindness, and to walk humbly with your God."

[264]   See Crump, *Encountering*, 61.

[265]   See Roger Mohrlang, *Matthew and Paul: A Comparison of Ethical Perspectives* (Cambridge: Cambridge University Press, 1984), 18, who argues that failing to observe the law can cost one the chance to enter the kingdom, but observing the law is not in itself what qualifies one to enter. Jesus' references to the law in the story of the rich man function only as a preface to his more radical demand to follow.

[266]   See Crump, *Encountering*, 62–69, who offers a helpful comparison between "command" and "corrective." Had Jesus' desire been to "correct" the rich man, then pointing him toward almsgiving may have been enough to qualify the rich man for eternal life. However, that Jesus then commands "follow me" is an indicator that "correction" was not the ultimate goal but rather moving the rich man beyond his place of self-reliance into fully devoted discipleship. Where the rich man saw a negative: give

is further indicated by the use of the term τέλειος (complete/whole, 19:21), a term not found in Mark's version, and in fact found only one other time in any of the Synoptic Gospels, in Matt 5:48. In Matt 5:48, the term τέλειος follows Jesus' commands to love one's enemies, and in Matt 19:21, it follows Jesus' command that the rich man sell his possessions, give to the poor, and follow him.[267] This sort of wholeness refers to following Jesus in the counterintuitive specifics of his own interpretations of kingdom obedience.[268] Teleiosity is a greater righteousness not easily described by law.

5) Certain rewards are promised to Jesus' core disciples, "the Twelve." At the "renewal," they will sit on twelve thrones "judging" (κρίνοντες) the twelve tribes of Israel. The story of the rich man deals with individual, rather than corporate, salvation. This is the case in Jesus' discourse with the rich man, as well as his statements regarding those who surrender their lives to the service of the kingdom.[269] "Inherit eternal life" is offered to individuals who commit themselves to Jesus and his mode of discipleship (though it is those disciples, collectively, who "inherit the earth" in Matt 5:5). This offer of reward to "the Twelve" is an outlier in this passage; it is an *additional* offer other than eternal life itself.[270] Although the nature of their judgment is difficult to determine, Konradt is persuasive that this refers to the rank of the twelve from within a renewed Israel at the eschatological restoration of the twelve tribes but that the outcomes of their judgments are left open and do not imply a condemnation of Israel.[271] The role of the disciples appears

---

up his possessions; Jesus saw a positive: offering the rich man a genuine opportunity to express his faith.

[267] Luz, *Studies*, 155, argues that the two uses of τέλειος refer to loving one's neighbor. In Matt 5:48 this is done by loving one's enemies, and in 19:21 this refers to assistance of the poor.

[268] Davies and Allison, *Matthew 19–28*, 47–48, discuss the circumstances of the two uses of the term and conclude that 19:21 could not refer to surrendering wealth as a universal path toward "completeness." In 5:48, it refers to love, and in 19:21, it refers to obedience. τέλειος is dependent on its situation. Therefore, to be complete is to "obey the divine word that comes to them." See also Garland, *Reading*, 203, τέλειος refers to total surrender to God.

[269] See Davies and Allison, *Matthew 19–28*, 41.

[270] See Burnett, "παλιγγενεσία," 63.

[271] Konradt, *Israel*, 259–63. So also Davies and Allison, *Matthew 19–28*, 55; Hagner, *Matthew 14–28*, 565. Different is France, *Matthew*, 744, who argues that Jesus' disciples will take Israel's place as a "new Israel," over against the "old, failed regime." It is argued in this study, however, that the disciples do not replace all Israel, but rather,

limited to their involvement over a renewed Israel, but Jesus also states that "everyone" (πᾶς) who follows him will inherit eternal life, implying a universality beyond Israel alone to eternal life in the kingdom.

6) The story of the rich man ends with Jesus stating that "Many who are first will be last, and the last will be first" (19:30). This statement follows the disciples' attempts to turn little children away from an audience with Jesus (19:13-15), as well as their surprise that wealthy people will have a difficult time entering the kingdom (19:23-26). This is a consistent theme throughout Matthew and in inheritance contexts: it is not those who appear well-to-do in the eyes of the world who will inherit but rather the meek (5:5) and those who have sacrificed and have been persecuted for Jesus' sake. Matthew 19:30 is "a caution against thinking oneself among the first."[272] In a story following shortly after the narrative of the rich man, particular disciples fall guilty of this and are reminded of this same warning (20:24-28).

5.2.1.3. Inheritance Traditions Antecedent to Matthew 19:29

The following discussion on antecedent traditions is not to suggest that each of these had a direct influence on inheritance in Matt 19:29. This discussion aims to draw attention to theological and thematic parallels that may assist in understanding the meaning of inheritance in Matt 19:29 and framing it in light of the Jewish concept history of inheritance. Some of these traditions have a greater potential for influence, direct or indirect, than others.

1. The Hexateuch

In section 5.1.2.2. aspects of the inheritance tradition in the Hexateuch are discussed that likely had an influence on Matt 5:5. In particular, both the Abrahamic promise and the land inheritance were relevant to

---

Israel's failed leaders, and therefore it is Israel's leadership who stands to be condemned rather than Israel as a whole. Most scholars argue that Dan 7 is the primary background to Matt 19:28, with Pss 122 and 110 as possible influences. On the influence of these HB passages on Matt 19:28, see Evans, *Matthew*, 347–48.

[272] Davies and Allison, *Matthew 19–28*, 60–61, list many of the suggestions offered by scholars as to the specific identities of "the last" and "the first" but rightly argue that the ambiguity is intended to serve as a warning against all who would assume the status of "the first," as well as a caution against all who would elevate themselves to such a status.

both the theology and the language of that verse. Although Matt 19:29 is related to Matt 5:5 in ways that are discussed above, and although it is argued here that inheritance in Matthew is a streamlined concept, in most ways the themes related to the language used regarding inheritance in the Hexateuch and Matt 19:29 could not be further apart. In particular, the Hexateuch focuses on the reception of land inheritance as a realized benefit of Israel's relationship with God. The land is a treasured possession, a means of security for God's people, and it must be maintained and passed down in perpetuity. Conversely, in Matt 19:29, it is precisely the surrender of his earthly possessions that is required for the rich man to devote himself to Christ as a disciple. Rather than a realized reward for covenant faithfulness, the eternal life in Matt 19:29 is a future-focused eschatological reward for those who surrender their security in order to commit themselves to being Jesus' disciples. While it is the case that the tribal land allotments described in the Hexateuch are no longer maintained by Jesus' time, and Matt 19:28 does envision a reconstitution for eschatological Israel, inheritance in the passage makes no mention of a restoration of land inheritance, but instead focuses on "life" as the inherited reward. The one point of thematic connection between the Hexateuch and Matt 19:29 may be the most important: both inheritances are guaranteed as an aspect of the inheritor's relationship and covenant faithfulness to the one who grants the inheritance. This has been the most common thread to inheritance contexts in Jewish literature.

2. Isaiah 65:17 and 66:22

A number of scholars have drawn attention to a possible connection between Matt 19:28 and Isa 65:17, 66:22, which further solidifies the argument that τῇ παλιγγενεσίᾳ refers not only to a new age but also to a recreated cosmos. As I argue above, Isa 56–66 stands in the background of Matt 5:5, so it is reasonable to assume that Isaiah's "new heavens and new earth" also stands in the background of 19:28-29.[273]

3. Titus 3:5

The term παλιγγενεσία is found in the NT literature only in Matt 19:28 and Titus 3:5. The dating of Titus in relationship to Matthew is an open question,[274] though it is unlikely that either text had a direct influence upon the other. And yet, reading the two passages side by side offers important

---

[273]   France, *Matthew*, 743; Keener, *Gospel*, 480; Sim, "Meaning," 5.

[274]   See the extensive discussion on the provenance of Titus in Donald A. Hagner, *The New Testament: A Historical and Theological Introduction* (Grand Rapids: Baker Academic, 2012), 614–38.

insights into the way the term was received in early Christianity. In Titus 3:5, the term παλιγγενεσίας refers to rebirth through baptism and renewal of the individual by the Holy Spirit. The term is not in itself eschatological, though the renewal referred to as παλιγγενεσίας leads to eschatological rewards; rewards specifically referred to in the same terms as Matt 19:28. Those who are renewed become "heirs" (κληρονόμοι) to the eschatological hope that is "eternal life" (ζωῆς αἰωνίου). Although, in Matthew, παλιγγενεσία is itself eschatological, and refers to the renewed earth as opposed to the reborn individual, it refers to the renewed earth where eternal life is to be lived by the individuals who have committed themselves to Jesus.[275] Between Matthew and Titus, the details of the term's use are somewhat different,[276] but both contexts view "renewal," "inheritance," and "eternal life" as eschatological hopes tied to Jesus as savior. This means that, in Matt 19, although the terms "eternal life" and "kingdom of God/heaven" are used somewhat interchangeably, it is more accurate to view "eternal life" as the life lived *within* the kingdom by individuals who have been qualified for the inheritance.

4. Psalms of Solomon 14:5-10

As discussed below, Pss. Sol. 17 has a particular relevance to Matt 21:38 and 25:35, so although the potential parallel between Pss. Sol. 14 and Matt 19:16-30 is less clear, possible points of connection to inheritance contexts in three separate Matthean passages heighten the probability that Matthew's writer was aware of at least portions of these psalms. In Pss. Sol. 3:12, the devout will be cleansed of their sins and granted "eternal life" (ζωὴν αἰώνιον). In Pss. Sol. 14:10, the devout "will inherit life in joy" (κληρονομήσουσιν ζωὴν ἐν εὐφροσύνῃ). In Pss. Sol. 14, the

---

[275]   See Davies and Allison, *Matthew 19–28*, 57, παλιγγενεσία refers not to a point in time, but rather "an extended period of time" in "the world in which Christ reigns."

[276]   That παλιγγενεσίας in Titus 3:5 refers to individual renewal and παλιγγενεσία in Matt 19:28 to cosmic renewal is not the only difference. James D. G. Dunn, *Unity and Diversity in the New Testament: An Inquiry into the Character of Earliest Christianity* (London: SCM Press, 2006), 171–74, argues that the gift of the Spirit was the decisive element in conversion-initiation leading to baptism, as the Spirit was viewed as "the expression of God's action towards humankind." In Titus 3:5 it is the Spirit that "regenerates and renews the inner nature and mind of the convert." In Matt 19 the Spirit and baptism are not in view, and conversion comes about by committing oneself as a disciple to the living Jesus in his ministry. Although these important differences are noted, the linguistic parallels between the two passages regarding renewal, heir/inherit, and eternal life are instructive.

devout are those who observe the law (14:1-3).[277] There are obvious linguistic connections between Pss. Sol. 14 and Matt 19:16-30: the future tense verb κληρονομέω is tied to ζωή, which is ζωὴν αἰώνιον in Pss. Sol. 3. The principal difference between the two is striking: whereas Pss. Sol. 14 promises the inheritance of life to those who observe the law, Jesus in Matt 19:16-30 challenges the rich man that law observance is not enough and that he must also commit himself to Jesus. A link between "life" and law observance is common in Jewish sources,[278] so using the law as a starting point for "having eternal life" would not have been surprising. However, Jesus connecting eternal life to himself was unprecedented and likely would have caught the rich man off guard.[279]

5. Instruction

The principal point of connection between Instruction and Matthew's story of the rich man concerns their worldviews regarding wealth. As argued in the discussion regarding Matt 5:5,[280] neither Matthew nor Instruction is particularly concerned with critiquing the wealthy as a social class, and considering their provenance in relationship to other texts that do contain such critiques, their restraint is surprising. However, both compositions view wealth as a stumbling block toward the acquisition of the audiences' divinely appointed *vocation* (in Instruction this refers to the addressee's path toward becoming a sage), and in Matthew's Gospel, no story portrays wealth as a stumbling block to discipleship more clearly than the story of the rich man. Moreover, in Instruction, the inheritance refers to a place among the heavenly community. By equating "inherit eternal life" with "enter the kingdom of heaven," Matt 19:16-30 situates the inheritance along the same lines.

5.2.2. The Meaning of "Inherit" in Matthew 19:29

The rich man asks Jesus what he must do to "have" eternal life. Jesus' response communicates to the rich man that eternal life is not something

---

[277] See Simon Gathercole, *Where Is Boasting? Early Jewish Soteriology and Paul's Response in Romans 1–5* (Grand Rapids: Eerdmans, 2002), 67.

[278] Evans, *Matthew*, 344, provides examples.

[279] Crump, *Encountering*, 55–62, lists three primary offenses that would likely be felt by the rich man: 1) the personal risk involved in giving up his wealth, 2) the transgression of cultural and religious norms, and 3) the question regarding whether Jesus would have had the authority to go beyond law observance and dictate the terms of eternal life. Jesus put himself in the center of the story in a way the rich man would not likely have expected.

[280] See 5.1.2.3.

he can possess through means, and in fact, his wealth would likely be a distraction to his ability to receive eternal life. In the words of Davies and Allison, in order for the rich man to inherit eternal life he must "make a pilgrimage instead of a purchase."[281] For Jesus, the entrance point is not law observance but "follow me" (ἀκολούθει μοι). Rather than simple obedience, greater righteousness is about following Jesus and living for the sake of Jesus' name. This call is made to Jesus' first disciples, who accept and follow (4:18-22), and also to the rich man, who rejects the call and goes away grieving (19:22). The rich man asks, "What do I still lack?" (19:20), but the disciples, having given up everything to follow Jesus, can ask "What then will we have?" (19:27). The answer is eternal life in the kingdom of God.

Throughout Matthew's Gospel God's grace, proffered through Jesus, motivates the disciples and presents offers of eschatological blessings, but this does not lessen the clear directives throughout the Gospel for the disciples to flourish by choosing to live righteously and in line with God's will. The story of the rich man contains the nature of true discipleship versus false discipleship, and I argue here that with the entire Matthean narrative in view, the rich man is at minimum a cipher for the neutral and inquisitive crowds, and it is possible that Matthew's writer shapes the narrative just enough to associate the rich man with the scribes, Pharisees, and other Jewish leaders who his Jesus opposes throughout the narrative and who do not follow Jesus into "greater righteousness."

Inheritance in 19:29 is closely connected to the themes discussed in Matt 5:5. It is not those who appear well-to-do in the eyes of the world who will inherit but rather the meek (5:5) and those who have sacrificed and been persecuted for Jesus' sake. Rather than a realized reward for covenant faithfulness, the eternal life in Matt 19:29 is a future focused eschatological reward for those who surrender their security in order to commit themselves to being Jesus' disciples. In both passages, the eschatological hope for Jesus' disciples motivates their active participation with Jesus, and such participation is then met with the guarantee of eschatological rewards. The sacrifices made by the disciples would be unnecessary in an ideal world but are ideal in a world that has not been fully reconciled to God. The disciples are required to be in a position that is both counterintuitive and countercultural when compared with the dispositions that are valued by those in the world in which they live, both in relationship to the Matthew's makarisms and in Jesus' demands made to the rich man.

---

[281]   Davies and Allison, *Matthew 19–28*, 43.

In both passages "inherit" is a relational term: it is guaranteed as an aspect of the inheritor's relationship and covenant faithfulness to the one who grants the inheritance—in this case, Jesus. The exact nature of "eternal life" is not made clear, but it refers to the life lived *within* the kingdom by individuals who have been qualified for the inheritance. The life is eschatological in nature, and although the timing of entrance into eternal life is not specified, it relates to the time of "the renewal" (τῇ παλιγγενεσίᾳ), which refers not only to the age to follow this one but also to the passing away and recreation/renewal of the cosmos.

5.3. Inheritance in Matthew 21:38

οἱ δὲ γεωργοὶ ἰδόντες τὸν υἱὸν εἶπον ἐν ἑαυτοῖς· οὗτός ἐστιν ὁ κληρονόμος· δεῦτε ἀποκτείνωμεν αὐτὸν καὶ σχῶμεν τὴν κληρο-νομίαν αὐτοῦ

But when the tenants saw the son, they said to themselves, "This is the heir; come, let us kill him and have his inheritance."

"The parable of the wicked tenants" has been the subject of considerable discussion in the past hundred or so years, but very few scholars have even mentioned the role of inheritance in the pericope, and those who have analyzed inheritance to some degree have not emphasized it as an important aspect in understanding the parable. An exception is James D. Hester, who focuses most of his discussion on inheritance and argues that it is "the central, generative theme of the parable."[282] One need not go so far as to regard inheritance as the "central" theme to still empha-size its importance. While the various aspects of the parable have been scrutinized in a number of important studies,[283] the focus here is limited

---

[282]   James D. Hester, "Socio-Rhetorical Criticism and the Parable of the Tenants," *JSNT* 45 (1992): 34.

[283]   Foundational studies of the parables as a whole include Adolf Jülicher, *Die Gleichnisreden Jesu* (repr.; Darmstadt: Wissenschaftliche Buchgesellschaft, 1963); Rudolf Bultmann, *Die Geschichte der synoptischen Tradition* (Göttingen: Vandenhoeck & Ruprecht, 1931); C. H. Dodd, *Parables of the Kingdom* (London: Fontana Books, 1961); Joachim Jeremias, *The Parables of Jesus* (London: SCM Press, 1954); Klyne Snodgrass, *Stories with Intent: A Comprehensive Guide to the Parables of Jesus* (Grand Rapids: Eerdmans, 2008). Extensive recent studies of the parable of the wicked tenants include Wesley G. Olmstead, *Matthew's Trilogy of Parables* (Cambridge: Cambridge University Press, 2003); John S. Kloppenborg, *The Tenants in the Vineyard: Ideology, Economics, and Agrarian Conflict in Jewish Palestine* (Tübingen: Mohr Siebeck, 2006). For a summary of research on the parable, see Klyne Snodgrass, "Recent Research on the Parable of the Wicked Tenants: An Assessment," *BBR* 8 (1998): 187–216, who sum-marizes no less than sixteen possible interpretations of the parable. Snodgrass reason-ably argues that the diversity of interpretations is driven largely by three factors: 1) ignoring the connection between the parable and its Israelite/Jewish contexts, 2) a desire

to aspects of the parable that inform an analysis of the meaning of inheritance both in the passage and toward the interpretation of inheritance in Matthew's Gospel.

The majority of scholars regard the parable as an allegory.[284] Most of the details are not controversial: the trilogy of parables (21:23–22:14) is addressed to the chief priests and the elders of the people (21:23), the landowner is God (21:33), the tenants refer to the Jewish leaders (21:45), the slaves are the prophets of God who have been sent to Israel (21:34-36),[285] the son and heir refers to Jesus as the son of God (21:37-38), and the killing of the son refers to the crucifixion (21:39).[286] The two

---

to avoid thoughts of judgment, and 3) a desire to avoid a connection to Jesus. Snodgrass argues that when one recognizes that the parable is linked to HB texts, references judgment, and is reflective of Jesus' message, then a number of possible interpretations are disqualified.

[284] However, a number of studies have focused on the possibility of a socio-historical foundation for the traditions that may have produced the earliest form of the parable. In line with this approach, the parable is best not read as an allegory but as "realistic fiction," which attempts to define the story by social, legal, and economic realities that would have concerned its earliest hearers in first-century Palestine. The root meaning of the parable is best understood through first-century Palestine's economics, tenancy, debt, conflict, family dynamics, etc. These studies recognize that allegory is present in the parable *in its synoptic form* but argue that the allegorical dynamics were supplied by the evangelists and not essential to the original meaning and intent of the parable. Studies that take this approach, albeit with different nuances, include: Dodd, *Parables*, 93–98; Jülicher, *Die Gleichnisreden Jesu*, 65–85; Hester, "Socio-Rhetorical," 27–57; Kloppenborg, *Tenants*; Martin Hengel, "Das Gleichnis von den Weingärtnern Mc 12 1-12 im Lichte der Zenonpapyri und der rabbinischen Gleichnisse," *ZNW* 59 (1968): 1–39. This approach is critiqued by, among others, George J. Brooke, "4Q500 1 and the Use of Scripture in the Parable of the Vineyard," *DSD* 2, no. 3 (1995): 268–94. Brooke argues that proponents of the sociohistorical approach base their views upon negative assumptions regarding the use of allegory in Scripture, assume a single type of audience member for the "original" form of the parable, and anchor their reconstructed "original" form of the parable on first-century Palestine rather than the scriptural allusions that are clear in the extant versions. Brooke argues instead that the parable as it is found in the triple tradition is best read as an allegory based upon the reliance of allegorical scriptural allusions in the LXX, such as Isa 5:1-7. A critique is also offered by Snodgrass, "Recent Research," 198, who argues that socio-critical approaches seek to usurp the parable by ignoring the context of the HB and Judaism and by showing no bridge between socio-critical reflections regarding Palestine and the actual message of Jesus.

[285] Cf. Jer 7:25-27; 20:2; 26:21-23; 2 Chr 24:21; Neh 9:26.

[286] See the summary by Jack Dean Kingsbury, "The Parable of the Wicked Husbandmen and the Secret of Jesus' Divine Sonship in Matthew: Some Literary-Critical Observations," *JBL* 105, no. 4 (1986): 645. The elements listed here are those largely agreed upon by scholars, though there have been various theories on other elements of the parable. For example, Davies and Allison, *Matthew 19–28*, 176, argue that the "fruit" in the story stands for "what is owed to God."

most controversial aspects of the parable that affect the interpretation of inheritance are: 1) to what does the "vineyard" refer? (21:33), and 2) who are the ἔθνει who receive the kingdom in replacement of the Jewish leaders? (21:43). An analysis of these features is required before inheritance in the parable can be interpreted.

5.3.1. The Vineyard

The majority of interpreters argue that the vineyard represents either Israel,[287] Jerusalem,[288] or the kingdom of God.[289] The vineyard as an allegory of Israel makes sense in light of the way the parable interacts with Isa 5:1-7, where Israel is in view. However, there are some important differences between Isa 5:1-7 and the parable. In Isaiah, the fruit itself fails. In Matthew, the tenants fail to produce the fruit for the landowner. In Isaiah, the vineyard is judged and destroyed, while in Matthew it is the tenants who are judged and the vineyard is given to new tenants precisely so it can be stewarded properly.[290] Although Isa 5:1-7 serves as an

---

[287]   So N. T. Wright, *Jesus and the Victory of God* (Minneapolis: Fortress, 1996), 178; Jeremias, *Parables*, 55; Evans, *Matthew*, 370; France, *Matthew*, 811; Daniel J. Harrington, *The Gospel of Matthew* (SP; Collegeville, Minn.: Liturgical Press, 1991), 304.

[288]   So Schweizer, *Matthew*, 441.

[289]   So Hagner, *Matthew 14–28*, 620; Douglas R. A. Hare, *The Theme of Jewish Persecution of the Christians in the Gospel According to Matthew* (Cambridge: Cambridge University Press, 1967), 151. Davies and Allison, *Matthew 19–28*, 176, argue that the vineyard is each of these at different points in the parable. In 21:33 the vineyard is Israel, in 21:39 it stands for Jerusalem, and in 21:43 it stands for the kingdom. The symbolism of the vineyard is "fluid" throughout the parable. An additional option is argued by Snodgrass, *Stories*, 293. The vineyard is "the privilege of being engaged with the purposes of God, or in other words, election and the promises of God." See also Klyne Snodgrass, *The Parable of the Wicked Tenants* (Tübingen: Mohr Siebeck, 1983), 73–77.

[290]   The majority of interpreters agree that Isa 5:1-7 stands in the background of the parable. The debate centers on whether Matthew uses the parable in a one-to-one correspondence or appropriates the parable for new symbolic meaning. On the differences between Isa 5:1-7 and Matthew's version of the parable, see W. J. C. Weren, "The Use of Isaiah 5:1-7 in the Parable of the Tenants (Mark 12:1-12; Matthew 21:33-46)," *Bib* 79, no. 1 (1998): 1–26. Weren argues that Matthew brings over the aspects of Isa 5:1-7 from Mark's version of the parable but also strengthens the association between the two passages by his own changes. In particular, Matthew heightens the juridical aspects of the parable through his focus on the conflict with the Jewish leaders. In Isaiah, the juridical aspects of the parable were "originally aimed at the house of Israel," whereas in Matthew they are "now leveled at Jesus' opponents" (26). This is also the view of Konradt, *Israel*, 175–76, who argues that Jesus' parable departs from the original intent of Isa 5:1-7, when he states, "the failure of the vineyard is not under discussion here but rather the failure of the vinedressers, who have no counterpart in Isa 5:1-7." See also Keener, *Gospel*, 510, who argues, "while Jesus borrows the imagery of Isaiah, he adapts it so that the primary evildoers represent not Israel but her leaders."

important background to the parable, it is evident that Matthew's writer appropriated its language and meaning for his own ends so that a direct correlation regarding the use of symbols cannot be assumed.

A convincing solution to the identity of the vineyard is offered by George Brooke. He argues that the casting out of the son from the vineyard (21:39) refers to the crucifixion of Jesus outside of the city of Jerusalem (cf. 27:31-33), which makes little sense if either the land of Israel, or its people, is in view. Brooke also points out that few interpreters have taken seriously the symbolism tied to the wine press and the watchtower (21:33). He argues that the watchtower refers to the sanctuary, and the winepress refers to the altar and its drainage system, which would fit nicely within the vineyard if it referred to Jerusalem.[291] Brooke supports his interpretation by pointing to the position of the parable within its overall narrative context. At the start of the trilogy of parables, Jesus enters the temple and engages in discussion with the chief priests and the elders of the people (21:23), who realize that the parables refer to them (21:45).[292] The vineyard symbolizes the city of Jerusalem with the temple as its particular focus. Wright also takes the position that the temple is an important concern of the parable. He argues that the story functions as a justification for Jesus' actions in the temple relayed just before the trilogy of parables (21:12-17). The temple, both in Isa 5:1-7 and the later chapters of Matthew, invited prophetic denunciation. Jesus' temple action was a symbol of judgment in line with prophetic tradition, and the parable provided a larger narrative framework by "claiming to bring that tradition to its climax."[293]

[291]   Brooke, "4Q500," 284–85.

[292]   Brooke, "4Q500," 289.

[293]   Wright, *Jesus*, 498. Matthew 21:42 quotes Ps 118:22-23. There has been considerable discussion regarding whether or not this quotation was original to the earliest form of the parable or was added by the early church as it interacted with the parable in an allegorical context. The majority of socio-critical interpreters have argued for the latter. Brooke, "4Q500," 287–88, and Wright, *Jesus*, 498–501, argue that the use of Ps 118 is indispensable to Jesus' understanding of the temple incident and his role within it. Brooke argues that the placement of the quote from the psalm in the triple tradition, as well as the version of the parable in Gos. Thom. 65–66, coupled with the integral role the psalm plays in the story's interpretation, puts the burden of proof on interpreters to prove that it was a late addition. Wright argues that Ps 118 was designed to be sung by pilgrims going into the temple and is about building the temple, celebrating it, and sacrificing within it. Thus, it is appropriated by Jesus in a way that is apposite with its original intent. This is designed as "a cryptic assertion of Jesus' Messiahship and a further explanation of his action in the Temple" (500). See also Keener, *Gospel*, 515, who argues that, by quoting Ps 118:22, Jesus was making himself part of "the architecture of the temple" and therefore challenging the temple authorities. The authenticity of the quote from Ps 118 as an integral aspect of the original form of the parable is defended at length by Gregory R. Lanier, "The Rejected Stone in the Parable

This interpretation is potentially supported by other aspects of the surrounding narrative. Jesus enters Jerusalem (21:1-11), judges the temple (21:12-17), and then curses the fig tree for not producing fruit, judging it by declaring that it will never produce fruit again (21:18-22). As the temple incident is a judgment against the temple itself, the cursing of the fig tree is likely a judgment against its leaders, as the following verse then places Jesus in the temple in dialogue with those same leaders (21:23). It is not only the effectiveness of the temple that is in question, but also the authority of Jesus, and therefore the authority of the Jewish leaders by contrast. This is supported by the parable itself; the vineyard has *the ability* to produce fruit but is not functioning properly due to those responsible to steward it. This is why it is possible for the vineyard to produce fruit if the tenants are replaced (21:40-41). Like the fig tree, it is the leaders in Jerusalem who fail to produce the fruit God requires. Jesus' difficulty with the temple and its leaders typifies his relationship with Jerusalem as a whole. He laments over the city (23:37-39) and then immediately foretells of the destruction of the temple (24:1-2). During the passion narrative, it is the same chief priests and elders from the trilogy of parables who convince the Jerusalem crowds to join them in persecuting Jesus (27:20).[294] That Jesus' contentious relationship with Jerusalem and the temple meets its climax in the antagonism of the formerly favorable crowds (cf. 21:46) may be one explanation as to why Matthew's Jesus meets with his disciples in Galilee after the resurrection, while Luke's resurrection stories all take place in and near Jerusalem (Luke 24:13-53).[295] Based on the narrative evidence, Jesus'

---

of the Wicked Tenants: Defending the Authenticity of Jesus' Quotation of Ps 118:22," *JETS* 56, no. 4 (2013): 733–51.

[294] Persuasive is the argument of Konradt, *Israel*, 139–66, that the crowds depicted in Matt 27:20 are specified as a crowd *from Jerusalem*, which serves a narrative purpose regarding the building conflict between Jesus and the city. Jerusalem is the city that murders prophets and therefore takes decisive actions against Jesus. The persuasive work of the authorities over this specific crowd was necessary to depict the city in an antagonistic relationship with Jesus, but this does not render these crowds as a symbol for all Israel. Konradt connects 27:20 to the parable of the wicked tenants specifically in the way that they depict Jerusalem's resistance to God's messengers. The differentiation between the response of the crowds to Jesus versus the response of the Jewish leaders throughout the Gospel is not revoked by 27:20-25, but the function of the crowds is modified by Jerusalem's role in the conflict between Jesus and the Jewish leaders.

[295] Aside from a very brief meeting immediately following the resurrection, where Jesus instructs his followers to go to Galilee (28:9-10). It is recognized that the different locations of the post-resurrection narratives between the Gospels is a complex problem and that many solutions have been offered related to the interests of the evangelists and the provenance of the compositions. This is not to suggest the sole or even primary reason but simply to suggest that the lack of meetings between Jesus and his followers within Jerusalem fits the narrative development of Matthew's Gospel. N. T. Wright, *The*

contention in the parable and the surrounding narrative material is with Jerusalem in particular, and the functioning of the temple within Jerusalem, not Israel as a whole.[296] Therefore, it is more convincing to view the vineyard as Jerusalem, with special reference to the functionality of the temple and the ability of the leaders to produce the fruits required.[297]

Although Jesus' discourse with the rich man takes place before Jesus enters Jerusalem, there is an important point of connection, other than inheritance language, between that story and Jesus' conflict with Jerusalem, the temple, and the temple's leaders. Among the reasons for Jesus' judgment against Jerusalem is the likelihood that he was angered by the vast economic divisions between rich and poor, between those who lived in luxury and those who lived in destitution. Jesus' vision for Israel was quite different. As Helen Bond argues, "the vision of the kingdom of God in Galilee was one in which economic divisions of rich and poor were dissolved, where widows and orphans could live in security, and where oppression and exploitation would have no place."[298] The ethical dimension of Matthew's Gospel emphasizes the disadvantaged, and Jesus placed the onus of extreme social injustice on the Jewish leaders. This is the primary intention of the parable of the wedding banquet (22:1-14), which directly follows and compounds the meaning of the parable of the wicked tenants. The parable of the wedding banquet refers to a community of people on the margins of society who would not previously have been invited to the banquet, and may refer directly to Jesus' disciples, who are meek and poor in spirit, and have abandoned their places in the social structure in order to follow Jesus (19:29).[299]

Resurrection of the Son of God (Minneapolis: Fortress, 2003), 642–45, argues that Jesus' meeting with his disciples in Matt 28:16 calls to mind major themes throughout the First Gospel, such as Galilee, discipleship, and the mountain. Bond, *Historical*, 172, suggests that the different locations speak to the commissioning of Jesus' followers at the beginnings of the new communities associated with each Gospel.

[296]   Though, as discussed throughout this chapter, Jesus' contention with the Jewish leadership is prevalent both within Jerusalem and throughout Israel more broadly.

[297]   So also Brooke, "4Q500," 294, the vineyard is "Jerusalem and its temple and all that takes place upon the altar." The parable refers to those who may "participate in the cult, in the right worship of God." An important detail of the parable that has occasioned considerable debate is the location of the landowner, who leased the vineyard to the tenants and went into ἀπεδήμησεν (another country, 21:33). Given Matthew's favor toward Galilee, condemnation of the functioning of the temple, and Jesus' entrance into Jerusalem from the surrounding regions *within Israel*, it makes sense to understand ἀπεδήμησεν as a reference to Israel outside of Jerusalem. Rather than a literal country, the allegorical nature of the parable appropriates the term to refer to geographic space outside of the vineyard, being Jerusalem, while confirming God's presence in, and favor toward, Israel at large.

[298]   Bond, *Historical*, 142.

[299]   Though this invitation may also refer to the offer for gentiles to join the people of God. Davies and Allison, *Matthew 19–28*, 202, argue that those invited in

Their invitation comes at the expense of the Jewish leaders, who had the opportunity to attend but spurned God instead. Both parables depict the imminent arrival of God and the judgment of Jerusalem,[300] and together with the story of the rich man, these stories contribute to the idea that the kingdom of God belongs to those who shake free of complacency and comfort in order to address injustice.

5.3.2. The ἔθνος of Matthew 21:43

The most controversial aspect of the parable of the wicked tenants has been the identity of the ἔθνος in 21:43. According to this verse, the kingdom of God will be taken away from the chief priests and Pharisees and given to an ἔθνος that will "produce its fruits" (ποιοῦντι τοὺς καρποὺς αὐτῆς). Stanton has been influential in arguing for what, until recently, has been the dominant view. The Jewish leaders symbolized in the parable represent not only themselves but the entirety of Israel.[301] It is all Israel, through its disobedience to God and rejection of Jesus, who will be replaced by an ἔθνος. Whether ἔθνος is translated as "nation"[302] or "people,"[303] the result is largely the same; Israel is being *replaced* and the kingdom of God is given to someone else.[304] The primary options

---

place of the Jewish leaders stand both for "the universal mission of the church" and for an offer to "the poor and maimed and blind and lame" mentioned in Luke 14:21. See also Keener, *Gospel*, 518, who argues that although Matthew's version focuses more on the judgment against the Jewish leaders, it may also address the marginalized group depicted by Luke 14:21.

[300] So Paul Foster, *Community, Law and Mission in Matthew's Gospel* (Tübingen: Mohr Siebeck, 2004), 232, the parable of the wedding feast is about "the demise of Jerusalem as the power base of the Jewish nation."

[301] So Luz, *Studies*, 246, "the behavior of Israel's leaders had dramatic consequences for the whole people under their charge." See also Jeremias, *Parables*, 55; Hare, *Theme*, 151; Hagner, *Matthew 14–28*, 617; France, *Matthew*, 816.

[302] So Olmstead, *Matthew 15–28*, 179; France, *Matthew*, 816. Stanton, *Gospel*, 11–12, 151–52, argues that the term ἔθνος is best translated as "nation," denoting a "new people," which refers to the self-understanding of Matthew's community as a "third-race over against both Jews and Gentiles." See also Georg Strecker, *Der Weg der Gerechtigkeit: Untersuchung zur Theologie des Matthäus* (Göttingen: Vandenhoeck & Ruprecht, 1971), 33; Hare, *Theme*, 157.

[303] So Luz, *Studies*, 246; Schweizer, *Matthew*, 414.

[304] Stanton, *Gospel*, 11–12, 151–52. Stanton's perspective derives from his socio-critical approach. He argues that the Matthean community is in view, which saw itself as a separate entity from Judaism. Matthew relates the quote of Ps 118:22 in Matt 21:42 to his own community, as a stone rejected by the Jewish leaders but accepted by God. The interpretation of Johannes Weiss, *Jesus' Proclamation of the Kingdom of God* (ed. Richard Hyde Hiers and David Larrimore Holland; London: SCM Press, 1971), 86–88, has not found traction in recent discussion but is worth noting. Weiss argues that 21:43 refers to the taking away of the kingdom from the Jewish leaders "unless some special

presented for the identity of the ἔθνος are either the gentiles[305] or the Christian church made up of both Jews and gentiles who are faithful to Jesus.[306] Stanton's position is supported by Wesley G. Olmstead, who argues that the parable of the wicked tenants is a "passion parable" that must be read in light of the passion narrative. In the passion narrative, the chief priests and elders have convinced the crowds to share in their responsibility for Jesus' execution; therefore, this responsibility is best read back into the parable. In this way, the crowds, representing Israel, lose their share in the kingdom along with the Jewish leaders. Israel has "filled up their cup of rebellion" and so elicited God's judgment.[307] Jesus is the fulfillment and climax of Israel's story in such a way that Israel loses its nationalistic privilege and is replaced and reconstituted along the lines of faith.[308]

---

deliverance occurs" but that the establishment of the kingdom of God was put on hold until the guilt of the people could be removed, which was done through Jesus' death as a ransom for the people. Weiss' interpretation does not take into account Jesus' conflict with the Jewish leaders as a theme in Matthew's Gospel.

[305]   So Dodd, *Parables*, 95; Jeremias, *Parables*, 55.

[306]   So France, *Matthew*, 817: the church is a "reconstituted Israel." See also Hagner, *Matthew 14–28*, 617, 623–24. Hagner recognizes that the parable is directed at the Jewish leaders specifically but argues that this is done only to highlight their culpability. Stanton, *Gospel*, 271, 276, argues that the vineyard in the parable refers to the kingdom of God, which is transferred from Israel to the church. In Stanton's socio-critical approach, the church more specifically refers to Matthew's community that replaced "rejected Israel." Pennington, *Sermon*, 95–96, follows Stanton, but without the socio-critical approach to a Matthean community. However, on this point, Pennington is contradictory. He argues in favor of Stanton's view that the ἔθνος of 21:43 refers to a "new people" who are given the kingdom but uses *negative* references to gentiles as ἔθνος and ἐθνικός throughout Matthew to demonstrate that these terms often refer not to ethnicity *per se* but to those who do not follow Jesus. He argues that this demonstrates that these terms are drawn not along ethnic lines but are instead based upon a faith response to Jesus. While the argument holds for much of Matthew, Pennington does not recognize that, in 21:43, ἔθνος is used *positively*, not for those who do not follow Jesus, but for those who receive God's favor and will be given the kingdom. Therefore, Pennington's argument regarding the use of ἔθνος throughout Matthew would not apply to 21:43. Furthermore, removing the ethnic connotations from the term also works against Stanton's view. If the ἔθνος who receives the kingdom is not an ethic group, then those who have the kingdom taken away from them are likely not an ethnic group either, making it unlikely that all Israel is in view. It is important to recognize that, while Pennington affirms Stanton's interpretation, he also engages positively with the views of Konradt (*Israel*, 97, n. 34), who argues that Israel has not been replaced by the church in 21:43. Pennington notes that he is sympathetic to Konradt's view regarding an ongoing mission to ethnic Israel but sides with Stanton regarding the replacement of Israel as the people of God.

[307]   See Jack Dean Kingsbury, *Matthew: Structure, Christology, Kingdom* (Minneapolis: Fortress, 1975), 152–57.

[308]   Wesley G. Olmstead, "A Gospel for a New Nation: Once More, the ἔθνος of Matthew 21.43," in Gurtner et al., *Jesus, Matthew's Gospel and Early Christianity:*

Two critiques can be made here regarding Olmstead's arguments. First, although Olmstead is persuasive that elements of the passion narrative are best read back into the parable of the wicked tenants, he does not distinguish between the crowds in each story, despite the fact that Matthew's writer does so explicitly. In the parable, the crowds are given a positive role as those who favored Jesus and regarded him as a prophet (21:46). It makes little narrative sense to read a negative role for the crowds into a parable where they are explicitly perceived in a positive way. Furthermore, Konradt persuasively argues that the crowds who turn against Jesus in the passion narrative serve the story as a cautionary tale within Jerusalem rather than a representative of Israel as a whole.[309]

Second, Olmstead's arguments regarding Jesus as the fulfillment and climax of Israel's story do not require a *rejection* of Israel, or a *replacement* of Israel,[310] but rather *rescue* and *redemption*. Olmstead convincingly argues that Israel in Matthew has been reconstituted in such a way that the community is redrawn along the lines of faith, which includes gentiles who are faithful to the Messiah. However, the inclusion of the gentiles and redefinition of God's people was always an eschatological expectation of the Jewish Scriptures, and an integral part of the Abrahamic promise, and existed in various textual traditions alongside the expectation of the salvation and redemption of Israel. That Israel is reconstituted along the lines of faith does not stem from judgment against it, but the opposite, it stems from a reaffirmation of Israel as Jesus brings the eschatological expectation of God's people into his own teaching and mission. Rather than Matthew's presentation of a new people of God "over against" Israel,[311] their reconstitution *extends from* Israel as the next soteriological stage of Israel's story based on the coming of the Messiah. The church is not born out of Israel's rejection but out of Jesus' activity on its behalf. When Matthew's writer, in the midst of recording Jesus' salvific-historical Israelite genealogy, wrote

---

Studies in Memory of Graham N. Stanton, 113–32, and Olmstead, *Trilogy*, 117, 161–62. See also W. G. Kümmel, *Introduction to the New Testament* (London: SCM Press, 1975), 116, "the unbelieving Jews are replaced by the eschatological people of God, who are identified by bringing forth fruits, so that the distinction between Jew and Gentile is no longer significant." Kümmel argues that the church is the "true" Israel. And according to Hare, *Theme*, 157, the church is not a continuation of Israel but replaces Israel.

[309]   See Konradt, *Israel*, 127, 160. Konradt argues persuasively that Matthew's writer goes to great lengths to emphasize the distance between the authorities and the people, and that it does not follow that the actions of certain members of the crowds in the passion narrative would serve to undermine this fact.

[310]   So Olmstead's language. See *Trilogy*, 117.

[311]   So Stanton's language. See *Gospel*, 151.

that Jesus would "save his people from their sins" (1:21), it is hard to imagine that he expected to record later in the narrative that this would be done by judging them and replacing them with another people. In the Matthean narrative, Jesus' fulfillment of the Israelite story is not *replacement* but rather *reaffirmation* through *redemption* as Jesus inaugurates Israel's eschatological potential. Matthew's Jesus did not come to reject Israel but to guarantee its future, and this is done precisely by gathering both Jews and gentiles around himself through faith and the pursuit of "greater righteousness." Jews and gentiles, or Israel and the church, are not competitive communities.[312] The goal of Matthew's Jesus is to recalibrate both Israel and the gentiles around his particular brand of discipleship through a successful mission both to his fellow Jews (10:5-6) and the nations (28:18-20). It is reading too much into the First Gospel to argue that its writer envisioned the replacement of Israel based upon its failure. The redemption of Israel was clearly on the writer's mind, and Israel becomes its truest self by being a light to the nations through the coming of its Messiah.[313]

The formerly dominant view epitomized by Stanton and Olmstead has given way in recent years to a counterproposal that some have described as an "emerging consensus."[314] Although the proponents of this new emerging consensus present their views with differing nuances, its most important tenet is that the parable of the wicked tenants is directed not toward all Israel, but the Jewish authorities

---

[312]   *Contra* Foster, *Community*, 234, who argues that Matthew's writer saw Christian communities as "the replacement for Israel" and that the goal of the writer was "an attempt to move them from an Israel based adherence to a more Gentile oriented mission."

[313]   It is recognized that much of this is similar to some of Olmstead's language. For example, in "Gospel," 124, Olmstead argues that Jesus sends out his apostles "to sweep the nations into the one people of God in fulfilment to his promise to Abraham." He also argues that Jesus' mission is *to Israel* in order to reconstitute the nation around himself. I affirm these conclusions. My disagreement comes in the particular way that Olmstead argues that the kingdom is taken away from all Israel as it is judged, rejected, and replaced. Such negative pronouncements are not required by the text, as will become clearer below. Noteworthy is that Olmstead, *Trilogy*, 162, admits that Matthew's Gospel does not allow one to conclude that all subgroups within Israel are equally culpable for Jesus' execution, that the crowds are a sympathetic group, and that the greater onus rests upon Israel's leaders. In light of this admission, it is difficult to follow his argument that all of Israel is judged and rejected in the same way. Finally, Olmstead argues that the loss of the kingdom refers to the *nation* but that the mission to Israel continues and that the Jews have a chance to respond in faith (162–63). However, there is no indication that those who lose the kingdom are offered a chance to regain it. To lose the kingdom is to lose a share in the eschatological future. It is difficult to reconcile the rhetoric of the parable with Olmstead's argument that all Israel is rejected but that a mission to Israel continues.

[314]   So Olmstead, "Gospel," 115.

alone, and therefore the kingdom of God will be taken from them alone and not from the nation as a whole. The vineyard has not failed and therefore is not judged. It is the leaders who have failed to steward the vineyard and produce the fruit required of them.[315] The trilogy of parables is directed at the leadership (21:23) and the leadership recognizes upon hearing the parable of the wicked tenants that Jesus was talking about them (21:45). The crowds view Jesus positively and are differentiated from the leadership (21:46).[316] It is the Jewish authorities, not all Israel, who have forfeited their role by opposing God's messengers,[317] culminating in their rejection of God's own son.[318] Rather than representing all Israel, the authorities are held responsible for their own actions, an idea that fits nicely with Jesus' conflicts with the authorities throughout the First Gospel. The consequence for the authorities is that the kingdom of God will be taken away from them (21:43), a judgment made about the Pharisees in 23:13.

The ἔθνος serves as the counterpart to those who lose the kingdom. If those who have the kingdom taken away refers to "the nation" of Israel, then it makes sense that, as a counterpart, the kingdom would then be given to a "nation" as well (either the gentiles or the church). However, as we have seen throughout this chapter, one of the core themes in all of Matthew's Gospel is the strong differentiation between, on the one hand, false disciples epitomized by the scribes, Pharisees, and other Jewish leaders, and, on the other hand, the "ideal" disciples, epitomized by those who sacrifice for Jesus' sake, develop kingdom-oriented dispositions, and pursue "greater righteousness." If the identity of those from whom the kingdom is taken away is the Jewish leadership, which fits both the direct context as well as the overall Matthean narrative, then it follows that the ἔθνος refers to the "ideal disciple" as their counterpart.[319] Rather than a "nation," the term ἔθνος

---

[315] So Davies and Allison, *Matthew 19–28*, 189; Snodgrass, *Stories*, 296; Gundry, *Matthew*, 430; Saldarini, *Matthew's*, 59–62; Sim, *Gospel*, 148–49; Keener, *Gospel*, 511; Konradt, *Israel*, 172–93; Markus Bockmuehl, *Seeing the Word: Refocusing New Testament Study* (Grand Rapids: Baker Academic, 2006), 218–19.

[316] Konradt, *Israel*, 183, points out that the specific identification of the chief priests and Pharisees in 21:45 is a Matthean addition in order to further differentiate the leadership from the crowds.

[317] Cf. Matt 21:34-36 and 23:31-32, where Jesus places the onus for the murder of the prophets on the Pharisees.

[318] See Konradt, *Israel*, 191.

[319] Similar is Konradt, *Israel*, 185, who refers to the ἔθνος as the "true followers" of Jesus. Although Olmstead, *Trilogy*, 117, argues for a different overall conclusion, his description of the contrary nature between those who lose the kingdom and the ἔθνος is apt: "this ethical description of the new people functions both as an indictment of those now rejected and as a warning to those who would not be rejected." There is a strong

refs to a "people,"[320] who are the ideal disciples who ποιοῦντι τοὺς καρποὺς (produce the fruits) of the kingdom.[321]

This interpretation is supported by the nature of the kingdom in the parable and its relationship to the other two passages discussed in this chapter. The kingdom in 21:43 is best understood as a reference to future salvation. To "produce the fruits" of the kingdom refers to its ethics.[322] It is those who develop and exhibit kingdom dispositions who have a part in the eschatological kingdom in 5:3-12[323] and those who sacrifice for Jesus' sake and live according to his standards as disciples who receive eternal life in the kingdom in 19:23-30. In each case, the ideal disciple receives a share in the kingdom of God. Jesus' closest disciples, "the Twelve," receive a special role of authority in the kingdom over redeemed Israel (19:28), which would be nonsensical if Israel lost its share in the kingdom.[324]

"in-group" and "out-group" dynamic in play, and the reception of the kingdom is used as an identifier of those in the "in-group."

[320]   Saldarini, *Matthew's*, 59–61, argues that the term ἔθνος has a wide range of meaning across various Greek sources and that "a people" is appropriate to the context. Olmstead, "Gospel," 127–31, attempts to invalidate this conclusion by arguing that ἔθνος in Matthew has a more limited range of meaning, is never without ethnic import, and should be rendered "nation." Konradt, *Israel*, 183, n. 90, argues that Olmstead does not account for all the evidence, especially regarding the potential differences in nuance between the singular and plural forms. Davies and Allison, *Matthew 19–28*, 189, and Kloppenborg, *Tenants*, 191, argue that the plural would be expected if ethnicity were in view and that the singular demands a different interpretation. See also Bockmuehl, *Seeing*, 219, who argues that the singular use of ἔθνος is decisive against viewing it as a reference against national Israel.

[321]   It could be argued that the ideal disciples who produce the fruits of the kingdom are the same group as those who make up the church. However, the church in Matthew has a limited (albeit important) role, and as Konradt, *Israel*, 178–79, 184, argues, the church is a *corpus mixtum* and that the term ἔθνος is poorly suited in Matthew to describe it. Although the church is undoubtedly something Matthew's Jesus intended to build toward, and although he explicitly associated the church with the kingdom (16:18-19), Jesus' development of ideal disciples is a far more dominant theme in the overall narrative of the Gospel, and the ideal disciple serves as a more logical counterpart to the false disciples depicted by the Jewish leaders. A similar argument is made by Sim, *Gospel*, 148–49, who recognizes that the church is a poor fit for the identification of the ἔθνος, though he argues that instead the term refers to Matthew's own community or Christian Judaism in general. Similar to Sim is Saldarini, *Matthew's*, 60, who argues that ἔθνος refers to Matthew's "own group in a restricted sense."

[322]   See Konradt, *Israel*, 178. See also Olmstead, *Trilogy*, 117, the nation God raises up in faithfulness is defined along ethical, not ethnic, lines.

[323]   See Jeremias, *Parables*, 60, who associates the parable of the wicked tenants directly with the "poor" and "meek" of Matt 5:3 and 5 and argues that the original intent of the parable "vindicates the offer of the gospel to the poor."

[324]   The connection between 19:28 and 21:43 is also made by Bockmuehl, *Seeing*, 218, who argues that the ἔθνος itself refers to the restored nation of Israel, and Reeves,

5.3.3. Inheritance Traditions Antecedent to Matthew 21:38

As previously stated regarding potential antecedents to Matt 5:5 and 19:29, the following is not to suggest that each of these traditions had a genetic influence on inheritance in Matt 21:38. The purpose of the following section is to survey antecedent traditions that may have contributed to the overall concept history of inheritance in ways that may have impacted, directly or indirectly, the role of inheritance in Matthew's version of the parable of the wicked tenants. Some of these traditions have a greater potential for influence than others.

1. The Hexateuch

Land inheritance contexts from the Hexateuch form the foundational background of inheritance and kingdom contexts in Matthew, and this may be evident more in the parable of the wicked tenants than in any other passage in Matthew's Gospel. Leviticus 25:23 depicts Yahweh as declaring his ownership of the land, and the passage refers to the Israelites as תושבים (tenants). God prepared the land before the Israelites took possession of it (Exod 23:20), and he directs the treatment and cultivation of the land to his own specifications (Exod 23:10-12). God is never depicted as surrendering his ultimate ownership and control. The land inheritance was a gift (Deut 4:21), and the community was tightly regulated for the strict purpose of maintaining the holiness of inherited land, including the offering of the first fruits of the land to God (Deut 26:1). God places a condition on the inheritance, namely, that if the Israelites will not be obedient to his commands, then they will not inherit the land (Deut 4:1; 12:9-12). When they enter the land, if they rebel against God, then the inheritance will not be retained. The story of the Hexateuch depicts the wilderness generation as rebellious, and it is said that their generation would not be allowed to partake in the inheritance (Num 32:10-15).

In the parable, God remains the landowner and specifies the required treatment of the vineyard (in this case, Jerusalem and its temple). Obedience, and the giving of the first fruits, is still required of the tenants. Jesus appropriates these foundational concepts to refer to the Jewish leadership as those who, like the rebellious wilderness generation, have forfeited their ability to "enter" the secured space of their expectations (the promised land/the promised kingdom). Although, in the Hexateuch, the Israelites were directed by God to "disinherit" the prior inhabitants

---

Matthew, 428, who argues that it is specifically "the twelve" who will replace Israel's failed leadership.

of the land by force,[325] the parable depicts the Jewish leaders as those who take a similar action *against God himself*, by virtue of their rejection and execution of his own son. Taking the inheritance away from the son, and therefore from God himself, would be unthinkable, but this sort of irrational behavior on the part of the Jewish leaders is consistent with Matthew's depiction of them both in Matt 23 and in the passion narrative.[326] The kingdom, like the land, is still regarded as given (δίδωμι) by God as a gift, but God exercises his right to take the kingdom from false shepherds and give it to those who are faithful.

2. The Books of Samuel

In the books of Samuel, the phrase נחלת יהוה (Yahweh's inheritance) is a "catch-all" phrase that refers to any and all things that belong to Yahweh. God entrusts his possessions, being his land and his people, to a king, whose role it is to maintain, protect, and steward God's inheritance. To be cut off from נחלת יהוה, as is so often the concern in passages where the phrase is found,[327] is much more about being cut off from a relationship to Yahweh himself than from his possessions.[328]

In the parable of the wicked tenants, the vineyard, and all contained therein, belongs to Yahweh, who entrusts the business of the vineyard to his son, who, throughout Matthew's Gospel, is depicted as the heir to the Davidic throne established in the books of Samuel.[329] The inheritance *belongs to the son*;[330] it is his to do with what he chooses, but rather than embrace the son and therefore have a share in the inheritance, and therefore the kingdom of God, the tenants commit an act of

---

[325]   See 2.2.1.2.

[326]   Attempts have been made to rationalize the actions of the tenants in their attempts to "disinherit" the son. Various theories are summarized by Davies and Allison, *Matthew 19–28*, 183, such as that the tenants may have believed the landowner already dead, leaving the land up for grabs. Hester, "Socio-Rhetorical," 36–48, arguing that the original version of the parable would have been about Palestinian land disputes, suggests that it is the tenants, not the landowner, who are the sympathetic figures. The tenant farmers are landless peasants who have lost their own land and are desperately trying to protect their livelihood. In Hester's view, it is precisely the inheritance contexts of the HB that explain that the tenant farmers had a right to the land and to protect it at all costs. However, in its Matthean form, and within the Matthean narrative, it is likely futile to rationalize the activities of the authorities. Such rationalizations push the details of the allegory too far. In the conclusion of Kloppenborg, *Tenants*, 334, the attempt by the tenants is "plainly unrealistic." The point is simply that Israel's false shepherds attempted to run the temple, and lead the people in Jerusalem, on their own terms rather than God's. See McNeile, *Gospel*, 310, the actions of the tenants "contribut[e] to the picture of their insensate hostility."

[327]   1 Samuel 26:19; 2 Sam 20:19; 21:3.

[328]   See 2.3.2.

[329]   See Willitts, *Matthew's*, 95–173.

[330]   See Gundry, *Matthew*, 427.

treachery and attempt to secure the entire inheritance for themselves.[331] As in the books of Samuel, having a share in the inheritance is primarily about having a special relationship to God, and to be cut off from the inheritance is to be cut off from God himself, which is evidenced by the tenants' loss of the kingdom (21:43). It is in this detail that a difference can be seen between the vineyard and the kingdom. The Jewish leaders targeted in the story were charged with producing fruits in the vineyard itself, referring to Jerusalem and the temple. However, the kingdom of God, referring to God's rule over all he possesses, is not signified by the vineyard alone, but by the inheritance of the son. It is not just the vocation of leadership in Jerusalem that is lost by the false shepherds but rather a share in the inheritance as a whole, which refers to the earth (5:5), eternal life (19:29), and an eschatological future in the kingdom of God (21:43). To embrace the son is to continue to have a role in his inheritance.[332] As is the case in inheritance contexts throughout Jewish literature, inheritance is primarily a relational term; to be cut off from the inheritance is to be cut off from God himself.

3. 1 Kings 21:19

Ahab's murder of Naboth, to take possession (ירש) of Naboth's vineyard, has obvious thematic links to the parable of the wicked tenants.[333] Naboth's intent was to protect the inheritance of his fathers (נחלת אבתי), and Ahab resorted to murder to take it by force. Ahab was rebuked by Elijah, and God relented of his judgment against Ahab because he repented (1 Kgs 21:27-29). Two main points can be drawn by parallels between the two passages. First, there was a precedent that, even when *performed* by an Israelite king, committing murder to abscond with another's inheritance was declared by God to be a vile act. Killing God's son would certainly be met with hostility by God.[334] Second, repentance could bring about a measure of favor by God, but hearing the parable only spiraled the Jewish leaders closer to committing the murder that the parable foretold.[335]

---

[331]   See Keener, *Gospel*, 513.

[332]   See McNeile, *Gospel*, 310. Early Christians worked out the idea that all God's sons can be united with Jesus as "coheirs" (Rom 8:17).

[333]   See 2.3.3.

[334]   So Keener, *Gospel*, 514.

[335]   Kloppenborg, *Tenants*, 39, also links the parable with 1 Kgs 21:19, noting that the Hellenistic and Roman contexts of the parable serve to heighten the importance of inheritance. In the Roman period, inheritance was even less secure due to confiscations by the state and a growing number of economic reasons that the security of an inheritance would come into question. He states, "the parable's underscoring of the legitimacy of inheritance is not simply an innocent reflection of an old Israelite practice of land tenure but an *assertion* of the importance of inheritance in a world where it could no longer be taken for granted."

5.3.4. The Meaning of Inheritance in Matthew 21:38

The inheritance in Matt 21:38 belongs to Jesus, the son of God. It refers to his stake in all that is owned by God (the landowner), depicted in the parable of the wicked tenants as the kingdom of God. The parable follows Hexateuchal traditions regarding God's perpetual ownership of the inheritance, the land-grant concept, and the need of God's people to produce the fruits required of those who take part in the inheritance. Throughout the HB, God's own inheritance often refers to any and all things owned by God, but especially his land and his people, and in Matthew's Gospel God's reign over the kingdom serves to encapsulate this concept. In the parable, the son's inheritance does not refer to the vineyard alone but to the whole of the kingdom, a kingdom the son shares with those who embrace him. To embrace the son is to continue to have a role in his inheritance. As is the case in inheritance contexts throughout Jewish literature, inheritance is primarily a relational term—to be cut off from the inheritance is to be cut off from God himself.

The parable concerns the loss of a share in the inheritance by the Jewish leaders in Jerusalem. It is the Jewish authorities, not all Israel, who have forfeited their role by opposing God's messengers, culminating in their rejection of God's own son. Despite their efforts, the inheritance continues to belong to the son, who will be vindicated by God in the resurrection (21:40, 42).[336] It is not just the vocation of leadership in Jerusalem that is lost by the false shepherds but also a share in the inheritance as a whole. Their share in the kingdom is given instead to an ἔθνος, which refers to Jesus' ideal disciples who sacrifice for Jesus' sake, develop kingdom-oriented dispositions, and pursue "greater righteousness." These "ideal disciples" are those same disciples who share in the inheritance of the earth (5:5) and eternal life in the kingdom (19:29). It is important to consider the striking juxtaposition between Jesus' ideal disciples and the Jewish leaders. The ideal disciple is one who is "meek" and who inherits the earth by relying on God following the son (5:5). As Stephen Westerholm writes, the meek "are those who renounce the world's pursuit of power, become like children, serve others, and bear their abuse."[337] The ideal disciple is humble and nonviolent. Conversely, the Jewish leaders are depicted as those who kill the son and attempt to secure the inheritance through violent force (21:38-39). Although Israel, as a whole, is not replaced, the challenge

---

[336]   See Garland, *Reading*, 219.

[337]   Stephen Westerholm, *Understanding Matthew: The Early Christian Worldview of the First Gospel* (Grand Rapids: Baker Academic, 2006), 131.

to its leaders does serve to reorient the Jewish conception of Israelite identity, requiring a new form of discipleship, centered upon Jesus, for those who hope to have a share in the inheritance.[338]

5.4. Inheritance in Matthew 25:34

Τότε ἐρεῖ ὁ βασιλεὺς τοῖς ἐκ δεξιῶν αὐτοῦ· δεῦτε οἱ εὐλογημένοι τοῦ πατρός μου, κληρονομήσατε τὴν ἡτοιμασμένην ὑμῖν βασιλείαν ἀπὸ καταβολῆς κόσμου.

Then the king will say to those on his right hand, "Come, those who are blessed by my father, inherit the kingdom prepared for you from the foundation of the world."

The judgment scene of Matt 25:31-46 is the climax of Matthew's five discourses.[339] The genre of the pericope is disputed,[340] though solving that dilemma is not necessary for evaluating the role of inheritance in this passage.[341] Jesus is the king who comes in glory to declare a judgment over "all the nations" (πάντα τὰ ἔθνη) who are gathered before him. He separates the sheep from the goats, the sheep being those who have found his favor and who will receive an eschatological reward, and the goats being those destined for eschatological punishment.[342] The sheep are those who were hospitable toward "the least of these," and the goats are those who showed no hospitality. The two most controversial

[338]   See Wright, *Jesus*, 178–79. See also Nolland, *Matthew*, 879, rather than national identity Jesus' disciples are those who respond to the message of the kingdom.

[339]   A well-known history of the interpretation of this passage is Sherman Gray, *The Least of My Brothers, Matthew 25:31-46: A History of Interpretation* (SBLDS 114; Atlanta: Scholars, 1989).

[340]   A number of scholars categorize the story as a parable in keeping with the structure of the previous three pericope (Matt 24:45–25:30). See, for example, Jeremias, *Parables*, 144; Reeves, *Matthew*, 477; Evans, *Matthew*, 422. Others argue that, despite some similarity to parables, the story does not contain enough parabolic elements to qualify and therefore functions as an "apocalyptic vision." Along these lines see France, *Matthew*, 960; Hagner, *Matthew 14–28*, 740; McNeile, *Gospel*, 368; Schweizer, *Matthew*, 475.

[341]   Though see Stanton, *Gospel*, 221–30, who argues that the genre of the pericope as an "apocalyptic discourse" presents a break with the preceding parables, necessitating a difference in interpretive approach and cutting off the meaning of the symbols of 25:31-46 from the themes and intent of the preceding passages. In Stanton's view, the break with the previous parables provided by the change in genre is vital to understanding the identity of those to whom the pericope refers. Even if Stanton is correct that 25:31-46 is not a parable, the change in genre does not guarantee a complete break in meaning and intent with the previous passages. As it stands, the interpretation of inheritance offered here is not dependent on the genre of the pericope.

[342]   On the imagery of sheep and goats in the pericope, see Kathleen Weber, "The Image of Sheep and Goats in Matthew 25:31-46," *CBQ* 59, no. 4 (1997): 657–78.

aspects of the passage are the most important for understanding inheritance: 1) who are πάντα τὰ ἔθνη (all the nations) in 25:32, and 2) who are τούτων τῶν ἀδελφῶν μου τῶν ἐλαχίστων (those who are my brothers, the least) in 25:40? Analyzing the second problem assists in analyzing the first, so they are discussed in reverse order. A treatment of these two issues is followed by consideration of possible traditions antecedent to Matt 25:31-46 that may have had an influence on the use of inheritance in this passage.

5.4.1. The "Least of These" in Matthew 25:40 and 45

There are two main approaches to understanding the identity of the "least of these" in Matt 25:31-46 (albeit with a number of variations). The first, the "universalist" approach, regards the "least of these" as all in the world who are needy. Therefore, those designated as sheep, who have found favor with the king, are those who have acted hospitably toward any who are in need.[343] The second, the "particularist" approach, regards the "least of these" as a particular group associated directly with Jesus, most commonly the church,[344] though some scholars argue in favor of a subset of the church, such as missionaries or Jewish Christians.[345]

The universalist approach is advocated by, among others, Davies and Allison. They argue that the generous deeds described in Matt 25:35-36 are not specific to any group and function as general deeds of mercy in various places in Jewish literature.[346] They argue that such works are a sign of salvation and therefore describe the deeds

---

[343] So Jeremias, *Parables*, 145; Schweizer, *Matthew*, 477; Davies and Allison, *Matthew 19–28*, 429.

[344] So Stanton, *Gospel*, 207–31; France, *Matthew*, 958; Hagner, *Matthew 14–28*, 744–45; Garland, *Reading*, 243.

[345] So Lamar Cope, "Matthew XXV: 31-46, The Sheep and the Goats Reinterpreted," *NovT* 11, no. 1 (1969): 32–44; Joong Suk Suh, "Das Weltgericht und die Matthäische Gemeinde," *NovT* 48, no. 3 (2006): 217–33; Gundry, *Matthew*, 514; Saldarini, *Matthew's*, 252. For a summary, see Davies and Allison, *Matthew 19–28*, 428–29. John R. Donahue, "The 'Parable' of the Sheep and Goats: A Challenge to Christian Ethics," *Theological Studies* 47 (1986): 3–31, cites the study of Johannes Friedrich, *Gott im Bruder? Eine methodenkritische Untersuchung von Redaktion, Überlieferung und Traditionen in MT 25,31-46* (Stuttgart: Calwer, 1977), who argued that the Matthean pericope was based on an original parable that referred to judgment based on the treatment of the poor and was then redacted by Matthew's writer toward concern for missionaries; he compares it with the study by Egon Brandenburger, *Das Recht des Welternrichters: Untersuchung zu Matthäus 25, 31-46* (Stuttgart: Katholisches Bibelwerk, 1980), who argued that the original parable was particularistic and that the Matthean redactor universalized it.

[346] See their chart of the relevant literature at Davies and Allison, *Matthew 19–28*, 426.

of a disciple but that the passage also makes clear the "just" includes those outside of the church who serve in that way.[347] They argue for a non-ecclesiological use of the term ἀδελφῶν, based upon its use in Matt 5:22-24 and 7:3-5, and that the passage simply describes Jesus giving mercy to all who are merciful in a general sense (cf. Matt 5:7).[348]

The particularist approach is advocated by, among others, Stanton, who argues that the "least of these" refers specifically to the church. Therefore, rather than the deeds of hospitality in 25:35-36 referring to the general treatment of the poor, the list refers to ways that Christians have been received by the rest of the world. For this reason, the genre matters greatly to Stanton, who recognizes that the parables preceding the judgment pericope envision accountability for Jesus' own disciples regarding their acts of service for the kingdom (cf. 24:45-51; 25:10-13, 28-30). Despite the immediate context, Stanton argues that the judgment pericope is not a parable, but rather an apocalyptic vision, and is therefore set apart from the preceding parables in such a way that accountability for the disciples is not in view. Instead, the pericope has the same particularist intention of many other apocalyptic writings: to offer consolation to a group of people oppressed by the dominant society—in this case, Jesus' (and ultimately Matthew's) own community.[349] This passage seeks to console anxious Christians who perceive themselves to be threatened by local Jewish leadership and gentile society at large. The "least of these" are not the poor and needy but rather Christians living as minorities in society. When the Son of Man comes in his glory, he will find favor with those who treated his people, Christians, with hospitality. Those who failed to do so will be punished.

---

[347]   The list is similar in this regard to that found in Isa 58:6-7, 10. The true worshiper shares their food with the hungry, brings the homeless into their home, covers the naked, and satisfies the needs of the afflicted. An example of the general application of such deeds as those mentioned in 25:35-36 may be found in *The Apology of Aristides*, who argues that first-century Christians were those who took strangers into their homes, visited the afflicted in prison, and fed the needy, therefore observing "the precepts of their Messiah with much care." See "The Apology of Aristides," in *Ante-Nicene Fathers*, vol. 9 (ed. Philip Schaff; Grand Rapids: Christian Classics Ethereal Library, 2004), 420–45, and J. Rendel Harris, ed., *The Apology of Aristides on Behalf of the Christians* (Cambridge: Cambridge University Press, 1893), especially page 49. The universalist approach to this passage has also been important to social and liberationist theologies. On this, see Gustavo Gutierrez, *A Theology of Liberation* (London: SCM Press, 1974), 151, 170, 197–98, the "least of these" refers not just to Christians but to all the needy, whoever they may be.

[348]   Davies and Allison, *Matthew 19–28*, 427–29.

[349]   Stanton, *Gospel*, 208. Stanton's approach is based on redaction-critical and socio-critical observations.

Each of these approaches is persuasive enough that it raises the possibility that it may be unnecessary, and undesirable, to choose between them. The particularist approach fits the overall narrative of Matthew more fluidly, offering more points of connection to other passages throughout the First Gospel. Persecution was a particular concern for Jesus (5:11-12; 10:16-25; 23:29-36; 24:9-14). Furthermore, although Davies and Allison might be correct that the phrase τῶν ἀδελφῶν *may* infer, however rarely, a non-ecclesial usage, it is used far more often to refer only to members of the Christian family (cf. Matt 12:46-50).[350] The connection between τῶν ἀδελφῶν and the "least of these" suggests that Christians are in view.[351]

Although Stanton argues that the particularist approach best understands the "least of these" as referring to Christians, I suggest a more specific referent is in view: the missionaries sent out by Jesus in both the missions to the Jews (10:1-42) and the gentiles (28:16-20).[352] In the mission to the Jews, Jesus instructs his disciples to proclaim that the kingdom has come near (10:7) and to take no extra money or provisions, including food and clothing (10:9-10). The towns who welcome

[350]   Stanton, *Gospel*, 216, notes that it appears in this context 18x, and that 12 of these instances are Matthean redactions.

[351]   Additionally, Stanton, *Gospel*, 214, argues that the phrase τῶν μικρῶν τού-των (these little ones; Matt 10:42-44; 11:11; 18:6, 10, 14) refers explicitly to disciples and that the superlative τῶν ἐλαχίστων of 25:40, 45 is a nearly synonymous phrase, therefore implying that the disciples are also in view. So too Nolland, *Matthew*, 1032, the "least of these" is "these little ones" in heightened form. This connects Matt 10:40-42 to 25:40, 45, passages that I argue below are connected in theme and intent. While this is possible, and supports the idea that Christians (or a subset of) are in view in 25:40, 45, other scholars have argued that the identification is not clear enough to make an obvious connection. In this vein, see W. G. Kümmel, *Promise and Fulfilment: The Eschatological Message of Jesus* (London: SCM Press, 1961), 94, and Davies and Allison, *Matthew 19–28*, 429. Schweizer, *Matthew*, 479, notes the extreme similarities but questions why Matthew's writer would use "these little ones" uniformly until this passage and then change the designation if he still had the disciples in mind. John P. Meier, *Matthew* (Dublin: Veritas Publications, 1980), 304, argues that passages referring to "these little ones" are different in nature and "lack the sweeping universalism of this scene." Although the similarities between the two phrases is striking, the identification between them is an open question, as is the relevance of their association to the identity of the "least of these" in 25:40, 45.

[352]   Hagner, *Matthew 14–28*, 744, argues that the difference between "Christians" and "Christian missionaries" is minimal, as all Christians were called to represent the Gospel. While there is a sense in which this is true, this ignores the way that Matt 25:31-46 interacts specifically with the act of "going" and being received in the missionary accounts of Matt 10 and 28:16-20. The connections between these passages make it likely that the judgment refers to the reception of those in the act of missionary vocation, and possibly the specific missionaries sent in Matt 10 and 28:16-20, rather than to all Christians regardless of activity.

them and listen to their message will be found favorable, and those who do not welcome the disciples will be condemned on the day of judgment (10:15). On their travels they will be persecuted by both Jews and gentiles (10:16-18; cf. 24:9-14), but the disciples are not to fear, for although they can be persecuted and killed, as long as they acknowledge Jesus on their travels they will ultimately be acknowledged before God the father (10:26-33). A detail of special importance is the way that Jesus explicitly identifies his missionaries *with himself*; those who welcome the missionaries welcome Jesus and therefore God (10:40-41). To welcome a messenger is to welcome the one the messenger represents, and all who welcome the disciples will receive a reward. Jesus states, "and whoever gives even a cup of water to one of these little ones in the name of a disciple—truly I tell you, none of these will lose their reward" (10:42). Although many of these details are not reiterated in the sending of missionaries to the nations (28:16-20), Jesus does reiterate that he is with them always, to the end of the age (28:20). Jesus is present with his missionaries in such a way that whoever receives them also receives him; his presence with them is an indication that treatment of the disciples extends to the treatment of Jesus himself. Beyond this, despite the lack of explicit restatement, it is reasonable to assume that many of the missionary commands of Matt 10 are still in place in 28:16-20, so that the disciples are sent out in reliance upon the hospitality of those with whom they engage.

Each of these features has direct relevance to Matt 25:31-46. Those who have been hospitable have provided food and clothing to the "least of these," Jesus' brothers.[353] Jesus associates himself directly with those

---

[353] Visiting those in prison is a feature of the list that has received particular attention regarding the interpretation of the "least of these." Davies and Allison, *Matthew 19–28*, 429, argue the unlikelihood that audiences of the missionaries would visit Christians in prison. Stanton, *Gospel*, 219–21, notes the difficulty but argues that the reverse side of this point is also true: if the list referred to the needy in general, then its omissions are more noteworthy than its inclusions. The list is far too specific to refer to helping the needy in a general sense. Stanton argues that treating prisoners well may not refer to visiting Christians who are imprisoned for their faith but instead refers to those who are charged with caring for them responsibly while they are imprisoned. He finds a parallel in Joel 3:3. While it is the case that there is no evidence that Christians were being imprisoned for their faith in Jesus' time, if the reference to visiting those in prison goes back to the historical Jesus, it may be anticipatory (cf. 24:9-14). Furthermore, there is evidence that Christians were being imprisoned by the time Matthew's Gospel was written, such as Acts 16:25-34, where a jailer is portrayed as showing hospitality to Christian missionaries and then accepts their message favorably. It is possible that Matthew's writer constructed his list based on an awareness of such incidents (cf. 1 Cor 11:23-29). See J. Ramsey Michaels, "Apostolic Hardships and Righteous Gentiles: A Study of Matthew 25:31-46," *JBL* 84, no. 1 (1965): 27–37.

who have received hospitality, as though the hospitable actions were done directly to him, and the hospitable ones stand to receive a blessing from the Father (25:34).[354] Preserved for those who lacked hospitality is condemnation at the final judgment (25:41). Although not explicitly stated in 25:31-46, it is reasonable to assume that those who responded to Jesus' missionaries hospitably also received the service and message of the missionaries favorably and therefore became disciples themselves.[355] This seems implied in the missionary discourse of Matt 10; those who receive the disciples hospitably do so in return for their works among them (10:10). In the context of the overall Matthean narrative, it is best to view the "least of these" as a reference to the disciples Jesus sent on mission to both the Jews and the gentiles. The sheep in the passage are those who have received the missionaries with hospitality, and therefore have likely become disciples themselves, while the goats are those who rejected the missionaries and their message and did not receive them

---

[354]   Even scholars who have argued in favor of the universalist approach have often recognized that Jesus identifies himself with his own disciples in Matthew's Gospel but never the poor and needy directly. This, then, would be a striking exception if the universalist approach were correct. Davies and Allison, *Matthew 19–28*, 429, recognize the problem but relate the passage to Prov 19:17, "Whoever is kind to the poor lends to the LORD, and will be repaid in full." McNeile, *Gospel*, 370, draws a parallel with the messianic interpretation of Isa 53 and says that Jesus will "identify himself with all sufferers." Meier, *Matthew*, 304, argues that Jesus identifies himself with the poor through the Emmanuel concept; he is with his church but "most especially with the no-accounts of this world." Stanton, *Gospel*, 217, argues that such an identification would be an "unprecedented step."

[355]   So Michaels, "Apostolic," 28, the sheep are those who demonstrate their own faith by works of love and hospitality to Jesus' messengers; Douglas R. A. Hare and Daniel J. Harrington, "Make Disciples of All Nations (Mt 28:19)," *CBQ* 37, no. 3 (1975): 365, "The thrust of the pericope is not simply that good deeds will receive and eschatological reward, but that the righteous of the pagan world have indeed formed a relationship with Jesus by their acts of love toward 'the least' with whom he has identified himself." Keener, *Gospel*, 606, cites comparisons with 4 Ezra 7:37, receiving Jesus' messengers involves embracing their message of the kingdom and treating Jesus' servants properly. George Eldon Ladd, *A Theology of the New Testament* (Grand Rapids: Eerdmans, 2000), 116, "The hospitality they receive at the hands of their hearers is a tangible evidence of people's reaction to their message." This view is *contra* France, *Matthew*, 958–59, who argues that a positive reception of the disciples does not indicate a positive reception toward Jesus himself. France argues that the sheep and goats did not know their actions were directed toward Jesus, and therefore their actions were judged as deeds of human kindness rather than as expressions of their attitude toward Jesus. In this regard France has read into the passage what is not plainly indicated. The surprise on the part of the sheep and the goats is only that they had not served Jesus directly through personal interaction ("When did we see/perceive you?" πότε σε εἴδομεν, 25:37), but it is not necessary to take this as an indicator that they had not responded to the message of the disciples in faith.

with hospitality.[356] In a direct sense, the actions of the Jewish leaders fit this narrative, as they have failed to receive God's messengers hospitably (23:29-36), though the goats in 25:31-46 appear to apply universally to any and all who do not receive the missionaries rather than to the Jewish leaders alone.

An important consideration regarding the particularist approach that views the "least of these" as Christian missionaries concerns the nature of final judgment. If the judgment in Matt 25:31-46 is the only one anticipated by Matthew's writer, then it would seem odd that it would concern only the treatment of missionaries rather than the works and/or faith response of people more generally. However, Matthew's Gospel does not offer a unified scenario for final judgment, including regarding the identities of those involved as judges as well as those being judged. The language of judgment throughout the First Gospel is evocative rather than prescriptive, so attempts at describing the final judgment with precision may be to pursue more than Matthew's Gospel permits. The varied descriptions throughout Matthew do not even make it clear how many judgments the writer had in mind (cf. 13:41-42, 49; 16:27; 19:28-29; 24:9-14, 29-31; 25:31-46). It is difficult to harmonize them into a uniform scenario, and none of them are best understood as snapshots of the future. This is not to say the various judgment scenes do not project a compelling reality upon their hearers/readers. As McKnight argues, "Jesus evidently used different images under different circumstances to enhance the vision he was seeking to impress upon what he considered to be a disobedient people."[357] There is uniformity in the fact that Jesus saw judgment as a process that he would enact in favor of those who exhibited "greater righteousness" and against those who did not, but the imagery and details in each judgment saying are varied enough that they are, at the very least, best viewed as instances of rhetoric in order to make a point to a given crowd in a given moment, and they open up the possibility that Matthew's Gospel imagines more than one judgment scene or event at the parousia. This diversity extends to the final discourse, as the trilogy of parables preceding the judgment scene (24:45–25:30) all envision accountability for the disciples for their

---

[356]   Cope, "Matthew," 40–41, argues that this makes the best sense of the nature of the list, in terms of potential acts of service included and excluded. The focus on hospitality specifically makes sense in light of receiving those who have been sent out on Jesus' behalf.

[357]   Scot McKnight, *A New Vision for Israel: The Teachings of Jesus in National Context* (Grand Rapids: Eerdmans, 1999), 146. For a discussion of judgment in the Gospels, see Marius Reiser, *Jesus and Judgment: The Eschatological Proclamation in Its Jewish Context* (Minneapolis: Fortress, 1997).

own acts of service for the kingdom, while in the judgment pericope of 25:31-46 they stand aside as others are judged based on how they have treated the disciples. The lack of uniformity regarding judgment scenes throughout Matthew indicates that it is possible to view 24:45–25:30 as a warning to the disciples themselves to remain vigilant, while also arguing that they are exempt from the judgment scene of 25:31-46, and both scenes are likely influenced by the First Gospel's anticipation of "imminence" regarding the end of the age. The timing of the parousia is uncertain, but the necessity for watchfulness regarding its imminence (24:36-44) heightens both the need of the disciples to be diligent, as well as the need of the nations to be hospitable. The linearity of the judgment scenes is difficult to determine, but the final discourse could possibly contain either 1) more than one judgment scene or 2) different events or stages of the one final judgment.[358]

Somewhat more uniform in the final discourse is its overall dominant theme: the judgment scenario is intended as "instruction on proper conduct prior to the final coming."[359] The scribes and Pharisees are held accountable as blind guides (23:1-36), the disciples themselves are warned to be watchful of the parousia and to remain diligent regarding their works for the kingdom (24:45–25:30), and the judgment scene of 25:31-46 stands in defense of those same disciples (or a subset thereof) against those who would treat them harshly. It is in this theme, the necessity of proper conduct, where the universalist and particularist interpretations come together. Twice in the pericope those who are blessed are referred to as δίκαιοι (just/righteous, 25:37, 46). As argued persuasively by John Donahue, such language provides a point of contact with themes of righteousness throughout Matthew's Gospel.[360] In the makarisms, those who hunger and thirst stand side by side with those who are merciful (5:6-7). Throughout Matthew, righteousness stands for "rightness," or what should happen, and concerns the behavior that should be exhibited by Jesus' followers. While the scribes and Pharisees are criticized for neglecting justice, mercy, and faith (23:23), the righteousness of the disciples is to exceed that of the scribes and Pharisees (5:20). The disciples are commanded to show hospitality not only to those so deserving but even to their enemies who persecute them (5:43-48). These visions of "rightness" come together in the final

---

[358]   On the difficulty of harmonizing the judgment scenes, see Konradt, *Israel*, 313–14.

[359]   See Donahue, "Parable," 12.

[360]   On the theme of righteousness in Matthew generally, see Benno Przybylski, *Righteousness in Matthew and His World of Thought* (SNTS 41; Cambridge: Cambridge University Press, 1980).

discourse so that its apocalyptic material can solve the problem of theodicy. Persecution and injustice is tolerable in light of the coming judgment, where sin will be unmasked, goodness will be rewarded, and "the world will be made 'right' again."[361] Matthew 25:31-46 is an apocalyptic moment in salvation history that stands in line with Jesus' prior commitments to these same ideals, so that the hospitality particularly applied to the disciples is best understood as universally required and acknowledged. Acts of mercy and loving kindness characterize the life of a disciple.[362] The criterion of hospitality described in the pericope, though not exhaustive, is one by which all people are to be judged and describes the norms by which they can be called righteous. In this way treatment of Christian missionaries becomes "the occasion by which the true meaning of justice is revealed." The passage is a "locus for the disclosure of God's will for all peoples."[363] Therefore, while Matt 25:31-46 deals with acts of mercy done to Jesus' own disciples who have been sent out on missionary journeys, the acts described are consistently viewed in Matthew's Gospel as consonant with the behavior of Jesus' own followers more generally and therefore are best understood as universal principles. These principles are supplied and applied by Matthew's Jesus in order to provide encouragement and protection to his disciples and to underscore the importance of their service for the kingdom.

5.4.2. All the Nations (πάντα τὰ ἔθνη) of Matthew 25:32

A number of positions have been proposed regarding the identity of the nations gathered for judgment in Matt 25:32, including: 1) all of humanity, without distinction,[364] 2) the gentiles,[365] 3) all non-Christians,[366]

---

[361]   Donahue, "Parable," 22–25.

[362]   Donahue, "Parable," 25. See also Ben Witherington III, *Jesus, Paul, and the End of the World: A Comparative Study in New Testament Eschatology* (Downers Grove, Ill.: InterVarsity Press, 1992). Jesus defined his followers on the basis of adherence to God's will, as opposed to the Pharisees, who were concerned over ceremonial issues.

[363]   Donahue, "Parable," 30.

[364]   So Davies and Allison, *Matthew 19–28*, 422; Schweizer, *Matthew*, 476; McNeile, *Matthew*, 369; Gundry, *Matthew*, 511; France, *Matthew*, 961; Hagner, *Matthew 14–28*, 742; Nolland, *Matthew*, 1024; Wolfgang Trilling, *Das Wahre Israel* (Leipzig: St. Benno-Verlag, 1959), 14. Kümmel, *Promise*, 94, argues that the inheritance of the kingdom in 25:34 requires that Christians are included in the judgment, as they stand to inherit the kingdom. His argument assumes that this scene depicts the one and only judgment where the inheritance can be granted. Donahue, "Parable," 16, "all the nations" stems from missionary discourse and refers to the "whole inhabited world."

[365]   So Hare and Harrington, "Make Disciples," 363; Saldarini, *Matthew's*, 71, 80–81, refers to gentiles who "join the house of Israel."

[366]   So Stanton, *Gospel*, 214.

and 4) the church.[367] Lamar Cope surveys the uses of ἔθνη in relevant antecedent and contemporary literature and argues that the data are inconclusive; it is impossible to identify the nations in Matt 25:32 based on linguistic considerations alone. The context of the passage is decisive, and it is in discussing the context that Cope makes an important observation: while it is difficult to say from the context who "all the nations" *are*, it is more possible to say who they *are not*. From the context it is clear that "those who have been given or refused hospitality are not a part of the judgment proceeding."[368] Therefore, identifying the "least of these" provides clarity to the role of the nations. Regardless of who is to be judged, the "least of these" stand to the side as nonparticipants.[369]

Although Cope is correct that it is difficult to identify "all the nations" with any certainty, if the interpretation of the "least of these" offered here is persuasive, then "all the nations" likely refers to those who were the intended audiences of the missionaries sent out by Jesus. In this case, both the Jews and the gentile nations are included, as both were the objects of missionary commissions. The judgment scene functions as the completion of both missions (cf. 24:14), and based on its position in the Matthean narrative, it precedes the commission to go to "the nations" (28:19) and therefore serves as a rhetorical device that motivates the disciples and warns those whom they encounter along the way. This reading also creates an inclusio: the first Matthean teaching discourse begins with a warning regarding persecution against the disciples (5:11-12) and a call for Jesus' disciples to be a light to the world (5:14-16), a call that alludes to the Abrahamic responsibility to be a light to all the nations. The last teaching discourse then ends with a scene describing accountability for the way that the nations received the disciples and reverses the condition for Jesus' enemies who persecuted him and his followers.

While the group of people left out of the judgment scene of Matt 25:31-46 likely refers to certain Christian missionaries in particular, this does not mean that all other Christians are then judged with "all the nations" on the basis of their own treatment of those missionaries. The rhetorical point of the pericope is less to describe the precise nature of judgment and more to describe who is "in" and who is "out" when

---

[367]   So Victor Paul Furnish, *The Love Command in the New Testament* (Nashville: Abingdon, 1972), 79–84. The judgment of the church would be consistent with the need of the disciples to remain diligent in good works until the parousia discussed in the three parables leading up to the judgment pericope. The Son of Man would call together the evangelized nations and judge them based on their actions as followers of Jesus.

[368]   Cope, "Matthew," 37.

[369]   See Garland, *Reading*, 243.

judged by a particular criterion. While it is possible that not all Christians are included among the "least of these" in this particular pericope, it is not likely that they are included among the nations either, because previously committed disciples are not likely those to whom the missionaries are sent. As discussed above, there is no indication that this is the only judgment scenario Matthew had in mind. A gathering of "the elect" from across the earth was depicted in Matt 24:31.[370] There is no reason to assume that any and all people must be depicted somewhere within Matt 25:31-46. The pericope is best understood as a narrative device providing a particular rhetorical function rather than a fully inclusive scene depicting the totality of final judgment. It is possible that Christians not included among the missionary groups are simply not depicted in this pericope.

5.4.3. Inheritance Traditions Antecedent to Matthew 25:34

Due to the genre and the narrative and rhetorical function of Matt 25:31-46, it is possible to detect a large number of antecedent traditions in the background of this pericope. While identifying possible antecedent traditions for each aspect of the pericope is helpful in its interpretation, the following discussion is limited to antecedent traditions that may have directly or indirectly influenced the use of κληρονομέω in verse 34.

1. The Hexateuch

Many of the ways that the Hexateuch may have influenced Matt 5:5 are relevant here.[371] The principal parallel concerns the foundations of God's role as Father. Although Matt 25:34 depicts God as the father of Jesus, it has been established in this chapter (as well as chapter 1) that God is depicted throughout Matthew as a father to his people, which in Matthew's text refers to Jesus' disciples, and it is the disciples who stand to receive his inheritance. God's role as "father" is connected directly in 25:34 to the giving of an inheritance, and as the inheritance is said to have been prepared at the dawn of the age, the implication is that God's role as a father who prepares such an inheritance stretches back to the beginning as well. That the inheritance was prepared ἀπὸ καταβολῆς

---

[370]   See Keener, *Gospel*, 586, "the elect" is a reference to Jesus' community. Davies and Allison, *Matthew 19–28*, 364, cite 1 Thess 4:17; Rev 7:1; Did. 9.4; 10.5, to argue that a gathering of Christians is in view but that the language recalls the Jewish hope that God will gather the Jews of the diaspora (cf. Isa 11:11; 27:12-13; Bar 4:36-37; 1 En. 57:2; Pss. Sol. 11:3) and that based on the Jewish background it is possible that the verse includes a gathering of faithful Jews.

[371]   See 5.1.2.3.

κόσμου (from the foundation of the world) signifies a permanence of the inheritance and ensures the permanence of the recipient's relationship to God. Conversely, to be cut off from the inheritance is to be cut off from God as Father. Jesus, the Son of Man (25:31), is depicted as the king and as God's son and is therefore the heir to David and the heir to God.[372] Therefore, he has authority over the inheritance and the responsibility to offer it universally, so that those who become υἱοὶ θεοῦ (Matt 5:9) are those who receive the inheritance.[373] In both contexts, the Hexateuch and Matt 25:34, the inheritance is guaranteed by God himself as a gift. In the Hexateuch this is illustrated by the consistent use of the verb נתן (to give), in conjunction with inheritance contexts,[374] and in Matt 25:34, this is illustrated by the use of the divine passive ἡτοιμασμένην ὑμῖν (prepared for you),[375] which indicates that God has prepared the place for the recipients of his blessing.[376]

2. The Latter Prophets

The influence of the Latter Prophets over Matthew's Gospel is pervasive, and this includes inheritance and the entirety of Matt 25:31-46. Although a positive attitude relating to gentiles can be found throughout all strands of the HB, as it pertains to inheritance, to gentile/alien acceptance as full coheirs to the land, and to their equal status with the Israelites in their relationship with Yahweh, there can be little doubt that these realities were not present until the Latter Prophets, as a need for a new social identity in Israel saw the liturgical community take precedent

---

[372]　In Jewish tradition God is usually depicted as the shepherd (Ezek 34:11-31; Zech 10:3; Ps 23:1-4; 74:1-2; 78:52; Isa 40:11; Jer 13:17; 31:10; Micah 7:14; 1 En. 89:18). In the Enochic literature he is the judge over the sheep (1 En. 89–90). However, Jesus as the Davidic king is consonant with his role as a shepherd in the imagery of the pericope, which also draws from Dan 7, particularly vv. 13-14. See Keener, *Gospel*, 602–3.

[373]　Cf. John 5:25-27, "Very truly, I tell you, the hour is coming, and is now here, when the dead will hear the voice of the Son of God, and those who hear will live. For just as the Father has life in himself, so he has granted the Son also to have life in himself; and he has given him authority to execute judgment, because he is the Son of Man."

[374]　See 2.2.1.1.

[375]　On the use of the divine passive in this verse, see Dale C. Allison Jr., *Constructing Jesus: Memory, Imagination, and History* (Grand Rapids: Baker Academic, 2010), 179.

[376]　The perf, mid, part term εὐλογημένοι indicates the divine passive enacted by God on behalf of the sheep. A similar usage is found in Ps 118:26, where the passive participle appears to pronounce blessing upon those who come in God's name. The term is less ethical, and therefore more theologically loaded, than μακάριος. On the use of εὐλογέω in Matt 25:34, see France, *Matthew*, 962. On the use of the term more generally, see *NIDNTTE*, 2:317.

over the ethnic one. The blessing of the gentiles was largely seen as a product of the gentiles' sojourn *into* Israel, as Israel served as an attractive source of salvation through God and the surrender of their former ways (cf. Jer 3:17; Isa 2:2-4; 49:6-7). A key aspect of gentile salvation in these writings was the gathering and repatriation of Israelites back into the land, where the gentiles who facilitated such repatriation share in Israelite blessings. The gradual development of gentile inclusion and the reshaping of Israelite identity to accept non-Israelites finds its fullest expression in restoration contexts. Isaiah 66:18-24 is an important passage in this regard, where God is depicted as gathering all the nations to come and see his glory. He sends representatives out to the nations to declare God's glory among them, and the nations respond by repatriating the Israelites back into the land. Serving the Israelites is regarded by God as an offering. God will make a new heavens and a new earth, of which those who worship him have a part, while those who have rebelled against God will be judged and their dead bodies left visible as a sign of their rebellion.[377] The culmination of gentile acceptance into the inheritance itself comes in Ezek 47:21-23, where resident aliens receive a share in the inheritance and are pronounced as citizens of Israel.

Rather than gentiles flowing *into* Israel, Matthew's Gospel depicts Jesus' disciples *going out* to the nations (cf. Isa 66:19). They do so in order to offer a share in the kingdom and accept them as equals through baptism (28:19). The hospitality required of the nations toward the disciples is similar to, and may have been influenced by, repatriation contexts that depict the nations as having a responsibility toward proper treatment of God's own. Not all depictions of gentiles in the Latter Prophets are positive; the wicked among the nations fall under judgment. The same is true of Matthew, where the nations are presented with an opportunity to respond favorably to God's messengers, but those who do not are liable to judgment (25:46). "Gathering" is an important element in each of these judgment scenes where the survivors of judgment are given a share of the eschatological kingdom.

3. Psalms of Solomon

Psalms of Solomon 14 depicts a chasm between the righteous and sinners who have forfeited their identity as Jews due to their disregard for the law. For the sinners, "their inheritance is Hades" (κληρονομία αὐτῶν ᾅδης, 14:9), but the devout "will inherit life in joy" (κληρονομήσουσιν ζωὴν ἐν εὐφροσύνῃ, 14:10). Eschatological judgment

---

[377] As discussed in 3.1.3, many of the themes associated with Isa 66:18-25 are also found in 1 En. 5:5-9 and 10:18–11:2.

is in view, and an inheritance is anticipated both for the righteous and the false shepherds of Israel who have neglected their responsibilities. To "inherit life" is not only found in Matt 19:29, but it is also implied in the connection between 25:34 and 46. Those found to be righteous inherit the kingdom in 25:34, and this is synonymous with receiving "eternal life" in 25:46, where the inhospitable are judged and sentenced to "eternal punishment."

Although intriguing, the connection between Matt 25:34 and Pss. Sol. 14:9-10 is general in nature. The connection becomes more probable when understood in light of the parallels between Matt 25:31-46 and Pss. Sol. 17. The psalm recounts both the illegitimacy of Israel's former leadership and the abuses of foreign rulers and casts them against the kingdom of God (ἡ βασιλεία τοῦ θεοῦ), which judges the nations (τὰ ἔθνη, 17:3). The Davidic king will rise (17:21-23) and drive sinners out from the inheritance (κληρονομίας), which, along with 7:2, is clearly a reference to Jerusalem. The Messiah will "gather" people for judgment (17:26).[378] As I argue in chapter 3,[379] although the first half of the psalm judges certain gentiles harshly and sees them cast from the presence of God's people, 17:28 is also a shifting point in the attitude of the psalm toward gentiles.[380] It is said of the messiah that he will judge all the nations (ἔθνη) in wisdom (σοφίᾳ), and the nations will serve him (17:29). The people of the nations will come from the ends of the earth to facilitate the pilgrimage of the Israelites back into the land, and he will be king over not only the Israelites but over the nations as well (cf. Isa 66:18-24). The Israelites and the nations together will be taught by God, and they will walk in his ways (17:32). The nations will stand before him, and he will have compassion on them (17:34). There is remarkable consistency with this section of the psalm and many repatriation passages in the Latter Prophets. Rather than being purged, the gentiles who assist in repatriating the Israelites will experience a change in position. If they repent of their old ways, they will be welcomed as servants of God, rather than rebuffed as foreigners. The negative depiction of certain gentiles in the psalm is not aimed at gentiles in total, but at the gentile *oppressors* who are

---

[378]   Compare Pss. Sol. 17:26, "He will gather" (συνάξει), with Matt 25:32, "All the nations will be gathered" (συναχθήσονται).

[379]   See 3.6.

[380]   Hare and Harrington, "Make Disciples," 364–65, argue that 17:27-28 envisions two separate judgments, one first for gentiles and then a second for Israelites and that this provides evidence that Matthew may have more than one judgment in view as well. Therefore, the single judgment scene of Matt 25:31-46 need not depict the judgment of any and all peoples.

exercising political domination over Israel. It is specifically the gentiles who have trampled upon Jerusalem and defiled the land that are to be destroyed.[381] The gentiles who facilitate the return of the Israelites to the land are received in a positive way.[382] It is specifically the sinners (oppressors) who are driven out from the inheritance, but this psalm appears to make a way for gentiles to be welcomed among the Israelites as they re-inherit their land. The messiah will "shepherd the Lord's flock" (17:40),[383] and lead the reconstituted nation in holiness and remove all avenues of oppression (17:41).[384]

Although Matthew depicts certain gentiles negatively in the context of judgment, this depiction refers to gentile *oppressors* (cf. Matt 24:9-14).[385] Those who respond well to Jesus' messengers and their message of the kingdom are given God's blessing and a share in the inheritance. As with Pss. Sol. 17, the issue regarding judgment for gentiles concerns *their treatment of God's own*. Furthermore, both Pss. Sol. 17 and Matthew's Gospel depict "a disdain for and disenfranchisement from the political and religious authorities centered in Jerusalem."[386] Among both Jews and gentiles, there are wayward ones who mistreat God's own and are liable to judgment, as well as salvation and an inheritance offered to those among both groups who find God's favor. In both Pss. Sol. 17 and Matt 25:31-46, those who find God's favor are depicted as his flock, shepherded by God's Davidic king.[387] Those who do not find his favor are denied a share in the inheritance. Although the issue in Matt 25:31-46 relates to the *sending* of God's people prior to judgment, rather than to repatriation, the language of "gathering," the universal inheritance of the kingdom, and the treatment of God's

---

[381]   See Joel Willitts, "Matthew and Psalms of Solomon's Messianism: A Comparative Study of First-Century Messianology," *BBR* 22, no. 1 (2012): 46–47.

[382]   *Contra* Kenneth Atkinson, "Enduring the Lord's Discipline: Soteriology in the *Psalms of Solomon*," in *This World and the World to Come: Soteriology in Early Judaism* (ed. David Gurtner; LSTS 74; London: T&T Clark, 2011), 160–61, who argues for a removal of gentiles in total.

[383]   Willitts, *Matthew's*, 88–89, makes a distinction between the present setting of the author of the psalm and the eschatological setting. In the present setting, "the flock of the Lord" refers to a subset of righteous Israelites. In the eschatological setting, the psalm envisions "the flock of the Lord" as comprising both a subset of Israel who form the nucleus of the political state of Israel, as well as "reverent Gentiles who pledge their allegiance to the kingship of Messiah when he judges the earth."

[384]   See Willitts, *Matthew's*, 81.

[385]   See Davies and Allison, *Matthew 19–28*, 344.

[386]   Willitts, *Matthew's*, 90.

[387]   Evans, *Matthew*, 423, "Righteous Gentiles will be added to the flock of Sheep destined for salvation. These Gentiles, just as surely as the righteous of Israel, will 'inherit the kingdom.'"

righteous ones places Matt 25:31-46 directly in the repatriation tradition of judgment scenes in Jewish literature.

5.4.4. The Meaning of Inherit in Matthew 25:34

God's good world is full of injustice. The apocalyptic contexts of Matthew's Gospel portray a scenario where God will one day take all that has been made wrong, and make it right again, not by ending the world, or by saving people from the world, but by restoring the world, by rewarding righteousness, and by judging evil.[388] The judgment scene of Matt 25:31-46 is in line with this scenario. The "least of these" is a reference to the disciples Jesus sent on mission to both the Jews and the gentiles to offer them a vision of greater righteousness and a share in God's kingdom. The sheep in the passage are those who have received the missionaries with hospitality, and therefore have likely become disciples themselves, while the goats are those who rejected the missionaries and their message and did not receive them with hospitality. Jesus the king offers the sheep a share in the inheritance of the kingdom of God, while the goats are condemned to eternal punishment.[389] The judgment scene is intended as a comfort to those who are just, as well as a warning regarding proper conduct prior to the final coming.[390] It is in this theme, the necessity of proper conduct, where the universalist and particularist interpretations come together. While Matt 25:31-46 deals with acts of mercy done to Jesus' own disciples who have been sent out on missionary journeys, the acts described are consistently viewed in Matthew's Gospel as consonant with the behavior of Jesus' own followers more generally and therefore are best understood as universal principles. These principles are supplied and applied by Matthew's Jesus in order to provide encouragement and protection to his disciples and to underscore the importance of their service for the kingdom.

God's role as "father" is connected directly in 25:34 to the giving of an inheritance, and as the inheritance is said to have been prepared at the dawn of the age, the implication is that God's role as a father who prepares such an inheritance stretches back to the beginning as well. The inheritance is guaranteed by God himself as a gift. That the inheritance was prepared ἀπὸ καταβολῆς κόσμου (from the foundation of the world) connects the kingdom to Israel's salvation history, signifies the permanence of the inheritance, and ensures the permanence of the

---

[388]   See Allison, *Constructing*, 32.

[389]   On Jesus' authority to offer eschatological judgment, see Allison, *Constructing*, 245–46.

[390]   See Donahue, "Parable," 12.

recipient's relationship to God.[391] Conversely, to be cut off from the inheritance is to be cut off from God as Father.

Although "inherit the kingdom" in 25:34 is synonymous with "eternal life" in 25:46,[392] this should not be understood to envision life as the only aspect or benefit of the kingdom. The language of "gathering" recalls contexts regarding repatriation into Israel and implies a spatial aspect of the kingdom of God.[393] The kingdom, as a reward for the righteous, looks forward to the age to come where the righteous benefit by living under God's rule as well as within God's realm (cf. Matt 5:5),[394] and this participation is open to all among the nations who are found to be just. Life is lived in a reconstituted world in relationship to God, as Father, who gifts his children with an inheritance in the age to come.[395]

5.5. Conclusions

Inheritance terms appear in Matthew four times; the verb κληρονο-μέω appears three times (5:5; 19:29; 25:34), and the noun κληρονομία appears once (21:38). It is important to understand that the four appearances of the term are not generic, unassociated uses solely relevant to their

---

[391] Schweizer, *Matthew*, 477, foundation of the world "underlines the certainty of the promise."

[392] See Gundry, *Matthew*, 513, the kingdom and eternal life are equivalent. Eternal life is portrayed as an inheritance "to indicate that Jesus' disciples will be compensated for the dispossessions they suffered in their persecutions. Eternal life is portrayed as a kingdom to indicate that they will be compensated for their disenfranchisement through persecution." Their reward "already exists, reserved for them. They suffer for a present reality, not for an uncertain hope." Allison, *Constructing*, 189, presents extensive parallels with rabbinic literature where eternal life and the kingdom of God are synonymous.

[393] Allison, *Constructing*, 179–81, kingdom based on Isa 61:7, in conjunction with Matt 5:3-12, and God's preparation of a place, which assumes a spatial aspect. See also Pennington, *Heaven*, 296–99.

[394] On the relationship between the kingdom and the age to come, see 2 En. 50:2; Allison, *Constructing*, 190–92; Dunn, *Unity*, 318.

[395] France, *Matthew*, 963, argues that the term βασιλείαν in 25:34, because it is not accompanied by "of God/heaven," is best translated "kingship" rather than "kingdom" and offers the recipients of the inheritance a share in God's rule. Therefore, when brought together with 5:3, 10; 19:28-29, the recipients of the inheritance are offered a co-rulership of the kingdom itself. The inheritance is not just a reward but the culmination of God's purpose for his disciples. So too Nolland, *Matthew*, 1028, who argues that 25:34 envisions at the very least an occupation of the royal realm but likely also includes "participation in royal rule." Olmstead, *Matthew 1–14*, 41, notes that the term can refer to either, or both, and that "rule" often implies "realm." Although being a full "coheir" is not entirely explicit in 25:34, it is consistent with images such as Matt 19:28-29, as well as with depictions elsewhere in early Christian literature of the co-ruling concept (cf. Rom 8:14-17).

independent contexts but are best understood as streamlined, consistently applied, and aimed at representing a single theological purpose. Each use of the term functions in its individual context to represent distinct facets of that one theological objective. In Matthew, inheritance consistently refers to the kingdom of God/heaven, though it reveals aspects of the kingdom rather than being merely synonymous with it. κληρονομία refers to the thing to be inherited, though rather than serving as an equivalent to the kingdom, the term serves to unveil a particular aspect of it, namely, that the kingdom is a gift, given by God, to his people, as a result of the particular, unique relationship that he has with them. God not only gives the kingdom to "subjects" of his rule, but his subjects are also his children who receive an inheritance from their father. This concept is not only assisted by explicit father/children language within inheritance contexts but also by familial language used of Jesus' followers throughout the Gospel (cf. 12:46-50). The inheritance ultimately belongs to Jesus, as God's unique son and the Davidic king, but he shares his inheritance with his followers as a reward for their commitment to him and their pursuit of his ideal, which is true discipleship and "greater righteousness." Jesus has authority over the inheritance, as well as authority to pass judgment upon all people with regard to who stands to receive it.

κληρονομέω then refers to the act of receiving or obtaining the inheritance. It is important to understand that, in one sense, "to inherit" from God (or Jesus) shares an important point of contact with patrimonial contexts of inheritance: both are based upon the uniqueness of the relationship between the descendent and the beneficiary. However, there is also an important difference; whereas in patrimonial contexts the decedent has passed away and grants an inheritance to be *received* by an heir, in Matthew's theological context God does not die, and Jesus rises from the dead, so that the inheritance is not only something *received* but it is also something *to be entered into*, where the beneficiaries' relationship with God continues unabated. In fact, the relationship not only continues, but builds in intensity, as rewards envisioned at the end of the age far outweigh the circumstances of present earthly status and conditions. Inheritance in Matthew is an egalitarian concept; to be an heir of God's inheritance is to take on an entirely new identity, which transcends ethnic and class distinction, and which guarantees one not only reception *of* the inheritance but entrance *into* the inheritance and eternal life therein.

The inheritance refers to the kingdom that belongs to Jesus (21:38) and is shared by Jesus with his followers (21:43), who are ideal disciples. The promises of the inheritance provided eschatological hope and comfort in the midst of persecution and guaranteed the disciples a reward that far surpassed the perilous circumstances they faced. The ideal disciples are those who develop kingdom-oriented dispositions of virtue (5:3-12), follow Jesus and make sacrifices for the sake of the kingdom (19:28-29), meekly wait upon God to deliver the inheritance rather than presuming upon it or taking it by force (5:5; 21:38), produce the fruits of the kingdom (21:43), and support the work and service of the kingdom's proclamation (25:31-46). Conversely, also important is the depiction of those who lose a share in the inheritance, namely, those who neglect "greater righteousness" (5:20) and the pursuit of justice (23:13, 23), those who are unwilling to meet the standards of the kingdom (19:22-23), those who presume upon their role in the kingdom (21:38),[396] and those who persecute Jesus' followers rather than serving them (5:11-12; 25:45-46).

The first two appearances of the verb κληρονομέω are in the future tense and suggest an eschatological kingdom benefit for present kingdom participation. In each case, the three individual instances of the verb portray a distinct aspect of the one reality of the kingdom. Matthew 5:5 details the spatial aspect of the kingdom by declaring that the disciples will receive a share in "the whole earth." Matthew 19:28-29 refers to the "renewal" of all things, which likely includes the eschatological earth itself, where life will be lived eternally by God's own. Matthew 25:34 and 46 confirm both the spatial aspect of the kingdom as well as the eternal nature of life lived within it, as a place that God has prepared before the foundation of the world. κληρονομήσουσιν in Matt 5:5 is addressed in the third-person plural, implying a characterization of the totality of Jesus' community: they are "meek," and they will inherit the earth. κληρονομήσει in Matt 19:29 is addressed in the third-person singular, implying the individualistic aspect of discipleship: although ideal disciples are characterized by certain virtues, each disciple must make individual decisions regarding their own attachment and commitment to Jesus. Finally, κληρονομήσατε is a second-person plural imperative; judgment has been passed and is final: Jesus gathers his sheep and those who are included among God's flock are collectively commanded to enter into their inheritance, which is a share in the kingdom, the reign and realm of God. The actual timing of the inheritance is left ambiguous throughout the Gospel, as is the possibility of stages of fulfillment and the precise relationship of the inheritance

---

[396] Konradt, *Israel*, 378, the kingdom is transferred from false shepherds to the true disciples, who take up their "missionary task" of conveying God's will and guiding people to the kingdom.

to the parousia.[397] Although Matt 5:5, 19:29, and 25:34 are more "forward-looking" toward the end of the age, 21:43 may envision a more immediate removal of false shepherds and a stewardship of the presently inaugurated aspects of the kingdom by Jesus' disciples. This may imply "entrance" into aspects of the inheritance as a lived reality rather than solely as an eschatological promise.

[397]   There are hints that Matthew's writer expected an imminent fulfillment of end-of-the-age expectations, though it is important to recognize that the First Gospel stresses watchfulness over the timing of fulfillment (parousia, renewal, consummation, etc.) per se (24:36-44). See Dunn, *Unity*, 350–52, Jesus' apocalyptic preaching did include an interval of time before the end, where his disciples would make an appeal and tribulation would occur, but it is also apparent that Jesus proclaimed "the final consummation of God's purpose for the world as imminent." Wright's caution is apt, that many discussions of such fulfillments, particularly regarding the parousia, "postpone the effectiveness" of the cross and misrepresent the historical, narrative, and literary-traditional contexts of the apocalyptic scenes in the Gospels in such a way that notions regarding timing and imminence are entirely dubious. While Wright's conclusions regarding historical referents to apocalyptic scenes are intriguing, it is possible that he reads more historical fulfillment into some of those scenes than is intended by the writers of the Gospels themselves. Although Wright questions the nature of parousia expectations, he does recognize the eschatological aspects of inheritance and its "whole-earth" fulfillment. See Wright, *Jesus*, 360–67, 470, 516, 525, 659–61.

6

Conclusion

Matthew and the Promise of Discipleship

Inheritance terms in Matthew are firmly rooted in, adopted from, and adapted beyond Jewish conceptions of inheritance as indicated by a comparison with the uses of inheritance terms and concepts across a broad range of ancient Israelite/Jewish textual sources. As Konradt begins the summary of his own study in Matthew's Gospel, "In investigating the intellectual-historical context that characterizes Matthew's theological thought, the fundamental significance of Israel's theological tradition emerges in the Gospel from beginning to end."[1] Konradt's comment refers to the writer/editor of Matthew's retelling of the Jewish story, his use of Scripture, and his characterization of Israel. His observation also holds true for an investigation into Matthew's use of inheritance concepts. The primary architect behind Matthew's Gospel was almost certainly Jewish, and he makes use of Jewish sources in a way that reflects a dutiful fondness for his own tradition. The writer's enthusiastic reliance on his Jewish tradition is a palpable and dynamic demonstration of his commitment to it, even if he views that tradition through adaptations brought on by the life, death, and resurrection of Jesus.

From Matthew's inheritance contexts it is difficult to determine the makeup of Matthew's community or to determine if such a community even existed—but that is not the point of Matthew's Gospel in the first place. Rather than a concern with the social conditions of his particular community, Matthew's writer examines the nature of ideal discipleship.

---

[1]   Matthias Konradt, *Israel, Church, and the Gentiles in the Gospel of Matthew* (Waco, Tex.: Baylor University Press, 2014), 369.

His Gospel does not envision discipleship of Jesus as a break from Judaism but as a move toward a universal mission that clearly captures a fundamental change in their Jewish context. Rather than portraying a conflict between Jesus' disciples and Judaism as a whole, the text frames the conflict between Jesus and the Jewish leaders and differentiates between the Jewish leaders and the Jewish crowds. Discipleship is a central concern of the First Gospel, and identity and inclusion are largely decided by the choice one makes in whom one will follow: Jesus or the wayward Jewish leaders. Furthermore, Matthew's use of the Abrahamic tradition as a starting point to his presentation of Jesus as Abraham's son is helpful to understanding the relevance of the promises as described in antecedent Jewish literature to both his application of inheritance terms as well as the mission of Jesus' disciples toward the nations.

In the HB, God himself is the foundation and stability of Israelite conceptions of theological inheritance, even when inheritance contexts refer to the patrimonial allotment and transfer of ancestral land. God is seen as the father of Israel and the ultimate ancestor of every tribe, and all inheritances were ultimately initiated by him. Inheritance signified something about God's relationship with, and disposition toward, those to whom he provided an inheritance. This positions the concept of inheritance as relational, especially when the term נחל is used regarding God and his interactions with his people. The Abrahamic promise served as a consistent reference point for inheritance as an identity marker, although the various aspects of the promise were applied and appealed to differently in separate sections of the HB. The first two key aspects, namely, that Abraham would be a father of many descendants and that his descendants would possess a land of their own, receive a great deal of attention in the Hexateuch and continue to be present in the Former Prophets. The third aspect, that Abraham's descendants would be a light to the nations, is all but neglected until the Latter Prophets, where it becomes a prominent feature.

While inheritance in the HB is largely confined to land, either promised, realized, or hoped for, in the Apocrypha and Pseudepigrapha inheritance refers to a wider range of items and realities, such as wisdom or the law. Inheritance can refer to the land, or more particularly Jerusalem or the temple. Rather than realized, the land is hoped for and often takes on an eschatological shape similar to the Latter Prophets. Inheritance in these texts is almost entirely corporate, rather than individualistic, as the regathering of the people is a key aspect of inheritance and restoration passages in the Second Temple period. What binds together the concept of inheritance in the Second Temple literature with the HB is that in the majority of cases these inheritances were viewed as a gift from God and signaled something specific about the relationship between God and his people. The inheritances were often linked to the Abrahamic promise, a feature shared with inheritance in the HB, and were frequently tied to God's providence in his people's lives, as well as their election and salvation. The connection between inheritance, the Abrahamic promise, election, and salvation solidified both the individual and shared identity of God's own. Because different compositions produced in the Second Temple period draw from the influence of various sections of the HB, inheritance can be presented either universally, to Jews and gentiles alike (1 Enoch, Sirach), particularly to Jews (Judith, 1 and 2 Maccabees), or feature a possible but ambiguous mixture of both universalist and particularistic language as it pertains to inheritance (Tobit, the Psalms of Solomon).

In the Qumran Scrolls, patrimonial contexts of inheritance and ancestral land are not in view; instead, inheritance terms more often refer to the gifts and blessings bestowed by God upon his covenant people. In other words, inheritance terms are more often theological than pragmatic; they are more often rooted in identity than property. Although much of inheritance terminology in the Qumran Scrolls often takes linguistic cues from the Hexateuch, the Hexateuchal literary traditions are usually appropriated toward new aims. Indicators of God's relationship to his people are largely the same between the Hexateuch and the Qumran Scrolls, but in the Scrolls more often the inheritance focuses on the community's membership boundaries, social identity, social status, ethical conduct, acquisition of wisdom, and eschatological postmortem fate (although land is in view in 1QM). The way that sapiential and apocalyptic themes come together is instructive in this regard: wisdom acquisition, ethical conduct, and ultimate fate take precedent over issues regarding basic property, to the point that poverty, in certain compositions, becomes the norm, while the pursuit of wisdom and righteousness become issues of central concern. Inheritance terms take on a rhetorical role and are important more for what they signify than what they provide in practical ways. Ultimately, the primary focus of inheritance in the Scrolls (esp. 4QInstruction, 4QMysteries, the Community Rule) is on the ability of those who pursue God and his wisdom and righteousness to become members of the heavenly community and have a share in God's dominion over the earth.

Many of these ideas come to bear on the theological, rhetorical, and narrative-critical exegesis of Matthew's Gospel. Some of these ideas came to Matthew's writer through organic written and oral traditions, whether in delineated or composite forms, while other ideas were likely

"in the air" at the time the First Gospel was written. A number of important observations can be drawn from the analysis in this book.

First, Matthew's Gospel relies on the historical and literary traditions of Israel and its literature, while appropriating those traditions
toward new aims in light of the teachings, life, death, and resurrection
of Jesus. Matthew's writer takes a number of important linguistic cues
from the Hexateuch, he appears aware of theological and legislative
contexts from the Former Prophets, and it is on the Latter Prophets that
he bases his theological and eschatological applications regarding universal inheritance and changes to the nature of the identity of God's
people. Anecdotally, the reception of the gentiles in Matthew functions
as a mirror to the story of the gentiles in the HB. The Hexateuch begins
with the Abrahamic promise and a call for the Israelites to be a light to
the nations, but it is not until the Latter Prophets that this theme is fully
developed and the gentiles are said to receive a share in the inheritance
(cf. esp. Ezek 47:21-23). Likewise, Matthew begins with a reference to
Jesus as the son of Abraham and offers early foreshadowing of a positive
attitude toward the gentiles, but this theme does not begin to take its
full shape until the First Gospel's final chapters. This is true of inheritance as well, as early uses of inheritance terminology hint at gentile
involvement and acceptance, but the full reception of the inheritance for
gentiles is not stated explicitly until the final appearance of the term in
25:31-46, just prior to the commission of a mission toward the gentiles.

The Matthean writer's reliance upon antecedent traditions is also
evident in his awareness of "gathering" and repatriation contexts, his
seamless utilization of sapiential and apocalyptic themes and motifs,
his employment and development of terms and concepts such as "the
kingdom" and "eternal life," and his understanding of the relationship
between poverty, wisdom, and ethical conduct. In terms of inheritance
concepts specifically, Matthew's writer betrays little use or awareness of
the majority of Second Temple sources surveyed in this study, but the
potential influence of sources such as 1 Enoch, Sirach, 4QInstruction,
and the Psalms of Solomon is palpable. The most striking example concerns the phrase "inherit the earth." It is often assumed that the Matthean
use of the phrase relates to eschatological reward alone, a sentiment of
comfort for those living meekly in a hostile environment, who are reliant on God's grace and are waiting on him for vindication. However, as
this study argues, the uses of the phrase "inherit the earth" in antecedent literature are found in ethical and vocational contexts. The inheritance of the earth does not solely relate to an anticipated possession of
a resplendent eschatological realm but belongs to those who walk upon

the earth in a particular way (e.g., the righteous in 1 Enoch, the faithful sage in 4QInstruction, the ideal disciple in Matthew). As such, the inheritance of the earth signals something about vocation—those who inherit the earth participate in God's plans and are given an authoritative role within God's heavenly community. Inheriting the earth is not just the reward of eschatological benefit, or receiving the earth as a gift, it is about vocational participation and authority upon the earth for those who follow Jesus' teachings. This understanding of the inheritance of the earth is an example of the convergence of the apocalyptic with the sapiential; it is a promise of authority and future blessing for those who live upon the earth in the pursuit of greater righteousness.

Among early Christians, this authority and vocational participation may have come to encompass undertones of stewardship and care for the earth. Haley Goranson Jacob argues (effectively, in my view) that such is the case for Paul in his letter to the Romans. Regarding the concept of "glory" in Rom 8, Jacob argues that, rather than the usual conceptions of radiance or eschatological resplendence, glory and conformity to Christ refers to union and participation—a partnering with Jesus in his vocation as the ruler of the earth. Paul uses the language of inheritance (κληρο-νόμος, 8:17) to assist in describing this reality. Those conformed to the image of God's son are those who have been adopted into God's family, with God as their father, and they share in the son's glory and vocation as coheirs. As with inheritance contexts in Matthew (especially 21:38), the inheritance in Rom 8 belongs to Jesus, as God's true firstborn, and is offered to Jesus' followers as his brothers and sisters (cf. Matt 12:49-50). Jacob states, "As children of God and therefore God's heirs, those adopted into God's eschatological family are given the privilege of sharing with the firstborn in the family inheritance." Like Matthew's writer, Paul connects his understanding of inheritance to the Abrahamic promises—Jesus fulfills God's promise to Abraham regarding his seed and his seed's inheritance of the entire world (cf. Rom 4). The adopted children of God, as coheirs with Christ, are recipients of the promises given to Abraham, and these promises are fulfilled in the inheritance of the reconstituted earth. By participating in Jesus' sonship, God's adopted children participate in his rulership over the inheritance.[2] God's adoption of his children, and his children's role as coheirs with Christ, concern their relationship to the earth in a powerful way. According to Jacob, Jesus' coheirs have a responsibility to participate in God's restoration project of the creation, and the Spirit intercedes on their behalf

---

[2]   Haley Goranson Jacob, *Conformed to the Image of His Son: Reconsidering Paul's Theology of Glory in Romans* (Downers Grove, Ill.: IVP Academic, 2018), 212–20.

as they do so (Rom 8:18-27). Therefore, in Rom 8, the inheritance and co-rulership of the earth is not only concerned with *walking upon the earth in a particular way*, but also *behaving in a particular way toward the earth itself*.[3] These ideas are not explicit in Matthew in precisely the same ways, but as is demonstrated in chapter 5 of this study, Matthew uses inheritance language to tie together the virtues of those who inherit (Matt 5:5), and the renewal of the creation, with glory and authority for those associated with Jesus (Matt 19:28-29). Romans 8 demonstrates that these ideas were being processed and presented in Christian writings outside of Matthew's Gospel and is instructive in helping interpreters in understanding Matthew's contribution to the development of these ideas. In Romans, God's people have failed in their rulership and stewardship of the earth, and sin has taken their place, ruling over the earth in an oppressive way that causes bondage and decay. God adopts a people, coheirs with Christ, to take sin's place as those who intercede on creation's behalf. In Matthew, it is the failed Jewish leaders who currently possess the inheritance and rule over it, and over God's people, in oppressive ways. These failed leaders will be replaced by the church, Jesus' ideal disciples, who will intercede with Jesus on behalf of God's people made up of both Israel and the nations.

Second, inheritance concepts in Matthew's Gospel assist in solidifying the new identity of Jesus' disciples, the "ideal disciples," as God's people. In the Matthean narrative, Jesus' fulfillment of the Israelite story is not *replacement* of Jews with gentiles but rather *reaffirmation* through *redemption* as Jesus inaugurates Israel's eschatological potential. Matthew's Jesus did not come to reject Israel but to guarantee its future, and this is done precisely by gathering both Jews and gentiles around himself through faith and the pursuit of "greater righteousness." Jews and gentiles, or Israel and the church, are not competitive communities. The goal of Matthew's Jesus is to recalibrate both Israel and the gentiles around his particular brand of discipleship through a successful mission both to his fellow Jews (10:5-6) and the nations (28:18-20). Jesus' disciples do not serve as a replacement for Israel but rather as the fulfillment of Israel's story; it is in Jesus that Israel finds her rescue, and this rescue, in line with the Abrahamic promise, is extended to include the nations. Therefore, all who understand what God has done, in Jesus, for Israel and the nations stand to have a share in the inheritance. The inheritance refers to the reception of and entrance into the kingdom of God, which

---

[3]   Jacob, *Conformed*, 244–45.

constitutes God's rule over Israel as it is extended to include the entirety of the created order.[4]

Third, inheritance terms in Matthew, as in all of Israelite/Jewish literature, are not only relational in nature but particularly signify one's status as a member of the heavenly community and as a child of God. To call upon God as Father (Matt 6:9) is to confess "God's redemptive and faithful love toward his people,"[5] and the nature of inheritance assists in this picture as it is presented in Matthew: God is a father who protects his people, offers them an inheritance, and secures their future. Because God is a father, he provides an inheritance, and because God is eternal, the inheritance takes on an eschatological shape and provides the hope of eternal life.

[4]   See N. T. Wright, *Jesus and the Victory of God* (Minneapolis: Fortress, 1996), 429: the expectation for restored land was refocused on restored human beings. The inheritance promised better than the possessions surrendered unto true discipleship, and the traditional symbol of sacred land was swallowed up in the eschatological promise that God was to be king "of all the earth."

[5]   Marianne Meye Thompson, *The Promise of the Father: Jesus and God in the New Testament* (Louisville: Westminster John Knox, 2000), 19.

Bibliography

Adams, Samuel L. *Wisdom in Transition: Act and Consequence in Second Temple Instructions*. SJSJ. Leiden: Brill, 2008.

Alexander, Loveday. "Ancient Book Production and the Circulation of the Gospels." Pages 71–112 in *The Gospels for All Christians: Rethinking the Gospel Audiences*. Edited by Richard Bauckham. Edinburgh: T&T Clark, 1998.

Alexander, Philip S., and Geza Vermes. *Qumran Cave 4: Serekh Ha Yaḥad and Two Related Texts*. DJD XXVI. Oxford: Clarendon, 1998.

Alexander, T. D. *From Paradise to the Promised Land*. Exeter: Paternoster Press, 2002.

Allegro, John M. "Wiles of the Wicked Woman: A Sapiential Work from Qumran's Fourth Cave." *PEQ* 96 (1964): 53–55.

Allen, Leslie C. *Ezekiel 20–48*. WBC 29. Nashville: Thomas Nelson, 1990.

Allison, Dale C., Jr. *Constructing Jesus: Memory, Imagination, and History*. Grand Rapids: Baker Academic, 2010.

———. "The Embodiment of God's Will: Jesus in Matthew." Pages 117–32 in *Seeking the Identity of Jesus: A Pilgrimage*. Grand Rapids: Eerdmans, 2008.

———. *The New Moses: A Matthean Typology*. Eugene, Ore.: Wipf & Stock, 1993.

———. *The Sermon on the Mount: Inspiring the Moral Imagination*. New York: Crossroad, 2016.

———. *Studies in Matthew: Interpretation Past and Present*. Grand Rapids: Baker Academic, 2005.

Anderson, A. A. *2 Samuel*. WBC 11. Nashville: Thomas Nelson, 1989.

Anderson, Janice Capel. *Matthew's Narrative Web: Over, and Over, and Over Again*. JSNTS 91. Sheffield: JSOT Press, 1994.

"The Apology of Aristides." Pages 420–45 in *Ante-Nicene Fathers*, vol. 9. Edited by Philip Schaff. Grand Rapids: Christian Classics Ethereal Library, 2004.

Argall, Randal A. *1 Enoch and Sirach: A Comparative Literary and Conceptual Analysis of the Themes of Revelation, Creation and Judgment*. Atlanta: Scholars Press, 1995.

Arnold, Russell C. D. *The Social Role of Liturgy in the Religion of the Qumran Community.* STDJ 60. Leiden: Brill, 2006.

Atkinson, Kenneth. "Enduring the Lord's Discipline: Soteriology in the *Psalms of Solomon.*" Pages 145–66 in *This World and the World to Come: Soteriology in Early Judaism.* Edited by Daniel Gurtner. LSTS 74. London: T&T Clark, 2011.

———. "Herod the Great, Sosius, and the Siege of Jerusalem (37 B.C.E) in Psalm of Solomon 17." *NovT* 38, no. 4 (1996): 313–22.

Auld, A. Graeme. *I & II Samuel.* Louisville: Westminster John Knox, 2011.

Aune, David E. "Greco-Roman Biography." Pages 107–26 in *Greco-Roman Literature and the New Testament: Selected Form and Genres.* Edited by David E. Aune. Atlanta: Scholars Press, 1988.

Aune, David E., with Eric Stewart. "From the Idealized Past to the Imaginary Future: Eschatological Restoration in Jewish Apocalyptic Literature." Pages 147–78 in *Restoration: Old Testament, Jewish, and Apocalyptic Perspectives.* Edited by James M. Scott. Leiden: Brill, 2001.

Baltzer, Klaus. *Deutero-Isaiah.* Hermeneia. Minneapolis: Fortress, 2001.

Barclay, John M. G. *Jews in the Mediterranean Diaspora: From Alexander to Trajan (323 BCE –117 CE).* Berkeley: University of California Press, 1996.

Barr, James. *The Semantics of Biblical Language.* London: SCM Press, 1961.

Bauckham, Richard, ed. *The Gospels for All Christians: Rethinking the Gospel Audiences.* Edinburgh: T&T Clark, 1998.

Baumgarten, Albert I. "The Perception of the Past in the Damascus Document." Pages 1–15 in *The Damascus Document: A Centennial of Discovery.* Leiden: Brill, 2000.

Beaton, Richard. *Isaiah's Christ in Matthew's Gospel.* Cambridge: Cambridge University Press, 2002.

Bedenbender, Andreas. "The Place of the Torah in the Early Enoch Literature." Pages 65–80 in *The Early Enoch Literature.* Edited by Gabriele Boccaccini and John J. Collins. Leiden: Brill, 2007.

Bergsma, John Sietze. *The Jubilee from Leviticus to Qumran: A History of Interpretation.* SVT 115. Leiden: Brill, 2007.

Berquist, Millard J. "The Meaning of δόξα in the Epistles of Paul." PhD diss., Southern Baptist Theological Seminary, 1941.

Betz, Hans Dieter. *Essays on the Sermon on the Mount.* Philadelphia: Fortress, 1985.

Bickermann, E., and J. Sykutris, "Speusipps Brief an König Philipp." *Berichte über die Verhandlungen der Sächsischen Akademie der Wissenschaften zu Leipzig: philologischhistorische Klasse* LXXX (1928).

Black, Matthew. *Apocalypsis Henochi Graece.* Leiden: Brill, 1970.

Blenkinsopp, Joseph. *Isaiah 1–39.* AB 19. New York: Doubleday, 2000.

———. *Isaiah 40–55.* AB 19A. New Haven: Yale University Press, 2002.

———. *Isaiah 56–66.* AB 19B. New York: Doubleday, 2003.

———. "Second Isaiah—Prophet of Universalism." In *The Prophets: A Sheffield Reader*. Edited by Philip R. Davies. Sheffield: Sheffield Academic, 1996.

———. *Wisdom and Law in the Old Testament: The Ordering of Life in Israel and Early Judaism*. Oxford: Oxford University Press, 1995.

Boccaccini, Gabriele, ed. *Enoch and the Messiah Son of Man: Revisiting the Book of Parables*. Grand Rapids: Eerdmans, 2007.

Bock, Darrell, L. *A Theology of Luke and Acts*. Grand Rapids: Zondervan, 2012.

Bockmuehl, Markus. *Seeing the Word: Refocusing New Testament Study*. Grand Rapids: Baker Academic, 2006.

Bond, Helen K. *The Historical Jesus: A Guide for the Perplexed*. London: T&T Clark, 2012.

Bornkamm, Gunter. "End-Expectation and Church in Matthew." Pages 15–51 in *Tradition and Interpretation in Matthew*. Edited by G. Bornkamm, G. Barth, and H. J. Held. London: SCM Press, 1963.

Boyce, Mark J. "The Poetry of the *Damascus Document* and Its Bearing on the Origin of the Qumran Sect." *RevQ* 14 (1990): 615–28.

Brandenburger, Egon. *Das Recht des Welternrichters: Untersuchung zu Matthäus 25, 31-46*. Stuttgart: Katholisches Bibelwerk, 1980.

Briggs, Charles Augustus, and Emilie Grace Briggs. *The Book of Psalms*. ICC. Edinburgh: T&T Clark, 1906.

Brooke, George J. "4Q500 1 and the Use of Scripture in the Parable of the Vineyard." *DSD* 2, no. 3 (1995): 268–94.

———. *The Dead Sea Scrolls and the New Testament*. London: SPCK, 2005.

———. *Reading the Dead Sea Scrolls: Essays in Method*. Atlanta: SBL, 2013.

———. "The Wisdom of Matthew's Beatitudes (4QBeat and Mt. 5:3-12)." *Scripture Bulletin* 19, no. 2 (1989): 35–41.

Brown, Raymond E. *The Birth of the Messiah: A Commentary on the Infancy Narratives in the Gospels of Matthew and Luke*. New Haven: Yale University Press, 1999.

Brueggemann, Walter. *The Land: Place as Gift, Promise, and Challenge in Biblical Faith*. Minneapolis: Fortress, 2002.

———. *Psalms*. Cambridge: Cambridge University Press, 2014.

Bruckner, J. K. "Ethics." In *Dictionary of the Old Testament: Pentateuch*. Edited by T. Desmond Alexander and David W. Baker. Downers Grove, Ill.: InterVarsity Press, 2003.

Budd, Philip J. *Numbers*. WBC 5. Columbia: Thomas Nelson, 1984.

Bultmann, Rudolf. *Die Geschichte der synoptischen Tradition*. Göttingen: Vandenhoeck & Ruprecht, 1931.

Burkes, Shannon. "Wisdom and Law: Choosing Life in Ben Sira and Baruch." *JSJ* 30, no. 3 (1999): 253–76.

Burnett, Fred W. "παλιγγενεσία in Matt 19:28: A Window on the Matthean Community?" *JSNT* 17 (1983): 60–72.

Burridge, Richard A. *What Are the Gospels? A Comparison with Graeco-Roman Biography*. Cambridge: Cambridge University Press, 1992.

Butler, Trent C. *Judges*. WBC 8. Nashville: Thomas Nelson, 2009.

Caird, George B. "The New Testament Concept of Doxa." PhD diss., Oxford University, 1944.

Carson, D. A. *Jesus' Sermon on the Mount: And His Confrontation with the World*. Grand Rapids: Baker Books, 1987.

Carter, Warren. "Narrative/Literary Approaches to Matthean Theology: The 'Reign of the Heavens' as an Example (Mt 4:17–5:12)." *JSNT* 67 (1997): 3–27.

———. *Telling Tales about Jesus: An Introduction to the New Testament Gospels*. Minneapolis: Fortress, 2016.

Charles, R. H. *The Book of Enoch*. Oxford: Clarendon, 1893.

———. *The Ethiopic Version of the Book of Enoch*. Oxford: Clarendon, 1906.

Charlesworth, James H., ed. *The Dead Sea Scrolls: Hebrew, Aramaic, and Greek Texts with English Translations*. Vol. 6B: *Pesharim, Other Commentaries, and Related Documents*. Tübingen: Mohr Siebeck, 2002.

———, ed. *The Old Testament Pseudepigrapha*. Vols. 1–3. New York: Doubleday, 1983.

———. *The Pseudepigrapha and Modern Research*. Ann Arbor: Scholars Press, 1981.

———. "The Qumran Beatitudes (4Q525) and the New Testament (Mt 5:3-1, Luke 6:20-26)." *RHPR* 80 (2000): 13–35.

Childs, Brevard S. *Isaiah*. Louisville: Westminster John Knox, 2001.

Chilton, Bruce. "God as 'Father' in the Targumim, in Non-Canonical Literatures of Early Judaism and Primitive Christianity, and in Matthew." Pages 151–69 in *The Pseudepigrapha and Early Biblical Interpretation*. Edited by James H. Charlesworth and Craig A. Evans. JSPS 14. Sheffield: Sheffield Academic, 1993.

Choi, Sungho. *The Messianic Kingship of Jesus: A Study of Christology and Redemptive History in Matthew's Gospel with Special Reference to the Royal-Enthronement Psalms*. Eugene, Ore.: Wipf & Stock, 2011.

Christensen, Duane L. *Deuteronomy 1–11*. WBC 6A. Dallas: Word Books, 1991.

Clements, Ronald E. *Old Testament Theology*. London: Marshall, Morgan & Scott, 1978.

Cogan, Mordechai. *1 Kings*. AB 10. New York: Doubleday, 2000.

Coggins, Richard J. *Sirach*. Sheffield: Sheffield Academic, 1998.

Cohn, Robert L. *2 Kings*. Berit Olam. Collegeville, Minn.: Liturgical Press, 2000.

Collins, John J. *The Apocalyptic Imagination: An Introduction to Jewish Apocalyptic Literature*. Grand Rapids: Eerdmans, 2016.

———. "Beyond the Qumran Community: Social Organization in the Dead Sea Scrolls." *DSD* 16, no. 3 (2009): 351–69.

———. "The Eschatologizing of Wisdom in the Dead Sea Scrolls." Pages 49–65 in *Sapiential Perspectives: Wisdom Literature in Light of the Dead Sea Scrolls*. Edited by John J. Collins, Gregory E. Sterling, and Ruth A. Clements. STDJ 51. Leiden: Brill, 2004.

———. "In the Likeness of the Holy Ones: The Creation of Humankind in a Wisdom Text from Qumran." Pages 609–18 in *The Provo International Conference on the Dead Sea Scrolls: Technological Innovations, New Texts, and Reformed Issues*. Edited by Donald W. Parry and Eugene Ulrich. STDJ 30. Leiden: Brill, 1999.

———. *Jewish Wisdom in the Hellenistic Age*. Louisville: Westminster John Knox, 1997.

———. *Scriptures and Sectarianism*. Tübingen: Mohr Siebeck, 2014.

———. *Seers, Sybils and Sages in Hellenistic-Roman Judaism*. SJSJ. Leiden: Brill, 1997.

———. "The *Yaḥad* and the 'Qumran Community.'" In *Biblical Traditions in Transmission: Essays in Honor of Michael A. Knibb*. Edited by C. Hempel and J. Lieu. Leiden: Brill, 2006.

Cook, G. A. *The Book of Ezekiel*. ICC. Edinburgh: T&T Clark, 1936.

Cooper, John M. *Reason and Human Good in Aristotle*. Cambridge, Mass.: Harvard University Press, 1975.

Cope, Lamar. "Matthew XXV: 31-46, The Sheep and the Goats Reinterpreted." *NovT* 11, no. 1 (1969): 32–44.

Cousland, J. R. C. *The Crowds in the Gospel of Matthew*. Leiden: Brill, 2002.

Craigie, Peter C. *The Book of Deuteronomy*. London: Hodder and Stoughton, 1976.

———. *Psalms 1–50*. WBC 19. Nashville: Thomas Nelson, 1983.

Craigie, Peter C., Page H. Kelley, and Joel F. Drinkard Jr. *Jeremiah 1–25*. WBC 26. Dallas: Word Books, 1991.

Crenshaw, James L. *The Psalms: An Introduction*. Grand Rapids: Eerdmans, 2001.

Crump, David. *Encountering Jesus, Encountering Scripture*. Grand Rapids: Eerdmans, 2013.

Davies, Eryl W. "Inheritance Rights and the Hebrew Levirate Marriage." *VT* 31, no. 2 (1981): 138–44.

Davies, Philip R. *1QM, the War Scroll from Qumran: Its Structure and History*. BibOr 32. Rome: Biblical Institute Press, 1977.

———. *The Damascus Covenant: An Interpretation of the "Damascus Document."* Sheffield: JSOT, 1982.

———. "The Judaism(s) of the Damascus Document." Pages 27–43 in *The Damascus Document: A Centennial of Discovery*. Edited by Joseph M. Baumgarten, Esther G. Chazon, and Avital Pinnick. Leiden: Brill, 2000.

———. *The Origins of Biblical Israel*. New York: T&T Clark, 2007.

Davies, W. D. *The Gospel and the Land: Early Christianity and Jewish Territorial Doctrine*. Berkeley: University of California Press, 1974.

Davies, W. D., and D. C. Allison Jr. *Matthew 1–7*. ICC. London: T&T Clark, 1998.

———. *Matthew 19–28*. ICC. London: Bloomsbury, 1997.

De Looijer, Gwynned. *The Qumran Paradigm: Critical Evaluation of Some Foundational Hypotheses in the Construction of the Qumran Sect*. Atlanta: SBL Press, 2015.

De Roo, Jacqueline C. R. "Is 4Q525 a Sectarian Document." Pages 338–67 in *The Scrolls and the Scriptures: Qumran Fifty Years After.* Edited by Stanley E. Porter and Craig A. Evans. Sheffield: Sheffield Academic, 1997.

Deutsch, Celia. *Lady Wisdom, Jesus, and the Sages: Metaphor and Social Context in Matthew's Gospel.* Valley Forge, Pa.: Trinity Press International, 1996.

———. "Wisdom in Matthew: Transformation of a Symbol." *NovT* 32 (1990): 13–47.

DeVries, Simon J. *1 Kings.* WBC 12. Waco, Tex.: Word Books, 1985.

Di Lella, A. A. "The Deuteronomic Background of the Farewell Discourse in Tob 14:3-11." *CBQ* 41, no. 3 (1979): 380–89.

Dixon, Thomas P. "Knowledge and Deeds in the Two Spirits Treatise." *JSP* 24, no. 2 (2014): 71–95.

Dodd, C. H. *Parables of the Kingdom.* London: Fontana Books, 1961.

———. *More New Testament Studies.* Manchester: Manchester University Press, 1968.

Donahue, John R. "The 'Parable' of the Sheep and Goats: A Challenge to Christian Ethics." *Theological Studies* 47 (1986): 3–31.

Doran, Robert. *2 Maccabees.* Hermeneia. Minneapolis: Fortress, 2020.

Driver, S. R. *Deuteronomy.* ICC. Edinburgh: T&T Clark, 1895.

Dugan, Elena. "Enochic Biography and the Manuscript History of 1 Enoch: The Codex Panopolitanus Book of the Watchers." *JBL* 140, no. 1 (2021): 113–38.

Duhaime, Jean. *The War Texts.* London: T&T Clark, 2004,

Dunn, James D. G. *The Theology of Paul the Apostle.* London: T&T Clark, 1998.

———. *Unity and Diversity in the New Testament: An Inquiry into the Character of Earliest Christianity.* London: SCM Press, 2006.

Durham, John I. *Exodus.* WBC 3. Columbia: Thomas Nelson, 1987.

Du Toit, Andrie B. "Revisiting the Sermon on the Mount: Some Major Issues." *Neot* 50 (2016): 59–91.

Ehorn, Seth M. *2 Maccabees 1–7: A Handbook on the Greek Text.* Waco, Tex.: Baylor University Press, 2020.

Eichrodt, Walther. *Ezekiel.* London: SCM Press, 1970.

Elgvin, Torleif. "The Mystery to Come: Early Essene Theology of Revelation" Pages 113–50 in *Qumran between the Old and New Testaments.* Edited by F. H. Cryer and T. L. Thompson. JSOT 290. Sheffield: Sheffield Academic, 1998.

———. "Priestly Sages? The Milieus of Origin of *4QMysteries* and *4QInstruction.*" Pages 67–87 in *Sapiential Perspectives: Wisdom Literature in Light of the Dead Sea Scrolls.* Edited by John J. Collins, Gregory E. Sterling, and Ruth A. Clements. STDJ 51. Leiden: Brill, 2004.

———. "The Reconstruction of Sapiential Work A." *RevQ* 16 (1995): 559–80.

Evans, Craig A. "Daniel in the New Testament: Visions of God's Kingdom." Pages 490–527 in *The Book of Daniel: Composition and Reception*. Vol. 2. Edited by John J. Collins and Peter W. Flint. Leiden: Brill, 2002.

———. *Matthew*. Cambridge: Cambridge University Press, 2012.

———. "The Synoptic Gospels and the Dead Sea Scrolls." Pages 75–96 in *The Bible and the Dead Sea Scrolls*. Vol. 3: *The Scrolls and Christian Origins*. Edited by James H. Charlesworth. Waco, Tex.: Baylor University Press, 2006.

Falk, Daniel K. "Prayer, Liturgy, and War." Pages 275–94 in *The War Scroll: Violence, War and Peace in the Dead Sea Scrolls*. Edited by Kipp Davis, Dorothy M. Peters, Kyung S. Baek, and Peter W. Flint. STDJ 115. Leiden: Brill, 2016.

Fitzmyer, Joseph A. *Tobit*. Berlin: de Gruyter, 2003.

Forman, Mark. *The Politics of Inheritance in Romans*. SNTS 148. Cambridge: Cambridge University Press, 2011.

Forshey, H. O. "The Construct Chain naḥalat YHWH / 'alōhîm." *BASOR* 220 (1975): 51–53.

Foster, Paul. *Community, Law and Mission in Matthew's Gospel*. Tübingen: Mohr Siebeck, 2004.

France, R. T. *The Gospel of Matthew*. Grand Rapids: Eerdmans, 2007.

Fredriksen, Paula. *When Christians Were Jews: The First Generation*. New Haven: Yale University Press, 2018.

Frey, Jörg. "Different Patterns of Dualistic Thought in the Qumran Library: Reflections on Their Background and History." Pages 275–335 in *Legal Texts and Legal Issues*. Edited by M. Bernstein, F. García Martínez, and J. Kampen. Leiden: Brill, 1997.

Friedrich, Johannes. *Gott im Bruder? Eine methodenkritische Untersuchung von Redaktion, Überlieferung und Traditionen in MT 25,31-46*. Stuttgart: Calwer, 1977.

Fritz, Volkmar. *I & II Kings*. Minneapolis: Fortress, 2003.

Furnish, Victor Paul. *The Love Command in the New Testament*. Nashville: Abingdon, 1972.

García Martínez, Florentino. *Qumran and Apocalyptic: Studies on the Aramaic Texts from Qumran*. Leiden: Brill, 1992.

García Martínez, Florentino, and Mladen Popović, eds. *Defining Identities: We, You, and the Other in the Dead Sea Scrolls*. Leiden: Brill, 2008.

García Martínez, Florentino, and Eibert J. C. Tigchelaar, eds. *The Dead Sea Scrolls Study Edition*. Leiden: Brill, 1999.

García Martínez, Florentino, and A. S. van der Woude. "A 'Groningen' Hypothesis of Qumran Origins and Early History." *RevQ* 14 (1989–1990): 521–41.

Garland, David E. *The Intention of Matthew 23*. Leiden: Brill, 1979.

———. *Reading Matthew: A Literary and Theological Commentary on the First Gospel*. New York: Crossroad, 1993.

Gathercole, Simon. *Where Is Boasting? Early Jewish Soteriology and Paul's Response in Romans 1–5*. Grand Rapids: Eerdmans, 2002.

Geyser-Fouché, Ananda. "Another Look at the Identity of the Wicked Woman in 4Q184." *HTS* 72 (2016): 1–9.

Glasson, T. F. "What Is Apocalyptic?" *NTS* 27, no. 1 (1980): 98–105.

Goff, Matthew J. *4QInstruction*. Atlanta: SBL, 2013.

———. "Discerning Trajectories: 4QInstruction and the Sapiential Background of the Sayings Source Q." *JBL* 124, no. 4 (2005): 657–73.

———. *Discerning Wisdom: The Sapiential Literature of the Dead Sea Scrolls*. Leiden: Brill, 2007.

———. "Hellish Females: The Strange Woman of Septuagint Proverbs and 4QWiles of the Wicked Woman (4Q184)." *JSJ* 39 (2008): 20–45.

———. *The Worldly and Heavenly Wisdom of 4QInstruction*. STDJ 50. Leiden: Brill, 2003.

Golb, Norman. *Who Wrote the Dead Sea Scrolls? The Search for the Secret of Qumran*. New York: Scribner's, 1994.

Goldingay, John, and David Payne. *Isaiah 40–55*. Vol. 2. ICC. London: T&T Clark, 2006.

Goldstein, Jonathan A. *1 Maccabees*. AB 41. New York: Doubleday, 1976.

———. *II Maccabees*. AB 41A. New York: Doubleday, 1984.

Goppelt, Leonhard. *Theology of the New Testament*. Vol. 1. Grand Rapids: Eerdmans, 1981.

Gray, George Buchanan. *Numbers*. ICC. Edinburgh: T&T Clark, 1956.

Gray, Sherman. *The Least of My Brothers, Matthew 25:31-46: A History of Interpretation*. SBLDS 114. Atlanta: Scholars Press, 1989.

Green, H. Benedict. *Matthew: Poet of the Beatitudes*. JSNT 203. Sheffield: Sheffield Academic, 2001.

Greenberg, Moshe. "The Design and Themes of Ezekiel's Program of Restoration." *Int* 38 (1984): 181–208.

Grossman, Maxine. *Reading for History in the Damascus Document: A Methodological Method*. Leiden: Brill, 2002.

Guelich, Robert A. "The Matthean Beatitudes: 'Entrance Requirements' or Eschatological Blessings?" *JBL* 95, no. 3 (1976): 415–34.

Grüneberg, Keith N. *Abraham, Blessing, and the Nations: A Philological and Exegetical Study of Genesis 12:3 in Its Narrative Context*. Berlin: de Gruyter, 2003.

Gundry, R. H. *Matthew: A Commentary on His Handbook for a Mixed Church under Persecution*. Grand Rapids: Eerdmans, 1994.

———. *The Use of the Old Testament in St. Matthew's Gospel: With Special Reference to the Messianic Hope*. NTS. Leiden: Brill, 1968.

Gurtner, Daniel M. "Matthew's Theology of the Temple and the 'Parting of the Ways': Christian Origins and the First Gospel." Pages 128–53 in *Built upon the Rock: Studies in the Gospel of Matthew*. Edited by Daniel M. Gurtner and John Nolland. Grand Rapids: Eerdmans, 2008.

———. "The Gospel of Matthew from Stanton to Present: A Survey of Some Research Developments." Pages 23–38 in *Jesus, Matthew's Gospel and Early Christianity: Studies in Memory of Graham N. Stanton*. Edited by

Daniel M. Gurtner, Joel Willitts, and Richard A. Burridge. LNTS 435. London: Bloomsbury, 2011.

——. "Interpreting Apocalyptic Symbolism in the Gospel of Matthew." *BBR* 22, no. 4 (2012): 525–45.

Gutierrez, Gustavo. *A Theology of Liberation*. London: SCM Press, 1974.

Haacker, Klaus. "What Must I Do to Inherit Eternal Life? Implicit Christology in Jesus' Sayings about Life and the Kingdom." Pages 140–53 in *Jesus Research: An International Perspective*. Edited by James H. Charlesworth and Petr Pokorný. Grand Rapids: Eerdmans, 2009.

Habel, Norman. *The Land Is Mine*. Minneapolis: Fortress, 1995.

Hagner, Donald A. "Apocalyptic Motifs in the Gospel of Matthew: Continuity and Discontinuity." *HBT* 7, no 2 (1985): 53–82.

——. *Matthew 1–13*. WBC 33A. Dallas: Word Books, 1993.

——. *Matthew 14–28*. WBC 33B. Nashville: Thomas Nelson, 1995.

——. "Matthew: Apostate, Reformer, Revolutionary?" *NTS* 49, no. 2 (2003): 193–209.

——. *The New Testament: A Historical and Theological Introduction*. Grand Rapids: Baker Academic, 2012.

Halpern, Baruch. *The First Historians: The Hebrew Bible and History*. University Park: Pennsylvania State University Press, 1988.

Hamlin, E. John. *At Risk in the Promised Land*. Grand Rapids: Eerdmans, 1990.

Hann, Robert R. *The Manuscript History of the Psalms of Solomon*. Chico, Calif.: Scholars Press, 1982.

Hanson, K. C. "How Honorable! How Shameful! A Cultural Analysis of Matthew's Makarisms and Reproaches." *Semeia* 68 (1994): 81–111.

Hare, Douglas R. A. *The Theme of Jewish Persecution of the Christians in the Gospel According to Matthew*. Cambridge: Cambridge University Press, 1967.

Hare, Douglas R. A., and Daniel J. Harrington. "Make Disciples of All Nations (Mt 28:19)." *CBQ* 37, no. 3 (1975): 359–69.

Harrington, Daniel J. *The Gospel of Matthew*. Sacra Pagina. Collegeville, Minn.: Liturgical Press, 1991.

——. "Two Early Jewish Approaches to Wisdom: Sirach and Qumran Sapiential Work A." *JSP* 16 (1997): 263–75.

——. *Wisdom Texts from Qumran*. London: Routledge, 1996.

Harris, J. Rendel, ed. *The Apology of Aristides on Behalf of the Christians*. Cambridge: Cambridge University Press, 1893.

Hays, Richard B. *Echoes of Scripture in the Gospels*. Waco, Tex.: Baylor University Press, 2016.

Hempel, Charlotte. *The Laws of the Damascus Document: Sources, Tradition and Redaction*. Leiden: Brill, 1998.

——. "Qumran Communities: Beyond the Fringes of Second Temple Society." Pages 43–53 in *The Scrolls and the Scriptures: Qumran Fifty Years After*. Edited by Stanley E. Porter and Craig A. Evans. Sheffield: Sheffield Academic, 1997.

———. "The Treatise on the Two Spirits and the Literary History of the Rule of the Community." Pages 102–20 in *Dualism in Qumran*. Edited by Géza G. Xeravits. London: T&T Clark, 2010.

Hengel, Martin. "Das Gleichnis von den Weingärtnern Mc 12 1-12 im Lichte der Zenonpapyri und der rabbinischen Gleichnisse." *ZNW* 59 (1968): 1–39.

———. *Judaism and Hellenism*. 2 vols. Philadelphia: Fortress, 1973.

Hertzberg, Hans Wilhelm. *I & II Samuel*. London: SCM Press, 1964.

Hester, James D. *Paul's Concept of Inheritance: A Contribution to the Understanding of Heilsgeschichte*. SJT 14. Edinburgh: Oliver and Boyd, 1968.

———. "Socio-Rhetorical Criticism and the Parable of the Tenants." *JSNT* 45 (1992): 27–57.

Hood, Jason B. "Matthew 23–25: The Extent of Jesus' Fifth Discourse." *JBL* 128, no. 3 (2009): 527–43.

Hicks-Keeton, Jill. "Already/Not Yet: Eschatological Tension in the Book of Tobit." *JBL* 132, no. 1 (2013): 97–117.

Himmelfarb, Martha. "Temple and Priests in the Book of the Watchers, the Animal Apocalypse, and the Apocalypse of Weeks." Pages 219–35 in *The Early Enoch Literature*. Edited by Gabriele Boccaccini and John J. Collins. Leiden: Brill, 2007.

Hogeterp, Albert. *Expectations of the End: A Comparative Traditio-Historical Study of Eschatological, Apocalyptic, and Messianic Ideas in the Dead Sea Scrolls and the New Testament*. STDJ 83. Leiden: Brill, 2009.

Holladay, Carl. R. "The Beatitudes: Happiness and the Kingdom of God." Pages 141–67 in *The Bible and the Pursuit of Happiness*. Edited by Brent A. Strawn. Oxford: Oxford University Press, 2012.

Holladay, William L. *Jeremiah 1*. Hermeneia. Minneapolis: Fortress, 1986.

Horsley, Richard A. "The Dead Sea Scrolls and the Historical Jesus." Pages 37–60 in *The Bible and the Dead Sea Scrolls*. Vol. 3: *The Scrolls and Christian Origins*. Edited by James H. Charlesworth. Waco, Tex.: Baylor University Press, 2006.

Hoyt, Thomas, Jr. "The Poor/Rich Theme in the Beatitudes." *JRT* 37, no. 1 (1980): 31–41.

Hummel, Reinhart. *Die Auseinandersetzung zwischen Kirche und Judentum im Matthäusevangelium*. Munich: Kaiser, 1963.

Jacob, Haley Goranson. *Conformed to the Image of His Son: Reconsidering Paul's Theology of Glory in Romans*. Downers Grove, Ill.: IVP Academic, 2018.

Jassen, Alex P. "Violent Imaginaries and Practical Violence in the *War Scroll*." Pages 175–203 in *The War Scroll: Violence, War and Peace in the Dead Sea Scrolls*. Edited by Kipp Davis, Dorothy M. Peters, Kyung S. Baek, and Peter W. Flint. STDJ 115. Leiden: Brill, 2016.

Jefferies, Daryl. *Wisdom at Qumran: A Form-Critical Analysis of the Admonitions in 4QInstruction*. Piscataway, N.J.: Gorgias, 2002.

Jeremias, Joachim. *The Parables of Jesus*. London: SCM Press, 1954.

Jobes, Karen H., and Moisés Silva. *Invitation to the Septuigint.* Grand Rapids: Baker Academic, 2000.

Johnson Hodge, Caroline. *If Sons, Then Heirs: A Study of Kinship and Ethnicity in the Letters of Paul.* Oxford: Oxford University Press, 2007.

Jokiranta, Jutta. "Sectarianism." Pages 1209–11 in *The Eerdmans Dictionary of Early Judaism.* Edited by John J. Collins and Daniel C. Harlow. Grand Rapids: Eerdmans, 2010.

———. *Social Identity and Sectarianism in the Qumran Movement.* STDJ. Leiden: Brill, 2013.

Jones, Scott C. "Wisdom's Pedagogy: A Comparison of Proverbs VII and 4Q184." *VT* 53 (2003): 65–80.

Jülicher, Adolf. *Die Gleichnisreden Jesu.* Repr. Darmstadt: Wissenschaftliche Buchgesellschaft, 1963.

Kaiser, Otto. *Isaiah 13–39.* London: SCM Press, 1974.

Kampen, John. "Aspects of Wisdom in the Gospel of Matthew in Light of the New Qumran Evidence." Pages 227–39 in *Sapiential, Liturgical and Poetical Texts from Qumran.* Edited by Daniel K. Falk, Florentino García Martínez, and Eileen M. Schuller. STDJ 35. Leiden: Brill, 2000.

———. *Wisdom Literature.* Grand Rapids: Eerdmans, 2011.

———. "Wisdom, Poverty, and Non-Violence in *Instruction.*" Pages 215–36 in *The War Scroll: Violence, War and Peace in the Dead Sea Scrolls.* Edited by Kipp Davis, Dorothy M. Peters, Kyung S. Baek, and Peter W. Flint. STDJ 115. Leiden: Brill, 2016.

———. *Matthew within Sectarian Judaism.* New Haven: Yale University Press, 2019.

Keefer, Kyle. *The New Testament as Literature: A Very Short Introduction.* Oxford: Oxford University Press, 2008.

Keener, Craig S. *The Gospel of Matthew: A Socio-Rhetorical Commentary.* Grand Rapids: Eerdmans, 2009.

Kingsbury, Jack Dean. *Matthew: Structure, Christology, Kingdom.* Minneapolis: Fortress, 1975.

———. "The Parable of the Wicked Husbandmen and the Secret of Jesus' Divine Sonship in Matthew: Some Literary-Critical Observations." *JBL* 105, no. 4 (1986): 643–55.

Kinney, Robert S. *Hellenistic Dimensions of the Gospel of Matthew.* Tübingen: Mohr Siebeck, 2016.

Kislev, Itamar. "Numbers 36, 1-12, Innovation and Interpretation." *ZAW* 122, no. 2 (2010): 249–59.

Kister, Menahem. "Wisdom Literature and Its Relation to Other Genres: From Ben Sira to *Mysteries.*" Pages 13–47 in *Sapiential Perspectives: Wisdom Literature in Light of the Dead Sea Scrolls.* Edited by John J. Collins, Gregory E. Sterling, and Ruth A. Clements. STDJ 51. Leiden: Brill, 2004.

Klein, Lillian R. *The Triumph of Irony in the Book of Judges.* Sheffield: Almond Press, 1988.

Kloppenborg, John S. *The Tenants in the Vineyard: Ideology, Economics, and Agrarian Conflict in Jewish Palestine.* Tübingen: Mohr Siebeck, 2006.

Knibb, Michael A. "The Book of Enoch or the Books of Enoch?" Pages 21–40 in *The Early Enoch Literature*. Edited by Gabriele Boccaccini and John J. Collins. Leiden: Brill, 2007.

———. *The Ethiopic Book of Enoch: A New Edition in Light of the Aramaic Dead Sea Fragments*. Vol. 2. Oxford: Clarendon, 1978.

Knowles, Michael P. "Scripture, History, Messiah: Scriptural Fulfillment and the Fullness of Time in Matthew's Gospel." Pages 59–82 in *Hearing the Old Testament in the New Testament*. Edited by Stanley E. Porter. Grand Rapids: Eerdmans, 2006.

Koch, Klaus. *The Growth of the Biblical Tradition: The Form-Critical Method*. London: Adam & Charles Black, 1969.

———. "What Is Apocalyptic? An Attempt at a Preliminary Definition." Pages 16–36 in *Visionaries and Their Apocalypses*. Edited by Paul D. Hanson. London: SPCK, 1983.

Konradt, Matthias. *Israel, Church, and the Gentiles in the Gospel of Matthew*. Waco, Tex.: Baylor University Press, 2014.

Kümmel, W. G. *Introduction to the New Testament*. London: SCM Press, 1975.

———. *Promise and Fulfilment: The Eschatological Message of Jesus*. London: SCM Press, 1961.

Ladd, George Eldon. *A Theology of the New Testament*. Grand Rapids: Eerdmans, 2000.

Lanier, Gregory R. "The Rejected Stone in the Parable of the Wicked Tenants: Defending the Authenticity of Jesus' Quotation of Ps 118:22." *JETS* 56, no. 4 (2013): 733–51.

Lange, Armin. "The Determination of Fate by the Oracle of the Lot in the Dead Sea Scrolls, the Hebrew Bible and Ancient Mesopotamian Literature." Pages 39–48 in *Sapiential, Liturgical and Poetical Texts from Qumran*. Edited by Daniel K. Falk, Florentino García Martínez, and Eileen M. Schuller. STDJ 35. Leiden: Brill, 2000.

Larsen, Matthew D. C. *Gospels before the Book*. Oxford: Oxford University Press, 2018.

Levine, Baruch A. *Numbers 21–36*. AB. New York: Doubleday, 2000.

Levenson, John Douglas. *Theology of the Program of Restoration of Ezekiel 40–48*. Missoula, Mont.: Scholars Press, 1976.

Lewis, Theodore J. "The Ancestral Estate (נַחֲלַת אלהים) in 2 Samuel 14:16." *JBL* 110, no. 4 (1991): 597–612.

———. "The Textual History of the Song of Hannah: 1 Samuel II:1-10." *VT* 44, no. 1 (1994): 18–46.

Linebaugh, Jonathan A. "Debating Diagonal Δικαιοσύνη: The Epistle of Enoch and Paul in Theological Conversation." *Early Christianity* 1 (2010): 107–28.

Longman, Tremper, III. *The Fear of the Lord Is Wisdom: A Theological Introduction to Wisdom in Israel*. Grand Rapids: Baker Academic, 2017.

Lundbom, Jack R. *Jeremiah 1–20*. AB 21A. New York: Doubleday, 1999.

———. *Jesus' Sermon on the Mount: Mandating a Better Righteousness.* Minneapolis: Fortress, 2015.

Luz, Ulrich. *Studies in Matthew.* Grand Rapids: Eerdmans, 2005.

———. *Matthew 1–7.* Hermeneia. Minneapolis: Fortress, 2007.

Macaskill, Grant. *Revealed Wisdom and Inaugurated Eschatology in Ancient Judaism and Early Christianity.* Leiden: Brill, 2007.

Malamat, Abraham. "Mari and the Bible: Some Patterns of Tribal Organization and Institutions." *Journal of the American Oriental Society* 82, no. 2 (1962): 143–50.

Manor, Dale W. "A Brief History of Levirate Marriage as It Relates to the Bible." *Restoration Quarterly* 27, no. 3 (1984): 129–42.

Marguerat, Daniel. *Le Jugment dans l'Evangile de Matthieu.* Geneva: Labor et Fides, 1981.

Marquis, Liane M. "The Composition of Numbers 32: A New Proposal." *VT* 63, no. 3 (2013): 408–32.

Matthews, Victor H. "Family Relationships." In *Dictionary of the Old Testament: Pentateuch.* Edited by T. Desmond Alexander and David W. Baker. Downers Grove, Ill.: InterVarsity Press, 2003.

———. *Judges and Ruth.* New Cambridge Bible Commentary. Cambridge: Cambridge University Press, 2004.

Mattison, William C, III. "The Beatitudes and Moral Theology: A Virtue-Ethics Approach." *Nova et Vetera*, English Edition 11, no. 3 (2013): 819–48.

McCarter, P. Kyle Jr. *II Samuel.* AB 9. New York: Doubleday, 1984.

McConville, J. G. *Deuteronomy.* Downers Grove, Ill.: InterVarsity Press, 2002.

McEleney, Neil J. "The Beatitudes of the Sermon on the Mount/Plain." *CBQ* 43, no. 1 (1981): 1–13.

McKane, William. *Jeremiah.* Vol. 1. ICC. Edinburgh: T&T Clark, 1986.

McKnight, Scot. *A New Vision for Israel: The Teachings of Jesus in National Context.* Grand Rapids: Eerdmans, 1999.

———. *Sermon on the Mount.* SGBC. Grand Rapids: Zondervan, 2013.

McNeile, Alan Hugh. *The Gospel According to St. Matthew.* Grand Rapids: Baker Book House, 1980.

Meeks, Wayne. *The Moral World of the First Christians.* Philadelphia: Westminster, 1986.

Meier, John P. *Matthew.* Dublin: Veritas Publications, 1980.

Menken, M. J. J. *Matthew's Bible: The Old Testament Text of the Evangelist.* Leuven: Leuven University Press, 2004.

Metso, Sarianna. "The Relationship between the Damascus Document and the Community Rule." Pages 85–94 in *The Damascus Document: A Centennial of Discovery.* Edited by Joseph M. Baumgarten, Esther G. Chazon, and Avital Pinnick. Leiden: Brill, 2000.

———. *The Serekh Texts.* London: T&T Clark, 2007.

———. *The Textual Development of the Qumran Community Rule.* STDJ 21. Leiden: Brill, 1997.

Metzger, Bruce M. *A Textual Commentary on the Greek New Testament.* Stuttgart: UBS, 1994.

Michaels, J. Ramsey. "Apostolic Hardships and Righteous Gentiles: A Study of Matthew 25:31-46." *JBL* 84, no. 1 (1965): 27–37.

Milik, J. T. *The Books of Enoch: Aramaic Fragments of Qumran Cave 4.* Oxford: Clarendon, 1976.

Minear, Paul S. "The Disciples and the Crowds in the Gospel of Matthew." Pages 28–44 in *Gospel Studies in Honor of Sherman Elbridge Johnson.* Edited by Massey H. Shepherd Jr. and Edward C. Hobbs. *Anglican Theological Review* Supplementary Series 3, 1974.

Mitchell, Gordon. *Together in the Land: A Reading of the Book of Joshua.* Sheffield: JSOT Press, 1993.

Mohrlang, Roger. *Matthew and Paul: A Comparison of Ethical Perspectives.* Cambridge: Cambridge University Press, 1984.

Moore, Carey A. *Judith.* AB 40. New York: Doubleday, 1985.

———. *Tobit.* AB 40A. New York: Doubleday, 1996.

Morgenstern, Matthew. "The Meaning of בין מולדים in the Qumran Wisdom Texts." *JJS* 51 (2000): 141–44.

Moyise, Steve. *Jesus and Scripture: Studying the New Testament Use of the Old Testament.* Grand Rapids: Baker Academic, 2010.

Murphy, C. M. *Wealth in the Dead Seas Scrolls and in the Qumran Literature.* STDJ 40. Leiden: Brill, 2001.

Murphy-O'Connor, Jerome. "The Critique of the Princes of Judah (CD VIII, 3–19)." *RB* 79 (1972): 200–216.

———. "An Essene Missionary Document? CD II, 14–VI, 1." *RB* 77 (1970): 201–29.

———. "The Essenes and Their History." *RB* 81 (1974): 215–44.

———. "A Literary Analysis of Damascus Document VI, 2–VIII, 3." *RB* 78 (1971): 210–32.

———. "A Literary Analysis of Damascus Document XIX, 33–XX, 34." *RB* 79 (1972): 544–64.

Najman, Hindy. "The Idea of Biblical Genre: From Discourse to Constellation." Pages 307–21 in *Prayer and Poetry in the Dead Sea Scrolls and Related Literature.* Edited by Jeremy Penner, Ken M. Penner, and Cecilia Wassen. STDJ 98. Leiden: Brill, 2012.

———. "Jewish Wisdom in the Hellenistic Period: Towards the Study of Semantic Constellation." Pages 459–72 in *Is There a Text in This Cave?* Edited by Ariel Feldman, Maria Cioata, and Charlotte Hempel. STDJ 119. Leiden: Brill, 2017.

New International Dictionary of New Testament Theology and Exegesis. 2nd ed. Edited by Moisés Silva. 5 vols. Grand Rapids: Zondervan, 2014.

New International Dictionary of Old Testament Theology and Exegesis. Edited by William A. VanGemeren. 5 vols. Grand Rapids: Zondervan, 1997.

Newport, Kenneth G. C. *The Sources and Sitz im Leben of Matthew 23.* JSNTS. Sheffield: Sheffield Academic, 1995.

Newsom, Carol A. "'Sectually Explicit' Literature from Qumran." Pages 167–88 in *The Hebrew Bible and Its Interpreters*. Edited by William Henry Propp, Baruch Halpern, and David Noel Freedman. Winona Lake, Ind.: Eisenbrauns, 1990.

———. *The Self as Symbolic Space: Constructing Identity and Community at Qumran*. Leiden: Brill, 2004.

Nickelsburg, George W. E. *1 Enoch 1*. Hermeneia. Minneapolis: Fortress, 2001.

———. "Enochic Wisdom and Its Relationship to the Mosaic Torah." Pages 81–94 in *The Early Enoch Literature*. Edited by Gabriele Boccaccini and John J. Collins. Leiden: Brill, 2007.

———. *Jewish Literature between the Bible and the Mishnah*. London: SCM Press, 1981.

———. "Wisdom and Apocalypticism in Early Judaism: Some Points for Discussion." Pages 17–38 in *Conflicted Boundaries in Wisdom and Apocalypticism*. Edited by Lawrence M. Wills and Benjamin G. Wright III. Atlanta: SBL, 2005.

Nickelsburg, George W. E., and James C. Vanderkam. *1 Enoch: The Hermeneia Translation*. Minneapolis: Fortress, 2012.

Nolland, John. *The Gospel of Matthew: A Commentary on the Greek Text*. New International Greek Testament Commentary. Grand Rapids: Eerdmans, 2005.

Noth, Martin. *The Deuteronomistic History*. Sheffield: JSOT Press, 1991.

———. *Numbers*. London: SCM Press, 1968.

Olmstead, Wesley G. "A Gospel for a New Nation: Once More, the ἔθνος of Matthew 21.43." Pages 113–32 in *Jesus, Matthew's Gospel and Early Christianity: Studies in Memory of Graham N. Stanton*. Edited by Daniel M. Gurtner, Joel Willitts, and Richard A. Burridge. LNTS 435. London: Bloomsbury, 2011.

———. *Matthew 1–14: A Handbook on the Greek Text*. Waco, Tex.: Baylor University Press, 2019.

———. *Matthew 15–28: A Handbook on the Greek Text*. Waco, Tex.: Baylor University Press, 2019.

———. *Matthew's Trilogy of Parables*. Cambridge: Cambridge University Press, 2003.

Orlinsky, Harry M. "The Biblical Concept of the Land of Israel: Cornerstone of the Covenant between God and Israel." In *The Land of Israel*. Notre Dame: University of Notre Dame Press, 1986.

Otzen, Benedikt. *Tobit and Judith*. Sheffield: Sheffield Academic, 2002.

Overman, J. Andrew. *Matthew's Gospel and Formative Judaism: The Social World of the Matthean Community*. Minneapolis: Fortress, 1990.

Parry, Donald W., and Emanuel Tov, eds. *The Dead Sea Scrolls Reader*. 6 vols. Leiden: Brill, 2004.

Pelikan, Jaroslav. *Divine Rhetoric: The Sermon on the Mount as Message and as Model in Augustine, Chrysostom, and Luther*. Crestwood: St. Vladimir's Seminary Press, 2006.

Pennington, Jonathan T. *Heaven and Earth in the Gospel of Matthew*. Grand Rapids: Baker Academic, 2009.

———. *The Sermon on the Mount and Human Flourishing: A Theological Commentary*. Grand Rapids: Baker Academic, 2017.

Perrin, Andrew B. "An Almanac of Tobit Studies: 2000–2014." *CBR* 13 no. 1 (2014): 107–42.

Petersen, A. Klostergaard. "Wisdom as Cognition: Creating the Others in the Book of Mysteries and 1 Cor 1–2." Pages 405–32 in *Wisdom Texts from Qumran*. Edited by C. Hempel, A. Lange, and H. Lichtenberger. Leuven: Leuven University Press, 2002.

Pickup, Martin. "Matthew's and Mark's Pharisees." Pages 67–112 in *In Quest of the Historical Pharisees*. Edited by Jacob Neusner and Bruce D. Chilton. Waco, Tex.: Baylor University Press, 2007.

Piovanelli, Pierluigi. "Sitting by the Waters of Dan, or the Tricky Business of Tracing the Social Profile of the Communities That Produced the Earliest Enochic Texts." Pages 257–81 in *The Early Enoch Literature*. Edited by Gabriele Boccaccini and John J. Collins. Leiden: Brill, 2007.

Popović, Mladen. "Light and Darkness in the Treatise on the Two Spirits (1QS III 13–IV 26) and in 4Q186." Pages 148–65 in *Dualism in Qumran*. Edited by Géza G. Xeravits. London: T&T Clark, 2010.

Powell, Mark Allen. "Matthew's Beatitudes: Reversals and Rewards of the Kingdom." *CBQ* 58, no. 3 (1996): 460–79.

———. Review of David C. Sim, *The Gospel of Matthew and Christian Judaism: The History and Social Setting of the Matthean Community*. *HBT* 22, no. 1 (2000): 85–88.

Provan, Iain, V. Philips Long, and Tremper Longman III. *A Biblical History of Israel*. Louisville: Westminster John Knox, 2003.

Przybylski, Benno. *Righteousness in Matthew and His World of Thought*. SNTS 41. Cambridge: Cambridge University Press, 1980.

Puech, Émile. "The Collection of Beatitudes in Hebrew and Greek (4Q525 1–4 and Mt 5:3-12)." Pages 353–68 in *Early Christianity in Context: Monuments and Documents*. Edited by F. Manns and E. Alliata. SBF 38. Jerusalem: Franciscan Printing Press, 1993.

Quarles, Charles. "The Blessings of the New Moses: An Examination of the Theological Purpose of the Matthean Beatitudes." *JSHJ* 13 (2015): 307–27.

———. *Sermon on the Mount: Christ's Message to the Modern Church*. Nashville: B&H, 2011.

Reeves, Rodney. *Matthew*. SGBC. Grand Rapids: Zondervan, 2017.

Reiser, Marius. *Jesus and Judgment: The Eschatological Proclamation in Its Jewish Context*. Minneapolis: Fortress, 1997.

Rey, Jean-Sébastien. *4QInstruction: Sagesse et eschatologie*. STDJ 81. Leiden: Brill, 2009.

Riches, John, and David C. Sim, eds. *The Gospel of Matthew in Its Roman Imperial Context*. London: T&T Clark, 2005.

Rofé, Alexander. "Revealed Wisdom: From the Bible to Qumran." Pages 1–11 in *Sapiential Perspectives: Wisdom Literature in Light of the Dead Sea Scrolls*. Edited by John J. Collins, Gregory E. Sterling, and Ruth A. Clements. STDJ 51. Leiden: Brill, 2004.

Römer, Thomas. *The So-Called Deuteronomistic History: A Sociological, Historical, and Literary Introduction*. London: T&T Clark, 2007.

Rowland, Christopher. "Apocalyptic, the Poor, and the Gospel of Matthew." *JTS* 45, no. 2 (1994): 504–18.

——. "Apocalypticism." Pages 345–48 in *The Eerdmans Dictionary of Early Judaism*. Edited by John J. Collins and Daniel C. Harlow. Grand Rapids: Eerdmans, 2010.

Runesson, Anders. "Judging Gentiles in the Gospel of Matthew: Between 'Othering' and Inclusion." Pages 133–51 in *Jesus, Matthew's Gospel and Early Christianity: Studies in Memory of Graham N. Stanton*. LNTS 435. Edited by Daniel M. Gurtner, Joel Willitts, and Richard A. Burridge. London: Bloomsbury, 2011.

Russell, Stephen C. "Ideologies of Attachment in the Story of Naboth's Vineyard." *BTB* 44 (2014): 29–39.

Saldarini, Anthony J. *Matthew's Christian-Jewish Community*. Chicago: University of Chicago Press, 1994.

Sanders, E. P. *Paul and Palestinian Judaism*. Minneapolis: Fortress, 1977.

——. *The Provenance of Deuteronomy 32*. Leiden: Brill, 1996.

Schiffman, Lawrence H. *Reclaiming the Dead Sea Scrolls: The History of Judaism, the Background of Christianity, the Lost Library of Qumran*. Philadelphia: JPS, 1994.

Schliesser, Benjamin. *Abraham's Faith in Romans 4*. Tübingen: Mohr Siebeck, 2007.

Schmid, Konrad, and Odil Hannes Steck. "Restoration Expectations in the Prophetic Tradition of the Old Testament." Pages 41–82 in *Restoration: Old Testament, Jewish, and Christian Perspectives*. Edited by James M. Scott. Leiden: Brill, 2001.

Schofield, Alison. "Rereading S: A New Model of Textual Development in Light of the Cave 4 *Serekh* Copies." *DSD* 15 (2008): 96–120.

Schultz, Brian. *Conquering the World: The War Scroll (1QM) Reconsidered*. Leiden: Brill, 2009.

Schweizer, Eduard. "Formgeschichtliches zu den Seligpreisungen Jesu." *NTS* 19, no. 2 (1973): 121–26.

——. *The Good News According to Matthew*. Atlanta: John Knox, 1975.

Scott, James M. *Paul and the Nations*. Tübingen: Mohr Siebeck, 1995.

Senior, Donald. "Between Two Worlds: Gentiles and Jewish Christians in Matthew's Gospel." *CBQ* 61, no. 1 (1999): 1–23.

Sim, David C. *Apocalyptic Eschatology in the Gospel of Matthew*. Cambridge: Cambridge University Press, 1996.

——. *The Gospel of Matthew and Christian Judaism: The History and Social Setting of the Matthean Community*. Edinburgh: T&T Clark, 1998.

———. "The Meaning of παλιγγενεσίᾳ in Matthew 19:28." *JSNT* 50 (1993): 3–12.

Sinnott, Alice M. *The Personification of Wisdom.* Aldershot: Ashgate, 2005.

Skehan, Patrick W., and Alexander A. Di Lella. *The Wisdom of Ben Sira.* AB 39. New York: Doubleday, 1987.

Snodgrass, Klyne. *The Parable of the Wicked Tenants.* Tübingen: Mohr Siebeck, 1983.

———. "Recent Research on the Parable of the Wicked Tenants: An Assessment." *BBR* 8 (1998): 187–216.

———. *Stories with Intent: A Comprehensive Guide to the Parables of Jesus.* Grand Rapids: Eerdmans, 2008.

Sparks, H. F. D. "The Doctrine of the Divine Fatherhood in the Gospels." Pages 241–62 in *Studies in the Gospels: Essays in Honor of R. H. Lightfoot.* Edited by D. E. Nineham. Oxford: Basil Blackwell, 1967.

Speiser, E. A. "Notes to Recently Published Nuzi Texts." *JAOS* 55 (1935): 432–43.

Spronk, Klaas. "Some Remarks on the Origin of the Book of Judges." Pages 137–50 in *The Land of Israel in Bible, History, and Theology: Studies in Honor of Ed Noort.* Edited by Jacques van Ruiten and J. Cornelis de Vos. Leiden: Brill, 2009.

Stager, Lawrence E. "Forging an Identity: The Emergence of Ancient Israel." In *The Oxford History of the Biblical World.* New York: Oxford University Press, 1998.

Stanton, Graham. *A Gospel for a New People: Studies in Matthew.* Louisville: Westminster John Knox, 1992.

Stegemann, Hartmut. "The Qumran Essenes: Local Members of the Main Jewish Union in Late Second Temple Times." Pages 83–166 in *The Madrid Qumran Congress.* Edited by J. Trebolle and L. Vegas Montaner. Leiden: Brill, 1992.

Stone, Michael E. "The Book of Enoch and Judaism in the Third Century B.C.E." *CBQ* 40, no. 4 (1978): 479–92.

Strecker, Georg. *The Sermon on the Mount: An Exegetical Commentary.* Edinburgh: T&T Clark, 1988.

———. *Der Weg der Gerechtigkeit: Untersuchung zur Theologie des Matthäus.* Göttingen: Vandenhoeck & Ruprecht, 1971.

Strugnell, John, Daniel J. Harrington, and Torleif Elgvin. *Discoveries in the Judaean Desert XXXIV: Sapiential Texts Part 2, 4QInstruction.* Oxford: Clarendon, 1999.

Stuckenbruck, Loren T. *1 Enoch 91–108.* Berlin: de Gruyter, 2007.

———. "4QInstruction and the Possible Influence of Early Enochic Traditions: An Evaluation." Pages 245–62 in *Wisdom Texts from Qumran and the Development of Sapiential Thought.* Leuven: Leuven University Press, 2002.

———. "Angels and God: Exploring the Limits of Early Jewish Monotheism." Pages 43–70 in *Early Jewish and Christian Monotheism.*

Edited by Loren T. Stuckenbruck and Wendy E. S. North. London: T&T Clark, 2004.

———. "The Dead Sea Scrolls and the New Testament." Pages 131–70 in *Qumran and the Bible: Studying the Jewish and Christian Scriptures in Light of the Dead Sea Scrolls*. Edited by Nóra Dávid and Armin Lange. Leuven: Peeters, 2010.

———. "The Interiorization of Dualism within the Human Being in Second Temple Judaism." Pages 145–68 in *Light against Darkness: Dualism in Ancient Mediterranean Religion and the Contemporary World*. Edited by Eric Myers, Armin Lange, and Randall Styers. Göttingen: Vandenhoeck & Ruprecht, 2010.

———. "The Plant Metaphor in Its Inner-Enochic and Early Jewish Context." Pages 210–12 in *Enoch and Its Qumran Origins: New Light on a Forgotten Connection*. Edited by Gabriele Boccaccini. Grand Rapids: Eerdmans, 2005.

Suggs, M. Jack. *Wisdom, Christology and Law in Matthew's Gospel*. Cambridge, Mass.: Harvard University Press, 1970.

Suh, Joong Suk. "Das Weltgericht und die Matthäische Gemeinde." *NovT* 48, no. 3 (2006): 217–33.

Suter, David W. "Temples and the Temple in the Early Enoch Tradition: Memory, Vision, and Expectations." Pages 195–218 in *The Early Enoch Literature*. Edited by Gabriele Boccaccini and John J. Collins. Leiden: Brill, 2007.

Sweeney, Marvin A. *I & II Kings*. Louisville: Westminster John Knox, 2007.

———. "Structure and Redaction in Isaiah 2–4." *HAR* 11 (1987): 407–22.

Talbert, Charles H. *Reading the Sermon on the Mount: Character Formation and Decision Making in Matthew 5–7*. Grand Rapids: Baker Academic, 2004.

Thompson, Marianne Meye. *The Promise of the Father: Jesus and God in the New Testament*. Louisville: Westminster John Knox, 2000.

Tigchelaar, Eibert J. C. "The Addressees of 4QInstruction." Pages 62–75 in *Sapiential, Liturgical and Poetical Texts from Qumran*. STDJ 35. Edited by Daniel K. Falk, Florentino García Martínez, and Eileen M. Schuller. Leiden: Brill, 2000.

———. *To Increase Learning for the Understanding Ones: Reading and Reconstructing the Fragmentary Early Jewish Sapiential Text 4QInstruction*. Leiden: Brill, 2001.

Tiller, Patrick A. "The 'Eternal Planting' in the Dead Sea Scrolls." *DSD* 4, no. 3 (1997): 312–35.

———. "The Sociological Settings of the Components of 1 Enoch." Pages 237–55 in *The Early Enoch Literature*. Edited by Gabriele Boccaccini and John J. Collins. Leiden: Brill, 2007.

Tooman, William A. "Wisdom at Qumran: Evidence from the Sapiential Texts." Pages 203–32 in *Wisdom and Torah: The Reception of Torah in the Wisdom Literature of the Second Temple Period*. Edited by Bernd U. Schipper and D. Andrew Teeter. Leiden: Brill, 2013.

Tov, Emanuel. *Textual Criticism of the Hebrew Bible*. Minneapolis: Fortress, 1992.

Trafton, Joseph L. "The Psalms of Solomon: New Light from the Syriac Version?" *JBL* 105, no. 2 (1986): 227–37.

———. *The Syriac Version of the Psalms of Solomon: A Critical Evaluation*. Atlanta: Scholars Press, 1985.

Trilling, Wolfgang. *Das Wahre Israel*. Leipzig: St. Benno-Verlag, 1959.

Tromp, Johannes. "The Davidic Messiah in Jewish Eschatology of the First Century BCE." Pages 179–202 in *Restoration: Old Testament, Jewish, and Christian Perspectives*. Edited by James M. Scott. Leiden: Brill, 2001.

———. "The Sinners and the Lawless in the Psalm of Solomon XVII." *NovT* 35, no. 4 (1993): 344–61.

Tsumura, David Toshio. *The First Book of Samuel*. NICOT. Grand Rapids: Eerdmans, 2007.

Tuell, Steven Shawn. *The Law of the Temple in Ezekiel 40–48*. Atlanta: Scholars Press, 1992.

Uusimäki, Elisa. "Happy Is the Person to Whom She Has Been Given: The Continuum of Wisdom and Torah in *4QSapiential Admonitions* (4Q185) and *4QBeatitudes* (4Q525)." *RDQ* 26, no. 3 (2014): 345–59.

———. *Turning Proverbs towards Torah*. Leiden: Brill, 2016.

Van Seters, John. *The Pentateuch: A Social Science Commentary*. Sheffield: Sheffield Academic, 1999.

Van Tilborg, Sjef. *The Jewish Leaders in Matthew*. Leiden: Brill, 1972.

Vermes, Geza. *The Complete Dead Sea Scrolls in English*. London: Penguin Books, 2011.

Viljoen, Francois P. "Righteousness and Identity Formation in the Sermon on the Mount." *HTS* 69, no. 1 (2013): 1–10.

Von Rad, Gerhard. *Genesis*. London: SCM Press, 1961.

———. *Old Testament Theology*. Vol 1. London: SCM Press Ltd, 1965.

———. "The Promised Land and Yahweh's Land in the Hexateuch." In *The Problem of the Hexateuch and Other Essays*. London: SCM Press, 1984.

———. *Wisdom in Israel*. London: SCM Press, 1972.

Wacholder, Ben Zion. *The New Damascus Document: The Midrash on the Eschatological Torah of the Dead Sea Scrolls; Reconstruction, Translation and Commentary*. STDJ 56. Leiden: Brill, 2007.

Walsh, Jerome T. *1 Kings*. Berit Olam. Collegeville, Minn.: Liturgical Press, 1996.

Wassén, Cecilia. "Visions of the Temple: Conflicting Images of the Eschaton." *Svensk exegetisk årsbok* 76 (2011): 41–59.

Watts, John D. W. *Isaiah 1–33*. WBC 24. Nashville: Thomas Nelson, 1985.

———. *Isaiah 34–66*. WBC 25. Columbia: Nelson Reference, 2005.

Wazana, Nili. "'Everything Was Fulfilled' versus 'The Land That Yet Remains.'" Pages 13–35 in *The Gift of the Land and the Fate of the Canaanites in Jewish Thought*. Edited by Katell Berthelot, Joseph E. David, and Marc Hirshman. Oxford: Oxford University Press, 2014.

Webb, Barry G. *The Book of Judges*. NICOT. Grand Rapids: Eerdmans, 2012.

Weber, Kathleen. "The Image of Sheep and Goats in Matthew 25:31-46." *CBQ* 59, no. 4 (1997): 657–78.

Weeks, Stuart. *An Introduction to the Study of Wisdom Literature.* London: T&T Clark, 2010.

Weeks, Stuart, Simon Gathercole, and Loren T. Stuckenbruck. *The Book of Tobit: Texts from the Principal Ancient and Medieval Traditions.* Berlin: de Gruyter, 2004.

Weinfeld, Moshe *Deuteronomy 1–11.* AB 5. New York: Doubleday, 1991.

———. *The Promise of the Land: The Inheritance of the Land of Canaan by the Israelites.* Berkeley: University of California Press, 1993.

Weiss, Johannes. *Jesus' Proclamation of the Kingdom of God.* Edited by Richard Hyde Hiers and David Larrimore Holland. London: SCM Press, 1971.

Welch, John W. *The Sermon on the Mount in the Light of the Temple.* Farnham: Ashgate, 2009.

Wenham, Gordon J. *Genesis 1–15.* WBC 1. Waco, Tex.: Word Books, 1987.

Weren, W. J. C. "The Use of Isaiah 5:1-7 in the Parable of the Tenants (Mark 12:1-12; Matthew 21:33-46)." *Bib* 79, no. 1 (1998): 1–26.

Werman, Cana. "What Is the Book of Hagu?" Pages 125–40 in *Sapiential Perspectives: Wisdom Literature in Light of the Dead Sea Scrolls.* Edited by John J. Collins, Gregory E. Sterling, and Ruth Clements. STDJ 51. Leiden: Brill, 2004.

Westerholm, Stephen. *Understanding Matthew: The Early Christian Worldview of the First Gospel.* Grand Rapids: Baker Academic, 2006.

Westermann, Claus. *Genesis 12–36.* London: SPCK, 1985.

———. *Isaiah 40–66.* Philadelphia: Westminster, 1969.

Williamson, H. G. M. *Isaiah 1–27.* Vol. 1. London: T&T Clark, 2006.

Willitts, Joel. "Matthew." Pages 82–100 in *Jesus Is Lord, Caesar Is Not: Evaluating Empire in New Testament Studies.* Edited by Scot McKnight and Joseph B. Modica. Downers Grove, Ill.: IVP Academic, 2013.

———. "Matthew and Psalms of Solomon's Messianism: A Comparative Study of First Century Messianology." *BBR* 22, no. 1 (2012): 27–50.

———. *Matthew's Messianic Shepherd-King: In Search of "The Lost Sheep of the House of Israel."* Berlin: de Gruyter, 2007.

———. "The Twelve Disciples in Matthew." Pages 166–79 in *Jesus, Matthew's Gospel and Early Christianity: Studies in Memory of Graham N. Stanton.* Edited by Daniel M. Gurtner, Joel Willitts, and Richard A. Burridge. LNTS 435. London: Bloomsbury, 2011.

Windisch, Hans. *The Meaning of the Sermon on the Mount.* Philadelphia: Westminster, 1951.

Witherington, Ben, III. *Jesus, Paul, and the End of the World: A Comparative Study in New Testament Eschatology.* Downers Grove, Ill.: InterVarsity Press, 1992.

———. *Matthew.* Macon, Ga.: Smyth & Helwys, 2006.

Wold, Benjamin G. *4QInstruction: Divisions and Hierarchies.* STDJ 123. Leiden: Brill, 2018.

———. *Women, Men, and Angels.* Tübingen: Mohr Siebeck, 2005.

Wright, Benjamin G. "The Categories of Rich and Poor in the Qumran Sapiential Literature." Pages 101–23 in *Sapiential Perspectives: Wisdom Literature in Light of the Dead Sea Scrolls*. Edited by John J. Collins, Gregory E. Sterling, and Ruth Clements. STDJ 51. Leiden: Brill, 2004.

Wright, Christopher J. H. *God's People in God's Land: Family, Land, and Property in the Old Testament*. Grand Rapids: Eerdmans, 1990.

Wright, N. T. *Finding God in the Psalms*. London: SPCK, 2014.

———. *Jesus and the Victory of God*. Minneapolis: Fortress, 1996.

———. *The New Testament and the People of God*. Minneapolis: Fortress, 1992.

———. *The Resurrection of the Son of God*. Minneapolis: Fortress, 2003.

———. *Virtue Reborn*. London: SPCK, 2010.

Wright, Robert B. "Psalms of Solomon." Pages 639–70 in *The Old Testament Pseudepigrapha*, vol. 2. Edited by James H. Charlesworth. New Haven: Yale University Press, 1985.

———. *The Psalms of Solomon: A Critical Edition of the Greek Text*. New York: T&T Clark International, 2007.

Yadin, Yigael. *The Scroll of the War of the Sons of Light against the Sons of Darkness*. Oxford: Oxford University Press, 1962.

Zimmerman, Frank. *The Book of Tobit: An English Translation with Introduction and Commentary*. New York: Harper and Bros, 1958.

Subject Index

Abraham, 33, 35, 37, 61, 63–67,
68, 71, 106, 135, 138, 219,
289–90, 305, 358, 360–61;
promise of, 33, 35–37, 63–67,
71–72, 88, 106, 107, 108, 136,
139, 150–51, 289–90, 302, 316,
329, 358–62
apocalypse/apocalyptic/apoca-
lypticism, 5, 7–12, 16–18, 23,
25, 120–25, 149–50, 157–61,
166, 168, 207–8, 210, 215,
237, 242–45, 250, 251–54,
260, 294, 301, 339, 345, 352,
359–61

covenant, 13, 25, 55, 63–67, 71–72,
76–77, 88, 91, 92, 94–95,
98–99, 107, 122, 131, 135–36,
139, 143–44, 218–22, 227–28,
231, 237, 263, 298, 317,
320–21, 359
crowds, 33, 34, 37, 257, 260,
265–68, 272–73, 296, 307, 312,
320, 325, 328–29, 331, 358

determinism, 9, 162–64, 166–70,
174, 180, 185–93, 197–98, 206,
208, 228
discipleship, 19, 21, 24, 32–37,
249–50, 251, 254, 257, 259–61,
265–76, 292, 296, 301, 302–5,
306–12, 315, 317, 319, 320,

331–32, 336, 341–42, 344–47,
349, 354–55, 357–63
dualism, 9, 25, 166–70, 174, 180,
185–93, 195, 197–98, 206, 208,
226, 228–31

election, 1, 9, 18, 29, 35, 49, 50,
58, 70–71, 95, 97, 110, 117,
118, 122, 124, 128, 130, 131,
150, 166–77, 179–84, 186–88,
196–98, 213, 227, 347, 359
eschatology, 8–9, 12, 13, 17, 28, 36,
96, 102–3, 108, 121, 124–27,
129, 130, 136, 138–39, 142,
144–45, 149–50, 163, 168, 177,
182–84, 193, 203–5, 207–8, 215,
227–28, 230–31, 233–34, 235,
236, 237, 240, 243–44, 246–51,
253–55, 258, 260–61, 268, 269,
284–87, 294, 298, 300–301,
302–5, 313–14, 316–18, 320–21,
329–30, 332, 337, 343–44, 349,
352, 355–56, 358–63
ethics, 6, 8, 68, 162–63, 166,
173–76, 185, 190, 192–97,
204–5, 229–30, 237, 240,
243–46, 248–50, 253, 255, 257,
258, 259–60, 265, 268, 272,
274, 276, 300–301, 305, 332,
359–62; virtue-ethics, 251–55,
259–60, 262, 265, 274–75, 288,
298, 303, 355

fatherhood of God, 18–20, 39, 47,
49, 92, 95, 137–38, 291–93,
347–48, 352–54, 358, 363

flourishing, 2, 4, 213, 240, 251–54,
260, 261–65, 269, 274, 288,
297–98, 302

glory, 124, 133–34, 140, 141, 171,
173–84, 191–94, 196, 197, 199,
202–4, 206–7, 215, 227, 235,
297, 302–3, 349, 361–62

kingdom of God, 5, 19, 23, 26–27,
28, 34, 36, 99, 142, 240,
244–45, 247–50, 251, 253–54,
259–60, 263, 265–66, 268, 269,
270, 272–74, 278–82, 288, 297,
301, 303, 309–10, 312–16, 318,
319, 320–21, 323, 326, 327–28,
331–32, 334–36, 339, 344,
349–55, 360, 362

land/earth, 1, 2, 5, 15, 19, 29,
40, 50, 64–67, 81–86, 91–95,
97, 100–101, 107–8, 110–30,
135–36, 137, 149, 203–4, 209,
218, 233, 234, 235, 237, 269,
278–88, 290, 292, 294, 297,
298–301, 303–5, 313, 315,
317–18, 334–36, 349, 355,
358–62; Israel, 45–47, 51–62,
76–77, 88, 97–98, 102, 105,
106, 121, 125, 130, 137–38,
139–40, 141–46, 148, 219–20,
222, 234–35, 237, 285–86, 288,
290, 298, 304, 317, 323–24,
333, 348–49, 351, 359, 362;
tribal, 48–50, 52–54, 55, 56–57,
68–69, 73, 78–79, 89, 91–92,
99, 104–5, 107, 201–2, 213, 317

mission, 20, 21–26, 29, 30, 32–37,
269, 329, 330, 338–47, 351–52,
360, 362

relationship to God, 1–2, 19–20, 33,
45–47, 49–50, 57, 58, 70–72,
76–77, 82, 88, 91, 94–95, 98,
107–8, 130, 135, 137, 140, 145,
149–50, 237, 242, 249–50, 257,
263, 299, 317, 321, 335–36,
348, 354, 358–59, 363

repatriation, 97, 126, 146–48,
349–51, 353

righteousness, 14–15, 25, 65, 99,
110, 114–16, 118–19, 121–22,
124, 126, 127, 128–30, 143,
184, 188, 211, 229–32, 237,
245, 250, 260, 265–66, 269–71,
273, 274, 276, 284, 286, 288,
294, 296, 302, 311, 314–15,
320, 330, 331, 343–45, 350,
352–55, 359, 361, 362

sectarian, 8, 13, 16, 23, 24, 25, 26,
153–57, 159–60, 212, 216–22,
234

Torah/law, 5, 13, 14, 23, 24, 25,
28, 29, 40, 55, 68, 120–24, 129,
130–36, 139, 141–43, 144,
151, 212–14, 265, 307, 311–12,
314–15, 319, 320, 349, 358

vocation, 174–76, 184–85, 196,
201–2, 206, 214, 259, 296–97,
319, 335–36, 360–61

wisdom/sapiential, 5–7, 16–18,
120–25, 128, 129, 130–36, 146,
150–51, 157–215, 231–32, 235,
236, 237, 242–43, 245, 251–54,
260, 262–63, 294, 298, 301,
302, 358–60

Ancient Sources Index

HEBREW BIBLE/OLD TESTAMENT

Genesis

1:1	125
1–3	125n51, 186n138, 205, 205n210
1:26	180n115, 189
2–4	160n28
4:14	81n117
10	106
12:1-7	63–64
15:1-8	62, 64–65
15:1-21	47
15:2	66, 68
15:4	66
15:7	283n167, 290n194
15:18	64–65
15:18-21	52n31
16:1-4	68
17:1-8	65–66
17:4-6	290n193
17:16	66
17:19	66
19:28	281
21:10	61
22:17	61
24:60	61
26:1-5	66
28:4	283n167, 290n194
28:10-15	66
31	68
45:11	61
45:13	174
47:27	283n167
48:4-6	66

Exodus

4:22-23	18, 49
6:1	81n117
6:7	47
10:11	81n117
12:39	81n117
15:1-18	251n47
15:17	57
19:5	57n50, 88n144
19:5-6	142n109
20:14	68
20:17	68
22:4	284
22:7	284
22:9	284
23:10-12	51, 333
23:20	51, 333
23:28	81n117
23:30	283n167, 290n194
23:30-31	51
23:31	52n31
32:12	66
32:13	290n193
33:18-23	141
34:9	57
34:24	60
35:10	57

Leviticus

18:5	144n116
18:26	106
19:33	105
20:10	68
20:24	60, 88n144, 203n203, 283n167
21:7	81n117

25:23	49, 51, 54, 333
25:23-28	89
25:46	61

Numbers

13:30	60
14:24	283n167
14:31	283n167
18:20	136, 201–3, 283n167
18:20-26	56, 57
21:35	283n167
22:6	81n117
26:52-56	53, 69n76, 89
26:53	283n167
26:55	221n273, 283n167
27:1-11	68
27:3	68n73
27:4	68
27:7	54
27:8	69n74
27:8-11	69
27:11	61
30:9	81n117
32	104
32:1-5	55
32:10-15	56, 333
32:28-42	55
33:50-56	59, 293
33:54	221n273
34	52n31
34:1-12	52
34:1-29	53
34:13	221n273
34:13-15	55n43
34:13-29	51
34:17	283n167
35:1-8	56
35:2	54
36	89
36:1-12	68, 69n77
36:2	221n273
36:5	69
36:8	62
36:8-9	69
36:54	53

Deuteronomy

1:8	66, 283n167
1:38-39	60
2:12-31	61
2:31	283n167
3:12	283n167
3:12-20	60
3:28	56
4	132n79
4:1	45, 55, 283n167, 290n194, 333
4:6-8	55
4:15-24	52
4:20	55, 88n144
4:21	52, 333
4:22	283n167
4:32-38	60
5:31-33	61
5:33	283n167
6:1	61
6:18	61
7:1-17	60
7:6	70
7:6-8	70
7:8	70
8:1	61, 66
9:1-23	60
9:4	53, 292
9:5	66, 220
9:6-8	53
9:13-21	52
9:24	57
9:25-29	52, 52n32, 53n35, 58, 71
9:29	88n144
10:9	57
10:11	61, 66
11:8-9	61, 66
11:10-12	45
12:1-7	52
12:9-12	55, 333
14:1	49
14:1-2	58n54, 71
14:2	70
14:21	70
14:27-29	54
15:4	61
15:6	55
16:20	62
17:14	62

18:1	56, 136
18:1-2	57
19:1-3	60
19:1-13	54
19:14	52, 54, 179, 219
20:10	54
20:16-18	54, 60
21:1	62
21:7	284
21:23	54
23:21	62
24:4	54
25:6	68n71
25:19	61
26:1	54, 61, 333
26:18-19	70
26:19	70
27–34	288n188
27:17	179
28:15-68	61
30:11-20	121
31:7	56, 61
31:7-8	66
31:13	61
32:4-6	18
32:5	49
32:6	49, 92
32:8-9	58, 70, 88n144, 92, 134n88
32:18	49
32:19	49
32:47	61
32:48-52	141
33:27-29	117

Joshua

1:6	56, 66
2–12	66
11:23	53, 73n88
13:1	74n88
13–19	66, 99, 104
14:2	221n273
14:6-15	140
14:9	54
14:12	60
14:13-15	136
15:63	60
16:10	60
17:4	68

17:12-18	60
17:14	221n273
18	56, 136
19:1	221n273
19:40-48	78n103
19:49-50	77
19:49-51	136
19:51	99
20	66
21:43-45	66, 73, 88, 120
23	75
24	75, 79
24:4	61
24:27	73
24:28	79
24:28-31	75–77
24:31	73

Judges

	74
1:1	75
1:1–2:5	75
1:34	78
2:1-5	74
2:4	74n91
2:6	74n89, 77, 79
2:6-10	75–77
2:11-13	76
3:1-6	76
6:9	81n117
8:27	80n110
11:1-3	77
14:5	74n89
17:6	72, 77
18	78
18:1	72, 77
18:7	74n89
19–20	78
19:1	72
20:6	78
20:26	74n91
20:34	80n110
21	79
21:23-24	78–79

Ruth

4:5-10	85

1 Samuel

2:1-10	80, 175
2:7	85n132

2:8	182–83
2:36	82n118
10:1	80–81, 85, 91, 291
24:6	89
26:11	89
26:19	81–82, 84–85, 334n327
28:13	84

2 Samuel

7:12-14	18
13–14	84
14:7	85
14:16	81, 84–86, 90n151
20:1	82n120
20:19	81–83, 334n327
21:3	81, 83, 334n327
23:17	89

1 Kings

8	87–88
8:35-40	83
8:36	18, 91
21	89–90, 104
21:3	91
21:19	335, 335n335
21:27-29	335

2 Kings

17	87
21	90

2 Chronicles

24:21	322n285

Ezra

7	132n79

Nehemiah

9:26	322n285
13	146n126

Job

19:19	174
26:5-6	145n117
30:7	82n118

Psalms

1	132n79, 263
6:5	145n117
8:5	174
19	132n79

23:1-4	348n372
24:13	284
33:12 (32, LXX)	286–87
34:18	275n131
37:1-34 (36, LXX)	2n5, 119–22, 203n203, 283n167, 284, 286–88, 298, 299n218, 304
37:9	293
37:11	278, 281, 283n167, 293
37:22	299
37:34-36	121
43:3-4	45
49:16-17	174
74:1-2	348n372
75:2	146n123
78:52	348n372
110	316n271
118:22	327n304
118:22-23	324n293
118:26	348n376
119	132n79
122	316n271

Proverbs

1–9	16, 210, 210n230, 211
2:6	134n87
3:13	240, 263n88
3:19	134, 185n131
3:35	133
5:5	211n232
6:3	171n78
7:7	211
8	134
8:22-31	133
9:16	211
9:18	211n232
19:17	342n354
30:7-9	191n158

Ecclesiastes/Qohelet

10:16-17	271n115

Isaiah

1:21-26	215n251
2:2-4	96, 97n171, 98, 138, 147, 284, 349
3:10-11	271n115

5:1-7	322n284, 323, 323n290, 324
5:7	200n191
8:19-20	84
8:23–9:1	285
9:7	293
11:11	347n370
11:11-12	126
13	97
14:1	82n118
14:1-2	97, 147, 284
16:14	174
19:16-25	98, 101n189, 284
21:16	175
25:6-9	293n206
26:8	293n206
27:12-13	347n370
30:15	293n206
30:18	293n206
40:11	348n372
40–55	97n169
40:30-31	293n206
42:1-7	285
43:5-7	97n174
46–47	97n172
49:1-8	284, 290n193
49:1-12	98–100
49:6-7	349
49:22-23	97n174
49:23	293n206
50:10-11	293n206
51:3	251n47
51:11	251n47
52:7	251n47
53	342n354
53:3-4	303n227
54:10	251n47
54:17	101n189
55:12-13	251n47
56–57	100–101, 284
56–66	284, 300, 305n233, 317
56:1-8	126
56:6-8	97n169
57:13	203n203, 283n167, 293n206
58:6-10	339n347
60	97n169
60:1-6	285
60:4	97n174
60:19-22	124
60:20	295n212
60:21	100, 101n190, 138, 200n191, 232, 232n310, 283, 283n167, 284–6, 285n177, 304n231
61	15, 255n61
61:1	278
61:1-7	193, 277n140, 277n141, 282–88, 295
61:3	200n191, 200n192, 232, 232n310
61:7	101n190, 203n203, 286n179, 299, 304n231, 353n393
61:7-9	18
63:16	18
64–66	285
64:4	293n206
64:8	18
64:8-9	124
65	300
65–66	100n185, 124–27
65:9	101n190
65:17	285, 300, 304n231, 317
65:17-25	150n132, 209, 251n47
66:10	295n212
66:12	251n47
66:18-21	97n169, 126
66:18-23	300
66:18-24	349, 350
66:18-25	349n377
66:19	349
66:22	317
66:22-23	126

Jeremiah

1:16-19	93
2:7	93
3:17	97n169, 98, 138, 147, 349
3:17-19	95–96
3:19	18

7:25-27	322n285
10:2	93
10:16	93
11:8-12	93
12	93–94
13:17	348n372
17:1	94
20:2	322n285
23:1-4	33n118
26:21-23	322n285
27:6	33n118
30:19	193
31:9	18, 49
31:10	348n372
31:33	94n163, 95n164
32–33	94
32:38	95n164
33:9	95n165
50:4-5	95
50:11	95
51:19	95

Ezekiel

1–39	101
5:5	45
8–11	102
20:40	102
22:17-22	215n251
30:3	96n167
34	33n118
34:11-31	348n372
34:25	251n47
35:15	101n191
36:12	101n191
36:35	251n47
37:24-28	102
37:26	251n47
40–48	101–8
47	218n261
47:21-23	148, 349, 360

Daniel

2–7	280
2:28	280n157
3:31–4:34	280n158
4:34-37	280n157
5:23	280n157
7	316n271, 348n372
12:1-13	175

12:12	242n12

Hosea

4:16	220n265
11:1	49

Joel

3:3	341n353

Micah

6:8	314n263
7:14	348n372

Habakkuk

2:15	82n118

Haggai

2:7-9	97n169

Zechariah

2:14-16	97n169
8:20-23	97n169
9:9	42
10:3	348n372
13:7	193
14:1	126n123

APOCRYPHA AND PSEUDEPIGRAPHA

1 Enoch

1–5	112n13, 114, 115, 119, 195
1:1	114, 117
1:3	117
1:4	123n43
1:7-9	114–15
1:8	117, 119, 124
2:1–5:3	115, 123n43
5	150, 205n209, 300, 302
5:4	122–23
5:5-9	110–27, 129–30, 150n132, 203, 203n203, 283n167, 299, 349n377
6–36	114
6:4	111
7–9	125
10:3	200n191
10:16	126, 200n191
10:17	126
10:18–11:2	126, 349n377

10:20-21	209	24:23	132n80, 142, 214
10:21-22	127	25:7-11	243n18
12:5	117	33:24	131n73
13:4-6	117	36:1-10	135
24–26	126n54	36:16	135n89
25:6	126	37:26	133
38:4	119n28	38:32	147
40:9	110, 127	44–50	135–36, 290
48:8	119n28	44:19-21	151
57:2	347n370	44:21	290
62:6	119n28	51:23-27	16
63:1	119n28	51:23-30	7
63:12	119n28		

Tobit

67:12	119n28

81:4	242n12	1:1	137
84:6	200n191	1:14	15n46
89–90	348n372	3:3-5	137–38
89:18	348n372	3:11	137
91–105	127n61	3:17	137
92:1	128	4:1-2	15n46
93:5	200n191	4:12	137–38, 203n203,
93:6-10	122		283n167, 299n218
93:10	118, 122n37,	6:12	137
	200n191	6:13	137
98:9	128	7:10-14	138
98:9–99:16	302	7:11	137
99	150	13–14	138n98
99:1	128	13:1-5	138
99:9	128	13:3-4	137
99:10	128, 302	13:5	139
99:10-16	271n115	13:8-11	138
99:11	128, 129	13:11	139
99:12-13	129	13:14	240, 242n12
99:14	110, 127–30, 302	13:16-17	138
99:16	128	14:5-7	138
100:6	128		

Judith

103:5-6	271n115

Sirach

4:12-15	133–34, 175, 183	4:12	139–40
4:16	134	5:15	139–40
4:19	133	5:18	139
7:32-36	177n103	6:19	280
10:11	131n73	8:22	140
14:20-27	213, 243n18	9:12	140
15:1	213	13:5	140
15:6	133	16:21	140
22:23	131n76		

1 Maccabees

24	134–35

1:32	140
2:19-20	129n69
2:57	140

6:24	140
15:33-34	140

2 Maccabees

2	214
2:1-5	142
2:4-5	141
2:17	141–42
2:18	141
7:9	142n110
7:23	142n110
15:3-4	280

The Psalms of Solomon

1:8	143
2:1-19	143
3	319
3:8-12	143
3:12	318
7:2	143, 350
8	144
9:1	144
11:3	347n370
12:6	127, 144
13	148n129
14	150n132, 318–19, 349
14:1-3	319
14:1-10	144–45
14:5	127
14:5-10	318
14:9	349
14:9-10	350
14:10	127, 318, 349
14:26	242n12
15	144n116
15:10-13	145
17	145–48, 150n132, 318, 350–51
17:3	350
17:21-23	350
17:26	350, 350n378
17:27-28	350n380
17:28	350
17:28-35	138
17:29	350
17:32	350
17:34	350
17:40	351
17:41	351
17:50	242n12
18:6	242n12

Testament of Job

43	133

Testament of Judah

25:4	194n168

Testament of Moses

1:8	129n69
2:1	129n69
9:6	129n69

Jubilees

17:3	203n203, 283n167
22:14	203n203, 283n167
23:30-31	194n168
23:31	177n104
32:19	203n203, 283n167

2 Enoch

42:6-14	242n12
50:2	303n226, 304n230, 353n394
52:1-16	242n12, 271n115

Baruch

4:36-37	347n370

2 Baruch

10:6	242n12
10:6-7	271n115
11:6	242n12
14:10	242n12

3 Maccabees

2:2	280

4 Ezra

7:37	342n355

QUMRAN/DEAD SEA SCROLLS

Ages of Creation

4Q180 1	206n215
4Q181 2	206n215

1 Enoch

4Q201 1ii 14–17	111
4Q202	111n9
4Q204	111n9

Songs of the Sabbath Sacrifice

4Q400 1 i 17	214n248

4QInstruction

1Q26	159n22
4Q415–18	159n22
4Q415 6 2	165
4Q415 11 11	193n166
4Q416 1	160n28, 181n118, 195
4Q416 2 ii	170–76
4Q416 2 ii 6	190, 296
4Q416 2 ii 12	188
4Q416 2 ii 13	198n183
4Q416 2 ii 18	191n159
4Q416 2 ii 20	164
4Q416 2 iii	176–85, 194, 195n172, 294
4Q416 2 iii 2	164
4Q416 2 iii 3–5	15n46
4Q416 2 iii 6–9	190
4Q416 2 iii 8	164
4Q416 2 iii 8–12	236
4Q416 2 iii 9	193–94
4Q416 2 iii 11	190
4Q416 2 iii 14–15	194
4Q416 2 iii 15–16	165
4Q416 2 iii 15–18	189
4Q416 2 iii 19	164
4Q416 2 iii 20	193n166
4Q416 3 2	202n201
4Q416 4 3	195n173
4Q417 1 i	185–92
4Q417 1 i 6–7	162, 194
4Q417 1 i 16	166, 206
4Q417 1 i 17	180n115
4Q417 2 i 7–18	192–94, 295
4Q417 2 i 10–12	177
4Q417 2 i 12	200, 295
4Q417 2 i 14	165
4Q417 2 i 17	236
4Q418 43 45 i 10	191n159
4Q418 55	181n119, 194–97
4Q418 55 12	200, 204n208
4Q418 69	181n119
4Q418 69 ii	165, 194–97, 236n324
4Q418 69 ii 13	200, 204n208
4Q418 77 3	188
4Q418 81	164, 207, 231, 295, 297, 301
4Q418 81+81a 1–14	197–205

4Q418 81+81a 3	191n159
4Q418 81+81a 14	300
4Q418 123 ii 3–4	162
4Q418 126 ii 7–8	177, 195n172
4Q418 177 5	165
4Q418 185a+b2	170n74
4Q418 251 1	170n74
4Q423	159n22, 160n28
4Q423 1 2	205
4Q423 1–2 i 7	200n191
4Q423 4 3	202n202
4Q423 5 3	205

Book of Mysteries

1Q27	163, 207n217
1Q27 1 i 1–12	209
1Q27 1 i 2	209n225
1Q27 1 i 5	208
1Q27 1 i 6	209
4Q299–301	163, 207n217
4Q299 1 1–9	209
4Q299 3a ii b 14	209
4Q299 8 6–7	208
4Q300 1b 2	209n225
4Q300 3 1–6	209

The Seductress

4Q184	210–12

4QBeatitutudes

4Q525	194n170, 212–15, 301–2
4Q525 2 ii	302n223
4Q525 13	302n223
4Q525 13 5	211n234
4Q525 14 i	302n223
4Q525 14 ii	302n223
4Q525 33	302n223

The Damascus Document

I 1–II 1	218–19
I 2	218
I 4	219
I 7	218
I 7–11	219
I 8	219
I 14–16	219–20, 222
I 15–17	129n69
I 16	218
III 7	191n159, 218, 220
XIII 7–XIV 2	221

XIII 12	218, 220–22
XIII 14	218, 220
XIX 9	193
XIX 27	218, 220

The Community Rule

1QS I 8–10	222n274
1QS III 13–VI 26	163, 222n275, 225–31
1QS III 15–16	185
1QS III 17	186n138
1QS III 17–26	222n274
1QS IV 3	275n131
1QS IV 7	194n168
1QS IV 13	211n236
1QS IV 22	232
1QS V 7–11	278n148
1QS V 23	221n272
1QS VIII 5	200n191, 232, 232n312
1QS IX 18	221n271
1QS XI	233
1QS XI 1	275n131
1QS XI 6	232
1QS XI 7	209n228, 231–33
1QS XI 8	200n191
1QS XI 16	196
1QSa I 6–8	163
1QSb III 22	199n189
1QSb IV 25–26	199n189
4QSa–j	222n276

The War Scroll

1QM X 10–15	235
1QM X 15	234n320
1QM XI 9	236
1QM XI 13	236
1QM XII 4	196
1QM XII 4–13	235
1QM XII 12	234n320
1QM XIV 7	15n44, 275n131
1QM XIX 4	234n320
4Q492 1 4	234n320

Thanksgiving Hymns

1QHa VI 3	15n44
1QHa XI 23–24	188n148
1QHa XIV 14–16	199, 199n189
1QHa XIV 15	200n191
1QHa XVI 6	200n191
1QHa XIX 12–18	199, 199n189
1QHa XXIII 16	193n164

Habakkuk Pesher

1QpHab V 4	196
1QpHab X 13	196, 211n236

Psalms Pesher

4Q171	121–22, 203n203, 304n230

Apocalypse of Joseph

4Q372 3	236n325

4QSongs of the Sage

4Q511 2 i	199n189

THE NEW TESTAMENT

Matthew

1:1	33, 35n124, 290, 290n193, 291n195, 292
1:1-17	26
1:2	289, 290n193
1:6	291n195
1:17	289, 290n193, 291n195
1:21	330
1:22-23	42n144
1:23	29
2:1-12	285
2:6	33
2:15-18	42n144
2:23	42n144
3:9	290n193
3:15	246n29
4:1-17	265
4:12-17	268, 285
4:14-16	42n144
4:15-16	35n124
4:17–11:1	33
4:18-22	259, 265, 320
4:23	267, 267n102, 268, 279n152
4:23-25	258, 265, 266, 268
4:23–5:2	248, 259
4:24	268
4:25	273, 304n229
5	263, 269n109, 270n111

5–7	6, 253n56, 271n114	5:10-12	17, 246, 269, 274, 303
5:1	268	5:11	291
5:1-2	265	5:11-12	239n1, 246, 256, 256n65, 277n138, 292n201, 340, 346, 355
5:3	15n44, 240, 241n6, 245, 246n28, 247, 249n41, 256n65, 258, 269, 272, 275–82, 285, 291, 294, 295, 295n211, 296, 297, 298, 304, 305n233, 332n323, 353n395		
		5:12	269, 291, 296
		5:13-14	35n124
		5:13-16	248, 265, 297
		5:14-16	346
		5:16	267
		5:17	23
5:3-5	255n62	5:17-20	213, 264, 265
5:3-10	256, 256n65, 258	5:18	285, 304, 313, 313n259
5:3-12	13, 17, 213, 239–303, 332, 353n393, 355		
		5:19	6, 18, 266
5:3–7:27	267	5:20	257, 260, 265, 266, 270–71, 275, 294, 310, 311, 344, 355
5:4	240n5, 255, 258, 277n138, 277n140, 277n141, 295n212		
		5:21–7:29	265
		5:22-24	339
5:4-9	247, 272	5:35	285, 304
5:5	2n5, 4, 18, 203n203, 213, 239, 241, 244, 246n28, 256, 257, 258, 259, 269, 275–305, 310, 315–17, 319, 320, 332n323, 333, 335, 336, 347, 353, 355, 356, 362	5:43-48	311, 344
		5:44-48	293n205
		5:45	292n200
		5:46-47	25n84
		5:47	21n66
		5:48	252, 264, 265, 315, 315n267, 315n268
5:6	250, 257, 258, 271, 277n138, 277n141, 297	6	311n246
		6:1-4	311
		6:1-5	275
		6:7	21n66
5:6-7	344	6:7-8	25n84
5:6-8	255n62	6:9	292n200, 363
5:7	269, 339	6:9-10	281
5:7-9	277n138	6:10	204n206, 282, 285, 297, 304
5:7-10	256		
5:8	246, 269, 270, 271	6:16	275
5:9	246, 255, 274, 287, 291, 292, 293, 348	6:19	285, 304
		6:19-21	297
5:9-12	255n62	6:20	311
5:10	247, 256n65, 258, 269, 272, 279, 291, 296, 297, 353n395	6:24	297
		6:25-34	297
		6:31-32	25n84
		6:32	21n66
5:10-11	310, 310n245	7	266n99

7:3-5	339	11:29	246n29, 256n67,
7:15-23	313		279, 303n226
7:24-27	267	12:6	23, 29
7:24-29	275	12:15-21	285
7:28	266, 268	12:17-21	42n144
7:28-29	267	12:18-21	35n124
8:1	268	12:38	309n241
8:1-4	267	12:38-42	29
8:1–9:34	267	12:42	29, 285, 304
8:5-13	23, 35n124	12:46-50	340, 354
8:10	29	12:49-50	361
8:11	290n193	13	6, 266n99
8:17	42n144	13:24-30	313
8:18-20	310n243	13:35	42n144
8:18-22	309	13:36-43	313
8:22	309n242	13:41-42	343
8:28-34	35n124	13:47-50	314
9:6	285, 304	13:49	297, 343
9:11	309n241	15:1-20	275
9:27	246n29	15:6-20	270
9:35	267, 267n102, 268	15:13	23
9:35–10:42	267	15:14	33, 266n98
9:36	267, 268	15:21-28	35n124
10	6, 340n352, 342	15:22	246n29
10:1	301	15:24	33, 266n98
10:1-42	340	15:28	29
10:5-6	20, 21, 22, 32, 33,	16:18-19	332n321
	35n126, 266n98,	16:19	36n131, 285, 304
	298, 330, 362	16:25	310n245
10:5-7	305n233	16:27	343
10:7	340	16:27-28	314
10:9-10	340	18	6
10:10	342	18:6	340n351
10:15	341	18:10	340n351
10:16-18	341	18:14	340n351
10:16-25	340	18:15-17	25n84
10:17-31	306n234	18:17	21n66
10:18	310n245	18:18-19	285, 304
10:26-33	341	19	318n276
10:32	29	19:3-12	307–8
10:39	310n245	19:10-12	308n238
10:40-41	341	19:13-15	309, 316
10:42	341	19:16	306, 312
10:42-44	340n351	19:16-30	296, 308, 308n238,
11:11	340n351		318, 319
11:19	7	19:20	309, 320
11:20-24	29	19:21	259n75, 309n242,
11:25	285, 304		311, 315, 315n267,
11:25-30	7, 17		315n268

19:22	309, 320	21:46	325, 329, 331
19:22-23	355	22:1-14	326
19:23	311	22:16	309n241
19:23-26	316	22:30	297, 297n215
19:23-30	332	23	34, 240, 263, 264,
19:24	296		264n94, 269,
19:27	320		269n109, 270n111,
19:28	5, 285, 291n195,		270n113, 275,
	298, 304, 309n242,		303, 311, 311n246, 334
	313–14, 316n271,	23–25	6, 271n114
	317–18,	23:1	34, 273
	332, 332n324	23:1-36	344
19:28-29	343, 353n395, 355,	23:6	312
	362	23:8-10	28
19:29	4, 296n214, 299,	23:8-12	312
	306–21, 326, 333,	23:9	285, 304
	335, 336, 350, 353,	23:12	260, 276n135
	355, 356	23:13	312, 331, 355
19:30	316	23:13-19	269
20:24-28	316	23:13-31	273
20:25-26	21n66	23:15	274
21:1-9	42	23:16-24	312, 312n250
21:1-11	325	23:16-26	33, 266n98
21:4-5	42n144	23:23	269, 312, 355
21:5	256n67, 279,	23:25	312, 312n251
	303n226	23:25-26	269
21:12-17	324, 325	23:25-28	270–71
21:14-15	33	23:29-36	340, 343
21:18-20	325	23:31-32	331n317
21:23	324, 325, 331, 344	23:34	269
21:23–22:14	322–23	23:37-39	261, 325
21:33	323n289, 324,	24–25	273
	326n297	24:1	273
21:33-46	23, 26, 34	24:1-2	325
21:34-36	331n317	24:3	273
21:38	4–5, 299, 318,	24:9-14	340, 341, 341n353,
	321–37, 353,		343, 351
	354–55, 361	24:14	346
21:38-39	336	24:29-31	343
21:38-43	36n131	24:30	285, 304
21:39	323n289, 324	24:31	347
21:40	336	24:35	313, 313n259
21:40-41	325	24:36-44	344, 356n397
21:41-43	23	24:45-51	339
21:42	327n304, 336	24:45–25:30	337n340, 343–44
21:43	26, 27n92,	25	266n99
	323n289, 327–32,	25:10-13	339
	335, 354–55, 356	25:28-30	339
21:45	324, 331, 331n316	25:31	348

25:31-40	291n195
25:31-46	314, 337, 337n341, 338, 340n352, 341–52, 355, 360
25:32	338, 345–47, 350n378
25:34	4–5, 299, 337–53, 355, 356
25:35	318
25:35-36	338–39, 339n347
25:37	342n355, 344
25:40	338, 340n351
25:41	342
25:45	338, 340n351
25:45-46	355
25:46	344, 350, 353, 355
26–27	246n29
26–28	273
26:1	273
26:8	273
26:10	273
26:20-21	273
26:26	273
26:31	273
26:36	273
26:36-45	246n29
26:38	273
26:45	273
26:56	42n144
27	266n100
27:4	246n29
27:15-26	260, 260n76
27:19	246n29
27:20	34, 273, 325, 325n294
27:20-25	325n294
27:24	273
27:31-33	324
27:45	304n232
28:9-10	325n295
28:15	23
28:16	326n295
28:16-20	298, 340, 340n352, 341
28:18	285, 304
28:18-19	29
28:19	29, 346

28:18-20	21, 22, 26, 30, 32, 33, 35n124, 35n126, 330, 362

Mark

10:17	306, 310n244, 312
10:17-31	306n234
10:30	312–13
11:1-10	42

Luke

3:23-28	289n191
6:20	241n6, 275, 280, 298
6:20-21	277n138
6:20-26	240, 271n115, 273
6:21	240n5
6:24	276n133
6:27-36	242n15
6:43-44	242n15
6:46-49	242n15
7:22	283n166
9:57	309
14:21	327n299
18:18-30	306n234
24:13-53	325

John

5:25-27	348n373

Acts

2:46	14n39
3:25	290n193
7:5	40n140
16:25-34	341n353
20:32	40n140

Romans

1	189n152
4	290n193, 304n230, 361
8	361
8:12-18	292n201
8:14-17	353n395
8:17	335n332, 361
8:18-27	362
8:21	292n201
8:27	292n201

1 Corinthians

11:23-29	341n353

Galatians
3   290n193

Colossians
3:24   40n141

1 Thessalonians
4:17   347n370

Titus
3:5   313n254, 317–18,
                                   318n276

Hebrews
9:15   40n141
11:8   40n141

1 Peter
3:4   256n67

Revelation
7:1   347n370
21:4   260, 295n212

Josephus
Ant. 12.7.3   264n92

Thucydides
2.35–36   140n102

EARLY CHRISTIAN TEXTS

Didache
9:4   347n370
10:5   347n370

Gospel of Thomas
65–66   324n293

GREEK AND ROMAN TEXTS

Demosthenes
12.21–23   140n102